Translational Research in Biomedical Sciences: Recent Progress and Future Prospects

Krupakar Parthasarathy
Radhakrishnan Manikkam
Editors

Translational Research in Biomedical Sciences: Recent Progress and Future Prospects

Springer

Editors
Krupakar Parthasarathy
Centre for Drug Discovery and Development
Sathyabama Institute of Science and Technology
Chennai, India

Radhakrishnan Manikkam
Centre for Drug Discovery and Development
Sathyabama Institute of Science and Technology
Chennai, India

ISBN 978-981-97-1776-7 ISBN 978-981-97-1777-4 (eBook)
https://doi.org/10.1007/978-981-97-1777-4

This Springer imprint is published by the registered company Springer Nature Singapore Pte Ltd.
The registered company address is: 152 Beach Road, #21-01/04 Gateway East, Singapore 189721, Singapore

Preface

Translational science is an interdisciplinary field of research that plays a vital role in bridging the gap between scientific discoveries and their real-time implementation in healthcare. As we enter a new era of biomedical advancement, the importance of efficiently translating research from bench to bedside has become increasingly crucial. Proof-of-concept studies have been numerous in the past decades. Each stage in translational research is built upon the outcome of previous studies, but the spectrum of the path is not linear or unidirectional but rather a multidirectional one. In biological sciences, it often involves collaboration between interdisciplinary researchers, clinicians, industry professionals, and other stakeholders to facilitate the seamless transfer of knowledge and technologies. It leads to the development of diagnostics, therapeutics, and aids that make the day-to-day life of patients a better one. It is a process that proceeds on a continuum mode, from the initial discovery phase to the development of interventions and their implementation in populations. The road map for this has three major milestones: the transition from lab to human use (Phase 1), assessment of efficacy (Phase 2) and finally, launching the product to clinical application, and evaluating the feasibility (Phase 3). Hence a deeper understanding of these processes and available tools is necessary for a researcher to translate the research outcomes to an application. *Translational Research in Biomedical Sciences: Recent Progress and Future Prospects* is a book that aims to guide aspiring scientists on how to conduct research in the field of clinical and translational science. It was nurtured by the technological and financial support that we received from the Scheme for Promotion of Academic and Research Collaboration (SPARC), an initiative of the Ministry of Human Resource Development (MHRD), Government of India. Our distinguished contributors from the Indo-Singapore Translational Research in Healthcare Conclave with decades of experience in basic and applied research share their experiences, inventions, and insights in a series of enlightening chapters, providing a complete view of the landscape of translational research. It covers multiple topics that include vaccine development, analytical methods, biological space research, gene manipulation, infectious disease diagnostics, and applications of artificial intelligence in clinical research. In the pages that follow, we will delve into the complexities of translational research, digging into its concepts, methodology, and the inherent problems that come with the path from discovery to implementation.

Chennai, India — Krupakar Parthasarathy
Chennai, India — Radhakrishnan Manikkam

Contents

1 Emerging Concepts in the Field of Vaccine Adjuvants

Shakila Harshavardhan, Vignesh Sounderrajan, Sam Ebenezer Rajadas, Krupakar Parthasarathy, and Rohini Tamilanban

1.1 Introduction

Vaccines are prophylactic as well as therapeutic agents that induce protective immune response through their active immunogenic compound, and broadly it has been classified into live, inactivated, or attenuated [1]. The immunogenic component may be a protein or polysaccharide or containing both with or without adjuvants. Vaccines induce immunity against specific pathogens, either as a prophylactic or therapeutic measure. Further, vaccines can be classified into live attenuated, heat-killed, subunit, recombinant, conjugated, toxoid, and polysaccharide vaccines. Live attenuated vaccines are modified forms of pathogenic organisms to reduce their virulence. These avirulent forms can be achieved by growing the pathogenic strain in laboratory conditions to lose its virulence property. Live attenuated vaccines are administered in low dosages to replicate slowly in the body to generate an immune response against that specific pathogen. Inactivated vaccines are mostly heat-killed forms of pathogens or fractions of dead microorganisms to evoke immunity against the administered pathogen. Usually, inactivated vaccines are needed to give boosters for effective immune response. Subunit vaccines contain a part of antigenic agents present in a pathogen which are highly immunogenic. Toxoids like tetanus, diphtheria, and pertussis are a type of subunit vaccine. Polysaccharides derived from the cell wall or capsule of pathogenic bacteria directly produce B cell immunity without the assistance of T helper cells. Since it produces T cell-independent immunity it loses its ability to protect children below two years. Compared to protein-based vaccines, polysaccharide vaccines are less protective because it produces Ig M antibodies and a lesser extent of Ig G antibodies. Polysaccharide-based vaccines are available for pneumococcal disease, meningococcal disease, and *Salmonella typhi*. Conjugated vaccines are polysaccharide combined with proteins which shows better immune response even in children due to the presence of protein which will process by T cells and produce both CMI and humoral response effectively. Recombinant vaccines are generated using genetic engineering. The active immunogenic antigens from pathogenic microorganisms are cloned into another host to produce the specific protein in high quantity or to make the avirulent

S. Harshavardhan (✉)
Department of Molecular Microbiology, School of Biotechnology, Madurai Kamaraj University, Madurai, India

V. Sounderrajan · S. E. Rajadas · K. Parthasarathy
Centre for Drug Discovery and Development, Sathyabama Institute of Science and Technology, Chennai, India
e-mail: vignesh.irc@sathyabama.ac.in; pkrupakar.cddd@sathyabama.ac.in

R. Tamilanban
Department of Microbiology, Mannar Thirumalai Naicker College, Madurai, India

K. Parthasarathy, R. Manikkam (eds.), *Translational Research in Biomedical Sciences: Recent Progress and Future Prospects*, https://doi.org/10.1007/978-981-97-1777-4_1

microorganism produce only one immunogenic part of the dominant antigen.

1.2 Adjuvants

Adjuvants are an active component first described in 1924 by Ramon as it has been used in vaccines in conjunction with antigens to improve immune response over the antigen alone [2]. Adjuvants come in different forms that include liposomes, derived products from microbes, cytokines, emulsions, inorganic mineral salts, saponins, polymers, and microparticles [3]. Adjuvants help to elicit immunity along with antigens by sustained release of antigens for constant immune response, by activating the upregulation of cytokines and chemokines, promoting antigen processing cells for increased uptake of antigens and presentations and infiltration into lymph nodes and activation of inflammasomes (Fig. 1.1) [4].

Adjuvants work by slowly releasing the antigen to obtain a sustained immune response of generating significant antibody titer. Alum, a well-known adjuvant, works in this way by absorbing the antigens by strong electrostatic interaction, avoiding precipitation, and facilitating the recruitment of immune cells like neutrophils, eosinophils, NK cells, $CD11b^+$ monocytes, and dendritic cells to carry the antigen to cells of humoral immune response [5]. Alum in combination with monophosphoryl lipid A along with AS04 showed better immune response by stabilizing the antigen and MPL-A. Another well-known adjuvant is Freund's adjuvant. It is a water-oil emulsion that is nontoxic and able to release antigens slowly for recruiting immune cells at the depot for effective immunogenicity. Two types of Freund's adjuvants are available, Freund's complete and Freund's incomplete adjuvants. Freund's incomplete adjuvant is a water-oil emulsion whereas the complete one is just an incomplete one that is added with dried cellular components of *Mycobacterium tuberculosis*. MF59 is another oil emulsion-based adjuvant that elicits a significant immune response of subunit vaccines by antigen-presenting cells, and improved phagocytosis. MF59 induces monocytes to express co-stimulatory molecules CD83 and CD86 that in turn promote MHC-II activation and response against bacteria by promoting DC-based T Cell propagation. Hence both the CMI and antibody response are modulated [6]. Freund's complete adjuvant, CpG-ODN, lipopolysaccharide (LPS), liposomes, MF59, AS04, and α-galactosylceramide (α-GAL) have all been shown to induce DC maturation to generate adaptive immunity. The unmethylated CpG dinucleotide flanked by two 5′ purines and two 3′ pyrimidines which encodes for TLR 9 mount the production of Th 1 immune response and generate CMI and humoral immune response. Cationic liposomal formulation preserves the vaccine nature of anionic antigens with assured sustained release. The activity of adjuvants relies on distinct molecular pathways including inflammation and activation of pattern recognition receptors, both intracellular (Poly:IC (toll-like receptor (TLR)3, TLR7/8, or CpG oligonucleotides (TLR9)) and extracellular (TLR2, 3-O-desacyl-4′-monophosphoryl lipid A (MPLA; TLR4), and Mincle) [7] (Fig. 1.1).

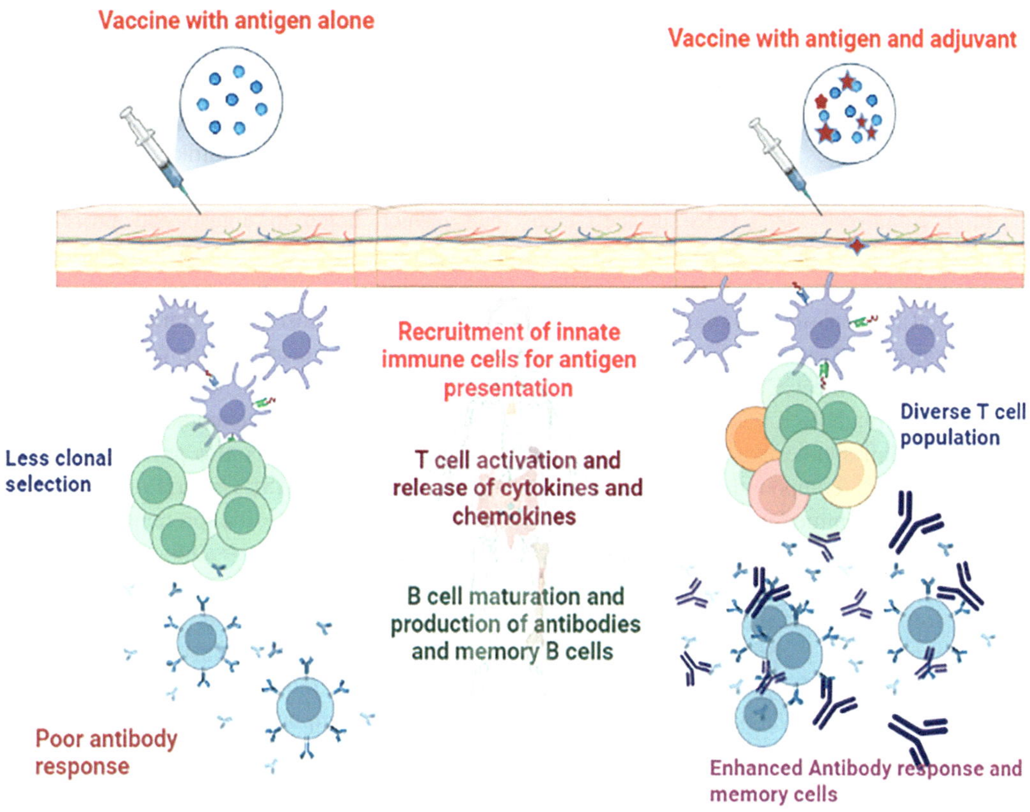

Fig. 1.1 Differentiation between vaccine with and without adjuvant. Vaccine with adjuvant enhances antigen uptake by APCs and induces long-lasting memory immune response

1.3 Carbohydrate-Based Adjuvant System

1.3.1 Cationic Lipid-Based Adjuvants for TB

Cationic liposomes are assembled vesicular lipid-based nanostructures that are compatible and are nontoxic in nature. It is used as an efficient vehicle for delivering vaccine [8]. As an adjuvant, liposomes improve the vaccine efficacy by regulating the binding with TLRs besides sustained release and immune stimulation [9]. The physio-chemical parameters like size, charge, and encapsulation efficiency enable it to entrap different types of antigens. Among various forms of liposome-based adjuvants, cationic liposome adjuvants are used in TB vaccines. It has the potential of inducing Th1 cells, which are essential for controlling MTB.

Many cationic lipids are available for using as adjuvants, which are DDA, dimethyl dioctadecyl ammonium, DOTAP, 1,2-dioleoyl-3-trimethylammonium-propane, DC-Chol, 3B-[N-(N0,N0-dimethylaminoethane)-carbamoyl] cholesterol, DOEPC, 2-dioleyl-sn-glycero-3-ethylphosphocholine, DOTIM, octa decanoyl oxy (ethyl-2-heptadecenyl-3-hydroxye-thyl) imidazolinium, CCS, N-palmitoyl-D-erythrospingosyl-1-O-carbamoyl spermine, diC14-amidine, 3-tetradecylamino-tert-butyl-N-tetradecylpropionamidine, DOTMA, and N-(1-[2,3-dioleyloxy] propyl)-N,N,N-trimethylammonium [10]. Among these cationic lipid-based adjuvants, the two adjuvants viz Adjuvant System 01 (AS01) and virosomes are in clinical phase [11]. M72 TB subunit vaccine harboring two antigens, namely Rv1196 and Rv0125 in combination with AS01, has been now in Phase II clinical trials which can be used as booster for BCG primed individuals for addressing latent TB infection.

Cationic liposomes make the maturation of dendritic cells causing expression of CD80/86 that binds to naïve CD4+ T cells surface CD26 and also shift naïve T cells to Th1 cells by upregulating the expression and secretion of IL-12 via activation of PI3 kinase and enhanced P38 activity [12]. Naïve $CD8^+$ cytotoxic T cells get induced and migrated by the CCL2 chemokine which upregulated through ERK1/2 pathway.

In 1960, Gall synthesized DDA, a synthetic amphiphilic lipid compound with a positively charged dimethylammonium head that is hydrophilic and two hydrophobic 18-carbon alkyl chains forming a tail resembling the lipid bilayer structure of cell membrane. Since DDA liposomes are unstable it is coupled with glycolipids like f trehalose 6,6V-dimycolate (TDM) derived from the cell wall of Mycobacteria or its analog trehalose 6,6V-dibehenate (TDB) [13]. Tuberculosis antigen coupled with DDA-TBM complex shows good CMI and humoral immune response.

TLR recognizes MTB antigens and paves way to Th1 immune response. The TLR9 recognizes unmethylated CpG motifs in bacterial DNA and induces dendritic cells (DCs) to produce IL-12 for effective Th1 responses [14]. The IC31 as a TLR inducing adjuvant has a Mixture of CpG motifs (CpG-ODNs) and positively charged synthetic peptide synthetic positively charged antimicrobial peptide KLKL5KLK gives significant protection by both CMI and humoral response [15]. TLR 2 ligand Lipokel conjugated with TB antigens showed increased dendritic cell activation and increased CD4+ and CD8+ population with significant IgG response [9].

An iron binding glyco protein lactoferrin has a potential of immunomodulatory effects by increasing the maturation of T and B lymphocytes for producing antigenic specific T cells [16]. Hence, this Lactoferrin is used as an adjuvant for TB. The protective immune response was found against TB when admixed BCG with Lactoferrin.

Dextran is a linear glucose molecule rich in α-1,6-linked units. It has been used as adjuvants because it has many features of sharing specific receptors with many pathogens. The dextron recognizing receptors are intracellular adhesion molecules and mannose receptors in dendritic cells which helps to uptake and process the pathogens effectively by antigen processing and presentation [17]. Dextran promotes the function of phagosomal-lysosomal fusion in macrophages and increases the death rate of the TB pathogen while it is administered along with Isoniazid. The upregulation of NADPH oxidase 2 after recognizing dextran by APCs also promotes the antimicrobial potential [18]. GamTBVac is a subunit vaccine containing fusion proteins along with dextran and CpG motifs as adjuvant.

Natural polymers stimulate immune cells including macrophages and T and B lymphocytes, and also it has the ability to modulate cytokine and chemokine factors. AD VAX is a delta inulin-based compound which induces cellular immune response against MTB [19]. The usage of $Advax^{CpG}$ significantly increases the triple-positive IFN-γ, IL-2, TNF cells and enhances chemotaxis of immune cells [20]. A formulation of Advax, CysVac2 comprising the fusion MTB antigens Ag85B (Rv1886c) and CysD (Rv1285) has shown significant protection in animal studies, and it was reported that it generates multifunctional CD4+ T cell (IFN-γ, TNF, IL-2) subsets [21, 22].

1.3.2 Oil Emulsion Adjuvants

MF59 is a squalene oil-based oil-in-water emulsion designed to be both safe and effective. Unlike Freund's adjuvants, Squalene exists in the pure form and can be easily metabolized. Fluad™ (Seqirus, Melbourne, Australia) recently licensed MF59 as a significant component of flu vaccination for the elderly, and it was later effectively utilized in infants and children. It was approved as a pandemic vaccination against H1N1 in children and pregnant women. MF59 adjuvant trivalent inactivated influenza vaccine (TIV) when administered with MF59 adjuvant elicited both humoral and cellular immune response in infants when compared with non-adjuvanted groups [23]. MF59 induces antigen-presenting cells to secrete the CCL 1–4 chemokines for the recruitment of Leukocytes for enhanced uptake of antigens. These APCs elicit an adaptive immune response in the lymph nodes. AS03 is a squalene, containing a-tocopherol, and polysorbate 80 in oil-in-water emulsion. The addition of a-tocopherol to the AS03 formulation distinguished it from previous oil-in-water emulsion adjuvants. It was first used as an malaria vaccine formulation. AS03 was found to elicit significant immune response in the pediatric population by activating nuclear factor kappa B (NF-kB), proinflammatory cytokine, and chemokines to stimulate immune cells like monocytes and macrophages. It is highly efficient at lower composition, i.e., 3.75 or 7.5 mg per strain, as compared to 15 μg per strain [24].

1.3.3 MPLA and RC-529 Adjuvant

MPL (Corixa) adjuvant is a derivative of lipopolysaccharide with significantly reduced toxicity by retaining the majority of lipopolysaccharide's immunostimulatory effect. MPLA has the property to induce and mature dendritic cells and macrophages expressing CD80, CD86, CD40, and CD83 [25]. MPLA has the ability to induce balanced Th1 and Th2 cytokines elicit the antigen-specific immune response by CTL cells. The MPLA is used as an adjuvant for hepatitis B vaccine formulation. RC-529 is an adjuvant system similar to MPLA, which mediates the immunity by TLR-4 signaling [26]. Rc-529-conjugated vaccine has the potential to induce significant humoral immune response [27, 28].

1.3.4 Virosomes

Virosomes are viral-like structures that provide adjuvant effects without any toxicity and are biodegradable. Structurally, virosomes are microscopic spherical unilamellar lipid membrane vesicles (150 nm) packed with neuraminidase and hemagglutinin viral envelope proteins such as those found in the influenza virus [29]. These virosomes are devoid of nucleocapsid and genetic material unless contaminated. The proteins found in virosomes help its membranes attach to cell receptors, allowing for pH-dependent fusion with immune cells. The virosomes with the adjuvants are capable of delivering their carrying vaccine antigens and elicit an antigen-specific immune response despite harboring a weak immunogenic antigen [30]. Virosomes are virus-like particles and present to both MHC classes I and II to produce CD4+, CD8+, and B cell response. It is defined by either the antigenic epitopes located outside or within the virosome. The well-established PeviPROTM has the potential to induce humoral immune response. PeviTER is a vital virosome that exhibits an enhanced CTL response with elicited CD4+ and CD8+ T cells. Epaxal and Inflexal are well-known virosomes successfully proven against influenza, widely used in many countries [31]. Virosome-based vaccines induce effective immunity and have high safety due to their non-replicative nature [32].

1.3.5 Mucosal Vaccine Adjuvants

Mucosal vaccinations have the potential to elicit strong protection against the pathogen. Mucosal adjuvants stimulate the host's innate immune system and improve in pathogen defense mechanism [33]. The majority of infections occurs by entry of pathogens into the host via intranasal or oral routes. Mucosal-based vaccines have many advantages, such as a lower risk of blood transmission of pathogen low-cost effectiveness. There are very few approved mucosal vaccines available due to their less availability of appropriate adjuvant. Mucosal adjuvants are able to induce immunostimulatory effect and effective delivery vehicle. Chitosan and their derivatives are effective adjuvant system with prolonged immune stimulatory potential and good vaccine carrier system [34, 35] exhibiting successful mucosal vaccination against numerous viral infections [36].

1.3.6 Molecular Adjuvants

Molecular adjuvants are a type of adjuvants in which regulatory immune-modulatory receptor ligands are directly fused to an antigen. Molecular adjuvants can also be defined as a immunostimulatory chemokine or cytokine expressed along with the vaccine epitope for their enhanced availability to the immune cells for effective vaccine potential. Molecular adjuvants are different from traditionally available adjuvants or liposomes and nanoparticles. Mostly, they are plasmid-encoded proteins that perform as adjuvants by directing innate immune receptors or regulating molecular signaling events. Few examples of molecular adjuvants include cytokines, chemokines, pathogen-recognition receptor (PRR) agonists, and immune-targeting genes. Granulocyte-macrophage colony-stimulating factor (GM-CSF) is a growth development factor able to induce cell differentiation, proliferation, and activation of various immune effector functions. GM-CSF also plays a most significant role in humoral and cell-mediated immunity, which makes GM-CSF a successful vaccine adjuvant. Several studies have shown GMCSF as an adjuvant to overcome the poor immunogenicity of antigens in the case of intracellular pathogens and cancer [37, 38] and enhance the activation of DCs. IgGFc is a most effective molecular adjuvant. It is a serum half-life enhancer as coordinated by the neonatal Fc receptor (FcRn). Besides these molecular adjuvants, C3d, a fragment of the complement component C3, functions by boosting the humoral immune response and exerts its adjuvant activity by targeting antigens to the C3d receptor (CD21/35) of B cells and follicular DCs.

1.4 Discussion

Vaccination is one of the most effective strategies of disease prevention. Continuous efforts have been put forward in the development of vaccine to increase its efficacy. Adjuvants are one such measure that are incorporated in the vaccine formulation to improve antigen transport and presentation for long-lasting protection, especially in the non-conventional modern era vaccines. Though inactive and live attenuated vaccines are frequently used, polysaccharide-toxoid conjugated vaccines and subunit vaccines are also important in the elimination of various infectious disease. A well-balanced Th1 and Th17 immune response is required to achieve protection against many infectious diseases like tuberculosis; this could be accomplished by TLR signaling. The development of new vaccine candidates and adjuvant formulations is required due to the rise of new infectious diseases, reemerging infectious diseases, and multi drug-resistant infections such as *Mycobacterium tuberculosis* and *Staphylococcus*.

References

1. Raghupathi V, Ren J, Raghupathi W. Studying public perception about vaccination: a sentiment analysis of tweets. Int J Environ Res Public Health. 2020;17(10):3464.
2. Ramon G. Floculation dans un élange neutre de toxin-antitoxine diphtériques. CR Soc Biol. 1922;86:6.
3. Guy B. The perfect mix: recent progress in adjuvant research. Nat Rev Microbiol. 2007;5(7):396–7.
4. Fraser CK, Diener KR, Brown MP, Hayball JD. Improving vaccines by incorporating immunological coadjuvants. Expert Rev Vaccines. 2007;6(4):559–78.
5. Glenny AT. The antigenic value of toxoid precipitated by potassium alum. J Pathol Bacteriol. 1926;29:38–40.
6. Dupuis M, McDonald DM, Ott G. Distribution of adjuvant MF59 and antigen gD2 after intramuscular injection in mice. Vaccine. 1999;18(5-6):434–9.
7. Stewart E, Triccas JA, Petrovsky N. Adjuvant strategies for more effective tuberculosis vaccine immunity. Microorganisms. 2019;7(8):255.
8. Alving CR, Beck Z, Matyas GR, Rao M. Liposomal adjuvants for human vaccines. Expert Opin Drug Deliv. 2016;13(6):807–16.
9. Xiong F, Mi Z, Gu N. Cationic liposomes as gene delivery system: transfection efficiency and new application. Pharmazie. 2011;66(3):158–64.
10. Christensen D, Agger EM, Andreasen LV, Kirby D, Andersen P, Perrie Y. Liposome-based cationic adjuvant formulations (CAF): past, present, and future. J Liposome Res. 2009;19(1):2–11.
11. Brito LA, O'Hagan DT. Designing and building the next generation of improved vaccine adjuvants. J Control Release. 2014;190:563–79.
12. Khademi F, Taheri RA, Momtazi-Borojeni AA, Farnoosh G, Johnston TP, Sahebkar A. Potential of cationic liposomes as adjuvants/delivery systems for

tuberculosis subunit vaccines. Rev Physiol Biochem Pharmacol. 2018;175:47–69.

13. Davidsen J, Rosenkrands I, Christensen D, Vangala A, Kirby D, Perrie Y, Agger EM, Andersen P. Characterization of cationic liposomes based on dimethyldioctadecylammonium and synthetic cord factor from M. tuberculosis (trehalose 6, 6′-dibehenate)—a novel adjuvant inducing both strong CMI and antibody responses. Biochim Biophys Acta. 2005;1718(1-2):22–31.
14. Tyne AS, Chan JG, Shanahan ER, Atmosukarto I, Chan HK, Britton WJ, West NP. TLR2-targeted secreted proteins from Mycobacterium tuberculosis are protective as powdered pulmonary vaccines. Vaccine. 2013;31(40):4322–9.
15. Schellack C, Prinz K, Egyed A, Fritz JH, Wittmann B, Ginzler M, Swatosch G, Zauner W, Kast C, Akira S, von Gabain A. IC31, a novel adjuvant signaling via TLR9, induces potent cellular and humoral immune responses. Vaccine. 2006;24(26):5461–72.
16. Hwang SA, Welsh KJ, Boyd S, Kruzel ML, Actor JK. Comparing efficacy of BCG/lactoferrin primary vaccination versus booster regimen. Tuberculosis. 2011;91:90–5.
17. van Kooyk Y, Geijtenbeek TB. DC-SIGN: escape mechanism for pathogens. Nat Rev Immunol. 2003;3(9):697–709.
18. Pustylnikov S, Sagar D, Jain P, Khan ZK. Targeting the C-type lectins-mediated host-pathogen interactions with dextran. J Pharm Pharm Sci. 2014;17(3):371.
19. Sun B, Yu S, Zhao D, Guo S, Wang X, Zhao K. Polysaccharides as vaccine adjuvants. Vaccine. 2018;36(35):5226–34.
20. Holten-Andersen L, Doherty TM, Korsholm KS, Andersen P. Combination of the cationic surfactant dimethyl dioctadecyl ammonium bromide and synthetic mycobacterial cord factor as an efficient adjuvant for tuberculosis subunit vaccines. Infect Immun. 2004;72(3):1608–17.
21. Counoupas C, Pinto R, Nagalingam G, Britton WJ, Petrovsky N, Triccas JA. Delta inulin-based adjuvants promote the generation of polyfunctional CD4+ T cell responses and protection against Mycobacterium tuberculosis infection. Sci Rep. 2017;7(1):1.
22. Wilkins AL, Kazmin D, Napolitani G, Clutterbuck EA, Pulendran B, Siegrist CA, Pollard AJ. AS03- and MF59-adjuvanted influenza vaccines in children. Front Immunol. 2017;8:1760.
23. Calabro S, Tortoli M, Baudner BC, Pacitto A, Cortese M, O'Hagan DT, De Gregorio E, Seubert A, Wack A. Vaccine adjuvants alum and MF59 induce rapid recruitment of neutrophils and monocytes that participate in antigen transport to draining lymph nodes. Vaccine. 2011;29(9):1812–23.
24. Alving CR, Peachman KK, Matyas GR, Rao M, Beck Z. Army liposome formulation (ALF) family of vaccine adjuvants. Expert Rev Vaccines. 2020;19(3):279–92.
25. Ismaili J, Rennesson J, Aksoy E, Vekemans J, Vincart B, Amraoui Z, Van Laethem F, Goldman M, Dubois PM. Monophosphoryl lipid A activates both human dendritic cells and T cells. J Immunol. 2002;168(2):926–32.
26. Evans JT, Cluff CW, Johnson DA, Lacy MJ, Persing DH, Baldridge JR. Enhancement of antigen-specific immunity via the TLR4 ligands MPL™ adjuvant and Ribi. 529. Expert Rev Vaccines. 2003;2(2):219–29.
27. Baldridge JR, McGowan P, Evans JT, Cluff C, Mossman S, Johnson D, Persing D. Taking a toll on human disease: toll-like receptor 4 agonists as vaccine adjuvants and monotherapeutic agents. Expert Opin Biol Ther. 2004;4(7):1129–38.
28. Cryz SJ, Que JU, Glück R. A virosome vaccine antigen delivery system does not stimulate an antiphospholipid antibody response in humans. Vaccine. 1996;14(14):1381–3.
29. Mischler R, Metcalfe IC. Inflexal® V a trivalent virosome subunit influenza vaccine: production. Vaccine. 2002;20:B17–23.
30. Alconcel SN, Baas AS, Maynard HD. FDA-approved poly (ethylene glycol)–protein conjugate drugs. Polym Chem. 2011;2(7):1442–8.
31. Saroja CH, Lakshmi PK, Bhaskaran S. Recent trends in vaccine delivery systems: a review. Int J Pharm Invest. 2011;1(2):64.
32. Aoshi T. Modes of action for mucosal vaccine adjuvants. Viral Immunol. 2017;30(6):463–70.
33. Zeng L. Mucosal adjuvants: opportunities and challenges. Hum Vaccin Immunother. 2016;12(9):2456–8.
34. Van der Lubben IM, Verhoef JC, Borchard G, Junginger HE. Chitosan and its derivatives in mucosal drug and vaccine delivery. Eur J Pharm Sci. 2001;14(3):201–7.
35. Lycke N. Recent progress in mucosal vaccine development: potential and limitations. Nat Rev Immunol. 2012;12(8):592–605.
36. Warren TL, Weiner GJ. Uses of granulocyte-macrophage colony-stimulating factor in vaccine development. Curr Opin Hematol. 2000;7(3):168–73.
37. Hartoonian C, Ebtekar M, Soleimanjahi H, Karami A, Mahdavi M, Rastgoo N, Azadmanesh K. Effect of immunological adjuvants: GM-CSF (granulocyte-monocyte colony stimulating factor) and IL-23 (interleukin-23) on immune responses generated against hepatitis C virus core DNA vaccine. Cytokine. 2009;46(1):43–50.
38. Saranya B, Saxena S, Saravanan KM, Shakila H. Comparative analysis of the molecular adjuvants and their binding efficiency with CR1. Interdiscip Sci: Comput Life Sci. 2016;8:35–40.

2 Applications of Optical Spectroscopic Techniques for In Situ Soft Tissue Analysis

Subitcha Jayasankar and Sujatha Narayanan Unni

2.1 Optical Spectroscopy: An Introduction

Observing light-tissue interactions (Fig. 2.1), viz reflection, absorption, scattering, transmission, or dispersion on a scale of involved wavelength range, is referred to as spectroscopy. Based on the energy of electromagnetic radiation, several spectroscopy modes are available, each catering to specific applications in medical diagnostics [1–4]. Examples include X-ray spectroscopy (0.001–1 nm), optical spectroscopy (100 nm to 2 × 10^4 nm), microwave spectroscopy (2 × 10^4 nm to 10^6 nm), and radiofrequency spectroscopy (greater than 10^6 nm).

Based on the active light-tissue interaction type, optical spectroscopy can further be mainly classified as absorption, diffuse reflectance, fluorescence and Raman spectroscopy. The typical wavelength range used for clinical diagnosis is 300–2500 nm, corresponding to the electromagnetic spectrum's ultraviolet (UV), visible and near-infrared regions (NIR). This window of the electromagnetic spectrum is particularly suitable for diagnosis owing to the unique optical properties exhibited by the tissues. Absorption and scattering are the significant interactions between light and tissues; hence the optical property of any tissue is defined by absorption and anisotropy-dependent scattering coefficient corresponding to the incident wavelength. The most common chromophores in the tissue that exhibit significant absorption in the visible and NIR range are given in Table 2.1. Table 2.2 shows the microstructures and their scattering effects for the UV and visible wavelength ranges. Many intrinsic molecules in the tissue are capable of fluorescence, referred to as endogenous fluorophores, as listed in Table 2.3.

Chromophore absorption in tissues is lower in wavelengths ranging from 700 nm to 1300 nm, while it is high in wavelengths below 700 nm. Hence for applications involving blood assessment that contain absorbing chromophores like hemoglobin (Hb), a wavelength below 700 nm will be helpful. On the other hand, scattering is inversely proportional to the fourth power of wavelength; hence scattering is reduced as the wavelength increases. Since decreased scattering will increase light penetration depth, wavelengths longer than 700 nm will benefit depth probing applications; therefore, it is crucial to understand and determine the optical properties of tissue under analysis before deciding on the measurement wavelength, technique, and parameters.

Scattering from the cell structure as a whole is considered Mie scattering, as the cell size is larger than the excitation wavelength (UV and visible). In contrast, Rayleigh scattering arises

S. Jayasankar · S. N. Unni (✉)
Biophotonics Lab, Department of Applied Mechanics and Biomedical Engineering, Indian Institute of Technology Madras, Chennai, India
e-mail: am19d004@smail.iitm.ac.in; nsujatha@iitm.ac.in

K. Parthasarathy, R. Manikkam (eds.), *Translational Research in Biomedical Sciences: Recent Progress and Future Prospects*, https://doi.org/10.1007/978-981-97-1777-4_2

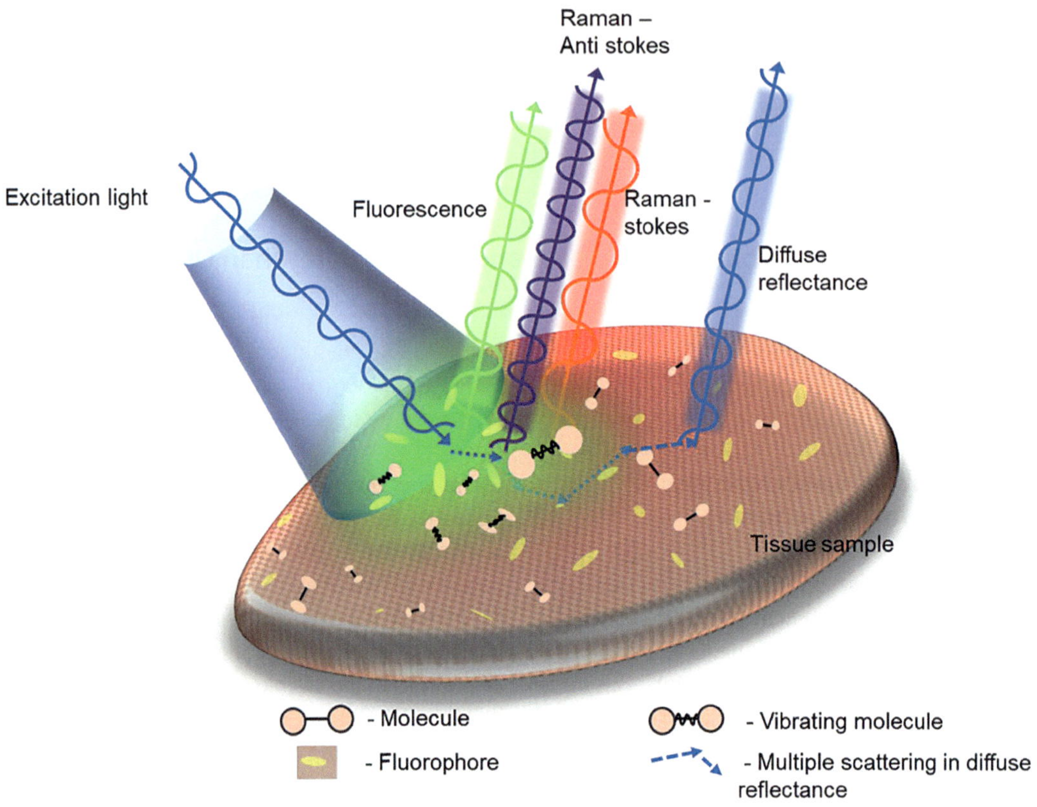

Fig. 2.1 Light-tissue interaction schematic

Table 2.1 Reported chromophores in the human body

Absorbers	Significant absorption wavelength (nm) [5]	Measurement site
Oxygenated hemoglobin	540, 576 [6]	Blood
Deoxygenated hemoglobin	550	Blood
Melanin	<400	Skin
Bilirubin	400–500	Skin, serum
β-Carotene	400–500	Tissues
Water	>900	Whole body
Lipid	762	Tissues

Table 2.2 Microstructures in the tissues and the type of scattering involved for the UV and visible light [5]

Microstructures in tissues	Approximate size (μm)	Scattering type
Cells	10	Mie
Nuclei	1–10	Mie
Mitochondria	1	Mie
Collagen fibrils	0.1	Rayleigh
Membranes	0.01	Rayleigh

Table 2.3 Reported endogenous fluorophores in the human body

Fluorophores [7]	Peak absorption wavelength (nm)	Peak emission wavelength (nm)	Organ site
Flavin adenine dinucleotide (FAD) (oxidized form)	365, 450	550, 510	Cells
Nicotinamide adenine dinucleotide (NADH) (reduced form)	290, 351	440, 460	Cells
Collagen	325, 360	400, 405	Stroma
Elastin	290, 325	340, 400	Dermis
Porphyrins	400 - 450	630, 690	Blood
Tryptophan	280	350	Proteins
Carotene	532	608	Liver and fatty tissue

from the subcellular structures, which are smaller than the wavelength (UV and visible), as shown in Table 2.2. Hence, tissue scattering can be considered a combination of Mie and Rayleigh scattering. In longer wavelengths, the scattering anisotropy (g) remains high, indicating that the scattering is unidirectional with domination from Mie scattering, while the scattering efficiency of the subcellular structures decreases with an increase in wavelength [5]. Though it is a common attribution that lower scattering aids good penetration depth in tissues, the penetration depth cannot be calculated as a strictly measured value due to multiple scattering and other experiment-specific parameters. The distribution of photons in the medium and their depth of origin with application-specific optical and experimental properties can be modeled and studied using analytical/numerical models before deciding on the experimental diagnostic technique for the medium under evaluation [8–10].

2.2 Advantages of Optical Spectroscopy

Optical spectroscopy techniques can provide real-time information on the functional state of the tissues to aid medical diagnosis, such as cancer. This technique is commonly referred to as optical biopsy. They can be used multiple times for measurements without tissue damage, as they predominantly utilize non-ionizing visible and IR wavelengths. Flexibility in tissue probing depth can be achieved by choosing an appropriate wavelength. When integrated with fiber optics, they provide easy tissue sampling from hard-to-access body regions. Moreover, with recent technological advancements in instrumentation and integration with artificial intelligence, they are quick, accurate, and highly sensitive, paving the way for commercialization. Among the several available spectroscopy varieties, diffuse reflectance spectroscopy (DRS), fluorescence spectroscopy (FS), and Raman spectroscopy (RS) are widely researched for their ability to probe unique diagnostic quality and will be discussed in this chapter. Combinations of these spectroscopic techniques are also explored to derive maximum advantage.

2.3 Physics of Optical Spectroscopy

2.3.1 Diffuse Reflectance Spectroscopy

As light is incident on a sample surface, a part of the light undergoes specular reflection from a smooth surface with the same angle as the incident angle. At the same time, diffuse reflection occurs from a rough surface, where the reflection angle is independent of the angle of incidence of the light. Also, in DRS, the broadband light incident on an uneven surface is refracted and undergoes multiple scattering in the sample medium before emerging from the surface. Therefore, analyzing DRS provides insight into the scattering and absorption properties of the medium.

A highly absorbing medium provides a diffuse reflectance spectrum with dips in absorption wavelengths, while a highly scattering medium with less absorption provides a diffuse reflectance spectrum with increased intensity. The size and concentration of particles in the medium influence the diffuse reflectance, which can provide information on the scattering coefficient. At the same time, the intensity of the acquired diffuse reflectance at specific wavelengths yields an insight into the absorption coefficient of the medium. Hence this method is suitable for probing samples with high scattering properties like fatty tissues and unsuitable for tissues with high broadband absorption properties [11, 12]. DRS is instrumental in gaining information on tissue structure and morphology. Larger penetration depth probing can be achieved in this technique by increasing the Source-Detector Separation (SDS).

2.3.2 Fluorescence Spectroscopy

After surface interaction, as light propagates through tissues, the energy of the incident radiation gets absorbed in the media subject to conditions of resonance with the energy band gap of the constituent molecules. Upon absorbing energy, the molecule goes to the higher vibrational level of the excited state. The electron then reaches the lower vibrational level of the excited state spontaneously with non-radiative energy loss. The remaining energy is emitted when the electron reaches the ground state from the lower vibrational level. The emitted light has a longer wavelength than the incident, commonly called Fluorescence, and the shift in wavelength, the Stoke's shift. The Frank Condon principle explains that nuclear vibrations determine the vibrational energy level to which the electron gets excited from the ground state and undergoes relaxation to the lower vibrational level [13].

FS depends on the fluorophore concentration, excitation wavelength, quantum yield, chemical environment, and sample optical properties. An appropriate choice of the fluorescent molecule can provide a contrast that is advantageous in marking and labeling the health state of the tissues, such as cancer or normal. The contrast agents can be exogenous or endogenous [14]. Exogenous contrast agents are mainly tailored to obtain stronger signals from the targeted molecules at a larger depth. Since most exogenous contrast agents emit light in the NIR region, their signal is unaffected by the autofluorescence from the endogenous fluorophores, which emit light in UV and visible wavelength.

2.3.3 Raman Spectroscopy

Along with absorption and emission, light encounters multiple scattering events in the particles while propagating through the tissues. A dominant part of the scattering process is elastic, which means that the scattering process does not involve any energy exchange between the molecule and the light, which translates to scattered light having the same wavelength as the incident light. At the same time, about 1 in 10^6 scattering events are inelastic. In inelastic scattering, an energy exchange occurs between incident light and the molecule, resulting in photons having higher or lower energy than the incident energy. The spectrum from RS shows the measure of the energy difference between the incident and inelastically scattered light, referred to as Raman shift in wavenumbers. This energy shift corresponds to the specific vibrational modes of the molecule, thereby providing a unique fingerprint spectrum for each molecule.

Due to the capability to provide a fingerprint spectrum for the molecules, RS plays a vital role in analyzing the biochemical composition of the tissues. RS demonstrates advantages like high resolution, chemical sensitivity, molecular specificity, non-destructive nature, zero or minimal sample preparation, and non-interference from water compared to other spectroscopy techniques elicited from light propagation in tissues. Raman signals are weak compared to other light-tissue interactions, which significantly hinders using this modality for various applications. The advent of lasers and highly sensitive spectrometers has increased their usage for multiple applications.

Raman spectrum is independent of the excitation wavelength; however, the choice of the excitation wavelength is vital to minimize autofluorescence background and to achieve optimal penetration depth. A shorter excitation wavelength (UV) provides an intense Raman spectrum because of the increased energy, but only surface-level characterization would be achievable. Visible wavelengths provide an optimal penetration depth and Raman spectral intensity, but autofluorescence from tissues significantly hinders using visible wavelengths for RS. NIR wavelengths can provide more significant penetration depth as scattering decreases with the fourth power of wavelength and a reduction in Raman scattered intensity. Interference from autofluorescence is minimal in the NIR region; hence the diminished Raman scattered intensity should suffice to make an analysis.

2.4 Instrumentation

2.4.1 Diffuse Reflectance Spectroscopy

The tissue DRS instrumentation includes a broadband light source such as a halogen or xenon lamp and optical fiber cables to deliver and collect the light. Silicon (Si) Photodiode and Photomultiplier tube can be employed for photon acquisition at a single wavelength, which can be integrated with an in-line bandpass filter or a monochromator [15]. Multi-channel Si CCD detectors can also acquire a spectrum concerning a broad range of wavelengths and are most preferred in portable systems. Single-channel detectors have good sensitivity compared to multi-channel detectors. In contrast, multi-channel detectors yield better resolution in visualizing intensity across several wavelengths, providing access to detailed information over the whole spectrum simultaneously. Higher sensitivity in multi-channel detectors can be acquired using thermoelectrically cooled or nitrogen cooled spectrometers, which, in turn, increases the cost of the spectrometer. The schematic of typical instrumentation required for fiber-optic optical spectroscopy experimentation is shown in Fig. 2.2.

2.4.2 Fluorescence Spectroscopy

The system requires a monochromatic wavelength source achieved by bandpass filtering from the broadband source or an LED/laser source of a particular wavelength. Conventionally, fluorescence is collected at a right angle from the incident light, effectively eliminating the transmitted excitation intensity. This method is more suitable for *ex-vivo* tissue imaging than *in-vivo* measurements. Optical fiber probes are advantageous for reaching inaccessible areas during *in-vivo* measurements. The close arrangement of the illumination and collection fiber cores provides better spatial resolution and efficient fluorescence collection in reflection mode. Since the reflection mode would collect the reflected incident light, optical filters are required for fluorescence collection. Photodiodes or photomultiplier tubes are used for single-channel acquisition. Alternatively, an edge pass or long pass filter with CCD can be utilized for multi-channel acquisition without excitation light interference.

2.4.3 Raman Spectroscopy

The instrumentation for RS is similar to the FS and DRS, with high-power laser and high-performance (sensitivity and resolution) spectrometer requirements. A tuned and sharp bandwidth excitation laser is required to acquire a countable number of Raman photons, which

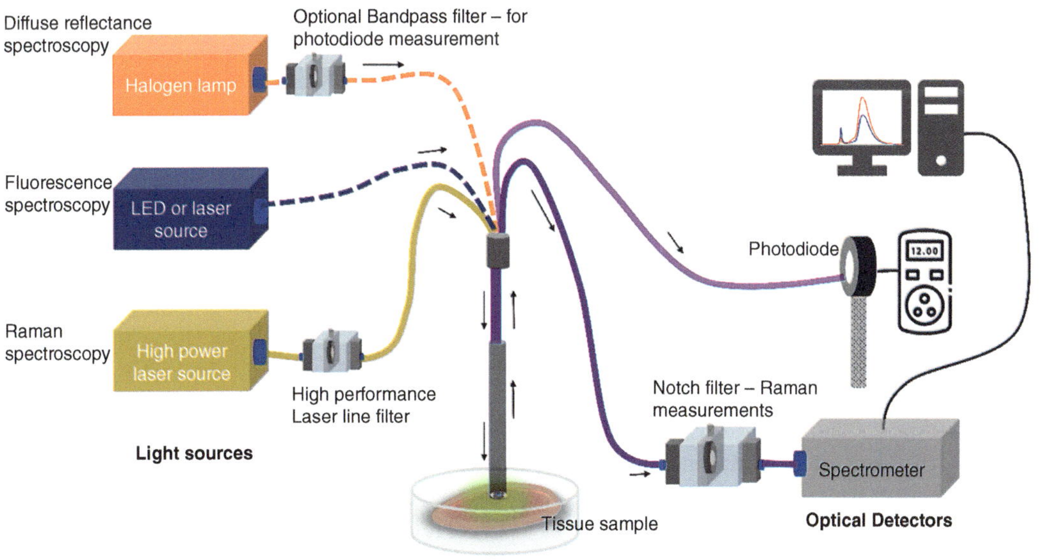

Fig. 2.2 Schematic of optical spectroscopy instrumentation

can be achieved by cleaning the laser line using a bandpass filter. A notch filter or an edge pass filter is necessary in the collection pathway to block the excited light from reaching the spectrometer. A compact and more robust setup can be achieved by incorporating the bandpass and edge pass filters in the fiber probe tip.

Raman spectrum remains unchanged irrespective of the excitation wavelength ranging from UV to NIR, and the choice of an excitation wavelength influences instrumental factors, like the detection limit of the spectrometer. As the excitation wavelength gets longer (>800 nm), the stokes-shifted Raman scattered photons would have a much longer wavelength, making detection difficult for Si-based spectrometers. An extensive range of CCDs used in the spectrometer is made of Si, whose Quantum Efficiency (QE) decreases as the wavelength gets longer than 900 nm. When using longer excitation wavelengths like 1064 nm, detectors made of InGaAs or other alternatives with high QE in the NIR region should be used for good signal acquisition.

2.5 Applications

Each optical spectroscopic technique measures the distinctive underlying principle of light-tissue interaction and can be utilized to gain anatomical and physiological information. Optical spectroscopic methods are widely explored in cancer management and have rapidly evolved as adjunct diagnostic tools for cancer diagnosis. These modalities can also provide quick information concerning physiological changes like oxygen and hemoglobin concentration, glucose estimation, water content analysis, biomarker presence, and anatomical changes like tumor structure, morphology, margin, and location. Exhaustive reviews of optical spectroscopy for cancer diagnosis, organized based on the anatomical sites, can be found here [2, 16]. More recent information focusing only on the point-based optical spectroscopy technique and their technological readiness level for cancer diagnosis are detailed elsewhere in a review, along with their future perspectives [17].

This chapter discusses application-based improvements in optical spectroscopic techniques involving physiological analysis. Recent technical advancements in optical spectroscopy-based cancer diagnosis are discussed with special attention.

2.5.1 Diffuse Reflectance Spectroscopy

2.5.1.1 Assessment of Tissue Hemoglobin and Oxygen

Physiological measurement using DRS represents an *in-vivo* application of optical biopsy techniques. Diffuse reflectance spectral intensity depends on the scattering and absorption properties of the tissues. Hence, DRS can provide insights into physiological parameters such as hemoglobin (Hb) concentration, an indirect measure of underlying microcirculation [18]. The shallow penetration depth of light in the visible region is suitable for collecting the reflectance spectrum from the microvasculature structures beneath the epithelium for Hb estimation. This technique could assess blood perfusion in the brain [19, 20], liver [21], gastric [22], breast [23], and cardiac [24] tissues.

Hb level variation causes a change in oxygen carrying capabilities of the blood, and hence, measurement of tissue oxygenation can also be carried out using DRS [25]. Blood oxygen saturation (SpO_2) is typically measured by processing the relative absorption of light intensity by the reduced and oxygenated hemoglobin (Hb and HbO_2) using a pulse oximeter. While a pulse oximeter can measure arterial blood oxygen saturation, it cannot provide oxygen saturation information on the tissues (StO_2). Measuring StO_2 levels can be used to understand tissue perfusion, classify cancerous lesions, and follow up on cancer treatment effectiveness as they indicate altered oxygenation. The method of DRS has extensively been used for tissue oxygenation (StO_2) measurements from the forearm [25], different regions of the foot [26], and forehead [27]. Calibration for StO_2 measurements is performed by taking the DRS intensity ratio ($I(\text{min})/I(\text{max})$)

at the wavelength where the difference in intensity among the oxygenated and deoxygenated blood samples is minimum to maximum. On validation, StO_2 levels were predicted with an average error as low as 2.29% from the forearm [25].

A significant application of pressure on the tissue by the reflectance probe during spectral measurements can modify the local blood volume, blood oxygenation, perfusion, tissue metabolism, and water content in the probed tissue volume leading to undesired variations in collected reflectance spectrum. Researchers recommend closely monitoring the probe contact pressure to maintain them at optimum calibrated levels during *in-vivo* acquisitions [28, 29]. The effects of the probe pressure are evaluated by intrinsic variations in the tissue's water content and scattering particles to counter its adverse effects during the calibration stage, thereby improving the accuracy of measurements.

2.5.1.2 Cancer Diagnosis

DRS has showcased its vital role in diagnosing cancers from varying etiology. DRS is utilized in analyzing cancers of breast [30–32], head and neck [33], colon [34], liver [12, 35], oral [36], and skin [37, 38]. *In vivo* DRS measurements in this direction pose specific challenges, such as the effect of probe pressure and the nature of tissues. Measurements on extracted tissue are carried out instead as they represent similar anatomical features as their *in-vivo* counterpart. *Ex-vivo* samples portrayed deoxygenation and reduced water content when measured within 5 min of excision [39]. However, to ensure *ex-vivo* data models can be reliably used for *in-vivo* analysis, researchers have analytically (single parameter fit model) extracted the tissue constituents of the *ex-vivo* and *in-vivo* samples from the diffuse reflectance spectrum for a more comprehensive understanding of the changes that occur in the *ex-vivo* samples after harvesting. Statistical analysis of the constituents from the *ex-vivo* and *in-vivo* samples indicates a significant increase in the blood and tissue oxygenation in the *ex-vivo* samples. This counterintuitive effect is explained by the increased blood volume in the capillaries and ambient air exposure with reduced oxygen consumption by the cells. Here, the measurements were taken about 1 hour from the time of excision. The *ex-vivo* samples also demonstrated a reduction in water content in agreement with the previous studies, with no notable change in the scattering parameters and diameter of blood vessels. The variations in blood and oxygenation show that the time between excision to measurement plays a vital role in the reliability of the *ex-vivo* analysis.

The extracted blood %, tissue oxygenation, water, and fat content from the above comparative study are then used to classify the healthy colorectal wall and fat, fat and tumor, and healthy colorectal wall and tumor using a linear Support Vector Machine (SVM). When the *ex-vivo* trained SVM classifier is used for *in-vivo* testing, the results were very similar to that obtained from *in-vivo* training and testing. This shows that *ex-vivo* analysis and algorithm training are reliable for *in-vivo* testing when parameters are carefully chosen based on their significance [40].

Optical spectroscopy techniques widely explore Tumor Margin Analysis (TMA), each having advantages and drawbacks for various types of tissues. However, one common problem in implementing any optical spectroscopy technique for TMA is localizing the region of probe contact to enable easy visualization of tumor margins. To overcome this, researchers have demonstrated an optical probe tracking technique during DRS acquisition in the resected upper gastrointestinal tract samples that provide the coordinates and orientation of the probe using color labels. The edges of the color-labeled DRS probe are detected by thresholding and tracked using the Kalman filter. The workflow of the probe tracking using DRS is shown in Fig. 2.3. The probe position is then annotated on the white light image, and the normal and tumor tissue probability markings are derived by classifying the diffuse reflectance spectrum. This technique has demonstrated a considerable leap in performance, enabling the utilization of the DRS in tumor margin resection applications [41].

In addition to probe positioning, TMA is also complicated by the inhomogeneous nature of the

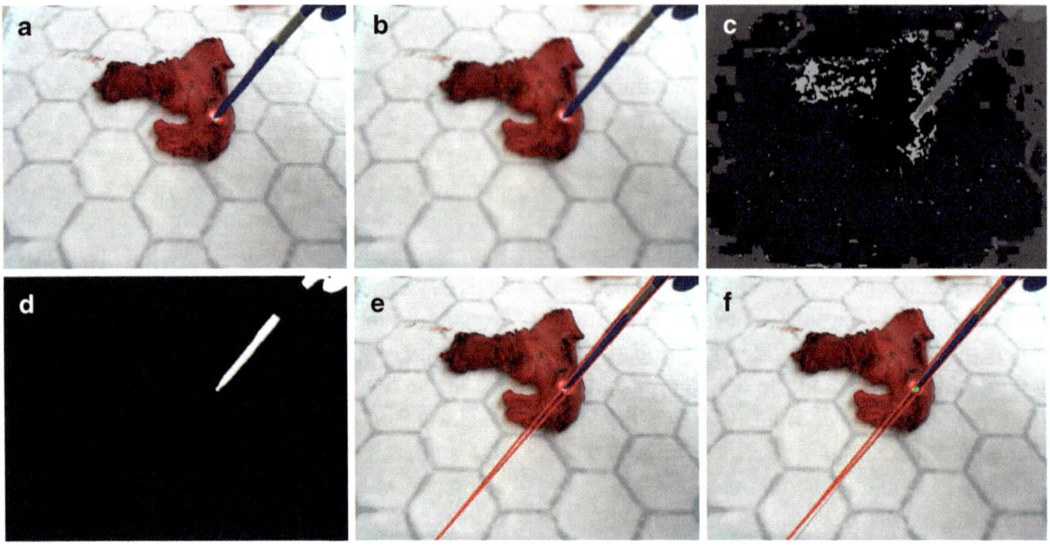

Fig. 2.3 Workflow of DRS probe detection. (**a**) Example of the input video frame. (**b**) The blurred frame. (**c**) Hue channel of the blurred input frame. (**d**) Binary mask result of the HSV segmentation. (**e**) Detected edge lines of the probe. (**f**) Detected tip point of the probe. Reprinted with permissions from Gkouzionis, Ioannis et al., "Real-time tracking of a diffuse reflectance spectroscopy probe used to aid histological validation of margin assessment in upper gastrointestinal cancer resection surgery". Journal of Biomedical Optics 27 (2), 025001 (February 2022). https://doi.org/10.1117/1.JBO.27.2.025001 © SPIE [41]

multi-layered tissue sample. Analysis of such complex tissue structures can be facilitated by identifying the top layer thickness and classifying multiple tissue layers using DRS analysis. The schematic representation of the phantom, its axial view from the CT scan, and the animal tissue used are shown in Fig. 2.4. Using the diffuse reflectance spectrum from multilayer phantoms and animal tissues, the thickness of the fat and muscle top layer is predicted with an accuracy of 0.58 ± 0.55 mm and 0.43 ± 0.42 mm, respectively. Additionally, the tissue type of the top and bottom layer is classified with an accuracy of 0.95 and a Matthews correlation coefficient of 0.90. These results showcase a critical milestone on the road to the independent deployment of DRS for tumor margin analysis in complex tissue environments [42].

Among the several treatment monitoring protocols for cancer, DRS is utilized to assess tissue thermal effects after radiofrequency (RF) ablation. Liver metastasis of colorectal cancer is treated using liver resection or RF ablation [43]. Complete ablation of the tissue is required to ensure thorough tumor removal. DRS acquired from the ablated tissues showed a decreased hemoglobin content and an overall reduction in the reflection due to protein denaturation and methemoglobin formation from Hb. The parameter Optical Ablation Ratio (OAR) (630 nm/675 nm) derived from the DRS increases with thermal damage. This could accurately discriminate the non-ablated and ablated tissue, irrespective of whether the tissue is healthy or a tumor. *In vivo* measurements of the OAR demonstrated a good correlation with the thermal damage in the tissue assessed by NADH staining, which provided real-time information to ensure the complete ablation of the tumor tissue during the surgery.

2.5.2 Fluorescence Spectroscopy

Fluorescence from the human body provides various biochemical, physiological, and anatomical insights. Tissue contains different fluorophores. As seen in Table 2.3, FAD and NADH are the electron-carrying endogenous fluorophores playing an integral part in cellular metabolism. Cellular metabolism abnormality in mitochon-

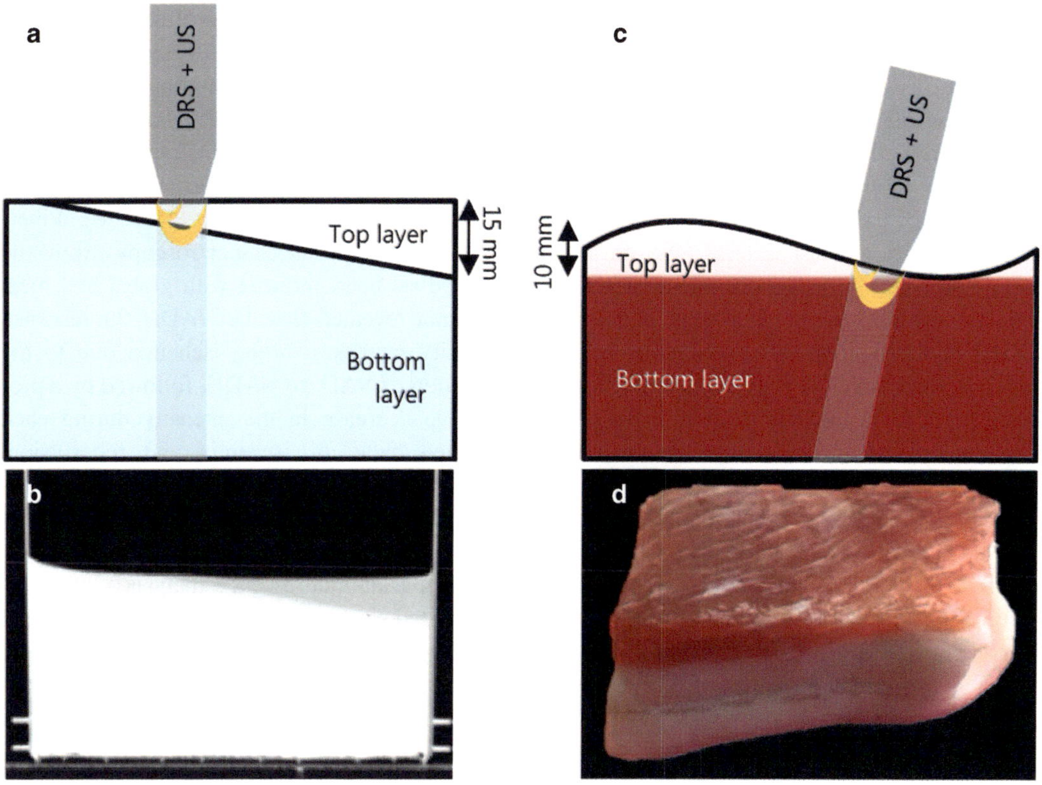

Fig. 2.4 (**a**) Schematic of an artificial phantom with two different homogeneous layers and a gradually increasing top layer thickness; (**b**) CT scan of the phantom in axial view; (**c**) two-layered animal tissue schematic, with varying top layer thickness; (**d**) picture of a piece of animal tissue, with a top layer of muscle tissue and a bottom layer of fat tissue. Figure reprinted from the article by Geldof, F., Dashtbozorg, B., Hendriks, B.H.W. et al., "Layer thickness prediction and tissue classification in two-layered tissue structures using diffuse reflectance spectroscopy". Scientific Reports 12, 1698 (2022) https://doi.org/10.1038/s41598-022-05751-5 published under Creative Commons (https://creativecommons.org/) by Springer Nature. Copyright (c) 2022, The Authors [42]

dria indicates various pathological conditions, including cancer, cardiovascular diseases, diabetes, and neurodegenerative diseases. The reduction-oxidation ratio of cells representing the reduction of NADH and oxidation of FAD, commonly referred to as the Optical Redox Ratio (ORR), is a powerful indicator of metabolic abnormality, differentiation, proliferation, invasion, apoptosis, migration, gene expression, and signaling [44–47], thereby providing directions for various diagnoses [48]. ORR is calculated by taking the ratio of FAD's fluorescence intensity to NADH's fluorescence intensity ($I_{FAD}/(I_{NADH})$). To achieve a statistically normal distribution of values, ORR is also calculated by dividing the fluorescence intensity of FAD or NADH by the sum of the fluorescence intensity of the FAD and NADH ($I_{FAD}/(I_{FAD} + I_{NADH})$). An excitation wavelength of 360 nm can provide fluorescence from both NADH and FAD simultaneously at 450 nm and 530 nm, respectively. In addition to FAD and NADH, fluorescence is also observed from the cellular components, tyrosine, tryptophan, collagen, and elastin, which play a significant role in pathological diagnosis [7].

2.5.2.1 Diabetes Detection

FS provides a comprehensive understanding of hyperglycemia and the development of diabetes mellitus by relating with NADH and Advanced Glycation End products (AGE) fluorescence, as their levels change when the glucose-related metabolism is disturbed. Hyperglycemia causes increased nonenzymatic glycation of proteins, which leads to the formation of AGE, and their collagen glycation is indicated by skin browning. In a study assessing the control and diabetes-induced rats, at 320 nm excitation, the autofluorescence from the blood plasma represented a fluorescence combination from three components, namely, tryptophan (383 nm), fluorescent cross-linking of plasma proteins (438 nm), and NADH (474 nm) [49]. The diabetic group exhibited a twofold elevation in the peak ratio of NADH to the fluorescent cross-linking plasma proteins. Substantial overlap between the fluorescence from AGE and NADH is also observed. This study confirms that fluorescence from AGE is a good indicator of diabetes mellitus.

AGE also induces vascular complications, and it is a more reliable indicator of the long-term effects of diabetes (retinopathy and nephropathy) as it demonstrates glucose exposure over several years compared to HbA_{1C} [50]. Diabetes accompanied by collagen glycation can produce fluorescent AGE and skin browning. Hence skin autofluorescence from AGE can be used as a noninvasive tool for screening diabetes mellitus and prediabetes. About 76% of the skin autofluorescence is contributed by the pentosidine of AGE, while the remaining is contributed by the cellular metabolites FAD and NADH [51]. The fluorescence spectrum acquired from the sequential excitation of skin in the forearm with wavelengths 375, 405, 420, 435, and 460 nm was processed using principal component analysis (PCA) and linear discriminant analysis (LDA). Skin autofluorescence was found to have higher sensitivity of 74.7% compared to the 58% and 63.8% sensitivity from fasting plasma glucose and HbA_{1C} testing [52]. A higher sensitivity of about 75.2% is also reported for abnormal glucose tolerance testing using skin autofluorescence compared to fasting plasma glucose and HbA_{1C} [53]. Good reproducibility is also demonstrated for inter-day and intraday testing of skin autofluorescence measurements [54] despite the fluorescence variations caused by skin color, diet-induced variations in AGE, and renal function, confirming the use of skin autofluorescence as a noninvasive screening and an adjunct tool for corroboration with the standard practice of diagnosis.

2.5.2.2 Assessment of Cardiac Ischemia

Cellular metabolism is also affected by variations in blood perfusion. Hence autofluorescence from the metabolic by-products (FAD and NADH) is also an indicator of the effects of anoxia caused by cardiac ischemia and reperfusion during cardiopulmonary bypass surgery [55, 56]. Fiber-optic autofluorescence spectroscopy from the isolated rat heart induced with global and local ischemia revealed that the NADH fluorescence intensity increases during ischemia due to the reduction of NAD^+ to NADH, followed by a progressive decrease in the intensity during each repeated cycle of ischemia and reperfusion. While in the case of FAD, a reduction in autofluorescence intensity is noted during the cycles of ischemia compared to perfusion [55]. This nondestructive autofluorescence analysis of the myocardial redox state is advantageous for studying myocardial perfusion after revascularization and optimizing the preconditioning protocols in cardiac surgery.

2.5.2.3 Cancer Detection

Owing to its ability to provide higher sensitivity, FS is one of the most widely explored methods for cancer detection and gross intraoperative tumor margin analysis. Similar to DRS, cancers of many etiologies can be diagnosed using varying methods of fluorescence acquisition from tissue sections and bulk tissues [7]. Genetic mutation causes cancer cells to produce energy by glycolysis, unlike normal cells, which utilize the citric acid cycle and oxidative phosphorylation for energy production. This alteration in the energy production cycle, known as the "Warburg effect," leads to abnormal metabolic co-enzymes (FAD and NADH) levels and redox ratio in the tumor cells [57]. Though autofluorescence can arise from any of the endogenous tissue fluorophores listed in Table 2.3 and can be utilized for cancer diagnosis if indicated [58], the Warburg effect forms the basis of the most commonly explored phenomenon for cancer diagnosis using fluorescence.

Thus far, the malignancy diagnostic potential of FS has been evaluated in the skin [59, 60], breast tissues [61, 62], esophagus [63, 64], stomach [65, 66], head and neck [67], oral tissues [68], and lungs [69, 70].

The first report that showcased the autofluorescence spectral profiles from normal and cancerous breast tissues displayed fluorescence emission between 514 nm and 520 nm corresponding to Flavins in the mitochondria. The spectral peak associated with porphyrin is also noticed around 592 nm with an excitation of 488 nm [71, 72]. Subsequent reports showed a classification sensitivity and specificity of 99.6% in discriminating malignant from benign and normal tissues using integrated autofluorescence intensity. The autofluorescence emission is around 390 nm, 430 nm, and 520 nm, corresponding to collagen and elastin, NADH, and Flavins (FAD), respectively, with an excitation wavelength of 337 nm. An enhancement in these fluorophore's concentration increased the cancerous tissue integrated fluorescence intensity at 337 nm excitation [73].

Continued research utilizing the metabolic by-products (FAD and NADH) and the ORR for cancer diagnosis transformed FS as an adjunct optical biopsy technique with conventional histopathological diagnosis. Quantitative extraction of the ORR from the snap-frozen breast tissues using calibration phantoms of FAD and NADH is achieved with a redox scanner. It has been noted that NADH and FAD concentrations in the cancerous breast tissues are about 2.6 and 3.7 times higher than the normal tissues, respectively. These results again confirmed the increased presence of these fluorophores in the cancerous tissues compared to normal tissues [74]. However, NADH and FAD concentration inconsistency is also expected concerning to patient's age, varying cell cultures, and the tumor microenvironment. To achieve *in-vivo* redox imaging and diagnosis, a novel fiber-optic needle redox imager is developed to fit in the 11 G coaxial biopsy needle. The device's performance characteristics are analyzed with phantoms containing synthetic metabolites and *in-vitro* tissues [75]. Commercialization of such hand-held devices will accelerate the usage of FS in intraoperative diagnosis.

The increased presence of the amino acid tryptophan also exhibits the presence of malignancy. Early works on analyzing fluorescence from breast tissues have shown peaks corresponding to tryptophan, and many other fluorophores, though their presence was not confirmed then [76]. Progressive research in these lines has demonstrated tryptophan's relatively increased presence in aggressive cancer cell lines upon a 300 nm excitation [77]. A prominent fluorescence peak corresponding to tryptophan is observed at 340 nm with a small NADH fluorescence peak around 460 nm. Using the fluorescence ratio from tryptophan to NADH, the Support Vector Machine (SVM) could classify the normal cells from cancerous ones with a sensitivity and specificity of 91.4% and 81.3%, respectively. In comparison, the non-aggressive cancer lines were classified from aggressive cell lines with a sensitivity and specificity of 88.9% and 90.9%, respectively. Further studies have correlated the tryptophan content to the histology grade and size of the tumor. A more aggressive and increased tumor size has portrayed an increase in the tryptophan content. These findings will help incorporate the histological grade in the cancer staging and patient prognosis [78]. At 280 nm and 300 nm excitation, fluorescence from NADH around 450 nm is also noted, which is established due to Forster Resonance Energy Transfer (FRET) from Tryptophan.

Recent developments in fluorescence-based diagnosis involve advanced spectral/image processing methods and subsequent classification strategies. A case study of oral cancer can demonstrate this evolvement. Several prototypes and devices capable of eliciting fluorescence in oral tissues are described and available. Studies and clinical trials have been conducted to evaluate such autofluorescence devices' performance in detecting malignant and benign oral tumors. Typically, the excitation light is in 400–460 nm wavelength range to excite the flavoproteins and collagen in the tissues. The absence of autofluorescence from the stromal collagen and FAD indicates malignancy and vice versa. Similar to malignancy, lack of fluorescence is also noticed in benign conditions like oral neoplasia and inflammation. Instruments incorporating tissue fluorescence imaging have demonstrated an overall sensitivity ranging from 33% to 100% across several studies with a specificity range of 12–88.6% [79] in discriminating malignant tissues from the controls.

Visual confirmation of fluorescence from the tissues aids in oral cancer diagnosis compared to white light images during preliminary assessment and diagnosis. A study on patients with premalignant oral lesions compared the diagnostic capability of fluorescence visualization and white light with biopsy. A 100% sensitivity is obtained in detecting malignancies using fluorescence instead of 17% with white light. Biopsy and subsequent analysis gave a higher specificity of 97% compared to 74% by autofluorescence imaging [80]. The sensitivity and specificity analysis of tissue fluorescence in cancer diagnosis is also available elsewhere [81, 82].

To improve the specificity of the diagnosis, quantitative analysis on the tissue autofluorescence images is carried out by extracting the average intensity (mean of RGB and gray channels) and heterogeneity (standard deviation of the image) of the image Region of Interest (ROI) as features for Quadratic Discriminant Analysis (QDA). Utilizing QDA to discriminate the precancerous lesions and oral cancer, a higher sensitivity and specificity of 0.970 and 0.923, respectively, are obtained compared to the previous studies using visual inspection analysis of autofluorescence images. However, the specificity of the diagnosis using QDA reduced from 0.923 to 0.776 when the normal gingiva mucosae and gingiva cancer cases were added to the dataset [83]. On using QDA for multiclass classification of normal, precancerous, and cancerous tongue lesions, an accuracy of 86% is obtained, while 84% is achieved for classifying buccal mucosa [84].

Representative autofluorescence images from patients with varying oral abnormalities and the marked ROI are shown in Fig. 2.5 [85]. The autofluorescence images' average intensity and heterogeneity (standard deviation) are calculated for the ROI selection and processed using QDA. Using the inputs such as NADH image heterogeneities, NADH intensities, FAD heterogeneities, FAD intensities, and redox ratio heterogeneity, the five-dimension QDA classified the cancerous lesions from the normal with a specificity and sensitivity of 0.898 and 0.974, respectively. The same algorithm portrayed a specificity and sensitivity of 0.755 and 0.919 in classifying the precancerous lesions from the normal. Hence, here, NADH-FAD combination fluorescence is used for tissue assessment with comparative sensitivity and specificity to collagen-FAD combination fluorescence commonly visualized in commercial devices [85].

The manual intervention and false positive rates of the diagnosis from the autofluorescence images can be reduced by automated mapping of ROIs for feature extraction. Researchers have utilized Quadtree and Gray Level Concurrence Matrix (GLCM) texture pattern analysis for automatic ROI selection for classifying the normal and abnormal regions in the autofluorescence images. About ten textural features extracted from GLCM are processed using Linear Discriminant Analysis (LDA) for feature selection. The selected features are utilized in K-Nearest Neighbor (KNN) classifier to differentiate the normal and abnormal regions. The highest accuracy of 83 ± 5% and sensitivity of 85 ± 5% is obtained when the first eight selected features are used for classification. The texture analysis method provided a reasonable specificity of about 84 ± 3% without manual intervention in image processing [86].

These methods show that we can rely on different endogenous fluorophores to support cancer diagnosis when processed and interpreted appropriately. While autofluorescence can be effectively utilized for diagnosis, it is challenging to probe them from deeper tissues. Such scenarios require application-specific tailored exogenous fluorophores with high quantum yield. Autofluorescence from the surrounding is considered an interference in such cases, and they can be removed in the processing stages. Although fluorescence provides good sensitivity in detecting cancers and lesions, it cannot be utilized as the standalone technique for cancer diag-

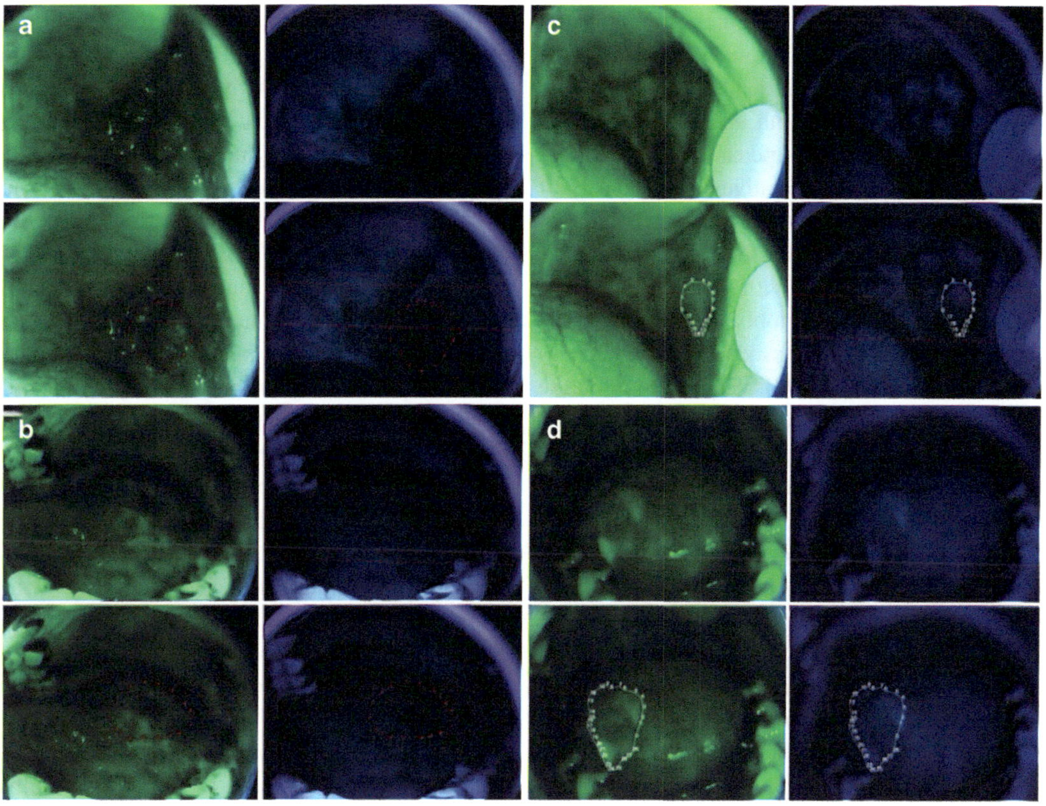

Fig. 2.5 Autofluorescence images. In each image quadrant, the upper left corresponds to 525 nm, the upper right corresponds to 479 nm, lower shows the ROI. (**a**) Buccal mucosa cancer, (**b**) tongue cancer, (**c**) buccal mucosa squamous hyperplasia, and (**d**) tongue squamous hyperplasia. Adapted from the article Tze-Ta Huang, et al., "Two-channel autofluorescence analysis for oral-cancer". Journal of Biomedical Optics 24 (5) 051402 (November 2018) DOI: https://doi.org/10.1117/1.JBO.24.5.051402 published under Creative Commons (https://creativecommons.org/) © SPIE [85]

nosis owing to limitations in specificity, even with considerable research carried out so far. But they rapidly evolve as a quick, noninvasive, preliminary adjunct diagnostic tool.

2.5.3 Raman Spectroscopy

Applications of RS in physiological measurements include blood glucose measurement, inflammatory response detection (C-reactive protein levels) [87], asthma detection [88], and malaria marker (hemoglobin and hemozoin) identification [89, 90], owing to its ability to probe the molecular fingerprint of the sample [91]. The pathophysiology of cancer development is also dealt with in detail using RS and will be discussed in the following section.

2.5.3.1 Blood Glucose Detection

Blood glucose level is one of the major physiological parameters measured using biochemical tests or glucometer strips with the sampled blood. Frequent blood sampling creates discomfort and increases the infection risk for patients who require continuous monitoring of blood glucose levels. Optical spectroscopic techniques offer noninvasive transcutaneous monitoring of blood glucose levels; however, they lack specificity and are overwhelmed by other tissue-interfering signals. RS provides excellent molecular specificity, thus making them a preferred and better optical spectroscopic technique for glucose monitoring. Researchers have demonstrated that the *in-vivo* NIR Raman spectrum measured from the blood vessel of the mice ear with an excitation wavelength of 785 nm shows peaks concerning glucose at 1125 cm^{-1}. The relative peak intensity of glucose (1125 cm^{-1}) normalized to hemoglobin peak (1549 cm^{-1}) correlates linearly with *in-vivo* glucose concentrations with a Mean Absolute error of 5.7%. As hemoglobin levels do not vary rapidly in blood, they are used as an internal standard for normalization [92]. While blood glucose levels can be measured using Raman peak intensity, challenges like interpatient variability due to unaccounted physiological activity and instrument response variations arise when the blood glucose levels in multiple subjects must be measured at different time points. To avoid direct dependency of glucose measurements on Raman peak intensity, in a glucose clamping study of dogs, researchers have utilized similarity between the *in-vivo* measured spectrum and the Raman spectrum of the known glucose solution using Partial Least Squares Regression without directly recognizing the Raman peak of glucose [93].

Additionally, optical spectroscopy measures glucose levels from the interstitial fluid. It can produce false results due to the physiological lag in glucose levels between the blood and the interstitial fluid (ISF). Owing to the factors mentioned above and several other physiological parameters, the chance correlation of the spectral data can give rise to a false prospective prediction of glucose concentrations. In vitro and *in-vivo* investigations of the Raman spectrum by assigning spurious glucose concentrations for the calibration model show that RS provides better robustness in prospective glucose predictions than NIR absorption spectroscopy, despite the chance correlations in the calibration model. However, the probability of chance correlation remains due to instrument drift and other physiological variations that can provide false predictions of glucose levels [94]. To overcome this, it has been recommended to use a double glucose tolerance study in the calibration to reduce the time-related correlations leading to false predictions.

The glucose level predictions using RS are carried out using the spectral information from the ISF of the tissues or by directly focusing on the blood vessels. So, the question arises on the possibility of making glucose predictions from the Raman spectrum acquired from the skin. Raman spectra obtained at 20 min intervals from the swine ear with two different glucose levels are subtracted to extract the glucose Raman peaks and remove the tissue Raman peaks. This showed that the glucose Raman spectrum can be extracted from the skin. The extracted glucose peaks maintained a linear relationship with the glucose concentration with an R-value of 0.95, demonstrating good prediction probability. To avoid using the spectrum at two different time points for subtraction, researchers have shown the usage of the band area ratio parameter, where the ratio of the area under the glucose peak (1125 cm^{-1}) to the area under the collagen peak (1450 cm^{-1}) is used as the variable for regression analysis with the prospective prediction R-value of 0.94. This approach is also extended to multiple peaks, where the R-value improved to 0.96 using multivariate linear regression analysis. The good level of prospective prediction from the direct observation of fingerprint peaks is mainly enabled using oblique excitation and multi-fiber collection geometry instrumentation [95].

2.5.3.2 Cancer Detection and Localization

The uniqueness of the vibrational spectrum has contributed to the widespread utilization of RS for cancer diagnosis of any etiology [91, 96]. RS provides high chemical specificity, thereby characterizing the biochemical progression of the disease, tumor grading, and even classification of benign and malignant forms of the tumor using the sample composition. Several modalities of RS are introduced, including Surface Enhanced Raman Spectroscopy, Transmission Raman Spectroscopy, Spatially Offset Raman Spectroscopy, and Stimulated Raman Spectroscopy to overcome the problem of weak Raman scattering. A comprehensive review of the varying modalities of RS and their application-specific advantages in oncology is given in the literature [97]. This section will cover the recent advancements and progression in conventional and Spatially Offset Raman Spectroscopy techniques that enable label-free RS breast cancer detection and management.

While preliminary breast cancer diagnosis and location can be identified using palpations and mammography, these techniques cannot distinguish between benign and malignant tumors. They also portray limitations in diagnosing dense breasts. They are unsuitable for intraoperative scenarios where a quick and sensitive diagnosis is expected. Among the optical spectroscopy techniques mentioned in this chapter, RS can be used as an adjunct tool for cancer detection using optical core needle biopsy owing to its high specificity. The *ex-vivo* studies [98, 99] for understanding the composition of the benign and cancerous breast tissues have led to the translation of the Raman spectroscopic technology to *in-vivo* studies during partial mastectomy, which demonstrated its potential for intraoperative tumor resection with an overall accuracy of 93.3% compared to pathological diagnosis [100]. The feasibility of breast cancer detection in animal models is also demonstrated with a continuous decrease in peak intensity of 1446 cm^{-1} in the tumor region compared to the normal region [101].

While RS is demonstrated to perform breast cancer diagnosis *ex-vivo* and *in-vivo*, the practicality of such techniques in intraoperative scenarios with time and cost limitations, assembly effort, and the technical expertise required for operation is a challenge to address. This problem is addressed using affordable, easy-to-use, portable, hand-held Raman spectrometers designed for multidisciplinary analysis. Researchers utilized commercial Raman spectrometers with a hand-held probe to show the possibility of rapid classification of invasive ductal carcinoma from normal tissues with an accuracy and specificity of 88% and 86%, respectively [102].

Small hand-held probes are quick and easy to handle, but they have the problem of missing residual tumors as it is operator dependent. Considering label-free techniques, selective sampling is another method to reduce the time consumption for large specimen TMA using RS. Selective sampling involves using a quick adjunct wide-field spectroscopic technique (like autofluorescence) with high sensitivity to rule out normal tissue regions (adipose tissues) and then prioritizing only suspicious regions for RS sampling, thereby scanning a larger area and improving the accuracy and specificity of the analysis in reduced time.

A 68-fold decrease in the number of Raman spectra required for histopathological mapping of 2×2 mm^2 tissue region is achieved using wide-field autofluorescence imaging and unsupervised clustering for selective sampling. This reduced the total spectral mapping time to 20 min while achieving high specificity in an intraoperative diagnostic time frame [103]. Though wide-field autofluorescence image segmentation effectively reduced the scanning time, it portrays poor specificity and leads to inefficient region selection for Raman spectral sampling. To improve the specificity of the region selection, wide-field High Wavenumber (HW) Raman spectral acquisition capturing the lipid bands at 2800 cm^{-1} to 3100 cm^{-1} is used for segmenting the adipose and non-adipose tissues as the adipose tissues portray a lesser probability of bearing a tumor. The high wavenumber Raman imaging, with the corresponding histopathological image, and segmented images with different thresholds for selective sampling are shown in Fig. 2.6. The non-adipose tissues are mapped using fingerprint RS for final diagnostic classification. An optimal wavelength excitation of 671 nm capable of providing a good Raman spectrum with minimal fluorescence interference in the fingerprint and high wavenumber region is chosen for initial mapping. However, the results concluded that 671 nm for high wavenumber mapping and 785 nm for fingerprint RS would be ideal to avoid autofluorescence interference for best results. Using the high wavenumber and fingerprint RS for selective sampling, the entire analysis is completed within 20–25 min, and it has been proposed that the analysis time can be reduced to as low as 10 min by optimizing the acquisition parameters and replacing the CCD with a single element detector [104].

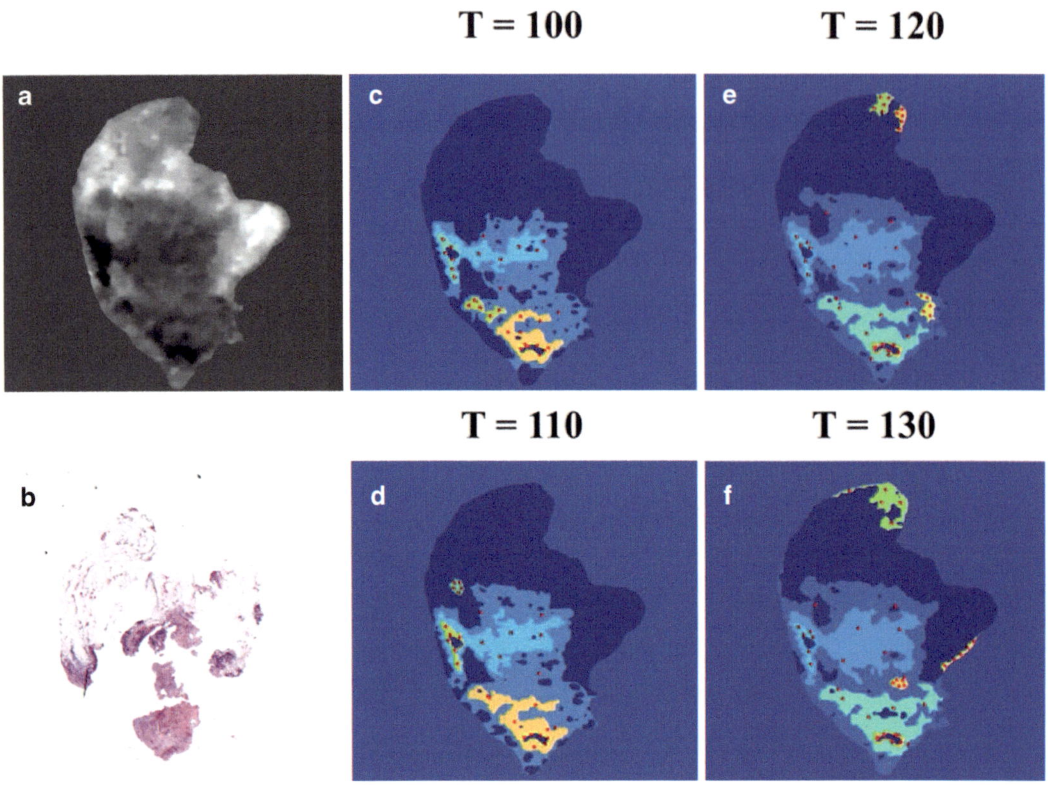

Fig. 2.6 Segmentation of HW-Raman imaging breast tumor tissue for selective sampling fingerprint RS. (**a**) HW-Raman image of size 2 × 2 cm^2; (**b**) H&E stained histopathological image; (**c–f**) segmented HW-Raman image with different intensity thresholds from 100 to 130. Figure adapted from Ioan Notingher, Emad Rakha, Hazem Khout, et al., Feasibility of integrated high wavenumber Raman imaging and fingerprint Raman spectroscopy for fast margin assessment in breast cancer surgery, Journal of Raman Spectroscopy, 51: 1986–1995 (2020) published under Creative Commons (https://creativecommons.org/). © The Authors. Journal of Raman Spectroscopy published by John Wiley & Sons Ltd [104]

Over the years, several works have been carried out to improve the classification accuracy of breast tumors using RS. Raman spectrum is loaded with extensive information, and it can be exploited to the fullest extent for cancer subtype classification using machine learning and deep learning techniques. Raman spectroscopic data of frozen breast tissue sections combined with a Convolutional Neural Network (CNN) deep learning model classified the normal tissue from breast tumors with an accuracy of 90%. The Raman spectral peaks that contribute significantly to the deep learning model are identified using permutation importance as 1002 cm^{-1}, 869 cm^{-1}, and 1309 cm^{-1}. Figure 2.7 shows the RGB mapping formed with the identified spectral peaks, which allows clear discrimination between normal, connective, and tumor tissue types and good correlation with Hematoxylin and Eosin-stained tissue slides demonstrating promising applicability in tumor margin analysis [105]. A similar study using a one-dimensional CNN on RS data from frozen tissues portrayed an overall classification accuracy of 92% and specificity of 86%, showcasing the potential of automated breast cancer diagnosis and tumor margin analysis using RS [106].

The depth of the spectral acquisition is also an essential parameter in TMA, especially in bulk tissue spectral acquisition, as the tumor regions are located below a normal tissue margin of about 1 or 2 mm in the excised tumor. Increasing the

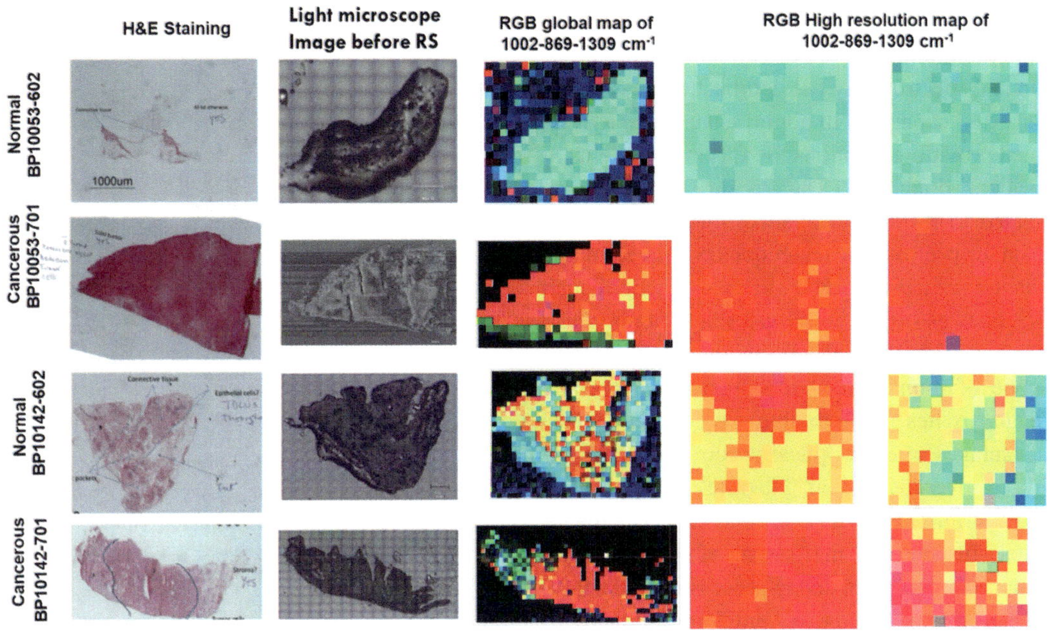

Fig. 2.7 Raman images of normal and cancerous tissues of breast. First panel shows the histopathological examination and the second panel shows the light microscope images before spectral acquisition. The RGB map of the selected Raman peaks (1002–869–1309 cm^{-1}) is shown in the third panel with red color indicating cancerous tissues, and the green and yellow colors indicating fatty and connective tissues, respectively. The high resolution RGB maps of the selected regions within the section are shown in the fourth and fifth panels. "Reprinted from Prostaglandins and Other Lipid Mediators, Vol. 151, S. Kiran Koya et al., Accurate identification of breast cancer margins in microenvironments of *ex-vivo* basal and luminal breast cancer tissues using Raman spectroscopy, 106475, Copyright (2020), with permission from Elsevier" [105]

separation between the source and detector in RS, commonly referred to as Spatially Offset Raman Spectroscopy (SORS), enables signal collection from deeper layers of the tissues. Using transfer learning-based CNN, accurate simultaneous predictions of the depth and thickness of the tumor with a respective Root Mean Square Error of 4.40% and 8.42% are also demonstrated by processing the Monte Carlo simulation results of Spatially Offset Raman scattering [107]. Attempts were also made to predict the size of the subsurface tumor from Monte Carlo simulations using Machine learning techniques with an RMSE lesser than 2% [108]. Fiber-optic probes incorporating Source-Detector Separation are designed to optimize the Signal to Noise Ratio (SNR) and the tumor signal collection from the deeper layers using Monte Carlo simulation and modeling.

Using the fiber-optic probes designed with Monte Carlo simulations to probe the tumor tissues located at a maximum of 2 mm depth from the surface, a 100% specificity and 95% sensitivity in identifying the margin status (positive or negative) are demonstrated [109]. The feasibility of utilizing these SORS probes for multidimensional scanning and margin status mapping in bulk excised tissue within the intraoperative timeframe is also evaluated by integrating the probe with a robotic scanner. Using the robotic scanner, samples as wide as 3–6 cm are probed to a depth of about 2 mm and reconstructed automatically within 7–15 min. On processing the averaged Raman spectra from the SORS fiber-optic probe using Sparse Multinomial Logistic regression, a 93% sensitivity and 85% specificity are obtained in classifying the fibroadenoma from fatty tissues [110].

2.6 Conclusion

Optical spectroscopy has demonstrated its versatility and capability in noninvasive tissue assessment providing solutions for varying problems in medical diagnosis. The recent advancements related to diffuse reflectance, fluorescence, and Raman spectroscopy techniques portrayed in this chapter are a testament to the evolvement of such practices as highly sensitive, quick, noninvasive adjunct clinical diagnostic methods. The future scope of improvement in optical spectroscopic diagnosis lies in combining the complementary advantages of each optical spectroscopy modality to overcome their inherent drawbacks to achieve improved diagnosis and cancer management. In addition, the advent of deep learning techniques in spectroscopy processing and analysis has demonstrated excellent diagnostic performance while opening up a new world of possibilities for improved medical diagnosis.

References

1. Kendall C, Isabelle M, Bazant-Hegemark F, et al. Vibrational spectroscopy: a clinical tool for cancer diagnostics. Analyst. 2009;134:1029–45.
2. Liu Q. Role of optical spectroscopy using endogenous contrasts in clinical cancer diagnosis. World J Clin Oncol. 2011;2:50. https://doi.org/10.5306/wjco.v2.i1.50.
3. Parrott EPJ, Sun Y, Pickwell-Macpherson E. Terahertz spectroscopy: its future role in medical diagnoses. J Mol Struct. 2011;1006:66–76. https://doi.org/10.1016/j.molstruc.2011.05.048.
4. Sahu RK, Mordechai S. Spectroscopic techniques in medicine: the future of diagnostics. Appl Spectrosc Rev. 2016;51:484–99. https://doi.org/10.1080/05704928.2016.1157809.
5. Jacques SL. Optical properties of biological tissues: a review. Phys Med Biol. 2013;58:37–61. https://doi.org/10.1088/0031-9155/58/11/R37.
6. Liu P, Zhu Z, Zeng C, Nie G. Specific absorption spectra of hemoglobin at different PO_2 levels: potential noninvasive method to detect PO_2 in tissues. J Biomed Opt. 2012;12:125002. https://doi.org/10.1117/1.JBO.17.12.125002.
7. Ramanujam N. Fluorescence spectroscopy of neoplastic and non-neoplastic tissues. Neoplasia. 2000;2:89–117. https://doi.org/10.1038/sj.neo.7900077.
8. Ash C, Dubec M, Donne K, Bashford T. Effect of wavelength and beam width on penetration in light-tissue interaction using computational methods. Lasers Med Sci. 2017;32:1909–18. https://doi.org/10.1007/s10103-017-2317-4.
9. Finlayson L, Barnard IRM, McMillan L, et al. Depth penetration of light into skin as a function of wavelength from 200 to 1000 nm. Photochem Photobiol. 2022;98:974–81. https://doi.org/10.1111/php.13550.
10. Li T, Xue C, Wang P, et al. Photon penetration depth in human brain for light stimulation and treatment: a realistic Monte Carlo simulation study. J Innov Opt Health Sci. 2017;10:5. https://doi.org/10.1142/S1793545817430027.
11. Hernández SE, Rodríguez VD, Pérez J, et al. Diffuse reflectance spectroscopy characterization of hemoglobin and intralipid solutions: in vitro measurements with continuous variation of absorption and scattering. J Biomed Opt. 2009;14:034026. https://doi.org/10.1117/1.3149864.
12. Reistad N, Nilsson J, Vilhelmsson Timmermand O, et al. Diffuse reflectance spectroscopy of liver tissue. In: Biophotonics South America. New York: SPIE; 2015. p. 95314E.
13. Mulliken RS. Role of kinetic energy in the Franck-Condon principle. J Chem Phys. 1971;55:309–14. https://doi.org/10.1063/1.1675522.
14. Pierce MC, Javier DJ, Richards-Kortum R. Optical contrast agents and imaging systems for detection and diagnosis of cancer. Int J Cancer. 2008;123:1979–90.
15. Yu B, Lo JY, Kuech TF, et al. Cost-effective diffuse reflectance spectroscopy device for quantifying tissue absorption and scattering in vivo. J Biomed Opt. 2008;13:060505. https://doi.org/10.1117/1.3041500.
16. Evers DJ, Hendriks BHW, Lucassen GW, Ruers TJM. Optical spectroscopy: current advances and future applications in cancer diagnostics and therapy. Future Oncol. 2012;8:307–20.
17. Kim JA, Wales DJ, Yang G-Z. Optical spectroscopy for in vivo medical diagnosis—a review of the state of the art and future perspectives. Prog Biomed Eng. 2020;2:042001. https://doi.org/10.1088/2516-1091/abaaa3.
18. Bender JE, Shang AB, Moretti EW, et al. Noninvasive monitoring of tissue hemoglobin using UV-VIS diffuse reflectance spectroscopy: a pilot study. Opt Express. 2009;17:23396. https://doi.org/10.1364/oe.17.023396.
19. Liebert A, Wabnitz H, Steinbrink J, et al. Bed-side assessment of cerebral perfusion in stroke patients based on optical monitoring of a dye bolus by time-resolved diffuse reflectance. NeuroImage. 2005;24:426–35. https://doi.org/10.1016/j.neuroimage.2004.08.046.
20. Rejmstad P, Johansson JD, Haj-Hosseini N, Wårdell K. A method for monitoring of oxygen saturation changes in brain tissue using diffuse reflectance spectroscopy. J Biophotonics. 2017;10:446–55. https://doi.org/10.1002/jbio.201500334.
21. Voulgarelis S, Fathi F, Stucke AG, et al. Evaluation of visible diffuse reflectance spectroscopy in liver tissue: validation of tissue saturations using extracor-

poreal circulation. J Biomed Opt. 2021;26:055002. https://doi.org/10.1117/1.jbo.26.5.055002.
22. Gareau D, Hunter J, Jacques S. Monitoring of tissue perfusion during esophagectomies with optical fiber probe spectroscopy. In: Advanced biomedical and clinical diagnostic systems VIII. New York: SPIE; 2010. p. 75551.
23. Brown JQ, Wilke LG, Geradts J, et al. Quantitative optical spectroscopy: a robust tool for direct measurement of breast cancer vascular oxygenation and total hemoglobin content in vivo. Cancer Res. 2009;69:2919–26. https://doi.org/10.1158/0008-5472.CAN-08-3370.
24. Häggblad E, Lindbergh T, Karlsson MGD, et al. Myocardial tissue oxygenation estimated with calibrated diffuse reflectance spectroscopy during coronary artery bypass grafting. J Biomed Opt. 2008;13:054030. https://doi.org/10.1117/1.2976433.
25. Sircan-Kucuksayan A, Uyuklu M, Canpolat M. Diffuse reflectance spectroscopy for the measurement of tissue oxygen saturation. Physiol Meas. 2015;36:2461–9. https://doi.org/10.1088/0967-3334/36/12/2461.
26. Anand S, Sujatha N, Narayanamurthy VB, et al. Diffuse reflectance spectroscopy for monitoring diabetic foot ulcer - a pilot study. Opt Lasers Eng. 2014;53:1–5. https://doi.org/10.1016/j.optlaseng.2013.07.020.
27. Quaresima V, Sacco S, Totaro R, Ferrari M. Noninvasive measurement of cerebral hemoglobin oxygen saturation using two near infrared spectroscopy approaches. J Biomed Opt. 2000;5(2):201–5.
28. Anand S, Sujatha N. Effects of probe placement on tissue oxygenation levels during reflectance measurements for different types of tissues in a clinical setting. In: 2015 International conference on biophotonics, BioPhotonics 2015. Piscataway: Institute of Electrical and Electronics Engineers Inc.; 2015.
29. Li C, Jiang J, Xu K. The variations of water in human tissue under certain compression: studied with diffuse reflectance spectroscopy. J Innov Opt Health Sci. 2013;6:1330002.
30. De Boer LL, Bydlon TM, Van Duijnhoven F, et al. Towards the use of diffuse reflectance spectroscopy for real-time in vivo detection of breast cancer during surgery. J Transl Med. 2018;16:367. https://doi.org/10.1186/s12967-018-1747-5.
31. Evers DJ, Nachabe R, Vranken Peeters MJ, et al. Diffuse reflectance spectroscopy: towards clinical application in breast cancer. Breast Cancer Res Treat. 2013;137:155–65. https://doi.org/10.1007/s10549-012-2350-8.
32. Soares JS, Barman I, Dingari NC, et al. Diagnostic power of diffuse reflectance spectroscopy for targeted detection of breast lesions with microcalcifications. Proc Natl Acad Sci USA. 2013;110:471–6. https://doi.org/10.1073/pnas.1215473110.
33. Rickard AG, Mikati H, Mansourati A, et al. A clinical study to assess diffuse reflectance spectroscopy with an auto-calibrated, pressure-sensing optical probe in head and neck cancer. Curr Oncol. 2023;30:2751–60. https://doi.org/10.3390/curroncol30030208.
34. Baltussen EJM, Snaebjornsson P, de Koning SGB, et al. Diffuse reflectance spectroscopy as a tool for real-time tissue assessment during colorectal cancer surgery. J Biomed Opt. 2017;22:1. https://doi.org/10.1117/1.jbo.22.10.106014.
35. Nilsson JH, Reistad N, Brange H, et al. Diffuse reflectance spectroscopy for surface measurement of liver pathology. Eur Surg Res. 2017;58:40–50. https://doi.org/10.1159/000449378.
36. Einstein G, Udayakumar K, Aruna PR, et al. Diffuse reflectance spectroscopy for monitoring physiological and morphological changes in oral cancer. Optik. 2016;127:1479–85. https://doi.org/10.1016/j.ijleo.2015.11.045.
37. Garcia-Uribe A, Zou J, Duvic M, et al. In vivo diagnosis of melanoma and nonmelanoma skin cancer using oblique incidence diffuse reflectance spectrometry. Cancer Res. 2012;72:2738–45. https://doi.org/10.1158/0008-5472.CAN-11-4027.
38. Zhang Y, Moy AJ, Feng X, et al. Diffuse reflectance spectroscopy as a potential method for nonmelanoma skin cancer margin assessment. Transl Biophotonics. 2020;2:e202000001. https://doi.org/10.1002/tbio.202000001.
39. Salomatina E, Yaroslavsky AN. Evaluation of the in vivo and ex vivo optical properties in a mouse ear model. Phys Med Biol. 2008;53:2797–807. https://doi.org/10.1088/0031-9155/53/11/003.
40. Baltussen EJM, Brouwer De Koning SG, Hendriks BHW, et al. Comparing in vivo and ex vivo fiber-optic diffuse reflectance spectroscopy in colorectal cancer. Transl Biophotonics. 2019;1:1–2. https://doi.org/10.1002/tbio.201900008.
41. Gkouzionis I, Nazarian S, Kawka M, et al. Real-time tracking of a diffuse reflectance spectroscopy probe used to aid histological validation of margin assessment in upper gastrointestinal cancer resection surgery. J Biomed Opt. 2022;27:025001. https://doi.org/10.1117/1.JBO.27.2.025001.
42. Geldof F, Dashtbozorg B, Hendriks BHW, et al. Layer thickness prediction and tissue classification in two-layered tissue structures using diffuse reflectance spectroscopy. Sci Rep. 2022;12:1698. https://doi.org/10.1038/s41598-022-05751-5.
43. Tanis E, Spliethoff JW, Evers DJ, et al. Real-time in vivo assessment of radiofrequency ablation of human colorectal liver metastases using diffuse reflectance spectroscopy. Eur J Surg Oncol. 2016;42:251–9. https://doi.org/10.1016/j.ejso.2015.12.005.
44. Cairns RA, Harris IS, Mak TW. Regulation of cancer cell metabolism. Nat Rev Cancer. 2011;11:85–95.
45. Chiarugi A, Dölle C, Felici R, Ziegler M. The NAD metabolome - a key determinant of cancer cell biology. Nat Rev Cancer. 2012;12:741–52.
46. Li LZ. Imaging mitochondrial redox potential and its possible link to tumor metastatic potential. J Bioenerg Biomembr. 2012;44:645–53.

47. Ying W. NAD+/NADH and NADP+/NADPH in cellular functions and cell death: regulation and biological consequences. Antioxid Redox Signal. 2007;10:179–206. https://doi.org/10.1089/ars.2007.1672.
48. And N, Fluorescence F, Chance B, et al. Oxidation-reduction ratio studies of mitochondria in freeze-trapped samples. J Biol Chem. 1979;254(11):4764–71.
49. Shirshin E, Cherkasova O, Tikhonova T, et al. Native fluorescence spectroscopy of blood plasma of rats with experimental diabetes: identifying fingerprints of glucose-related metabolic pathways. J Biomed Opt. 2015;20:051033. https://doi.org/10.1117/1.jbo.20.5.051033.
50. Singh VP, Bali A, Singh N, Jaggi AS. Advanced glycation end products and diabetic complications. Korean J Physiol Pharmacol. 2014;18:1–14.
51. Smit AJ, Gerrits EG. Skin autofluorescence as a measure of advanced glycation endproduct deposition: a novel risk marker in chronic kidney disease. Curr Opin Nephrol Hypertens. 2010;19:527–33.
52. Maynard JD, Rohrscheib M, Way JF, et al. Noninvasive type 2 diabetes screening: superior sensitivity to fasting plasma glucose and A1C. Diabetes Care. 2007;30:1120–4. https://doi.org/10.2337/dc06-2377.
53. Hull EL, Matter NI, Olson BP, et al. Noninvasive skin fluorescence spectroscopy for detection of abnormal glucose tolerance. J Clin Transl Endocrinol. 2014;1:92–9. https://doi.org/10.1016/j.jcte.2014.06.003.
54. Olson BP, Matter NI, Ediger MN, et al. Noninvasive skin fluorescence spectroscopy is comparable to hemoglobin A1c and fasting plasma glucose for detection of abnormal glucose tolerance. J Diabetes Sci Technol. 2013;7(4):990–1000.
55. Papayan G, Petrishchev N, Galagudza M. Autofluorescence spectroscopy for NADH and flavoproteins redox state monitoring in the isolated rat heart subjected to ischemia-reperfusion. Photodiagn Photodyn Ther. 2014;11:400–8. https://doi.org/10.1016/j.pdpdt.2014.05.003.
56. Ranji M, Kanemoto S, Matsubara M, et al. Fluorescence spectroscopy and imaging of myocardial apoptosis. J Biomed Opt. 2006;11:64036. https://doi.org/10.1117/1.2400701.
57. Warburg O. On the origin of cancer cells. Science. 1956;123:309–14. https://doi.org/10.1126/science.123.3191.309.
58. Gill EM, Palmer GM, Ramanujam N. Steady-state fluorescence imaging of neoplasia. In: Methods in enzymology. New York: Academic; 2003. p. 452–81.
59. Kollias N, Zonios G, Stamatas GN. Fluorescence spectroscopy of skin. Vib Spectrosc. 2002;28:17–23.
60. Panjehpour M, Julius CE, Phan MN, et al. Laser-induced fluorescence spectroscopy for in vivo diagnosis of non-melanoma skin cancers. Lasers Surg Med. 2002;31:367–73. https://doi.org/10.1002/lsm.10125.
61. Alchab L, Dupuis G, Balleyguier C, et al. Towards an optical biopsy for the diagnosis of breast cancer in vivo by endogenous fluorescence spectroscopy. J Biophotonics. 2010;3:373–84. https://doi.org/10.1002/jbio.200900070.
62. Choi J, Gupta S, Park I, et al. Breast cancer diagnosis from fluorescence spectroscopy using support vector machine. In: Optical tomography and spectroscopy of tissue VII. New York: SPIE; 2007. p. 64340.
63. Panjehpour M, Overholt BF, Vo-Dinh T, et al. Endoscopic fluorescence detection of high-grade dysplasia in Barrett's esophagus. Gastroenterology. 1996;111:93–101. https://doi.org/10.1053/gast.1996.v111.pm8698231.
64. Pfefer TJ, Paithankar DY, Poneros JM, et al. Temporally and spectrally resolved fluorescence spectroscopy for the detection of high grade dysplasia in Barrett's esophagus. Lasers Surg Med. 2003;32:10–6. https://doi.org/10.1002/lsm.10136.
65. Chen W, Wei G. Ultraviolet laser-induced fluorescence spectroscopy diagnosis of human stomach malignant tissues. Lasers Med Sci. 1998;13:209–13.
66. Silveira L, Betiol Filho JÂ, Silveira FL, et al. Laser-induced fluorescence at 488 nm excitation for detecting benign and malignant lesions in stomach mucosa. J Fluoresc. 2008;18:35–40. https://doi.org/10.1007/s10895-007-0232-y.
67. Dhingra JK, Zhang X, McMillan K, et al. Diagnosis of head and neck precancerous lesions in an animal model using fluorescence spectroscopy. Laryngoscope. 1998;108:471–5. https://doi.org/10.1097/00005537-199804000-00002.
68. Gillenwater A, Jacob R, Ganeshappa R, et al. Noninvasive diagnosis of oral neoplasia based on fluorescence spectroscopy and native tissue autofluorescence. Arch Otolaryngol Head Neck Surg. 1998;124(11):1251–8.
69. Uspenskiĭ LV, Kuzin MI, Ablitsov IA, et al. Laser fluorescence spectroscopy in intraoperative diagnosis and staging of lung cancer. Khirurgiia. 1996;3:31–3.
70. Wang M, Long F, Tang F, et al. Autofluorescence imaging and spectroscopy of human lung cancer. Appl Sci. 2017;7:32. https://doi.org/10.3390/app7010032.
71. Alfano RR, Tang GC, Pradhan A, et al. Fluorescence spectra from cancerous and normal human breast and lung tissues. IEEE J Quantum Electron. 1987;23:1806–11.
72. Alfano RR, Tata DB, Cordero J, et al. Laser induced fluorescence spectroscopy from native cancerous and normal tissue. IEEE J Quantum Electron. 1984;20:1507–11. https://doi.org/10.1109/JQE.1984.1072322.
73. Kumar Gupta P, Kumar Majumder S, Uppal A. Breast cancer diagnosis using N 2 laser excited autofluorescence spectroscopy. Lasers Surg Med. 1997;21(5):417–22.
74. Xu HN, Tchou J, Feng M, et al. Optical redox imaging indices discriminate human breast cancer from

normal tissues. J Biomed Opt. 2016;21:114003. https://doi.org/10.1117/1.jbo.21.11.114003.
75. Kanniyappan U, Tang Q, Liu Y, et al. Novel needle redox endoscopy imager for cancer diagnosis. SPIE Int Soc Optical Eng. 2018;10489:18.
76. Yang Y, Katz A, Celmer EJ, et al. Optical spectroscopy of benign and malignant breast tissues. Lasers Life Sci. 1996;7:115–27. https://doi.org/10.1117/12.237597.
77. Zhang L, Pu Y, Xue J, et al. Tryptophan as the fingerprint for distinguishing aggressiveness among breast cancer cell lines using native fluorescence spectroscopy. J Biomed Opt. 2014;19(3):37005.
78. Sordillo LA, Sordillo PP, Budansky Y, et al. Differences in fluorescence profiles from breast cancer tissues due to changes in relative tryptophan content via energy transfer: tryptophan content correlates with histologic grade and tumor size but not with lymph node metastases. J Biomed Opt. 2014;19:125002. https://doi.org/10.1117/1.jbo.19.12.125002.
79. Lima IFP, Brand LM, de Figueiredo JAP, et al. Use of autofluorescence and fluorescent probes as a potential diagnostic tool for oral cancer: a systematic review. Photodiagn Photodyn Ther. 2021;33:102073.
80. Rana M, Zapf A, Kuehle M, et al. Clinical evaluation of an autofluorescence diagnostic device for oral cancer detection: a prospective randomized diagnostic study. Eur J Cancer Prev. 2012;21:460–6. https://doi.org/10.2307/48503060.
81. Ganga RS, Gundre D, Bansal S, et al. Evaluation of the diagnostic efficacy and spectrum of autofluorescence of benign, dysplastic and malignant lesions of the oral cavity using VELscope. Oral Oncol. 2017;75:67–74. https://doi.org/10.1016/j.oraloncology.2017.10.023.
82. Hanken H, Kraatz J, Smeets R, et al. The detection of oral pre-malignant lesions with an autofluorescence based imaging system (VELscope™) - a single blinded clinical evaluation. Head Face Med. 2013;9:23. https://doi.org/10.1186/1746-160X-9-23.
83. Huang TT, Huang JS, Wang YY, et al. Novel quantitative analysis of autofluorescence images for oral cancer screening. Oral Oncol. 2017;68:20–6. https://doi.org/10.1016/j.oraloncology.2017.03.003.
84. Jeng MJ, Sharma M, Chao TY, et al. Multiclass classification of autofluorescence images of oral cavity lesions based on quantitative analysis. PLoS One. 2020;15:0228132. https://doi.org/10.1371/journal.pone.0228132.
85. Huang T-T, Chen K-C, Wong T-Y, et al. Two-channel autofluorescence analysis for oral cancer. J Biomed Opt. 2018;24:1. https://doi.org/10.1117/1.JBO.24.5.051402.
86. Awais M, Ghayvat H, Krishnan Pandarathodiyil A, et al. Healthcare professional in the loop (HPIL): classification of standard and oral cancer-causing anomalous regions of oral cavity using textural analysis technique in autofluorescence imaging. Sensors. 2020;20:1–25. https://doi.org/10.3390/s20205780.
87. Bergholt MS, Hassing S. Quantification of C-reactive protein in human blood plasma using near-infrared Raman spectroscopy. Analyst. 2009;134:2123–7. https://doi.org/10.1039/b903089a.
88. Sahu A, Dalal K, Naglot S, et al. Serum based diagnosis of asthma using Raman spectroscopy: an early phase pilot study. PLoS One. 2013;8:e0078921. https://doi.org/10.1371/journal.pone.0078921.
89. Bonifacio A, Finaurini S, Krafft C, et al. Spatial distribution of heme species in erythrocytes infected with *Plasmodium falciparum* by use of resonance Raman imaging and multivariate analysis. Anal Bioanal Chem. 2008;392:1277–82. https://doi.org/10.1007/s00216-008-2414-0.
90. Hobro AJ, Konishi A, Coban C, Smith NI. Raman spectroscopic analysis of malaria disease progression via blood and plasma samples. Analyst. 2013;138:3927–33. https://doi.org/10.1039/c3an00255a.
91. Kong K, Kendall C, Stone N, Notingher I. Raman spectroscopy for medical diagnostics - from in-vitro biofluid assays to in-vivo cancer detection. Adv Drug Deliv Rev. 2015;89:121–34.
92. Shao J, Lin M, Li Y, et al. In vivo blood glucose quantification using Raman spectroscopy. PLoS One. 2012;7:e0048127. https://doi.org/10.1371/journal.pone.0048127.
93. Shih W-C, Bechtel KL, Rebec MV. Noninvasive glucose sensing by transcutaneous Raman spectroscopy. J Biomed Opt. 2015;20:051036. https://doi.org/10.1117/1.jbo.20.5.051036.
94. Dingari NC, Barman I, Singh GP, et al. Investigation of the specificity of Raman spectroscopy in non-invasive blood glucose measurements. Anal Bioanal Chem. 2011;400:2871–80. https://doi.org/10.1007/s00216-011-5004-5.
95. Woong Kang J, Sang Park Y, Chang H, et al. Direct observation of glucose fingerprint using in vivo Raman spectroscopy. Appl Sci Eng. 2020;6:5206.
96. Pence I, Mahadevan-Jansen A. Clinical instrumentation and applications of Raman spectroscopy. Chem Soc Rev. 2016;45:1958–79.
97. Jermyn M, Desroches J, Aubertin K, et al. A review of Raman spectroscopy advances with an emphasis on clinical translation challenges in oncology. Phys Med Biol. 2016;61:R370–400.
98. Haka AS, Shafer-Peltier KE, Fitzmaurice M, et al. Diagnosing breast cancer by using Raman spectroscopy. Proc Natl Acad Sci USA. 2005;102:12371–6. https://doi.org/10.1073/pnas.0501390102.
99. Shafer-Peltier KE, Haka AS, Fitzmaurice M, et al. Raman microspectroscopic model of human breast tissue: implications for breast cancer diagnosis in vivo. J Raman Spectrosc. 2002;33:552–63. https://doi.org/10.1002/jrs.877.
100. Haka AS, Volynskaya Z, Gardecki JA, et al. In vivo margin assessment during partial mastectomy breast surgery using Raman spectroscopy. Cancer Res. 2006;66:3317–22. https://doi.org/10.1158/0008-5472.CAN-05-2815.

101. Bitar R, Martins MA, Ribeiro D, et al. In vivo Raman spectroscopy for breast cancer: diagnosis in animal model. In: Biomedical optical spectroscopy. New York: SPIE; 2008. p. 685300.
102. Zúñiga WC, Jones V, Anderson SM, et al. Raman spectroscopy for rapid evaluation of surgical margins during breast cancer lumpectomy. Sci Rep. 2019;9:14639. https://doi.org/10.1038/s41598-019-51112-0.
103. Kong K, Zaabar F, Rakha E, et al. Towards intra-operative diagnosis of tumours during breast conserving surgery by selective-sampling Raman micro-spectroscopy. Phys Med Biol. 2014;59:6141–52. https://doi.org/10.1088/0031-9155/59/20/6141.
104. Liao Z, Lizio MG, Corden C, et al. Feasibility of integrated high-wavenumber Raman imaging and fingerprint Raman spectroscopy for fast margin assessment in breast cancer surgery. J Raman Spectrosc. 2020;51:1986–95. https://doi.org/10.1002/jrs.5937.
105. Koya SK, Brusatori M, Yurgelevic S, et al. Accurate identification of breast cancer margins in microenvironments of ex-vivo basal and luminal breast cancer tissues using Raman spectroscopy. Prostaglandins Other Lipid Mediat. 2020;151:106475. https://doi.org/10.1016/j.prostaglandins.2020.106475.
106. Ma D, Shang L, Tang J, et al. Classifying breast cancer tissue by Raman spectroscopy with one-dimensional convolutional neural network. Spectrochim Acta A Mol Biomol Spectrosc. 2021;256:119732. https://doi.org/10.1016/j.saa.2021.119732.
107. Jayasankar S, Bajhaiya D, Narayanan Unni S. Deep learning-enabled soft tissue tumor localization using spatially offset Raman spectral analysis: in-silico investigations. J Phys D Appl Phys. 2022;55:394006. https://doi.org/10.1088/1361-6463/ac8126.
108. Jayasankar S, Unni SN. Soft tissue tumor size prediction using precise fiber-optic Raman probes: in silico investigations. Proc SPIE. 2022;12144:1214404.
109. Keller MD, Vargis E, de Matos GN, et al. Development of a spatially offset Raman spectroscopy probe for breast tumor surgical margin evaluation. J Biomed Opt. 2011;16:077006. https://doi.org/10.1117/1.3600708.
110. Thomas G, Nguyen TQ, Pence IJ, et al. Evaluating feasibility of an automated 3-dimensional scanner using Raman spectroscopy for intraoperative breast margin assessment. Sci Rep. 2017;7:1–14. https://doi.org/10.1038/s41598-017-13237-y.

Space Biosciences: Translational Research for Space, Benefitting Life on Earth

3

K. G. Sreejalekshmi

3.1 Introduction

Life is an exciting phenomenon and hard to explain despite several definitions, all built on the context of life on Earth. All through its evolution into the present highly complex hierarchical setup, the membrane-bound, carbon-based life on this planet evolved and thrived under the influence of the ubiquitous force of gravity, the only constant environmental parameter. Hence, it is no wonder that depriving living beings of this directional force, as in space, triggers a cascade of biological events manifesting from the organ to the molecular level [1]. The broad domain of space biosciences addresses the modalities of response and adaptations of life forms when displaced far from the "gravity pull" as well as other "protective blankets" like the magnetosphere of the Earth, into space. Through several experiments conducted in space using live specimens, new scientific discoveries emerged which helped in understanding the fundamental life processes and ushered technological developments in the biological sciences [2–5]. Importantly, the "zero gravity" or altered gravity offers distinct advantages that can be put to use in both earth- and space-based applications [6]. Considering the imminent strides in space explorations including space tourism, addressing the health risks on the crew imparted by spaceflights and supporting life in space to get the best benefits from the missions have become more crucial than ever before. The environmental transition from "terrestrial to extraterrestrial" imposes multidimensional stressors [7] on life (Table 3.1), which calls for protection from radiation hazards, and developing countermeasures towards reduced gravity, life support systems, medical care, and consideration of several other human factors.

From the initial phases of the human spaceflights to the current space commercialization age where plans are on for building outposts in space to support deep space missions, the harsh and unseen domains of space challenged researchers by posing risks to health and life at every stage of the flight. A quick glance at the historical evolutions of human spaceflights can shed light on the systematic efforts from space researchers to accumulate scientific wisdom and practical knowledge which culminated in a multidisciplinary domain called bioastronautics, the study and support of life in space. From the design of human-rated launch vehicles and conducive habitat to the postflight care for astronauts, research in bioastronautics is typically translational and covers all human and nonhuman factors of space life science, including crew protection, performance, and life support as well as the effect of space on biological processes [12].

K. G. Sreejalekshmi (✉)
Department of Chemistry, Indian Institute of Space Science and Technology, Department of Space, Government of India, Thiruvananthapuram, India
e-mail: sreeja@iist.ac.in

K. Parthasarathy, R. Manikkam (eds.), *Translational Research in Biomedical Sciences: Recent Progress and Future Prospects*, https://doi.org/10.1007/978-981-97-1777-4_3

Table 3.1 Characteristics of the space environment in the LEO and their impact on crew health and safety (adapted from Thirsk et al. 2009 and modified)

Unique features of space environment	Impact on crew health and safety
Microgravity	Alterations in body functions
Temperature extremes [8] • –100 to 100 °C	• Damage to spacecraft structural components • Thermal injury to astronauts on EVA
Circadian dyssynchrony	• Disruption of circadian rhythms • Deprived/reduced quality sleep
High vacuum • 10^{-7} torr	• Damage to space suits • Astronauts on EVA at the risk of space decompression sickness
Ionizing radiations [9–11] • 425 μSv/day • For 1 year stay on the lunar surface: 100–120 mGy • For a ~3-year Mars mission 300–450 mGy	Long-term medical risks • Cancer, cataract • Cardiovascular and late neurodegenerative disorders
Micrometeoroids and orbital debris • ~25,000 space debris objects are large enough (>10 cm) to be tracked and cataloged • Including non-trackable high velocity objects (orbital velocities 8–70 km/s), the number rises to millions	• Threat to currently healthy and operating space systems • Damage to space crafts and space shuttles, calling for emergency situations
Ionospheric plasma • High level charging of spacecraft surfaces occurs in GEO and LEO polar orbits • Spacecraft may develop an induced charge up to –140 V	Arcing can disrupt EVA and cause damages to the astronaut
Acoustic noise (on orbiting laboratories) • Ambient noise level on ISS is 60 dB • 58 dB in the working areas and 49 dB in the sleeping areas (Tiangong space station)	Impaired concentration, sleep disruptions, hearing loss, and fatigue

The long-term goal remains the bioengineering of spacecraft and habitats to stabilize the ecosystem of plants, microbes, crops, animals, and humans for sustained multi-planetary life.

3.2 Spaceflights with "Life Onboard": Challenging Researchers on Earth?

Tracing back the early years of space research to the late 1940s, or more precisely to the time when rocket science was evolving, no one knew for certain what it takes for a successful spaceflight with "life on board." Launching life into space was an activity by engineers who flew several living beings including dogs, monkeys, chimps, fruit flies, newts, worms, beetles, fish, spiders, rabbits, ants, frogs, mice, jellyfish, guinea pigs, cockroaches, among many others [13, 14]. Through these animal astronauts (thanks to their selfless sacrifices and quiet contributions to space biosciences), rocketry started addressing a new challenge and grew an extra domain which focused on understanding how to launch life into space and bring living beings safely back to Earth. From these historic flights up to the ongoing research in the ISS, which has been hosting life continuously for over two decades, and in other recently established orbiting laboratories in space, the body of scientific knowledge about life in space has grown substantially. It is worth emphasizing that a huge part of data accumulated on space biosciences was gathered through studies on model organisms—flies, worms, mice, fish, and more providing us with valuable insights into the myriad effects of spaceflights on the body, including muscle atrophy and bone loss, neuronal changes, aging, immune system alterations, microbiome shifts, microbe-pathogen interactions, sleep disruptions, and many more. Model organism research is key to translational science, refining the direction of human health research and driving the design of life support systems [4]. In sharp contrast to the planning, design, and execution of experiments in Earth laboratories, the physical limitations on in-orbit laboratories have made selected organisms and plants that could comply with the size and habitat restrictions as regular travelers to space. Once life scientists make the choice of an animal/plant model, the challenge is handed over to engineers to build the functional habitat in line with the requirements of the chosen animal models and the science objectives of the planned experiment [15]. Needless to mention, the challenging demands for customized hardware support for space life science research have made huge engineering strides and spun-off several automated and semi-automated devices. However, this aspect is beyond the scope of this chapter and will be reviewed elsewhere [16]. Furthermore, the post splashdown events for a mission containing biological samples are a race against time with meticulously scheduled events. From the retrieval of the samples from the module to the transportation to the lab, the activities need to be completed before any live subjects re-acclimate to the effects of Earths' gravity or frozen samples start to thaw. From an extremely rare opportunity, the recent advancements in launch vehicle technology have imparted momentum to the on-going orbital research on ISS by providing several Commercial Resupply Service missions (CRS). These missions bring in new experiments at the space laboratory, thus partly meeting the challenge of reduced spaceflight opportunities and adding up diversity to space biosciences [17]. Currently, the number of life science experiments conducted in space laboratories and/or researchers directly working on space bioscience research from Earth laboratories around the world are in the thousands. Many universities, research institutions, and space agencies have focused programs and dedicated facilities for space biosciences research, and collaborations between researchers from different countries and disciplines are common. It is also imperative to note that since the *modus operandi* of conducting bioscience research in spaceflight presents unique technical and biological challenges that are rarely anticipated or met before in their Earth counterparts, specific attention by the international space biology community is extremely important to ensure its success. Furthermore, to enthuse upcoming researchers and thus expand the space biosciences community, the potential and the benefits of space biosciences research, especially the translational nature, need to be spread across a large lot of the future research community. Towards this goal, let us ponder a bit over the question—what are the exact benefits from spaceflight research? Starting with the options to view our planet in a whole new light, these space laboratories support a wide range of disciplines from atmospheric sciences, disaster management, and human health to high-powered computing and hence impact everyday life on Earth. This chapter provides a bird's eye view of the health benefits for Earth from space, typically the offshoots from research addressing the physiological challenges of a spaceflight. Further, attempts are made to demonstrate the space laboratories as a proving ground for new technologies through marvelous examples for translational research.

3.3 Physiological Challenges of a Spaceflight

On Earth, under normal conditions, any abnormal physiological conditions are classified as illness whereas for space travelers, the normal physiology is challenged by the abnormalities of space. The knowledge and experience accumulated over several years of biosciences research in the space laboratories attest that life in space is constantly subjected to unique conditions, operating both inside and outside of the crew capsule/cabin including microgravity, absence of the day and night cycle, radiations, and hypoxic conditions to mention a few. While these environmental stressors destabilize the homeostatic state in multiple ways, the body unleashes mechanisms for its recovery and stabilization, thus triggering a series of physical and biological adaptive changes. Hence, from a physiological point of view, spaceflights can impart a broad spectrum of changes in the biofunctions, spanning from temporary or adaptive alterations to life-threatening manifestations. These changes and their impact on life processes are typically dependent on the duration of the spaceflights. In particular, long-term exposure to microgravity is known to cause several physiological and biochemical changes in humans including the loss of bone density, atrophy of antigravity muscles, decreased plasma volume, and cardiovascular deconditioning to highlight a few. The timelines of space acclimation (short-term exposure) and acclimatization (long-term missions) experienced by astronauts from launch to after return to earth were tabulated by Williams et al. [18], and a modified version is presented in Table 3.2. The risks of spaceflights can be broadly classified into two—environmental centric and individual centric, in which the latter is considered critical during crew selection and training by different space agencies. Further, since crews do not experience environmental stressors independently, their combined impact on human physiology and performance, called "space exposome," needs to be considered while devising countermeasures (Fig. 3.1).

The agencies which are into human space programs have dedicated divisions and research teams in bioastronautics for understanding the physiologic effects of spaceflight and to develop countermeasures to nullify/reduce the detrimental effects of spaceflights on human health and performance. Bioastronautics is a multidisciplinary field that focuses on understanding and addressing the physiological, psychological, and environmental factors that impact human health and performance in space. From the past experiences with piloted missions, it has been shown that gradual breakdown in bone and muscle tissue, together with fluid losses, despite a vigorous exercise regimen can ultimately lead to increased occurrences of renal stones, musculoskeletal injuries, and bone fractures [20]. Over longer periods of time, the biological effects of radiation can increase the risk of cancer development. Preflight countermeasures involve physical fitness, exercise, and physiologic adaptation training whereas inflight countermeasures concern nutritional health, medications, and sensory-motor training protocols along with physical fitness. Yet another important step is the assessment of medical standards, ratings of launch vehicles, space suits, and design countermeasures accordingly to ensure crew health and safety during all phases of flight. Postflight countermeasures focus on rehabilitation strategies. Importantly, ground-based studies and testing precede flight testing, which are crucial in the development and refinement of countermeasures and technologies. In an interesting study conducted in 2018, the National Aeronautics and Space Administration (NASA) selected a pair of monozygotic (identical) twin astronauts to assess the impact of long-duration spaceflight on the human body, brain, and overall physiology. One of the candidate subjects remained on earth as a ground-based control whereas the other one spent almost a year on the ISS. Longitudinal assessments of the yearlong accumulated multiomic, molecular, physiological, and behavioral datasets identified spaceflight-specific changes in these subjects. The specific ones noted in the astronaut included reduced body mass, telomere elongation, genome instability, carotid artery distension and increased intima-media thickness, altered ocular structure, changes in transcriptional, metabolic, and DNA methylation [21, 22]. The study also indicated postflight alterations in oxidative stress–related pathways, and gastrointestinal microbiota along with some cognitive decline. Though some of these changes, for instance, the average telomere length, global gene expression, and microbiome changes, restored to near preflight levels within 6 months after return to Earth, some factors persisted even beyond this time span. These include expression levels of some genes, increased numbers of short telomeres, increased DNA damage from chromosomal inversions, and attenuated cognitive function. This landmark Twins Study provided the first integrated molecular picture of the human body's adaptation to the spaceflight environment. Findings from the study were analyzed by multiple research groups which revealed the dynamic nature of the responses to spaceflight (Fig. 3.2) and the multitude of changes happening inside a human body. Many of the findings are consistent with previously recorded data, thus

Table 3.2 The timelines of space acclimation and acclimatization experienced by astronauts from launch to after return to earth

Physiologic effects	Launch	Inflight duration				Landing	Postflight duration		
		1 day	2 days	2 weeks	>1 month		1–2 days	1–2 months	>1 year
Fluid redistribution	• Fluid shift to torso and head • 10% decreased fluid volume in the legs	• 17% reduction in plasma volume	• Gradual reduction in erythropoietin secretion • 10% reduction in blood volume			• Pooling of blood in the legs leading to orthostatic hypotension	• Restoration of normal fluid distribution		
Neurovestibular effects	• Space motion sickness					• Space motion sickness			
Bone demineralization	• Increased (60–70%) calcium loss (urine, fecal) • Decreased parathyroid hormone and vitamin D production • Gradual loss of bone density (1–2% per month)								• Almost complete restoration of bone density
Muscle changes	• Gradual decrease in muscle mass (by 20%)			• Gradual decrease in muscle mass (by 30%)		• Muscle soreness and tightness		• Full recovery of muscle mass and strength	
Immune dysregulation	• Reactivation (most probable) of latent herpes viruses and impairment of cell-mediated immunity					• Impaired immunity		• Gradual improvement in immunity	
Spaceflight-associated neuro-ocular syndrome (SANS)	• Diagnosed during or immediately after long-duration missions (>30 days) • Signs have been discovered as early as 10 days during missions [19]								
Psychosocial effects	Fatigue, isolation, insomnia, emotional effects, acclimatizing with multicultural crew, stress to family								

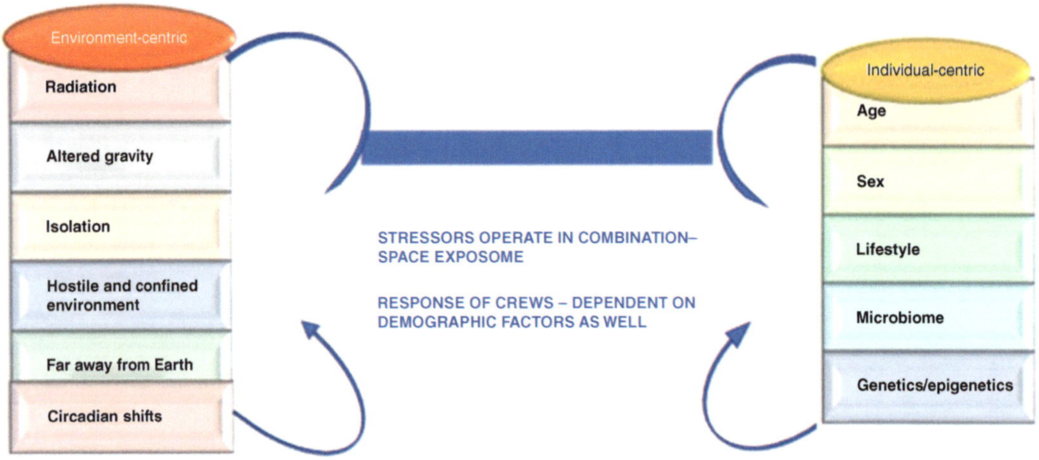

Fig. 3.1 The main hazards of spaceflight: environment-centric and individual-centric

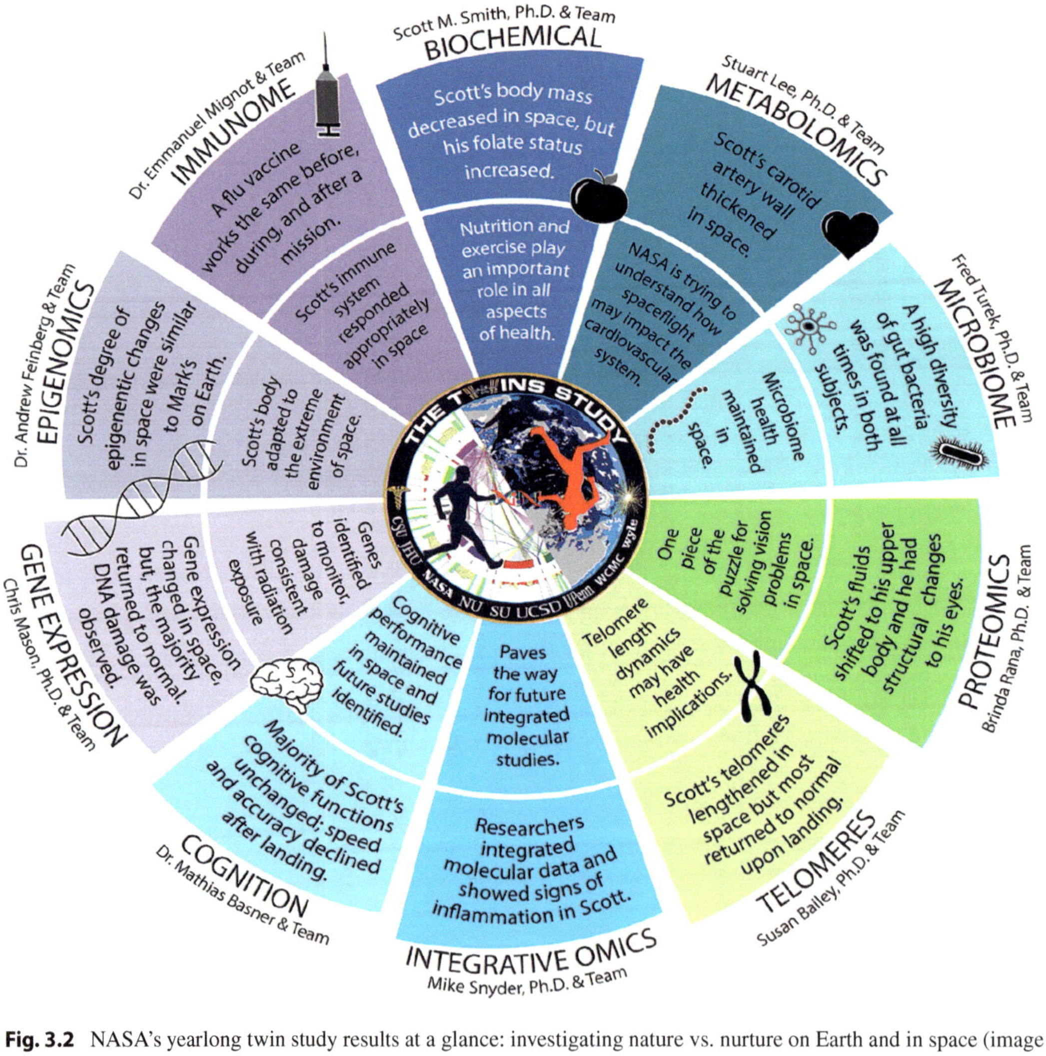

Fig. 3.2 NASA's yearlong twin study results at a glance: investigating nature vs. nurture on Earth and in space (image courtesy: NASA)

confirming the research already being pursued. Additionally, the study demonstrated how a human body remains robust and resilient even after spending a year in space, thus encouraging space agencies to venture into interplanetary voyages.

As more and more countries venture into human space programs, and a few have already started aiming for interplanetary missions, space biosciences are receiving more attention, an outcome of coherent efforts to solve the issues anticipated from long duration missions. For instance, the Program Science Forum (PSF) of ISS, partnered by seven leading space agencies, National Aeronautics and Space Administration (NASA), European Space Agency (ESA), Canadian Space Agency (CSA), Japan Aerospace Exploration Agency (JAXA), State Space Corporation ROSCOSMOS (ROSCOSMOS), and the Italian Space Agency (ASI), stride together to bring new scientific discoveries in space biosciences to propel human curiosity forward. Space omics studies are gaining prominence to make the best use of data from the space laboratories and to develop countermeasures for safe and effective crewed space missions. Of late, the critical requirement of standardization of data from spaceflight experiments was recognized. To facilitate the optimal extraction of scientific insight from such data through improved standardization, ISSOP (International Standards for Space Omics Processing), an international consortium of scientists and space researchers to enhance benchmarks between space biologists globally, was recently formulated [23]. The idea is to formulate protocols and other standards, including for interoperable metadata needed to average out the noise surrounding a particular experiment, to make sure that all researchers, regardless of their geographical locations, can speak the same space science language [14].

3.4 Space Biosciences and Spin-Offs: Impacting Life on Earth

In a broad sense, spin-offs from space research refer to technologies or innovations that were originally developed for use in space exploration, but have since been adapted for use in other fields. When space exploration began in the early 1960s, outer space was looked upon as a new destination to potentially new resources and a habitat for life, the extraterrestrial ones. After surviving serious criticisms regarding the expenditure versus benefits of spaceflights, the space agencies started succeeding in improving the appreciation levels by the governments and the society at large owing to the vast accumulation of new technology and novel techniques from the first decade of space exploration. For example, the wireless communication headsets initially developed for astronauts during the Apollo Program were refined, miniaturized, and put for use with airline pilots during the 1970s. This technology has continued to develop over the decades and is ubiquitous in our modern world, where mobile headsets offer greater efficiency and flexibility for the users.

There are some unprecedented and rather strange benefits documented from space research as well [24]. One such example dates back to 1968, when a bullet lodged in the head of a man named Barrios, making a critical surgery inevitable. However, before performing the surgery to remove the shot, doctors hit on the idea to attempt a repositioning of it to a less critical area, using a centrifuge capsule used to train astronauts. By accelerating the man to six times the force of gravity for 5 s in the centrifuge, the bullet was dislodged to a less critical region eliminating the need for a complex surgery. Truly in line with the "off the Earth, for the Earth" motto upheld by space researchers, one could find several offshoots from space research which found direct use for humanity, both in developed and developing countries, including an array of new materials, products, and processes, significant progress in electronics, computer technology, and a host of benefits from space applications (Fig. 3.3). The capabilities in communications, weather forecasting, novel research in food and agriculture, innovations in education, health and medicine, industry and manufacturing, transportation and commerce, among many other domains in the applied sciences achieved by many countries owe a lot to space research. These benefits also keep

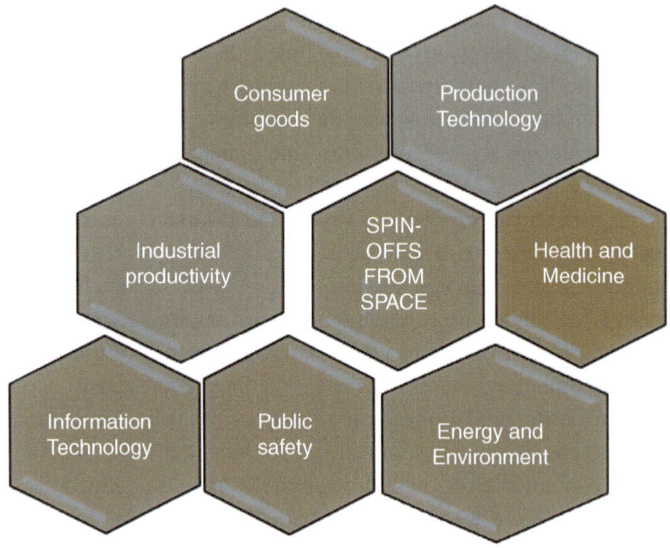

Fig. 3.3 For Earth from space: impact of spin-off technologies is far reaching

the future generation motivated to pursue research in space in the years to come as evidenced from the few examples to signify the impact of space biosciences research and its spin-offs in improving the healthcare sector across the globe.

The common goal of confronting the biological challenges of spaceflight has imparted a multidisciplinary nature to space biosciences research which has resulted in several new findings augmenting our knowledge in functional biology and considerable technological progress, specifically in the biomedical field. From experiments conducted to understand how life survives the extreme environments of space and the physiological changes imparted by a spaceflight, the focus has been now shifted towards equipping humans and systems to endure long and deep space missions. Due to the highly demanding nature of space bioscience experiments, the research and development programs continuously sought high-end technical solutions for handling life in extreme environments. This, in many cases, led to significant improvements in existing or the creation of new production methods or technologies, instruments, and products. For instance, the demand for conducting physiological routine measurements and experiments by astronauts has driven the development of small, compact, light, and easy-to-handle equipment that finds immense applications for health monitoring on Earth, be it in hospitals or in isolated environments like submarines or less inhabited regions of our planet. Another new technology developed and designed by a NASA engineer during the mid-1970s was the cochlear implants. Inspired by the frustration with his own poor hearing, Adam completed a prototype in 1977 and received a patent for his device which converted speech acoustic signals into electrical impulses. These electric signals were transferred to the auditory nerve of the patient, thereby completely bypassing the patients' defective natural hearing apparatus.

More importantly, several equipment and existing technologies already available on Earth have been improved, tested, and applied in the harsh and challenging conditions of spaceflight, thus promoting their commercial success, portable ultrasound machines and prosthetics being typical examples. Importantly, these achievements play crucial roles in stimulating new markets, industries, and opportunities along with improving the general quality of life. Readers who wish to gain an even broader view on the accomplishments that are currently delivered by the research and development activities specifically on the International Space Station are directed to the publications by the ISS partners, "ISS Benefits for Humanity" (latest issue can be downloaded) [25]. An impressive number of spin-offs have led to advancements in medical technology, and a few are selectively presented to highlight the impact of space biosciences on life on Earth. As part of crew health monitoring, for space station inhabitation, many investigations of crew viral shedding were initiated, especially in the early days of human spaceflights. This has led to the identification of reactivation (subclinical) of latent herpes viruses in crew as a potential health risk, especially during long-duration missions. The technologies for saliva and urine testing developed for the crew during the research were patented and currently used in the rapid virus-detection tests for diagnosing common ailments on Earth such as mononucleosis, herpes, and chicken pox. To solve the critical issues with disease diagnosis when the physical distance separates the doctor and the patient, telemedicine technology was introduced. Telemedicine allows doctors to remotely monitor and diagnose patients in remote locations. This has proven particularly useful in rural and under-served areas, where access to medical care is limited. NASA, ROSCOSMOS, and ISRO have successfully utilized telemedicine networks, a spin-off from space research, and connected remote and under-served areas to specialized medical care. Considering the requirements of palliative care for astronauts during long-term interplanetary missions, telemedicine strategies are currently being expanded by including exploratory three-dimensional projection-based technology [26]. Such advances will certainly bring benefits for palliative care on Earth in the years to come.

NASA's Jet Propulsion Laboratory (JPL) developed a miniature heart pump for the Viking spacecraft that landed on Mars in 1976. This technology was later used to develop the first artificial heart pump for humans, which has since saved countless lives. Similarly, ISRO's expertise in device miniaturization has led to the development of a low-cost heart pump called the "Chitra Heart Valve." This tilting disc valve with an integrally machined cobalt alloy cage, an ultra-high molecular weight polyethylene disc, and a polyester suture ring has been used in over 10,000 cardiac surgeries in India, making cardiac surgery more affordable for patients [27]. Yet another interesting breakthrough invention to benefit the health sector came from NASA when Space Shuttle fuel pumps inspired the development of Artificial Hearts and miniaturized ventricular assist pumps. The ventricular assist device (VAD) functions as a "bridge to heart transplant" by pumping blood throughout the body to keep critically ill patients alive until a donor's heart is available.

The widely used noninvasive medical imaging technology, magnetic resonance imaging (MRI) scanners, is an offshoot from space research. NASA's Jet Propulsion Laboratory (JPL) developed a new type of magnet for use in space missions that was later adapted for use in magnetic resonance imaging. This technology has revolutionized medical imaging and allowed doctors to diagnose a wide range of conditions without the need for invasive procedures. ROSCOSMOS' research on the effects of microgravity on the human body has led to advances in MRI technology. JAXA's research on autonomous robots for use in space has led to the development of advanced artificial intelligence (AI) technology that can be used to analyze medical images and assist with diagnosis. The technology uses machine learning algorithms to identify patterns and anomalies in medical images, which can help doctors to make more accurate and timely diagnosis of disease conditions. The portable ultrasound system for use in space was developed by ESA and has since been adapted for use in remote and under-served areas on Earth. The technology has allowed doctors to perform noninvasive diagnostic imaging in the field and has tremendously helped to improve maternal and infant health in developing countries. Further, a range of wearable health monitors, developed by ESA, can be used to track vital signs, such as heart rate and blood pressure. These devices are now widely used by athletes, first responders, and people with chronic health conditions to monitor their health in real time.

JAXA's research on space radiation has led to the development of a new type of radiation detector that is more sensitive and accurate than traditional detectors. This technology has been adapted for use in diagnostic imaging and has allowed doctors to detect cancer and other diseases at an earlier stage. Roscosmos has developed technology for radiation therapy that is used to treat cancer. This technology uses a cyclotron to produce a beam of high-energy particles that can destroy cancer cells while minimizing damage to surrounding healthy tissue. NASA's research into LED lighting for plant growth in space has led to the development of new LED lighting technologies that are used to treat a range of medical conditions, including skin disorders and seasonal affective disorder. A two yearlong clinical trial has reported to have successfully reduced the painful side effects resulting from chemotherapy and radiation treatment in bone marrow and stem cell transplant patients. The HEALS (High Emissivity Aluminiferous Luminescent Substrate) device known as the WARP 75 light delivery system is expected to provide a cost-effective therapy since the device itself is less expensive than a day at the hospital [28].

The ESA has partnered with industry leaders to develop surgical robotics technology that can be used to perform minimally invasive surgery. The technology has been used to perform complex surgical procedures with greater precision and has helped to reduce the risk of complications and recovery time for patients. NASA's research into new materials for use in spacecraft seating, "a material that could mold and fit the astronaut's shape and return to a 'rest' position when not in use," led to the development of memory foam, which is now used in a range of medical applications, including hospital beds, wheelchair cushions, and prosthetics. As for advanced prosthetic limbs, ESA partnered with industry leaders to develop more responsive and intuitive prosthetics than the traditional ones. The technology uses sensors and machine learning algorithms to interpret signals from the user's muscles and nerves, allowing for more natural movement and greater functionality. ISRO's lightweight materials technology has also been applied to the development of low-cost prosthetic limbs. These prosthetics are made of lightweight carbon fiber composites and have been used to help amputees in India.

Water being a precious commodity in space, all the agencies working towards human space missions have put extra efforts in purifying and harvesting even a single drop possible. NASA's research into water filtration systems for use on spacecraft has led to the development of new water filtration technologies that are used in many medical applications, including kidney dialysis machines. ROSCOSMOS's technology for water purification has been adapted for use in medical settings, where it is used to purify water for surgical procedures and other medical applications. ISRO has developed a water purification system that uses solar energy to purify water. This system has been used in disaster relief efforts and in rural areas to provide clean drinking water. The ESA has developed technology for monitoring food safety in space that has since been adapted for use on Earth. The technology uses spectral analysis to detect the presence of harmful bacteria and toxins in food and has helped to improve food safety and reduce the risk of foodborne illnesses. Another interesting spinoff is baby formula, a good dietary supplement highly beneficial to mental and visual development of infants. When NASA was conducting an experiment as part of CELSS (Closed Environment Life Support System), using algae as a recycling agent for long-duration space travel, they identified the formula containing two essential polyunsaturated fatty acids—docosahexaenoic acid (DHA) and arachidonic acid (ARA)—to be highly beneficial to support infants' growth and within a decade it reached the households as Formulaid in 1994.

It is now well known that without effective countermeasures, prolonged spaceflights result in marked muscle and bone atrophy. The molecular and physiological mechanisms of this atrophy under microgravity conditions were revealed through several spaceflight experiments conducted by the JAXA using a variety of model organisms, including both aquatic and terrestrial animals. Apart from gaining an understanding of how to prevent muscle and bone atrophy in humans undergoing long-term space voyages, these studies also would help understand countermeasures against age-related locomotive syndrome in the elderly [29]. JAXA's research on muscle atrophy in astronauts has led to the development of a new drug that blocks the activity of a protein that is responsible for muscle breakdown. This can help to prevent and treat muscle wasting in patients with conditions such as muscular dystrophy and amyotrophic lateral sclerosis (ALS). Yet another important research by space agencies on balance and coordination in microgravity has led to the development of a new type of rehabilitation technology that can be used to improve balance and mobility in patients with conditions such as Parkinson's disease and stroke. The technology uses virtual reality and body-worn sensors to provide targeted feedback and training [30]. Currently, as space exploration becomes increasingly common, palliative care for astronauts is also a growing concern where all aspects of palliative care need to be specifically adapted for astronauts [31].

Initial research conducted in collaboration between NASA and the Russian agency over the course of the Foton M2 and M3 missions on tissue regeneration suggested that microgravity is responsible for the inhibition of the transition from progenitor cells to differentiated adult cells [32]. This suggests that prolonged exposure to microgravity may result in a decrease in the tissue regeneration capacity. With the emergence of 3D Bioprinting, microgravity experiments on the ISS have led to the development of 3D bioprinting technology that can be used to create human tissue and organs for transplant. The microgravity environment allows for the creation of more complex and uniform tissue structures, which could help to address the shortage of donor organs and improve transplant outcomes.

Another health problem of astronauts in space is skin deterioration. Until recently, wound healing has not been considered as a severe health concern for crew members. This can change with deep space exploration missions and commercial spaceflights together with space tourism [33]. Roscosmos developed a fibrin glue based on the technology used to seal wounds in space. The glue, which is made from blood plasma, is used to seal wounds and promote healing in surgery [34].

3.5 Outlook

Space is vast and largely unknown, but exploration of space is severely challenged by limitations in transportation technologies and health risks to human crews. But along with quenching curiosity and tackling the challenges of space endeavors, humankind has made enormous progress on many aspects that are directly relevant to daily life on Earth, from communication to healthcare to transportation. They have also contributed to the advancement of science and technology and helped to drive economic growth and innovation. Spin-offs from space research have led to the creation of new industries and job opportunities, particularly in the fields of technology and engineering. While venturing to deep space with life onboard, the delivery of healthcare becomes one of the most important obstacles to be overcome. The operational concepts of healthcare, crew performance, and life support need to be reworked through seamless integration of expertise from physicians, biomedical engineers, human factors specialists, materials scientists, and radiation experts. Ideally, the onboard medical resources must include imaging, laboratory analysis of routine biospecimens, surgery, and emergency care. An artificial intelligence-assisted health informatics network onboard to assist with autonomous, and point of care health could be the goal. Translational research is a critical component of advancing space exploration, as it enables the development of innovative solutions to the challenges associated with long-duration spaceflight and supports the exploration of new frontiers beyond Earth. More and more young researchers need to be sensitized on the research prospects of space biosciences and bioastronautics, and how it benefits life on Earth.

Translational research has the potential to advance space exploration by enabling the development of innovative technologies, interventions, and approaches to overcome the challenges associated with long-duration spaceflight. One area of translational research that has received significant attention is the development of countermeasures to mitigate the adverse effects of spaceflight on human health, such as muscle and bone loss, immune dysfunction, and radiation exposure. Researchers in bioastronautics are exploring various approaches, such as exercise interventions, nutritional supplementation, and pharmacological treatments, to address these issues and enhance the well-being of astronauts during space missions. Another area of focus is the development of advanced technologies that can support long-duration space missions, such as autonomous systems, artificial intelligence, and additive manufacturing. These technologies can enhance the efficiency and safety of space missions while reducing the reliance on Earth-based support systems. In addition, translational research is also being used to advance our understanding of the fundamental principles underlying space exploration, such as the physics of space propulsion, space weather, and planetary science. This knowledge can inform the design of new space exploration missions and enable the exploration of new frontiers beyond our solar system.

Acknowledgment The author thanks IIST Thiruvananthapuram for the resources and support.

References

1. Afshinnekoo E, Scott RT, MacKay MJ, Pariset E, et al. Fundamental biological features of spaceflight: advancing the field to enable deep-space exploration. Cell. 2020;183(5):1162–84.
2. Krishnamurthy RS, Hatton J. Space science and technologies to advance health-related sustainable development goals. Bull World Health Organ. 2018;96(1):3. PMID: 29403092; PMCID: PMC5791876.
3. Kanapskyte A, Hawkins EM, Liddell LC, Bhardwaj SR, Gentry D, Santa Maria SR. Space biology research and biosensor technologies: past, present, and future. Biosensors. 2021;11(2):38. PMID: 33572823; PMCID: PMC7912197.
4. Alwood JS, et al. From the bench to exploration medicine: NASA life sciences translational research for human exploration and habitation missions. NPJ Micrograv. 2017;3:5. PMID: 28649627; PMCID: PMC5460236.
5. Asrar FM, Saint-Jacques D, Chapman HJ, et al. Can space-based technologies help manage and prevent pandemics? Nat Med. 2021;27:1489–90.
6. Pletser V, Thais R. Research in microgravity in physical and life sciences: an introduction to means and methods. In: Preparation of space experiments. London: IntechOpen; 2020. https://doi.org/10.5772/intechopen.93463.
7. Thirsk R, Kuipers A, Mukai C, Williams D. The space-flight environment: the International Space Station and beyond. CMAJ. 2009;180(12):1216–20. PMID: 19487390; PMCID: PMC2691437.
8. Newman DJ. Life in extreme environments: how will humans perform on Mars? Gravit Space Biol Bull. 2000;13:35–47.
9. Soares C, Mikatarian R, Schmidl R, et al. Natural and induced space environments effects on the International Space Station. In: Proceedings of the 56th International Astronautical Congress, Fukuoka, Japan, 2005.
10. Wilson JW, Badavi FF, Kim MY, et al. Natural and induced environment in low earth orbit [technical report]. Washington: National Aeronautics and Space Administration; 2002. Report no. NASA/TM—2002-211668.
11. Norbury JW, et al. Galactic cosmic ray simulation at the NASA Space Radiation Laboratory. Life Sci Space Res. 2016;8:38–51.
12. Simon NE. Overview of bioastronautics. In: Musgrave GE, Larsen AM, Sgobba T, editors. Safety design for space systems. Oxford: Butterworth-Heinemann; 2009. p. 105–61.
13. Sonnenfeld G. Use of animal models for space flight physiology studies, with special focus on the immune system. Gravit Space Biol Bull. 2005;18(2):31–5.
14. Neff EP. Animal models, open science, & space-omics. Lab Anim. 2021;50:143–5. https://doi.org/10.1038/s41684-021-00776-1.
15. Kern VD, Bhattacharya S, Bowman RN, Donovan FM, Elland C, Fahlen TF, Girten B, Kirven-Brooks M, Lagel K, Meeker GB, Santos O. Life sciences flight hardware development for the International Space Station. Adv Space Res. 2001;27(5):1023–30.
16. Sreejalekshmi KG, et al. Customising hardware for space biology experiments.
17. https://www.issnationallab.org/spacex-crs-25-mission-overview/. Accessed 25 March 2023.
18. Williams D, Kuipers A, Mukai C, Thirsk R. Acclimation during space flight: effects on human physiology. CMAJ. 2009;13:1317–23. PMID: 19509005; PMCID: PMC2696527.
19. Macias B, et al. Anterior and posterior ocular structures change during long-duration spaceflight and one year after landing. Invest Ophthalmol Vis Sci. 2018;59:722.
20. Thirsk RB. Health care for deep space explorers. Ann ICRP. 2020;49(1):182–4.
21. Garrett-Bakelman, et al. Science. 2019;364(6436):eaau8650.

22. Lobrich M, Jeggo PA. Science. 2019;364(6436): 127–8.
23. Rutter L, Barker R, Bezdan D, Cope H, et al. A new era for space life science: International standards for space omics processing. Patterns. 2020;1(9):100148.
24. Gregory G. Spin-off: the fruit of space research. In: The UNESCO courier: a window open on the world, vol. XXIII. Paris: UNESCO; 1970. p. 1–38. https://unesdoc.unesco.org/ark:/48223/pf0000078253.
25. https://www.nasa.gov/sites/default/files/atoms/files/iss_benefits_for_humanity_2022_book.pdf.
26. Garcia M. Innovative 3D telemedicine to help keep astronauts healthy. National Aeronautics and Space Administration (NASA), 2022. https://www.nasa.gov/feature/innovative-3d-telemedicine-to-help-keep-astronauts-healthy. Accessed 10 April 2023.
27. Bhuvaneshwar GS, Muraleedharan CV, Vijayan GA, Kumar RS, Valiathan MS. Development of the Chitra tilting disc heart valve prosthesis. J Heart Valve Dis. 1996;4:448–58.
28. https://www.nasa.gov/topics/nasalife/features/heals.html. Accessed 15 March 2023.
29. Furukawa S, Chatani M, Higashitani A, Higashibata A, et al. Findings from recent studies by the Japan Aerospace Exploration Agency examining musculoskeletal atrophy in space and on Earth. NPJ Micrograv. 2021;7(1):18. PMID: 34039989; PMCID: PMC8155041.
30. Carpinella I, Cattaneo D, Bonora G, Bowman T, et al. Wearable sensor-based biofeedback training for balance and gait in Parkinson disease: a pilot randomized controlled trial. Arch Phys Med Rehabil. 2017;98(4):622–30.
31. Tan S, Tran V, Stretton B, Gupta A, et al. The final frontier: palliative care in space is an inevitability. J Palliat Care. 2023;38(4):405–6. https://doi.org/10.1177/08258597231159839.
32. Blaber E, Sato K, Almeida EAC. Stem cell health and tissue regeneration in microgravity. Stem Cells Dev. 2014;23:73–8. https://doi.org/10.1089/scd.2014.0408.
33. Riwaldt S, Corydon TJ, Pantalone D, Sahana J, et al. Role of apoptosis in wound healing and apoptosis alterations in microgravity. Front Bioeng Biotechnol. 2021;9:679650. PMID: 34222218; PMCID: PMC8248797.
34. Aliberti F, Paolin E, Benedetti L, Cusella G, Ceccarelli G. 3D bioprinting and Rigenera® micrografting technology: a possible countermeasure for wound healing in spaceflight. Front Bioeng Biotechnol. 2022;10:937709. PMID: 36110324; PMCID: PMC9468613.

4 Progress and Prospects in CRISPR Genome Engineering Nucleases

Kalpana Surendranath, Khalid Akram, Radhakrishnan Kanagaraj, Munuse C. Savash Ishanzadeh, Sana Khan, Jessica Pantuzcek, Mugdha Karri, Shashwat Guha, Sneha Latha Rangan, Ekam Kour, Kevin Roshan Amalanathan, and John J. Murphy

4.1 CRISPR a Breakthrough in Basic Research

CRISPR is an acronym for clustered regularly interspaced short palindromic repeats, has impacted several areas of biological, biomedical, and biotechnology in this decade. CRISPR-Cas9 is a result of extensive research into the acquired immune systems of archaea and bacteria by researchers across the globe spanning several decades. The origins of CRISPR date back to a series of discoveries starting in 1987 in Japan. During an investigation of the *iap* gene in *Escherichia coli's* phosphate metabolism, Ishino et al. identified a unique structure in the 3′ flanking region of the gene [1]. This structure consisted of five homologous sequences of 29 nucleotides arranged as direct repeats with 32 nucleotides spacing between them. Francisco Mojica, a researcher from the University of Alicante, used the term "CRISPR" in 1990 to describe the structure and organization of these sequences in bacteria, known as clustered regularly interspaced short palindromic repeats [2].

Further studies conducted in the early 2000s revealed the prevalence of CRISPR sequences in

K. Surendranath (✉)
Genome Engineering Laboratory, School of Life Sciences, University of Westminster, London, UK

Centre for Drug Discovery and Development, Sathyabama Institute of Science and Technology, Chennai, India
e-mail: k.surendranath1@westminster.ac.uk

K. Akram · S. Khan · M. Karri · S. Guha · S. L. Rangan · E. Kour · K. R. Amalanathan · J. J. Murphy
Genome Engineering Laboratory, School of Life Sciences, University of Westminster, London, UK

R. Kanagaraj
Institute of Medical, Biomedical and Allied Health Education, St. George's University of London, London, UK

Genome Engineering Laboratory, School of Life Sciences, University of Westminster, London, UK

Centre for Drug Discovery and Development, Sathyabama Institute of Science and Technology, Chennai, India

M. C. Savash Ishanzadeh
Genome Engineering Laboratory, School of Life Sciences, University of Westminster, London, UK

Nuffield Department of Women's and Reproductive Health, Institute of Reproductive Sciences (IRS), Oxford, UK

J. Pantuzcek
Genome Engineering Laboratory, School of Life Sciences, University of Westminster, London, UK

Faculty of Medicine, Department of Metabolism, Digestion and Reproduction, Imperial College London, South Kensington Campus, London, UK

K. Parthasarathy, R. Manikkam (eds.), *Translational Research in Biomedical Sciences: Recent Progress and Future Prospects*, https://doi.org/10.1007/978-981-97-1777-4_4

archaea and bacteria, frequently accompanied by specific sequences identified as CRISPR-associated (Cas) genes. Jansen et al. discovered that these structures were found in multiple copies within the chromosomes of archaea and bacteria, suggesting their potential mobility. The study also identified the presence of Cas genes adjacent to the CRISPR loci and proposed a functional relationship in prokaryotes [3]. The four Cas proteins they identified contained motifs commonly found in helicases of superfamily 2 and the RecB family of exonucleases, indicating their possible roles in DNA metabolism or gene expression. Groundbreaking studies conducted in 2005 independently by Francisco Mojica and Christine Pourcel shed light on the spacer regions within CRISPR loci and proved that these DNA fragments were derived from genomes of bacteriophages [4]. In addition, these non-bacterial DNA elements were found to be associated with the antiviral immunity of bacteria serving similar roles as eukaryotic RNA interference (RNAi) systems. Studies on *Streptococcus thermophilus* have further established the link between CRISPR sequences and resistance to bacteriophage infection [5]. Subsequent investigations identified that the integration of new spacers derived from the DNA sequence of infecting bacteriophage played a crucial role in bacterial resistance to infections by the same strain of the virus and the absence of Cas proteins in bacteria was found to lead to susceptibility to viral infections [6]. Collectively, these findings demonstrate that the CRISPR immune memory mechanism enables bacteria to defend against viral infections that pose a threat to their survival [4].

4.2 The CRISPR Arm of Bacterial Adaptive Immunity

Bacteria employ various defence mechanisms to combat viral infections, including cell surface modification to prevent bacteriophage access, induction of cell apoptosis to control infection spread, and restriction-modification systems [7–9]. Among these mechanisms, CRISPR-Cas systems serve as natural prokaryotic adaptive immune systems that store foreign DNA as a genomic memory to protect against viral invasions [10].

In an ongoing molecular race for survival, both bacteriophages and bacteria evolve through point mutations in the protospacers and the protospacer adjacent motifs (PAM), a conserved sequence that determines the targeting of CRISPR immune mechanisms. In a coculture of *S. thermophilus* with phages, they are shown to evolve asynchronously, as evidenced by the variations in the spacer repertoire [11]. CRISPR systems work in conjunction with other defence mechanisms, such as restriction-modification systems, abortive infections, and adsorption blocks, to safeguard prokaryotic populations from phage infections. The spacers, which are DNA segments derived from invading bacteriophages, play a crucial role in this process. Decades of research on the repetitive sequences, their organization, and their functions within the densely packed bacterial genome have significantly advanced our understanding of CRISPR systems [1, 11, 12].

As depicted in detail in Fig. 4.1, an incoming bacteriophage is cut into fragments by a series of Cas enzymes, leading to the integration of a snippet into the bacterial genome. During the adaptation phase, the section of the viral DNA excised through double-stranded breaks, serves as a protospacer that is inserted into the bacterial genome between two repeat sequences at the beginning of the CRISPR array. This stored DNA fragment serves as a memory of the specific wave of infection and is maintained while the corresponding viral strain prevails. During a subsequent infection, the expression of virus-specific CRISPR RNAs is activated in the expression stage. The entire CRISPR array is transcribed into a single long precursor CRISPR RNA (pre-crRNA). This pre-crRNA is then processed into mature crRNAs by a distinct complex of Cas proteins and nucleases, or sometimes by external RNases [13]. The CRISPR array consists of a sequence of 20–50 base pairs direct repeats preceded by an AT-rich leader region and

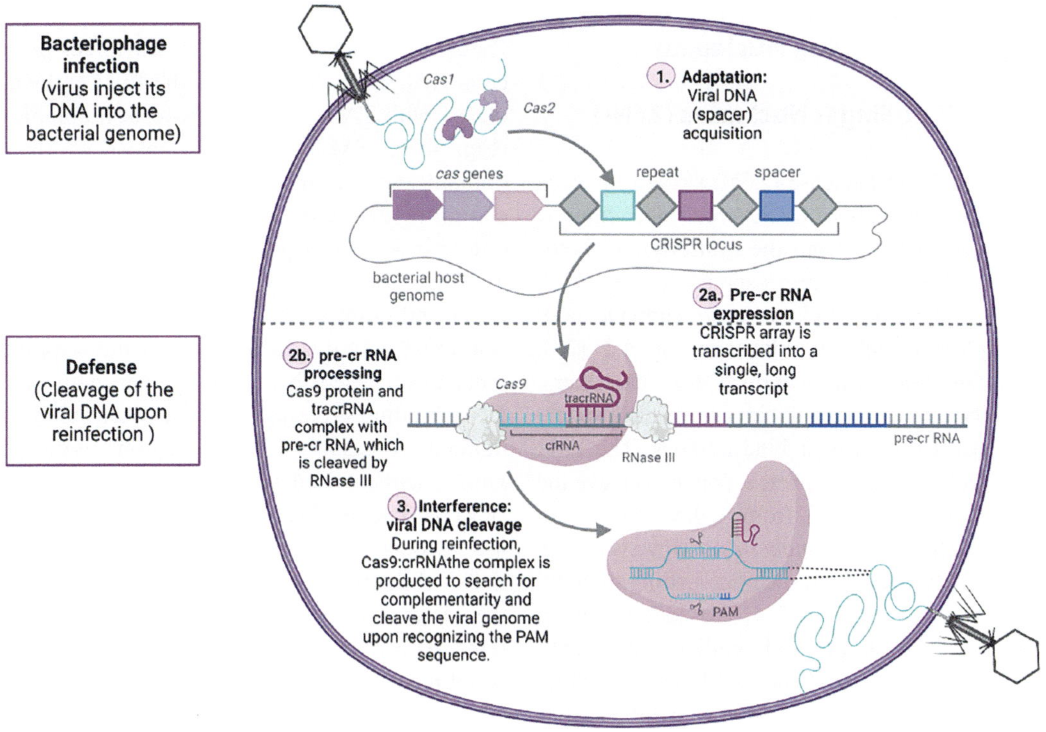

Fig. 4.1 A schematic representation of CRISPR-Cas9 system in bacterial immune system. CRISPR-induced immune response in bacteria consists of three main stages: adaptation (1), pre-crRNA expression (2a) and processing (2b), and interference (3). During adaptation, bacteria harvest viral DNA and incorporate it into CRISPR locus, this allows the cell to store a "memory" of that infection. The expression of CRISPR locus produces a long strand of pre-crRNA, which is then processed in preparation for the defence, to produce a functioning Cas9:crRNA complex. During the interference stage the Cas9:sgRNA complex searches for the viral DNA molecule, and upon recognition induces DSBs at target sites effectively destroying the viral genome

is typically used to define CRISPR-Cas systems. These arrays can contain approximately 2 to 100 repeats, usually palindromic, with lengths of 25–35 base pairs each. Spacers, which are typically 30–40 base pairs long, are situated between the repeats. The CRISPR array also includes a set of Cas genes encoding the adaptation and effector modules, along with accessory genes [14, 15]. A wealth of information on CRISPRs and Cas genes is now available online through databases and tools [16].

Anti-CRISPR (Acr) proteins showcase the ongoing battle for survival between bacteria and viruses [17]. They are a diverse group of small protein inhibitors that effectively hinder the immune function of CRISPR-Cas systems at different stages. So far, researchers have discovered 50 distinct non-homologous anti-CRISPR proteins [18]. These proteins equip phages with the ability to overcome the powerful CRISPR-Cas immune response deployed by bacteria. Mutating the anti-CRISPR genes in bacteriophages that *target Pseudomonas aeruginosa* renders them ineffective against bacteria while introducing the same genes into a targeted phage allows it to evade the CRISPR/Cas system [19]. AcrIIA4 hinders Cas9 binding to the PAM site, while AcrIIC3 induces Cas protein dimerization, thereby blocking PAM recognition [20, 21]. AcrIIC2 disrupts the assembly of the crRNA-Cas complex, leading to interference with crRNA loading and AcrIIC1 binds specifically to Cas9's HNH endonuclease domain, preventing DNA cleavage at the target site [22].

4.3 Pre-CRISPR Genome Engineering Nucleases

4.3.1 Zinc Finger Nucleases (ZFNs)

The zinc finger nuclease (ZFN) system involves two main domains: C2H2-type zinc fingers, which are derived from the transcription factor ZIF268/EGR1 and are responsible for DNA binding, and the FokI bacterial endonuclease, which is responsible for cleavage (Fig. 4.3) [23]. Each zinc finger can recognize 9–18 base pairs, and when paired, the zinc fingers cleave a spacer sequence between their binding sites. The FokI endonuclease which acts as a dimer to cleave the DNA is derived from the bacterium *Flavobacterium okeanokoites*. However, the cleavage by FokI is nonspecific, leading to undesired cleavage of DNA [24]. To address this, a modified version of FokI, called a half FokI endonuclease, is used. The half FokI endonuclease is an inactive form of FokI that exhibits activity only when it forms a dimer, reducing the nonspecific cleavage. Despite its potential, ZFNs has limitations due to their complex multimeric protein with structures, making engineering, producing, and achieving sufficient selectivity with larger proteins challenging [25]. Moreover, target-site overlapping binding specificities of individual zinc fingers can interfere with adjacent zinc fingers, with the potential to introduce difficulties in applications of this method. ZFN-mediated inactivation of genes such as PTEN, NF1, and TET2 exhibited adverse effects. For example, inactivating tumour suppressor genes PTEN and NF1 can result in nf1a or nf1b loss of function, reported as lethal in zebrafish. Inactivation of transcriptional regulator TET2 involved in DNA demethylation can lead to myelodysplastic syndromes [23].

4.3.2 Transcription Activator-Like Effector Nucleases (TALENS)

Transcription Activator-Like Effector Nucleases (TALENs) are derived from bacteria of the genus Xanthomonas, belonging to the Pseudomonadaceae family, which infect plant cells [26]. TALENs combine the FokI endonuclease with TALE proteins to form a complex (Fig. 4.3). TALE proteins consist of three domains: an N-terminal translocation domain, a central repeat domain for DNA binding, and a C-terminal transcriptional activation domain. TALENs function by "wrapping" around the DNA and employing a one-dimensional, non-rotational activity, in contrast to the hopping mechanism used by other sequence-specific DNA-binding proteins [27]. The TALE binding domain consists of repeat regions with 34 amino acids, called repeat variable diresidues (RVDs). The residues at position 13 of the RVD are associated with base-specific DNA contacts, while the residues at position 12 stabilize the interaction between DNA and TALE proteins. The repeat region also includes a truncated repeat with 20 residues that, collectively, allow TALENs to interact with DNA and induce conformational changes leading to DNA cleavage through recognition of individual nucleotides [28, 29]. TALENs possess distinct advantages as they can recognize both normal target sequences and sequences with one base pair deletion stemming from an aberrant repeat. Additionally, specific RVDs can differentiate between methylated and unmethylated cytosine, allowing TALENs to distinguish between two sequences with one nucleotide methylation difference. This specificity enables application of TALENs in gene manipulation through methylation [27]. Delivery of TALENs can be optimized using various techniques, including physical methods such as biolistic transformation, microinjection, or electroporation, as well as bacterial or viral delivery and chemical methods involving liposomes, transfection reagents, or polyethylene gycol (PEG) [27]. Compared to CRISPR and ZFNs, TALENs tend to favour deletions greater than one base pair (Fig. 4.2). Heterodimerization of TALENs and two amino acid additions in FokI further improve target specificity and nuclease activity while decreasing toxicity [27].

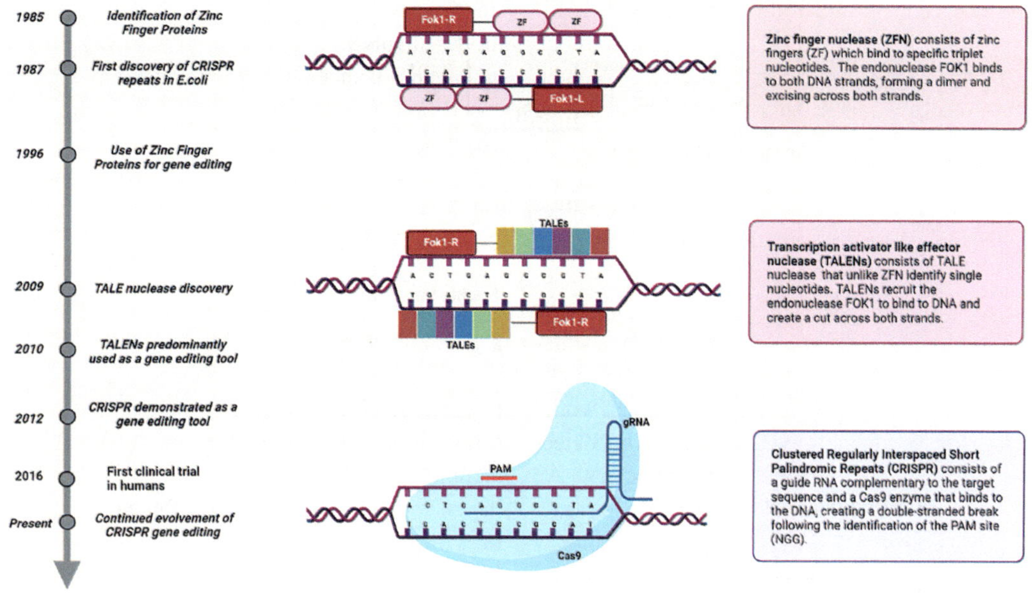

Fig. 4.2 A timeline showing the progression, development, and continuous refinement of genome engineering nucleases. The three major types of nucleases discussed are represented: clustered regularly interspaced short palindromic repeats (CRISPR), zinc finger nucleases (ZFNs), and transcription activator-like effector nucleases (TALENs)

4.4 First-Generation Genome Editing Technologies

Genome editing technologies, developed over a decade from 2002 to 2012, include ZFNs, TALENs, and the RNA-guided CRISPR-Cas nuclease system, belonging to the first-generation genome editing methods. ZFNs and TALENs employ complexes of modular DNA-binding proteins and endonuclease domains, enabling precise DNA targeting and the generation of DSBs [23]. Protospacer adjacent motif enables sequence recognition by the widely used CRISPR-Cas9 system capable of generating double-strand breaks at the target site [30]. Double-strand breaks are targeted for repair through error-prone non-homologous end joining (NHEJ) or homology-directed repair (HDR) mechanisms (Fig. 4.3). However, a limitation of CRISPR-Cas9 is the potential for off-target mutagenesis which led to the development of approaches such as CRISPRHIDE and CRISPR guard to evade off-target effects [31, 32].

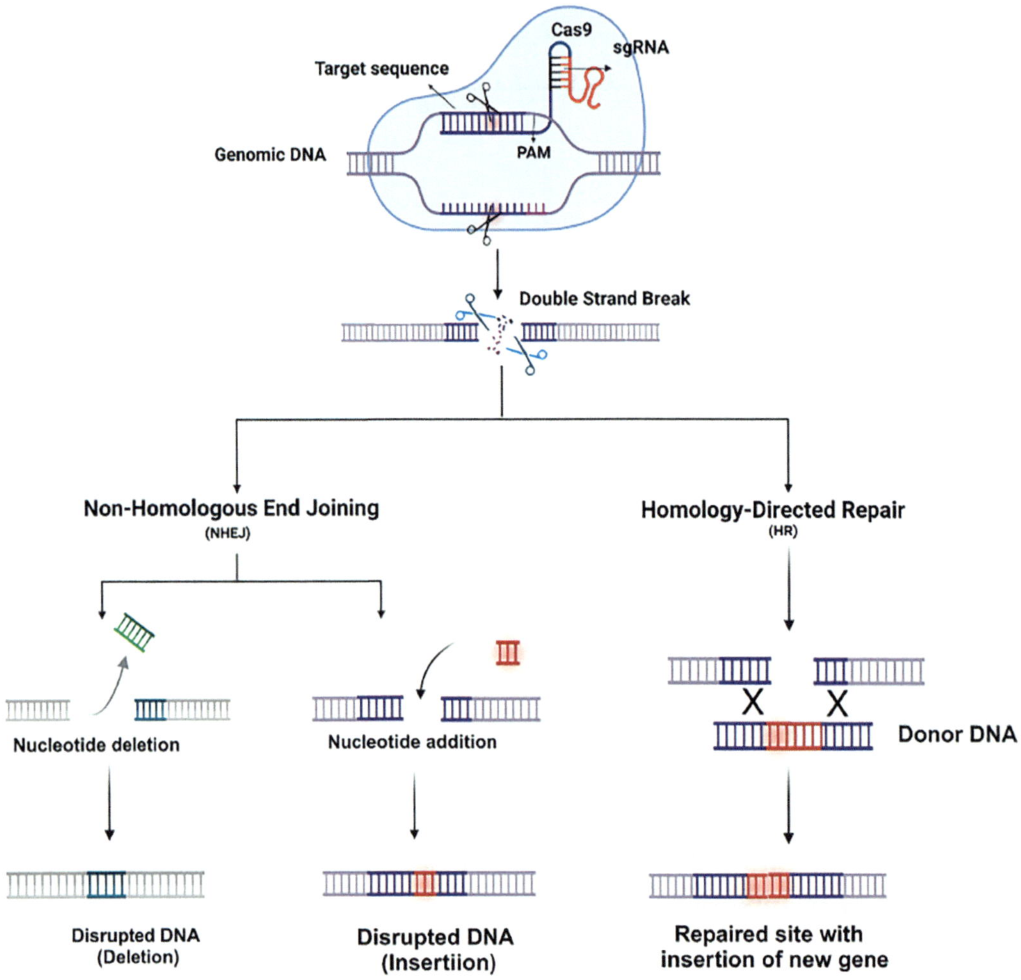

Fig. 4.3 CRISPR-Cas9 mediated gene editing and double-stranded break repair. Gene editing through CRISPR-Cas9 technology relies on the cell's DNA repair mechanisms to facilitate the repair of double-stranded breaks (DSBs). Two primary DSB repair pathways are involved: non-homologous end joining (NHEJ) and homology-directed repair (HDR). (a) NHEJ is an error-prone DNA repair mechanism that often introduces insertions or deletions of bases at the double-strand break site leading to frameshifts, resulting in the disruption or knockout of the target gene. (b) HDR employs a homologous template DNA with the correct sequence to repair the DSB. By providing a template, specific mutations can be repaired or introduced

4.5 CRISPR-Cas Systems

Since their discovery, CRISPR-Cas systems have attracted interest leading to the identification of numerous new variants. The complexity of these systems suggests a long evolutionary history and the classification of the variants has been challenging due to their high diversity and lack of phylogeny markers. Phylogenetic studies show that mobile genetic elements (MGEs) have significantly shaped the evolution of CRISPR-Cas systems [33]. CRISPR-Cas systems identified so far are divided into two classes based on the molecular mechanisms and structure of the effector proteins. Class 1 and Class 2 complexes are comprised of multi-subunit effector and single-unit effector complexes respectively. Class 1 is predominantly found in bacteria and archaea, while Class 2 is restricted to bacteria which are further categorized into types I, III, and IV belonging to Class 1, and types II, V, and VI belonging to Class 2. Each type is characterized by distinct effector protein architecture and can be further divided into subtypes based on specific variations (Fig. 4.4).

Recent research suggests that casposons, which are found in bacteria and archaea, serve as ancestors to the adaptation module of CRISPR-Cas systems. Casposons are transposable elements with terminal inverted repeats (TIRs) and encode a casposase protein that shares similarities with Cas1, a protein involved in CRISPR spacer acquisition [34]. Cas1 and Cas2 are components of heterotetrameric complexes that play crucial roles in integrating spacers into the CRISPR array during the adaptation phase. Cas6 endoribonuclease is responsible for cleaving repeat sequences within the pre-crRNA structure and recognizing hairpins within palindromic sequences in the repeats. CrRNA processing in Subtype I-C CRISPR-Cas systems involves Cas5d, while Class 1 type IV systems employ Csf5 for crRNA maturation. In Class 2 type II systems, RNase III and tracrRNA are used for the same purpose. Additionally, Cas5, Cas2, and Csy2 participate in pre-crRNA processing in various organisms. The diversity of processing endoribonucleases of different Cas systems is currently being investigated [35]. The impact of type IV systems on DNA or RNA remains unclear. Type VI systems can edit RNA, while type III systems can edit both DNA and RNA. Types I, II, and V systems are capable of detecting and cleaving DNA. Table 4.1 provides a summary of the different CRISPR-Cas systems, highlighting their key features and applications.

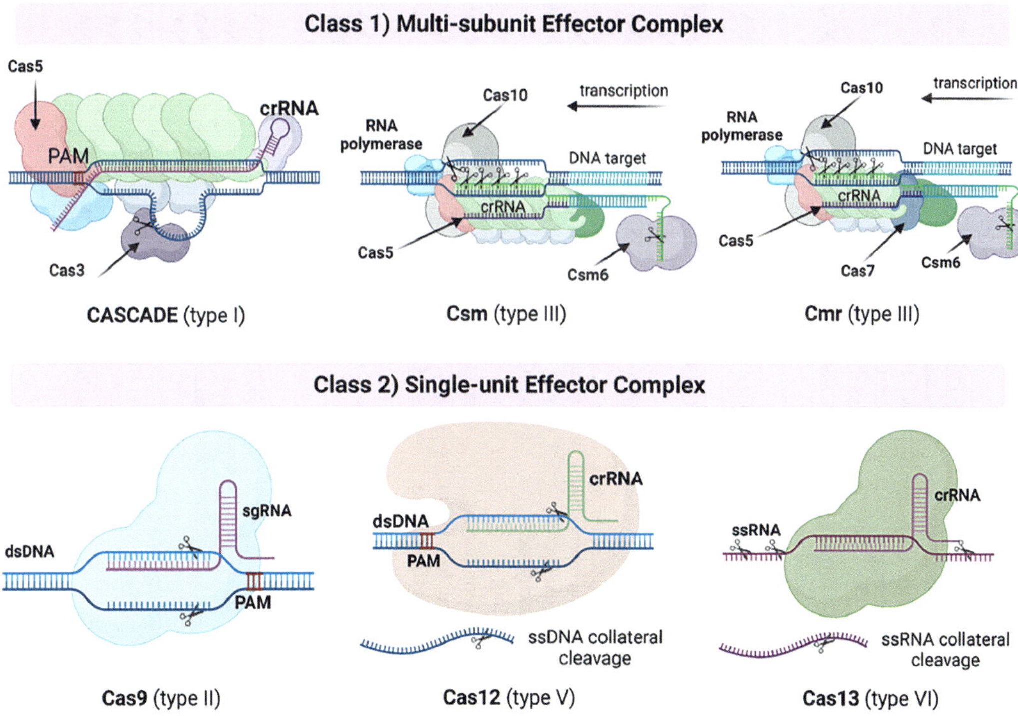

Fig. 4.4 Class 1 and class 2 CRISPR systems. Class 1 CRISPR systems feature multi-subunit effector complexes like cascade and Csm work together using crRNA-guided surveillance and interference to target foreign DNA or RNA, while Class 2 CRISPR systems involve single-effector proteins, e.g., Cas9 or Cas12a guided by a single guide RNA (sgRNA) and cleave target DNA

Table 4.1 A comprehensive summary of CRISPR-Cas systems

Type/subtype	Key features	Cas proteins	PAM/PFS	Target and efficiency	Domain	TracrRNA/ scoutRNA	Applications in disease research
I-subtypes—A, B, C, D, E, F, U	Multi-subunit effector complexes, long-range DNA cleavage	Cascade—Cas3, Cas7, Cas5, Cas6, Cas8	–	dsDNA/ high	HD fused to Cas3	No	Functional genomics studies to identify cancer-associated genes and pathways transcriptional regulation, antimicrobial therapy
II-subtype A	Single-component RNA-guided system, simple and versatile	SpCas9	NGG	dsDNA/ high	RuvC, HNH	Yes (TracrRNA)	Gene editing, genome-wide screens, gene regulation, diagnostics and disease modelling, drug target screens
II-subtype A		SaCas9	NNGRRT	dsDNA	RuvC, HNH	Yes (TracrRNA)	
II-subtype B		FnCas9	NGG	dsDNA/ ssRNA	RuvC, HNH	Yes (TracrRNA)	
II-subtype C		NmCas9	NNNNGATT	dsDNA	RuvC, HNH	Yes (TracrRNA)	
III-subtypes A, B, C, D	Targeting both DNA and RNA, cyclic oligoadenylate signalling	Cascade—Cas10, Cas6, Cas7, Cas5, Cas11	–	ssRNA/ moderate	HD fused to Cas10	No	RNA editing, gene regulation, antiviral defence, epigenetic regulation of cancer-related genes
IV-subtypes A, B	Single-component RNA-guided system, smaller effector size	Cascade—Cas12, Cas5, Cas6, Cas8	–	dsDNA/ high	HD fused to Cas10-like	No	Gene editing, diagnostics, gene regulation, synthetic biology, molecular imaging, cancer immunotherapy
V-subtype A	Single-component RNA-guided system, collateral RNA cleavage	Cas12a	5′ AT-rich (TTV)	dsDNA/ ssDNA high	RuvC, Nuc	No	RNA editing, antiviral defence, transcriptome engineering
V-subtype B		Cas12b	5′ AT-rich (TTN)	dsDNA/ ssDNA	RuvC	Yes (TracrRNA)	
V-subtype C		Cas12c	5′ AT-rich (TG/ TN)	dsDNA/ ssDNA	RuvC	Yes (scoutRNA)	
V-subtype D		Cas12d	TA/TG	dsDNA/ ssDNA	RuvC	Yes (scoutRNA)	
V-subtype E		Cas12e	TTCN	dsDNA	–	Yes (TracrRNA)	

Type/subtype	Key features	Cas proteins	PAM/PFS	Target and efficiency	Domain	TracrRNA/ scoutRNA	Applications in disease research
V-subtype C	F	Cas14	–	ssDNA	–	Yes (TracrRNA)	Detects specific sequences via fluorescence screening and SNPs detection in targets. HUDSON-viral screening, epidemiology, phylogenetic studies.
V-subtype G		Cas12g	–	ssRNA	REC2, Nuc	Yes (TracrRNA)	
V-subtype H		Cas12h	RTR	dsDNA/ ssDNA	–	No	
V-subtype I		Cas12i	TTN	dsDNA/ ssDNA	RuvC	No	
V-subtype K		Cas12k	GTN	dsDNA	Inactive RuvC & Tn7-like transposon	Yes (TracrRNA)	
V	Φ	Cas12j	–	dsDNA/ ssDNA	–	No	
VI-subtype A	Single-component RNA-guided system, target RNA cleavage	Cas13a	3′PFS: Non-G	ssRNA	2xHEPN	No	Modulation of non-coding RNAs in cancer progression
VI-subtype B		Cas13b	5′PFS: Non-C; 3′PFS: NAN/ NNA	ssRNA	2xHEPN	No	
VI-subtype C		Cas13c	–	ssRNA	2xHEPN	No	
VI-subtype C	D	Cas13d	–	ssRNA	2xHEPN	No	

4.6 Genome Engineering Nucleases

With a few exceptions like Cas1 and Cas3, the sequences of most Cas proteins are not conserved due to the rapid evolution of defence systems. The molecular weight of CRISPR-Cas proteins identified so far falls in the range of approximately 100–400 kDa.

4.6.1 Cas9

CRISPR-associated protein 9 (Cas9) belonging to the class II type II CRISPR system is an RNA-guided DNA endonuclease composed of two distinct domains: a recognition domain that binds to the guide RNA (gRNA) and a nuclease domain responsible for cleaving the target DNA. The recognition domain comprises two RNase H-like domains that form a structural unit facilitating binding to the gRNA [36]. The nuclease domain consists of two important components: a RuvC-like domain, a structure-specific endonuclease that binds exclusively to the Holliday structure, an intermediate formed during the late stage of homologous recombination, and an HNH-like domain with the characteristic Histidine and Asparagine residues responsible for cleaving the target DNA. Specifically, the HNH-like domain cleaves the complementary strand to the gRNA, while the RuvC-like domain cleaves the non-complementary strand [37, 38]. In addition, Cas9 possesses a PAM-interacting domain, which recognizes a specific DNA sequence adjacent to the target site known as the protospacer adjacent motif (PAM). The PAM sequence is crucial for the recognition and binding of Cas9 to the target DNA [30]. Cas9 binds to the gRNA to effectively target and cleave specific DNA sequences 3 bases away from the PAM site. The gRNA has 2 crucial parts, CRISPR RNA (crRNA), a 20-nt sequence that is complementary to the target DNA, and a trans-activating CRISPR RNA (tracrRNA) sequence with affinity to bind to the recognition domain of Cas9 [38]. The gRNA and Cas9 protein binding to the target DNA sequence changes the confirmation of Cas9 enabling the nuclease domains to cut the DNA on both the strands precisely. The resulting double-strand break in human cells can be repaired through two main cellular mechanisms: non-homologous end joining (NHEJ) or homology-directed repair (HDR) [30]. The interplay between the DSB repair pathways NHEJ and HDR determines the outcomes of Cas9-mediated genome editing. Also, several factors, including the cell type, availability of suitable repair templates, and regulatory factors that influence the activity of these repair mechanisms are vital for optimized outcomes of CRISPR-Cas9-mediated genome editing [39].

4.6.2 dCas9

Structurally, dCas9 shares the same protein architecture as Cas9, comprising two distinct domains: the recognition domain and the nuclease domain. However, specific mutations in the nuclease domain, such as D10A and H840A, render the RuVC and HNH sub-domains inactive, thereby preventing dCas9 from introducing DSBs [38]. The modification allows dCas9 to function as a programmable DNA-binding protein, capable of specifically targeting DNA sequences without inducing DNA cleavage [38]. This unique characteristic of dCas9 makes it a valuable tool for various genome editing applications that require precise DNA targeting without altering the genetic information. Additionally, dCas9 can be utilized for cleavage-free knock-in of sequences by creating a single-strand nick and facilitating insertion with the help of single-strand annealing proteins (SSAPs) [40] (Fig. 4.5). Interestingly, dCas9 without a cutting activity can be employed to mask access to the target DNA sequence for instance promoter regions by other proteins, or to recruit additional proteins to the target site including differential regulation of gene expression and imaging [41–43]. This is achieved by fusing dCas9 with a transcriptional repressor domain, such as SRDX, or an activator domain, such as VP64 [44], respec-

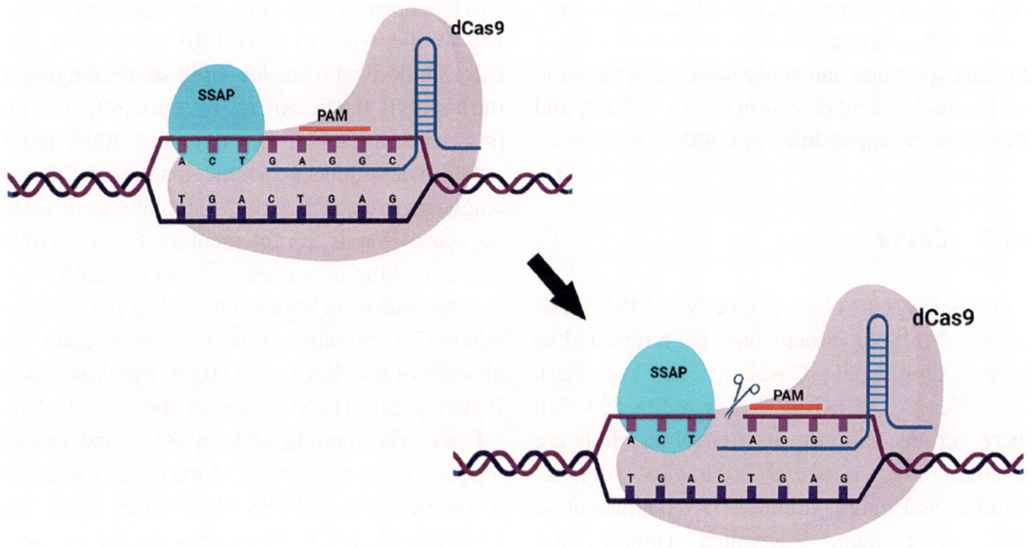

Fig. 4.5 Dead Cas9 based gene editing. The figure shows the action of fusion protein of dead Cas9 (dCas9) enzyme and single-strand annealing (SSAP) protein, where they collaboratively perform a precise "nick" on a single strand of DNA after recognizing the PAM site

tively. dCas9-fusion repressor protein can inhibit the binding of the cell's transcription machinery, including RNA polymerase, to the promoter region, thereby suppressing gene expression. Alternatively, when dCas9 is fused to an activator domain, it can activate gene expression without introducing changes to the DNA sequence [41].

4.6.3 Cas10

CRISPR-associated protein 10 (Cas10) also known as Csm, Cmr or Csx is a multifunctional protein belonging to the class I type III CRISPR-Cas system plays a crucial role in the adaptive immune systems of bacteria and archaea [45]. Unlike the guide RNA in type II systems, the guide RNA in Type III systems consists of a fusion between CRISPR RNA (crRNA) and trans-activating RNA (tracrRNA). Unlike Cas9, Cas10 is a larger protein consisting of multiple domains including the CRISPR-associated Rossmann fold (CARF) domain, histidine-aspartate (HD) domain, palm domain, and RuvC-like nuclease domain. The CARF domain, unique to Cas10, is involved in RNA binding and processing through the RNA recognition motif (RRM). Unlike Cas9 and Cas3, Cas10 actively participates in RNA binding. The HD domain is responsible for metal ion binding and the cleavage of nucleic acids, specifically single-stranded DNA. The palm domain plays a role in binding and stabilizing the guide RNA, while the RuvC-like nuclease domain is responsible for cleaving the target DNA [46]. Cas10 exhibits versatility in targeting both double-stranded DNA (dsDNA) and single-stranded RNA (ssRNA) through the formation of distinct effector complexes. In type III-A systems, Cas10 forms Csm effector complexes that target and degrade dsDNA. In type III-B systems, it forms Cmr effector complexes that target and degrade ssRNA [47]. Cas10 effector complexes have two functions: the generation of cyclic oligoadenylate and RNA-guided nucleic acid cleavage. Upon binding to the target RNA, cyclase activity is activated, leading to DNA degradation. However, subsequent RNA cleavage deactivates cyclase activity and suppresses DNase activity [45, 48]. This dual targeting and cleavage ability of Cas10 plays a vital role in bacterial immunity against phages. In addition to its role in bacterial immunity, Cas10 has been found to have non-immune functions such as regulation of gene expression and hence serves as a valuable tool for nucleic acid detection due to its RNA and DNA tracking capabilities [45, 49].

4.6.4 Cas12

Cas12 belongs to class 2 type V CRISPR-Cas systems. Multiple variants have been reported so far including Cpf1 (Cas12a), c2c1 (Cas12b), c2c3 (Cas12c), Cas12e, and Cas12I [50–52]. These variants differing in their N-terminus are classified based on their ability to cleave double-stranded and single-stranded DNA adjacent to PAM using their C-terminal endonuclease domain and the HNH-like domain similar to Cas9 [53, 54]. Cas12 specifically recognizes PAM regions rich in T-content, limiting its target range. However, a new family, Cas12I, has been reported to recognize C-rich PAM sequences [50]. Unlike the CRISPR-Cas9 system, which utilizes single guide RNA (sgRNA) in combination with a crRNA-tracrRNA duplex, Cas12a (type V-A) functions with a single CRISPR RNA (crRNA) along with repeat and spacer sequences. This complex guides the staggered double-stranded DNA cleavage at the target site by the endonuclease Cas12A [55]. The small protein-crRNA complex derived from Cas12, found in bacteria such as *Francisella novicida* and *Lachnospiraceae* sp., offers a convenient system for inducing DNA interference with either a single nuclease domain or a dual-nuclease domain (Cas12a, Cas12I, Cas12j, and Cas12c) [56–58]. The unique characteristics of the CRISPR-Cas12 protein system make it suitable for applications such as enhanced multiplexing ability, epigenome editing, and detection of minimal amounts of single-stranded DNA in a mixture [59].

4.6.5 Cas 13

Cas13 is a recently discovered Cas protein that plays a crucial role in the defence mechanisms of archaea and bacteria specifically against invasive RNA. There are two distinct subtypes of Cas13: Cas13a, derived from *Leptotrichia shahii* (belonging to the type VI CRISPR/Cas system), and Cas13b, derived from *Prevotell* sp. (belonging to the type III CRISPR/Cas system) [60]. Cas13a precisely and selectively degrades RNA molecules in a sequence-specific manner. It cleaves single-stranded RNA by recognizing a target sequence that is complementary to the crRNA spacer making it an excellent tool for RNA interference and gene regulation studies [61]. Unlike other Cas proteins, Cas13a can tolerate the absence of tracrRNA, as it targets the Protospacer Flanking Site (PFS) region at the 3′-end of the ssRNA. The binding of LshCas13a and crRNA together leads to cleavage of the target RNA with a completely paired PFS (Adenosine, uracil, and Cytosine) [62]. Cas13b exhibits greater precision compared to its subtype counterpart Cas13a. It recognizes target RNA with a PFS flanking the 5′-end of the RNA sequence with A, U, or G, and a PAM at the 3′-end [62]. The nuclease activity responsible for cleaving the target RNA is mediated by the HEPN (higher prokaryotic and eukaryotic nucleotide-binding) domain present in Cas13 [60]. For efficient cleavage of the target RNA, a complementary sequence to the crRNA guide is required. However, a fully paired 3′-end PFS region with the 5′-tag of the crRNA inhibits the cleavage process [62, 63]. Cas13a possesses a bilobed structure comprising the REC and NUC lobes, which are connected and contribute to single nucleotide detection within target sequences [52, 64]. The NUC lobe, housing the HEPN domains, is responsible for both targeting and nonspecific cleavage of RNA. On the other hand, the REC lobe contains three helix-rich domains that facilitate recognition of the crRNA-target RNA helix and guide RNA hairpin loop [64]. The binding of LbuCas13 and its related target RNA brings the two HEPN domains to proximity, forming a catalytic site for cleavage [64]. In the presence of a fully paired 3′-PFS and crRNA in a target-bound LshCas13a complex, the structure required for cleavage formation is inhibited, primarily due to the suppression of the HEPN2 domain [64, 65]. Notably, the activated HEPN domains cleave RNA in a non-specific manner, targeting a region far from the crRNA and rich in uridine [61].

4.6.6 CasΦ

Cas12j2, also known as CasΦ, is a hypercompact effector protein belonging to the type V CRISPR-Cas system. It is derived from large phages and has a length of approximately 750 amino acids [66]. Unlike Cas9 and Cas12a, CasΦ is relatively small, with a size of about 70–80 kDa [66]. This compact size, together with its unique characteristics, makes CasΦ suitable for modifying a wide range of target sites through vector-mediated entry into cells [57]. CasΦ can perform both DNA cleavage and pre-crRNA processing, facilitated by a C-terminal RuvC domain that shares homology with TnpB [57, 66]. It cleaves double-stranded DNA guided by crRNA and PAM sequences. Interestingly, CasΦ requires minimal T-rich sequences in the target site, enabling it to efficiently modify a wide range of targets [57]. Although CasΦ exhibits high specificity, variants such as nCas12j2 and vCas12j2 have been reported to improve in vitro nuclease kinetics compared to CasΦ [57]. CasΦ has been used for genetic manipulation in plants, including applications in epigenome editing to enhance the expression of genes of interest [67]. Unique characteristics, such as an affinity for editing non-dividing cells and tolerance to a range of temperatures, contribute to the robustness of this protein [67]. Furthermore, CasΦ's characteristic PAM, consisting of minimal T-rich sequences, provides an added advantage for successful plant genome engineering [68]. Studies on CasΦ-mediated editing in Arabidopsis have demonstrated minor deletions (~9 base pairs) and induced staggered cuts of 8–12 nucleotides in the target cells [57, 68].

4.6.7 Cas 3

Cas3 nuclease, also known as Csm1, is a signature component of class I type I CRISPR systems, which are more prevalent compared to class II systems. Class I CRISPR systems, specifically the class 1 cascade-Cas3 systems, are highly efficient at inducing large unidirectional genomic deletions [69, 70]. Cas3 functions as a multidomain helicase-nuclease responsible for the degradation of invading viral DNA. Unlike Cas9, which breaks the target DNA specifically, Cas3 shreds the target DNA, resulting in degradation [69, 70]. The Cas3 nuclease is comprised of two main domains: an N-terminal HD (histidine-aspartate) domain and a C-terminal helicase domain connected by a linker. The HD domain contains a conserved metal-dependent endonuclease, cleaving the phosphodiester bonds in the backbone with high specificity while the helicase domain unwinds the double-stranded DNA (dsDNA) substrate [71, 72]. Furthermore, the helicase domain of Cas3 belongs to the superfamily 2 (SF2) of helicases and contains seven conserved motifs responsible for ATP hydrolysis and DNA unwinding. It possesses two RecA-like domains that bind to single-stranded DNA (ssDNA) substrates and a wedge domain that aids in separating the two strands of the dsDNA substrate [71]. The HD domain contains a cluster of four metal ions, coordinated by conserved histidine and aspartate residues, which are crucial for its catalytic activity [71, 72]. Cas3 nuclease is a crucial component of the CRISPR I-E system, found in E. coli, where it works in conjunction with other Cas proteins. Cas6 processes precursor RNA into mature crRNA, with Cas5 and Cas7 involved in handling the 5′ and backbone regions of the crRNA, respectively. Cas11 (Cse2) supports the crRNA structure and the target strand DNA loop (R-loop) structure, while Cas8 (Cse1) recognizes PAM sequences and directs Cas3 to the target [70]. The degradation of viral DNA by Cas3 nuclease occurs in two steps. Firstly, the HD domain cleaves the ssDNA, producing nucleotide fragments that act as signals to recruit additional Cas proteins. In the second step, the helicase domain binds to the ssDNA fragments and utilizes ATP hydrolysis to unwind the dsDNA substrate in the 3′–5′ direction followed by degradation [70, 71]. Owing to the nature of Cas3 nuclease activity, the enzyme is not primarily used for precise cuts in DNA but deployed to regulate gene expression by inducing large-scale deletions or modifying specific regulatory sequences [70].

> Cas3 is like Cas9 with a motor—after finding its specific DNA target, it runs on DNA and chews it up like a Pac-Man. Unlike Cas9, when Cas3 binds to its precise DNA target it begins chewing up one strand of the double-stranded DNA in both directions, leaving a single strand exposed.—Joseph Bondy-Denomy [73]

4.6.8 Off-Target Activity and Recent Developments

The stable interaction between the gRNA/Cas9 ribonucleoprotein complex and target DNA, along with the shielding effect of Cas9 on significant portions of the target DNA, including the PAM sequence, has both advantages and disadvantages. On the one hand, it provides a strong and long-lasting binding for efficient editing. On the other hand, prolonged interaction can increase the risk of recutting and unintended modifications [37]. The progress in the application of CRISPR systems is hindered by two major challenges, namely, poor efficiency and off-target effects. While advancements in recent years have improved on-target efficiency through high-fidelity Cas9 variants and engineered nucleases, the accurate prediction, detection, and mitigation of off-target effects remain a challenge [74, 75]. Researchers are exploring computational and experimental methods to refine off-target detection and minimize unintended genetic alterations. Addressing these challenges is crucial for maximizing the precision and safety of CRISPR-based applications. Certain off-target prediction software including CasOT, Cas-OFFinder, and FlashFry generate data on the alignment of sgRNA sequences with potential off-target sites in the genome [76–78]. On the other hand, algorithms such as MIT score, CCTop, and CROP-IT consider mismatch positions or distances from the PAM sequence [79–81].

In addition to off-target prediction several methods have been tested to reduce off-target activity in Cas9-mediated genome editing including using dual guide RNAs for DSB induction, truncating the guide RNA, and modifying the Cas9 protein itself [30, 82–84]. These strategies aim to enhance the specificity of Cas9 and minimize unintended off-target effects. One such method is CRISPR Guide RNA Assisted Reduction of Damage (CRISPR GUARD) (Fig. 4.6), which leverages the ability of guide RNAs approximately 16 bases in length to direct Cas9 to complementary sites on the target DNA. By co-delivering short guide RNAs that compete with the on-target guide RNA, CRISPR GUARD safeguards off-target sites [31]. The method reported by Harmsen et al. utilized regular guide RNAs alongside trimmed guide RNAs with shortened spacers of >15 nt that allow Cas9 binding to the target site without nuclease activity termed as hide RNAs. The study reports a remarkable increase in the recovery of precise single base-pair substitution events in the presence of both regular guide RNA and hide RNA [32].

RNA-mediated targeting of Cas9 confers exceptional flexibility in selecting target sites, except for the requirement of the NGG protospacer adjacent motif (PAM) positioned alongside the target, despite its prevalence across genomes. The emerging generation of CRISPR effectors significantly broadens the scope of potential targets by introducing alternative PAM motifs [85].

Fig. 4.6 The figure highlights the significance of PAM site mutation and the potential application of CRISPR guard in modulating CRISPR-Cas activity. (**a**) In the wild-type scenario, the Cas protein recognizes the protospacer adjacent motif site on the target DNA, enabling efficient binding and subsequent double-strand break formation. (**b**) Mutation of the PAM site disrupts the Cas protein's recognition, leading to reduced binding and cleavage activity. Interestingly, PAM site mutations have also been shown to improve homology-directed repair efficiency, potentially by altering DNA repair dynamics or favouring HDR over non-homologous end joining. (**c**) The introduction of CRISPR guard method deploys competing guide RNAs that effectively inhibit the binding and cutting of Cas protein at the target DNA. CRISPR guard acts as a safeguard against off-target sites and provides an additional layer of control to enhance the specificity and safety of CRISPR-Cas applications

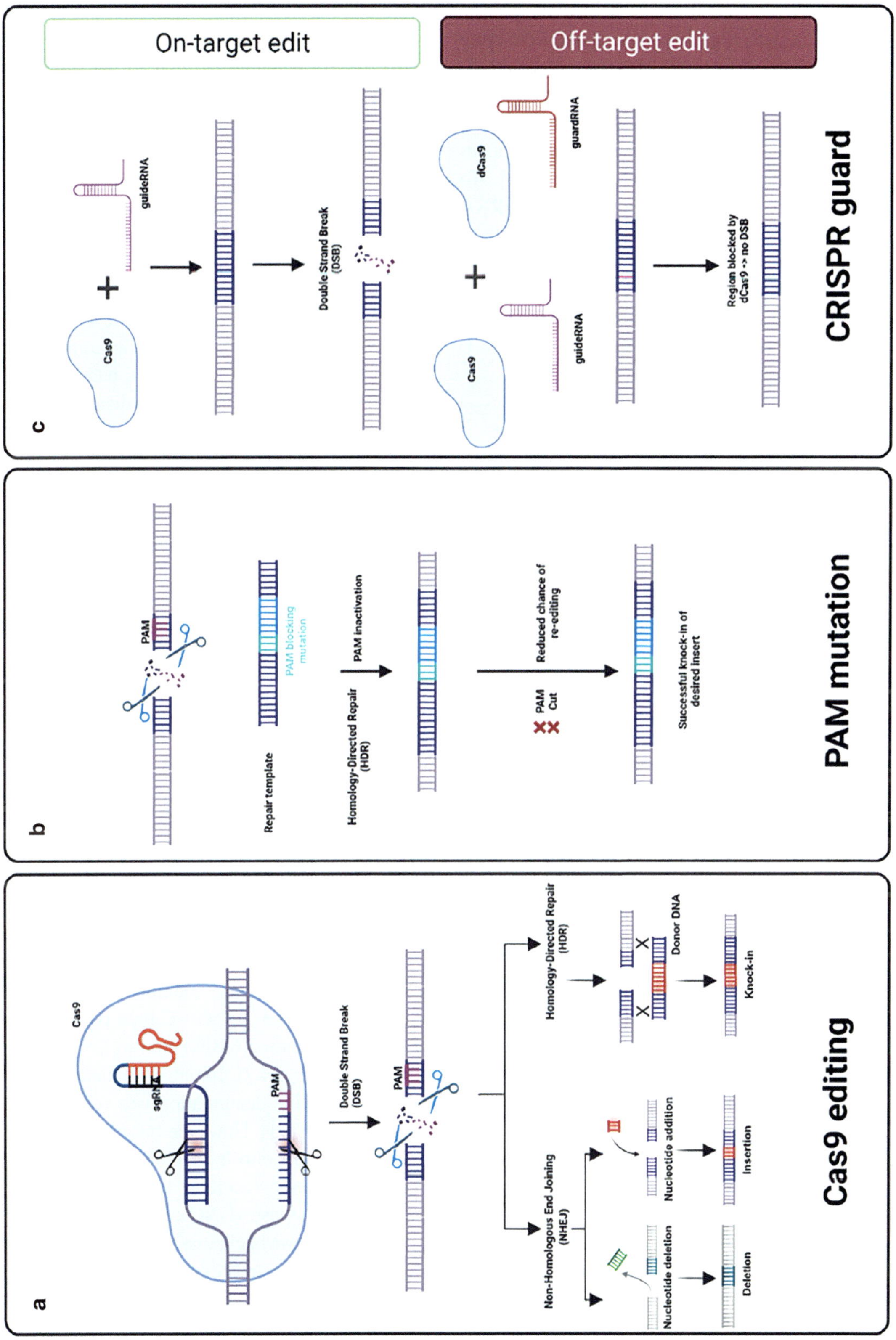
a
Cas9
sgRNA
PAM
Double Strand Break (DSB)
PAM
Non-Homologous End Joining (NHEJ)
Homology-Directed Repair (HDR)
Nucleotide deletion
Nucleotide addition
Donor DNA
Deletion
Insertion
Knock-in
Cas9 editing
b
PAM
Repair template
PAM blocking mutation
Homology-Directed Repair (HDR)
PAM inactivation
PAM Cut
Reduced chance of re-editing
Successful knock-in of desired insert
PAM mutation
c
On-target edit
Off-target edit
Cas9
guideRNA
Double Strand Break (DSB)
Cas9
guideRNA
dCas9
guardRNA
Region blocked by dCas9 -> no DSB
CRISPR guard

The EXTRA-CRISPR method enables precise microRNA detection in bodily fluids, delivering results within 20 min to 3 h. This one-pot technique utilizes Cas12a and Cas13a enzymes to amplify signals and pinpoint microRNA sequences. These sequences can be detected using a smartphone-based fluorescence detection method [86]. To address reduced editing efficiency due to gRNA complexities, an elongated tracrRNA's first hairpin with the stable C(UUCG)G loop motif has been introduced to reduce misfolding, enhancing gRNA efficiency and revolutionizing genome editing capabilities [87].

4.7 Second-Generation Genome Editing

The rapid advancement of genome editing tools with CRISPR technology at the forefront, has transformed research in areas such as human medicine, animal breeding, and disease diagnosis. However, the inherent risk of nonspecific mutations at unintended sites due to DSBs during the editing process remains a challenge. To address this limitation, scientists have developed base editors (BEs), which offer a solution for precise single nucleotide change without inducing DSBs. By utilizing enzymes like cytosine deaminase or adenosine deaminase, BEs enable targeted modifications of individual nucleotides, reducing the risk of unintended mutations [88]. The emergence of prime editors (PEs) in recent years has further enhanced the capabilities of genome editing by using a fused version of Cas9 protein with a reverse transcriptase enzyme, harnessing the power of a prime editing guide RNA (pegRNA) as a repair template to achieve precise gene editing [89]. Further advancements in genome editing tools, from CRISPR to BEs and PEs, hold great promise for revolutionizing the research and treatment of human diseases.

4.7.1 Base Editing

Traditional genome editing methods involved the induction of double-stranded breaks in DNA, followed by random insertions and deletions caused by error-prone DNA repair mechanisms such as NHEJ. NHEJ available through all the stages of the cell cycle often introduces errors, while HDR which primarily occurs during the G2 and S phases of the cell cycle, allows precise and accurate modifications in DNA [88]. As an alternative to traditional approaches, the base conversion technique offers precise modification of individual bases without inducing DSBs. This technique involves the use of a complex comprising a catalytically inactive dCas9 and a cytidine or adenine deaminase enzyme, which is programmed by guide RNA to perform irreversible base conversions. The fusion of catalytically disabled Cas9 with a base modification enzyme enables editing on single-stranded DNA rather than double-stranded DNA [88]. By binding to the DNA target locus, BE allows the target DNA strand to pair with guide RNA, leading to the displacement of the ssDNA into an R loop. The deaminase enzyme then modifies the bases in the displaced ssDNA inserting point mutations without causing DSBs, using a DNA donor template, and bypassing the need for HDR in DNA and circular RNA editing [88]. Also, they do not yield potentially undesired by-products commonly associated with Cas9, such as insertions, deletions, rearrangements, and translocations. Single nucleotide polymorphisms (SNPs) contribute to approximately 50% of known genetic diseases and the discovery of BEs has the potential to revolutionise current approaches to the treatment of diseases associated with SNPs [90].

Based on the outcome of editing there are two types of base editors, adenine base editors (ABEs) convert A • T to G • C base pairs, while cytosine base editors (CBEs) convert C • G to A • T base pairs (Fig. 4.7). Initially, efficient CBE1-mediated cytosine deamination was reported by in vitro in 2016 [91]. However, this efficiency did not translate well into in vivo studies due to the recognition of the resulting U•G mismatch by uracil N-glycosylase (UNG), which cleaves the uracil-deoxyribose backbone glycosidic bond. To overcome this, Liu and colleagues fused an uracil DNA glycosylase inhibitor (UGI) to the C-terminal of BE1, creating BE2. Though UNG

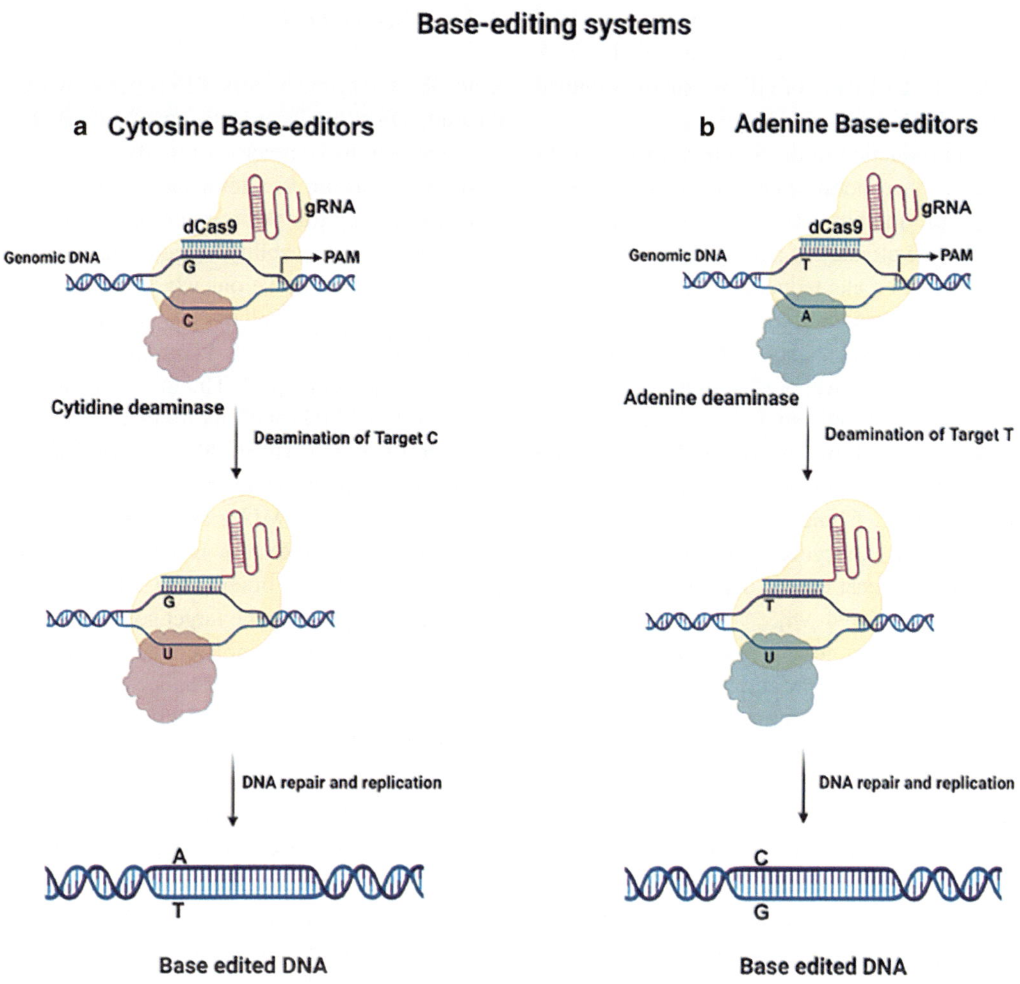

Fig. 4.7 Schematic representation of base editors in CRISPR-based genome editing. Base editors utilize cytidine deaminase or adenine deaminase to enable the conversion of specific bases in the genome. (**a**) Cytidine base editors (CBEs) incorporate cytidine deaminase, allowing the targeted conversion of C•G base pairs into A•T base pairs. (**b**) Adenine base editors (ABEs) incorporate adenine deaminase, enabling the precise conversion of A•T base pairs into C•G base pairs

inhibition was achieved by BE2 leading to successful cytosine editing, BE2 can operate on only one DNA strand at a time. To ensure repair of the unedited strand, catalytically impaired Cas9 nuclease causing a nick in the unedited DNA strand was deployed. Further improvements in BE technology led to the development of BE3, which enabled efficient nicking of the unedited DNA strand at the U•G mismatch, favouring U•A conversion [92] which significantly improved editing efficiency in mammalian cells. CBE-induced knockout of a programmed cell death protein (PDCD1) with over 90% efficiency has been reported in T cells [93]. The development of ABEs facilitated the reversal of A•T to G•C, enabling the correction of the most common single nucleotide polymorphisms (SNPs) associated with various disease pathologies [88]. Liu and colleagues synthesized a deoxyadenosine deaminase to function on single-stranded DNA (ssDNA). In the presence of Cas9-guide RNA, ABE catalyses deamination of the target locus, resulting in the conversion of A•T to G•C. This conversion is proposed to occur within the 4–7 protospacer window. Currently, there are six BEs available for editing double-stranded DNA (dsDNA) and 12 BEs for editing single-stranded DNA (ssDNA) [88].

The introduction of third-generation base editors, which incorporate a nickase and uracil DNA glycosylase inhibitor (UGI), has significantly enhanced the efficacy of permanent base editing. Single-strand breaks induced by nickases trigger DDR mechanisms for accurate changes in the target sequence. UGI enhances editing efficiency by preventing the removal of uracil bases. Extensive studies have demonstrated the effectiveness of advanced base editors in organisms and laboratory models, including bacteria, rice, wheat, zebrafish, mice, Chinese hamster ovary (CHO) cells, human embryonic kidney (HEK293T) cells, human breast cancer cell line (HCC1954), and yeast [91, 92, 94–98].

Despite challenges such as maintaining an optimal editing window and potential off-target editing, base editors offer numerous advantages that outweigh these limitations. Base editors minimize or eliminate the occurrence of deletions, translocations, and DNA damage response activation (p53) [90, 99–101]. Base editors have proven offer safe correction of mutations in disease models including but not limited to hereditary genetic disorders like sickle cell disease, blindness, progeria as well as certain types of cancer [99, 102, 103]. Furthermore, the application of base editing has expanded to encompass the modification of single nucleotide polymorphisms (SNPs) associated with asthma in human CD4 T cells, highlighting its potential to address genetic variations linked to disease [104]. BEs can recognize relaxed or alternative PAMs, allowing for broader applications [105]. The efficiency of BEs is influenced by the DNA deaminase enzyme's activity, which can be altered by using different cytidine deaminase orthologs and mutants. CBE with human A3A cytidine deaminase or mutant A3A-Y130F has shown enhanced editing capabilities across various sequences and a wide editing window in both monocot and dicot plants [106–108].

4.7.2 Prime Editing

Both BEs and prime editors (PEs) operate without creating DSBs and can efficiently edit specific genomic regions by precisely modifying stretches of bases according to a template. Although BEs can induce four transition mutations (C.T, G.A, A.G, and T.C), the ability to generate the other types transversion mutations which are crucial in conditions like sickle cell disease (T.A to A.T) led to the discovery of versatile PEs capable of inducing all 12 mutations [89]. The first generation of prime editors (PE1) with an efficiency of up to 5.5% consists of Cas9-H840A nickase fused to reverse transcriptase (RT) from Moloney murine leukaemia virus (M-MLV) and a pegRNA. The multifunctional pegRNA is 100 nucleotides long possessing the primer binding site (PBS), a protospacer for recognizing the target sequence, and a reverse transcriptase template that contains the desired edit [89] (Fig. 4.7). The mechanism of this system involves the binding of protospacer to the complementary DNA strand while leaving the non-complementary strand. Subsequently, nCas9 nicks the PAM strand to hybridize with primer binding site of pegRNA. The 3′ flap, which contains the edited sequence interacts with the "primer binding site" of the pegRNA, forming an RNA/DNA hybrid and is extended by action of RT using rest of the pegRNA as a template [89, 109].

To enhance the efficiency of PE1, researchers have developed engineered variants with improved functionality at higher temperatures and enhanced binding to the template-PBS complex of M-MLV reverse transcriptase. This second-generation system (PE2) has shown a 1.6 to 5.1 fold improvement over PE1 [89, 110]. In the third generation of prime editors (PE3), a strategy involving the nicking of the non-edited strand by a single guide RNA (sgRNA) directs the damaged template for the DNA repair process. The PE3 system has been further modified (PE3b) to prevent DSBs by nicking the non-edited strand after the synthesis of the edited strand efficiently reducing the average number of indels without altering the efficiency [89,

109]. Prime editors have been successfully used in human cell lines such as HEK293T [89], zebrafish [111], mouse models [112–114], and Drosophila [115]. Twin prime editing (twinPE) comprising of PE protein and two pegRNAs, consists of templates for both complementary DNA flaps, when coupled with serine recombinase twin PE facilitated the integration of more than 5000 base pair-long-DNA plasmids and inversion of up to 40 kilobases at the target site of human cells [116]. With more optimisations and further modifications in PEs, it is imperative that a viable method for studying and analysing genetic disease models for the development of potential gene therapy could be on the horizon [117]. Engineered pegRNAs (epegRNAs) contain structured RNA motifs at the 3′ terminus at flaps rendering enhanced stability of the 3′ extension of pegRNAs exhibit improved editing efficiency (Fig. 4.8). In various cell cultured lines and primary human fibroblasts, epegRNAs have demonstrated a three- to four-fold increased efficiency without a significant impact on the specificity [118].

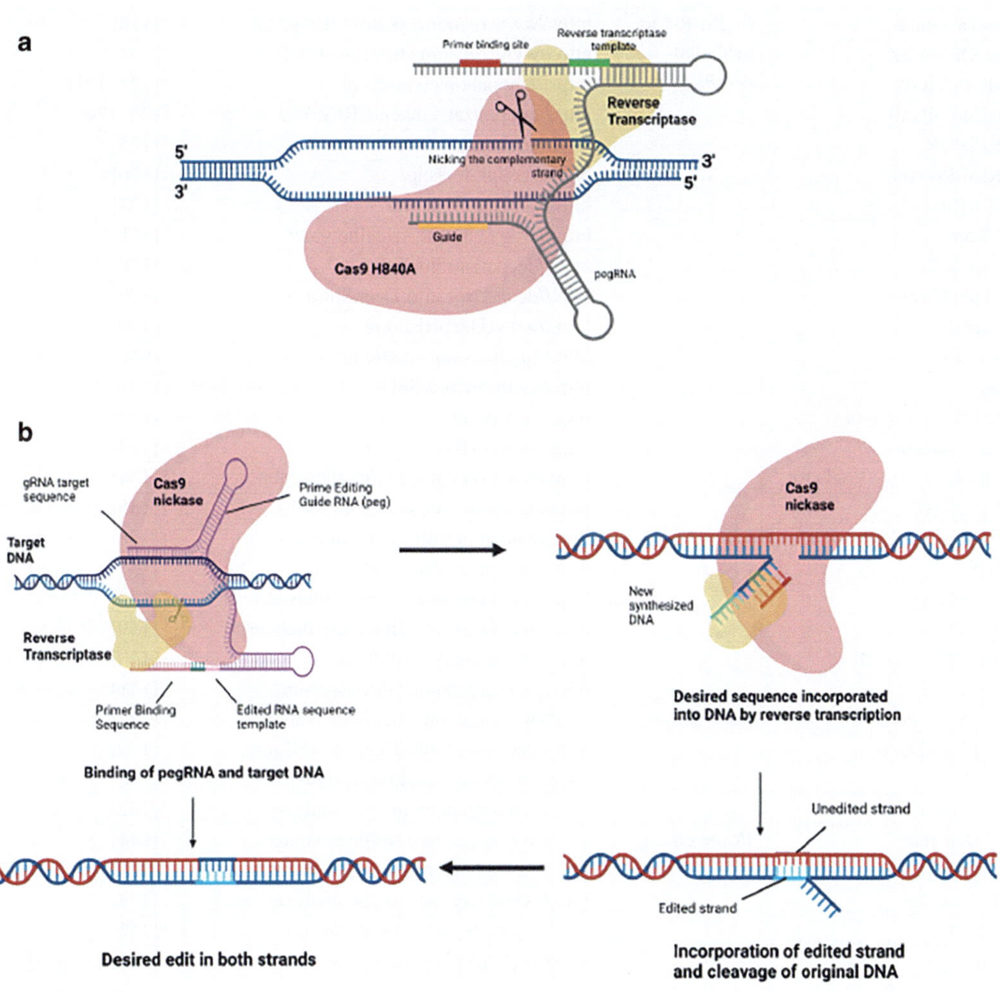

Fig. 4.8 The prime editing system. (**a**) Components of the prime editing system. (**b**) The prime editing system comprises a Cas9 nickase enzyme fused to a reverse transcriptase and a multifunctional prime editing guide RNA (pegRNA). The Cas9 nickase creates a single-strand break in the target DNA, and the reverse transcriptase utilizes the pegRNA as a template for reverse transcription. The pegRNA contains the desired edit sequence and a primer binding site for binding with the target DNA

4.8 Programming the CRISPR Tools

An array of software tools and analytical methods has emerged, facilitating the simplification of planning and assessing CRISPR-Cas experiments [119]. These resources offer the ability to create precise guide RNAs customized for a wide range of manipulation strategies, as well as to scrutinize the results of editing experiments. Notably, there is particular emphasis on constructing comprehensive workflows to handle the extensive datasets generated by genetic screenings. As the field continues its rapid advancement, to overcome the challenges a range of innovative methods have been developed that underscore the constant evolution of cutting-edge computational resources available for CRISPR-Cas applications. A list of the current tools available for precise genome engineering is provided in Table 4.2.

Table 4.2 Web tools for precise genome engineering

Algorithm	Editing	URL	References
Cas-Designer	CRISPR-Cas mediated editing	http://www.rgenome.net/cas-designer/	[120]
Cas-OFFinder		http://www.rgenome.net/cas-offinder/	[76]
CHOPCHOP		https://chopchop.cbu.uib.no/	[121–123]
CRISPR-P 2.0		http://crispr.hzau.edu.cn/CRISPR2/	[28, 124]
CRISPOR		http://crispor.tefor.net/	[125]
CRISPRdirect		https://crispr.dbcls.jp/	[126]
E-CRISP		http://www.e-crisp.org/	[127]
CCTop		http://crispr.cos.uni-heidelberg.de/	[81]
DeepCpf1		http://deepcrispr.info/	[128]
DeepSpCas9		http://deepcrispr.info/DeepSpCas9	[129]
DeepHF		http://www.DeepHF.com/	[130]
CINDEL		http://big.hanyang.ac.kr/cindel	[94]
SSC		http://cistrome.org/SSC/	[131]
Prediction web tool		https://crispr.ml	[132]
CRISPRscan		https://www.crisprscan.org	[133]
Microhomology-Predictor		http://www.rgenome.net/michcalculator	[134]
FORECasT		https://partslab.sanger.ac.uk/FORECasT	[135]
inDelphi		https://indelphi.giffordlab.mit.edu	[136]
TIDE		http://shinyapps.datacurators.nl	[137]
Cas-Analyzer		http://www.rgenome.net/cas-analyzer/	[138]
CRISPResso2		https://crispresso.pinellolab.partners.org/	[139]
CRISPRAnalyzeR		http://crispr-analyzer.dkfz.de/	[140]
CRISPR-Sub		http://www.rgenome.net/crispr-sub	[141]
BE-Designer	Base editing	http://www.rgenome.net/be-designer/	[142]
DeepBaseEditor		http://deepcrispr.info/DeepBaseEditor	[100]
BE-Hive		https://www.crisprbehive.design/	[143]
BE-Analyzer		http://www.rgenome.net/be-analyzer/	[142]
PE-Designer	Prime editing	http://www.rgenome.net/pe-designer	[144]
PrimeDesign		https://drugthatgene.pinellolab.partners.org/	[105]
PE-Analyzer		http://www.rgenome.net/pe-analyzer/	[144]
DeepPE		http://deepcrispr.info/DeepPE/	[145]
pegFinder		http://pegfinder.sidichenlab.org	[146]

4.9 Delivering the CRISPR Tools

Advancements in CRISPR technology have revolutionized genome editing; however, efficiently delivering gene editing tools in target tissues/cells remains a significant challenge due to extracellular and intracellular barriers and the complexity of organism (Fig. 4.9). CRISPR/Cas systems tools consist of two parts: the payload (Cas9 and single guide RNA) and the carrier. Although different methods including physical (microinjection, electroporation) and viral (adenoviruses, lentiviruses) techniques, as well as non-viral approaches, e.g., lipids, polymers, have been studied [147–149] there are considerations such as transfection efficiency, off-target effects, payload size, and immunogenicity. Recent advancements, such as cationic lipid-based systems and gold nanoparticles have shown promise in improving transfection efficiency and enhanced genome editing [150].

The first strategy utilizes an all-in-one plasmid-based system encoding both the Cas9 protein and the sgRNA which allows the expression and assembly of the Cas9 gene and sgRNA *in vivo* offering a long-lasting expression of Cas9 and sgRNA and thereby eliminating the need for multiple transfections. However, its major limitation lies in the efficient delivery of the plasmid into the nucleus of target cells [151].

Therapeutic editing has showcased successful outcomes in CD34+ human haematopoietic stem cells through the utilization of ribonucleoproteins (RNPs), formed by complexing sgRNA with Cas9 [152]. Another approach involves mRNA delivery of CRISPR tools, which although susceptible to rapid degradation, offers several advantages, including immediate translation into proteins, enhanced chemical stability, increased on-target effects, and reduced off-target effects [152]. The co-transfection of mRNA and sgRNA

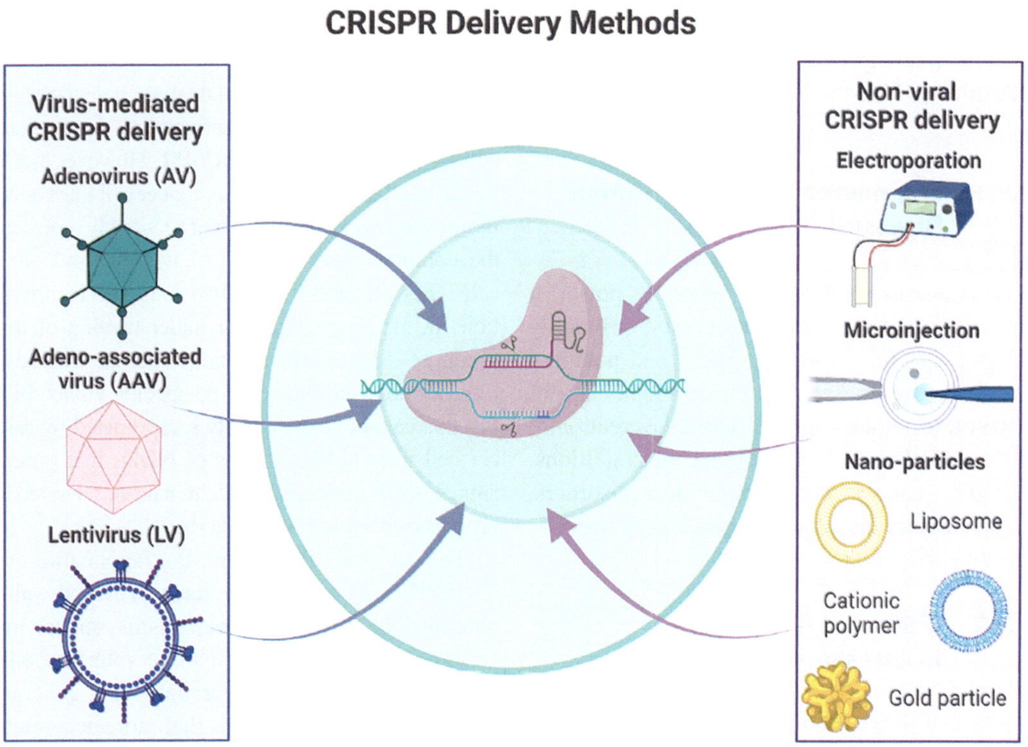

Fig. 4.9 Viral and non-viral delivery methods for CRISPR gene editing. AAV efficiently delivers CRISPR tools to target tissues, while lentiviral vectors enable CRISPR-Cas9 complex delivery for *in vitro* and *in vivo* applications. Non-viral delivery methods include techniques such as lipofection, electroporation, and direct injection of CRISPR components

enables the targeting of multiple genes in primary cells and induced pluripotent stem cells through techniques such as lipofection. Alternatively, for model organisms, mRNAs and sgRNAs can be directly injected to facilitate CRISPR component delivery.

Viral delivery methods commonly involve adeno-associated viruses (AAVs) and lentiviruses [152]. AAVs are used to deliver genome editing tools into local tissues, although the delivery of Cas9 BEs can be challenging because of the cargo size constraints of these vectors [153]. Splitting AAV BE sequences into two different AAV vectors has successful achieved BE expression after delivery and AAV protein product splicing [152]. Lentiviral vectors enable the delivery of CRISPR-Cas9 complexes for inducing cancer-driving mutations in cell cultures and *in vivo* models [154]. BEs can be delivered using various methods such as plasmids, ribonucleoprotein, lipofection, electroporation, and viral vectors [152]. However, it is important to note that extended exposure to plasmids may be toxic to certain cell types and can cause undesirable side effects [155, 156].

4.9.1 Engineered Models of Human Diseases

Human disease models have served as powerful tools to replicate disease processes, providing insights into mechanisms, targets, and potential treatment responses. The development of CRISPR technology has bolstered the creation of disease models for a wide range of conditions, including cancer, neurodegenerative disorders, cardiovascular diseases, and genetic syndromes.

4.9.2 iPSCs and Prospects in Disease Research

Pluripotent embryonic stem cells (ESCs), originally derived from the inner cell mass of an embryo, have long been recognized for their remarkable ability to self-renew and differentiate into any cell type of the developing and adult organism. However, the use of ESCs in research and drug development has faced significant ethical limitations [157]. The extraction of ESCs requires the destruction of embryos raising ethical concerns and limiting the widespread adoption of ESCs in scientific research and therapeutic applications. The discovery of induced pluripotent stem cells (iPSCs) by Shinya Yamanaka in 2006 revolutionized the field of regenerative medicine and disease modelling [157]. iPSCs are generated by reprogramming adult somatic cells, such as skin cells, into an embryonic-like state. This reprogramming allows cells to regain pluripotency and differentiate into various cell types, resembling ESCs in their capabilities (Fig. 4.10). The development of iPSCs has opened new avenues for research, drug development, and disease modelling offering a valuable near-physiology tool for studying human diseases as they can be derived from patients with specific conditions. Most importantly, iPSCs provide a more ethically acceptable source of pluripotent stem cells, as they can be generated from adult individuals without the need for embryo destruction.

Given their genetic origins, many neuronal developmental disorders (NDDs) are potential candidates for therapeutic interventions using gene editing technologies like CRISPR. However, traditional cellular models, such as cancer cell lines commonly used in research, may not accurately represent the complex characteristics of neurons and other cell types affected in NDDs posing severe limitations in the progress of our understanding of this group of diseases. In addition, neurodegenerative diseases often exhibit cell-type-specific vulnerabilities that cannot be adequately recapitulated by cancer cell lines [158]. Studies of NDDs that pose a significant threat to global health have accelerated in progress with the IPSC methods.

The use of iPSCs and the application of CRISPR/Cas9 technology have provided valuable insights into the mechanisms underlying NDDs and potential therapeutic interventions. By utilizing iPSCs, researchers can generate disease-specific cell models that more accurately reflect the characteristics of neurons and other affected cell types in NDDs. Mutations in the amyloid precursor protein (APP) increase the

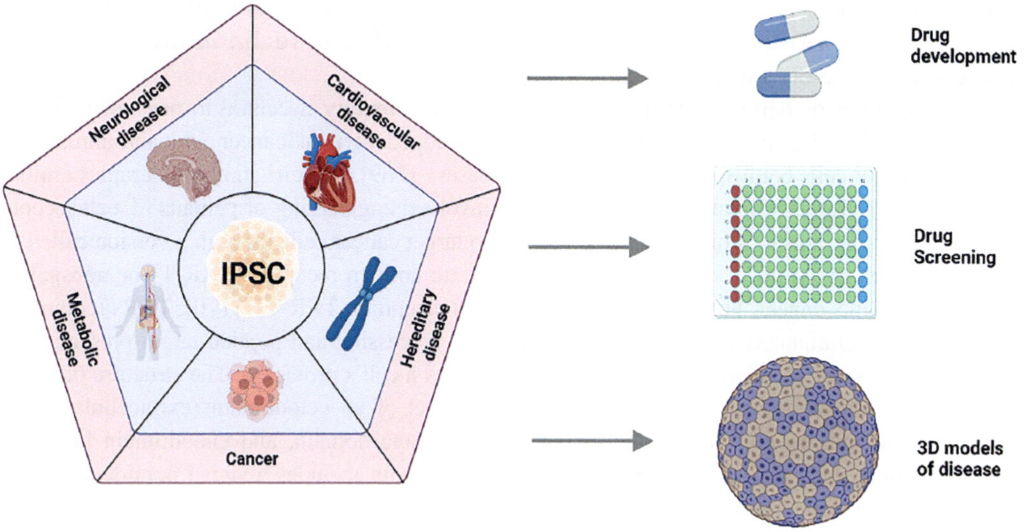

Fig. 4.10 Application of induced pluripotent stem cells (iPSCs) as a tool for modelling human diseases with CRISPR/Cas9 technology. iPSCs can be derived from patient samples or healthy individuals, serving as a renewable and customizable source of human cells for disease modelling. iPSCs are generated by reprogramming adult cells to an embryonic-like state, allowing them to differentiate into various cell types relevant to the disease under study

levels of Aβ in the brain and peripheral tissues It was also observed that CRISPR/Cas9 mediated knockout was sufficient to cause a reduction in the secretion of Aβ rescuing cells from plaque formation and subsequent cell death [159, 160].

4.9.3 CRISPR and Advanced Cancer Modelling

Genes involved in cancer growth, tumour suppression, metabolism, and therapy resistance have been precisely targeted and edited, resulting in significant constraints on tumour progression and growth. Therefore, targeting oncogenic mutations is a potent strategy to disrupt cancer-related mutations. Employing knockout (KO) and knock-in (KI) strategies, researchers have revealed the intricate underpinnings of the genesis of certain tumours. In hepatocellular carcinoma (HCC), targeted gene alterations, exemplified by NSD1, PHGDH, and LIN28B-AS1 modifications, have yielded remarkable outcomes by halting tumour advancement, augmenting tumour cell demise, and reduction of growth. Likewise, in colorectal cancer (CRC), the precision editing of genes such as CCAT1, MUC5AC, and DACH1 has shed light on pathways responsible for anchorage-independent growth, tumourigenesis, and organoid formation [161]. Furthermore, breast cancer genes like FASN, miR-23b/miR-27b, GPVI, and others have unveiled crucial facets of metastasis, radiosensitivity, and proliferation dynamics [162].

CRISPR/Cas9 gene editing can be employed to target tumour-suppressor genes for treatment purposes. In lung adenocarcinoma, knockout of Keap1 led to overactivation of Nrf2 and tumour promotion [163]. Knockout of the tumour-suppressor gene *MFN2* in lung cancer cells enhanced survival, cell viability, growth, invasion, and metastasis through the mTORC2/AKT pathway [164]. Genetic knockout of the tumour-suppressor miR-1304 increased HO-1 expression, promoting cell survival and growth [165]. Lung cancer-associated proto-oncogenes include MYC, *RAS*, *ERBB1*, *ERBB2*, *ROS1*, *FOS*, *JUN*, *RAF1*, and SRC. CRISPR/Cas9 gene editing is utilized to target oncogenes such as *EGFR*, *FAK*, *NESTIN*, *RSF1*, *CTNND2*, and *IGF1R* in lung cancer [166].

The effectiveness of nutlin, an anticancer drug, was shown to be dependent on the presence of functional p53, as demonstrated in cells where p53 was modified or deficient. Inducing mutations in the p53 gene using CRISPR-Cas9 in colorectal cancer cells confirmed the dependence of nutlin on p53. Target validation with CRISPR-Cas9 revealed that nutlin, which blocks the p53 binding pocket of Mdm2, induces cell cycle arrest and prevents cancer, but only in cells with functional and unmutated p53 [167]. Fanconi anaemia, a recessive Mendelian disorder characterized by chromosome instability, sensitivity to DNA crosslinking agents, increased chromosomal breakage, and poor DNA repair, shares similarities with reactivating p53 and inducing tumour apoptosis (RITA)-sensitive colorectal cancer cells. By using CRISPR knockout models, it was discovered that inhibiting the Fanconi anaemia gene *FANCD2* can restore RITA drug sensitivity [167].

In a bladder cancer cellular model, sgRNA and Cas9 were selectively expressed using cancer-specific promoters: hTERT (human telomerase reverse transcriptase) for sgRNA and hUP II (human uroplakin II) for Cas9. This approach activated suppressor genes, including p21, E-cad, and hBax which suppressed growth and induced apoptosis specifically in bladder cancer cells. Similarly, a study by Aubrey et al. demonstrated that the lentiviral CRISPR-Cas9 system induced apoptosis in human Burkitt lymphoma (BL) cells by targeting the MCL-1 gene leading to impairment of tumour growth in a human BL xenograft model through repeated induction of sgRNA [154]. The insights gleaned from genome-wide CRISPR screens on thousands of cancer cell lines cultivated in conventional conditions underscore the value of CRISPR pooled screens. Comparable genome-wide CRISPR screens conducted on three-dimensional spheroid cultures will prove crucial for future biological revelations [168].

4.9.4 Overview of CAR-T, TCR-T, and CRISPR Technologies

T-cell immunity is central to new methodologies developed to treat cancer and autoimmune diseases [169]. T-cell immunotherapies initially involved engineering of patients' T cell receptors to target cancer cells through a version called chimeric antigen receptor (CAR-T) or transgenic T cell receptors (TCR-Ts) [170]. TCRs require antigen processing and peptide target presentation to access a cell's proteome. The structure of CAR-T consists of an ectodomain (extracellular), transmembrane domain, and endodomain [171]. The ectodomain includes a signal peptide, an antigen recognition region, and a spacer. The signal peptide (scFv) recognizes antigens and the transmembrane domain contains a membrane-spanning hydrophobic α-helix and a native CD3-zeta transmembrane, enabling TCR conversion. The endodomain, which contains immunoreceptor tyrosine-based activation motifs (ITAMs), is responsible for receptor function.

CAR-Ts have undergone four major generations of development [171]. First-generation CAR-Ts have a single CD3 ζ-chain or FcεRIγ structure in the intracellular domain, serving as the primary endogenous TCR signal transmitter. CAR-Ts with CD3ζ-chains containing three ITAMs showed greater potency as T cell activators and inducers of tumour necrosis compared to CAR-Ts with FcεRIγ-chain, which has only one ITAM. However, first-generation CAR-Ts demonstrated insufficient proliferation, poor cytokine secretion, and short lifespans *in vivo*. Second-generation CAR-Ts utilize dual signalling through three different receptor types: T-cell antigen receptors, co-stimulatory receptors (such as CD28/B7), and cytokine receptors [171]. The first signal is initiated by TCR-induced recognition of MHC-complex peptide on the APC surface. The second signal is provided by co-stimulatory molecules like CD28/B7, which are required for T-cell activation, memory, and effector cell establishment.

These molecules upregulate IL2 signalling, leading to increased T-cell activation, function, and prevention of apoptosis. CD28ζ-CAR-Ts have properties that promote stimulation, growth, and proliferation. Transfection of single-chain receptors combined with IL2 administration improved tumour necrosis. The third generation involved combinations of multiple signalling domains, such as CD3ζ-CD28-41BB and CD3ζ-CD28-OX40, to improve cytokine release and apoptotic activity [172]. However, HER2-CAR-T cells and CD20-CD28-CD137-CD3ζ-CAR-T cells did not demonstrate enhanced outcomes compared to second-generation CAR-Ts, likely due to limited cases [171]. Fourth-generation CAR-Ts, known as T cell redirects for universal cytokine-mediated killing (TRUCKs), were engineered by adding IL12 to the base of second-generation CAR-Ts [171]. It was concluded that this amplifies T cell and innate immune cell activation against cancer cells without requiring antigen presentation in target lesions [173].

Tisagenlecleucel CAR-T therapy successfully prevented relapse in 52 out of 63 patients under 25 years old over 6-months after treatment. Axicabtagene ciloleucel CAR-T therapy against refractory large B cell lymphoma led to tumour suppression in 54% of patients and deceleration or cessation of tumour growth in 82% of patients. Han et al. targeted natural killer group 2 member D (NKG2D) ligands on ex vivo triple-negative breast cancer (TNBC) cells using CAR therapy. NKG2DL expression was enhanced using lentiviral vectors. T-cell-enhanced tumour regression was observed. Based on clinical observations, Han et al. proposed auto-stimulation following T cell-induced NKG2D, leading to long-term cell culture enrichment [155].

Limitations of CAR-T and TCR-T therapies include life-threatening conditions such as cytokine release syndrome (CRS) due to hyperinduction of inflammatory molecules such as IL1 and IL6 [174, 175]. Systemic inflammation can lead to neurotoxicity [175]. Off-target effects can arise due to a lack of antigen specificity. Although CAR-T cells are engineered to recognize antigens specific to tumours, certain non-tumour cells may also express these antigens, resulting in "on-target, off-tumour toxicity" where CAR-T cells recognize antigens on the wrong cells. CAR-Ts with multiple antigen complexes can increase antigen specificity and ensure CAR-Ts recognize only antigens typically expressed by target tumours. Engineering "suicide/elimination" genes into CAR-Ts can selectively mediate and diminish CAR-T cells to prevent off-target toxicity. T cell exhaustion, resulting from a lack of the Nr4a gene transcription regulator, has been identified in murine models but has not yet been translated into human models [173, 176]. Multi-pathway resistance severely hinders prolonged CAR-T efficacy through changes in G1 regulatory protein expression, inhibitor release (e.g., IL-10, indoleamine 2,3-dioxygenase, transforming growth factor-beta), Treg recruitment, and overexpression of immunosuppressive receptors like PD-L1. The cost of CAR-T therapies, such as Kymriah and Yescarta, can be very high. However, efforts such as CAR-TXpress™ by ThermoGenesis aim to culture high-quality CAR-T cells quickly for immediate commercialization, thereby reducing the cost of therapy [177].

Since 2016, CRISPR technology has been utilized in the generation of CAR-T cells which marked the beginning of alternatives to autologous CAR cell therapies and personalised therapies. Most importantly, CRISPR gene editing enhances 'Off-the-shelf' CAR-T cells reducing graft versus host disease (GVHD), and improving survival. Alternatives to autologous CAR-T cell therapies receive a further boost through PD-1 disruption and increase effectiveness against tumours. In addition, CRISPR/Cas9 aids in cytokine control, reducing CRS and improving tumour resistance. CRISPR-edited universal CAR-T cells show remarkable resistance to immune suppression, offering immediate availability and flexibility for large-scale clinical use [178].

4.9.5 TCR-Ts

In TCR-T therapies, T lymphocytes recognize HLA-peptides on tumour cells and use immune tyrosine-based activation motifs (ITAM) to induce antigen-stimulating signals for T cell activation and subsequent tumour necrosis [179]. TCR-Ts express one α and one β chain alongside the original chain to aid in tumour specificity in T cells [170]. TCRs use TCR-CD3 clusters to identify MHC complexes. Subsequent TCR-MHC interactions trigger downstream protein recruitment in the plasma membrane for signal transduction and propagation. TCR-Ts have also undergone four generations of development. The first generation involved isolating T cells specific to tumour antigens and re-infusing them into patients, to expand cell cultures *in vitro*. This approach relied on unique gene expressions in individuals but was challenging to replicate in industrial settings. The second generation aimed to improve the methodology to make it easier to implement in industry for T cell production and treatment. TCRs specific to tumour antigens were cloned, and the gene sequences were identified for transduction into patient T cell samples. The third generation increased the affinity of tumour-TCRs for improved therapeutic effects, while the fourth generation further enhanced TCR specificity for neoantigens to improve patient safety and tumour responses [180]. TCR-T therapy can be personalized by CRISPR targeting neoantigens and somatic mutations specific to tumours. Selecting suitable substrate cells can improve TCR-T transportation, replication, resilience, and memory. Insufficient T cell activation can lead to immune escape, decreasing the efficacy of immunotherapy [179].

CRISPR technology has also simplified TCR-T engineering by providing efficient and precise tools for genetic modifications, enabling stable expression of the engineered receptors, effective targeting of cancer cells, and knockout of endogenous receptor expression. The technology allows the editing of TCRs to recognise neoantigens, personalising TCR-T cells to target unique tumour markers effectively. The ability to perform multiplex editing enables simultaneous modifications of multiple genes to improve the survival and robustness of T cells in an immunosuppressive tumour microenvironment [181].

As we enter the second decade of the CRISPR revolution, remarkable progress has been made in developing precise genome editing technologies, placing CRISPR in a strong position to transform basic, clinical, and biotechnological research [182, 183] (Fig. 4.11). In the world's first attempt, CRISPR therapy Casgevy was approved by the Medicines & Healthcare products Regulatory Agency on November 16th, 2023, for the treatment of blood conditions like sickle-cell disease and β-thalassaemia, followed by FDA approval in the same year. A thorough understanding of the differences presented by cells in the diseased microenvironment will create more opportunities to deliver gene-editing tools in novel and specific ways. The identification of new Cas9 variants not recognized by the human immune system and new gene editing systems could address the problem of immunogenicity [182]. Additionally, there is a significant need to create ethical guidelines for responsible use and to increase accessibility for the benefit of wider human society.

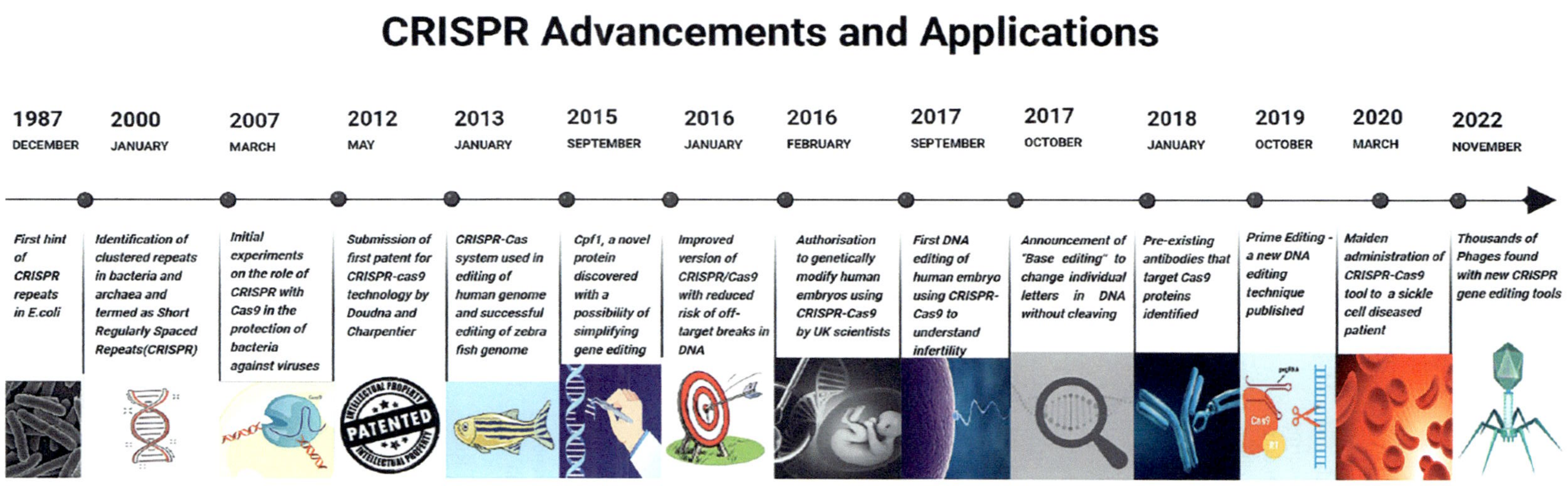

Fig. 4.11 The figure summarizes the remarkable progress in precise gene editing, from its identification including invention of different gene editing modalities and disease therapies

Acknowledgements: We thank Ms. Harshana Chaurasia and Ms. Magdalena Ruiz Perez for critically proofreading this book chapter and for their support in coordinating Gene Editors of the Future sessions. Our sincere gratitude goes to the University of Westminster and the Quintin Hogg Trust for supporting the Gene Editors of the Future, a vertically integrated, research-engaged extracurricular program since 2020, as well as to our alumni donor Mr. Raj Sitlani and Ms Simay Sali Sevik of the development team at Westminster for supporting the research and knowledge activities of the Genome Engineering Laboratory. All figures were created with BioRender.com, and the publication license is available at https://help.biorender.com/en/articles/3619405-how-do-i-cite-biorender.

References

1. Ishino Y, Shinagawa H, Makino K, Amemura M, Nakata A. Nucleotide sequence of the *iap* gene, responsible for alkaline phosphatase isozyme conversion in *Escherichia coli*, and identification of the gene product. J Bacteriol. 1987;169:5429–33. https://doi.org/10.1128/jb.169.12.5429-5433.1987.
2. Gostimskaya I. CRISPR–Cas9: a history of its discovery and ethical considerations of its use in genome editing. Biochemistry. 2022;87(8):777–88.
3. Jansen R, van Embden JDA, Gaastra W, Schouls LM. Identification of genes that are associated with DNA repeats in prokaryotes. Mol Microbiol. 2002;43(6):1565–75.
4. Ishino Y, Krupovic M, Forterre P. History of CRISPR-Cas from encounter with a mysterious repeated sequence to genome editing technology. J Bacteriol. 2018;200(7):e00580-17.
5. Bolotin A, Quinquis B, Sorokin A, Ehrlich SD. Clustered regularly interspaced short palindrome repeats (CRISPRs) have spacers of extrachromosomal origin. Microbiology. 2005;151(8):2551–61.
6. Barrangou R, Fremaux C, Deveau H, Richards M, Boyaval P, Moineau S, Romero DA, Horvath P. CRISPR provides acquired resistance against viruses in prokaryotes. Science. 2007;315(5819):1709–12. https://www.ncbi.nlm.nih.gov/pubmed/17379808/.
7. Cumby N, Edwards AM, Davidson AR, Maxwell KL. The bacteriophage HK97 gp15 moron element encodes a novel superinfection exclusion protein. J Bacteriol. 2012;194(18):5012–9. https://jb.asm.org/content/194/18/5012.short. Accessed 19 May 2020.
8. Molineux IJ. Host-parasite interactions: recent developments in the genetics of abortive phage infections. New Biol. 1991;3(3):230–6. https://europepmc.org/article/med/1831658. Accessed 24 Mar 2023.
9. Tock MR, Dryden DT. The biology of restriction and anti-restriction. Curr Opin Microbiol. 2005;8(4):466–72. https://www.sciencedirect.com/science/article/pii/S1369527405000779. Accessed 25 Oct 2021.
10. Ipoutcha T, Tsarmpopoulos I, Talenton V, Gaspin C, Moisan A, Walker CA, Brownlie J, Blanchard A, Thebault P, Sirand-Pugnet P. Multiple origins and specific evolution of CRISPR/Cas9 systems in minimal bacteria (Mollicutes). Front Microbiol. 2019;10:2701.
11. Mohanraju P, Makarova KS, Zetsche B, Zhang F, Koonin EV, van der Oost J. Diverse evolutionary roots and mechanistic variations of the CRISPR-Cas systems. Science. 2016;353(6299):aad5147.
12. Mojica FJM, Díez-Villaseñor C, García-Martínez J, Soria E. Intervening sequences of regularly spaced prokaryotic repeats derive from foreign genetic elements. J Mol Evol. 2005;60:174–82. https://doi.org/10.1007/s00239-004-0046-3.
13. Karvelis T, Gasiunas G, Miksys A, Barrangou R, Horvath P, Siksnys V. crRNA and tracrRNA guide Cas9-mediated DNA interference in Streptococcus thermophilus. RNA Biol. 2013;10(5):841–51.
14. Grissa I, Vergnaud G, Pourcel C. The CRISPRdb database and tools to display CRISPRs and to generate dictionaries of spacers and repeats. BMC Bioinformatics. 2007;8(1):172. https://www.ncbi.nlm.nih.gov/pmc/articles/PMC1892036/.
15. Grissa I, Vergnaud G, Pourcel C. CRISPRcompar: a website to compare clustered regularly interspaced short palindromic repeats. Nucleic Acids Res. 2008;36:W145–8.
16. Tang Z, Chen S, Chen A, He B, Zhou Y, Chai G, Guo F, Huang J. CasPDB: an integrated and annotated database for Cas proteins from bacteria and archaea. Database (Oxford). 2019;2019:baz093. https://doi.org/10.1093/database/baz093. PMID: 31411686; PMCID: PMC6693189.
17. Borges AL, Davidson AR, Bondy-Denomy J. The discovery, mechanisms, and evolutionary impact of anti-CRISPRs. Annu Rev Virol. 2017;4:37–59.
18. Marino ND, Pinilla-Redondo R, Csörgő B, Bondy-Denomy J. Anti-CRISPR protein applications: natural brakes for CRISPR-Cas technologies. Nat Methods. 2020;17(5):471–9.
19. Bondy-Denomy J, Pawluk A, Maxwell KL, Davidson AR. Bacteriophage genes that inactivate the CRISPR/Cas bacterial immune system. Nature. 2013;493(7432):429–32.
20. Dong D, Guo M, Wang S, Zhu Y, Wang S, Xiong Z, Yang J, Xu Z, Huang Z. Structural basis of CRISPR-SpyCas9 inhibition by an anti-CRISPR protein. Nature. 2017;546(7658):436–9.
21. Harrington LB, Doxzen KW, Ma E, Liu JJ, Knott GJ, Edraki A, Garcia B, Amrani N, Chen JS, Cofsky JC, Kranzusch PJ, Sontheimer EJ, Davidson AR, Maxwell KL, Doudna JA. A broad-spectrum inhibitor of CRISPR-Cas9. Cell. 2017;170(6):1224–33.e15. https://doi.org/10.1016/j.cell.2017.07.037.
22. Zhu Y, Gao A, Zhan Q, Wang Y, Feng H, Liu S, Gao G, Serganov A, Gao P. Diverse mechanisms of

CRISPR-Cas9 inhibition by type IIC anti-CRISPR proteins. Mol Cell. 2019;74(2):296–309.
23. Raby L, Völkel P, Le Bourhis X, Angrand P-O. The polycomb orthologues in teleost fishes and their expression in the zebrafish model. Genes. 2020;11(4):362.
24. Li H, Yang Y, Hong W, et al. Applications of genome editing technology in the targeted therapy of human diseases: mechanisms, advances and prospects. Sig Transduct Target Ther. 2020;5(1):1. https://doi.org/10.1038/s41392-019-0089-y.
25. Carroll D. Genome engineering with zinc-finger nucleases. Genetics. 2011;188(4):773–82. https://www.ncbi.nlm.nih.gov/pmc/articles/PMC3176093/.
26. Mussolino C, Cathomen T. TALE nucleases: tailored genome engineering made easy. Curr Opin Biotechnol. 2012;23(5):644–50.
27. Becker S, Boch J. TALE and TALEN genome editing technologies. Gene Genome Ed. 2021;2: 100007.
28. Lei Y, Lu L, Liu HY, Li S, Xing F, Chen LL. CRISPR-P: a web tool for synthetic single-guide RNA design of CRISPR-system in plants. Mol Plant. 2014;7(9):1494–6.
29. Moore R, Chandrahas A, Bleris L. Transcription activator-like effectors: a toolkit for synthetic biology. ACS Synth Biol. 2014;3(10):708–16. https://doi.org/10.1021/sb400137b.
30. Ran FA, Hsu PD, Wright J, Agarwala V, Scott DA, Zhang F. Genome engineering using the CRISPR-Cas9 system. Nat Protoc. 2013;8(11):2281–308. https://doi.org/10.1038/nprot.2013.143.
31. Coelho MA, De Braekeleer E, Firth M, et al. CRISPR GUARD protects off-target sites from Cas9 nuclease activity using short guide RNAs. Nat Commun. 2020;11:4132. https://doi.org/10.1038/s41467-020-17952-5.
32. Harmsen TJW, Pritchard CEJ, Riepsaame J, et al. HideRNAs protect against CRISPR-Cas9 re-cutting after successful single base-pair gene editing. Sci Rep. 2022;12:9606.
33. Koonin EV, Makarova KS. Mobile genetic elements and evolution of CRISPR-Cas systems: all the way there and back. Genome Biol Evol. 2017;9(10):2812–25.
34. Krupovic M, Shmakov S, Makarova KS, Forterre P, Koonin EV. Recent mobility of casposons, self-synthesizing transposons at the origin of the CRISPR-Cas immunity. Genome Biol Evol. 2016;8(2):375–86.
35. Behler J, Hess WR. Approaches to study CRISPR RNA biogenesis and the key players involved. Methods. 2020;172:12–26. https://doi.org/10.1016/j.ymeth.2019.07.015.
36. Nishimasu H, Ran FA, Hsu PD, Konermann S, Shehata SI, Dohmae N, Ishitani R, Zhang F, Nureki O. Crystal structure of Cas9 in complex with guide RNA and target DNA. Cell. 2014;156(5):935–49. https://doi.org/10.1016/j.cell.2014.02.001. Epub 2014 Feb 13. PMID: 24529477; PMCID: PMC4139937.
37. Jiang F, Doudna JA. CRISPR-Cas9 structures and mechanisms. Annu Rev Biophys. 2017;46:505–29. https://doi.org/10.1146/annurev-biophys-062215-010822. Epub 2017 Mar 30. PMID: 28375731.
38. Jinek M, Chylinski K, Fonfara I, Hauer M, Doudna JA, Charpentier E. A programmable dual-RNA-guided DNA endonuclease in adaptive bacterial immunity. Science. 2012;337(6096):816–21.
39. Xue C, Greene EC. DNA repair pathway choices in CRISPR-Cas9-mediated genome editing. Trends Genet. 2021;37(7):639–56. https://doi.org/10.1016/j.tig.2021.02.008. Epub 2021 Apr 22. PMID: 33896583; PMCID: PMC8187289.
40. Wang C, Qu Y, Cheng JKW, Hughes NW, Zhang Q, Wang M, Cong L. dCas9-based gene editing for cleavage-free genomic knock-in of long sequences. Nat Cell Biol. 2022;24(2):268–78. https://doi.org/10.1038/s41556-021-00836-1.
41. Bikard D, et al. Programmable repression and activation of bacterial gene expression using an engineered CRISPR-Cas system. Nucleic Acids Res. 2013;41(15): 7429. https://doi.org/10.1093/nar/gkt520.
42. Chen B, Gilbert LA, Cimini BA, Schnitzbauer J, Zhang W, Li GW, Park J, Blackburn EH, Weissman JS, Qi LS, Huang B. Dynamic imaging of genomic loci in living human cells by an optimized CRISPR/Cas system. Cell. 2013;155(7):1479–91.
43. Larson MH, Gilbert LA, Wang X, Lim WA, Weissman JS, Qi LS. CRISPR interference (CRISPRi) for sequence-specific control of gene expression. Nat Protoc. 2013;8(11):2180–96. https://doi.org/10.1038/nprot.2013.132.
44. Maeder ML, et al. CRISPR RNA-guided activation of endogenous human genes. Nat Methods. 2013;10(10):977. https://doi.org/10.1038/nmeth.2598.
45. Lin J, Feng M, Zhang H, et al. Characterization of a novel type III CRISPR-Cas effector provides new insights into the allosteric activation and suppression of the Cas10 DNase. Cell Discov. 2020;6:29. https://doi.org/10.1038/s41421-020-0160-4.
46. Zhu X, Ye K. Crystal structure of Cmr2 suggests a nucleotide cyclase-related enzyme in type III CRISPR-Cas systems. FEBS Lett. 2012;586(6):939–45. https://doi.org/10.1016/j.febslet.2012.02.036.
47. Tamulaitis G, Kazlauskiene M, Manakova E, Venclovas Č, Nwokeoji AO, Dickman MJ, Horvath P, Siksnys V. Programmable RNA shredding by the type III-A CRISPR-Cas system of Streptococcus thermophilus. Mol Cell. 2014;56(4):506–17. https://doi.org/10.1016/j.molcel.2014.09.027.
48. Kazlauskiene M, Tamulaitis G, Kostiuk G, Venclovas Č, Siksnys V. Spatiotemporal control of type III-A CRISPR-Cas immunity: coupling DNA degradation with the target RNA recognition. Mol Cell. 2016;62(2):295–306.

49. Wang L, Mo CY, Wasserman MR, Rostøl JT, Marraffini LA, Liu S. Dynamics of Cas10 govern discrimination between self and non-self in Type III CRISPR-Cas immunity. Mol Cell. 2019;73(2):278–90.e4. https://doi.org/10.1016/j.molcel.2018.11.008.
50. Urbaitis T, Gasiunas G, Young JK, Hou Z, Paulraj S, Godliauskaite E, Juskeviciene MM, Stitilyte M, Jasnauskaite M, Mabuchi M, Robb GB, Siksnys V. A new family of CRISPR-type V nucleases with C-rich PAM recognition. EMBO Rep. 2022;23(12):e55481. https://doi.org/10.15252/embr.202255481.
51. Xu Y, Li Z. CRISPR-Cas systems: overview, innovations and applications in human disease research and gene therapy. Comput Struct Biotechnol J. 2020;18:2401–15.
52. Zetsche B, Gootenberg JS, Abudayyeh OO, Slaymaker IM, Makarova KS, Essletzbichler P, Volz SE, Joung J, van der Oost J, Regev A, Koonin EV, Zhang F. Cpf1 is a single RNA-guided endonuclease of a class 2 CRISPR-Cas system. Cell. 2015;163(3):759–71. https://doi.org/10.1016/j.cell.2015.09.038.
53. Chen JS, Ma E, Harrington LB, Da Costa M, Tian X, Palefsky JM, Doudna JA. CRISPR-Cas12a target binding unleashes indiscriminate single-stranded DNase activity. Science. 2018a;360(6387):436–9.
54. Shmakov S, Smargon A, Scott D, Cox D, Pyzocha N, Yan W, Abudayyeh OO, Gootenberg JS, Makarova KS, Wolf YI, Severinov K, Zhang F, Koonin EV. Diversity and evolution of class 2 CRISPR-Cas systems. Nat Rev Microbiol. 2017;15(3):169–82. https://doi.org/10.1038/nrmicro.2016.184.
55. Dong D, Ren K, Qiu X, Zheng J, Guo M, Guan X, Liu H, Li N, Zhang B, Yang D, Ma C, Wang S, Wu D, Ma Y, Fan S, Wang J, Gao N, Huang Z. The crystal structure of Cpf1 in complex with CRISPR RNA. Nature. 2016;532(7600):522–6.
56. Harrington LB, et al. A scoutRNA is required for some type V CRISPR-Cas systems. Mol Cell. 2020;79(3):416–24.e5.
57. Pausch P, Soczek KM, Herbst DA, Tsuchida CA, Al-Shayeb B, Banfield JF, Nogales E, Doudna JA. DNA interference states of the hypercompact CRISPR-CasΦ effector. Nat Struct Mol Biol. 2021;28(8):652–61. https://doi.org/10.1038/s41594-021-00632-3.
58. Yan WX, Hunnewell P, Alfonse LE, Carte JM, Keston-Smith E, Sothiselvam S, Garrity AJ, Chong S, Makarova KS, Koonin EV, Cheng DR, Scott DA. Functionally diverse type V CRISPR-Cas systems. Science. 2019;363(6422):88–91. https://doi.org/10.1126/science.aav7271.
59. López-Calleja AC, Vizuet-de-Rueda JC, Alvarez-Venegas R. Chapter 5—CRISPR-Cas epigenome editing: improving crop resistance to pathogens. In: Abd-Elsalam KA, Lim K-T, editors. Nanobiotechnology for plant protection, CRISPR and RNAi systems. Amsterdam: Elsevier; 2021. p. 65–106.
60. Hillary VE, Ceasar SA. A review on the mechanism and applications of CRISPR/Cas9/Cas12/Cas13/Cas14 proteins utilized for genome engineering. Mol Biotechnol. 2023;65(3):311–25.
61. Abudayyeh OO, et al. RNA targeting with CRISPR–Cas13. Nature. 2017;550(7675):280–4.
62. Smargon AA, Cox DBT, Pyzocha NK, Zheng K, Slaymaker IM, Gootenberg JS, Abudayyeh OA, Essletzbichler P, Shmakov S, Makarova KS, Koonin EV, Zhang F. Cas13b is a type VI-B CRISPR-associated RNA-guided RNase differentially regulated by accessory proteins Csx27 and Csx28. Mol Cell. 2017;65(4):618–30.e7. https://doi.org/10.1016/j.molcel.2016.12.023.
63. Cox DBT, Gootenberg JS, Abudayyeh OO, Franklin B, Kellner MJ, Joung J, Zhang F. RNA editing with CRISPR-Cas13. Science. 2017;358(6366):1019–27.
64. Das A, Goswami HN, Whyms CT, Sridhara S, Li H. Structural principles of CRISPR-Cas enzymes used in nucleic acid detection. J Struct Biol. 2022;214(1):107838.
65. Wang B, Zhang T, Yin J, Yu Y, Xu W, Ding J, Patel DJ, Yang H. Structural basis for self-cleavage prevention by tag:anti-tag pairing complementarity in type VI Cas13 CRISPR systems. Mol Cell. 2021;81(5):1100–5.e5. https://doi.org/10.1016/j.molcel.2020.12.033.
66. Al-Shayeb B, Sachdeva R, Chen LX, Ward F, Munk P, Devoto A, Castelle CJ, Olm MR, Bouma-Gregson K, Amano Y, He C, Méheust R, Brooks B, Thomas A, Lavy A, Matheus-Carnevali P, Sun C, Goltsman DSA, Borton MA, Sharrar A, Jaffe AL, Nelson TC, Kantor R, Keren R, Lane KR, Farag IF, Lei S, Finstad K, Amundson R, Anantharaman K, Zhou J, Probst AJ, Power ME, Tringe SG, Li WJ, Wrighton K, Harrison S, Morowitz M, Relman DA, Doudna JA, Lehours AC, Warren L, Cate JHD, Santini JM, Banfield JF. Clades of huge phages from across Earth's ecosystems. Nature. 2020;578(7795):425–31.
67. Liu S, Sretenovic S, Fan T, Cheng Y, Li G, Qi A, Tang X, Xu Y, Guo W, Zhong Z, He Y, Liang Y, Han Q, Zheng X, Gu X, Qi Y, Zhang Y. Hypercompact CRISPR-Cas12j2 (CasΦ) enables genome editing, gene activation, and epigenome editing in plants. Plant Commun. 2022a;3(6):100453. https://doi.org/10.1016/j.xplc.2022.100453.
68. Li Z, Zhong Z, Wu Z, Pausch P, Al-Shayeb B, Amerasekera J, et al. Genome editing in plants using the compact editor CasΦ. Proc Natl Acad Sci U S A. 2023;120(4):e2216822120. https://doi.org/10.1073/pnas.2216822120.
69. Csörgő B, et al. A compact Cascade–Cas3 system for targeted genome engineering. Nat Methods. 2020;17(12):1183–90. https://doi.org/10.1038/s41592-020-00980-w.
70. Morisaka H, Yoshimi K, Okuzaki Y, Gee P, Kunihiro Y, Sonpho E, Xu H, Sasakawa N, Naito Y, Nakada S, Yamamoto T, Sano S, Hotta A, Takeda J, Mashimo T. CRISPR-Cas3 induces broad and unidirectional

genome editing in human cells. Nat Commun. 2019;10(1):5302.
71. Sinkunas T, Gasiunas G, Fremaux C, Barrangou R, Horvath P, Siksnys V. Cas3 is a single-stranded DNA nuclease and ATP-dependent helicase in the CRISPR/Cas immune system. EMBO J. 2011;30(7):1335–42. https://doi.org/10.1038/emboj.2011.41.
72. Sun S, He Z, Jiang P, Baral R, Pandelia ME. Metal dependence and functional diversity of type I Cas3 nucleases. Biochemistry. 2022;61(5):327–38. https://doi.org/10.1021/acs.biochem.1c00779.
73. Mayer K. Minimal CRISPR-Cas3 system makes substantial deletions. GEN—Genetic Engineering and Biotechnology News. 2020. https://www.genengnews.com/news/minimal-crispr-cas3-system-makes-substantial-deletions/. Accessed 23 Mar 2023.
74. Fu Y, Foden JA, Khayter C, Maeder ML, Reyon D, Joung JK, Sander JD. High-frequency off-target mutagenesis induced by CRISPR-Cas nucleases in human cells. Nat Biotechnol. 2013;31(9):822–6.
75. Pacesa M, Lin CH, Cléry A, Saha A, Arantes PR, Bargsten K, et al. Structural basis for Cas9 off-target activity. Cell. 2022;185(22):4067–81.e21. https://doi.org/10.1016/j.cell.2022.09.026.
76. Bae S, Park J, Kim JS. Cas-OFFinder: a fast and versatile algorithm that searches for potential off-target sites of Cas9 RNA-guided endonucleases. Bioinformatics. 2014a;30(10):1473–5.
77. McKenna A, Shendure J. FlashFry: A fast and flexible tool for large-scale CRISPR target design. BMC Biol. 2018;16(1):74.
78. Xiao A, Cheng Z, Kong L, Zhu Z, Lin S, Gao G, et al. CasOT: A genome-wide cas9/gRNA off-target searching tool. Bioinformatics. 2014;30(8):1180–2.
79. Haeussler M, Schonig K, Eckert H, Eschstruth A, Mianne J, Renaud JB, et al. Evaluation of off-target and on-target scoring algorithms and integration into the guide RNA selection tool CRISPOR. Genome Biol. 2016;17(1):148.
80. Hsu PD, Scott DA, Weinstein JA, Ran FA, Konermann S, Agarwala V, et al. DNA targeting specificity of RNA-guided Cas9 nucleases. Nat Biotechnol. 2013;31(9):827–32.
81. Stemmer M, Thumberger T, Del Sol Keyer M, Wittbrodt J, Mateo JL. CCTop: an intuitive, flexible and reliable CRISPR/Cas9 target prediction tool. PLoS One. 2015;10(4):e0124633.
82. Ran FA, Hsu PD, Lin CY, Gootenberg JS, Konermann S, Trevino AE, Scott DA, Inoue A, Matoba S, Zhang Y, Zhang F. Double nicking by RNA-guided CRISPR Cas9 for enhanced genome editing specificity. Cell. 2013b;154:1380–9.
83. Slaymaker IM, Gao L, Zetsche B, Scott DA, Yan WX, Zhang F. Rationally engineered Cas9 nucleases with improved specificity. Science. 2016;35:84–8.
84. Tsai SQ, Wyvekens N, Khayter C, Foden JA, Thapar V, Reyon D, Goodwin MJ, Aryee MJ, Joung JK. Dimeric CRISPR RNA-guided FokI nucleases for highly specific genome editing. Nat Biotechnol. 2014;32:569–76.
85. Tong B, Dong H, Cui Y, Jiang P, Jin Z, Zhang D. The versatile type V CRISPR effectors and their application prospects. Front Cell Dev Biol. 2021;8:622103. https://doi.org/10.3389/fcell.2020.622103.
86. Yan H, Wen Y, Tian Z, Hart N, Han S, Hughes SJ, Zeng Y. A one-pot isothermal Cas12-based assay for the sensitive detection of microRNAs. Nat Biomed Eng. 2023;7(12):1583–601. https://doi.org/10.1038/s41551-023-01033-1.
87. Riesenberg S, Helmbrecht N, Kanis P, et al. Improved gRNA secondary structures allow editing of target sites resistant to CRISPR-Cas9 cleavage. Nat Commun. 2022;13:489. https://doi.org/10.1038/s41467-022-28137-7.
88. Rees HA, Liu DR. Base editing: precision chemistry on the genome and transcriptome of living cells. Nat Rev Genet. 2018;19(12):770–88. https://doi.org/10.1038/s41576-018-0059-1.
89. Anzalone AV, Randolph PB, Davis JR, Sousa AA, Koblan LW, Levy JM, Chen PJ, Wilson C, Newby GA, Raguram A, Liu DR. Search-and-replace genome editing without double-strand breaks or donor DNA. Nature. 2019;576:149–57. https://doi.org/10.1038/s41586-019-1711-4.
90. Gaudelli NM, Komor AC, Rees HA, Packer MS, Badran AH, Bryson DI, Liu DR. Programmable base editing of A•T to G•C in genomic DNA without DNA cleavage. Nature. 2017;551(7681):464–71. https://doi.org/10.1038/nature24644.
91. Komor AC, Kim YB, Packer MS, Zuris JA, Liu DR. Programmable editing of a target base in genomic DNA without double-stranded DNA cleavage. Nature. 2016;533(7603):420–4. https://doi.org/10.1038/nature17946.
92. Rees H, Komor A, Yeh WH, et al. Improving the DNA specificity and applicability of base editing through protein engineering and protein delivery. Nat Commun. 2017;8:15790. https://doi.org/10.1038/ncomms15790.
93. Robbins GM, Wang M, Pomeroy EJ, Moriarity BS. Nonviral genome engineering of natural killer cells. Stem Cell Res Ther. 2021;12(1):350.
94. Kim HK, Song M, Lee J, Menon AV, Jung S, Kang Y-M, Choi JW, Woo E, Koh HC, Nam J-W, Kim H. In vivo high-throughput profiling of CRISPR-Cpf1 activity. Nat Methods. 2017;14(2):153–9.
95. Nishida K, Arazoe T, Yachie N, Banno S, Kakimoto M, Tabata M, Mochizuki M, Miyabe A, Araki M, Hara KY, Shimatani Z, Kondo A. Targeted nucleotide editing using hybrid prokaryotic and vertebrate adaptive immune systems. Science. 2016;353(6305):aaf8729. https://doi.org/10.1126/science.aaf8729.
96. Komor AC, Badran AH, Liu DR. CRISPR-based technologies for the manipulation of eukaryotic genomes. Cell. 2017;168(1-2):20–36. https://doi.org/10.1016/j.cell.2016.10.044.

97. Satomura A, Nishioka R, Mori H, Sato K, Kuroda K, Ueda M. Precise genome-wide base editing by the CRISPR Nickase system in yeast. Sci Rep. 2017;7(1):2095. https://doi.org/10.1038/s41598-017-02013-7.
98. van der Meer D, Barthorpe S, Yang W, Lightfoot H, Hall C, Gilbert J, Francies HE, Garnett MJ. Cell Model Passports—a hub for clinical, genetic and functional datasets of preclinical cancer models. Nucleic Acids Res. 2019;47(D1):D923–9. https://doi.org/10.1093/nar/gky872.
99. Newby GA, Yen JS, Woodard KJ, Mayuranathan T, Lazzarotto CR, Li Y, Sheppard-Tillman H, Porter SN, Yao Y, Mayberry K, Everette KA, Jang Y, Podracky CJ, Thaman E, Lechauve C, Sharma A, Henderson JM, Richter MF, Zhao KT, Miller SM, Wang T, Koblan LW, McCaffrey AP, Tisdale JF, Kalfa TA, Pruett-Miller SM, Tsai SQ, Weiss MJ, Liu DR. Base editing of haematopoietic stem cells rescues sickle cell disease in mice. Nature. 2021;595(7866):295–302.
100. Song M, Kim HK, Lee S, Kim Y, Seo S-Y, Park J, Choi JW, Jang H, Shin JH, Min S, Quan Z, Kim JH, Kang HC, Yoon S, Kim HH. Sequence-specific prediction of the efficiencies of adenine and cytosine base editors. Nat Biotechnol. 2020;38(9):1037–43.
101. Webber BR, Lonetree CL, Kluesner MG, Johnson MJ, Pomeroy EJ, Diers MD, Lahr WS, Draper GM, Slipek NJ, Smeester BA, Lovendahl KN, McElroy AN, Gordon WR, Osborn MJ, Moriarity BS. Highly efficient multiplex human T cell engineering without double-strand breaks using Cas9 base editors. Nat Commun. 2019;10(1):5222. https://doi.org/10.1038/s41467-019-13007-6.
102. Choi EH, Suh S, Foik AT, et al. In vivo base editing rescues cone photoreceptors in a mouse model of early-onset inherited retinal degeneration. Nat Commun. 2022;13:1830. https://doi.org/10.1038/s41467-022-29490-3.
103. Koblan LW, Erdos MR, Wilson C, Cabral WA, Levy JM, Xiong ZM, Tavarez UL, Davison LM, Gete YG, Mao X, Newby GA, Doherty SP, Narisu N, Sheng Q, Krilow C, Lin CY, Gordon LB, Cao K, Collins FS, Brown JD, Liu DR. In vivo base editing rescues Hutchinson-Gilford progeria syndrome in mice. Nature. 2021;589(7843):608–14. https://doi.org/10.1038/s41586-020-03086-7.
104. Weng N, Miller M, Pham AK, Komor AC, Broide DH. Single-base editing of rs12603332 on chromosome 17q21 with a cytosine base editor regulates ORMDL3 and ATF6α expression. Allergy. 2021;77(4):1139–49. https://doi.org/10.1111/all.15092.
105. Hsu JY, Grünewald J, Szalay R, Shih J, Anzalone AV, Lam KC, Shen MW, Petri K, Liu DR, Joung JK, Pinello L. PrimeDesign software for rapid and simplified design of prime editing guide RNAs. Nat Commun. 2021;12(1):1034–6.
106. Cheng H, Hao M, Ding B, Mei D, Wang W, Wang H, Zhou R, Liu J, Li C, Hu Q. Base editing with high efficiency in allotetraploid oilseed rape by A3A-PBE system. Plant Biotechnol J. 2021;19(1):87–97. https://doi.org/10.1111/pbi.13444. Epub 2020 Aug 4. PMID: 32640102; PMCID: PMC7769242.
107. Ren Q, Sretenovic S, Liu G, Zhong Z, Wang J, Huang L, Tang X, Guo Y, Liu L, Wu Y, Zhou J, Zhao Y, Yang H, He Y, Liu S, Yin D, Mayorga R, Zheng X, Zhang T, Qi Y, Zhang Y. Improved plant cytosine base editors with high editing activity, purity, and specificity. Plant Biotechnol J. 2021;19(10):2052–68. https://doi.org/10.1111/pbi.13635. Epub 2021 Jun 7. PMID: 34042262; PMCID: PMC8486236.
108. Zong Y, Song Q, Li C, Jin S, Zhang D, Wang Y, Qiu JL, Gao C. Efficient C-to-T base editing in plants using a fusion of nCas9 and human APOBEC3A. Nat Biotechnol. 2018;36:950–3. https://doi.org/10.1038/nbt.4261. PMID: 30272679.
109. Kantor A, McClements ME, MacLaren RE. CRISPR-Cas9 DNA base-editing and prime-editing. Int J Mol Sci. 2020;21(17):6240. https://doi.org/10.3390/ijms21176240.
110. Baranauskas A, Paliksa S, Alzbutas G, Vaitkevicius M, Lubiene J, Letukiene V, Burinskas S, Sasnauskas G, Skirgaila R. Generation and characterization of new highly thermostable and processive M-MuLV reverse transcriptase variants. Protein Eng Des Sel. 2012;25(10):657–68. https://doi.org/10.1093/protein/gzs034.
111. Petri K, Zhang W, Ma J, Schmidts A, Lee H, Horng JE, Kim DY, Kurt IC, Clement K, Hsu JY, Pinello L, Maus MV, Joung JK, Yeh J-RJ. CRISPR prime editing with ribonucleoprotein complexes in zebrafish and primary human cells. Nat Biotechnol. 2021;40:189–93. https://doi.org/10.1038/s41587-021-00901-y.
112. Gao P, Lyu Q, Ghanam AR, Lazzarotto CR, Newby GA, Zhang W, Choi M-H, Slivano OJ, Holden K, Walker JE, Kadina AP, Munroe RJ, Abratte CM, Schimenti JC, Liu DR, Tsai SQ, Long X, Miano JM. Prime editing in mice reveals the essentiality of a single base in driving tissue-specific gene expression. BMC. 2021;22(1):83. https://doi.org/10.1186/s13059-021-02304-3.
113. Liu Y, Li X, He S, Huang S, Li C, Chen Y, Liu Z, Huang X, Wang X. Efficient generation of mouse models with the prime editing system. Cell Discov. 2020;6:27. https://doi.org/10.1038/s41421-020-0165-z.
114. Park S-J, Jeong TY, Shin SK, Yoon DE, Lim S-Y, Kim SP, Choi J, Lee H, Hong J-I, Ahn J, Seong JK, Kim K. Targeted mutagenesis in mouse cells and embryos using an enhanced prime editor. Genome Biol. 2021;22(1):170. https://doi.org/10.1186/s13059-021-02389-w.
115. Bosch JA, Birchak G, Perrimon N. Precise genome engineering in Drosophila using prime editing. Proc Natl Acad Sci U S A. 2020;118(1):e2021996118. https://doi.org/10.1073/pnas.2021996118.
116. Anzalone AV, Koblan LW, Liu DR. Genome editing with CRISPR–Cas nucleases, base editors, transposases and prime editors. Nat Biotechnol. 2020;38(7):824–44. https://doi.org/10.1038/s41587-020-0561-9.

117. Scholefield J, Harrison PT. Prime editing—an update on the field. Gene Ther. 2021;28(7):396–401. https://doi.org/10.1038/s41434-021-00263-9.
118. Nelson JW, Randolph PB, Shen SP, Everette KA, Chen PJ, Anzalone AV, An M, Newby GA, Chen JC, Hsu A, Liu DR. Engineered pegRNAs improve prime editing efficiency. Nat Biotechnol. 2022;40(3):402–10. https://doi.org/10.1038/s41587-021-01039-7.
119. Tao J, Bauer DE, Chiarle R. Assessing and advancing the safety of CRISPR-Cas tools: from DNA to RNA editing. Nat Commun. 2023;14:212. https://doi.org/10.1038/s41467-023-35886-6.
120. Park J, Bae S, Kim JS. Cas-Designer: a web-based tool for choice of CRISPR-Cas9 target sites. Bioinformatics. 2015;31(24):4014–6.
121. Labun K, et al. CHOPCHOP v2: a web tool for the next generation of CRISPR genome engineering. Nucleic Acids Res. 2016;44(W1):W272–6. https://doi.org/10.1093/nar/gkw398.
122. Labun K, Montague TG, Krause M, Torres Cleuren YN, Tjeldnes H, Valen E. CHOPCHOP v3: expanding the CRISPR web toolbox beyond genome editing. Nucleic Acids Res. 2019;47(W1):W171–4.
123. Montague TG, Cruz JM, Gagnon JA, Church GM, Valen E. CHOPCHOP: a CRISPR/Cas9 and TALEN web tool for genome editing. Nucleic Acids Res. 2014;42:W401–7.
124. Liu H, Ding Y, Zhou Y, Jin W, Xie K, Chen LL. CRISPR-P 2.0: an improved CRISPR-Cas9 tool for genome editing in plants. Mol Plant. 2017;10(3):530–2.
125. Concordet JP, Haeussler M. CRISPOR: intuitive guide selection for CRISPR/Cas9 genome editing experiments and screens. Nucleic Acids Res. 2018;46:W242–5.
126. Naito Y, Hino K, Bono H, Ui-Tei K. CRISPRdirect: software for designing CRISPR/Cas guide RNA with reduced off-target sites. Bioinformatics. 2015;31(7):1120–3.
127. Heigwer F, Kerr G, Boutros M. E-CRISP: fast CRISPR target site identification. Nat Methods. 2014;11(2):122–3.
128. Kim HK, Min S, Song M, Jung S, Choi JW, Kim Y, Lee S, Yoon S, Kim HH. Deep learning improves prediction of CRISPR-Cpf1 guide RNA activity. Nat Biotechnol. 2018;36(3):239–41.
129. Kim HK, Kim Y, Lee S, Min S, Bae JY, Choi JW, Park J, Jung D, Yoon S, Kim HH. SpCas9 activity prediction by DeepSpCas9, a deep learning-based model with high generalization performance. Sci Adv. 2019;5(11):eaax9249.
130. Wang D, Zhang C, Wang B, Li B, Wang Q, Liu D, Wang H, Zhou Y, Shi L, Lan F, Wang Y. Optimized CRISPR guide RNA design for two high-fidelity Cas9 variants by deep learning. Nat Commun. 2019;10(1):4284–14.
131. Xu H, Xiao T, Chen C-H, Li W, Meyer CA, Wu Q, Wu D, Cong L, Zhang F, Liu JS, Brown M, Liu XS. Sequence determinants of improved CRISPR sgRNA design. Genome Res. 2015;25(8):1147–57.
132. Doench JG, Fusi N, Sullender M, Hegde M, Vaimberg EW, Donovan KF, Smith I, Tothova Z, Wilen C, Orchard R, Virgin HW, Listgarten J, Root DE. Optimized sgRNA design to maximize activity and minimize off-target effects of CRISPR-Cas9. Nat Biotechnol. 2016;34(2):184–91.
133. Moreno-Mateos MA, Vejnar CE, Beaudoin JD, Fernandez JP, Mis EK, Khokha MK, Giraldez AJ. CRISPRscan: designing highly efficient sgRNAs for CRISPR-Cas9 targeting in vivo. Nat Methods. 2015;12(10):982–8.
134. Bae S, Kweon J, Kim HS, Kim JS. Microhomology-based choice of Cas9 nuclease target sites. Nat Methods. 2014b;11:705–6.
135. Allen F, Crepaldi L, Alsinet C, Strong AJ, Kleshchevnikov V, De Angeli P, Páleníková P, Khodak A, Kiselev V, Kosicki M, Bassett AR, Harding H, Galanty Y, Muñoz-Martínez F, Metzakopian E, Jackson SP, Parts L. Predicting the mutations generated by repair of Cas9-induced double-strand breaks. Nat Biotechnol. 2019;37(1):64–72.
136. Shen MW, Arbab M, Hsu JY, Worstell D, Culbertson SJ, Krabbe O, Cassa CA, Liu DR, Gifford DK, Sherwood RI. Predictable and precise template-free CRISPR editing of pathogenic variants. Nature. 2018;563(7733):646–51.
137. Brinkman EK, Chen T, Amendola M, van Steensel B. Easy quantitative assessment of genome editing by sequence trace decomposition. Nucleic Acids Res. 2014;42(22):e168.
138. Park J, Lim K, Kim JS, Bae S. Cas-analyzer: an online tool for assessing genome editing results using NGS data. Bioinformatics. 2017;33(2):286–8.
139. Clement K, Rees H, Canver MC, Gehrke JM, Farouni R, Hsu JY, Cole MA, Liu DR, Joung JK, Bauer DE, et al. CRISPResso2 provides accurate and rapid genome editing sequence analysis. Nat Biotechnol. 2019;37:224–6.
140. Winter J, Schwering M, Pelz O, Rauscher B, Zhan T, Heigwer F, Boutros M. CRISPRAnalyzeR: interactive analysis, annotation and documentation of pooled CRISPR screens. bioRxiv. 2017.
141. Hwang GH, Yu J, Yang S, Son WJ, Lim K, Kim HS, Kim JS, Bae S. CRISPR-sub: analysis of DNA substitution mutations caused by CRISPR-Cas9 in human cells. Comput Struct Biotechnol J. 2020;18:1686–94.
142. Hwang GH, Park J, Lim K, Kim S, Yu J, Yu E, Kim ST, Eils R, Kim JS, Bae S. Web-based design and analysis tools for CRISPR base editing. BMC Bioinformatics. 2018;19(1):542.
143. Arbab M, Shen MW, Mok B, Wilson C, Matuszek Z, Cassa CA, Liu DR. Determinants of base editing outcomes from target library analysis and machine learning. Cell. 2020;182(2):463–80.e30.
144. Hwang G-H, Jeong YK, Habib O, Hong S-A, Lim K, Kim J-S, Bae S. PE-Designer and PE-Analyzer: web-based design and analysis tools

for CRISPR prime editing. Nucleic Acids Res. 2021;49(W1):W499–504.
145. Kim HK, Yu G, Park J, Min S, Lee S, Yoon S, Kim HH. Predicting the efficiency of prime editing guide RNAs in human cells. Nat Biotechnol. 2021;39(2):198–206.
146. Chow RD, Chen JS, Shen J, Chen S. A web tool for the design of prime-editing guide RNAs. Nat Biomed Eng. 2021;5:190–4.
147. Chen S, Lee B, Lee AY, Modzelewski AJ, He L. Highly efficient mouse genome editing by CRISPR ribonucleoprotein electroporation of zygotes. J Biol Chem. 2016;291(28):14457–67.
148. Qin W, et al. Efficient CRISPR/Cas9-mediated genome editing in mice by zygote electroporation of nuclease. Genetics. 2015;200(2):423–30. https://doi.org/10.1534/genetics.115.176594.
149. Rahimi H, Salehiabar M, Charmi J, Barsbay M, Ghaffarlou M, Razlighi MR, Davaran S, Khalilov R, Sugiyama M, Nosrati H, Kaboli S, Danafar H, Webster TJ. Harnessing nanoparticles for the efficient delivery of the CRISPR/Cas9 system. Nano Today. 2020;34:100895., ISSN 1748-0132. https://doi.org/10.1016/j.nantod.2020.100895.
150. Duan L, Ouyang K, Xu X, Xu L, Wen C, Zhou X, Qin Z, Xu Z, Sun W, Liang Y. Nanoparticle delivery of CRISPR/Cas9 for genome editing. Front Genet. 2021;12:673286. https://doi.org/10.3389/fgene.2021.673286. PMID: 34054927; PMCID: PMC8149999.
151. Ghosh D, Venkataramani P, Nandi S, Bhattacharjee S. CRISPR-Cas9 a boon or bane: the bumpy road ahead to cancer therapeutics. Cancer Cell Int. 2019;19:12. https://doi.org/10.1186/s12935-019-0726-0. PMID: 30636933; PMCID: PMC6325665.
152. Pal M, Herold MJ. CRISPR base editing applications for identifying cancer-driving mutations. Biochem Soc Trans. 2021;49(1):269–80. https://portlandpress.com/biochemsoctrans/article/49/1/269/227608/CRISPR-base-editing-applications-for-identifying.
153. Xu CL, Ruan MZC, Mahajan VB, Tsang SH. Viral delivery systems for CRISPR. Viruses. 2019;11(1):28. https://www.ncbi.nlm.nih.gov/pmc/articles/PMC6356701/.
154. Aubrey BJ, Kelly GL, Kueh AJ, Brennan MS, O'Connor L, Milla L, Wilcox S, Tai L, Strasser A, Herold MJ. An inducible lentiviral guide RNA platform enables the identification of tumour-essential genes and tumour-promoting mutations in vivo. Cell Rep. 2015;10(8):1422–32.
155. Han X, Wang Y, Wei J, Han W. Multi-antigen-targeted chimeric antigen receptor T cells for cancer therapy. J Hematol Oncol. 2019;12(1):128. https://doi.org/10.1186/s13045-019-0813-7.
156. Han HA, Pang JKS, Soh BS. Mitigating off-target effects in CRISPR/Cas9-mediated in vivo gene editing. J Mol Med. 2020;98(5):615–32. https://doi.org/10.1007/s00109-020-01893-z.
157. Omole AE, Fakoya AO. Ten years of progress and promise of induced pluripotent stem cells: historical origins, characteristics, mechanisms, limitations, and potential applications. PeerJ. 2018;6:e4370. https://doi.org/10.7717/peerj.4370.
158. Bock C, Datlinger P, Chardon F, Coelho MA, Dong MB, Lawson KA, Lu T, Maroc L, Norman TM, Song B, Stanley G, Chen S, Garnett M, Li W, Moffat J, Qi LS, Shapiro RS, Shendure J, Weissman JS, Zhuang X. High-content CRISPR screening. Nat Rev Methods Primers. 2022;2(1):9. https://doi.org/10.1038/s43586-022-00098-7.
159. György B, Lööv C, Zaborowski MP, Takeda S, Kleinstiver BP, Commins C, Kastanenka K, Mu D, Volak A, Giedraitis V, Lannfelt L, Maguire CA, Joung JK, Hyman BT, Breakefield XO, Ingelsson M. CRISPR/Cas9 mediated disruption of the Swedish APP allele as a therapeutic approach for early-onset Alzheimer's disease. Mol Ther Nucleic Acids. 2018;11:429–40.
160. Spires-Jones TL, Hyman BT. The intersection of amyloid beta and tau at synapses in Alzheimer's disease. Neuron. 2014;82(4):756–71.
161. Liu X, Xie T, Mao X, et al. Knockdown of long non-coding RNA CCAT1 suppresses proliferation and EMT of human colorectal cancer cells by downregulating microRNA-27a. Biosci Rep. 2020;40(1) https://doi.org/10.1042/BSR20193569.
162. Yang J, Yu J, Jia X. Fatty acid synthase promotes breast cancer metastasis by mediating changes in fatty acid metabolism. Oncol Lett. 2018;15(4):4706–12. https://doi.org/10.3892/ol.2018.7901.
163. Daisy PS, Shreyas KS, Anitha TS. Will CRISPR-Cas9 have cards to play against cancer? An update on its applications. Mol Biotechnol. 2021;63(2):93–108. https://doi.org/10.1007/s12033-020-00289-1.
164. Xu K, Chen G, Li X, Wu X, Chang Z, Xu J, Zhu Y, Yin P, Liang X, Dong L. MFN2 suppresses cancer progression through inhibition of mTORC2/Akt signaling. Sci Rep. 2017;7(1):41718. https://doi.org/10.1038/srep41718.
165. Li C, Pu M, Li C, Gao M, Liu M, Yu C, Yan H, Peng C, Zhao Y, Li Y, Ma Z, Qi X, Wang Y, Miao L, Ren J. MicroRNA-1304 suppresses human non-small cell lung cancer cell growth in vitro by targeting heme oxygenase-1. Acta Pharmacol Sin. 2016;38(1):110–9. https://doi.org/10.1038/aps.2016.92.
166. Khajuria O, Sharma N. Epigenetic targeting for lung cancer treatment via CRISPR/Cas9 technology. Adv Cancer Biol Metastasis. 2021;3:100012. https://doi.org/10.1016/j.adcanc.2021.100012.
167. Wanzel M, Vischedyk JB, Gittler MP, Gremke N, Seiz JR, Hefter M, Noack M, Savai R, Mernberger M, Charles JP, Schneikert J, Bretz AC, Nist A, Stiewe T. CRISPR-Cas9–based target validation for p53-reactivating model compounds. Nat Chem Biol. 2015;12(1):22–8.
168. Rodríguez TC, Dadafarin S, Pratt HE, Liu P, Amrani N, Zhu LJ. Genome-wide detection and analysis of

CRISPR-Cas off-targets. Prog Mol Biol Transl Sci. 2021;181:31–43.
169. Tsuji T, Yoneda A, Matsuzaki J, Miliotto A, Ryan C, Koya RC, Odunsi K. Rapid construction of antitumor T-cell receptor vectors from frozen tumors for engineered T-cell therapy. Cancer Immunol Res. 2018;6(5):594–604. https://doi.org/10.1158/2326-6066.CIR-17-0434.
170. Ellis GI, Sheppard NC, Riley JL. Genetic engineering of T cells for immunotherapy. Nat Rev Genet. 2021;22:1–21.
171. Zhang Z, Zhang Y, Gao F, Han S, Cheah KS, Tse HF, Lian Q. CRISPR/Cas9 genome-editing system in human stem cells: current status and future prospects. Mol Ther Nucleic Acids. 2017;9:230–41. https://doi.org/10.1016/j.omtn.2017.09.009.
172. Marín O, Valiente M, Ge X, Tsai L-H. Guiding neuronal cell migrations. Cold Spring Harbor Perspect Biol. 2010;2(2):a001834. https://www.ncbi.nlm.nih.gov/pmc/articles/PMC2828271/.
173. Zhao L, Cao YJ. Engineered T cell therapy for cancer in the clinic. Front Immunol. 2019;10:2250. https://www.ncbi.nlm.nih.gov/pmc/articles/PMC6798078/.
174. Norelli M, Camisa B, Barbiera G, Falcone L, Purevdorj A, Genua M, Sanvito F, Ponzoni M, Doglioni C, Cristofori P, Traversari C, Bordignon C, Ciceri F, Ostuni R, Bonini C, Casucci M, Bondanza A. Monocyte-derived IL-1 and IL-6 are differentially required for cytokine-release syndrome and neurotoxicity due to CAR T cells. Nat Med. 2018;24(6):739–48. https://www.ncbi.nlm.nih.gov/pubmed/29808007/. Accessed 29 Mar. 2020.
175. Wang Z, Han W. Biomarkers of cytokine release syndrome and neurotoxicity related to CAR-T cell therapy. Biomark Res. 2018;6:4. https://doi.org/10.1186/s40364-018-0116-0.
176. Chen J, López-Moyado IF, Seo H, Lio CJ, Hempleman LJ, Sekiya T, Yoshimura A, Scott-Browne JP, Rao A. NR4A transcription factors limit CAR T cell function in solid tumors. Nature. 2019;567(7749):530–4. https://doi.org/10.1038/s41586-019-0985-x.
177. Hernandez I, Prasad V, Gellad WF. Total costs of chimeric antigen receptor T-cell immunotherapy. JAMA Oncol. 2018;4(7):994.
178. Dimitri A, Herbst F, Fraietta JA. Engineering the next-generation of CAR T-cells with CRISPR-Cas9 gene editing. Mol Cancer. 2022; 21(1):78.
179. Liu Y, Yan X, Zhang F, Zhang X, Tang F, Han Z, Li Y. TCR-T immunotherapy: the challenges and solutions. Front Oncol. 2022;11:794183. https://www.ncbi.nlm.nih.gov/pmc/articles/PMC8822241/.
180. Zhao L, Cao YJ. Engineered T cell therapy for cancer in the clinic. Front Immunol. 2019;10:1708. https://doi.org/10.3389/fimmu.2019.01708.
181. Ottaviano G, Georgiadis C, Gkazi SA, Syed F, Zhan H, Etuk A, Preece R, Chu J, Kubat A, Adams S, Veys P, Vora A, Rao K, Qasim W, TT52 CRISPR-CAR Group. Phase 1 clinical trial of CRISPR-engineered CAR19 universal T cells for treatment of children with refractory B cell leukemia. Sci Transl Med. 2022;14(668):eabq3010. https://doi.org/10.1126/scitranslmed.abq3010.
182. Villiger L, Joung J, Koblan L, Weissman J, Abudayyeh OO, Gootenberg JS. CRISPR technologies for genome, epigenome and transcriptome editing. Nat Rev Mol Cell Biol. 2024;25(6):464–87. https://doi.org/10.1038/s41580-023-00697-6.
183. Kim D, Luk K, Wolfe SA, Kim JS. Evaluating and enhancing target specificity of gene-editing nucleases and deaminases. Annu Rev Biochem. 2019;88:191–220. https://doi.org/10.1146/annurev-biochem-013118-111730.

Mycobacterial F-ATP Synthase: From Structures to Target Sites to Inhibitors

5

Amaravadhi Harikishore, Chui Fann Wong, Priya Ragunathan, Shin Joon, Thomas Dick, and Gerhard Grüber

5.1 Introduction

Mycobacterial infections are mainly spread through tuberculoid-infected aerosols or liquid droplets from running nose or mouth and lead to lung to skin infections. Based on the presence of tubercular bacilli as infectious agents, mycobacteria can be grouped into tuberculoid and non-tuberculoid infections. *Mycobacteria tuberculosis* (*Mtb*) complex (MTC) infections or tuberculosis (TB) is manifested with the presence of tuberculoid bacillus in the lungs. *M. leprae* complex (MLC) infections in addition to tuberculous bacilli show the presence of lepromatous skin lesions. In contrast to these tuberculoid infections, non-tuberculous mycobacteria (NTM) like the *M. abscessus* (*Mab*) or *M. avium* complex (MAC) strains are responsible for non-tuberculoid lung/skin infections (NTI) [1]. Unlike MTC/MLC infections, NTI infections do not need tuberculoid-infected aerosols and can be transmitted or acquired from environmental sources. Co-incidentally, in recent years, infection rates of NTI in patients with comorbidities were alarmingly high paralleling the MTC infections [2–4]. Both *Mtb* and NTM are responsible for more deaths than any other bacteria [2–4]. The lethality of mycobacterial infections is due to their innate ability to adapt their metabolic respiration in response to their microenvironments to persist, survive, and infect at a latent stage [5].

This fundamental adaptation enables the mycobacterium to regenerate its reducing equivalents which are vital to conduct its basal respiration for sustenance of energy currencies like adenine triphosphate (ATP). Such ATP homeostasis is regulated by an ensemble of oxidative phosphorylation enzymes in the electron transport chain (ETC). The cytochrome oxidases of the ETC efficiently reduce oxygen to water, releasing electrons that are coupled to the genesis of a proton motive force (PMF) and ultimately synthesis of ATP from ADP + P_i by the F_1F_O-ATP synthase [6]. Co-incidentally, the very nonreplicative dormant phase with low basal levels of ATP also represents a metabolically vulnerable and susceptible phase of mycobacteria. This stage is sensitive to anti-TB drugs that target the ATP homeostasis mechanisms [7]. This observation suggests that drugs that inhibit oxidative

A. Harikishore · C. F. Wong · P. Ragunathan · S. Joon
G. Grüber (✉)
School of Biological Sciences, Nanyang Technological University, Singapore, Republic of Singapore
e-mail: amaravadhi@ntu.edu.sg; CHUIFANN001@e.ntu.edu.sg; rpriya@ntu.edu.sg; SHINJOON@ntu.edu.sg; ggrueber@ntu.edu.sg

T. Dick
Center for Discovery and Innovation, Hackensack Meridian Health, Nutley, NJ, USA

Medical Sciences, Hackensack Meridian School of Medicine, Nutley, NJ, USA

Department of Microbiology and Immunology, Georgetown University, Washington, DC, USA

K. Parthasarathy, R. Manikkam (eds.), *Translational Research in Biomedical Sciences: Recent Progress and Future Prospects*, https://doi.org/10.1007/978-981-97-1777-4_5

phosphorylation could contribute to shortening the duration of therapy for drug-resistant TB or NTM diseases. This working model was corroborated by the anti-TB drug Sirturo® (Bedaquiline, BDQ), which targets the *Mtb*- [8, 9] and *Mab* F_1F_O ATP synthase [10], as well as novel targets and inhibitors which have been identified recently [11–19].

The mycobacterial F_1F_O ATP synthase is composed of a cytoplasmic F_1 and a membrane-bound F_O domain. The F_1 sector, also referred to as F_1-ATPase (Fig. 5.1), is constituted by the catalytic headpiece formed by alternating α_3,β_3 subunits arranged in a hexameric form and the central and rotary stalk subunits γ and ε. The catalysis of ATP synthesis or ATP hydrolysis occurs on catalytic β subunits upon the rotary motion ignited by the F_O domain [20]. The F_1 and F_O parts are held together by the peripheral stalk subunits *b*, *b′*, and δ (Fig. 5.1). The F_O domain consists of the *a* and the c_9 subunits, which are organized to form a c_9 ring, and in part by the peripheral stalk subunits *b*, *b′* (Fig. 5.1). During the rotary motions, subunit *a* and the *c* subunits converge to form half channels to translocate protons from the intermembrane to the plasma side [21]. In the case of ATP synthesis, such rotation drives the rotational movement of the central γ-ε stalk in a clockwise direction, which is coupled to the three catalytic centers located at the three αβ-interfaces. In contrast to most bacterial and mitochondrial F_1F_O ATP synthase, the mycobacterial enzyme shows very low, latent ATP hydrolysis, and therefore does not promote ATP-driven proton translocation [12, 22]. This prevents wastage of ATP and a strict regulation of the membrane potential, an important regulation under hypoxia conditions [7].

Combining genetic, structural, microbiological, and biochemical studies has provided insights into the main mechanistic and regulatory elements of the engine, which are pathogen-specific

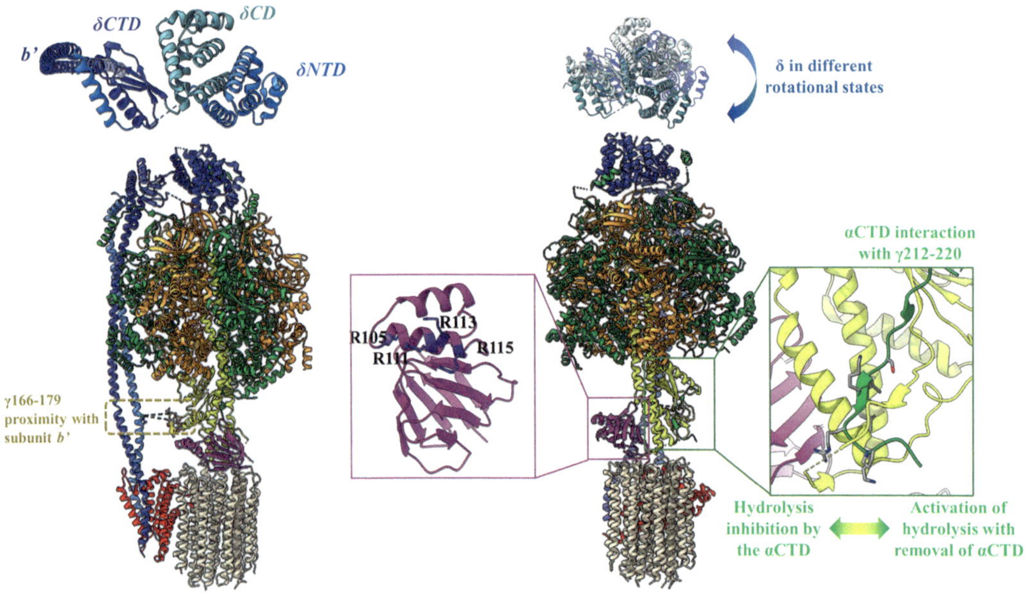

Fig. 5.1 (*left*) Structural traits of the mycobacteria specific γ-loop, which comes in close proximity to subunit *b′* and engages in salt bridge interactions. The three domains of subunit δ are shown on the top with the extended N-terminal domain (*δNTD*), which are uniquely seen in the mycobacterial enzyme. (*right*) The *M. smegmatis* F_1F_O-ATP synthase enzyme represented in a different rotary position, highlighting the compact state of subunit ε and its C-terminal arginine residues, which interact with the N-terminal β-barrel domain. A second zoom-in shows the interplay of the C-terminus of subunit α with the central and rotating γ subunit, leading to reduced ATP hydrolysis activity of the enzyme. On top, the three different conformations of subunit δ, which enable the transfer of elastic energy within the engine, are illustrated

and not present in the human mitochondrial counterparts [12–16, 19]. These studies provided the platform for the identification of new targets and structure-based inhibitor designs against this essential enzyme. Such novel structure-based anti-TB and anti-*Mab* inhibitors together with anti-TB compounds, identified by high-throughput screening (HTS) approaches, will be highlighted in the chapter below.

5.2 The C-terminal Subunit α Extension Inhibits ATP Hydrolysis

Mitochondria, bacteria, chloroplasts, and algae have designed a variety of tools for regulating ATP hydrolysis by their F-ATP synthases, which prevents the wastage of biological energy in the form of ATP. Chloroplasts have evolved a unique β-hairpin in the rotating γ subunit, which communicates with the catalytic β-subunit and suppresses ATP cleavage [23]. In mitochondria, ATP hydrolysis by the molecular engine is regulated by the inhibitor protein IF_1 that binds to a catalytic α-β interface [24]. In a related manner, most α-proteobacteria have evolved an additional subunit called ζ, which binds to a catalytic α-β interface [25]. Interestingly, latent ATP hydrolysis of the mycobacterial F-ATP synthase has its major regulatory element within the mycobacterium-specific C-terminal domain (~3.5 kDa; αCTD) of the nucleotide-binding subunit α (Fig. 5.1) [12, 13, 16, 19, 21]. This αCTD binds to a mycobacterium-specific sequence of the central stalk subunit γ [19, 21, 26], resulting in an intramolecular lock as shown by single molecule rotational assays [19]. Structural and biochemical insights paved the way for a protein-based pharmacophore model, virtual screening, and characterization of the novel inhibitor N-(2-chloro-5-methoxy-4-((3-(2-oxopyrrolidin-1-yl)propyl)carbamoyl) phenyl)-2-methyl-5,6-dihydro-1,4-oxathiine-3-carboxamide (Fig. 5.2), called AlMF1 [27]. The inhibitor reduces NADH-driven ATP synthesis of *Mycobacterium smegmatis* inverted membrane vesicles and the recombinant and reconstituted F_1F_O-ATP synthase in a μM range [27].

5.3 Targeting the Mycobacterium-Specific Loop of Subunit γ

To adapt to diverse environmental niches, critical mechanistic elements of essential enzymes like the F-ATP synthase show variations of extra features to improve the enzymatic processes of ion transport and ATP synthesis. Like in the anaerobic acetogenic bacterium *Acetobacterium woodii*, an extra insertion of 17 residues in the rotary γ subunit is important for proper ion transport and ATP synthesis [28]. In the mycobacterial counterpart, an insertion of 12–14 residues has been observed, which does not exist in the human homologue. This extra-loop has been shown to be critical for ATP formation and the regulation of ATP-driven proton pumping [12, 19]. The structure of the *M. smegmatis* F-ATP synthase revealed a conformation in which polar amino acids of the γ-loop form a salt bridge with an arginine of subunit *b′* while rotating (Fig. 5.1) [26]. In silico virtual screening studies targeting this mycobacterial γ-loop resulted in the identification of the compound diaminopyrimidine, GaMF1 [29]. GaMF1 was shown to inhibit ATP formation, driven by NADH or succinate oxidation of mycobacterial inside-out vesicles with an inhibitory concentration (IC_{50}) of 0.5 ± 0.1 μM [29]. In contrast to BDQ, which exerts bactericidal activity only upon extended treatment duration, GaMF1 shows immediate bactericidal activity in vitro. Furthermore, GaMF1 is bactericidal against isoniazid or rifampicin resistant clinical isolates and even against isoniazid plus rifampicin resistant *Mtb* strains [29]. Further medical chemistry studies led to the lead molecule GaMF1-8, which showed an 18-fold enhancement compared to GaMF1 [29]. Interestingly, GaMF1 was also found to be bactericidal against the NTM species *M. abscessus* by targeting the F-ATP synthase [30].

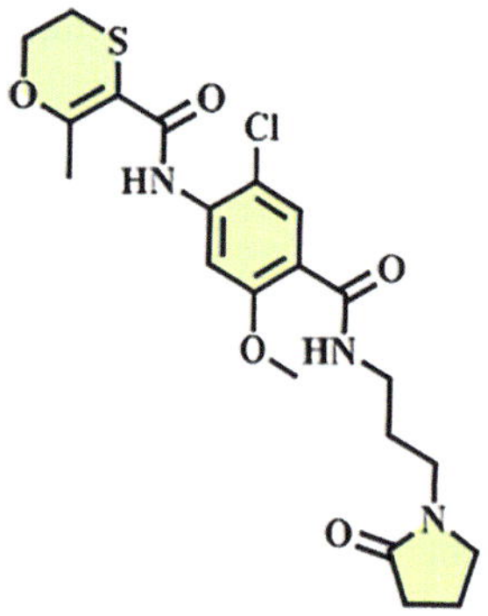

AlMF1

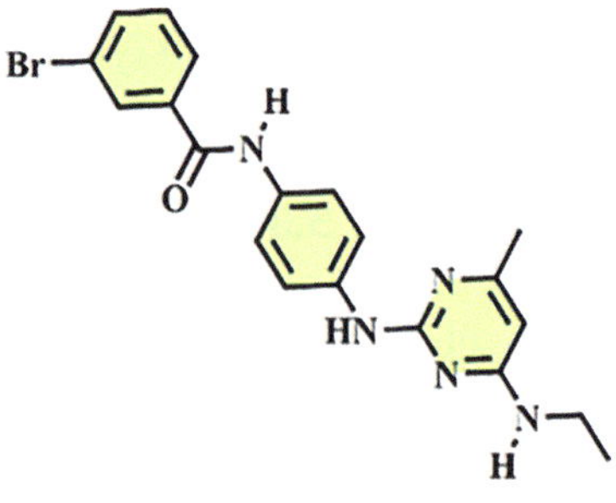

GaMF1

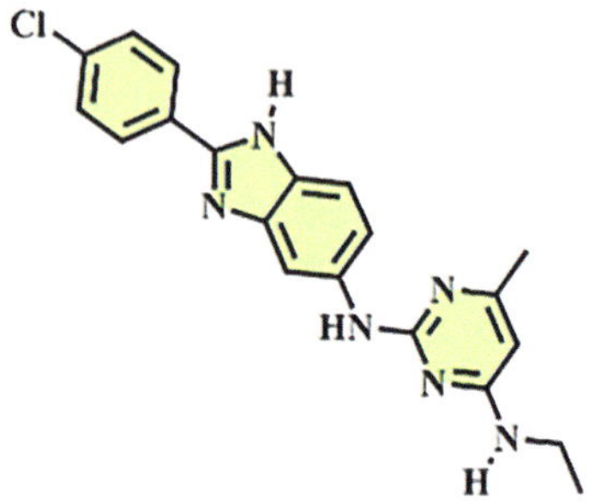

GaMF1.8

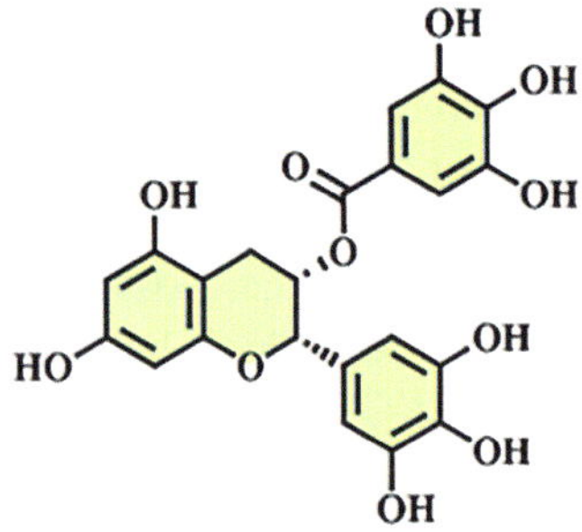

EGCG/EpMF1

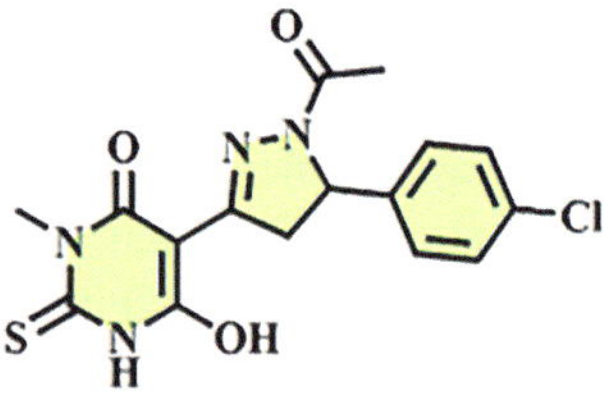

EpNMF1

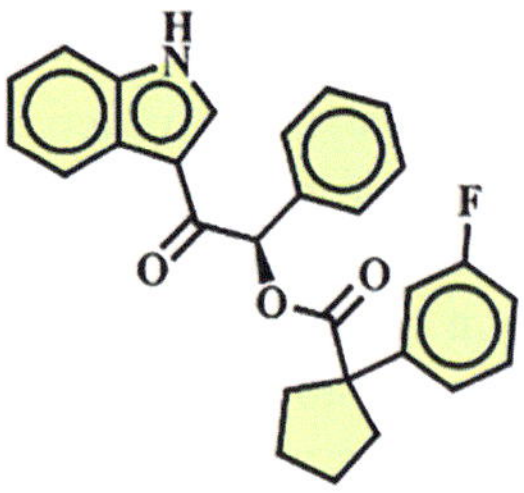

DeMF1

Fig. 5.2 F_1-ATP synthase inhibitors targeting mycobacteria-specific epitopes of subunit α (AlMF1), γ (GaMF1 and its lead GaMF1-8), ε (EpMF1/EGGC and EpNMF1), and δ (DeMF1)

5.4 Insights into Energy Coupling by Subunit ε Led to Novel Inhibitors

The number and composition of residues of the mycobacterial subunit ε differs significantly from the other bacterial or mitochondrial counterparts [14]. It consists of a β-barrel structure at its N-terminus (Fig. 5.1), which like a spring connects the *c*-ring rotary movements in the F_O part to the catalytic $α_3$:$β_3$ domain. The *spring mechanism* is coupled by ε's C-terminal α-hairpin domain, whose helices are significantly shorter compared to the mitochondrial and other bacterial counterparts [14].

Multiple arginine (R105, R109, R111, R113, R115) residues in $α_2$ helix of the ε hairpin structure are involved in salt bridge interactions with the linker region residues εA81-E87 and D98 on the C-terminal helix (Fig. 5.1). Chromosomal mutation of the four arginine residues R105, R111, R113, R115 into alanine (ε4A) diminished whole cell ATP synthesis [15]. The ε4A mutant showed low growth yield on non-fermentable carbon sources, exhibited defective colony morphology, and was hypersensitive to cell wall inhibitors and BDQ. In addition, this mutant strain revealed a dysregulated oxidative phosphorylation with a significant increase in cellular respiration and metabolism. These results brought the mycobacterial ε subunit into the focus for a virtual screening campaign using the C-terminal arginine residues, which identified the green tea ingredient epigallocatechin gallate (EGCG; Fig. 5.2) as a potent binder to subunit ε and an ATP synthesis inhibitor (IC_{50} = 0.16 μM) [15].

Recent characterization of an overexpressed *M. smegmatis* F_1-ATPase ($α_3$:$β_3$:γ:e), the ε-free

α_3:β_3:γ complex as well as N-terminal ($F_1\alpha\beta\gamma\varepsilon_{\Delta 2\text{-}5}$) and C-terminal ($F_1\alpha\beta\gamma\varepsilon_{\Delta 121}$, *Ms*$F_1\alpha\beta\gamma\varepsilon_{\Delta 103\text{-}121}$) deletion mutants provided further insights into ε's residues being important for coupling and stability [17]. Likewise, the N-terminal residues A_2-L_4 are needed to maintain structural stability. Such data have been used in an in silico screening, leading to the new anti-TB inhibitor EpNMF1 (IC_{50} of 0.2 μM; Fig. 5.2) [17]. NMR titration and molecular docking studies confirmed EpNMF1's binding to the N-terminal β-barrel of ε [17].

5.5 Inhibiting Elastic Energy Transmission by Targeting Subunit δ

As described for the *α*, *γ*, and *ε* subunits above, specific residue composition and structural features of the mycobacterial engine opened the door for novel inhibitors targeting the mycobacterial energy converter. In line with these, the mycobacterial peripheral stalk subunit *δ*, which is located at the tip of the F-ATP synthase (Fig. 5.1), displays a unique noncanonical N-terminal domain (NTD; 111-amino acids extension) [20, 31]. Atomic structures of the *M. smegmatis* F-ATP synthase described significant movements of subunit *δ* (Fig. 5.1) with its NTD (α3–α8), the central domain (CD; α9–α14), and the C-terminal domain (CTD; β1–β4 as well as α15–α16) (Fig. 5.1) [19, 26], which enable coupling of elastic energy caused by the rotational movements of the *c*-ring and the F_1-domain [19, 26]. Mutational and enzymatic studies revealed that the δ residues δR171, δR171G, δR177Q, and δQ178R of α-helices 3 and 4, which are in proximity to the catalytic α_3:β_3 part, are important for ATP synthesis of the recombinant enzyme [18]. These results were used for a δ receptor-based pharmacophore, resulting in the identification of the potent subunit δ inhibitor DeMF1 (2–(1H-indol–3–yl)–2–oxo–1-phenylethyl 1–(3–fluorophenyl) cyclopentane–1–carboxylate) (Fig. 5.2), which inhibits NADH-driven ATP formation of mycobacterial IMVs and overexpressed F-ATP synthase in proteoliposomes with an IC_{50} of about 0.5 μM [18]. Target specificity and mechanism of action studies identified the δ residues involved in DeMF1 binding [18]. The novel structural and mechanistic results of the mycobacterial δ subunit demonstrate the potential to foster δ's flexible coupling as a target for the development of mycobacterial F-ATP synthase compounds.

5.6 Characteristics of BDQ and Its Improved Analogs

In a whole-cell approach, the anti-TB drug BDQ (Fig. 5.3) was discovered [8] and became FDA-approved for clinical use in cases of extremely drug-resistant (XDR)/multidrug-resistant TB in 2012 [32]. The drug consists of a 6-bromo-2-methoxyquinoline and a butan-1-yl moiety with a 1-phenyl (Ar_1), 2-naphthalen-1-yl (Ar_2) ring, and 4-dimethyl amino (DMA) substitutions (Fig. 5.3). Although with a delay [33], BDQ is bactericidal against nonreplicating subpopulations [34]. It was shown to bind to subunit ε [35] and three sites of the F_O domain, including the so-called *c*-ring only, lagging sites as well as the leading site with higher affinity [21] (Fig. 5.4). The leading site is the deepest and proposed to be the most important one as it inhibits the rotation of the turbine *c*-ring in ATP synthesis direction [21]. The *a*-subunit and c_9-ring of the F_O domain function as half channels to conduct the protons from the periplasm to the cytoplasm. During the rotary motions in synthesis direction, the leading sites could be primarily involved in the entry of protons from the periplasmic half channel, while the lagging site on the cytoplasmic half channel coordinates the egress of protons into cytoplasm [21].

BDQ's high lipophilicity is associated with nonspecific inhibition of the hERG channel linked to cardiotoxicity, mitochondrial F-ATP synthase inhibition [36], and more worryingly, the incidence of nonspecific clinical resistance [37] could thwart the success story of this anti-TB drug.

Attempts to reduce lipophilicity of BDQ derivatives and increase potency by varying the phenyl (Ar_1) and naphthyl (Ar_2) ring resulted in the derivatives TBAJ-876 and TBAJ-587 [38,

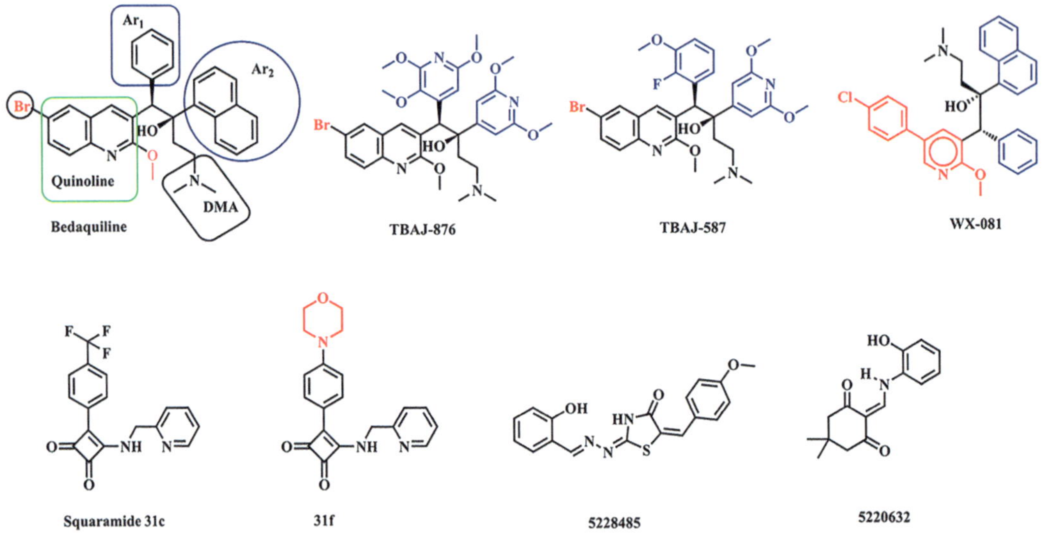

Fig. 5.3 Inhibitors targeting the mycobacterial F_O domain: Bedaquiline with its key pharmacophore groups comprising 6-bromo-2-methoxyquinoline (green) and phenyl (Ar_1), naphthyl (Ar_2) rings (purple), and a dimethyl amine (DMA, orange) substitution(s) on 1, 2, and 4th position of butane moiety, respectively. Shown are the newer BDQ derivatives TBAJ876, TBAJ587. WX-081, bearing a 5-(4-Chloro-phenyl)-2-methoxypyridin-3-yl scaffold (red) instead of a quinoline ring, maintained BDQ's potency

Fig. 5.4 Binding traits of BDQ at the membrane-embedded *c*-ring, leading and lagging sites. Top panel highlights the importance of the c_9 ring (F69)-*a* subunit interface (F221, F213), which plugs the 6-bromo-quinoline. Bottom panel shows BDQ's binding at the lagging site and highlights the possible additional interaction anchored by *a*-subunit residues V176, I173, P172

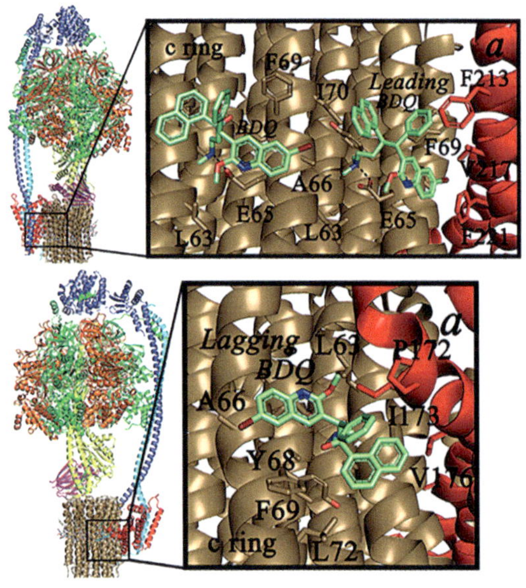

39], which entered early clinical development (Fig. 5.3). Simulation studies via molecular dynamics and free energy calculations showed an increased affinity of TBAJ-876 to the F_O part compared to BDQ [40]. Most recent substitutions of the quinoline ring of BDQ with 5-(4-Chloro-phenyl)-2-methoxypyridin-3-yl group led to the discovery of sudapyridine (WX-081; Fig. 5.3), which is in clinical phase 2 development [41]. The analog shows improved pharmacokinetic properties compared to BDQ, low cytotoxicity, and a similar efficacy to that of BDQ [41].

Interestingly, BDQ [10] and TBAJ-876 [42] are also potent against *M. abscessus* by inhibiting

ATP formation although, in contrast to *Mtb*, the two compounds do not show nanomolar bactericidal activity level against the non-tuberculous mycobacterium. Therefore, BDQ can, at best, be used as salvage therapy against *M. abscessus*-caused lung infections [43].

5.7 Further Anti-TB Compounds Targeting the F_O Subunits *a* and *c*

HTS campaigns also identified the anti-TB compounds 5228485 and 5220632, which reduce ATP formation with an IC_{50} of 0.34 μM and 4 μM, respectively [44] (Fig. 5.5). Spontaneous resistant mutants at subunits *a* and *c* indicated that the compounds target the F_O part of the mycobacterial engine. In addition, a novel scaffold Squaramide (31c, Fig. 5.5) was unraveled that potently inhibits ATP synthesis with an IC_{50} of 0.3 μM and shows growth inhibition of *Mtb* with an MIC_{50} of 6.2 μM [45]. SAR results showed that modifications on the morpholine ring of the phenyl moiety (31f, Fig. 5.5) yielded analogs with an IC_{50} of 0.03 μM and an MIC of 0.5 μM. Spontaneous resistant mutations generated by this class of molecules revealed binding at the subunits *a*-*c* interface.

5.8 Concluding Comment

The oxidative phosphorylation pathway with its ETC and the F-ATP synthase catalyzes (1) the oxidation of the electron carriers NADH and $FADH_2$, thereby facilitating NAD^+/NADH and FAD/$FADH_2$ balance, (2) driving a PMF, which is needed for maintaining transmembrane electrochemical gradients, which regulate PMF-driven pumps, and (3) forming ATP for metabolic and replication processes of the mycobacterial pathogen. New paradigms of regulating the F_1F_O-ATP synthase in ATP formation and ATPase activity led to new inhibitors targeting subunit *a*, *γ*, *δ*, or *ε* of the F_1 domain, which is soluble, and attractive for the identification of compounds with favorable physicochemical properties. In parallel, a significant number of potent anti-TB compounds have been unraveled by mycobacterial whole cell or inside-out membrane assays and improved by SAR efforts, which target the membrane-embedded F_O domain with its half channel forming subunits *a* and *c*. Anti-TB inhibitors like GaMF1, BDQ, or TBAJ-876 have been shown to also inhibit the growth of the NTM *M. abscessus* or, in the case of GaMF1, to even kill the pathogen. These data underscore the attractiveness of this molecular engine, as a rich target for the discovery of broad-spectrum anti-mycobacterials.

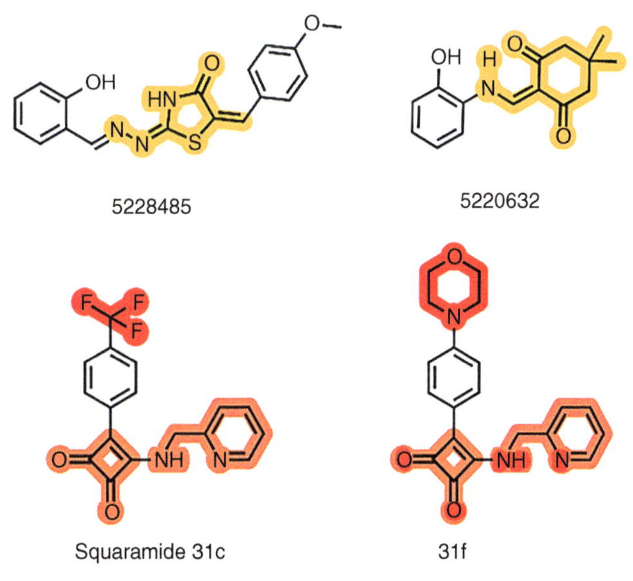

Fig. 5.5 Newer potent inhibitors that target the membrane-embedded F_O domain: 5228485, 5220632 with their respective core groups highlighted in yellow. Squaramide (31c) and its derivative (31f) have squaramide and amino methyl pyrid-2-yl groups as common scaffold (light red), while the morpholine group (red) afforded the highest potency

Acknowledgments The team was supported by the National Research Foundation (NRF) Singapore, NRF Competitive Research Programme (CRP), Grant Award Number NRF-CRP27-2021-0002.

References

1. WHO. Global tuberculosis report 2022.
2. Wu M-L, Aziz DB, Dartois V, Dick T. NTM drug discovery: status, gaps and the way forward. Drug Discov Today. 2018;23(8):1502–19.
3. Johansen MD, Herrmann JL, Kremer L. Non-tuberculous mycobacteria and the rise of *Mycobacterium abscessus*. Nat Rev Microbiol. 2020;18(7):392–407.
4. Winthrop KL, Marras TK, Adjemian J, Zhang H, Wang P, Zhang Q. Incidence and prevalence of non-tuberculous mycobacterial lung disease in a large U.S. managed care health plan, 2008-2015. Ann Am Thorac Soc. 2020;17(2):178–85.
5. Cook GM, Hards K, Vilchèze C, Hartman T, Berney M. Energetics of respiration and oxidative phosphorylation in mycobacteria. Microbiol Spectr. 2014;2(3):6.
6. Lu P, Lill H, Bald D. ATP synthase in mycobacteria: special features and implications for a function as drug target. Biochim Biophys Acta. 2014;1837(7):1208–18.
7. Rao SP, Alonso S, Rand L, Dick T, Pethe K. The protonmotive force is required for maintaining ATP homeostasis and viability of hypoxic, nonreplicating *Mycobacterium tuberculosis*. Proc Natl Acad Sci USA. 2008;105(33):11945–50.
8. Andries K, Verhasselt P, Guillemont J, Gohlmann HW, Neefs JM, Winkler H, et al. A diarylquinoline drug active on the ATP synthase of *Mycobacterium tuberculosis*. Science. 2005;307(5707):223–7.
9. Hards K, Robson JR, Berney M, Shaw L, Bald D, Koul A, et al. Bactericidal mode of action of bedaquiline. J Antimicrob Chemother. 2015;70(7):2028–37.
10. Dupont C, Viljoen A, Thomas S, Roquet-Baneres F, Herrmann JL, Pethe K, et al. Bedaquiline inhibits the ATP synthase in *Mycobacterium abscessus* and is effective in infected zebrafish. Antimicrob Agents Chemother. 2017;61(11):e01225.
11. Priya R, Biuković G, Manimekalai MS, Lim J, Rao SP, Grüber G. Solution structure of subunit gamma (gamma(1-204)) of the *Mycobacterium tuberculosis* F-ATP synthase and the unique loop of gamma(165-178), representing a novel TB drug target. J Bioenerg Biomembr. 2013;45(1-2):121–9.
12. Hotra A, Suter M, Biuković G, Ragunathan P, Kundu S, Dick T, et al. Deletion of a unique loop in the mycobacterial F-ATP synthase gamma subunit sheds light on its inhibitory role in ATP hydrolysis-driven H(+) pumping. FEBS J. 2016;283(10):1947–61.
13. Ragunathan P, Sielaff H, Sundararaman L, Biuković G, Subramanian Manimekalai MS, Singh D, et al. The uniqueness of subunit alpha of mycobacterial F-ATP synthases: an evolutionary variant for niche adaptation. J Biol Chem. 2017;292(27):11262–79.
14. Joon S, Ragunathan P, Sundararaman L, Nartey W, Kundu S, Manimekalai MSS, et al. The NMR solution structure of *Mycobacterium tuberculosis* F-ATP synthase subunit ε provides new insight into energy coupling inside the rotary engine. FEBS J. 2018;285(6):1111–28.
15. Saw W-G, Wu M-L, Ragunathan P, Biuković G, Lau A-M, Shin J, et al. Disrupting coupling within mycobacterial F-ATP synthases subunit ε causes dysregulated energy production and cell wall biosynthesis. Sci Rep. 2019;9(1):16759.
16. Wong CF, Grüber G. The unique C-terminal extension of mycobacterial F-ATP synthase subunit α is the major contributor to its latent ATP hydrolysis activity. Antimicrob Agents Chemother. 2020;64(12):e01568–20.
17. Wong CF, Lau AM, Harikishore A, Saw WG, Shin J, Ragunathan P, et al. A systematic assessment of mycobacterial F(1)-ATPase subunit ε's role in latent ATPase hydrolysis. FEBS J. 2021;288(3):818–36.
18. Harikishore A, Saw WG, Ragunathan P, Litty D, Dick T, Müller V, et al. Mutational analysis of mycobacterial F-ATP synthase subunit δ leads to a potent δ enzyme inhibitor. ACS Chem Biol. 2022;17(3):529–35.
19. Wong CF, Saw WG, Basak S, Sano M, Ueno H, Kerk HW, et al. Structural elements involved in ATP hydrolysis inhibition and ATP synthesis of tuberculosis and nontuberculous mycobacterial F-ATP synthase decipher new targets for inhibitors. Antimicrob Agents Chemother. 2022;66(12):e0105622.
20. Kamariah N, Huber RG, Nartey W, Bhushan S, Bond PJ, Grüber G. Structure and subunit arrangement of Mycobacterial F1FO ATP synthase and novel features of the unique mycobacterial subunit delta. J Struct Biol. 2019;207(2):199–208.
21. Guo H, Courbon GM, Bueler SA, Mai J, Liu J, Rubinstein JL. Structure of mycobacterial ATP synthase bound to the tuberculosis drug bedaquiline. Nature. 2021;589(7840):143–7.
22. Haagsma AC, Driessen NN, Hahn MM, Lill H, Bald D. ATP synthase in slow- and fast-growing mycobacteria is active in ATP synthesis and blocked in ATP hydrolysis direction. FEMS Microbiol Lett. 2010;313(1):68–74.
23. Hahn A, Vonck J, Mills DJ, Meier T, Kühlbrandt W. Structure, mechanism, and regulation of the chloroplast ATP synthase. Science. 2018;360(6389):eaat4318.
24. Cabezón E, Arechaga I, Jonathan P, Butler G, Walker JE. Dimerization of bovine F1-ATPase by binding the inhibitor protein, IF1. J Biol Chem. 2000;275(37):28353–5.
25. Morales-Rios E, de la Rosa-Morales F, Mendoza-Hernandez G, Rodriguez-Zavala JS, Celis H, Zarco-Zavala M, et al. A novel 11-kDa inhibitory subunit in the F1FO ATP synthase of *Paracoccus denitrificans* and related alpha-proteobacteria. FASEB J. 2010;24(2):599–608.

26. Montgomery MG, Petri J, Spikes TE, Walker JE. Structure of the ATP synthase from *Mycobacterium smegmatis* provides targets for treating tuberculosis. Proc Natl Acad Sci USA. 2021;118:47.
27. Harikishore A, Wong CF, Ragunathan P, Litty D, Müller V, Grüber G. Targeting mycobacterial F-ATP synthase C-terminal α subunit interaction motif on rotary subunit γ. Antibiotics. 2021;10(12):1456.
28. Bogdanović N, Trifunovic D, Sielaff H, Westphal L, Bhushan S, Müller V, et al. The structural features of *Acetobacterium woodii* F-ATP synthase reveal the importance of the unique subunit gamma-loop in Na(+) translocation and ATP synthesis. FEBS J. 2019;286(10):1894–907.
29. Hotra A, Ragunathan P, Ng PS, Seankongsuk P, Harikishore A, Sarathy JP, et al. Discovery of a novel mycobacterial F-ATP synthase inhibitor and its potency in combination with diarylquinolines. Angew Chem Int Ed Engl. 2020;59(32):13295–304.
30. Ragunathan P, Dick T, Grüber G. Anti-*mycobacterium abscessus* activity of tuberculosis F-ATP synthase inhibitor GaMF1. Antimicrob Agents Chemother. 2022;66(5):e0001822.
31. Gajadeera CS, Weber J. *Escherichia coli* F1Fo-ATP synthase with a b/δ fusion protein allows analysis of the function of the individual b subunits. J Biol Chem. 2013;288(37):26441–7.
32. FDA. SIRTURO™ (bedaquiline). 2012.
33. Koul A, Vranckx L, Dhar N, Gohlmann HW, Ozdemir E, Neefs JM, et al. Delayed bactericidal response of *Mycobacterium tuberculosis* to bedaquiline involves remodelling of bacterial metabolism. Nat Commun. 2014;5:3369.
34. Koul A, Vranckx L, Dendouga N, Balemans W, Van den Wyngaert I, Vergauwen K, et al. Diarylquinolines are bactericidal for dormant mycobacteria as a result of disturbed ATP homeostasis. J Biol Chem. 2008;283(37):25273–80.
35. Sarathy JP, Ragunathan P, Shin J, Cooper CB, Upton AM, Grüber G, et al. TBAJ-876 retains Bedaquiline's activity against subunits c and epsilon of *Mycobacterium tuberculosis* F-ATP synthase. Antimicrob Agents Chemother. 2019;63(10):e01191.
36. Luo M, Zhou W, Patel H, Srivastava AP, Symersky J, Bonar MM, et al. Bedaquiline inhibits the yeast and human mitochondrial ATP synthases. Commun Biol. 2020;3(1):452.
37. Veziris N, Bernard C, Guglielmetti L, Le Du D, Marigot-Outtandy D, Jaspard M, et al. Rapid emergence of *Mycobacterium tuberculosis* bedaquiline resistance: lessons to avoid repeating past errors. Eur Respir J. 2017;49(3):1601719.
38. Sutherland HS, Tong AST, Choi PJ, Conole D, Blaser A, Franzblau SG, et al. Structure-activity relationships for analogs of the tuberculosis drug bedaquiline with the naphthalene unit replaced by bicyclic heterocycles. Bioorg Med Chem. 2018;26(8):1797–809.
39. Sutherland HS, Tong AST, Choi PJ, Blaser A, Conole D, Franzblau SG, et al. 3,5-Dialkoxypyridine analogues of bedaquiline are potent antituberculosis agents with minimal inhibition of the hERG channel. Bioorg Med Chem. 2019;27(7):1292–307.
40. Krah A, Grüber G, Bond PJ. Binding properties of the anti-TB drugs bedaquiline and TBAJ-876 to a mycobacterial F-ATP synthase. Curr Res Struct Biol. 2022;4:278–84.
41. Huang Z, Luo W, Xu D, Guo F, Yang M, Zhu Y, et al. Discovery and preclinical profile of sudapyridine (WX-081), a novel anti-tuberculosis agent. Bioorg Med Chem Lett. 2022;71:128824.
42. Sarathy JP, Ganapathy US, Zimmerman MD, Dartois V, Gengenbacher M, Dick T. TBAJ-876, a 3,5-dialkoxypyridine analogue of bedaquiline, is active against *Mycobacterium abscessus*. Antimicrob Agents Chemother. 2020;64(4):e02404–19.
43. Philley JV, Wallace RJ Jr, Benwill JL, Taskar V, Brown-Elliott BA, Thakkar F, et al. Preliminary results of bedaquiline as salvage therapy for patients with nontuberculous mycobacterial lung disease. Chest. 2015;148(2):499–506.
44. Kumar S, Mehra R, Sharma S, Bokolia NP, Raina D, Nargotra A, et al. Screening of antitubercular compound library identifies novel ATP synthase inhibitors of *Mycobacterium tuberculosis*. Tuberculosis. 2018;108:56–63.
45. Tantry SJ, Markad SD, Shinde V, Bhat J, Balakrishnan G, Gupta AK, et al. Discovery of imidazo[1,2-a]pyridine ethers and squaramides as selective and potent inhibitors of Mycobacterial adenosine triphosphate (ATP) synthesis. J Med Chem. 2017;60(4):1379–99.

6 Unravelling the Microbiome of Diverse Industrial Effluents Through NGS Platforms: An Overview

Renuga Devi Navaneethan, Suganya Thangaiyan, Subasri Balaraman, and Arul Ananth Devanesan

6.1 Introduction

The primary cause of water pollution, which also affects and modifies the microbial environment, is industrial effluents. A group of microbial community that metabolise organic and inorganic compounds to produce energy and cellular components as well as to adapt with peripheral osmotic pressure of industrial wastewater environments [1, 2].

Microbes are the most dominant and diverse group of life on earth and have a vital role in biogeochemical cycling of compounds which is important to the function of ecosystem [3]. Moreover, this microbiome has the capacity to be exploited as a resource for the generation of new biotransformations, bioremediation processes, and bioenergy production [4]. Cultivating these untapped microbes in formulated laboratory atmosphere needs the information about their optimum growth condition. Actually, this has been influencing the development of several approaches to study the microbial resource [5, 6]. Out of the procedures to assess both culturable and unculturable bacteria majorly based on marker genes, like 16S rRNA or recA genes [7]. The quantity of 16S rRNA gene fragments from a sample gives an idea of species richness, and relative abundance (structure or evenness) reflects relative pressures that shape variety within biological groups [8].

Next-generation sequencing (NGS) may determine the DNA sequence of a whole bacterial genome in a single sequence run (Fig. 6.1). This information can be used to target research by allowing for the determination of resistance and virulence features as well as knowledge of grouping [9]. Bacteria, in particular, serve as bioindicators of highly polluted effluents [10]; this prompted researchers to examine the native bacterial population in the effluent and exploit it for biodegradation.

The massive amounts of data generated by NGS have increased our understanding of structural and functional genomics and given us new insight into the mechanisms and significance of genetic diversity and conservation in living things. These concepts of "omics" range from basic genomics to integrated systeomics. NGS investigates how many animals use genetic information and molecular biology to live and reproduce both with and without disease, variability within their population networks, and in response

R. D. Navaneethan (✉) · S. Balaraman
Department of Zoology, G.T.N. Arts College, Dindigul, Tamil Nadu, India

S. Thangaiyan
Department of Medical Biotechnology and Integrative Physiology, Saveetha School of Engineering, Chennai, Tamil Nadu, India

A. A. Devanesan
Department of Biotechnology, The American College, Satellite Campus, Madurai, Tamil Nadu, India
e-mail: arulananth@americancollege.edu.in

K. Parthasarathy, R. Manikkam (eds.), *Translational Research in Biomedical Sciences: Recent Progress and Future Prospects*, https://doi.org/10.1007/978-981-97-1777-4_6

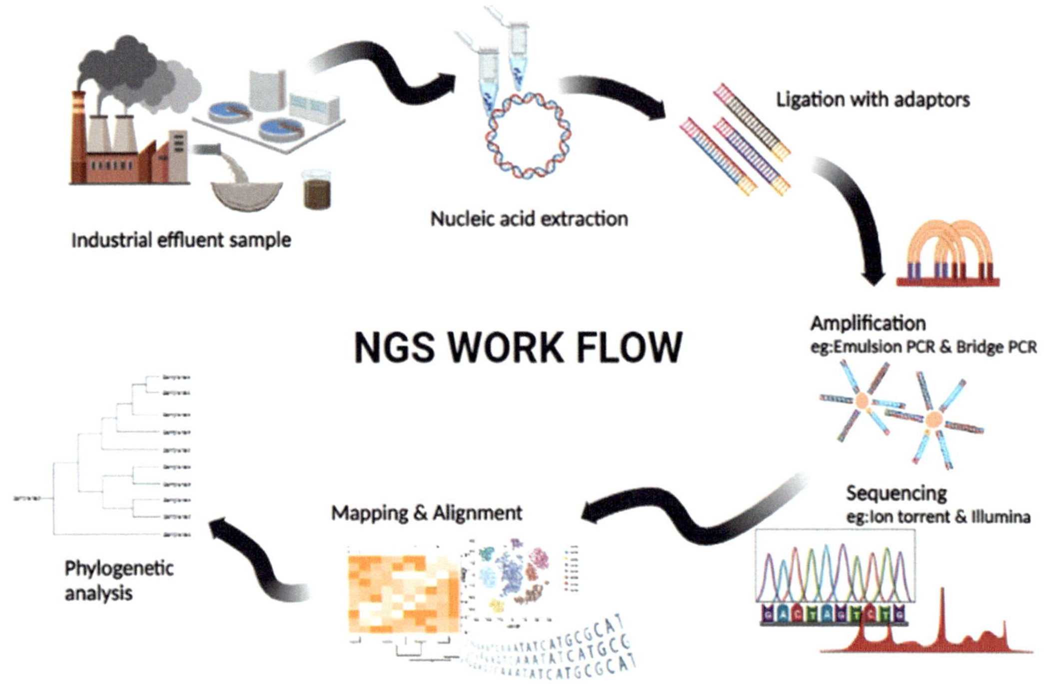

Fig. 6.1 Workflow of NGS from sample extraction of polluted sample to sequencing

to changing environmental conditions more than ever [11]. This chapter will change the way we think about how bacterial assemblages are distributed differently in various industrial effluents. It will also provide more information about how resilient these bacterial communities are to pollution.

6.2 Resistance of Bacterial Species Against Pollutants

One of the main reasons for declining water quality is chemical pollution [12]. Toxic chemicals can be removed or trapped by stimulation of the local microbial community for bioremediation [13]. According to Tan et al. [14], the occurrence of pollutants creates selected pressures which favour microbial communities to get adapt with the stresses they cause or it can use contaminants as a source of carbon, nutrients, or an electron acceptor for the purpose of respiration. Likewise, microbial communities and gene expression profiles in polluted waterways reveal pathways for contaminant transformation which acting as a marker for in situ biodegradation and exhibiting metabolic pathways to accelerate pollutant degradation [15–18].

Chief microbial mechanisms involved in contamination tolerance and transformation have been identified by analysis of microbial populations and genes enriched in polluted locations using "-omics" enabled techniques. For example, metagenomics assessment of a severely contaminated underground water system with heavy metals, nitric acid, and organic solvents showed a limited diversity of Beta- and Gammaproteobacteria with efficient metabolic competences, as well as the capacity to exploit heavy metal ions for lithotrophy process [19].

In bioreactors major roles of several members of an intricate microbial community have been studied through comparative metagenomics and genomecentric metagenomics [20, 21]. For microbially mediated processes, like the dechlorination of chlorinated compounds, to play supporting roles, like the production of essential nutrients, such as H_2, corrinoid, and methionine, which are needed by primary degraders, like *Dehalococcoides*, in substrate mineralisation, it is frequently necessary for a mixed community to exist. Hug et al.'s [22] analysis of the metagenomes of three enrichment cultures used to produce chlorinated ethene led to the discovery of genes required for the production of nutrients essential to *Dehalococcoides* during dechlorination. Using a homology-approach to assign these genes to taxa revealed a mutualistic interaction between a variety of microbes, which is difficult to detect using traditional microbiology techniques that involve separation. The roles of major players involved in the degradation of pollutants can be inferred using targeted genome enrichment techniques like stable-isotope probing (SIP), which use tagged recalcitrant chemicals to enrich essential degraders. The analysis followed by sequencing of the (meta)genome, allowing research into the genetic potential or metabolic modelling of uncultivated pollution degraders [23].

The Czc efflux system of bacteria has the ability to remove Cd (II), Zn (II), and Co (II) from cells, is due to well-studied the genetic mechanism of its metal resistance [24]. Widespread host genera for CzcA in activated sludge included *Herminiimonas arsenicoxydans*, *Oxalobacteraceae* sp., *Azoarcus* sp., and *Zobellia galactanivorans* [25]. The microbial conversion of organic and inorganic pollutants to meet nutritional needs causes the reduction in BOD and COD [26]. The changes in the makeup of the microbial community were more significantly correlated with variations in environmental restrictions than with changes in geographical proximity [27]. For evaluating the community structure in wastewater treatment, CFU is an essential qualitative data point [28].

6.3 Tannery Effluent

Among all, tanneries are chiefly known as the highwater consumption industry with hefty effluent discharge. Nearly 20% of the chemicals used up are exploited in the tanning method; rest 80% remnants pollute the environment. The physico-chemical findings showed that the level of contaminants decreased at each stage of CETP. It was proposed that the bacterial community, apart from chemical treatment, is crucial in the decrease of chemical load and heavy metals. In order to investigate the unculturable bacterial community, which is accountable for pollution reduction, the V6 hyper-variable segment of the 16S rRNA gene was produced and sequenced through ion torrent PGM platform. The MG-RAST server was used to analyse the sequence data, and the results showed that proteobacteria (4.3–34.6%) predominated in all CETP phases (Fig. 6.2). *Actinobacteria* was dominantly exist in secondary treated (10.6%) and tertiary treated (5.1%) effluent, while bacteroidetes abundant in primary treated (36.7%) and raw effluent (51.9%). The findings amply demonstrated the taxonomic changes that occurred during each CETP stage and were in line with physico-chemical alterations. Results confirm that the bacterial thriving and species richness in all CETP stage could be act as marker to find the pollution concentration and suitable functioning of treatment plant [29].

A fizzy microbial consortium known as CETP is home to diverse bacteria, fungi, archaea, algae, protozoa, and viruses. The predominant phylum in aeration systems that are in charge of digesting and removing contaminants during treatment are bacteria [30]. The small subunit ribosomal RNA molecule is encoded by the 16S rRNA gene, found to be the most versatile and reliable marker gene for the evaluation of bacterial populations. It is made up of nine highly variable sections (C1–C9) flanked by nine hypervariable regions (V1–V9) [Baker]. By measuring the V6 hypervariable region, which corresponds to 100 bp, the bacterial community was evaluated. Even though it is a smaller region, the phylogeny was clearly explained [31].

Phylum level relative richness varies dramatically between different samples. The examination of these sequence data revealed that Actinobacteria, Bacteroidetes, Firmicutes, Proteobacteria, and unclassified bacteria were the most prevalent bacterial taxa in these CETP treatment systems. In contrast to Actinobacteria and Bacteroidetes, which were abundant in all stages of therapy

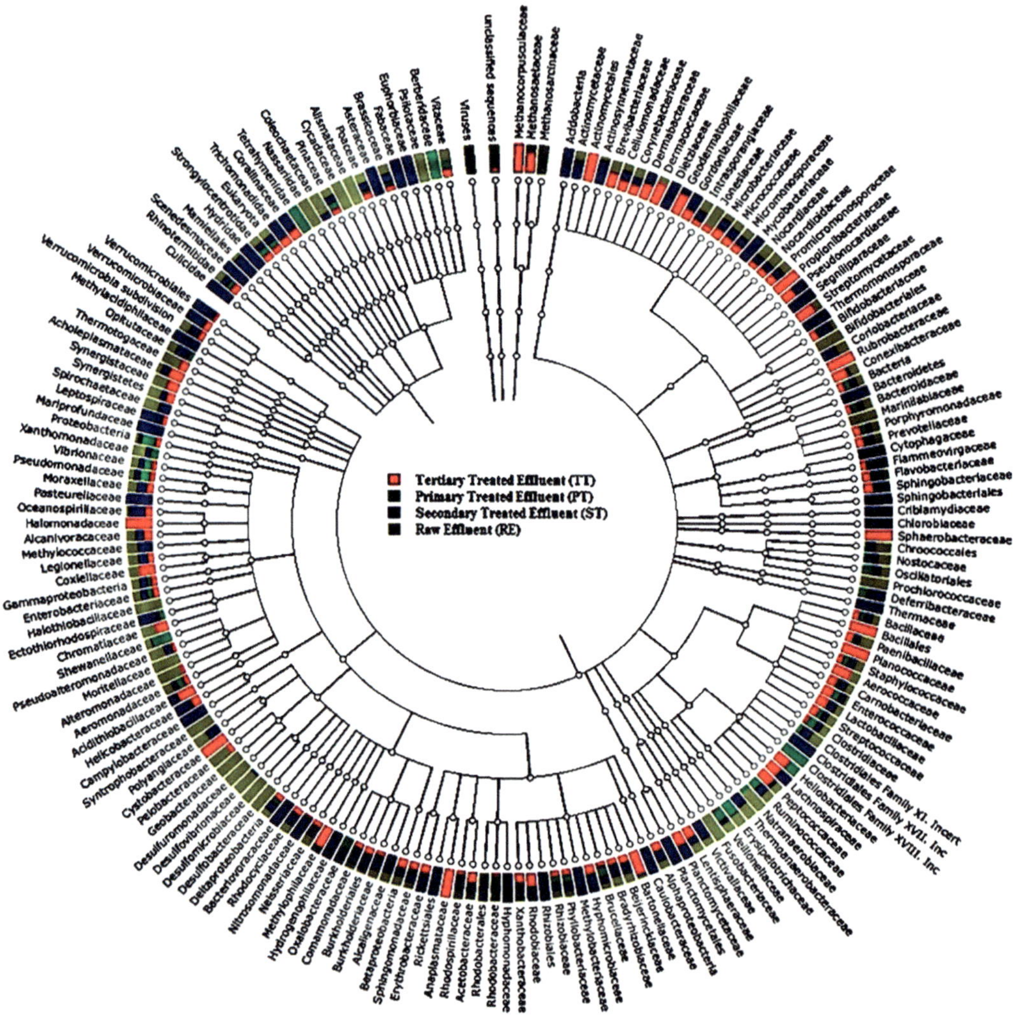

Fig. 6.2 Phylogenetic tree showing the abundance of Proteobacteria in the all the four stages of tannery effluent treatment plant (Courtesy: Krishnan et al., Expert Opin Environ Biol. 2016; 5: 3. https://doi.org/10.4172/2325-9655.1000136)

except the primary treatment stage, proteobacteria, firmicutes, and unclassified bacteria were clustered with a high abundance in all four stages of treatment. At the raw effluent stage, cyanobacteria and spirochaetes were moderately abundant, declining in the subsequent phases [29].

Chemoautotrophic microorganisms utilise the organic sulphates in the sludge as a source of energy [32]. A notable decrease in indices like TSS (more than 95%), TS (more than 10%), and TDS (more than 1%) was observed over the subsequent treatments. The successful breakdown of complex organic and inorganic contaminants by the bacterial community was demonstrated by the steady lowering of all physico-chemical parameters [33]. Additionally, microbial detoxification of industrial wastewater is economical, secure, and long-lasting. In tanneries, raw skins are processed using over 40 acids and heavy metals [34]. Metal bioaccumulation within bacterial cells or interaction with lipopolysaccharides of the extracellular membrane may be to blame for the decrease in metal concentration [26]. Prokaryotes are superior to eukaryotes in terms of resistance against Cr, few gram +ve bacteria have the capacity to detoxify Chromium (VI); by reducing it to less lethal Chromium (III) [35, 36].

By using Illumina HiSeq to analyse the microbial diversity in tannery effluent, it was discovered that *Proteobacteria, Firmicutes, Bacteroidetes, Actinobacteria,* and *Planctomycetes* predominated. The key functional categories that KEGG and SEED annotated included protein, amino acid, and carbohydrate metabolism. These metagenomes demonstrated the ability to degrade proteinaceous waste due to the presence of diverse serine- and metallo-proteases enzymes present in bacterial families such as *Bacillaceae, Clostridiaceae, Xanthomonadaceae, Flavobacteraceae*, and *Chitinophagaceae* [37].

6.4 Heavy Metal Outlet

Heavy metals have recently been released into the environment in substantial levels due to overused manufacturing and urbanisation operations. In the electroplating manufacturing, metal ion contamination of water has been a significant issue, particularly when it comes to dangerous metals like nickel (II), which is widely used. Aguilar et al. reported extracting Ni(II) from actual industrial effluent using a bioreactor infected with a heterotrophic consortium as the bioadsorbent. Kosmotogae, Firmicutes Ruminococcus, and Clostridium predominated the bacterial genus, although high-throughput sequencing of 16S rRNA genes revealed significant changes in their bacterial diversity and structural composition throughout the bioreactor treatment area. The absence of Fervidobacterium and Geobacter species towards the end of the bioreactor treatment, however, suggests that they are essential at the start of the anaerobic treatment for Ni(II) removal [38].

In order to meet the throughput requirements of soil microbial ecology studies, 16S rRNA hypervariable gene stretch was used [39, 40]. Promisinly, Illumina sequencing generates millions of fractional 16S rRNA gene segment reads at a lower cost which allows researchers access to organisms with low relative abundances that cannot be evaluated by culture-dependent approaches or clone library building. The Cauvery River's concentration of uranium (U) and other heavy metals has recently dramatically grown as a result of recent continuous pesticide spraying to agricultural regions and accumulation of quartz that enters the river. The impact of uranium on the variety of bacteria in the Cauvery River was investigated using metagenomic analysis of the V3 region of the 16S rDNA by Illumina sequencing. Taxonomic analysis showed that bacteroidetes (27.7%) and firmicutes (25.9%) dominated the unpolluted sample, whereas proteobacteria (47.5%), bacteroidetes (22.4%), and firmicutes (14.6%), respectively, predominated in the sediment sample from the highly polluted site. Results of the study showed how uranium and metal accumulation affected bacterial populations, and they also supported the potential of some particular bacterial species to serve as bioindicators of contamination [29].

The effectiveness of remediation in bacteria is one of the obstacles preventing bioremediation from being used in the treatment of tanneries' waste, despite the fact that it has proven a promising strategy for treating potentially dangerous metals. Shotgun sequencing made it possible to identify the operational factors that affect the microbiome's composition and capacity to lower Chromium (Cr) levels. To investigate the taxonomic community structure, phylogenetic relationships, and functional profile, metagenomic deoxyribonucleic acid (DNA) was isolated. In the structural biodiversity, bacteria (83%) archaebacteria (14%), and viruses (3%) were found. Bacteria were grouped into phyla, with proteobacteria (52%) being the most prevalent group. The following groups were the most frequent: Bacteriodetes (15%), Chloroflexi (15%), Spirochaetes (7%), Thermotogae (5%), Actinobacteria (4%), and Firmicutes (1%), in that order. After being cloned, the OXR genes' capacity to reduce Cr concentration was evaluated. A decrease in Cr content from 700 ppm to 24 ppm in 72 h (96.51% reduction) was seen during in situ testing of the OXR8 gene. According to the findings, there are a vast number of unknown chromate reductase genes and microorganisms [41].

6.5 Dairy Effluents

The microbial population in dairy effluents was investigated using next-generation sequencing technologies. Heterotrophic nitrifiers were said to be responsible for nitrification. The primary possibilities for the nitrification process are bacteria from the genera *Niabella* and *Diaphorobacter* as well as the order *Planctomycetales*. The co-treatment of dairy and ammonium-rich wastewater is a potential technique for the biological treatment of dairy wastewaters [42].

6.6 Electronic Effluent

The microbial population dynamics of a full-scale activated sludge process that treated opto-electronic wastewater were assessed using NGS of 16 S rRNA amplicons and the Illumina HiSeq platform. Indicator taxa analysis revealed that bacterial genera that could degrade aromatic compounds, including Acinetobacter, as well as those that could withstand extremely high levels of ionising radiation, had much reduced diversity and abundance during the low-performance phase compared to the high-performance period. The low-performance group was also deficient in bacterial species like Nitrospira, which are crucial to the nitrification process. Additionally, co-occurrence network analysis showed that during the high-performance period, microbial taxa's average path length and network diameter were much lower, indicating effective information diffusion among taxa. Collectively, these discoveries might help with system design and/or optimisation improved performance in treating optoelectronic industrial wastewater [43].

6.7 Future Opportunities

Unexpectedly, during the 1990s, a wide range of applications of microscopic and molecular techniques have provided engineers with access to the "black box" of microbiology housed in artificial microbial communities employed in biotechnological processes, offering direction for process design and optimisation. The advent of next-generation sequencing (NGS) is changing how conventional methods of microbiology and ecological research are conducted, as well as how quickly costs are falling. The primary research costs are currently migrating away from dealing with the computationally expensive and bioinformatically demanding analysis of large and relevant NGS data and towards dealing with traditional labour-intensive laboratory experiments [44].

In comparison to Illumina and Roche 454, next-generation sequencing technologies for single molecule real-time sequencing technology (SMRT; for instance, Pacific Biosciences and Oxford Nanopore Technologies) can produce sequences with read lengths larger than 1000 bp. These technologies are also desirable integration targets for sensors that monitor environmental sequence data due to real-time data gathering. These techniques have not yet been regularly utilised for surveys of extremely diverse bacterial communities due to large percentages of randomly distributed sequencing mistakes, which would unnaturally increase community diversity [45].

Genome sequencing has largely relied on Pacific Bioscience (PacBio) sequencing up until this point. Microbial genomes can commonly be closed in a single run due to the high coverage and lengthy sequence read length that enable production of highly contiguous consensus sequences with low error rates [46]. Due of its affordability and portability in a pocket, MinION, a more recent SMRT built on Nanopore technology [47]. In order to evaluate the device in a variety of sequencing applications, hundreds of units were sent to participants in the MinION Access Programme. The sequencing results from some of the labs showed that MinION could produce single read lengths of up to 5500 bp in a single run despite having many faults while having a high sequence error rate [48, 49]. Nanopore sequencing holds particular promise for the real-time identification of aquatic nucleic acids because of its high potential mobility and real-time data output. This will make it possible to build real-time sensors for monitoring water quality in the future.

6.8 Conclusion

The distribution and diversity of site-specific bacterial consortia are strongly influenced by the type of pollutant. Environmental contaminants may modify physico-chemical characteristics, which may influence the diversity and function of the microbial community [50]. The number of competitors changes over time as a result of differences in the battling potential across species, with the better contending species becoming more prevalent [51]. NGS, however, gives information about how the bacterial community of a contaminated sample is changing. Therefore, understanding the geomicrobiology of contaminated areas by researching the local microbial populations is crucial for developing effective bioremediation strategies as well as monitoring the influence of contamination on microbial indicators [52, 53]. Due to the emergence of various NGS platforms there is a massive development in the assessment of microbial community from any tough environment sample. Obviously, researchers can narrow down downstream studies rapidly in cost effective way.

References

1. Bramucci M, Kane H, Chen M, Nagarajan V. Bacterial diversity in an industrial wastewater bioreactor. Appl Microbiol Biotechnol. 2003;62:594–600.
2. Roberts MF. Organic compatible solutes of halotolerant and halophilic microorganisms. Saline Syst. 2005;1:5.
3. Whitman WB, Coleman DC, Wiebe WJ. Prokaryotes: the unseen majority. PNAS. 1998;95:6578–83.
4. Lee M, Kim MK, Singleton I, Goodfellow M, Lee ST. Enhanced biodegradation of diesel oil by a newly identified Rhodococcus baikonurensis EN3 in the presence of mycolic acid. J Appl Microbiol. 2006;100:325–33.
5. Handelsman J. Metagenomics: application of genomics to uncultured microorganisms. Microbiol Mol Biol Rev. 2004;68:669–85.
6. Green D, Keller M. Capturing the uncultivated majority. Curr Opin Biotechnol. 2006;17:236–40.
7. Weisburg WG, Barns SM, Pelletier DA, Lane DJ. 16S ribosomal DNA amplification for phylogenetic study. J Bacteriol. 1991;2:697–703.
8. Paul D, Pandey G, Meier C, Van der Meer JR, Jain RK. Bacterial community structure of a pesticide-contaminated site and assessment of changes induced in community structure during bioremediation. FEMS Microbiol Ecol. 2006;57:116–27.
9. Deurenberg RH, Bathoorn E, Chlebowicz MA, Couto N, Ferdous M, García-Cobos S, Kooistra-Smid AMD, Raangs EC, Rosema S, Veloo ACM, Zhou K, Friedrich AW, Rossen JWA. Application of next generation sequencing in clinical microbiology and infection prevention. J Biotechnol. 2017;243:16–24. https://doi.org/10.1016/j.jbiotec.2016.12.022.
10. Farag S, Zaki S. Identification of bacterial strains from tannery effluent and reduction of hexavalent chromium. J Environ Biol. 2010;3(5):867–72.
11. Kulski JK. Next-generation sequencing—an overview of the history, tools, and "omic" applications. In: Next-generation sequencing. London: IntechOpen; 2016. https://doi.org/10.5772/61964.
12. Schwarzenbach RP, Egli T, Hofstetter TB, von Gunten U, Wehrli B. Global water pollution and human health. Annu Rev Environ Resour. 2010;35:109–36. https://doi.org/10.1146/annurev-environ-100809-125342.
13. Koenig J, Lee M, Manefield M. Aliphatic organochlorine degradation in subsurface environments. Rev Environ Sci Biotechnol. 2014;14:49–71. https://doi.org/10.1007/s11157-014-9345-3.
14. Tan B, Jane Fowler S, Laban NA, Dong X, Sensen CW, Foght J, et al. Comparative analysis of metagenomes from three methanogenic hydrocarbon degrading enrichment cultures with 41 environmental samples. ISME J. 2015;9:2028–45. https://doi.org/10.1038/ismej.2015.22.
15. Kimes NE, Callaghan AV, Aktas DF, Smith WL, Sunner J, Golding B, et al. Metagenomic analysis and metabolite profiling of deep–sea sediments from the Gulf of Mexico following the Deepwater Horizon oil spill. Front Microbiol. 2013;4:50. https://doi.org/10.3389/fmicb.2013.00050.
16. Engel AS, Gupta AA. Regime shift in sandy beach microbial communities following deepwater horizon oil spill remediation efforts. PLoS ONE. 2014;9:e102934. https://doi.org/10.1371/journal.pone.0102934.
17. Lamendella R, Strutt S, Borglin S, Chakraborty R, Tas N, Mason OU, et al. Assessment of the deepwater horizon oil spill impact on gulf coast microbial communities. Front Microbiol. 2014;5:130. https://doi.org/10.3389/fmicb.2014.00130.
18. Mason OU, Scott NM, Gonzalez A, Robbins-Pianka A, Bælum J, Kimbrel J, et al. Metagenomics reveals sediment microbial community response to deepwater horizon oil spill. ISME J. 2014;8:1464–75. https://doi.org/10.1038/ismej.2013.254.
19. Hemme CL, Deng Y, Gentry TJ, Fields MW, Wu L, Barua S, et al. Metagenomic insights into evolution of a heavy metal contaminated groundwater microbial community. ISME J. 2010;4:660–72. https://doi.org/10.1038/ismej.2009.154.
20. Albertsen M, Hugenholtz P, Skarshewski A, Nielsen KL, Tyson GW, Nielsen PH. Genome sequences of rare, uncultured bacteria obtained by differential

coverage binning of multiple metagenomes. Nat Biotechnol. 2013;31:533–8. https://doi.org/10.1038/nbt.2579.
21. Haroon MF, Hu S, Shi Y, Imelfort M, Keller J, Hugenholtz P, et al. Anaerobic oxidation of methane coupled to nitrate reduction in a novel archaeal lineage. Nature. 2013;500:567–70. https://doi.org/10.1038/nature12375.
22. Hug LA, Beiko RG, Rowe AR, Richardson RE, Edwards EA. Comparative metagenomics of three dehalococcoides-containing enrichment cultures: the role of the non-dechlorinating community. BMC Genomics. 2012;13:327. https://doi.org/10.1186/1471-2164-13-327.
23. Saidi-Mehrabad A, He Z, Tamas I, Sharp CE, Brady AL, Rochman FF, et al. Methanotrophic bacteria in oilsands tailings ponds of northern Alberta. ISME J. 2013;7:908–21. https://doi.org/10.1038/ismej.2012.163.
24. Martínez-Huitle CA, Ferro S. Electrochemical oxidation of organic pollutants for the wastewater treatment: direct and indirect processes. Chem Soc Rev. 2006;35:1324–40.
25. Chandra R, Bharagava RN, Kapley A, Purohit HJ. Bacterial diversity, organic pollutants and their metabolites in two aeration lagoons of common effluent treatment plant (CETP) during the degradation and detoxification of tannery wastewater. Bioresour Technol. 2010;102:2333–41.
26. Srinath T, Verma T, Ramteke PW, Garg SK. Chromium (VI) biosorption and bioaccumulation by chromate resistant bacteria. Chemosphere. 2002;48:427–35.
27. Intorne AC, de Oliveira MV, de Pereira ML, de Souza Filho GA. Essential role of the CZC determinant for cadmium, cobalt and zinc resistance in Gluconacetobacter diazotrophicus PAl 5. Int Microbiol. 2012;15:69–78.
28. Jia S, Wang Z, Zhang XX, Liu B, Li W, et al. Metagenomic analysis of cadmium and copper resistance genes in activated sludge of a tannery wastewater treatment plant. J Environ Biol. 2013;34:375–80.
29. Suriya J, Shekar MC, Nathani NM, Suganya T, Bharathiraja S, Krishnan M. Assessment of bacterial community composition in response to uranium levels in sediment samples of sacred Cauvery River. Appl Microbiol Biotechnol. 2017;101:831–41. https://doi.org/10.1007/s00253-016-7945-2.
30. Sanapareddy N, Hamp TJ, Gonzalez LC, Hilger HA, Fodor AA, Clinton SM. Molecular diversity of a North Carolina wastewater treatment plant as revealed by pyrosequencing. Appl Environ Microbiol. 2009;75:1688–96.
31. Liu Z, Lozupone C, Hamady M, Bushman FD, Knight R. Short pyrosequencing reads suffice for accurate microbial community analysis. Nucleic Acids Res. 2007;35:e120.
32. Calheiros CS, Rangel AO, Castro PM. Evaluation of different substrates to support the growth of Typha latifolia in constructed wetlands treating tannery wastewater over long-term operation. Bioresour Technol. 2008;99:6866–77.
33. Gupta K. Modulation of antioxidant defence system for detoxification of oxidative stress caused by tannery effluent in Eichhornia crassipes. Int J Environ. 2014;3:101–10.
34. Eccles H. Removal of heavy metals from effluent streams. Why select a biological process? Int Biodeterior Biodegrad. 1995;35:5–16.
35. Fujii E, Toda K, Ohtake H. Bacterial reduction of toxic hexavalent chromium using a fed-batch culture of Enterobacter cloacae strain HO1. J Ferment Bioeng. 1990;69:365–7.
36. Basu M, Bhattacharya S, Paul AK. Isolation and characterization of chromium-resistant bacteria from tannery effluents. Bull Environ Contam Toxicol. 1997;58:535–42.
37. Verma SK, Sharma PC. NGS-based characterization of microbial diversity and functional profiling of solid tannery waste metagenomes. Genomics. 2020;112(4):2903–13.
38. Parades-Aguilar J, Reyes-Martínez V, Bustamante G, Almendáriz-Tapia FJ, Martínez-Meza G, Vílchez-Vargas R, Link A, Certucha-Barragán MT, Calderón K. Removal of nickel(II) from wastewater using a zeolite-packed anaerobic bioreactor: bacterial diversity and community structure shifts. J Environ Manag. 2021;279:111558.
39. Bartram AK, Lynch MD, Stearns JC, Moreno-Hagelsieb G, Neufeld JD. Generation of multimillion-sequence 16S rRNA gene libraries from complex microbial communities by assembling paired-end Illumina reads. Appl Environ Microbiol. 2011;77:3846–52. https://doi.org/10.1128/AEM.02772-10.
40. Wu JY, Jiang XT, Jiang YX, Lu SY, Zou F, Zhou HW. Effects of polymerase, template dilution and cycle number on PCR based 16 S rRNA diversity analysis using the deep sequencing method. BMC Microbiol. 2010;10:255. https://doi.org/10.1186/1471-2180-10-255.
41. Singh A, Varma A, Prasad R, Porwal S. Bioprospecting uncultivable microbial diversity in tannery effluent contaminated soil using shotgun sequencing and bio-reduction of chromium by indigenous chromate reductase genes. Environ Res. 2022;215(2):114338. https://doi.org/10.1016/j.envres.2022.114338.
42. Bucci P, Coppotelli B, Morelli I, Zaritzky N, Caravelli A. Simultaneous heterotrophic nitrification and aerobic denitrification of wastewater in granular reactor: microbial composition by next generation sequencing analysis. J Water Process Eng. 2020;36:101254. https://doi.org/10.1016/j.jwpe.2020.101254.
43. Gao J, Yang N, Liao H, Yuan H, Zhu J. Activated sludge microbial communities influencing the performance of a full-scale wastewater treatment plant treating optoelectronic wastewater. J Environ Chem Eng. 2022;10(1):106833. https://doi.org/10.1016/j.jece.2021.106833.

44. Ju F, Zhang T. 16S rRNA gene high-throughput sequencing data mining of microbial diversity and interactions. Appl Microbiol Biotechnol. 2015;99:4119–29. https://doi.org/10.1007/s00253-015-6536-y.
45. Schloss PD, Westcott SL, Jenior ML, Highlander SK. Sequencing 16S rRNA gene fragments using the PacBio SMRT DNA sequencing system. PeerJ. 2015;3:e778. https://doi.org/10.7287/peerj.preprints.778v1.
46. Koren S, Harhay GP, Smith TPL, Bono JL, Harhay DM, McVey SD, et al. Reducing assembly complexity of microbial genomes with single molecule sequencing. Genome Biol. 2013;14:R101. https://doi.org/10.1186/gb-2.
47. Venkatesan BM, Bashir R. Nanopore sensors for nucleic acid analysis. Nat Nanotechnol. 2011;6:615–24. https://doi.org/10.1038/nnano.2011.129.
48. Ashton PM, Nair S, Dallman T, Rubino S, Rabsch W, Mwaigwisya S, et al. MinION nanopore sequencing identifies the position and structure of a bacterial antibiotic resistance island. Nat Biotechnol. 2014;33:296–300. https://doi.org/10.1038/nbt.3103.
49. Madoui M-A, Engelen S, Cruaud C, Belser C, Bertrand L, Alberti A, et al. Genome assembly using nanopore-guided long and error-free DNA reads. BMC Genomics. 2015;16:327. https://doi.org/10.1186/s12864-015-1519-z.
50. Zeglin LH. Stream microbial diversity in response to environmental changes: review and synthesis of existing research. Front Microbiol. 2015;6:454. https://doi.org/10.3389/fmicb.2015.00454.
51. Pfennig DW, Pfennig KS. Character displacement and the origins of diversity. Am Nat. 2010;176(1):26–44. https://doi.org/10.1086/657056.
52. Mondani L, Benzerara K, Carrière M, Christen R, Mamindy-Pajany Y, Février L, Marmier N, Achouak W, Nardoux P, Berthomieu C, Chapon V. Influence of uranium on bacterial communities: a comparison of natural uranium-rich soils with controls. PLoS One. 2011;6:e25771. https://doi.org/10.1371/journal.pone.0025771.
53. Morcillo F, Gonzalez-Munoz MT, Reitz T, Romero-Gonzalez ME, Arias JM, Merroun ML. Biosorption and biomineralization of U(VI) by the marine bacterium Idiomarina loihiensis MAH1: effect of background electrolyte and pH. PLoS One. 2014;9:e91305. https://doi.org/10.1371/journal.pone.0091305.

Biofilm: A Bane to the Food Industry and Its Control Measures

7

Saranya Somasundaram, Vignesh Sounderrajan, and Rohini Tamilanban

7.1 Introduction

The biofilm is formed by a cluster of unicellular microorganism predominantly bacteria that exists in both living surface such as dental plaque, food products and in non-living exteriors such as food contact surface and medical devices, etc. [1]. The cluster of microorganism in the biofilm is encased by extracellular matrix which is composed mainly of protein content, the exogenous DNA, and polysaccharides, which can act as an obstacle during the antimicrobial treatment, and develop resistance against the most of the antibiotics currently available in the market. The biofilm acquire resistance mainly due to the inadequate penetration of antibiotics in to the glycocalyx matrix, a vital part of biofilm, then by interaction of antimicrobial drug with the biofilm matrix reduces the activity of the drug, enzymes-mediated resistance, amendment in metabolic activity of bacterial cells inside the biofilm, genetic alteration in the target sites of the bacteria present in the biofilm, nature of the outer membrane, and efflux pumps that extrudes antibiotic agents from the biofilm matrix [2]. Genetic diversification of the bacterial community in the biofilm matrix also leads to the development of resistance against the antibiotics because of the existence of different bacterial species in close proximity, so they can transfer their resistance genes more effectively and rapidly [3]. The development of resistance against the antibiotics in the biofilm matrix leads to several deleterious health defects worldwide.

At present, the outbreak of food borne pathogens leads to increase in morbidity and mortality rate all around the world [4]. The World Health Organization reported that disease caused due to food borne pathogens will be the major issues in both privileged and under privileged countries. The outbreak of the food borne pathogens is mainly due to the attachment of the microbes as biofilm matrix on the food contact surface or to the food products [5].

The aspiration for this chapter is to stipulate the knowledge on biofilm formation, resistant development, and the infections caused by the biofilm in the food industries and the control measures to overcome the cross contamination caused by the food borne pathogens present in the food contact surfaces, food handler or directly on the food substance. The food borne pathogens leads to the food poisoning and other illness such as vomiting and nausea.

S. Somasundaram (✉)
Department of Biotechnology, Dr. N.G.P. Arts and Science College, Coimbatore, India

V. Sounderrajan
Centre for Drug Discovery and Development, Sathyabama Institute of Science and Technology, Chennai, India
e-mail: vignesh.irc@sathyabama.ac.in

R. Tamilanban
Department of Microbiology, Mannar Thirumalai Naicker College, Madurai, India

K. Parthasarathy, R. Manikkam (eds.), *Translational Research in Biomedical Sciences: Recent Progress and Future Prospects*, https://doi.org/10.1007/978-981-97-1777-4_7

7.2 Biofilm Formation by Various Microbes in the Food Industry

7.2.1 *Bacillus* Species

Around the world, food borne illness related to *Bacillus* species was recorded as 1.4–12% [6]. Kwon et al. [7] study revealed that *Bacillus cereus* were able to form higher biofilm matrix in the presence of glucose as a carbon source along with NaCl at 30 °C in TSB broth. The growth of *Bacillus cereus* in glucose and NaCl specify that it can promote higher biofilm formation in the food contact surfaces such as stainless steel, glass, and plastic surfaces that lead to the contamination of food substance. The *Bacillus* species were able to produce biofilm matrix with distinct spatial arrangements in the inert surface of the synthetic equipment such as storage tanks, pipelines, and stainless steel vessels. The endospores of *Bacillus* species in the biofilm matrix of the equipment spoiled the quality of food products and promote food borne illness [8]. The food borne illness due to *Bacillus species* was predominantly due the release of toxins. The food substance such as soups, sauce, poultry meat, and vegetable when consumed with vegetative cells of *Bacillus* species make contact and effectively grow in the gut and release numerous toxic substance. For instance, the release of toxins, namely, hemolytic and non-hemolytic enterotoxins (NHE), cytotoxin K (CytK) leads to the diarrhea, abdominal pain, and nausea [9]. Another toxin, namely, cereulide, a cyclic peptide which is preformed in the food substance such as rice and dairy products produced by the *Bacillus* species causes emetic syndrome. The emetic syndrome results due to nerve stimulation of cereulide and leads to nausea and vomiting [10].

7.2.2 *Salmonella* Species

European Food Safety Authority reported that the main substrates for the growth of *Salmonella* are the meat and egg products from the poultry, fish, and Porcine. *Salmonella* species is one of the scrupulous microbes, accountable for most of the food borne disease worldwide. Most of the *Salmonella* species uses food residues as the substrate and develop the biofilm matrix that consists of polysaccharides [11]. The study by Paz-Mendez et al. [11] also stated that biofilm formation by *Salmonella* species depend up on the high temperature (22 °C) and flagella mediated motility. If the temperature lowers, the growth of *Salmonella* species was considered to be sluggish and as a result there was alteration in the metabolism followed by the inability of *Salmonella* species to produce biofilm matrix. The consequence of lower temperature leads to the decrease synthesis of flagella by *Salmonella* species, and as an outcome the motility and attachment of *Salmonella* species to the food contact surface is diminished. *Salmonella* species can contaminate the raw food substance as well as the processed food substance. The *Salmonella* species was considered to be resistance to most of the antibiotics and hence causes a serious deleterious effect when associated with biofilm matrix present in the biotic and abiotic equipment surfaces of the food industry [12]. *Salmonella* species in the biofilm matrix can manifest the infections such as gastroenteritis, septicemia, and typhoid fever [13]. The cell wall of *Salmonella* species endose lipopolysaccharide that function as virulence factor and responsible were inducing fever and altering the functions of lymphocyte. The prolonged infection of *Salmonella* species with the dissemination of endotoxin substance results in septic shock [14].

7.2.3 *Escherichia coli*

Carter et al. [15] reported that *E. coli* species can adhere to a diversified surfaces which includes food contact surfaces also. Biofilm formed by *E. coli* O157:H7 species on glass materials and stainless steel surface was strong compared to the formation on polypropylene because of the hydrophobic nature. The *E. coli* can form biofilm in both processing and production instruments and even lead to the destruction of equipment related to the food industry [16]. Taketo Kawarai et al.

[17] reported that adhesion of the *E. coli* K-12 was inhibited by the high osmolarity of NaCl but *E. coli* K-12 produces a higher biofilm matrix when cultured in 1M sucrose. The *E. coli* K-12 at the high osmolarity lack the FtsZ rings that is responsible for septum formation, which is mainly involved in formation of biofilm matrix. The *Escherichia coli* producing shiga-toxin (STEC) can form biofilm in the food processing environment such as milk storage tank, pipelines, and stainless steel vessels. The biofilm formation in the processing unit will become resistance to disinfectants and sanitizers that will question the food safety and quality. The infections manifested by Shiga toxin–producing *Escherichia coli* (STEC) were mainly human enteric infections that results in symptoms such as abdominal cramps, bloody diarrhea, and then diarrhea [18]. Ma et al. [19] reported that Shiga toxin-producing *Escherichia coli* (STEC) produces the biofilm at 22 °C at 24 h incubation and then oxygen is the main media for the formation of biofilm matrix. When the temperature decreased to 13 °C, there was diminished biofilm formation, but increases over time period. From this study it was stated that environmental conditions such as temperature, incubation time period, and oxygen play a significant role in biofilm formation in the processing and production units related to the food industry. Nesse et al. [20] reported the biofilm forming ability of three *E. coli* serotypes O26:H11, O103:H2, and O103:H25 at different temperature (12 °C, 20 °C, and 37 °C) and different surfaces such as stainless steel containers, glass materials, and polystyrene surface. The *E. coli* serotype O103:H2 exhibits higher biofilm forming capacity compared to two other serotypes. The report also stated that temperature plays a predominant role in the hydrobocity of the serotypes. The hydrophobicity helps in the attachment of the *E. coli* cells to the surface and after attachment to the surface it does not have ability to form biofilm. The *E. coli* with eae gene, which codes for intimin, a cell adhesion-mediating protein produced a reduced amount of biofilm compared to the isolates without eae gene. From the above study, it was clear that *E. coli* has the ability to form biofilm in various food contact surfaces.

7.2.4 *Listeria monocytogenes*

Among the other food borne pathogens, *Listeria monocytogenes* is accountable for about 1% of foodborne disease but the mortality rate due to *Listeria monocytogenes* is very high, compared to other food borne pathogens [21]. *Listeria monocytogenes* have the ability to attach on different surfaces and the attachment differs based on the materials used in food industry such as polystyrene used to construct drains, polytetrafluoroethylene material used in the conveyor belts, stainless steel containers, polyester, glass, and rubber [22]. The *Listeria monocytogenes* can grow or form biofilm in the food products such as processed food materials, milk and milk products, and finally in the marine food items. The *Listeria monocytogenes* can resist and survive in the environmental conditions such as low temperature, UV radiation, very low pH, and even at high osmolarity [23]. The growth of *Listeria monocytogenes* on those food materials attribute to the mild or severe gastroenteritis compared to other food borne pathogens [24]. Listeriosis is the ford borne disease manifested by with symptoms such as septicemia, meningitis, miscarriage that crucially affects the pregnant women, new born children's, the older age people and the individuals who are also immunocompromised [25]. The cross contamination and the ability to produce biofilm among the *Listeria monocytogenes* increases at low temperatures. The low temperature in food industry is mainly maintained during food processing and also during the storage of the food substance making the food safety a concern [26]. Gram et al. [27] reported that *Listeria monocytogenes* were not able to form the strong biofilm matrix with several layers, but slightly attached to the different food contact surfaces. The adherence of *Listeria monocytogenes* to the food contact surface is majorly owing to the existence of flagella, pilli, and the membrane proteins present in the cell [28]. The *Listeria monocytogenes* have the ability to adhere to different food contact surface with response to temperature, pH, nutrients, and the materials used in the surface. At 37 °C, the *Listeria monocytogenes* can form a high amount of biofilm in stainless steel container and glass compared to the polystyrene material.

7.2.5 *Staphylococcus* Species

Food poisoning in recent years is mainly due to the capability of *Staphylococcus aureus* to form biofilm matrix in food contact surfaces such as equipment, tanks, and pipelines. Improper sanitation of the equipment associated with food contact surface and the unhygienic practice followed by food handlers leads to the development of biofilm formation. The biofilm formed by *Staphylococcus* specie*s can* cause severe food borne illness. Giaouris et al. [29] reported that *Staphylococcus aureus* is a human opportunistic pathogen that lives in a human beings and synthesis a toxic substance known as enterotoxins. *Staphylococcus aureus* can proliferate in the skin and mucous membrane of the person who are in touch with food contact surfaces and those who handle food product. Oniciuc et al. [30] study revealed that *Staphylococcus aureus* produces profusion number of exopolysaccharides that leads to the formation of strong biofilm matrix in the food processing units. Lee [31] reported the development of resistance by *Staphylococcus* species against the β-lactam antibiotics such as penicillins, cephalosporins carbapenems, and monobactams possess a sky-scraping threat mostly in the food industry. Gutierrez et al. [32] reported the presence of *Staphylococcus aureus* in food products sites such as meat, dairy, and sea food sites. The study also revealed that *Staphylococcus* species harbor a numerous microbiota identified by PCR-DGGE fingerprinting techniques. The co-existing microbiota was *Leuconostoc citreum* that was present in all three meat, dairy, and seafood sector. The other microbiota which coexist with *Staphylococcus aureus* are *Enterococcus faecium*, *Pseudomonas* sp., *Acinetobacter*, *Lactobacillus plantarum,* and finally *Macrococcus caseolyticusi.* The co-existence of *Staphylococcus aureus* along with other bacterial species can form a strong biofilm matrix in the food industries, which will lead to the contamination and spoilage of the food products. The biofilm matrix formed by wild type *Staphylococcus aureus* varies in their constituents and diversification when exposed to variety of stress conditions. For example, protein substrate enhance the structure of biofilm formation in the food substance, sometimes carbon sources such as lactose, a simple carbohydrate can stimulate the synthesis of polysaccharide intercellular adhesins in the biofilm matrix [33]. The attachment of *Staphyloccus aureus* to the food contact surface or any other surface is possible only when the *Staphyloccus aureus* secrete fibronectin-binding proteins that are crucial for pathogenicity and also enhance the bacterial adhesion to any of the surfaces [34].

7.3 Biofilm Infections in Food Industry and Its Control Measures

The biofilm formed in the food industry is mainly associated with the pathogens that are harmful to the human beings. A total of 600 million people around the world were considered to suffer by the disease caused by food borne pathogens. The food borne pathogens possess stern challenge in a wide range of food industries, including meat processing, beverage industry, and dairy and poultry industries [35].

The impacts associated with biofilm formation in the food industry were mainly pathogenicity especially causing food poisoning. The main microorganism that causes pathogenicity are *Bacillus cereus and Staphylococcus aureus*, *E. coli,* and *Salmonella enterica.* The biofilm formed on the food contact surfaces such as stainless steel, pipeline, and chilling units causes metal corrosion and modifications in the organoleptic characteristic such as rancid and bitter taste. The changes in the organoleptic character are mainly due to the excretion of enzymes mainly proteases and Lipases by the *Bacillus* species and *Pseudomonas* species present in the biofilm matrix [36].

7.4 Ultrasonication Treatment

In the dairy industry, the biofilm growth was inhibited by the physical method, namely, ultrasonication. Ultrasonication is used when the food materials or food contact surface cannot undergo heat or stress conditions to eradicate the biofilm matrix. The biofilm dispersion by ultrasonication depends upon the types of frequency used (high or low frequency), incubation period, and intensity of the ultrasound used. The ultrasonication can absolutely eradicate the biofilm matrix formed on the surface using low-frequency ultrasound with 0.4 MHz for 5 min at 37 °C [37]. Ultrasonication can inhibit the growth of the microorganism in the biofilm matrix, in a safe and mild approach and then increase the shelf-life of the food substance.

7.5 Chemical Treatment

The physical treatment becomes sluggish, once the biofilm matrix reaches the maturation stage. A total of about 76% of biofilm matrix survive on the surface even after the physical treatment, so in order to eradicate the biofilm matrix, chemical agent or compounds should be included [38]. Chemical compounds such as ClO_2, sodium hypochlorite, quaternary ammonium salts, peracetic acid, and hydrogen peroxide were used to inhibit the biofilm growth. The strong growth of *Staphylococcus aureus* in the pipelines of the food industry can be eradicated by using strong alkaline acidic acids as cleaning agents. The ClO_2 was mainly used to inhibit the endospoes of *Bacillus* species in biofilm adhered to the steel surfaces of the food industry. Sodium hypochlorite can be used to eradicate the *Staphylococcus aureus* and *Salmonella enteric* bacterial species in the biofilm attached to the stainless steel surfaces. Hydrogen peroxide when used at 3% and 5% concentration can completely eradicate the biofilm formed by the *Staphylococcus* species at 5 min incubation time. Hydrogen peroxide are able to generate the free radicals that can neutralize or inhibit the growth of the *L. monocytogenes* and *Staphylococcus aureus* in the water pipelines [39]. The application 0.5 ppm concentration of ozone will inhibit the growth of microorganism such as *Pseudomonas fluorescens* and *Alcaligenes faecalis* on the milk contact surfaces and protect the quality of milk [40].

7.6 Biosurfactants

The biosurfactants, a natural bioactive compound with enhanced surface activity and amphipathicity, were secreted by the microbial sources during their metabolism. The biosurfactants because of their ability to decrease the interfacial tension are used to inhibit the biofilm matrix formed on the food contact surfaces. The biosurfactants of microbial origin have low toxicity and therefore there is increasing in need of biosurfactants [41]. The biosurfactants such as nonribosomal lipopeptide, lichenysin synthesized by the *Bacillus licheniform,* and lactic acid bacteria (LAB) derived glycolipid can be used as coatings in food contact surface that will inhibit the biofilm formation by altering the binding and adhesion properties of the bacterial cell in the biofilm matrix [42]. The biosurfactants posses' antimicrobial activity, which prevents the adherence of bacterial cells to the food contact surface and thereby preventing biofilm formation on their surface.

7.7 Bacteriophages

The biofilm formed in the food used industry can be controlled by the bacteriophages, which is considered as green biocontrol technology. It is a virus particle that can kill the bacterial cells in the biofilm matrix. The bacteriophages infect and eradicate the specific bacterial species, the bacteriophage after infection will replicate by its own and they are compatible with the living species without causing any damage to the environment or health, so its consider as a suitable candidate for eradication of biofilms [43]. The higher specificity of bacteriophages toward the single species or specific strain in the species, stipulate the bacteriophages as an effective control agent in the food industries. In the food industry, the bacteriophages have a significant role in eradicating the biofilm matrix at three stages, namely, primary production, biosanitization, and finally biopreservation. In the process of biosanitation, the phages secrete enzyme that will not allow the bacterial cells to adhere to the food contact surface. On the other hand, biopreservation is a process in which the shelf-life period of the food substance is increased [44]. The lytic proteins secreted by bacteriophage particle have the ability to remove biofilm formed on the food contact surface. For example, endolysin, endolysin SAL-2, and endolysin lysH5 produced by diversified bacteriophages have the ability to remove biofilm formed by *Staphylococcus aureus* on the surface [32].

7.8 Enzymatic Treatment

Enzymatic treatment is yet another milestone of green technology to remove the biofilm formed on the surfaces. The enzymatic treatment to eradicate biofilm has become a promising treatment in food industry mainly because of its biodegradability and low toxicity. Most of the enzymes are proteinaceous in nature and have the ability to remove the biofilm matrix. The enzymes were especially proteases, serine proteases, and proteinase K, etc. and glycosidases group enzyme molecules such as amylases, dextranase, and pectinase [45]. The biofilm formation in the meat industry is suppressed by the enzymatic treatment especially Papain enzyme. The papain enzyme destructs the structure of biofilm by disrupting the carbohydrate and protein molecules present in the matrix [46]. Enzymes were able to remove biofilm formed by *Pseudomaonas* species on the glass surfaces. Kuyukina et al. [47] reported that sophorolipids, an enzyme were able to remove the biofilm matrix of *Bacillus* species and *Staphylococcus* species. From this study, it was revealed that sophorolipids can be a promising candidate for anti-biofilm activity. The adhesion property of *Listeria monocytogenes* and *Pseudomonas fluorescens* bacterial cell on the polystyrene surface can be eradicated up to 79% and 54% by the rhamnolipids and surfactin enzymes, similarly the biofilm formation by *Listeria monocytogenes* decreases up to 83% and *Pseudomonas fluorescens* on stainless steel also decreases up to 73%, respectively, by rhamnolipids and surfactin enzymes [48].

7.9 Essential Oils

A plant derived compound, namely, essential oils is used in the clearance of the biofilm formed by diversified microbiota on different surfaces. It is considered to be the secondary metabolite synthesized by the plant cells and can act as a natural antimicrobial against the broad spectrum of bacterial species. Essential oils can prevent several food borne pathogens by inhibiting its metabolic activity [49]. Kalemba et al. 50 reported the ingredients such as terpenes, phenols, aldehydes, ketones, alcohols, ethers, hydrocarbons, and terpenoids present in the essential oils derived from plant secondary metabolites. Among these ingredients, phenol has the highest antimicrobial activity and can inhibit the biofilm formation. The single active ingredient of essential oil cannot clear the biofilm formed, so the combination of different ingredients of essential oils were used to eradicate the biofilm formation. The essential oil ingredients of *C. cyminum* and *A. sativum* can be combined and used as an effective tool against planktonic and biofilm *formed by Salmonella typhimurium* [51].

7.10 Nanoparticles as a Control Agent

Nanotechnology is used in the removal of biofilm formed in the stainless steel. The nanoparticle because of its large surface volume ratio can interact with the microbiota and results in the eradication of biofilms more easily. Nanowires made up of vanadium pentoxide is used to inhibit the biofilm formed by *Staphylococcus aureus* (reduction up to 96%) and in *E. coli* the reduction was up to 78%, respectively, without affecting any other marine microbiota [52]. Ghasemian et al. [53] reported that copper nanoparticle can clear the biofilm formation due to its antibacterial effects. The antimicrobial activity is mainly because of large surface area where copper–bacteria interaction can occur. Based on the surface area and interaction to the microbes tends to increase the cytotoxic activity of the bacterial cell. Hence nanoparticles can eradicate the biofilm formed on the surface in an effective manner.

7.11 Conclusion

Biofilm formation in the food industry leads to many food borne disease and also economic issues in both developed and under developed countries. The microbiota present in the biofilm matrix of the food industries are *Bacillus species*, *Staphylococcus aureus*, *Listeria* species, *E. coli* species, etc. The presence of the diversified microbiota in the biofilm matrix enhances the surveillance of the biofilm stronger on the food contact surfaces and as a result there is an outbreak of food associated illness. The adhesion of bacterial cells to the surface depends up on the types of materials used along with internal and external environmental factors such as temperature, pH, osmolarity, and oxygen. The adhesion of the bacterial cells to the food contact surface is also mediated by the adhesion proteins like intimin produced by the bacteria cells. Conventional methods to eradicate biofilm is considered to be time consuming and laborious. In order to overcome these drawbacks new effective methods should be implemented. New bioactive molecule targeting the genes that is responsible for the production of adhesion proteins should be identified. If the synthesis of adhesion protein is blocked, then there will be lower affinity of bacterial cells attaching to surface of the food contact surfaces. The food contact surfaces can be coated with nanoparticles that exhibits antimicrobial activity so that growth of microbes at the initial stage will be prevented. The inhibition of flagella, Pilli, and fimbriae of the bacterial cells also diminish the adherence of the bacterial cell to the food contact surface. The food contact surfaces must be coated with anti-adhesive substance enabling the non-adherence of bacterial cells to the surface can be achieved. Overall, the control measures are essential for the dispersion and eradication of the biofilm formed in the food contact surfaces. When effective control measures were followed, there is no question of cross contamination by the microbiota and the safety of the food standard was also assured. Economic issues and other health problems will also be reduced while using the contamination free equipment. Finally, the sustainable development of the food safety and food quality can be achieved by effective control measures that is eco-friendly, cost effective, and efficient working.

References

1. Donlan RM. Biofilms: microbial life on surfaces. Emerg Infect Dis. 2002;8(9):881–90. https://doi.org/10.3201/eid0809.020063.
2. Singh S, Singh SK, Chowdhury I, Singh R. Understanding the mechanism of bacterial biofilms resistance to antimicrobial agents. Open Microbiol J. 2017;28(11):53–62. https://doi.org/10.2174/1874285801711010053.
3. Balcazar JL, Subirats J, Borrego CM. The role of biofilms as environmental reservoirs of antibiotic resistance. Front Microbiol. 2015;6:1216.
4. Zhao X, Lin CW, Wang J, Oh DH. Advances in rapid detection methods for foodborne pathogens. J Microbiol Biotechnol. 2014;24(3):297–312. https://doi.org/10.4014/jmb.1310.10013.
5. Aarnisalo K, Lunden J, Korkeal H, Wirtanen G. Susceptibility of *Listeria monocytogenes* strains to disinfectants and chlorinated alkaline cleaners at cold temperatures. LWT Food Sci Technol. 2007;6:1041–8. https://doi.org/10.1016/j.lwt.2006.07.009.
6. Grutsch AA, Nimmer PS, Pittsley RH, Kornilow KG, McKillip JL. Molecular pathogenesis of *Bacillus* spp., with emphasis on the dairy industry. Fine Focus. 2018;4:203–22. https://doi.org/10.33043/FF.4.2.203-222.
7. Kwon M, Hussain MS, Oh DH. Biofilm formation of *Bacillus cereus* under food-processing-related conditions. Food Sci Biotechnol. 2017;26(4):1103–11. https://doi.org/10.1007/s10068-017-0129-8.
8. Lin Y, Briandet R, Kovacs AT. *Bacillus cereus sensu lato* biofilm formation and its ecological importance. Biofilms. 2022;4:100070. https://doi.org/10.1016/j.bioflm.2022.100070.
9. Jessberger N, Dietrich R, Granum PE, Martlbauer E. The *Bacillus cereus* food infection as multifactorial process. Toxins. 2020;12:701.
10. Tirloni E, Stella S, Celandroni F, Mazzantini D, Bernardi C, Ghelardi E. *Bacillus cereus* in dairy products and production plants. Foods. 2022;11:2572. https://doi.org/10.3390/foods11172572.
11. Paz-Mendez AM, Lamas A, Vázquez B, Miranda JM, Cepeda A, Franco CM. Effect of food residues in biofilm formation on stainless steel and polystyrene surfaces by Salmonella *enterica* strains isolated from poultry houses. Foods. 2017;6(12):106. https://doi.org/10.3390/foods6120106.
12. Harrell JE, Hahn MM, D'Souza SJ, Vasicek EM, Sandala JL, Gunn JS, McLachlan JB. *Salmonella* biofilm formation, chronic infection, and immunity within the intestine and hepatobiliary tract. Front

Cell Infect Microbiol. 2021;2(10):624622. https://doi.org/10.3389/fcimb.2020.624622.
13. Gamazo C, Solano C, Lasa I. Biofilm formation by *Salmonella* in food processing environments. In: Biofilms in the food and beverage industries. Sawston: Woodhead Publishing; 2009. p. 226–49.
14. Hagar JA, Powell DA, Aachoui Y, Ernst RK, Miao EA. Cytoplasmic LPS activates caspase-11: implications in TLR4-independent endotoxic shock. Science. 2013;341:1250–3. https://doi.org/10.1126/science.1240988.
15. Carter MQ, Louie JW, Feng D, Zhong W, Brandl MT. Curli fimbriae are conditionally required in *Escherichia coli* O157: H7 for initial attachment and biofilm formation. Food Microbiol. 2016;57:81–9. https://doi.org/10.1016/j.fm.2016.01.006.
16. Kang JW, Lee HY, Kang DH. Synergistic bactericidal effect of hot water with citric acid against *Escherichia coli O157:H7* biofilm formed on stainless steel. Food Microbiol. 2020;95:103676.
17. Kawarai T, Furukawa S, Narisawa N, Hagiwara C, Ogihara H, Yamasaki M. Biofilm formation by *Escherichia coli* in hypertonic sucrose media. J Biosci Bioeng. 2009;107(6):630–5. https://doi.org/10.1016/j.jbiosc.2009.01.018.
18. Fakhouri F, Zuber J, Fremeaux-Bacchi V, Loirat C. Haemolytic uraemic syndrome. Lancet. 2017;390:681–96.
19. Ma Z, Bumunang EW, Stanford K, Bie X, Niu YD, McAllister TA. Biofilm formation by Shiga toxin-producing *Escherichia coli* on stainless steel coupons as affected by temperature and incubation time. Microorganisms. 2019;7:95. https://doi.org/10.3390/microorganisms7040095.
20. Nesse LL, Sekse C, Berg K, Johannesen KC, Solheim H, Vestby LK, Urdahl AM. Potentially pathogenic *Escherichia coli* can form a biofilm under conditions relevant to the food production chain. Appl Environ Microbiol. 2013;80(7):2042–9. https://doi.org/10.1128/AEM.03331-13.
21. Gomez D, Azon E, Marco N, Carraminana JJ, Rota C, Arino A, Yanguela J. Antimicrobial resistance of *Listeria monocytogenes* and *Listeria innocua* from meat products and meat-processing environment. Food Microbiol. 2014;2:61–5. https://doi.org/10.1016/j.fm.2014.02.017.
22. Mazaheri T, Cervantes-Huaman BRH, Bermudez-Capdevila M, Ripolles-Avila C, Rodriguez-Jerez JJ. *Listeria monocytogenes* biofilms in the food industry: is the current hygiene program sufficient to combat the persistence of the pathogen? Microorganisms. 2021;9(1):181. https://doi.org/10.3390/microorganisms9010181.
23. Chaturongakul S, Raengpradub S, Wiedmann M, Boor KJ. Modulation of stress and virulence in *Listeria monocytogenes*. Trends Microbiol. 2008;16:388–96. https://doi.org/10.1016/j.tim.2008.05.006.
24. Radoshevich L, Cossart P. *Listeria monocytogenes*: towards a complete picture of its physiology and pathogenesis. Nat Rev Microbiol. 2018;16:32–46.
25. Carpentier B, Cerf O. Review—persistence of *Listeria monocytogenes* in food industry equipment and premises. Int J Food Microbiol. 2011;145:1–8. https://doi.org/10.1016/j.ijfoodmicro.2011.01.005.
26. Colagiorgi A, Bruini I, Di Ciccio PA, Zanardi E, Ghidini S, Ianieri A. *Listeria monocytogenes* biofilms in the wonderland of food industry. Pathogens. 2017;6(3):41. https://doi.org/10.3390/pathogens6030041.
27. Gram L, Bagge-Ravn D, Ng YY, Gymoese P, Vogel BF. Influence of food soiling matrix on cleaning and disinfection efficiency on surface attached *Listeria monocytogenes*. Food Control. 2007;18(10):1165–71.
28. Lemon KP, Higgins DE, Kolter R. Flagellar motility is critical for *Listeria monocytogenes* biofilm formation. J Bacteriol. 2007;189:4418–24. https://doi.org/10.1128/JB.01967-06.
29. Giaouris, Efstathios, et al. "Intra-and inter-species interactions within biofilms of important foodborne bacterial pathogens." Frontiers in microbiology 2015;6:144151.
30. Oniciuc EA, Cerca N, Nicolau AI. Compositional analysis of biofilms formed by *Staphylococcus aureus* isolated from food sources. Front Microbiol. 2016;30(7):390. https://doi.org/10.3389/fmicb.2016.00390.
31. Lee JH. Methicillin (oxacillin)-resistant *Staphylococcus aureus* strains isolated from major food animals and their potential transmission to humans. Appl Environ Microbiol. 2003;69:6489–94.
32. Gutierrez D, Delgado S, Vazquez-Sanchez D, Martinez B, Cabo ML, Rodriguez A, Herrera JJ, Garcia P. Incidence of *Staphylococcus aureus* and analysis of associated bacterial communities on food industry surfaces. Appl Environ Microbiol. 2012;78(24):8547–54. https://doi.org/10.1128/AEM.02045-12.
33. Xue T, Chen X, Shang F. Short communication: effects of lactose and milk on the expression of biofilm associated genes in *Staphylococcus aureus* strains isolated from a dairy cow with mastitis. J Dairy Sci. 2014;97(10):6129–34. https://doi.org/10.3168/jds.2014-8344.
34. Shanks RM, Meehl MA, Brothers KM, Martinez RM, Donegan NP, Graber ML, O'Toole GA. Genetic evidence for an alternative citrate-dependent biofilm formation pathway in *Staphylococcus aureus* that is dependent on fibronectin binding proteins and the GraRS two-component regulatory system. Infect Immun. 2008;76:2469–77.
35. Jung T, Jung Y, Ahn J, et al. Continuous, rapid concentration of foodborne bacteria (*Staphylococcus aureus, Salmonella typhimurium, and Listeria monocytogenes*) using magnetophoresis-based microfluidic device. Food Control. 2020;114:107229.
36. Mizan MF, Jahid IK, Ha S. Microbial biofilms in seafood: a food-hygiene challenge. Food Microbiol. 2015;49:41–55. https://doi.org/10.1016/j.fm.2015.01.009.

37. Karosi T, Sziklai I, Csomor P. Low-frequency ultrasound for biofilm disruption in chronic rhinosinusitis with nasal polyposis: in vitro pilot study. Laryngoscope. 2013;123:17–23.
38. Zhao X, Zhao F, Wang J, Zhong N. Biofilm formation and control strategies of food borne pathogens: food safety perspectives. RSC Adv. 2017;7:36670–83.
39. Galie S, Garcia-Gutierrez C, Miguelez EM, Villar CJ, Lombo F. Biofilms in the food industry: health aspects and control methods. Front Microbiol. 2018;9:898. https://doi.org/10.3389/fmicb.2018.00898.
40. Varga L, Szigeti J. Use of ozone in the dairy industry: a review. Int J Dairy Technol. 2016;69:157–68. https://doi.org/10.1111/1471-0307.12302.
41. Zhu T, Yang C, Bao X, Chen F, Guo X. Strategies for controlling biofilm formation in food industry. Grain Oil Sci Technol. 2022;5(4):79–186. https://doi.org/10.1016/j.gaost.2022.06.003.
42. Patel M, Siddiqui AJ, Hamadou WS, Surti M, Awadelkareem AM, Ashraf SA, Alreshidi M, Snoussi M, Rizvi SMD, Bardakci F, Jamal A, Sachidanandan M, Adnan M. Inhibition of bacterial adhesion and antibiofilm activities of a glycolipid biosurfactant from *Lactobacillus rhamnosus* with its physicochemical and functional properties. Antibiotics. 2021;10(12):1546. https://doi.org/10.3390/antibiotics10121546.
43. Garvey M. Bacteriophages and the one health approach to combat multidrug resistance: is this the way? Antibiotics. 2020;9:414. https://doi.org/10.3390/antibiotics9070414.
44. Polaska M, Sokolowska B. Bacteriophages-a new hope or a huge problem in the food industry. Microbiology. 2019;5(4):324–46. https://doi.org/10.3934/microbiol.2019.4.324.
45. Huang H, Ren H, Ding L, GengJ XK, Zhang Y. Aging biofilm from a full-scale moving bed biofilm reactor: characterization and enzymatic treatment study. Bioresour Technol. 2014;154:122–30. https://doi.org/10.1016/j.biortech.2013.12.031.
46. Manohar CM, Prabhawathi V, Sivakumar PM. Design of a papain immobilized antimicrobial food package with curcumin as a crosslinker. PLoS One. 2015;10:e0121665.
47. Kuyukina MS, Ivshina IB, Korshunova IO. Diverse effects of a biosurfactant from *Rhodococcus ruber* IEGM 231 on the adhesion of resting and growing bacteria to polystyrene. AMB Express. 2016;6:14.
48. de Araujo LV, Guimaraes CR, da Silva Marquita RL, et al. Rhamnolipid and surfactin: anti-adhesion/antibiofilm and antimicrobial effects. Food Control. 2016;63:171–8.
49. Burt SA. Essential oils: their antibacterial properties and potential applications in foods—a review. Int J Food Microbiol. 2004;94:223–53.
50. Kalemba DAAK, Kunicka A. "Antibacterial and antifungal properties of essential oils." Current medicinal chemistry 2003;10(10):813–29.
51. Alni RH, Ghorban K, Dadmanesh M. Combined effects of *Allium sativum* and *Cuminum cyminum* essential oils on planktonic and biofilm forms of *Salmonella typhimurium* isolates. Biotech. 2020;10:315.
52. Natalio F, Andre R, Hartog AF, Stoll B, Jochum KP, Wever R, Tremel W. Vanadium pentoxide nanoparticles mimic vanadium haloperoxidases and thwart biofilm formation. Nat Nanotechnol. 2012;7:530–5.
53. Ghasemian E, Naghoni A, Rahvar H, Kialha M, Tabaraie B. Evaluating the effect of copper nanoparticles in inhibiting *Pseudomonas aeruginosa* and *Listeria monocytogenes* biofilm formation. Jundishapur J Microbiol. 2015;8:e17430.

An Emerging Artificial Intelligence Tool for the Advancement of Modern Health Care in Tuberculosis

8

Jayanthi Palanivel, Radhakrishnan Manikkam, Vignesh Sounderrajan, Sakthivel Jayaraj, Sudhanarayani S. Rao, T. Thangam, and Krupakar Parthasarathy

8.1 Introduction

Tuberculosis is the deadly infectious disease from ancient days, but that is still persisting as an unresolved condition in healthcare field across the universe even in the twenty-first century. The detection and treatment of contagious and active TB patients is critical to establishing tuberculosis control and breaking the transmission chain of *Mycobacterium tuberculosis* [1]. Robert Koch identified *Mycobacterium tuberculosis* (MTB) in 1882, about 150 years ago. Tuberculosis (TB) is still a dangerous human infection that poses a threat to the entire world. In many places, it is so pervasive that it poses a risk to healthcare workers on the field. TB has historically been one of the top ten causes of death worldwide due to its high incidence including both immune-competent and immune-compromised patients. In 2019, India (27%, 2.8 million cases yearly, 150,000 MDR-TB cases yearly), China (14%), and the Russian Federation (8%), accounted for the biggest proportion of the worldwide burden. According to estimates, around ten million individuals will contract TB globally in 2020. In comparison to levels in 2015, the aims for 2030 include a 90% decrease in TB deaths and an 80% decrease in new cases annually. By 2050, the targets aim for new cases to be at or below 1 per million people [2]. Hence, it is necessary to establish accurate, precise, rapid, and novel diagnostic as well as therapeutic tools for the optimal prevention and eradication of tuberculosis.

Extensive use of tuberculosis screening tools and newer screening technology, powered by artificial intelligence, along with novel biological markers, have recently emerged and are now ready for expanded investigation and application in tuberculosis-endemic nations [1]. Artificial intelligence (AI) models serve as an emerging tool, which uses machine learning (ML), deep learning (DL) algorithms incorporating computer-aided detection (CAD), and diagnosis methods for the advancement of modern health care in tuberculosis.

J. Palanivel · R. Manikkam · V. Sounderrajan · S. Jayaraj · S. S. Rao · T. Thangam · K. Parthasarathy (✉)
Centre for Drug Discovery and Development, Sathyabama Institute of Science and Technology, Chennai, India
e-mail: radhakrishnan.cddd@sathyabama.ac.in; vignesh.irc@sathyabama.ac.in; sudhanarayani.cddd@sathyabama.ac.in; thangam.t.cddd@sathyabama.ac.in; pkrupakar.cddd@sathyabama.ac.in

K. Parthasarathy, R. Manikkam (eds.), *Translational Research in Biomedical Sciences: Recent Progress and Future Prospects*, https://doi.org/10.1007/978-981-97-1777-4_8

8.2 Artificial Intelligence

AI has influenced medical research, beginning in the 1950s and it was developed by John McCarthy in 1956. Artificial intelligence is a burgeoning computational technologies and statistics domain with the goal of creating systems that resemble human behaviours [3] like reasoning, in-depth learning, resilience, involvement, and sensory perception but need human intelligence for assistance. These techniques are multidisciplinary approaches that are effective in a variety of other domains, including medicine and healthcare. Research and developments in the applications of AI in medicine have increased recently because of the significantly increased computational power of the enormous amount of digital information and contemporary computing accessible for consumption and collection. AI is evolving gradually altering medical procedures. There are various AI technologies in medicine that have a wide range of potential uses such as therapeutic, diagnostic, and rehabilitation, operative and prognostic techniques. Healthcare system is a crucial field of medicine where AI is having an impact in making decisions and identifying diseases. Large volumes of data from various modalities can be ingested, analysed, and reported using AI technology to identify disease and direct clinical actions [4].

8.3 Machine Learning

In 1959, Arthur Samuel first used the term machine learning (ML) [5]. Machine learning is a branch of artificial intelligence that emphasises on the learning element of AI by constructing algorithms that truly describe a collection of data [6]. The field of machine learning (ML) in medicine is expanding. ML typically employs four learning techniques supervised, reinforcement, unsupervised, semi-supervised learning, each of which is effective for resolving a distinct problem [7]. Algorithms that use the labelled data as their training dataset are known as supervised learning. Labelled data are those that contain a specific outcome of interest. The algorithm will therefore select the best model to anticipate the desired outcome. Using data without a predetermined desirable outcome is known as unsupervised learning. Even without expert labelling, algorithms remain left to sift through data on their own to discover patterns and extract underlying structure. The main use of unsupervised learning in medicine is clustering, with the goal of identifying natural grouping in the data, such as clusters of patients with similar clinical characteristics [5–8]. Semi-supervised learning is a combination of supervised and unsupervised machine learning that can analyse a significant amount of unlabelled (unclassified) data while supplementing its pattern identification abilities with a small portion of labelled (pre-classified) data. Semi-supervised learning can speed up and improve the accuracy of information retrieval from huge data sets [5]. Through trial and error, reinforcement learning algorithms uncover activities that provide the greatest rewards. In this classification, the algorithm is set to take survival or a reduced hospital stay as a reward. The approach employs a training dataset to run several tests in order to generate the model with the highest reward. The limitations of expert systems were addressed by the development of machine learning (ML). In machine learning, engineers create algorithms that can create their unique guidelines from data. This enables ML systems to know new conditions and learn from existing information. Since the quantity and calibre of the data supplied determine the performance and capacity of machine to learn, ML systems are sometimes referred to as data-intensive systems. Clinical decision support systems (CDSS) are software programmes that use a patient's unique attributes to provide suggestions or assessments that are particular to that patient to a doctor. Expert systems make up the majority of CDSS now used in computer-assisted diagnosis or therapy, but interest in machine learning-clinical decision support systems (ML-CDSS) is expanding [7].

Two broad prediction pipelines was developed in machine learning. The first pipeline was created entirely using traditional machine learning (CML) techniques such as Bernoulli Naive Bayes, random forest, AdaBoost decision tree, linear logistic regression, and support vector machine. All CML models incorporated into this pipeline were built, tuned, and validated using the ML Python library. The secondary pipeline was developed using Keras, a deep learning toolkit, with TensorFlow as the backend, employing deep neural networks (DNN) generating models of various complexity [9].

8.4 Deep Learning

The term "Deep Learning" was initially used by Igor Aizenberg and his colleagues in the early twentieth century while discussing the artificial neural network (ANN). The progression goes AI to ML to DL because DL is a subclass of ML, which is a subfield of AI [10].

Machines can learn to execute classification directly from input data using a method of machine learning called deep learning. A mixture of signals with various weights is needed to create deep learning models with high accuracy, and the results are passed down successive layers of the multi-layer architecture of neural networks until they reach the output layer. This method is more suited to solving complicated problems since it has multiple learning stages. In this context, "deep" refers to the networks total number of hidden layers, meaning that it can have more hidden layers than more conventional neural networks. Bioinformatics and computational science both have made extensive use of deep learning. The creation of more complex algorithms, such as deep learning models, which enabled clinicians to carry out their duties with a high degree of precision. A number of easy procedures have been developed using deep learning in combination with fuzzy logic, artificial immune system, and the genetic algorithms increasing the specificity and effectiveness of TB diagnosis [11].

8.5 AI in Tuberculosis

Innovative strategies like digital health (electronic and mobile health) to support patient care, surveillance, programme management, training, and communication are required promptly to reduce their tuberculosis (TB) burden by 2035. The incorporation of artificial intelligence to new operating system holds the possibility of improving the effectiveness and efficiency of procedures. Many of the digital technologies that are now on the market aware of one or more of these responsibilities, but greater widespread use of these tools is required to meet the End TB strategy's lofty objectives [12].

8.6 Applications of Artificial Intelligence in Tuberculosis (Fig. 8.1)

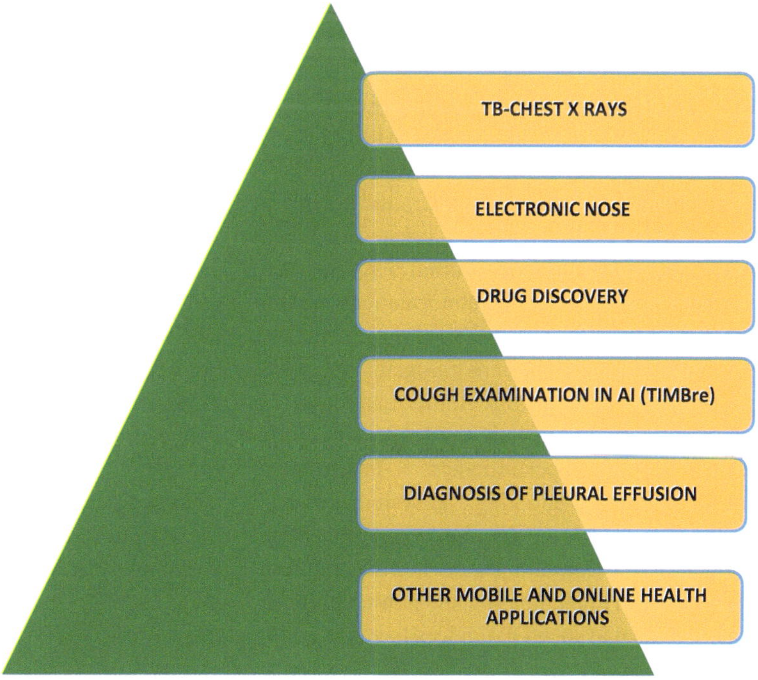

Fig. 8.1 AI in Tuberculosis-drug development, and diagnosis

8.7 TB Chest X-rays

The application of chest X-rays (CXR) in the identification of tuberculosis (TB) dates back to the days of widespread examinations, and more recently, prevalence studies and active cases finding programmes. CXR is only of limited utility for TB diagnosis. Chest radiography (CXR) interpretation using deep learning (DL) neural networks has just recently been used to screen and prioritise patients for pulmonary tuberculosis. In the past few years, a number of deep learning (DL) structures have been created to analyse digital chest radiographs for TB-related disorders that may address current issues, such as lowering human inter-reader variance and reproducibility and providing radiologic services in areas where radiographers are not readily available. The goal of neural networks is to automatically infer rules to recognise patterns. Neural networks are a collection of algorithms arranged into nodes and layers to replicate human cognitive capabilities. After being trained on labelled datasets, neural networks assist us in clustering and classifying images, sound, text, and time series. By obtaining over one hidden layer, deep learning networks differ from earlier iterations of neural networks because each layer learns a unique set of traits and aggregates and manages to combine input data from the preceding layer to comprehend as well as accomplish more complicated features and functions, such as reading images and autonomous driving. Three DL systems with solid version controls were identified such as CAD4TB, qXR created by Qure AI (India), and for Chest Radiography Lunit INSIGHT created by Lunit (South Korea). This is the initial assessment of various DL systems for TB abnormality detection in CXR and studies found that all three technologies outperformed human radiologists in terms of performance. In numerous studies and stratifications, the three DL techniques displayed comparable overall performance. Practitioners considering about adopting DL system for chest X-ray monitoring should also consider service, simplicity of use, maintenance, and price all crucial criteria in implementing any new technology. This reveals that such DL devices have the ability to boost capacity and assist TB diagnosis, particularly in environments where there is a dearth of qualified human readers, which has been identified as a drawback in the use of CXR [13]. Jaeger et al. suggested that Automated TB detection system uses a local binary pattern to extract texture and shape data from CXRs. The retrieved features are then used to create a normality-pathology diagnostic by feeding them into a binary classifier [14]. Lakhani et al. used the Shenzhen Hospital CXR database and the Montgomery County CXR dataset to categorise the chest radiography as pulmonary Tuberculosis with a healthy case. They designed two deep CNN methods, AlexNet and GoogLeNet [15]. Pasa et al. demonstrated a deep CNN with a shortcut connection than an automated diagnosis with the localisation of TB within the same two datasets [16]. Zimic et al. studies identified a CNN for automated evaluation of digital pictures from microscopic observed drug susceptibility (MODS) cultures has been trained and tested. The MODS test involves visual detection of particular *Mycobacterium tuberculosis* growth cording patterns in a broth culture to detect active tuberculosis and drug sensitivity directly from the sputum sample taken in 7–10 days with excellent sensitivity and specificity. Despite its benefits, MODS remains limited in distant, low-resource areas since its image-based diagnostics require permanent, skilled technical staff [17]. In order to deal such unbalanced, less-category X-ray images, Liu et al. proposed an innovative technique employing CNN. Their approach significantly increases classification accuracy for a variety of TB symptoms. In their investigation of the efficiency and effectiveness of shuffling sample with cross-validation in network training, they discovered that it had a particularly notable impact on the classification of medical images. Their approaches and results point to a possible route for a more precise and speedy TB diagnosis in low- and middle-income countries health centres [18]. Norval et al. studies looked into the precision of two techniques for pulmonary TB detection based on patient CXR pictures [19]. Guo et al. used deep CNN models like (VGG16, VGG19, Inception V3, ResNet34,

ResNet50, ResNet101) to study the identification of lung abnormality as well as the diagnosis of certain TB symptoms in seven TB-related lung disorders such as consolidation, effusion, fibrosis, infiltration, mass, nodules, and pleural thickening [20].

Bade et al. provides a method for TB diagnosis utilising contrast-enhanced canny edge detected (CEED-Canny) X-ray pictures and deep learning. The edge identified images were produced using the CEED-Canny algorithm, a modified version of Canny that is used to determine the edges of X-ray images. The first type feature was taken out from Enhanced X-ray images, whereas the second type from the edge detected photos. Their study predicted that employing ensemble classifiers and various types of features will increase the TB detection accuracy, sensitivity, and specificity [21].

Nafisah and Muhammad developed a deep learning-based automated system for TB early detection and also described a transfer learning method employing deep CNNs to detect TB automatically from CXRs. U-Net is indeed a CNN architecture which emerges with a specific objective that is learning from a set of images how to recognise the necessary components in testing images. The semantic segmentation architecture is called U-Net. Medical image segmentation is the major goal of U-Net. As input images, original and segmented images that contained the desired portion of the original image were used. Then, features from each image were extracted using pretrained CNN models, including ResNet, Inception, Xception, MobileNet, and EfficientNet. The efficacy of the models was assessed based on their ability to identify TB in CXRs, and their efficacy was contrasted using several measures [22]. Ahmed et al. discussed the five different AI algorithms such as JF CXR-1 (edition 2), Lunit INSIGHT CXR (edition 4.9.0), qXR (version 3), and CAD4TB (version 7) and assessed AI algorithms performed in comparison to one another, to radiologists, and to the WHO's Target Product Profile (TPP) set triage tests. The five AI algorithms maintained their sensitivity levels above 90% while reducing the amount of Xpert tests needed by 50%. They also concluded that in high-burden areas, AI systems can detect tuberculosis with greater accuracy and effectiveness than human readers [23].

8.8 Electronic Nose

Since 2000 BC, both the Greeks as well as the Chinese have been using odour to diagnose diseases [24, 25]. New developments in gas sensor technology and artificial intelligence are rediscovering the diagnostic power of odours, a classical technique. Rapid tuberculosis detection is one area of medical diagnostics where "artificial nose" technology has been used [24–26]. Omelianski was the first to examine and research naturally released microbial odours in 1923, such as the sweet or pleasant odour of dangerous species like Mycobacterium TB. Moncrieff created the very first mechanical olfactory device in 1961 [24] 20 years later, Persaud and Dodd described the invention of the first intelligent artificial nose model in 1982 [24, 26]. The term electronic nose refers to a device containing chemical sensors and a pattern recognition system. In order to evaluate and classify complex scents without dissecting the mixture into its component parts, an EN uses a combination of non-specific gas sensors and a pattern recognition algorithm to resemble the human olfactory system [24, 25]. The so-called bio-electronic noses are a new class of smart gas detecting devices that utilise entire olfactory cells or protein receptors [24].

Fend et al. studied an electronic nose gas sensor array made of 14 conducting polymers could be used to identify various Mycobacterium species [25]. Principal-component analysis, artificial neural networks, and discriminant function analysis were all used to examine the data [25, 26]. In culture and spiked sputum samples, the EN distinguished between various mycobacteria species that are between mycobacteria and also other lung pathogens. In accordance to the culture, the described approach has an aggregate 91% specificity and 89% sensitivity, respectively. Recently, researchers found that electronic noses might be used as a diagnosing tool for detecting *Mycobacterium bovis* in cattle and badgers. In comparison with molecular or serologically based assays, electronic nose technology has some advantages, including a low limit of detection (5 to 0.1 ppm) [21], cost- and time effectiveness, resilience, simplicity, and operator independence [25].

Saktiawati et al. described the breath tests could be used to detect tuberculosis (TB) through the detection of particular volatile organic chemicals produced by MTB or the infected host, breath tests may be used to diagnose tuberculosis (TB). Chemical and physical methods can also be used to examine breath samples. Chemical methods include, for instance, immunosensor and bio-optical technique, gas chromatography with mass spectrometry (GC/MS), and electronic nose with sensors that detect chemical reactions between VOCs and the sensor surfaces. Physical methods measure a molecule's physical characteristics, such like field asymmetric ion mobility spectrometry (FAIMS), which examines the mobility of ionised breath molecules [27]. Teixeira et al. studied that electronic nose demonstrated significant specificity and negative predictive value, and might thus be used as a TB rule-out test for groups that are more susceptible to the disease. With the advancement of a triage test such as EN, more affordable diagnostics can be avoided while utilising health economic resources more effectively. shorter test duration and instant results analysis using a portable cloud database platform attached to a EN would transform it into authentic "Point of Care" test [28].

8.9 Drug Discovery

The pharmaceutical sector's productivity has been declining. After treatments are studied in model organisms, clinical trial failure rates reach 90%, and the price to develop a new medicine approaches $2.6 billion. Recent developments in artificial intelligence could assist in reversing this trend and enhancing pharmaceutical research and development. Although deep learning and artificial intelligence are still not new, newer developments in greater computing, the availability of sizable annotated data sets needed for training, and new frameworks for incorporating deep neural networks have caused an extraordinary acceleration of the field. Drug repurposing leveraging the large amount of data sets accessible from high-throughput research including gene expression profiles is one of the primary potentials of AI in drug discovery [29]. Intense global efforts to create novel treatments to combat resistance for first- and second-line antibiotics continue to be focused on TB. It is crucial to find new TB medication candidates with cutting-edge mechanisms of action and shorter course of treatment [9].

The main goal for drug design and research is to develop a molecule that can focus on a specific region in a protein and prevent its enzymatic activity. Compared to conventional drug design procedures, which are tedious and time-consuming, new methodologies, which incorporate computational and analytical tools, increased the chances of drug discovery and a greater knowledge of the statistically significant relationship among structure and biological activity has resulted in the creation of computer-aided drug design (CADD) techniques in the development of new anti-TB treatments. The application of artificial intelligence and machine learning to CADD was recognised as a novel approach to TB medication management. The screening of many libraries of compounds against various significant proteins believed to be necessary for MTB survival was made possible using computational techniques. About 73 proven outcomes and 10 possible targets in the search for new anti-tubercular medicines exist despite the discovery of more than 500 important MTB proteins. In order to find new, effective MTB drugs, it is therefore necessary to investigate the inhibition of a number of other important proteins. Computational drug discovery methods are usually Structure Based Drug Design (SBDD) and ligand-based drug design (LBDD), based on availability of protein structures. Target proteins accelerated drug development, creating the foundation for structure-based drug design. SBDD is becoming a more significant part of both academic and commercial drug development endeavours. It is a more accurate, quick, and practical method of lead identification and optimisation. Instead of depending on protein structural information, LBDD creates forecasting model of hit and lead optimisation using data from a wide range of ligands with demonstrated activity. Quantum computing's development as well as the development of Clustered Regularly Interspaced Short Palindromic Repeats (CRISPR) are two more crucial areas of CADD. With the hybrid integration of machine learning, artificial intelligence, quantum computing, and CRISPR, SBDD approaches to TB drug discovery and development will bring about a paradigm shift in the future [30].

8.10 Cough Examination in AI (TIMBre)

Cough examination is critical in the therapeutic management of respiratory illnesses such as tuberculosis (TB), however, techniques to quantify cough accurately and unobtrusively are inadequate. Coughing is a typical TB symptom; thus, it is commonly used to diagnose TB and evaluate the efficacy of treatment. With the goal of improving health outcomes for persons with respiratory infections connected to coughing, the field of acoustic epidemiology uses technology to track cough patterns and detect cough noises. The prospective use of artificial intelligence (AI) for more sophisticated applications, such as using the sounds of coughing as a biomarker for illness screening, is being widely explored in this field [31].

The visual analogue scale (VAS), cough symptom score (CSS), and cough diaries are examples of questionnaire-based techniques. Based on how a patient feels about their cough, the VAS and CSS both make an effort to quantify the intensity of coughing. There are several different types of cough diaries, but they all require patients to monitor the intensity and frequency of their coughs over time [32]. The Leicester Cough Questionnaire (LCQ) is a validated self-administered survey that assesses the quality of life of people who have a chronic cough. It has previously been used to assess cohorts of TB patients receiving anti-TB medicine [33]. Loudon and Spohn began counting the coughs of TB patients at night in the 1960s using tape [34]. There are now 24 h recording equipment that are more sophisticated. The VitaloJak, the Cayetano Cough Monitor, and the Leicester Cough Monitor are a few examples of such recording devices [35, 36]. A sophisticated Microphone Array was employed to record the cough as a harmless and contactless screening technique under a strict infection control strategy. Now, the "TimBre" solution, which seamlessly conducts bidirectional testing with one recording of cough and also provides insights into Non-Communicable diseases as part of differential diagnosis, can be added to the toolkit of healthcare professionals in situations where an RT-PCR or the CXR is not available [37].

8.11 AI in Diagnosis of Pleural Effusion

The condition pleural effusion (PE) is defined by substantial fluid accumulations in the pleural cavity [38]. Pleural effusion is a common symptom of tuberculous pleurisy. The clinical issue of TBPE is prevalent in several countries and is particularly important in nations with a high prevalence of HIV. As an effect of a delayed hypersensitivity reaction, TBPE develops when macrophages' antimicrobial activity increases capillary permeability and hinders lymphatic drainage, leading to PE [39].

Pathogenic diagnosis with smears or cultures of the respiratory system or pleural fluid specimens has poor positive rates as well as extensive culturing times. Pathological diagnosis with thoracoscopic pleural biopsy is traumatic, risky, and expensive, with prohibitive technical limits. As a result, tuberculous pleural effusion (TPE) diagnosis remains difficult. Pleural fluid adenosine deaminase (pfADA) is the most often utilised diagnostic biomarker for TPE in clinical practice. Pleural effusion can be diagnosed as TPE when lymphocyte is predominant in exudative pleural fluid with a raised level of pfADA and no sign of other illnesses. The study of artificial intelligence (AI)'s potential applications in medicine has grown in recent years. K-nearest neighbour (KNN), random forest (RF), and support vector machine (SVM) are a few examples of machine learning algorithms (MLAs) that can be used to build highly effective, unbiased, and precise disease diagnostic models. RF outperforms logistic regression, KNN, SVM, and pfADA in this aspect. The development of an idea for the diagnosis of TPE using RF may give a more effective, cost-effective, and time-efficient diagnostic tool based on routine clinical data that helps doctors in making appropriate diagnoses and treatment decisions [40].

8.12 Other Mobile and Online Health Applications

The field of mobile health, or "mHealth," is one that is fast developing and has been used in many different disease-related contexts. mHealth apps can make a significant contribution to the development of tuberculosis treatment. Tuberculosis is still one of the leading infectious disease causes of mortality worldwide. The emergence of drug-resistant tuberculosis or its recurrence can be prevented in particular by using apps that facilitate dose individualisation, adherence monitoring, or the dissemination of knowledge and awareness about the disease. The following factors are used to categorise mHealth apps that are description, targeted end user, cost, available languages, downloads, store, country of development, and qualification as a medical device. All recognised mHealth apps were evaluated using information from the app stores, the product's website, or supporting publications.

VOT video directly observed treatment defines the daily remote monitoring of drug intake through the use of a smartphone app. MiDOT is a drug adherence software developed by emocha Mobile Health Inc, with the ability to filter patients who have difficulty with adherence or encountering adverse effects. AiCure is a mHealth software that uses artificial intelligence to confirm drug consumption. The other apps include SureAdhere, Wisepill evriMED, Adhere2Tx-TB, Stop TB, TBmCure, and Sembuh TB, TB Doctor, Medical Management of MDR-TB, DoseMeRx, MwPharm, InsightRx, TDMx [41]. TB Mobile is an easy-to-use tool that provides handy features for viewing and modifying data regarding compounds having Mtb activity, their targets, and other relevant information [42]. To categorise chest X-Ray (CXR) pictures as TB suspicion, multiple effusion, or normal, the dataset was expanded using the augmentation approach. To make the procedure easier, DIGITS UI was used to train CXR pictures. Caffe framework was used to generate the model. To train CXR pictures, the GoogLeNet network was chosen. The model was transformed to an IOS model using coreML tools and IOS-based picture categorisation app. The IOS mobile App correctly classified the Tuberculosis (CXR) photos. The accuracy of GoogLeNet was 98.39% [43]. The number of tuberculosis-related mHealth apps has grown during the last three years. Though some of the uncovered apps appear promising, several were proven to contain flaws or to deliver hazardous or incorrect information. Furthermore, the vast majority of mHealth apps now available on the market are aimed towards disseminating tuberculosis information [41].

8.13 Conclusion

According to the World Health Organization's Global Tuberculosis Report 2021, there are around 1.4 million mortalities and 10 million new cases per year. According to the Global TB Report 2022, India accounts for around 28% of all TB cases worldwide. The advisory board on Hazardous Pathogens classifies MTB as a group 3 Hazard, which is a biological agent that can cause significant human disease and could be a substantial risk to workers could spread to the neighbourhood, handling the appropriate containment facilities is necessary to ensure public safety. Diagnostics that are quick, sensitive, accurate, and portable are essential in modern medicine.

The diagnostic tools for tuberculosis have undergone significant advancements, but they are sometimes error-prone, costly, lack the essential sensitivity or accuracy, and, most importantly, are not sufficiently portable to be used in the distant, rural areas where they are most required. In order to solve this, a number of companies are creating computational algorithms and employing AI for interpretation. While these recent advancements show promise in addressing many of the challenges in TB diagnostics, they will require investments as well as time to attain full potential and penetrate worldwide markets. While scientific progress is being made, it is vital to keep vigilance and continue to use TB monitoring programmes in order to continue the fight to combat this ancient illness [44].

Ending tuberculosis is a development challenge as well as an opportunity. Every year on March 24, organisations observe World Tuberculosis Day to promote public awareness about the catastrophic health, social, and economic effects of TB and to intensify efforts to stop the global TB epidemic. World TB Day under the themes for every year intends to inspire hope and motivate high-level leadership, higher funding, faster implementation of new WHO guidelines, adoption of innovations, expedited action, and international cooperation to combat the pandemic of TB. "YES! We Can End Tb", 2023-year theme draws attention to tuberculosis and our collective ability to abolish tuberculosis by 2030 and thereby achieve the Sustainable Development Goals. The Stop TB Partnership and all members are urging everyone involved in the TB battle to band together under one overarching theme. Global leaders must step up their efforts to eradicate tuberculosis and save lives.

References

1. Koegelenberg CF, Schoch OD, Lange C. Tuberculosis: the past, the present and the future. Respiration. 2021;100(7):553–6.
2. Merchant SA, Shaikh MJS, Nadkarni P. Tuberculosis conundrum-current and future scenarios: a proposed comprehensive approach combining laboratory, imaging, and computing advances. World J Radiol. 2022;14(6):114.
3. Tran NK, Albahra S, May L, Waldman S, Crabtree S, Bainbridge S, Rashidi H. Evolving applications of artificial intelligence and machine learning in infectious diseases testing. Clin Chem. 2022;68(1):125–33.
4. Secinaro S, Calandra D, Secinaro A, Muthurangu V, Biancone P. The role of artificial intelligence in healthcare: a structured literature review. BMC Med Inform Decis Mak. 2021;21(1):1–23.
5. Handelman GS, Kok HK, Chandra RV, Razavi AH, Lee MJ, Asadi H. eDoctor: machine learning and the future of medicine. J Intern Med. 2018;284(6):603–19.
6. Choi RY, Coyner AS, Kalpathy-Cramer J, Chiang MF, Campbell JP. Introduction to machine learning, neural networks, and deep learning. Transl Vis Sci Technol. 2020;9(2):14.
7. Peiffer-Smadja N, Rawson TM, Ahmad R, Buchard A, Georgiou P, Lescure FX, Holmes AH. Machine learning for clinical decision support in infectious diseases: a narrative review of current applications. Clin Microbiol Infect. 2020;26(5):584–95.
8. Deo RC. Machine learning in medicine. Circulation. 2015;132(20):1920–30.
9. Lane T, Russo DP, Zorn KM, Clark AM, Korotcov A, Tkachenko V, Ekins S. Comparing and validating machine learning models for *Mycobacterium tuberculosis* drug discovery. Mol Pharm. 2018;15(10):4346–60.
10. Gupta R, Srivastava D, Sahu M, Tiwari S, Ambasta RK, Kumar P. Artificial intelligence to deep learning: machine intelligence approach for drug discovery. Mol Divers. 2021;25(3):1315–60.
11. Singh M, Pujar GV, Kumar SA, Bhagyalalitha M, Akshatha HS, Abuhaija B, Gandomi AH. Evolution of machine learning in tuberculosis diagnosis: a review of deep learning-based medical applications. Electronics. 2022;11(17):2634.
12. Doshi R, Falzon D, Thomas BV, Temesgen Z, Sadasivan L, Migliori GB, Raviglione M. Tuberculosis control, and the where and why of artificial intelligence. ERJ Open Res. 2017;3(2):56.
13. Qin ZZ, Sander MS, Rai B, Titahong CN, Sudrungrot S, Laah SN, Creswell J. Using artificial intelligence to read chest radiographs for tuberculosis detection: a multi-site evaluation of the diagnostic accuracy of three deep learning systems. Sci Rep. 2019;9(1):1–10.
14. Xue Z, Jaeger S, Antani S, Long LR, Karargyris A, Siegelman J, Thoma GR. Localizing tuberculosis in chest radiographs with deep learning. In: Medical imaging 2018: imaging informatics for healthcare, research, and applications, vol. 10579. Bellingham: SPIE; 2018. p. 185–91.
15. Lakhani P, Sundaram B. Deep learning at chest radiography: automated classification of pulmonary tuberculosis by using convolutional neural networks. Radiology. 2017;284(2):574–82.
16. Pasa F, Golkov V, Pfeiffer F. Efficient deep network architectures for fast chest X-ray tuberculosis screening and visualization. Sci Rep. 2019;9:6268.
17. Zimic M, Sheen P, Lopez-Garnier S. Automatic diagnostics of tuberculosis using convolutional neural networks analysis of MODS digital images. PLoS One. 2019;14(2):e0212094.

18. Tx-Cnn: detecting tuberculosis in chest X-ray images using convolutional neural network.
19. Norval M, Wang Z, Sun Y. Pulmonary tuberculosis detection using deep learning convolutional neural networks. In: Proceedings of the 3rd international conference on video and image processing. New York: ACM; 2019. p. 47–51.
20. Guo R, Passi K, Jain CK. Tuberculosis diagnostics and localization in chest X-rays via deep learning models. Front Artif Intell. 2020;3:583427.
21. Hwa SKT, Bade A, Hijazi MHA, Jeffree MS. Tuberculosis detection using deep learning and contrast enhanced canny edge detected X-ray images. IAES Int J Artif Intell. 2020;9(4):713.
22. Nafisah SI, Muhammad G. Tuberculosis detection in chest radiograph using convolutional neural network architecture and explainable artificial intelligence. Neural Comput & Applic. 2022;36:111–31.
23. Qin ZZ, Ahmed S, Sarker MS, Paul K, Adel ASS, Naheyan T, Creswell J. Tuberculosis detection from chest X-rays for triaging in a high tuberculosis-burden setting: an evaluation of five artificial intelligence algorithms. Lancet Digital Health. 2021;3(9):e543–54.
24. Pavlou AK, Turner APF. Sniffing out the truth: clinical diagnosis using the electronic nose. Clin Chem Lab Med. 2000;38(2):99–112.
25. Fend R, Kolk AH, Bessant C, Buijtels P, Klatser PR, Woodman AC. Prospects for clinical application of electronic-nose technology to early detection of Mycobacterium tuberculosis in culture and sputum. J Clin Microbiol. 2006;44(6):2039–45.
26. Turner AP, Magan N. Electronic noses and disease diagnostics. Nat Rev Microbiol. 2004;2(2):161–6.
27. Saktiawati AM, Putera DD, Setyawan A, Mahendradhata Y, van der Werf TS. Diagnosis of tuberculosis through breath test: a systematic review. EBioMedicine. 2019;46:202–14.
28. Coronel Teixeira R, Ijdema D, Gómez C, Arce D, Roman M, Quintana Y, Magis-Escurra C. The electronic nose as a rule-out test for tuberculosis in an indigenous population. J Intern Med. 2021;290(2):386–91.
29. Zhavoronkov A. Artificial intelligence for drug discovery, biomarker development, and generation of novel chemistry. Mol Pharm. 2018;15(10):4311–3.
30. Ejalonibu MA, Ogundare SA, Elrashedy AA, Ejalonibu MA, Lawal MM, Mhlongo NN, Kumalo HM. Drug discovery for Mycobacterium tuberculosis using structure-based computer-aided drug design approach. Int J Mol Sci. 2021;22(24):13259.
31. Zimmer AJ, Ugarte-Gil C, Pathri R, Dewan P, Jaganath D, Cattamanchi A, Grandjean Lapierre S. Making cough count in tuberculosis care. Commun Med. 2022;2(1):83.
32. Wang Z, Wang M, Wen S, Yu L, Xu X. Types and applications of cough-related questionnaires. J Thorac Dis. 2019;11(10):4379.
33. Suzuki T, et al. Improved cough- and sputum-related quality of life after initiation of treatment in pulmonary tuberculosis. Respir Investig. 2019;57:252–9.
34. Loudon RG, Spohn SK. Cough frequency and infectivity in patients with pulmonary tuberculosis. Am Rev Respir Dis. 1969;99(1):109–11.
35. Matos S, Birring SS, Pavord ID, Evans DH. An automated system for 24-h monitoring of cough frequency: the Leicester cough monitor. IEEE Trans Biomed Eng. 2007;54(8):1472–9.
36. Birring SS, Fleming T, Matos S, Raj AA, Evans DH, Pavord ID. The Leicester Cough Monitor: preliminary validation of an automated cough detection system in chronic cough. Eur Respir J. 2008;31(5):1013–8.
37. Pathri R, Jha S, Tandon S, GangaShetty S. Acoustic epidemiology of pulmonary tuberculosis (TB) & Covid19 leveraging AI/ML. medRxiv, 2022-02. 2022.
38. Li Y, Tian S, Huang Y, Dong W. Driverless artificial intelligence framework for the identification of malignant pleural effusion. Transl Oncol. 2021;14(1):100896.
39. Ren Z, Hu Y, Xu L. Identifying tuberculous pleural effusion using artificial intelligence machine learning algorithms. Respir Res. 2019;20(1):1–9.
40. Ferreiro L, Toubes ME, San José ME, Suárez-Antelo J, Golpe A, Valdés L. Advances in pleural effusion diagnostics. Expert Rev Respir Med. 2020;14(1):51–66.
41. Keutzer L, Wicha SG, Simonsson US. Mobile health apps for improvement of tuberculosis treatment: descriptive review. JMIR Mhealth Uhealth. 2020;8(4):e17246.
42. Ekins S, Clark AM, Sarker M. TB mobile: a mobile app for anti-tuberculosis molecules with known targets. J Chem. 2013;5:1–14.
43. Hendrick H, Zhi-Hao W, Hsien C, Pei-Lun C, Gwo-Jia J. IOS mobile APP for tuberculosis detection based on chest X-ray image. In: 2019 2nd international conference on applied information technology and innovation (ICAITI). IEEE: Piscataway; 2019. p. 122–5.
44. MacGregor-Fairlie M, Wilkinson S, Besra GS, Goldberg Oppenheimer P. Tuberculosis diagnostics: overcoming ancient challenges with modern solutions. Emerg Top Life Sci. 2020;4(4):435–48.

Role of Artificial Intelligence in the Diagnosis and Therapy of Gynecological Disorders: Opportunities and Challenges

9

Savithri Vemulavada, Shriya Karthikvatsan, Anchana Babu, B. Kadalmani, T. Ramani Devi, T. Sasipraba, Radhakrishnan Manikkam, Krupakar Parthasarathy, and V. Hari Balaji

9.1 Introduction

Artificial intelligence (AI) is a branch of computer science that aims to create machines or systems that can perform tasks that normally require human intelligence, such as learning, reasoning, perception, decision making, or natural language processing. AI has been widely applied in various fields of medicine and healthcare, such as disease diagnosis, drug discovery, patient risk assessment, and personalized treatment [1–3]. AI has been revolutionizing discovery, diagnosis, and treatment designs in various fields of medicine, including gynecology. AI can aid not only in the detection of gynecological disorders but also in therapy design, identification of new therapeutic targets with accelerating drug discovery, and in improving treatment outcomes [4, 5].

Artificial Intelligence (AI), machine learning, deep learning, and neural networks are some of the terms that are often used to describe the use of advanced computational methods to analyze large and complex data sets, such as those generated by clinical research (Table 9.1) [4, 6]. These methods can help researchers and clinicians to better understand the underlying mechanisms of the disorder, identify biomarkers for diagnosis and prognosis, and predict the optimal treatment for each patient based on their individual characteristics and preferences [7–9]. AI is a broad concept that encompasses any system that can perform tasks that would normally require human intelligence, such as perception, reasoning, decision making, and natural language processing. Machine learning is a subset of AI that focuses on creating algorithms and models that can learn from data and improve their performance without

S. Vemulavada · V. H. Balaji (✉)
VivagenDX Labs, Centre for Advanced Studies, Sathyabama Institute of Science and Technology, Chennai, Tamil Nadu, India

S. Karthikvatsan
Bouve College of Health Sciences, Northeastern University, Boston, Massachusetts (MA), USA
e-mail: karthikvatsan.s@northeastern.edu

A. Babu
PG & Research Department of Biotechnology, Women's Christian College, Chennai, Tamil Nadu, India

B. Kadalmani · T. R. Devi
Department of Animal Science, Bharathidasan University, Tiruchirappalli, India
e-mail: kadalmani@bdu.ac.in

T. Sasipraba · R. Manikkam · K. Parthasarathy
Centre for Drug Discovery and Development, Sathyabama Institute of Science and Technology, Chennai, Tamil Nadu, India
e-mail: vc@sathybama.ac.in; radhakrishnan.cddd@sathyabama.ac.in; pkrupakar.cddd@sathyabama.ac.in

K. Parthasarathy, R. Manikkam (eds.), *Translational Research in Biomedical Sciences: Recent Progress and Future Prospects*, https://doi.org/10.1007/978-981-97-1777-4_9

Table 9.1 Artificial intelligence, machine learning, and deep learning

Artificial intelligence	Machine learning	Deep learning
A broad term that encompasses machine learning and deep learning as subsets	A subset of AI that uses statistical methods to enable machines to improve with experience	A subset of machine learning that uses deep neural networks to enable machines to solve more complex problems
Examples: search engines, voice assistants, chess programs, self-driving cars	Examples: spam filters, recommendation systems, face recognition, natural language processing	Examples: image classification, speech recognition, text generation, computer vision

explicit programming. Deep learning is a type of machine learning that uses multiple layers of artificial neural networks to learn from large amounts of data and extract complex features and patterns. Neural networks are computational models that mimic the structure and function of biological neurons, which are the basic units of the nervous system [10–12].

Artificial Intelligence (AI) in healthcare is the use of artificial intelligence (AI) to perform tasks that are related to medical services and health care. AI can help improve the efficiency, accuracy, and quality of various processes and outcomes in the healthcare industry. AI can help with administrative workflow, such as documentation, coding, billing, and information sharing. AI can also provide virtual nursing assistants that can answer questions, monitor patients, and schedule appointments. This can save time and resources for health care workers and improve the patient experience. AI can help with diagnosis and treatment, such as analyzing medical images, detecting diseases, recommending drugs, and creating personalized treatment plans. AI can also help with dosage error reduction, by identifying errors in how patients self-administer medications. This can enhance the accuracy and effectiveness of medical interventions and reduce the risk of adverse effects [13–15].

AI can help with research and innovation, such as discovering new drugs, developing new therapies, and predicting outcomes. AI can also help with data analysis, such as finding patterns, trends, and insights from large and complex data sets. This can accelerate the scientific discovery and clinical decision making processes. AI can help with safer surgeries, such as assisting surgeons with robotic equipment, providing real-time information, and reducing physical fluctuations. AI can also help with post-operative care, such as monitoring recovery, detecting complications, and providing feedback. This can improve the precision and quality of surgical procedures and outcomes [16, 17] and as shown in Fig. 9.1.

Although AI in healthcare has the potential to transform the healthcare industry and improve the health and well-being of people around the world. However, there are also some challenges and limitations that need to be addressed, such as ethical issues, data privacy and security, human-AI interaction, regulation and governance, and social impact. Therefore, it is important to balance the benefits and risks of AI in healthcare and ensure that it is used responsibly and appropriately [18, 19].

In this review we will annotate the emerging and well established role of AI within the gynecological setting with special focus on gynecological cancers, hormonal disorders and infection. Although AI has other emerging roles in women's sexual health and care, these are beyond the ambit of the current review.

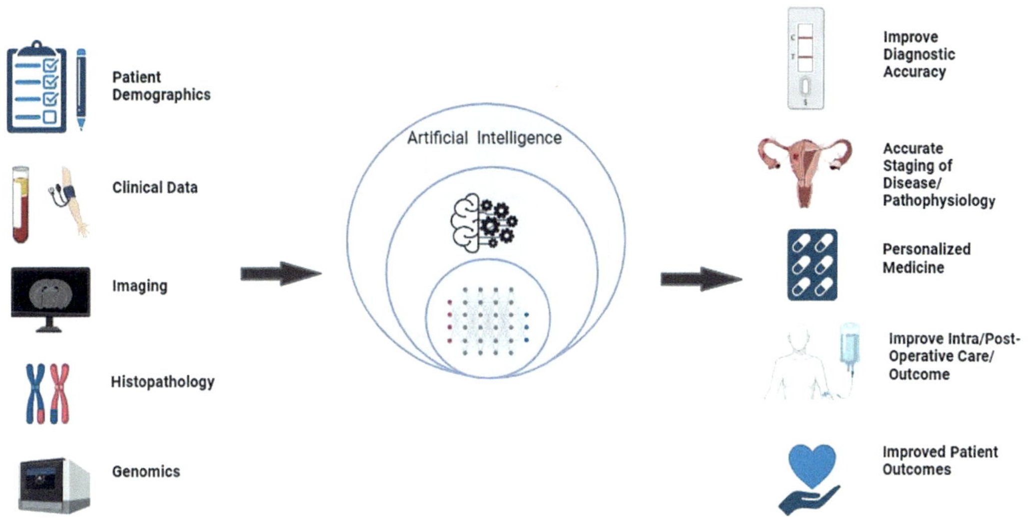

Fig. 9.1 Potential roles of artificial intelligence in healthcare

9.2 Artificial Intelligence and Gynecological Oncology

AI in gynecological oncology is the use of artificial intelligence (AI) to perform tasks that are related to the diagnosis, treatment, and prognosis of gynecological cancers, such as cervical, uterine, and ovarian cancers. AI can help improve the efficiency, accuracy, and quality of various processes and outcomes in the gynecological oncology field. AI can help with screening and diagnosis, such as analyzing medical images, detecting lesions, recommending biopsies, and classifying tumors. AI can also help with risk assessment, such as predicting the likelihood of developing or having gynecological cancers based on genetic, environmental, and lifestyle factors. This can enhance the early detection and prevention of gynecological cancers. AI in recent times has revolutionized treatment and prognosis, such as creating personalized treatment plans, recommending drugs, optimizing dosages, and monitoring responses [20, 21]. AI can also help with outcome prediction, such as estimating survival rates, recurrence risks, and quality of life. This can improve the effectiveness and safety of medical interventions and reduce the side effects and complications. AI can dramatically enhance research and innovation, such as discovering new biomarkers, developing new therapies, and evaluating clinical trials. AI can also help with data analysis, such as finding patterns, trends, and insights from large and complex data sets. This can accelerate the scientific discovery and clinical decision making processes [22, 23] and as shown in Fig. 9.2.

9.2.1 Artificial Intelligence and Diagnosis and therapy in Ovarian Cancer

9.2.1.1 Disease Diagnostics

AI is a powerful technology that can help in the diagnosis of ovarian cancer, which is a challenging and deadly disease. AI can analyze various types of data, such as blood tests, patient background, imaging tests, and genomic sequencing, to identify the features, subtypes, and complications of ovarian cancer. AI can also provide interactive and tailored information to the patients and clinicians through chatbots or virtual assistants. Here are some examples of the role of AI in the diagnosis of ovarian cancer [24, 25]. AI can predict the pathological diagnosis of ovarian tumors using patient information and data from preoperative examinations. A study used five machine learning classifiers, including support vector

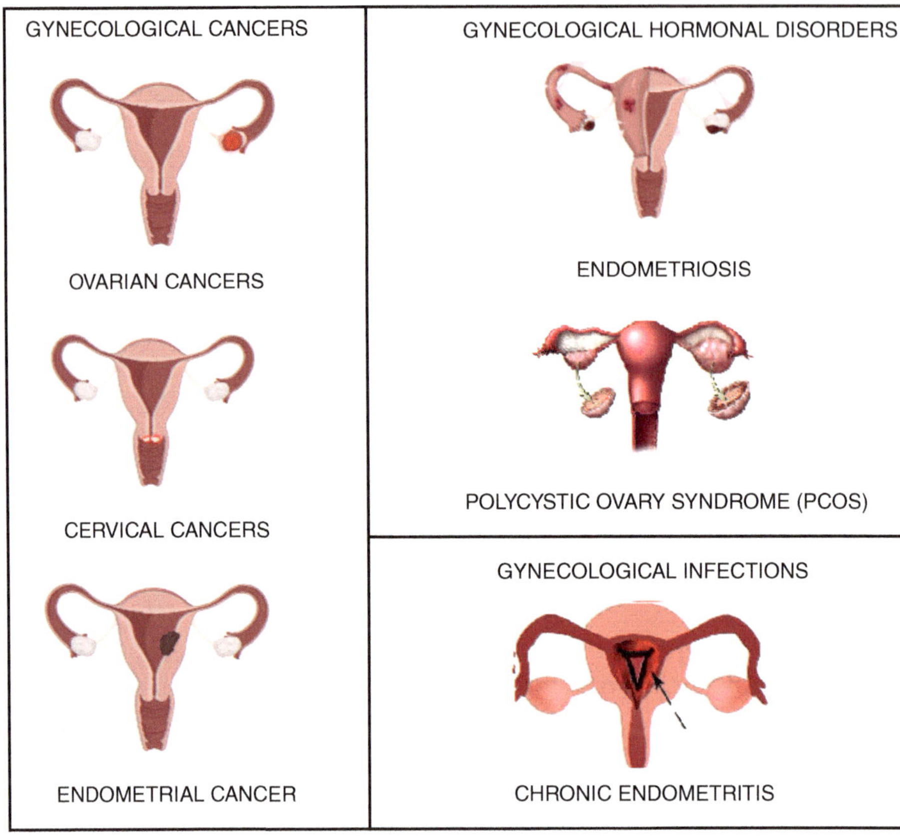

Fig. 9.2 Examples of gynecological cancers, hormonal disorders, and infection that benefit from artificial intelligence (AI) mediated interventions

machine, random forest, naive Bayes, logistic regression, and XGBoost, to derive diagnostic results from 16 features, commonly available from blood tests, patient background, and imaging tests. The highest accuracy was 0.80 in the machine learning algorithm of XGBoost [26]. AI can enhance ovarian cancer diagnostics by integrating multiple data sources and using deep learning methods. A study led by Dr. Ali Bashashati, a UBC and Vancouver Coastal Health Research Institute researcher, revealed how AI can aid in the diagnosis of ovarian cancer to improve patient outcomes. The study used a deep learning framework to analyze data from clinical records, pathology reports, immunohistochemistry results, gene expression profiles, and copy number profiles of 768 ovarian cancer patients. The framework was able to classify the patients into four subtypes of ovarian cancer with high accuracy and consistency [27]. For example, one study used a deep learning approach to segment ovarian regions from ultrasound images and measure ovarian volume using a U-Net model. The study reported an accuracy of 97.5% for ovarian volume measurement using the U-Net model [28]. Another study used a machine learning approach to classify ovarian images into benign or malignant based on texture features extracted from gray-level co-occurrence matrices (GLCMs). The study reported an accuracy of 92.5% for ovarian cancer detection using a support vector machine (SVM) classifier [29] (Fig. 9.3).

9.2.1.2 Biomarker Discovery

AI can discover new biomarkers for ovarian cancer using image analysis techniques. A study applied AI methods to ovarian cancer, pancre-

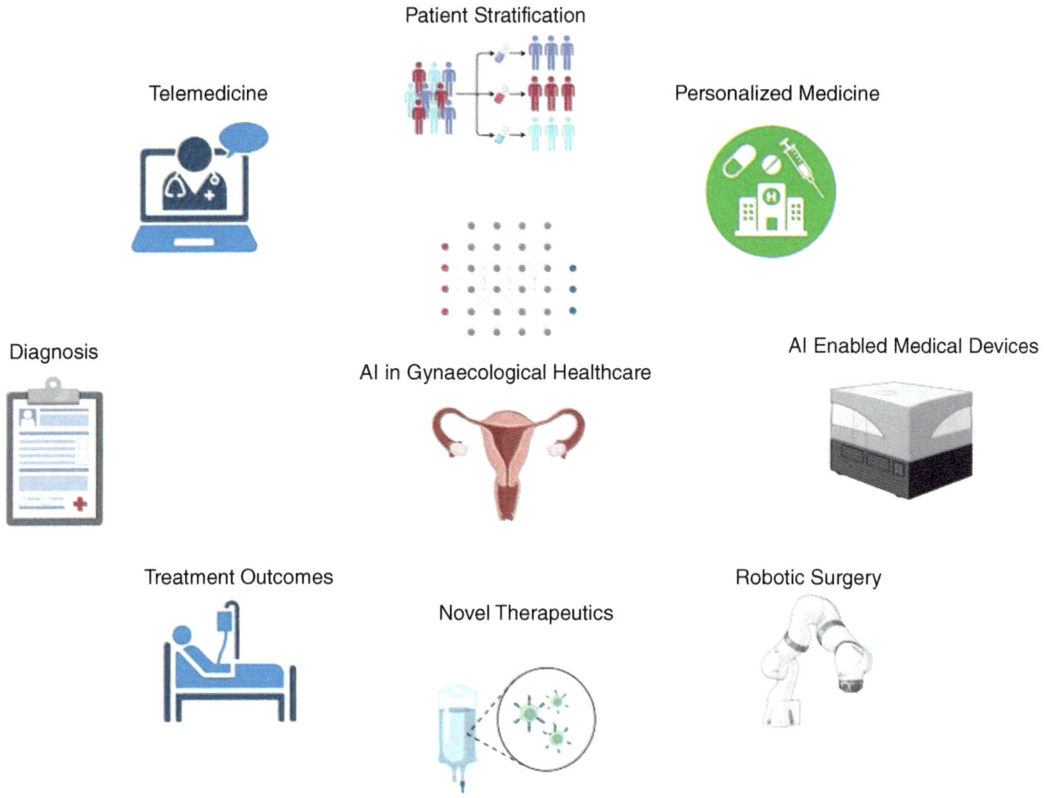

Fig. 9.3 Potential roles of artificial intelligence in gynecological disorders such as gynecological cancers and hormonal disorders

atic cancer, and image biomarker discovery [30, 31]. One study used convolutional neural networks (CNNs) to analyze histopathological images of ovarian tumors and identify features that are associated with survival outcomes. The study also used generative adversarial networks (GANs) to generate synthetic images of ovarian tumors that can be used for training and testing AI models [32]. One of the applications of AI in biomarker discovery is for ovarian cancer, which is a rare but lethal disease that often lacks early symptoms and detection [33, 34]. Ovarian cancer has a high mortality rate, with only about 47% of patients surviving 5 years after diagnosis. Biomarkers can help in improving the diagnosis, prognosis, and treatment of ovarian cancer by providing information about the molecular characteristics of the tumor, the response to therapy, and the risk of recurrence [35–37].

Deep learning models that can analyze histopathological images of ovarian tumors and classify them into different subtypes based on their morphology and molecular features [38, 39]. These models can also identify novel image biomarkers that are associated with clinical outcomes, such as survival or recurrence. Machine learning models that can integrate multiple types of data, such as gene expression, DNA methylation, copy number variation, and clinical information, and identify biomarkers that can predict the survival or response to chemotherapy of ovarian cancer patients. These models can also discover new subgroups of patients with distinct molecular profiles and clinical behaviors [40, 41]. Machine learning models that can analyze liquid biopsy samples, such as blood or ascites fluid, and detect biomarkers that can diagnose ovarian cancer at an early stage or monitor its progression. These models can also identify biomarkers that can indicate the presence of drug resistance or minimal residual disease [42]. AI can predict the pathological diagnosis of ovarian tumors using patient information and data from preoperative examinations. A study used five machine learning classifiers, including support vector machine, random forest, naive Bayes, logistic regression, and XGBoost, to derive diagnostic results from 16 features, commonly available from blood tests, patient background, and imaging tests. The highest accuracy was 0.80 in the machine learning algorithm of XGBoost [43].

AI can enhance ovarian cancer diagnostics by integrating multiple data sources and using deep learning methods. A study led by Dr. Ali Bashashati, a UBC and Vancouver Coastal Health Research Institute researcher, revealed how AI can aid in the diagnosis of ovarian cancer to improve patient outcomes. The study used a deep learning framework to analyze data from clinical records, pathology reports, immunohistochemistry results, gene expression profiles, and copy number profiles of 768 ovarian cancer patients. The framework was able to classify the patients into four subtypes of ovarian cancer with high accuracy and consistency [44]. AI can discover new biomarkers for ovarian cancer using image analysis techniques. A study applied AI methods to ovarian cancer, pancreatic cancer, and image biomarker discovery. The study used convolutional neural networks (CNNs) to analyze histopathological images of ovarian tumors and identify features that are associated with survival outcomes. The study also used generative adversarial networks (GANs) to generate synthetic images of ovarian tumors that can be used for training and testing AI models [45].

9.2.1.3 Therapy

AI can also improve the prognosis and treatment of ovarian cancer by using genomic analysis or natural language processing to detect the molecular subtypes or biomarkers of ovarian cancer from endometrial samples or electronic health records [46, 47]. Genomic analysis is a technique that uses high-throughput sequencing or microarray technologies to analyze the genetic material of organisms or cells [48, 49]. Natural language processing is a subfield of AI that involves creating algorithms that can understand, generate, or manipulate natural language, such as text or speech [50, 51].

For example, one study used a genomic analysis approach to identify the molecular subtypes of ovarian cancer based on gene expression profiles using a deep neural network (DNN). The study reported that the DNN model could classify ovarian cancer into four subtypes (immunoreactive, differentiated, proliferative, and mesenchymal) with an accuracy of 94.4% [52]. Another study used a natural language processing approach to extract clinical features of ovarian cancer from electronic health records using a rule-based system. The study reported that some clinical features, such as age, stage, grade, histology, and survival time, were significantly associated with ovarian cancer subtypes, thereby impacting treatment options [53].

AI can also optimize the treatment of ovarian cancer by using reinforcement learning or decision support systems to recommend the best drug regimen or alternative therapy for each patient based on their molecular profile and clinical characteristics [54]. Reinforcement learning is a subfield of AI that involves creating algorithms that can learn from their own actions and rewards in an environment and optimize their behavior to achieve a goal [55]. Decision support systems are computer-based systems that can provide information, analysis, or recommendations to help users make decisions in complex situations [56]. For example, one study used a reinforcement learning approach to optimize the drug dosage for treating ovarian cancer using a deep Q-network (DQN). The study reported that the DQN model could learn to adjust the drug dosage according to the tumor size and minimize the treatment duration and toxicity [57]. Another study used a decision support system approach to recommend alternative therapies for treating ovarian cancer using a fuzzy logic system. The study reported that the fuzzy logic system could provide personalized suggestions based on the patient's symptoms and multimodal datasets comprising clinical symptoms, histopathological and genomic test data [58].

9.2.2 Artificial Intelligence and Diagnosis, Treatment, and Therapy in Cervical Cancer

9.2.2.1 Disease Diagnostics

Artificial intelligence (AI) has improved cervical cancer diagnosis and treatment in several ways. AI can help automate the evaluation of dual-stain tests, which measure the presence of two proteins (p16 and Ki-67) in cervical samples to predict the risk of precancer. This can reduce the time and cost of screening, as well as increase the accuracy and efficiency of diagnosis [59]. AI can also help analyze images of cervical cells or tissues, such as Pap cytology or histopathology, using complex algorithms that can automatically recognize, extract, and classify features. This can improve the sensitivity and specificity of detecting precancerous or cancerous changes and reduce the variability and subjectivity of human interpretation [60].

In an AI-based tool for colposcopy examinations, a novel machine learning-based diagnostic tool for colposcopy examinations was shown to improve the accuracy of diagnosing cancerous and precancerous cervical lesions, including cervical intraepithelial neoplasia (CIN), according to a retrospective validation study presented at the 2023 ASCO Breakthrough meeting in Yokohama, Japan [61]. The investigators reported that the tool can also be used to identify appropriate biopsy sites in the cervix. The tool was trained on 60 cases of cervical cancer and CIN3 and validated on 150 cases. The tool identified severe lesions in CIN3 cases with a sensitivity of 85%, a specificity of 73%, an AUC of 0.89 for lesion area, and an accuracy of 95% for the number of lesions identified. It predicted abnormal colposcopy findings in CIN1 cases with a sensitivity of 87%, a specificity of 70%, an AUC of 0.81 for lesion area, and an accuracy of 97% for the number of lesions identified [62]. In another AI-based lesion-detection model, NCI researchers have built and tested a deep learning algorithm that can identify cervical precancers that should be removed or treated. In some low-resource settings, health workers screen for cervical precancer by inspecting the cervix with a small camera. Although this method is simple and sustainable, it is not very reliable or accurate. The algorithm was trained on more than 60,000 cervical images from Costa Rica and tested on more than 9000 images from a different study in Guatemala. The algorithm correctly identified 91% of women who needed treatment [63]. AI can use deep learning algorithms to analyze digital images of the cervix and classify them according to the severity of cervical lesions. For example, a study by Hu et al. developed a computer algorithm that can accurately identify precancerous changes in the cervix using a smartphone camera and a low-cost microscope. The algorithm was trained on more than 60,000 cervical images from Costa Rica, India, South Korea, and Zambia, and achieved an accuracy of 91% in detecting cervical intraepithelial neoplasia grade 2 or higher [64].

9.2.2.2 Biomarker Discovery

Artificial intelligence (AI) is a powerful tool that can help in the discovery of novel biomarkers for cervical cancer. Biomarkers are biological indicators that can be used for the diagnosis, treatment, and prognosis of cervical cancer [65]. AI can analyze large and complex data sets generated by high-throughput omics technologies, such as genomics, transcriptomics, proteomics, and metabolomics, and identify patterns and associations that are relevant for cervical cancer [66]. AI can also assist in the screening and diagnosis by analyzing digital images of the cervix and detecting precancerous changes that require medical attention [67].

AI can integrate multi-omics data to better understand the molecular mechanisms of cervical cancer and identify novel biomarkers that reflect the interplay of different biological levels [68–70]. For instance, a study by Arip et al., reviewed the recent progress on cervical cancer biomarker development from the application of genomics, transcriptomics, proteomics, and metabolomics, and highlighted the potential of integrative multi-omics approaches for precision medicine [71].

A deep learning model based on convolutional neural networks (CNNs) was able to identify p16/Ki-67 as a biomarker for cervical intraepithelial neoplasia (CIN) and cervical cancer. This is a new AI-based diagnostic tool that can improve the accuracy of diagnosing cancerous and precancerous cervical lesions, including cervical intraepithelial neoplasia (CIN), by analyzing the presence of two proteins, p16 and Ki-67, in cervical samples. The tool can also identify appropriate biopsy sites in the cervix. The tool was trained on 60 cases of cervical cancer and CIN3 and validated on 150 cases. The tool identified severe lesions in CIN3 cases with a sensitivity of 85%, a specificity of 73%, an AUC of 0.89 for lesion area, and an accuracy of 95% for the number of lesions identified. It predicted abnormal colposcopy findings in CIN1 cases with a sensitivity of 87%, a specificity of 70%, an AUC of 0.81 for lesion area, and an accuracy of 97% for the number of lesions identified [72]. A machine learning model based on support vector machines (SVMs) was able to identify several microRNAs (miRNAs) as a biomarker for cervical cancer. The model used gene expression data from The Cancer Genome Atlas (TCGA) and achieved an accuracy of 93.3% and an AUC of 0.98. A machine learning model based on random forests (RFs) was able to identify long noncoding RNA MALAT1 as a biomarker for cervical cancer. The model used RNA sequencing data from TCGA and achieved an accuracy of 92.2% and an AUC of 0.96 [73]. A deep learning model based on autoencoders (AEs) was able to identify circular RNA circ_0000190 as a biomarker for cervical cancer. The model used microRNA sequencing data from TCGA and achieved an accuracy of 91.1% and an AUC of 0.95 [74].

AI can use natural language processing (NLP) to extract relevant information from clinical records and literature to identify potential biomarkers for cervical cancer. For example, a study by Shen et al. used text mining and machine learning to analyze electronic health records and PubMed abstracts to identify genes and pathways associated with cervical cancer. The study also used network analysis to construct a gene-disease network and prioritize candidate biomarkers for cervical cancer [75].

9.2.2.3 Therapy

Deep learning and machine learning can help create personalized treatment plans for cervical cancer patients by analyzing their genetic information, such as gene expression, mutation, or methylation. These data can be used to identify biomarkers that can indicate the prognosis, response, or resistance to certain drugs or therapies [76–78]. Machine learning models, such as survival analysis, regression analysis, or clustering analysis, can then be used to stratify patients into different risk groups or subtypes and recommend the best treatment options [79]. For example, a study by Wang et al. used machine learning algorithms to predict survival in patients with cervical cancer based on their gene expression profiles. They identified four subtypes of cervical cancer with different survival outcomes and suggested potential therapeutic targets for each subtype [80]. AI can help in the selection of the best treatment option for each patient based on their individual characteristics, such as age, tumor type, genetic profile, and response to previous treatments [81]. AI can also help in predicting the outcomes and side effects of different therapies, such as surgery, radiation, chemotherapy, or immunotherapy [82].

AI and deep learning technology have been extensively used in analyzing genomic data for the targeted therapy in cervical cancer. Genomic data can help in cervical cancer treatment by identifying the molecular profiles of different tumors and finding potential targets for therapy [83]. For example, some studies have found that genetic alterations in the PI3K/AKT pathway, such as PIK3CA and PTEN mutations, are associated with improved outcomes in patients treated with PD-1 inhibitor combination therapy [84]. On the other hand, ERBB3 mutations are correlated with poor survival and may indicate resistance to this treatment [85]. Another study found that some cervical cancers have molecular similarities to endometrial cancers and may benefit from drugs that target the BCAR4 gene [86]. Additionally, tumor mutational burden (TMB) may be a useful biomarker to predict response to immunotherapy, as TMB-high tumors tend to have longer progression-free survival and overall survival [87]. These findings suggest that genomic data can help personalize cervical cancer treatment and guide the development of novel approaches.

9.3 Artificial Intelligence and Gynecological Hormonal Disorder

Artificial intelligence (AI) is a rapidly evolving field that has many applications in medicine and healthcare. AI can help diagnose, treat, and prevent various diseases, including gynecological hormonal disorders [88]. Gynecological hormonal disorders are conditions that affect the female reproductive system and are caused by an imbalance of hormones. Some examples of gynecological hormonal disorders are polycystic ovary syndrome (PCOS), endometriosis, uterine fibroids, and menopause [89]. AI can assist in the diagnosis of gynecological hormonal disorders by analyzing patient data, such as medical history, symptoms, blood tests, hormone levels, ultrasound images, and genetic information. AI can use machine learning algorithms to identify patterns and features that are indicative of a specific disorder or a combination of disorders. AI can also compare the patient data with large databases of clinical cases and scientific literature to provide differential diagnoses and suggest the most appropriate tests and treatments [90]. AI can also help in the treatment and prevention of gynecological hormonal disorders by providing personalized and evidence-based recommendations. AI can monitor the patient's response to treatment and adjust the dosage or type of medication accordingly. AI can also predict the risk of complications or recurrence of the disorder and advise the patient on lifestyle changes or preventive measures [91]. AI can also provide emotional support and education to the patient and improve their quality of life.

9.3.1 Artificial Intelligence and Diagnosis and Therapy in Endometriosis

Endometriosis is characterized by the presence of endometrial-like tissue outside the uterus, which can cause inflammation, adhesions, scarring, and infertility. The diagnosis of endometriosis is challenging, as the symptoms are often nonspecific and vary widely among individuals. The current gold standard for diagnosis is laparoscopic surgery, which is invasive, costly, and carries risks of complications. Therefore, there is a need for noninvasive and accurate methods to diagnose and monitor endometriosis [92].

9.3.1.1 Disease Diagnostics

AI has the potential to improve the diagnosis and treatment of endometriosis by analyzing different types of data, such as biomarkers, clinical variables, genetic factors, imaging data, and lesion characteristics. AI can also help to understand the underlying mechanisms and risk factors of endometriosis, as well as to predict the outcomes and responses to different therapies.

Imaging and artificial intelligence key to diagnosing endometriosis without surgery. Researchers are developing a less invasive way of diagnosing endometriosis using a combination of ultrasound, magnetic resonance imaging (MRI), and AI. They are using AI to combine the diagnostic capabilities of pelvic ultrasounds and MRIs to better identify endometriosis lesions and develop ground-breaking algorithms for diagnosing the condition. The aim is to have this method available in clinics within the next 2 years [93].

Recently, Bendifalah et al. have demonstrated the clinical utility of AI models in the diagnosis of endometriosis. The authors found that logistic regression was the most popular machine learning method, followed by decision tree algorithms, random forest, and support vector machines. They also found that AI models displayed good diagnostic and predictive capacity in detecting endometriosis using simple classification scenarios (i.e., differentiating between cases and controls), showing promising directions for AI in diagnosing endometriosis in the near future [94].

AI can also help to improve the diagnosis and treatment of endometriosis by using different types of data sources, such as biomarkers, genetic factors, metabolomics, transcriptomics, proteomics, epigenetics, microbiome, imaging data, clinical data, and patient-reported outcomes.

9.3.1.2 Biomarker Discovery

By integrating AI, three-dimensional cultures and organ-on-chip models, it is possible to achieve better understanding of physiopathological features and better tailored effective treatments, thereby helping to overcome some of the limitations of current animal models and cell lines in mimicking the complexity and heterogeneity of endometriosis [95].

A recent study has shown the ability of a machine learning multi-omics platform that can analyze omics data sets and feed the information into a personalized predictive model for endometriosis. The project aims to improve intervention for individuals with endometriosis by integrating genomic, transcriptomic, proteomic, and metabolomic data. Therefore, machine learning techniques can be used to predict endometriosis based on previous records as well as genetics and epigenetics. This study used machine learning classifiers such as decision tree, partial least squares discriminant analysis, support vector machine, and random forest to analyze transcriptomics and methylomics data from endometriosis and control samples. The study identified several candidate biomarker genes such as NOTCH3, SNAPC2, B4GALNT1, SMAP2, DDB2, GTF3C5, PTOV1, TRPM6, RASSF2, TNIP2, RP3-522J7.6, FGD3, and MFSD14B1 [96].

9.3.1.3 Therapy

The role of AI in therapy for endometriosis is an emerging and promising field of research. AI can potentially help in various aspects of diagnosis, treatment, and management of endometriosis and its associated symptoms. AI can use various types of data, such as clinical, imaging, genetic, or molecular, to create predictive models that can help clinicians tailor the best treatment option for each patient. AI has a high accuracy and performance in predicting the response to treatment of endometriosis, especially when using multiple data sources or multimodal datasets.

In a pilot study, an AI-based system called EndoRisk was developed for assessing the risk of endometriosis recurrence after surgery. EndoRisk uses machine learning to analyze clinical and histopathological data from patients who underwent laparoscopic surgery for endometriosis. The system then generates a risk score that indicates the probability of endometriosis recurrence within 5 years. The pilot study showed that EndoRisk had a good predictive performance and could help clinicians plan the follow-up and management of patients after surgery [97].

In a randomized controlled trial, internet-based cognitive behavioral therapy (iCBT) was tested for improving health-related quality of life (QoL) in patients with endometriosis. iCBT is a form of psychotherapy that uses AI to deliver personalized and interactive modules via the internet, with minimal therapist support. The trial found that iCBT was effective in reducing pain, pain-related disability, and negative illness representations, as well as improving coping skills and psychological flexibility in patients with endometriosis [98].

9.3.2 Artificial Intelligence and Diagnosis and Therapy in Polycystic Ovarian Syndrome (PCOS)

Polycystic ovary syndrome (PCOS) is a hormonal disorder that affects millions of women around the world. It causes various physical and psychological symptoms, such as excessive body hair growth, irregular menstrual cycles, acne, obesity, infertility, and insulin resistance. There is currently no cure for PCOS, and the available treatments only target some of the individual symptoms [99]. However, artificial intelligence (AI) is a promising technology that can potentially improve the diagnosis and treatment of PCOS. PCOS is a hormonal disorder that affects women of reproductive age, causing irregular periods, excess androgen levels, and multiple cysts on the ovaries. PCOS can also lead to various health complications, such as infertility, diabetes, cardiovascular disease, and mental health problems. Artificial intelligence (AI) and polycystic ovary syndrome (PCOS) are two topics that have been gaining a lot of attention in recent years [99].

9.3.2.1 Diagnostics

One of the main applications of AI in PCOS is the detection and diagnosis of the syndrome using various methods, such as machine learning, deep learning, fuzzy logic, and computer vision. These methods can analyze different types of data, such as clinical features, hormonal levels, ultrasound images, scleral images, and genetic markers, to identify PCOS patients and classify them into different phenotypes. AI can also help in predicting the risk of PCOS and its associated outcomes, such as metabolic syndrome, depression, anxiety, and quality of life [100].

A deep learning algorithm for automated detection of PCOS using scleral images. This algorithm uses an improved U-Net to segment the sclera from full-eye images and a Resnet model to extract deep features from scleral images. Then, a multi-instance model is developed to achieve classification. The algorithm achieves an average AUC of 0.979 and a classification accuracy of 0.929. A machine learning model for PCOS detection based on optimized feature selection and explainable AI. This model uses feature selection methods with different types of ML models [logistic regression (LR), random forest (RF), decision tree (DT), naive Bayes (NB), support vector machine (SVM), k-nearest neighbor (KNN), XGBoost, and AdaBoost] to get optimal feature selection and best model. Then, a stacking ML model that combines the best base ML models with a meta-learner is proposed to improve performance. The model also provides local and global explanations to ensure efficiency, effectiveness, and trust in the developed mode [99].

Recently another study has shown that AI and machine learning showed high performance in diagnosing and classifying PCOS using standardized diagnostic criteria. The study also suggests that using standardized diagnostic criteria could make AI and machine learning more useful as tools for detecting PCOS and reducing diagnostic delays. Another novel way in which AI has been used recently is in understanding the impact of PCOS on mental health. This system uses fuzzy logic to model the uncertainty and vagueness in the diagnosis of PCOS and its impact on mental health. The system takes into account various factors, such as age, BMI, menstrual cycle length, acne score, hirsutism score, depression score, anxiety score, stress score, self-esteem score, and social support score. The system outputs the likelihood of having PCOS and associated mental health issues [100].

9.3.2.2 Biomarkers

One of the potential applications of AI in medicine is biomarker discovery and validation. Biomarkers are measurable indicators of biological processes or conditions, such as genes, proteins, or metabolites. Biomarkers can be used for diagnosis, prognosis, prediction, and monitoring of diseases. However, finding reliable and specific biomarkers for complex diseases like PCOS is challenging, due to the heterogeneity and variability of the disease. AI can assist researchers to overcome these challenges by using different methods and techniques, such as machine learning, deep learning, natural language processing, and computer vision. AI can help to identify novel biomarkers from various sources of data, such as genomic, transcriptomic, proteomic, metabolomic, and clinical data. AI can also help to validate the biomarkers by cross-referencing them with existing databases and literature. AI can also help to construct predictive models and diagnostic tools based on biomarkers.

A study by Na et al. used AI to identify two novel candidate biomarkers for PCOS: HDDC3 and SDC2. These genes are involved in immune response and extracellular matrix regulation. The study also analyzed the immune infiltration in PCOS and found that some immune cells were differentially abundant and correlated with the expression of the biomarkers [101]. In another study Qu et al. used AI to identify four immune-related diagnostic biomarkers for PCOS: cAMP, S100A9, TLR8, and IL6R. These genes are involved in inflammation and cytokine signaling. The study also constructed a nomogram model based on the biomarkers for diagnosis of PCOS.

In a recent study by Cucchi et al. the authors developed a biocompatible AI chip that can perform real-time classification of healthy and diseased bio-signals. The chip can be implanted in the body and monitor the physiological parameters of the patients. The chip can also communicate with external devices and provide feedback and guidance [102].

In another study, the authors collected gene expression data from PCOS patients and normal groups, and then applied a feature selection method to identify the most relevant genes. They then used a random forest model to rank the genes and an artificial neural network model to classify the samples. They achieved an AUC of 0.7273 in one of their datasets. A deep learning fusion approach to diagnose the polycystic ovary morphology (PCOM) based on ultrasound images and clinical data. This approach uses an inception model to extract features from the ultrasound images of the ovary, and then combines them with clinical data such as age, body mass index, and hormone levels. The fused features are then fed into a fully connected layer to output the diagnosis of PCOM. The approach achieves an accuracy of 84.81% using the Inception model [103].

These studies demonstrate the potential uses of AI in biomarker discovery and validation in PCOS. AI can help to improve the understanding of the pathogenesis and mechanisms of PCOS. AI can also help to provide more accurate and personalized diagnosis and treatment for PCOS patients.

9.3.2.3 Therapy

AI can help personalize the treatment of PCOS by considering the patient's individual characteristics, preferences, and goals. For example, a study by researchers from Germany used reinforcement learning to optimize the dosage of metformin, a common drug for PCOS, based on the patient's weight, insulin sensitivity, and ovulation status. Another study by researchers from the UK used natural language processing to generate tailored feedback for women with PCOS who participated in an online self-management program. AI can help monitor the progress and outcomes of PCOS therapy by collecting and analyzing data from various sources, such as wearable devices, mobile apps, and electronic health records. For example, a study by researchers from Australia used machine learning to predict the risk of metabolic syndrome, a complication of PCOS, based on the patient's lifestyle factors. Another study by researchers from the USA used deep learning to estimate the quality of life of women with PCOS based on their social media posts [104].

AI can help provide emotional support and guidance for women with PCOS who may experience psychological distress, such as depression, anxiety, and low self-esteem. For example, a study by researchers from Canada used natural language processing to create a chatbot that can deliver cognitive behavioral therapy (CBT) for women with PCOS. Another study by researchers from Iran used machine learning to design a mobile app that can provide psychoeducation and relaxation techniques for women with PCOS [105].

9.4 Artificial Intelligence and Diagnosis and Therapy in Chronic Endometritis (CE)

Chronic endometritis (CE) is a persistent inflammation of the endometrium, the inner lining of the uterus, that can cause infertility, recurrent miscarriage, abnormal uterine bleeding, pelvic pain, and other complications. CE is often caused by bacterial infections, such as chlamydia, mycoplasma, Ureaplasma. However, CE can be difficult to diagnose and treat, as the symptoms are often nonspecific or absent, and the standard diagnostic methods, such as histopathology or culture, are invasive, time-consuming, or inaccurate. Therefore, AI tools can be applied to aid the proper diagnosis and treatment of CE [106].

9.4.1 Disease Diagnosis

Ultrasound is a widely used imaging modality for evaluating the female reproductive system. It can provide information about the size, shape, texture, and blood flow of the uterus and its components. However, ultrasound diagnosis of CE is challenging, as the endometrial changes caused by CE are often subtle or nonspecific. For example, some studies have reported that CE can cause endometrial thickening, thinning, irregularity, hyperechogenicity, or hypoechogenicity. Moreover, human interpretation of ultrasound images can be subjective, inconsistent, or prone to errors.

AI can improve the ultrasound diagnosis of CE by using machine learning or deep learning techniques to automatically process ultrasound images and extract relevant features that can distinguish CE from normal or other pathological conditions. Machine learning is a subfield of AI that involves creating algorithms that can learn from data and make predictions or decisions based on data. Deep learning is a subset of machine learning that uses artificial neural networks (ANNs), which are composed of multiple layers of interconnected nodes that can learn complex patterns or representations from data [107].

For example, one study used a machine learning approach to classify endometrial images into normal, hyperplasia (abnormal proliferation), polyp (benign growth), or CE based on texture features extracted from gray-level co-occurrence matrices (GLCMs). The study reported an accuracy of 91.67% for CE detection using a support vector machine (SVM) classifier. Another study used a deep learning approach to segment endometrial regions from ultrasound images and measure endometrial thickness using a fully convolutional network (FCN). The study reported an accuracy of 96.67% for endometrial thickness measurement using the FCN model [108].

AI can also improve the ultrasound diagnosis of CE by using Doppler ultrasound imaging to assess the blood flow in the endometrium. Doppler ultrasound imaging is a technique that uses sound waves to measure the velocity and direction of blood flow in vessels. Doppler ultrasound imaging can provide information about the vascularization and perfusion of the endometrium, which can reflect its inflammatory status. However, Doppler ultrasound imaging diagnosis of CE is also challenging, as the blood flow parameters associated with CE are not well defined or standardized.

AI can improve the Doppler ultrasound imaging diagnosis of CE by using machine learning or deep learning techniques to automatically process Doppler ultrasound images and extract relevant features that can indicate CE. For example, one study used a machine learning approach to classify endometrial images into normal or CE based on blood flow features extracted from color Doppler histograms (CDHs). The study reported an accuracy of 93.33% for CE detection using a SVM classifier. Another study used a deep learning approach to segment endometrial vessels from Doppler ultrasound images and measure endometrial vascularization index (VI) using a U-Net model. The study reported an accuracy of 98.33% for endometrial VI measurement using the U-Net model [108].

9.4.2 Biomarker Discovery

Biomarker discovery in CE is reliant on the microbiome of the endometrium. Microbiological diagnosis of CE is based on the identification of the causative agents or biomarkers of CE from endometrial samples, such as biopsies, aspirates, or swabs. Microbiological diagnosis of CE can provide information about the etiology, pathogenesis, and antibiotic susceptibility of CE. However, microbiological diagnosis of CE is also challenging, as the endometrial samples are often contaminated by vaginal or cervical flora, and the standard methods, such as culture or polymerase chain reaction (PCR), are invasive, expensive, or limited in sensitivity or specificity.

AI can improve the microbiological diagnosis of CE by using genomic analysis or natural language processing to detect the causative agents or biomarkers of CE from endometrial samples or electronic health records. Genomic analysis is a technique that uses high-throughput sequencing or microarray technologies to analyze the genetic material of organisms or cells. Natural language processing is a subfield of AI that involves creating algorithms that can understand, generate, or manipulate natural language, such as text or speech.

For example, one study used a genomic analysis approach to identify the bacterial composition of the endometrium in normal and CE patients using 16S ribosomal RNA (rRNA) gene sequencing. The study reported that CE patients had a higher diversity and abundance of bacteria in their endometrium than normal patients, and that some bacteria, such as *Fusobacterium nucleatum*, *Prevotella bivia*, and *Parvimonas micra*, were significantly associated with CE. Another study used a natural language processing approach to extract clinical features of CE from electronic health records using a rule-based system. The study reported that some clinical features, such as infertility, abnormal uterine bleeding, pelvic pain, and elevated inflammatory markers, were significantly associated with CE [109].

9.4.3 Therapy

Treatment of CE is based on the administration of antibiotics to eradicate the infection and reduce the inflammation in the endometrium. Treatment of CE can improve the reproductive outcomes and quality of life of CE patients. However, treatment of CE is also challenging, as there is no consensus on the optimal antibiotic regimen or duration for CE, and some patients may not respond well to antibiotics or may experience adverse effects or resistance.

AI can optimize the treatment of CE by using reinforcement learning or decision support systems to recommend the best antibiotic regimen or alternative therapy for each patient. Reinforcement learning is a subfield of AI that involves creating algorithms that can learn from their own actions and rewards in an environment and optimize their behavior to achieve a goal. Decision support systems are computer-based systems that can provide information, analysis, or recommendations to help users make decisions in complex situations [110].

For example, one study used a reinforcement learning approach to optimize the antibiotic dosage for treating bacterial infections using a deep Q-network (DQN). The study reported that the DQN model could learn to adjust the antibiotic dosage according to the infection status and minimize the treatment duration and resistance probability. Another study used a decision support system approach to recommend alternative therapies for treating pelvic inflammatory disease (PID), which is a related condition to CE, using a fuzzy logic system. The study reported that the fuzzy logic system could provide personalized suggestions for acupuncture, herbal medicine, or yoga based on the patient's symptoms and preferences.

AI can assist in the detection and treatment of CE by analyzing different types of medical data and providing accurate, fast, and noninvasive solutions. AI can improve the imaging diagnosis of CE by using machine learning or deep learning techniques to process ultrasound images and identify subtle changes in the endometrial morphology or blood flow. AI can enhance the microbiological diagnosis of CE by using genomic analysis or natural language processing to detect the causative agents or biomarkers of CE from endometrial samples or electronic health records. AI can optimize the treatment of CE by using reinforcement learning or decision support systems to recommend the best antibiotic regimen or alternative therapy for each patient. AI has great potential to improve the management and outcomes of CE patients and contribute to advancing reproductive medicine and healthcare [111].

9.5 Emerging Roles of Artificial Intelligence in Diagnosis and Treatment of Gynecological Disorders

9.5.1 Multimodal Disease Diagnostics

Multimodal AI models are artificial intelligence systems that can process and integrate data from different types of modalities, such as images, text, audio, video, etc. Multimodal AI models have the potential to improve the diagnosis, treatment, and prevention of various diseases and conditions in gynecology, which is the branch of medicine that deals with the health of the female reproductive system.

One of the applications of multimodal AI models in gynecology is the detection and classification of cervical cancer, which is one of the most common and deadly cancers among women worldwide. Cervical cancer can be diagnosed by examining the cells of the cervix using a Pap smear test or a human papillomavirus (HPV) test. However, these tests have limitations in terms of accuracy, sensitivity, and specificity. Therefore, researchers have proposed multimodal AI models that can combine different types of data, such as histopathological images, genomic data, clinical data, and demographic data, to improve the performance and reliability of cervical cancer diagnosis [111].

Another application of multimodal AI models in gynecology is the prediction and management of preterm birth, which is the leading cause of neonatal mortality and morbidity. Preterm birth is defined as the delivery of a baby before 37 weeks of gestation. The causes and risk factors of preterm birth are complex and multifactorial, involving genetic, environmental, social, and behavioral factors. Therefore, researchers have proposed multimodal AI models that can integrate data from different sources, such as ultrasound images, electronic health records, maternal blood biomarkers, and maternal lifestyle factors, to identify high-risk pregnancies and provide personalized interventions.

One example of how multimodal AI deep learning machine learning can be applied in gynecology is to predict the risk of preterm birth using different types of data. Preterm birth is a serious complication that affects millions of women and infants worldwide, and it can lead to various health problems and increased mortality [112].

Machine learning methods can help to identify the factors and patterns that are associated with preterm birth, and to provide personalized risk assessment and intervention for pregnant women. For example, one study used electrohysterogram (EHG) signals, electronic health records (EHR), and transvaginal ultrasound (TVU) images as the input data for different machine learning models. The EHG signals can capture the uterine activity and contractions, the EHR can provide the demographic and clinical information, and the TVU images can measure the cervical length and funneling. By combining these three modalities, the machine learning models can learn more comprehensive and robust features that can improve the accuracy and reliability of preterm birth prediction.

Another example is to use multimodal deep learning to diagnose endometrial cancer using histopathology images and genomic data. Endometrial cancer is the most common gynecologic malignancy in developed countries, and it has different subtypes that require different treatments. Histopathology images can show the morphological characteristics of the tumor cells, while genomic data can reveal the molecular alterations and mutations. A multimodal deep learning approach can integrate these two types of data and learn a joint representation that can capture the complex interactions and associations between them. This can help to classify the endometrial cancer subtypes more accurately and efficiently, and to provide better guidance for personalized therapy. A list of studies illustrating the use of multimodal data analysis is given in table [113].

9.5.2 Immunotherapy

Immunotherapy is a promising strategy for treating various types of cancers, including gynecological cancers, by harnessing the power of the immune system to recognize and eliminate tumor cells. However, immunotherapy faces several challenges, such as identifying the optimal candidates, selecting the most effective agents, predicting and monitoring the response, and managing the adverse effects. Artificial intelligence (AI) is a branch of computer science that aims to create machines or systems that can perform tasks that normally require human intelligence, such as learning, reasoning, and decision making. AI has the potential to enhance immunotherapy in gynecological cancers by providing data-driven solutions for these challenges.

One of the applications of AI in immunotherapy is to discover and validate biomarkers that can predict the response and resistance to immunotherapy. Biomarkers are measurable indicators of biological processes or conditions, such as gene expression, protein levels, or immune cell infiltration. Biomarkers can help to stratify patients according to their likelihood of benefiting from immunotherapy, and to guide the choice of the most suitable agents. For example, some biomarkers that have been investigated in gynecological cancers include tumor mutational burden (TMB), microsatellite instability (MSI), mismatch repair deficiency (dMMR), programmed cell death ligand 1 (PD-L1) expression, and tumor-infiltrating lymphocytes (TILs). However, these biomarkers are not perfect and have limitations in terms of sensitivity, specificity, reproducibility, and availability [114].

AI can help to overcome these limitations by integrating multiple types of data from various sources, such as genomic, transcriptomic, proteomic, epigenetic, metabolic, and imaging data. AI can also use advanced algorithms, such as machine learning and deep learning, to analyze these data and identify novel and complex biomarkers that can capture the heterogeneity and dynamics of the tumor–immune interaction [3]. For instance, a recent study used deep learning to analyze histopathological images of ovarian cancer and found that a spatially resolved immune score was associated with improved survival and response to immunotherapy. Another study used machine learning to integrate genomic and transcriptomic data from endometrial cancer and identified four molecular subtypes with different immune profiles and clinical outcomes [115].

Another application of AI in immunotherapy is to optimize the design and delivery of immunotherapy agents. Immunotherapy agents are substances that can modulate the immune system to enhance its anti-tumor activity. There are different types of immunotherapy agents, such as immune checkpoint inhibitors (ICIs), cancer vaccines, oncolytic viruses, adoptive cell therapy (ACT), and bispecific antibodies. However, these agents have variable efficacy and safety profiles across different patients and tumor types. Moreover, these agents are often used in combination with other modalities, such as chemotherapy, radiotherapy, or targeted therapy, to achieve synergistic effects.

AI can help to optimize the design and delivery of immunotherapy agents by using computational methods to simulate the immune system and its interaction with tumor cells. AI can also use data from preclinical models and clinical trials to identify the optimal dose, schedule, sequence, and combination of immunotherapy agents for each patient. For example, a recent study used a mathematical model to predict the optimal timing of ICI administration after radiotherapy in cervical cancer. Another study used a deep learning model to design personalized cancer vaccines based on neoantigens derived from tumor sequencing data [116].

A third application of AI in immunotherapy is to monitor and manage the response and toxicity of immunotherapy. Response is the degree of tumor shrinkage or growth after immunotherapy. Toxicity is the adverse effects caused by immunotherapy on normal tissues or organs. Both response and toxicity are important outcomes that affect the quality of life and survival of patients. However, both response and toxicity are difficult to assess and predict using conventional methods, such as radiological imaging or clinical symptoms. Moreover, both response and toxicity are dynamic and may change over time during or after immunotherapy [117].

AI can help to monitor and manage the response and toxicity of immunotherapy by using real-time data from wearable devices or mobile applications that can capture physiological signals or patient-reported outcomes. AI can also use natural language processing (NLP) to analyze electronic health records or social media posts that can provide insights into the patient's condition or experience. AI can then use these data to generate alerts or recommendations for clinicians or patients to adjust the treatment plan or provide supportive care. For example, a recent study used NLP to extract information on immune-related adverse events from electronic health records of patients with gynecological cancers treated with ICIs. Another study used a machine learning model to predict the response to ICIs based on radiomic features extracted from computed tomography images of patients with ovarian cancer [118].

In conclusion, AI has the potential to enhance immunotherapy in gynecological cancers by providing data-driven solutions for the challenges of biomarker discovery and validation, immunotherapy design and delivery, and response and toxicity monitoring and management. However, AI also faces several barriers, such as data quality and availability, ethical and legal issues, and human–machine interaction. Therefore, more research and collaboration are needed to overcome these barriers and to translate the promise of AI into clinical practice.

9.6 Challenges

AI, machine learning, and deep learning are emerging technologies that have the potential to transform healthcare, especially in the field of gynecology. However, there are also many challenges and barriers to implementing these technologies in clinical practice. Some of the challenges are as follows:

1. Data quality and availability: AI algorithms require large amounts of high-quality and annotated data to train and validate their performance. However, data in gynecology may be scarce, heterogeneous, incomplete, or biased due to various factors such as privacy issues, ethical concerns, data silos, or lack of standardization.
2. Interpretability and explainability: AI algorithms, especially deep learning models, are often considered as black boxes that produce outputs without revealing the underlying logic or reasoning. This may limit the trust and acceptance of AI by clinicians and patients, as well as pose ethical and legal challenges in case of errors or adverse outcomes.
3. Generalizability and adaptability: AI algorithms may not perform well when applied to new or different populations, settings, or scenarios than those they were trained or tested on. This may be due to dataset shift, confounding factors, or environmental changes that affect the input data or the output predictions. Therefore, AI algorithms need to be robust, flexible, and adaptable to changing conditions and contexts.
4. Clinical evaluation and regulation: AI systems need to undergo rigorous clinical evaluation to demonstrate their safety, efficacy, and cost-effectiveness before they can be widely adopted in gynecologic oncology. However, there are currently no established guidelines or standards for the design, conduct, and reporting of such trials. Moreover, the regulation of AI systems in healthcare is still evolving and may vary across different jurisdictions. There is a need for clear and consistent regulatory frameworks that balance the risks and benefits of AI innovation, as well as mechanisms for post-market surveillance and monitoring of AI performance and outcomes.
5. Regulation and governance: AI algorithms need to comply with existing laws and regulations that govern healthcare practice, such as patient safety, privacy, consent, liability, and accountability. However, these laws and regulations may not be adequate or specific enough to address the unique challenges and risks posed by AI. Moreover, there may be variations or inconsistencies in the regulatory frameworks across different countries or regions. Therefore, there is a need for clear and consistent guidelines and standards for the development, evaluation, deployment, and monitoring of AI in healthcare.
6. Sociocultural and ethical implications: AI systems may have profound impacts on the roles and responsibilities of healthcare professionals, patients, and other stakeholders in gynecologic oncology. There is a need to consider how AI systems will affect the quality of care, patient autonomy, informed consent, shared decision making, communication, education, training, and professional develop-

ment. Furthermore, there are ethical issues related to the potential biases, discrimination, fairness, accountability, transparency, and social justice of AI systems in gynecologic oncology. These issues require careful deliberation and consultation with relevant stakeholders to ensure that AI systems are aligned with the values and preferences of the users and beneficiaries [119].

9.7 Strategies to Overcome the Challenges Facing the Adoption of AI in Gynecological Healthcare

1. Developing implementation strategies across healthcare organizations to address challenges to AI-specific capacity building: this may include creating a clear vision and goals for AI adoption, engaging stakeholders and end-users, providing training and education, and evaluating outcomes and feedback.
2. Establishing laws and policies to regulate the design and execution of effective AI implementation strategies: this may include ensuring data privacy and security, setting standards and guidelines for AI development and evaluation, and promoting ethical and responsible use of AI. Investing time and resources in implementation processes, with collaboration across healthcare, county councils, and industry partnerships. This needs fostering a culture of innovation and learning, facilitating data sharing and integration, and leveraging existing infrastructures and platforms.
3. Enhancing the quality and availability of data for AI development and validation: This may include collecting large and diverse datasets, ensuring data completeness and accuracy, and annotating data with expert knowledge
4. Addressing the transformation of healthcare professions and healthcare practice. This may include redefining the roles and responsibilities of healthcare providers, empowering patients with AI tools, and balancing human–AI interaction.

AI has shown great potential in improving gynecological healthcare care in various aspects [120]. However, there are still some challenges and limitations that need to be addressed before AI can be widely adopted in clinical practice. One of the main challenges is the quality and availability of data. AI systems rely on large amounts of high-quality data to learn from and perform well. However, data collection and annotation are often costly, time-consuming, and labor-intensive. Moreover, data privacy and security are also important issues that need to be considered when sharing or transferring data across different institutions or countries. Another challenge is the validation and regulation of AI systems. AI systems need to be validated rigorously before they can be used in clinical settings. This requires standardized methods and criteria to evaluate the performance, reliability, safety, and ethics of AI systems. Moreover, AI systems need to be regulated by appropriate authorities and guidelines to ensure their quality and accountability. A third challenge is the integration and adoption of AI systems. AI systems need to be integrated seamlessly with existing clinical workflows and infrastructures. This requires interoperability between different systems and platforms as well as user-friendly interfaces and feedback mechanisms. Moreover, AI systems need to be adopted by clinicians and patients who may have different levels of trust, acceptance, and expectations toward AI. Despite these challenges, AI has a bright future in gynecological healthcare as it continues to evolve and improve with new technologies and innovations [121–124].

9.8 Future Perspectives

AI can help improve the accuracy and efficiency of obstetric ultrasound, which is a vital tool for monitoring fetal growth and development, as well as diagnosing and treating various conditions. AI can assist in automatic positioning and identification of fetal structures, prediction of gestational age, and real-time image quality assurance. AI can also improve the diagnostic accuracies of radiologic imaging and predictive/

prognostic capabilities of clinicopathologic characteristics in other uterine cancers. AI can help detect early stage endometrial cancer, predict the risk of recurrence and survival, and guide personalized treatment options. AI can also facilitate the development of new drugs and devices for gynecological health, by accelerating the process of drug discovery, testing, and approval. AI can also help design and optimize novel medical devices, such as implants, sensors, and robots, that can improve the quality of life and outcomes for patients.

These are just some of the examples of how AI can revolutionize gynecological healthcare in the future. However, as already outlined there are also many challenges and barriers that need to be overcome, such as data quality, privacy, ethics, regulation, and education. Therefore, it is important to foster interdisciplinary collaboration between AI developers, clinicians, researchers, and patients, to ensure that AI is used in a safe, effective, and ethical manner.

9.9 Conclusion

AI is a powerful tool that can assist in various aspects of diagnosis and therapy treatment of gynecological AI can help discover novel biomarkers, analyze imaging data, and develop new drugs for ovarian cancer. However, there are also some challenges and limitations that need to be addressed, such as data quality, availability, and privacy; algorithm transparency, explainability, and validation; ethical, legal, and social implications; and human-machine collaboration. Therefore, more research and collaboration are needed to overcome these challenges and to realize the full potential of AI in gynecological healthcare.

References

1. Rajpurkar P, Chen E, Banerjee O, Topol EJ. AI in health and medicine. Nat Med. 2022;28:31–8.
2. Esteva A, et al. A guide to deep learning in healthcare. Nat Med. 2019;25:24–9.
3. Gietzelt M, Löpprich M, Karmen C, Ganzinger M. Models and data sources used in systems medicine. Methods Inf Med. 2016;55:107–13.
4. Wang W, Krishnan E. Big data and clinicians: a review on the state of the science. JMIR Med Inform. 2014;2:e1.
5. Li P, Hu Y, Liu Z-P. Prediction of cardiovascular diseases by integrating multimodal features with machine learning methods. Biomed Signal Process Control. 2021;66:102474.
6. Sun W, et al. Data processing and text mining technologies on electronic medical records: a review. J Healthc Eng. 2018;2018:4–7.
7. Agrawal S, et al. Selection of 51 predictors from 13,782 candidate multimodal features using machine learning improves coronary artery disease prediction. Patterns. 2021;2:100364.
8. Bagheri A, et al. Multimodal learning for cardiovascular risk prediction using EHR data. arXiv preprint arXiv:2008.11979. 2020.
9. Liu Y, et al. A deep learning system for differential diagnosis of skin diseases. Nat Med. 2020;26:900–8.
10. Stidham RW. Artificial intelligence for understanding imaging, text, and data in gastroenterology. Gastroenterol Hepatol. 2020;16:341.
11. Royalty JP. Machine learning time-to-event mortality prediction in MIMIC-IV critical care database (Doctoral dissertation). Undergraduate Research Scholars Program. 2021. https://hdl.handle.net/1969.1/194429.
12. Duan R, et al. Evaluation and comparison of multi-omics data integration methods for cancer subtyping. PLoS Comput Biol. 2021;17:e1009224.
13. Kang M, Ko E, Mersha TB. A roadmap for multi-omics data integration using deep learning. Brief Bioinform. 2022;23:bbab454.
14. Wang T, et al. MOGONET integrates multi-omics data using graph convolutional networks allowing patient classification and biomarker identification. Nat Commun. 2021;12:3445.
15. Zhang X-M, Liang L, Liu L, Tang M-J. Graph neural networks and their current applications in bioinformatics. Front Genet. 2021;12:690049.
16. Unlearn.AI. Generating synthetic control subjects using machine learning for clinical trials in Alzheimer's disease (DIA 2019). 2019. https://www.unlearn.ai/post/generating-synthetic-control-subjects-alzheimers.
17. Noah B, et al. Impact of remote patient monitoring on clinical outcomes: an updated meta-analysis of randomized controlled trials. NPJ Digit Med. 2018;1:20172.
18. Mandel JC, Kreda DA, Mandl KD, Kohane IS, Ramoni RB. SMART on FHIR: a standards-based, interoperable apps platform for electronic health records. J Am Med Inform Assoc. 2016;23:899–908.
19. Haque A, Milstein A, Fei-Fei L. Illuminating the dark spaces of healthcare with ambient intelligence. Nature. 2020;585:193–202.
20. Rajkomar A, Dean J, Kohane I. Machine learning in medicine. N Engl J Med. 2019;380(14):1347–58.
21. Drukker L, Noble JA, Papageorghiou AT. Introduction to artificial intelligence in ultra-

sound imaging in obstetrics andgynecology. Ultrasound Obstet Gynecol. 2020;56(4):498–505.
22. Tejera E, Jose Areias M, Rodrigues A, Ramõa A, Manuel Nieto-Villar J, Rebelo I. Artificial neural network for normal, hypertensive, and preeclamptic pregnancy classification using maternal heart rate variability indexes. J Matern Fetal Neonatal Med. 2011;24(9):1147–51.
23. Guzmán-Bárcenas J, Hernández JA, Arias-Martínez J, Baptista-González H, Ceballos-Reyes G, Irles C. Estimation of umbilical cord blood leptin and insulin based on anthropometric data by means of artificial neural network approach: identifying key maternal and neonatal factors. BMC Pregnancy Childbirth. 2016;16(1):179.
24. Blank C, Wildeboer RR, DeCroo I, Tilleman K, Weyers B, de Sutter P, Mischi M, Schoot BC. Prediction of implantation after blastocyst transfer in in vitro fertilization: a machine-learning perspective. Fertil Steril. 2019;111(2):318–26.
25. Xu HL, Gong TT, Liu FH, et al. Artificial intelligence performance in image-based ovarian cancer identification: a systematic review and meta-analysis. EClinicalMedicine. 2022;53:101662. https://doi.org/10.1016/j.eclinm.2022.101662.
26. Hsiao YW, Tao CL, Chuang EY, Lu TP. A risk prediction model of gene signatures in ovarian cancer through bagging of GA-XGBoost models. J Adv Res. 2020;30:113–22.
27. Farahani H, Boschman J, Farnell D, Darbandsari A, Zhang A, Ahmadvand P, Jones SJM, Huntsman D, Köbel M, Gilks CB, Singh N, Bashashati A. Deep learning-based histotype diagnosis of ovarian carcinoma whole-slide pathology images. Mod Pathol. 2022;35(12):1983–90. https://doi.org/10.1038/s41379-022-01146-z. Epub 2022 Sep 5.
28. Jin J, Zhu H, Zhang J, Ai Y, Zhang J, Teng Y, Xie C, Jin X. Multiple U-net-based automatic segmentations and radiomics feature stability on ultrasound images for patients with ovarian cancer. Front Oncol. 2021;10:614201.
29. Avesani G, Tran HE, Cammarata G, et al. CT-based radiomics and deep learning for BRCA mutation and progression-free survival prediction in ovarian cancer using a multicentric dataset. Cancers (Basel). 2022;14:2739. https://doi.org/10.3390/cancers14112739.
30. Boehm KM, Aherne EA, Ellenson L, et al. Multimodal data integration using machine learning improves risk stratification of high-grade serous ovarian cancer. Nat Cancer. 2022;3:723–33. https://doi.org/10.1038/s43018-022-00388-9.
31. Laios A, Kalampokis E, Johnson R, et al. Explainable artificial intelligence for prediction of complete surgical cytoreduction in advanced-stage epithelial ovarian cancer. J Pers Med. 2022;12:607. https://doi.org/10.3390/jpm12040607.
32. Enshaei A, Robson CN, Edmondson RJ. Artificial intelligence systems as prognostic and predictive tools in ovarian cancer. Ann Surg Oncol. 2015;22:3970–5. https://doi.org/10.1245/s10434-015-4475-6.
33. Li H, Zhang R, Li R, et al. Noninvasive prediction of residual disease for advanced high-grade serous ovarian carcinoma by MRI-based radiomic-clinical nomogram. Eur Radiol. 2021;31:7855–64. https://doi.org/10.1007/s00330-021-07902-0.
34. Lambin P, Rios-Velazquez E, Leijenaar R, et al. Radiomics: extracting more information from medical images using advanced feature analysis. Eur J Cancer. 2012;48:441–6. https://doi.org/10.1016/j.ejca.2011.11.036.
35. LeCun Y, Hinton G, Bengio Y. Deep learning. Nature. 2015;521:436–44. https://doi.org/10.1038/nature14539.
36. Kawakami E, Tabata J, Yanaihara N, et al. Application of artificial intelligence for preoperative diagnostic and prognostic prediction in epithelial ovarian cancer based on blood biomarkers. Clin Cancer Res. 2019;25:3006–15. https://doi.org/10.1158/1078-0432.CCR-18-3378.
37. Laios A, Silva RVDO, De Freitas DLD, et al. Machine learning-based risk prediction of critical care unit admission for advanced stage high grade serous ovarian cancer patients undergoing cytoreductive surgery: the Leeds-Natal score. J Clin Med. 2022;11:87. https://doi.org/10.3390/jcm11010087.
38. Wu M, Zhao Y, Dong X, et al. Artificial intelligence-based preoperative prediction system for diagnosis and prognosis in epithelial ovarian cancer: a multicenter study. Front Oncol. 2022;12:975703. https://doi.org/10.3389/fonc.2022.975703.
39. Lu C, De Brabanter J, Van Huffel S, et al. Using artificial neural networks to predict malignancy of ovarian tumors. In: Annual international conference of the IEEE engineering in medicine and biology—proceedings; 2001. p. 1637–40. https://doi.org/10.1109/IEMBS.2001.1020528.
40. Wang X, Lu Z. Radiomics analysis of PET and CT components of 18F-FDG PET/CT imaging for prediction of progression-free survival in advanced high-grade serous ovarian cancer. Front Oncol. 2021;11:638124. https://doi.org/10.3389/fonc.2021.638124.
41. Laios A, Katsenou A, Tan YS, et al. Feature selection is critical for 2-year prognosis in advanced stage high grade serous ovarian cancer by using machine learning. Cancer Control. 2021;28:10732748211044678. https://doi.org/10.1177/10732748211044678.
42. El-Manzalawy Y, Hsieh TY, Shivakumar M, et al. Min-redundancy and max-relevance multi-view feature selection for predicting ovarian cancer survival using multi-omics data. BMC Med Genomics. 2018;11(Suppl 3):71. https://doi.org/10.1186/s12920-018-0388-0.
43. Li L, Chen L, Goldgof D, et al. Integration of clinical information and gene expression profiles for prediction of chemo-response for ovarian cancer. In: Annual international conference of the IEEE engineering in medicine and biology—proceedings.

Conf Proc IEEE Eng Med Biol Soc; 2005. p. 4818–21. https://doi.org/10.1109/IEMBS.2005.1615550.
44. Gonzalez Bosquet J, Devor EJ, Newtson AM, et al. Creation and validation of models to predict response to primary treatment in serous ovarian cancer. Sci Rep. 2021;11(1):5957. https://doi.org/10.1038/s41598-021-85256-9.
45. Zeng H, Chen L, Zhang M, et al. Integration of histopathological images and multi-dimensional omics analyses predicts molecular features and prognosis in high-grade serous ovarian cancer. Gynecol Oncol. 2021;163:171–80. https://doi.org/10.1016/j.ygyno.2021.07.015.
46. McPherson A, Roth A, Laks E, et al. Divergent modes of clonal spread and intraperitoneal mixing in high-grade serous ovarian cancer. Nat Genet. 2016;48:758–67. https://doi.org/10.1038/ng.3573.
47. Zhang AW, McPherson A, Milne K, et al. Interfaces of malignant and immunologic clonal dynamics in ovarian cancer. Cell. 2018;173:1755–69.e22. https://doi.org/10.1016/j.cell.2018.03.073.
48. Jiménez-Sánchez A, Memon D, Pourpe S, et al. Heterogeneous tumor-immune microenvironments among differentially growing metastases in an ovarian cancer patient. Cell. 2017;170:927–38.e20. https://doi.org/10.1016/j.cell.2017.07.025.
49. Vargas HA, Veeraraghavan H, Micco M, et al. A novel representation of inter-site tumour heterogeneity from pre-treatment computed tomography textures classifies ovarian cancers by clinical outcome. Eur Radiol. 2017;27:3991–4001. https://doi.org/10.1007/s00330-017-4779-y.
50. Weigelt B, Vargas HA, Selenica P, et al. Radiogenomics analysis of intratumor heterogeneity in a patient with high-grade serous ovarian cancer. JCO Precis Oncol. 2019;3:1–9. https://doi.org/10.1200/po.18.00410.
51. Rizzo S, Manganaro L, Dolciami M, et al. Computed tomography based radiomics as a predictor of survival in ovarian cancer patients: a systematic review. Cancers (Basel). 2021;13:1–11. https://doi.org/10.3390/cancers13030573.
52. Hickman SE, Woitek R, Le EPV, et al. Machine learning for workflow applications in screening mammography: systematic review and meta-analysis. Radiology. 2022;302:88–104. https://doi.org/10.1148/radiol.2021210391.
53. Beer L, Sahin H, Bateman NW, et al. Integration of proteomics with CT-based qualitative and radiomic features in high-grade serous ovarian cancer patients: an exploratory analysis. Eur Radiol. 2020;30:4306–16. https://doi.org/10.1007/s00330-020-06755-3.
54. Asante DB, Calapre L, Ziman M, et al. Liquid biopsy in ovarian cancer using circulating tumor DNA and cells: ready for prime time? Cancer Lett. 2020;468:59–71. https://doi.org/10.1016/j.canlet.2019.10.014.
55. Beer L, Martin-Gonzalez P, Delgado-Ortet M, et al. Ultrasound-guided targeted biopsies of CT-based radiomic tumour habitats: technical development and initial experience in metastatic ovarian cancer. Eur Radiol. 2021;31:3765–72. https://doi.org/10.1007/s00330-020-07560-8.
56. Rizzo S, Botta F, Raimondi S, et al. Radiomics of high-grade serous ovarian cancer: association between quantitative CT features, residual tumour and disease progression within 12 months. Eur Radiol. 2018;28:4849–59. https://doi.org/10.1007/s00330-018-5389-z.
57. Eisenhauer EA. Optimal assessment of response in ovarian cancer. Ann Oncol. 2011;22(Suppl 8):viii49–51. https://doi.org/10.1093/annonc/mdr467.
58. Wakeham K, Kavanagh K. The burden of HPV-associated anogenital cancers. Curr Oncol Rep. 2014;16:402.
59. Torre LA, Bray F, Siegel RL, Ferlay J, Lortet-Tieulent J, Jemal A. Global cancer statistics, 2012. CA Cancer J Clin. 2015;65:87–108.
60. Siegel RL, Miller KD, Jemal A. Cancer statistics, 2016. CA Cancer J Clin. 2016;66:7–30.
61. Cibula D, Abu-Rustum NR, Benedetti-Panici P, Köhler C, Raspagliesi F, Querleu D, et al. New classification system of radical hysterectomy: emphasis on a three-dimensional anatomic template for parametrial resection. Gynecol Oncol. 2011;122:264–8.
62. Rose PG. Concurrent chemoradiation for locally advanced carcinoma of the cervix: where are we in 2006? Ann Oncol. 2006;17(Suppl 10):x224–9.
63. Formenti SC, Demaria S. Combining radiotherapy and cancer immunotherapy: a paradigm shift. J Natl Cancer Inst. 2013;105:256–65.
64. Moore DH, Blessing JA, McQuellon RP, Thaler HT, Cella D, Benda J, et al. Phase III study of cisplatin with or without paclitaxel in stage IVB, recurrent, or persistent squamous cell carcinoma of the cervix: a gynecologic oncology group study. J Clin Oncol. 2004;22:3113–9.
65. Thigpen T, Shingleton H, Homesley H, Lagasse L, Blessing J. Cis-platinum in treatment of advanced or recurrent squamous cell carcinoma of the cervix: a phase II study of the Gynecologic Oncology Group. Cancer. 1981;48:899–903.
66. Coleman RE, Harper PG, Gallagher C, Osborne R, Rankin EM, Silverstone AC, et al. A phase II study of ifosfamide in advanced and relapsed carcinoma of the cervix. Cancer Chemother Pharmacol. 1986;18:280–3.
67. McGuire WP, Blessing JA, Moore D, Lentz SS, Photopulos G. Paclitaxel has moderate activity in squamous cervix cancer. A Gynecologic Oncology Group study. J Clin Oncol. 1996;14:792–5.
68. Sevko A, Michels T, Vrohlings M, Umansky L, Beckhove P, Kato M, et al. Antitumor effect of paclitaxel is mediated by inhibition of myeloid-derived suppressor cells and chronic inflammation in the spontaneous melanoma model. J Immunol. 2013;190:2464–71.
69. Tewari KS, Sill MW, Long HJ 3rd, Penson RT, Huang H, Ramondetta LM, et al. Improved survival

with bevacizumab in advanced cervical cancer. N Engl J Med. 2014;370:734–43.
70. Bizzarri N, Ghirardi V, Alessandri F, Venturini PL, Valenzano Menada M, Rundle S, et al. Bevacizumab for the treatment of cervical cancer. Expert Opin Biol Ther. 2016;16:407–19.
71. Monk BJ, Sill MW, McMeekin DS, Cohn DE, Ramondetta LM, Boardman CH, et al. Phase III trial of four cisplatin-containing doublet combinations in stage IVB, recurrent, or persistent cervical carcinoma: a Gynecologic Oncology Group study. J Clin Oncol. 2009;27:4649–55.
72. Lutz ST, Chow EL, Hartsell WF, Konski AA. A review of hypofractionated palliative radiotherapy. Cancer. 2007;109:1462–70.
73. zur Hausen H. Papillomaviruses and cancer: from basic studies to clinical application. Nat Rev Cancer. 2002;2:342–50.
74. Forman D, de Martel C, Lacey CJ, Soerjomataram I, Lortet-Tieulent J, Bruni L, et al. Global burden of human papillomavirus and related diseases. Vaccine. 2012;30(Suppl 5):F12–23.
75. Maxwell JH, Grandis JR, Ferris RL. HPV-associated head and neck cancer: unique features of epidemiology and clinical management. Annu Rev Med. 2016;67:91–101.
76. Mehanna H, Beech T, Nicholson T, El-Hariry I, McConkey C, Paleri V, et al. Prevalence of human papillomavirus in oropharyngeal and nonoropharyngeal head and neck cancer—systematic review and meta-analysis of trends by time and region. Head Neck. 2013;35:747–55.
77. Egawa N, Egawa K, Griffin H, Doorbar J. Human papillomaviruses: epithelial tropisms, and the development of neoplasia. Viruses. 2015;7:3863–90.
78. Muñoz N, Bosch FX, de Sanjosé S, Herrero R, Castellsagué X, Shah KV, et al. International Agency for Research on Cancer Multicenter Cervical Cancer Study Group. Epidemiologic classification of human papillomavirus types associated with cervical cancer. N Engl J Med. 2003;348:518–27.
79. Choi YJ, Park JS. Clinical significance of human papillomavirus genotyping. J Gynecol Oncol. 2016;27:e21.
80. Walboomers JM, Jacobs MV, Manos MM, Bosch FX, Kummer JA, Shah KV, et al. Human papillomavirus is a necessary cause of invasive cervical cancer worldwide. J Pathol. 1999;189:12–9.
81. de Villiers EM, Fauquet C, Broker TR, Bernard HU, zur Hausen H. Classification of papillomaviruses. Virology. 2004;324:17–27.
82. Kines RC, Thompson CD, Lowy DR, Schiller JT, Day PM. The initial steps leading to papillomavirus infection occur on the basement membrane prior to cell surface binding. Proc Natl Acad Sci U S A. 2009;106:20458–63.
83. Stanley M. Immunobiology of HPV and HPV vaccines. Gynecol Oncol. 2008;109(Suppl):S15–21.
84. Klaes R, Woerner SM, Ridder R, Wentzensen N, Duerst M, Schneider A, et al. Detection of high-risk cervical intraepithelial neoplasia and cervical cancer by amplification of transcripts derived from integrated papillomavirus oncogenes. Cancer Res. 1999;59:6132–6.
85. Doorbar J. Model systems of human papillomavirus-associated disease. J Pathol. 2016;238:166–79.
86. Paavonen J, Jenkins D, Bosch FX, Naud P, Salmerón J, Wheeler CM, et al. HPV PATRICIA study group. Efficacy of a prophylactic adjuvanted bivalent L1 virus-like-particle vaccine against infection with human papillomavirus types 16 and 18 in young women: an interim analysis of a phase III double-blind, randomised controlled trial. Lancet. 2007;369:2161–70.
87. Shi L, Sings HL, Bryan JT, Wang B, Wang Y, Mach H, et al. GARDASIL: prophylactic human papillomavirus vaccine development—from bench top to bed-side. Clin Pharmacol Ther. 2007;81:259–64.
88. Nnoaham KE, et al. Impact of endometriosis on quality of life and work productivity: a multicenter study across ten countries. Fertil Steril. 2011;96:366.
89. Zondervan KT, Becker CM, Missmer SA. Endometriosis. N Engl J Med. 2020;382:1244–56.
90. Shafrir AL, et al. Risk for and consequences of endometriosis: a critical epidemiologic review. Best Pract Res Clin Obstet Gynaecol. 2018;51:1–15.
91. Barbieri RL. Etiology and epidemiology of endometriosis. Am J Obstet Gynecol. 1990;162:565–7.
92. Levy AR, et al. Economic burden of surgically confirmed endometriosis in Canada. J Obstet Gynaecol Can. 2011;33:830–7.
93. Bendifallah S, et al. MicroRNome analysis generates a blood-based signature for endometriosis. Sci Rep. 2022;12:4051.
94. Parlatan U, et al. Raman spectroscopy as a non-invasive diagnostic technique for endometriosis. Sci Rep. 2019;9:1–7. https://doi.org/10.1038/s41598-019-56308-y.
95. Ghazi N, et al. 1H NMR-based metabolomics approaches as non-invasive tools for diagnosis of endometriosis. Int J Reprod BioMed. 2016;14:1–8.
96. Akter S, Xu D, Nagel SC, Bromfield JJ, Pelch K, Wilshire GB, Joshi T. Machine learning classifiers for endometriosis using transcriptomics and methylomics data. Front Genet. 2019;10:766.
97. Fassbender A, et al. Proteomics analysis of plasma for early diagnosis of endometriosis. Obstet Gynecol. 2012;119:276–85; Fassbender A, et al. Combined mRNA microarray and proteomic analysis of eutopic endometrium of women with and without endometriosis. Hum Reprod. 2012;27:2020–9; Dutta M, et al. A metabonomics approach as a means for identification of potential biomarkers for early diagnosis of endometriosis. Mol Biosyst. 2012;8:3281–7.
98. Carmina E, Lobo RA. Polycystic ovary syndrome (PCOS): arguably the most common endocrinopathy is associated with significant morbidity in women. J

Clin Endocrinol Metab. 1999;84(6):1897–9. https://doi.org/10.1210/jcem.84.6.5803.
99. Bharati S, Podder P, Hossain Mondal MR. Diagnosis of polycystic ovary syndrome using machine learning algorithms, In: 2020 IEEE region 10 symposium (TENSYMP). 2020. p. 1486–9.
100. Cahyono B, Adiwijaya K, Mubarok MS, Wisesty UN. An implementation of convolutional neural network on PCO classification based on ultrasound image. In: 2017 5th international conference on information and communication technology (ICoIC7); 2017.
101. Castro V, Shen Y, Yu S, Finan S, Pau CT, Gainer V, et al. Identification of subjects with polycystic ovary syndrome using electronic health records. Reprod Biol Endocrinol. 2015;13:116. https://doi.org/10.1186/s12958-015-0115-z.
102. Cucchi M, Gruener C, Petrauskas L, Steiner P, Tseng H, Fischer A, Penkovsky B, Matthus C, Birkholz P, Kleemann H, Leo K. Reservoir computing with biocompatible organic electrochemical networks for brain-inspired biosignal classification. Sci Adv. 2021;7(34):eabh0693.
103. Rodriguez EM, Thomas D, Druet A, Vlajic-Wheeler M, Lane KJ, Mahalingaiah S. Identifying women at risk for polycystic ovary syndrome using a mobile health app: virtual tool functionality assessment. JMIR Form Res. 2020;4(5):e15094.
104. Purnama B, Adiwijaya Wisesti UN, Nhita F, Gayatri A, Mutiah T. A classification of polycystic ovary syndrome based on follicle detection of ultrasound images. In: 2015 3rd international conference on information and communication technology (ICoICT), Nusa Dua, Bali, Indonesia; 2015. p. 396–401.
105. Prapty AS, Shitu TT. An efficient decision tree establishment and performance analysis with different machine learning approaches on polycystic ovary syndrome. In: 2020 23rd international conference on computer and information technology (ICCIT); 2020. p. 1–5.
106. Chauhan P, Patil P, Rane N, Raundale P, Kanakia H. Comparative analysis of machine learning algorithms for prediction of PCOS. In: 2021 international conference on communication information and computing technology (ICCICT), Mumbai, India; 2021. p. 1–7.
107. Kitaya K, Matsubayashi H, Yamaguchi K, Nishiyama R, Takaya Y, Ishikawa T, et al. Chronic endometritis: potential cause of infertility and obstetric and neonatal complications. Am J Reprod Immunol. 2016;75:13–22.
108. Alonso L, Carugno J. Chronic endometritis: three-dimensional ultrasound and hysteroscopy correlation. J Minim Invasive Gynecol. 2020;27(5):993–4. https://doi.org/10.1016/j.jmig.2019.08.028. Epub 2019 Sep 3.
109. Singh N, Sethi A. Endometritis—diagnosis, treatment and its impact on fertility—a scoping review. JBRA Assist Reprod. 2022;26(3):538–46.
110. HogenEsch E, Hojjati R, Komorowski A, Maniar K, Pavone ME, Bakkensen J, Bernardi L. Chronic endometritis: screening, treatment, and pregnancy outcomes in an academic fertility center. J Assist Reprod Genet. 2023;40(10):2463–71.
111. Puente E, Alonso L, Laganà AS, Ghezzi F, Casarin J, Carugno J. Chronic endometritis: old problem, novel insights and future challenges. Int J Fertil Steril. 2020;13(4):250–6.
112. Hosny A, Parmar C, Quackenbush J, Schwartz LH, Aerts HJWL. Artificial intelligence in radiology. Nat Rev Cancer. 2018;18(8):500–10.
113. Liu X, Faes L, Kalc AU, et al. A comparison of deep learning performance against health-care professionals in detecting diseases from medical imaging: a systematic review and meta-analysis. Lancet Digit Heal. 2019;1(6):e271–97.
114. Xie J, Luo X, Deng X, Tang Y, Tian W, Cheng H, Zhang J, Zou Y, Guo Z, Xie X. Advances in artificial intelligence to predict cancer immunotherapy efficacy. Front Immunol. 2023;13:1076883.
115. Nishino M, Ramaiya NH, Hatabu H, Hodi FS. Monitoring immune-checkpoint blockade: response evaluation and biomarker development. Nat Rev Clin Oncol. 2017;14(11):655–68.
116. Anagnostou V, Landon BV, Medina JE, Forde P, Velculescu VE. Translating the evolving molecular landscape of tumors to biomarkers of response for cancer immunotherapy. Sci Transl Med. 2022;14(670):eabo3958.
117. Benjamens S, Dhunnoo P, Mesko B. The state of artificial intelligence-based FDA-approved medical devices and algorithms: an online database. NPJ Digit Med. 2020;3:118.
118. Angell H, Galon J. From the immune contexture to the immunoscore: the role of prognostic and predictive immune markers in cancer. Curr Opin Immunol. 2013;25(2):261–7.
119. Biomedical Data Translator Consortium. Toward a universal biomedical data translator. Clin Transl Sci. 2019;12(2):86–90; Ghoshal B, Tucker A, Sanghera B, Lup Wong W. Estimating uncertainty in deep learning for reporting confidence to clinicians in medical image segmentation and diseases detection. Comput Intell. 2021;37:701–34.
120. Shickel B, Tighe PJ, Bihorac A, Rashidi P. Deep EHR: a survey of recent advances in deep learning techniques for electronic health record (EHR) analysis. IEEE J Biomed Health Inform. 2017;22(5):1589–604.
121. Kaissis GA, Makowski MR, Rückert D, Braren RF. Secure, privacy-preserving and federated machine learning in medical imaging. Nat Mach Intell. 2020;2(6):305–11.
122. Unni DR, Moxon SAT, Bada M, et al. The Biomedical Data Translator Consortium. Biolink model: a universal schema for knowledge graphs in clinical, biomedical, and translational science. Clin Transl Sci. 2022;15:1848–55.

123. Yu KH, Beam AL, Kohane IS. Artificial intelligence in healthcare. Nat Biomed Eng. 2018;2(10):719–31.
124. Manickam P, Mariappan SA, Murugesan SM, Hansda S, Kaushik A, Shinde R, Thipperudraswamy SP. Artificial intelligence (AI) and internet of medical things (IoMT) assisted biomedical systems for intelligent healthcare. Biosensors (Basel). 2022;12(8):562.

10 Translational Research in Microbial Healthcare Products with Special Reference to Anticancer Drug Discovery from Actinobacteria

Radhakrishnan Manikkam, Geetha Saravanan Thenmozhli, Singaraj Ranjani, Annamalai Kishore Kumar, Selvaraj Azhagesan, Kaari Manigundan, Venugopal Gopikrishnan, Krupakar Parthasarathy, Thangavel Shanmugasundaram, Shanmugam Sasirekha, and Ramasamy Balagurunathan

10.1 Introduction

Cancer is a disorder which is caused due to uncontrolled division of cells. The average human body is made up of 37.2 trillion cells [1]. Each cell in the body maintains its integrity by communicating to the adjacent cells through well-orchestrated signaling pathways. The growth and division of cells begin with a signaling molecule such as a growth factor that binds to the receptor on the cell surface followed by a flow of cellular actions leading to activation of genes involved in cell division and growth [2]. Normally the cells grow and divide when required and to replace dead cells. In a normal cell, the growth and division are controlled by checkpoint proteins like p53 and MYC. Cells that have mutations in these genes lose control and divide rapidly leading to a disorder called cancer. The most mutated gene in cancers is p53 which serves as the guardian of cancerous cells [3, 4]. The cancerous cells gain unique characteristics and do not abide by controlled signaling [5, 6]. The hallmarks of cancer include sustaining proliferative signaling, evading growth suppressors, activating invasion and metastasis, enabling replicative immortality, inducing angiogenesis, and resisting cell death [7]. The host immune system usually removes the cancerous cells from the system by deploying cytotoxic T cells which target the cells infected with cancer-causing viruses and other damaged cells. However, the cancer cells or the cells surrounding cancer produce immune-

R. Manikkam (✉) · G. S. Thenmozhli · S. Ranjani · A. Kishore Kumar · K. Manigundan · V. Gopikrishnan · K. Parthasarathy
Centre for Drug Discovery and Development, Sathyabama Institute of Science and Technology, Chennai, Tamil Nadu, India
e-mail: radhakrishnan.cddd@sathyabama.ac.in; pkrupakar.cddd@sathyabama.ac.in

S. Azhagesan
Department of Biotechnology, Bharathidasan University, Tiruchirappalli, Tamil Nadu, India

T. Shanmugasundaram
Centre for Life Sciences, DRDO – Bharathiar University, Coimbatore, Tamil Nadu, India

S. Sasirekha
Aurigene Discovery Technologies Limited, Bangalore, Karnataka, India

R. Balagurunathan
Department of Microbiology, Periyar University, Salem, Tamil Nadu, India

K. Parthasarathy, R. Manikkam (eds.), *Translational Research in Biomedical Sciences: Recent Progress and Future Prospects*, https://doi.org/10.1007/978-981-97-1777-4_10

suppressive cytokines that cripple the immune system. Thus, cancer cells survive by evading immune surveillance in the host.

The causes of cancer are the external environment and internal genetic changes. The environmental causes of cancer are lifestyle, exposure to viruses, UV radiation, X-ray, a carcinogen, and the use of tobacco. The exposure to these environmental factor damages DNA. The cells usually repair the damaged DNA by recruiting DNA damage repairing enzymes. The faulty repair induces mutations in the genetic makeup of the cells which lead to cancer. Somatic and germinal mutations are the two types of mutations induced by environmental factors. The somatic mutations are not passed on to the progeny while the germinal mutations are inherited by the progeny. Some examples of inherited mutations are BRCA1 and BRCA2 in the case of breast cancer [8, 9]. Sickle cell anemia which is caused due to the mutation in the hemoglobin gene, retinoblastoma in children which is a type of cancer in the eye is caused due to the mutation in the gene called RB1which is inherited from the parent.

The molecular mechanisms involved in cancer are the same whether the source of genetic change was induced externally or inherited by the cell. The three main types of genes which contribute to cancer when mutated are proto-oncogenes, tumor suppressors, and DNA repair genes. Proto-oncogenes are involved in normal cell growth and division. When there is a mutation in the proto-oncogene, it turns into an oncogene which drives cancer. Mutations in the tumor suppressor genes lead to uncontrolled division of cells. DNA repair genes are involved in repairing the damaged DNA. The mutations in these genes introduce additional mutations leading to cancer. Hence these genes are called driver genes for cancer. Translocations, mutations, deletion, and overexpression of genes involved in cellular growth and metabolism are some of the key molecular mechanisms involved in cancer genetics [10].

Cancer is classified based on the tissue from which it originated. For example, carcinoma (skin cancer), leukemia (blood cancer), sarcoma (cancer of connective tissues like bone, cartilage), and lymphoma (cancer of immune system like T cells and B cells). There are over 100 types of cancers are listed by the National Cancer Institute (NCI, USA). The most common cancer types listed include bladder cancer, breast cancer, colon and rectal cancer, endometrial cancer, kidney cancer, Leukemia, liver cancer, lung cancer, melanoma, non-Hodgkin lymphoma, pancreatic cancer, prostate cancer, and thyroid cancer. The type of cancer is named after their organ of origin, for example, cancer originated from the breast is called breast cancer and the one originated from the lung is called lung cancer. Further cancer is classified as benign if the tumor stays at the site of origin or malignant if it can metastasize and invade neighboring tissues [10]. Benign tumors are differentiated cells and malignant tumors are undifferentiated cells. Common benign tumors are moles and uterine fibroids which do not spread nor invade other tissues. Metastatic cancer causes more damage to the body and it is reported that 80% of the cancer deaths are due to metastasis.

10.2 Cancer Chemotherapy—Need for Novel Drugs

"Cancer is emerging as a major problem globally, both in more developed and in less developed countries," says the recent 2020 WHO report. Currently, there are 10 million cases reported worldwide and likely to increase to 20 million in 17 years [11] if control measures are not taken. Chemotherapy or chemo is one of the widely used therapies to treat cancer which involves the usage of powerful drugs to kill fast-growing cells or slow down the growth rate of cells. The growth and multiplying of cells are usually governed by a phenomenon called "central dogma" that begins with replication of the genetic material DNA which is packed in the form of chromosomes followed by transcribing the information into ribonucleic acid (RNA) and finally translated into functional proteins. The proteins cater to the metabolic needs of the cells to grow in size and divide. The growth and dividing of cells take place as a cycle which is called a cell cycle.

The four phases of cell cycle include the G1 phase (cell grow in size), S phase (DNA is duplicated), G2 phase (Prepares for cell division), and M phase (Cell divides). Chemotherapy involves drugs that primarily disrupt the central dogma of the cell by inhibiting DNA replication, RNA synthesis, and protein synthesis. The drug binds to the single-stranded DNA or intercalates between the double-stranded DNA and interferes with the enzymes involved in the replication of DNA such as topoisomerases. RNA synthesis is inhibited by inhibiting DNA dependent RNA polymerases. Chemotherapeutic drugs also inhibit DNA synthesis by acting as antimetabolites. Drugs inhibiting cell cycle are classified as cytotoxic drugs.

Chemotherapy approach to treat cancer dates to 1942 where the first patient was administered a cytotoxic drug at Yale, USA [12]. Since then, several anticancer agents which target cell cycle has been identified and developed as chemotherapeutic drugs. Chemo drugs are classified as alkylating agents, alkaloids, antimetabolites, and antibiotics. The alkylating agents inhibit the synthesis of DNA and RNA, antimetabolites inhibit the synthesis of nucleic acid building blocks, and alkaloids target the cytoskeleton and mitosis. Chemotherapy has been used as a standalone therapy, combination with radiation, neoadjuvant therapy, adjuvant therapy and to kill cells which have spread to other parts of the body after surgery [13].

The class of actinobacteria has been a significant contributor to chemotherapeutic drugs since the 1960s [14]. The secondary metabolites from the genus *Streptomyces* such as actinomycin, anthracyclines, and antibiotic glycopeptides are developed as drugs such as actinomycin D, doxorubicin daunorubicin and bleomycin. The discovery of anticancer drugs progressed from drugs which inhibit cell cycle to targeted therapy where small molecule inhibits particular signaling molecule (e.g., Imatinib which inhibits protein BCR-Abl tyrosine kinase), antitumor antibodies (trastuzumab, targets HER2), oncolytic viruses (RNA viruses). Though the drugs which act on cell cycle inhibition has been used successfully as first-line drugs for cancer, drug-induced cytotoxicity is observed even after the treatment is stopped [13]. The chemotherapeutic drugs also contribute to the formation of genome structural variants leading to mutations and recurrence of cancer [15]. The continuous exposure to chemotherapeutic drugs also leads to resistance to drugs [16]. According to the WHO, the intensity of toxicity can be classified as grade 1 (mild)), grade 2 (moderate), grade 3 (severe), and life-threatening or disabling. Certain chemotherapeutic drugs induce carcinogenicity and infertility. The growing cases of drug resistance and drug-induced cytotoxicity demands ongoing need to explore various resources for novel anticancer molecules.

The success of cancer treatment always depends on the type and stage of cancer. Among the various treatment options for cancer, widely used approach include surgical removal of cancerous tissues/tumors, radiation therapy, chemotherapy, and immunotherapy. Even these approaches are effective on its own or in combination with other treatment options, they have their limitations such as disease recurrence and noncompliance owing to severe adverse effects. Most synthetic chemotherapeutic agent developed earlier is failed during clinical trials. Therefore, a dire need for novel, promising, and low-cost anticancer drugs. Herbal medicines are now focused by global scientific community for the cancer prevention and treatment. Several studies revealed that the toxicity associated with chemotherapeutic agents has been growing over the years.

10.3 Natural Products in Cancer Therapy

Natural products are a huge family of different and multifaceted chemical molecules that are synthesized by various organisms through their primary and secondary metabolism. More than 210,000 natural products have been described from different organisms such as microbes, plants, marine organisms, and animals. The majority of anticancer compounds in clinical practice are mainly derived from the members of the actinobacterial phylum. For the past several decades, natural product discovery and development have played significant roles in the fields of human medicine [17] including for cancer therapy [18]. Approximately >60% of anticancer drugs that are in clinical use originates from natural products derived from plants, marine organisms, and microorganisms. Most of the natural molecules exhibit their anticancer property by interfering with the immune function regulation, apoptosis or autophagy, or cell proliferation inhibition [19].

There are numerous compounds, now in the preclinical stage, are plant-derived or -inspired compounds which shows their significance in cancer therapy [20]. Table 10.1 showing the list of selected medicinal plants and their molecules exhibiting anticancer properties.

Living marine resources such as sponges and its associated microbes, microbes, marine plants, corals, and ascidians, etc. have been investigated in detail for their anticancer properties [29]. Over the past decade, there are several new anticancer compounds isolated from marine organisms has reached the clinical and preclinical level. The nucleosides spongouridine and spongothymidine from the *Cryptotethya crypta* (sponge) can be considered as the first steps in the development of marine-inspired anticancer drugs [30]. Despite a range of anticancer compounds that have been produced from the marine organisms, still there are numerous marine organisms are yet to be explored for anticancer drug discovery. Selected anticancer compounds reported from marine organisms are given in Table 10.2.

Some of the most promising anticancer drugs produced mainly by marine bacteria include the Discodermolide, Sarcodictyin, and Eleutherobin [36]. Compounds like cytarabine (Ara C) and Trabectedin (ET-743) isolated from marine organisms are approved for clinical use [29]. Although some success stories of anticancer drugs from marine organisms, several compounds are failed at the stage of preclinical or clinical trials due to their physicochemical properties like limited bioavailability and/or their toxicity to the normal cells.

Table 10.1 List of some important anticancer compounds reported from medicinal plants

Compounds	Plants	Target cancer type	References
5-Fluorouracil	*Withania somnifera*	Human cervical cancer	[21]
Vincristine	*Catharanthus roseus*	Lymphocytic leukemia	[22]
Vinblastine	*Catharanthus roseus*	Lymphocytic leukemia	[22]
Paclitaxel	*Taxus brevifolia*	Breast and ovarian cancer	[22]
Lycopene	*Solanum lycopersicum*	Prostate, colon cancer	[23]
Rasveratrol	*Polygonum cuspidatum*	Colorectal, skin, liver cancer	[24]
Luteolin	*Capsicum annum*	Colorectal cancer	[25]
Curcumin	*Curcuma longa*	Colon adenocarcinoma	[26]
Thymoquinone	*Nigella sativa*	Colon, prostate, breast, pancreatic cancer	[27]
Artemisinin	*Artemesia annua*	Liver, breast and ovarian cancer	[28]

Table 10.2 List of some important anticancer compounds reported from marine organisms

Compounds	Plants	Target cancer type	References
Bryostatins	*Bugula neritina* (marine animal)	Murine P388 lymphocytic leukemia	[31]
Ascididemin	*Cystodytes dellechiajei* (ascidian)	HL-60; P388 leukemia cells	[32]
Lamellarin D	*Lamellaria* (Mollusc)	Anticancer	[33]
Laurenditerpenol	*Laurencia intricate* (red algae)	Anticancer	[34]
Heteronemin	*Hyrtios* sp. (sponge)	Myelogenous leukemia cells	[35]

10.4 Actinobacteria—A Gold Mine for Drug Discovery

Members of the phylum Actinobacteria are the Gram-positive bacteria which are existing in different morphologies. According to the recent report by Salam et al. (2020) [37], based on the 16S rRNA gene sequences, there are more than 425 genera are reported under six classes, 46 orders and 79 families. The six actinobacterial classes include the Acidomicrobiia, Actinomycetia, Coriobacteria, Nitriliruptoria, Rubrobacteria, and Thermoleophilia. In general, the majority of the actinobacterial genera are aerobic whereas some genera are reported as facultative or obligatory anaerobes. They are metabolically chemoheterotrophic and they utilize diverse substrates. Most of the *Actinobacteria* are free-living saprophytes in a wide range of habitats. However, the actinobacterial distribution was also reported in the extreme habitats like the greatest depth of the ocean, Antarctica, Caves, high altitude Mountain, and desert soil [38, 14]. Also, some are pathogens for humans, animals, and plants [39]. It has been reported that actinobacterial population decreases gradually with increasing the depth of soil (Fig. 10.1).

Biogeo chemical cycling of dead and decade matters and also the degradation of hard to degrade recalcitrant chemicals in the environment are the vital roles played by the actinobacterial members in the environment. The genus *Streptomyces* remains as top among the actinobacterial genera in several ecosystem. Other than the genus *Streptomyces,* all other genera come under the phylum actinobacteria are called as rare actinobacteria which are difficult to isolate [39].

Due to their ability to produce diverse chemical structures with multifaceted biological activities, actinobacteria remains top among the natural resources in drug discovery research [14]. To date, about two third of the antibiotics used in medicine are produced members of the genus *Streptomyces* [38, 40]. However, still the genus *Streptomyces* remains as the potential source for novel drug discovery research [41, 42]. Actinobacterial secondary metabolites exhibit diverse biological activities such as antibacterial, antifungal, antiviral, anticancer, anti-diabetic, immunosuppressive, etc. [43, 44, 45]. The antibiotics produced by actinobacteria are divided into numerous classes based upon their structure such as aminoglycosides, ansamycins, anthracyclines, β-lactam, macrolides, and tetracycline [39]. In recent years there are several rare actinobacteria from rare habitats are reported to produce new bioactive molecules (Table 10.3).

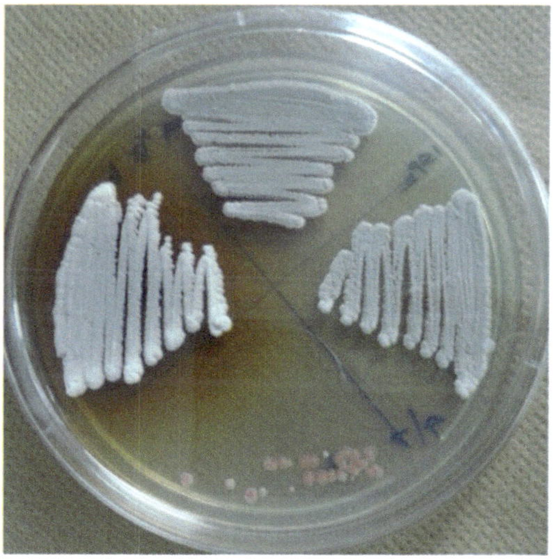

Fig. 10.1 Cultural growth of actinobacteria

Table 10.3 List of bioactive metabolites reported from actinobacteria isolated from extreme habitats

Ecosystem	Actinobacteria	Bioactive metabolite	Biological activity	References
Caves	*Streptomyces tendae* strain HKI 0179	Cervimycins A, B, C, and D	Antibacterial	[46]
Caves	*Streptomyces* sp. CC8-201	Xiakemycin A	Antibacterial; anticancer	[47]
Caves	*Streptomyces* sp. IB 2014/I/78-8	Chaxalactin B	Antibacterial	[48]
Caves	*Nonomuraea* sp.	Hypogeamicin A	Anticancer	[49]
Caves	*Streptomyces* sp. CB09001	Huanglongmycin [HLM] A	Anticancer	[50]
Desert	*Streptomyces* sp. strain DB634	Abenquines A-E	Antibacterial, antifungal	[51]
Desert	*Streptomyces* sp. C34	Chaxalactins A-C	Antibacterial	[52]
Desert	*Streptomyces* sp. TK-VL_333	4-[4-hydroxyphenoxy] butan-2-one	Antibacterial and antifungal	[53]
Deep sea	*Dermacoccus abyssi*	Dermacozines H-J	Radical scavenging activity	[54]
Deep sea	*Marinactinospora thermotolerans*	Marinacarbolines A–D	Antiplasmodial	[55]
Deep sea	*Microbacterium sediminis* sp. *nov.*	Microbacterins A and B	Anticancer	[56]
Deep sea	*Micromonospora* sp.	Levantilides A and B	Anticancer	[57]
Deep sea	*Streptomyces niveus* SCSIO 3406	Marfuraquinocins	Cytotoxic, antibacterial activity	[58]

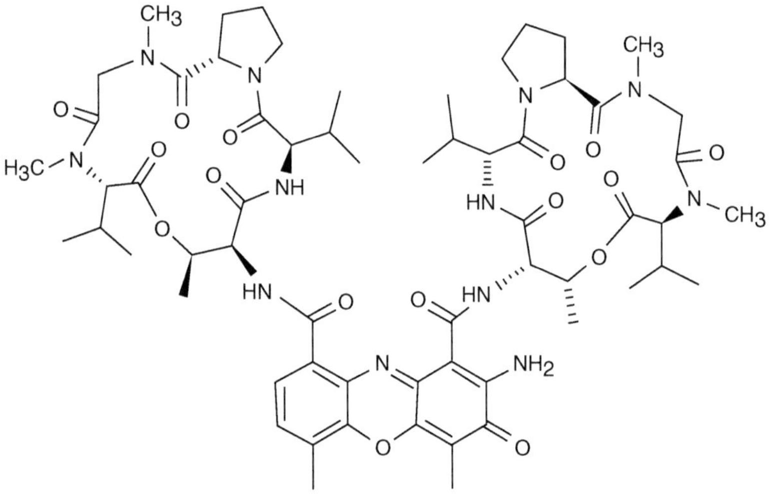

Fig. 10.2 Chemical structure of Actinomycin D

10.5 Actinobacteria—Pioneer in Anticancer Metabolite Production

Actinobacterial members playing a vital role in providing anticancer metabolites for several decades. In the early days, the normal terrestrial actinomycetes especially the genus *Streptomyces* are well explored for anticancer drugs. Actinomycin, a class of chromopeptide antibiotic was isolated in the 1940s from *Streptomyces antibioticus* and used for the treatment of several types of cancers notably leukemia (Fig. 10.2).

Doxorubicin and daunorubicin, a class of anthracycline antibiotics from *Streptomyces peuceticus used for the treatment of* severe leukemia, lymphoma, breast and ovarian cancer, and other solid tumors.

10.6 Anticancer Compounds from Marine Actinobacteria

Marine ecosystems are under extensive investigation over the past 3–4 decades for the actinobacterial diversity and their bioprospecting potentials. In the recent decades, marine derived actinobacteria are recognized as newly added source for bioactive secondary metabolites [59]. In the recent years, there were several new metabolites discovered from marine actinobacteria when compared to actinobacteria from terrestrial ecosystems, even with the limited screening efforts (Table 10.4).

Table 10.4 List of anticancer compounds reported from marine actinobacteria

Anticancer compounds	Producing actinobacteria	Target cancer type	References
Avreoverticillactam	*Streptomyces aureoverticillatus*	Colorectal adenocarcinoma, melanoma, leukemia	[60]
Manumycin A, B	*Streptomyces* sp. M045	Renal, memory cancer, melanoma	[61]
Daryamides A, B	*Streptomyces* sp. CNQ-085	Colon carcinoma	[62]
Marinomycin A, B, C, D	*Marinispora* sp. CNQ140	Melanoma	[63]
Arenicolides A	*Salinispora arenicola* CNR-005	Colon adenocarcinoma	[64]
Chalcomycin A, B	*Streptomyces* sp. M491	Cervix carcinoma	[65]
Marmycin A, B	*Streptomyces* sp. CNH990	Colon adenocarcinoma, breast, prostate cancer	[66]
Cyanogrisides A, B, C, D	*Actinoalloteichus cyanogriseus*	Brast, human epidermoid carcinoma	[67]
Saccharopyrone	*Saccharothrix xinjiangensis* Act24Zk	Cervical cancer	[68]
Ala—Geninthiocin	*Streptomyces* sp. ICN19	Lung cancer	[69]
Akazamycin	*Nonomuraea* sp. AKA32	Murine B16 melanoma	[70]
Thiasporines A-C	*Actinomycetospora chlora* SNC-032	Non-small cell lung cancer cell line H2122	[71]
Dibohemamines A-C	*S. spinoverucosus* SNB032	Non-small cell lung cancer cell line A549	[71]
Chartreusin	*Streptomyces* sp. QD518	Murine P388 and L1210 leukemia, and B16 melanoma cells	[72]
Resistoflavine	*Streptomyces chinaensis* AUBN1/7	Human colorectal adenocarcinoma, HT-29, Jurkat leukemia	[73]
Nonactin	*Streptomyces* sp. KORDI-3238	Human erythroleukemia cell line K-562	[74]
Piperazimycins	*Streptomyces* sp. strain CNQ-593	Human colon carcinoma HCT-116 cell line	[75]
Lajollamycin	*Streptomyces nodosus* strain NPS007994	Murine melanoma cell line B16-F10	[76]
Bohemamines	*Streptomyces* sp. CNQ-583	Human colon adenocarcnioma HCT-116 cell line	[77]
Butenolids	*Streptoverticillium* sp.	Murine lymphoma P388 and human leukemia K562 cell lines	[78]
Caboaxamycin	*Streptomyces* sp. NTK 937	Gastric adenocarcinoma [AGS], hepatocellular carcinoma [Hep G2] and breast carcinoma cells [MCF7]	[79]
Ammosamides	*Streptomyces* sp. CNR-698	HCT-116 colon carcinoma	[80]
Salinisporamide A	*Salinispora tropica CNB-440 and CNB476*	Human colon carcinoma HCT-116	[81]
Arenamides	*Salinispora arenicola CNT-088*	Human colon carcinoma HCT-116	[82]

Table 10.5 List of anticancer compounds reported from endophytic actinobacteria

Anticancer compounds	Producing actinobacteria	Target cancer type	References
Coronamycin	*Streptomyces* sp. (MSU 2110)	HMEC, BT20	[88]
4 Aryl coumarin analogs	*S. aureofaciens* CMUAc130	Transplanted Lewis lung carcinoma (LLC) in mice	[85]
Brartemicin	*Micromonospora* sp.	Colon carcinoma	[89]
Lupinacidins	*Micromonospora lupine*	Murine colon 26-L5 carcinoma	[90]
Pterocidin	*S. hygroscopicus* TP-A0451	NCI-H522; OVCAR 3 SF539	[91]
Kakadumicin A	*Streptomyces*	Breast cancer	[92]
Paclitaxel	*Kitasatospora* sp.	Anticancer	[93]

10.7 Anticancer Compounds from Endophytic Actinobacteria

Several actinobacterial genera residing inside the healthy plants as endophytes are recognized as a promising source for novel bioactive metabolites and enzymes [83]. Next to antimicrobial properties, endophytic actinobacterial extracts and metabolites are reported to exhibit promising anticancer activity against different cancer cell lines. Janaki et al. (2019) [84] reported that the endophytic *Streptomyces cocoi* M20 isolated from *Avicennia marina* was found to inhibit the breast cancer cell lines at the concentration of 200 μg/ml (IC_{50}value). Two biphenyls, 3′ hydroxyl-5-methoxy-3,4-methylenedioxyphenyl and 3′ hydroxyl −5-5′-dimethoxy-3,4-methylenedioxyphenyl isolated from the *Streptomyces* sp. of *Boesenbergia rotunda* root tissue was found to inhibit three human cancer cell lines (HeLa, Hep G2, and Huh7) at an IC_{50} value of 30.04–20.30 μg/ml [85]. Among the endophytic actinobacteria recovered from the rain forest medicinal plants in Yunnan, China, 41 strains were showed anticancer activity, 31% of the strains were active against A549 cells, 29.3% on HL-60 cells, and 85.4% on BEL-7404 cells whereas 90.02% of strains on P388Dl cells [86]. Salam et al. (2017) [87] reported that out of 17 anthracyclines producing endophytic actinobacteria isolated from *Dracaena cochinchinensis* extracts, three strains exhibited anticancer activity against MCF-7 and HepG2 cells with IC_{50} values range between 3 and 33 μg/mL. Some anticancer compounds reported from endophytic actinobacteria are given in Table 10.5.

10.8 Anticancer Compounds from Marine Organism Associated Actinobacteria

Actinobacteria associated with the marine organisms can also reported to produce diverse and novel natural products including anticancer [40]. Bryostatin 1, a polyketide isolated initially from Bryozoa, is now known to be produced by its bacterial symbiont, Candidatus *Endobugulasertula* [94]. *Penicillium chrysogenum* isolated from the *Ircinia fasciculata* (marine sponge) was also reported to produce an antileukemic agent Sorbicillactone - A [95]. Recent studies revealed that actinobacteria associated with sponges, corals, mollusks, ascidians, seaweeds, seagrasses, and mangroves [96] are the most important producers for bioactive natural products [97]. Apart from antibacterial compounds, there are several anticancer compounds are isolated from marine organism associated actinobacteria (Table 10.6).

Table 10.6 List of anticancer compounds isolated from marine organism associated Actinobacteria

Marine host	Anticancer compounds	Producing actinobacteria	Target cancer type	References
Chondrilla caribensis (sponges)	22′-deoxythiocoraline, thiochondrilline A-C, and 12′-sulfoxythiocoraline	*Verrucosispora* sp. WMMA107	Anticancer	[98]
Cinachyra sp. (sponges)	Squalene	*Micromonospora* sp. SpC080624GE-05	Anticancer	[99]
Demospongiae sponge	Salicylamide derivative, JBIR-58	*Streptomyces* sp.	Anticancer	[100]
Halichondria panacea (sponges)	Mayamycin	*Streptomyces* sp. HB202	Anticancer	[101]
Hymeniacidon sp. (sponges)	Lobophorin C and D	*Streptomyces carnosus* AZS17	Anticancer	[102]
Unidentified sponge	Ulbactin	*Brevibacillus*	Anticancer	[103]
Unidentified soft coral	Thiocoraline (Depsipeptide)	*Micromonospora* sp. ACM2–092	Anticancer	[104]
Unidentified mollusk	Aburatubolactam A (macrolactams)	*Streptomyces* sp. SCRC-A20	Anticancer	[105]
Unidentified tunicate	Barmumycin	*Streptomyces* sp. BOSC-022A	Anticancer	[106]
Penquins excreta	Trisindolal	*Arthrobacter psychrochitiniphilus*	Human breast cancer and melanoma	[107]

10.9 Anticancer Drugs from Actinobacteria in Clinical Trials

Actinobacteria derived secondary metabolites belonging to macrolide, indole bipyrrole, and γ-lactam-β-lactone class is developed into anticancer drugs with the varied mechanism of action. Some of the actinobacterial derived drugs in clinical trials are Marizomib (NPI-0052, Salinosporamide), Sirolimus (Rapamycin derivative), and Obatoclax (Prodiginin family derivative). Salinosporamide A (NPI-0052, Marizomib) is a naturally occurring proteasome inhibitor derived from the obligate marine actinomycetes *Salinispora tropica* and *Salinispora arenicola* [108]. Proteosomes are protein complexes that dispose of all the unwanted proteins in the cellular system. Inhibition of the proteasomal activity leads to the accumulation of toxic protein which kills the cells ultimately. Proteosome inhibitors are used widely for hematological malignancies. Salinosporamide A inhibits proteasome activity by irreversibly binding to all three subunits [b1(caspase-like; C-L), b2 (trypsin-like; T-L), and b5 (chymotrypsin-like; CT-L)] of the 20S proteasome. Salinosporamide A has shown significant activity in patients with metastatic solid tumors and advanced hematological malignancies. The clinical trial studies conducted with Marizomib are phase I in patients with metastatic solid tumors and refractory lymphoma (NPI-0052-100, NCT00396864). Phase 1/11 trials (NPI-0052-100, NCT00396864) were conducted in the USA. The clinical trial conducted in Australia and Estonia (NCT00629473) demonstrated that Marizomib does not possess any severe peripheral neuropathy or hematological toxicity as observed with other proteasome inhibitors. The superior characteristics of Marizomib compel additional investigation of this drug.

Prodigiosin is a red-pigmented secondary metabolite secreted by several bacterial species. The *Streptomyces* species having this pigment are *Streptomyces coelicolor* [109], *Streptomyces griseoviridis* [110]. Prodigiosin has been a molecule of interest since the early twentieth century and it has reported acting through several mechanisms of action. Prodigiosin and its derivatives are known for its immunomodulatory, antibacterial, antimalarial, and anticancer activity. Prodigiosin is effective against multiple can-

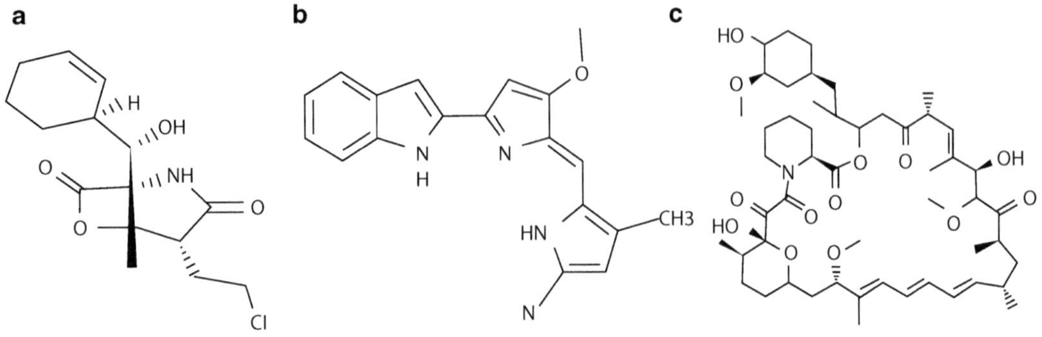

Fig. 10.3 Chemical structure of (**a**). Salinosporamide, (**b**). Obatoclax, and (**c**). Sirolimus

cers and not toxic to normal cells. Activating p53 for cancer chemotherapy is gaining attention recently and prodigiosin is reported to induce apoptosis by activating p53 signaling [111]. One of its derivative obatoclax was used in clinical trials in patients with chronic lymphocytic leukemia.

Rapamycin was a secondary metabolite isolated from *Streptomyces hygroscopicus* from the soil sample of Easter Island (Rapa Nui) in 1972. It was found to have immunosuppressive and antiproliferative activities in mammalian cells. It was cytostatic rather than cytotoxic and attracted further exploration of the mechanism of action of this molecule. Rapamycin was one of the earliest secondary metabolites of *Streptomyces* origin which was reported to have its mechanism of action through a signaling pathway. The target modulated by rapamycin was named as the mammalian target of rapamycin (mTOR). The mTOR signaling pathway has mTORC1 and mTORC2 complexes which are the master regulators that control the growth of cells. mTOR signaling is involved in RNA, protein, and lipid synthesis and autophagy.

Enhanced mTOR signaling is the driver for many cancers. Hence it makes rapamycin an interesting anticancer agent. Derivatives of rapamycin such have everolimus, temsirolimus was clinically tested in a wide range of cancers [112]. The setback with rapamycin's mechanism of action is a relapse of tumors, as compensatory mechanisms come in place for the survival of tumors. Rapamycin analog sirolimus is currently in clinical trials in pancreatic cancer (NCT03662412) and a combination drug in lung cancer (NCT04348292) (Fig. 10.3).

10.10 Molecular Mechanism of Action of Anticancer Drugs from Actinobacteria

The molecular mechanism of cancer is complex and heterogenous where the uncontrolled cell division is the common outcome. The growth and division of cells commence with an extracellular signal which triggers signaling events to replicate DNA, synthesis of RNA, and proteins. Several signaling pathways in the cells govern the growth and development of cells. Some key signaling pathways in the cells which govern the growth and cell development are PI3K/ATK/mTOR, MAP/ERK, JAK/STAT, AKT/PKB, and TGF beta signaling pathways. The activation of these pathways varies depending on the type of cancers. Anticancer drugs can stall any of the events leading to the arrest of growth and division of cells. Certain drugs called targeted drugs to inhibit these signaling molecules directly. Molecular mechanisms of action of some important anticancer drugs are described below.

10.10.1 Actinomycin D (Chromopeptide)

Actinomycin D, a chromopeptide compound produced mainly from several *Streptomyces* species, has been widely used in clinical practice since 1954 as an anticancer drug. Actinomycin D exhibits anticancer action through several modes. Which are primarily being associated with DNA functionality, leading to RNA and, protein synthesis inhibition. Majorly the two mechanisms involving in anticancer activity are the intercalation to DNA and the stabilization of cleavable complexes of topoisomerases I and II with DNA. During the process of action, a phenoxazone ring of actinomycin D localizes between GpC base pair sequence in DNA and polypeptide lactones rings occupy a position in the minor groove of the DNA helix or the drug penetrates to a place in the DNA structure where topoisomerase binds with DNA, respectively. Moreover, the biological activity of actinomycin D is greatly influenced by its slow dissociation from DNA complexes, its photodynamic activity, and free radical formation [113].

10.10.2 Mitomicin C

The mitomycins are another important anticancer antibiotic that are in clinical practice for the past 60 years. Mitomycin C (MMC) is the best-investigated subtype that serves as a prototype for drugs with bio reductive alkylation, a unique feature of this class. MMC has a wide clinical antitumor spectrum with efficacy in various tumor types such as gastric cancer, pancreatic cancer, breast cancer, non-small cell lung cancer, cervical cancer, prostate cancer, and bladder cancer. The main toxicities of MMC are thrombocytopenia and leukocytopenia [114].

10.10.3 Bleomycin (Glycopeptide)

Bleomycin is a glycopeptide molecule discovered in 1962 from *Streptomyces verticillus*. This anticancer medicine effective in treating lymphoma, testicular cancer, ovarian cancer, etc. It acts with a unique mechanism of action in which the drug binds to guanosine-cytosine-rich portions of DNA. A group of five nitrogen atoms arranged in a square-pyramidal conformation binds divalent metals including iron, the active ligand, and copper, an inactive ligand. Molecular oxygen, bound by the iron, can produce highly reactive free radicals and Fe (III). The free radicals produce DNA single-strand breaks at 3′-4′ bonds in deoxyribose. This yields free base propenals, especially of thymine [115].

10.10.4 Anthracyclines

Doxorubicin is a WHO classified essential anticancer drug derived from *Streptomyces peucetius* and it was approved by FDA in the year 1974 for cancer therapy. Doxorubicin is an anthracycline antibiotic and several mechanisms of action are postulated for this drug over the years. Some of the mechanisms of action of doxorubicin include the intercalation of doxorubicin into DNA strands and inhibiting DNA and RNA synthesis, inhibiting DNA unwinding enzyme topoisomerase II, and free radical generation. There is a recent report which proposes that doxorubicin acts through regulated intramembrane proteolysis. Daunorubicin an analog of doxorubicin has a similar mechanism of action which is used in chemotherapy. Komodoquinone A is a unique anthracycline produced from marine *Streptomyces* sp. KS3 was active against neuroblastoma [116, 117].

10.10.5 Anthraquinones

Several compounds such as parimycin, trioxacarcins, and gutingimycin of the anthraquinone family are produced by actinomycetes. It has been shown that trioxacarcin A forms a stable complex with dsDNA and the cleavage of these complexes provided the natural product gutingimycin by guanine abstraction [118]. Parimycin showed activity against human tumor cell lines of stomach cancer GXF 251L, lung cancer H460, LXFA 629L, and LXFL 529L, breast cancer MCF-7 and MAXF 401NL, melanomas MEXF 462NL and MEXF 514L with IC70 values ranging from 0.9 to 6.7 μg/mL [119].

10.10.6 Non-ribosomal Peptides [NRP]

Proximicins are non-ribosomal peptides produced by marine *Verrucosispora* strain MG-37 and *V. maris* AB-18-032. Proximicins A, B, and C showed significant growth inhibitory activities toward human gastric adenocarcinoma AGS and hepatocellular carcinoma Hep G2 [120]. Thiocoraline produced by *Micromonospora* sp. L-13-ACM2-092 isolated from a soft coral collected at the Indian Ocean [121, 122] was showed promising anticancer activity against murine leukemia (P388), human lung adenocarcinoma (A549), and melanoma (MEL288). Besides, on both LOVO and SW620 human colon cancer cell lines, thiocoraline caused an arrest in the G1 phase of the cell cycle and a decrease in the rate of S phase progression toward G2/M phases, due to its DNA bis intercalative properties and its DNA polymerase α inhibition [104].

Three new cyclohexadepsipeptides, arenamides were isolated from marine *Salinispora arenicola* CNT-088. Arenamides A and B exhibited weak in vitro cytotoxicity against human colon carcinoma HCT-116 with IC50 values of 13.2 and 19.2 μg/mL, respectively [82]. Also, arenamides have been associated to chemoprevention of carcinogenesis by suppressing the activation of NFκB regulates the expression of several genes, the products of which are involved in tumorigenesis [123, 124].

10.10.7 Salinosporamide

A mixed polyketide, non-ribosomal peptide Salinosporamide A, produced by the obligate marine actinobacterium, *Salinispora tropica*, is a highly potent anticancer compound which acts on the 20S proteasome [125]. Salinosporamide A displayed potent in vitro cytotoxicity against HCT-116 (human colon carcinoma) with an IC50 value of 11 ng/mL. The greatest potency was observed against human cell lines of non-small cell lung cancer (NCI-H226), central nervous system cancer (SF-539), melanoma (SK-MEL-28), and breast cancer (MDA-MB-435) with LC50 values less than 10 nM. When salinosporamide A was tested against purified rabbit muscle 20S proteasome, it inhibited proteasomal chymotrypsin-like proteolytic activity [108].

10.11 Actinobacterial Enzymes with Anticancer Properties

Enzymes can act as powerful agents in this respect, as demonstrated by asparaginase, which has been included in the treatment of acute lymphoblastic leukemia for half a century [126]. L-asparaginase is an important enzyme as therapeutic agents used in combination with other drugs in the treatment of acute lymphoblastic leukemia [127]. L-Glutaminase is another therapeutic enzyme recognized for its use as a potent antileukemic agent. There is a continuous search for L-asparaginase and L-glutaminase since these enzymes differ from different sources greatly in their properties such as anticancer activity, immunogenicity, cytotoxicity, activity at physiological conditions, plasma clearance rate, substrate specificity, temperature, pH and salt tolerance, etc., [128]. Anticancer therapeutic exploitation of L-methionase (MGL) from *Pseudomonas putida* to deplete plasma methionine has been extensively investigated. The MGL was tested as a potent antiproliferative enzyme toward Lewis lung and human colon carcinoma, glioblastoma, and neuroblastoma [129].

There are very few studies reported the anticancer activity of enzymes from actinobacteria. El-Naggar et al. (2016) [130] reported that the L-asparaginase enzyme purified from alkaliphilic *Streptomyces fradiae* NEAE-82 was found to exhibit anti-colon cancer activity. In another study, L-asparaginase produced from the endophytic *Streptomyces* sp. ALP03 was found to exhibit anticancer activity against diverse cancer cell lines [131]. Reda et al. (2015) [132] reported that L-glutaminase isolated from *Streptomyces canaries* showed significant inhibition against Hep-G2 cell (IC50, 6.8 μg/mL) and HeLa cells (IC50, 8.3 μg/mL). Awad et al. (2019) [133] isolated and studied the anticancer properties of L-glutaminase from rhizosphere soil

Streptomyces rochei SAH2_CWMSG. The results showed that the pure enzyme has significant efficiency against Hep-G2 cell (100%), MCF-7 cells (97.5%), and HCT-116 cells (100%) at 1000 μg/ml with IC50 of 279.7, 405.1, and 354.2 μg/ml, respectively. Even there are several reports on the isolation and characterization of L-asparaginase, and L-glutaminase from actinobacterial genera, they are least investigated for their anticancer properties.

10.12 Actinobacterial Nanomedicines for Cancer Treatments

Nanotechnology to monitor, maintain, prevent, treat diseases and control human biological systems at the nanometer size range, using nanostructures and engineered nanodevices. Several features of nanoparticles make them well suited for a wide range of biomedical applications. A medical branch that practices nanotechnology tools and proficiency to prevent and treat disease is called nanomedicine. Nanomedicine is an enormously developing area of science present alternate treatment approaches over conventional methods for disease therapy and diagnosis [134]. Nanomedicine is always applying into three main areas: therapeutics, diagnostics, and theranostics [135]. Nanomedicine is usually seen as having huge potential to carry profits to many areas of research and application and is attracting quickly increasing investments from governments and private sectors in many parts of the world.

Cancer nanomedicine is one of the most important areas in nowadays [136, 137]. Cancer nanomedicines are usually improving the therapeutic efficiency of currently available chemotherapeutic agents by combining them with a nanoscale delivery component. However, the overall potential use of nanomaterials in oncology also includes therapeutics, diagnostics, medical devices and theragnostic for personalized medicine [138, 139]. For instance, the nanoparticles can develop the target-specificity or tissue dispersal of a diagnostic probe, thus allowing earlier detection of malignancy in the cancer patient. Similarly, theragnostic assistance from nanoscience in the development of multifunctional clinical products that permit real-time pursuing of the targeted delivery of cancer therapeutics [140, 141].

Microorganisms have been revealed to be significant nano-factories that hold massive potential as eco-friendly and cost-effective methods, avoiding high energy and toxic chemicals required for physiochemical synthesis. Microorganisms can reduce the metal nanoparticles from corresponding metal salts using various reductase enzymes, with narrow size distribution and less polydispersity. Over the past few decades, microorganisms, including bacteria, actinobacteria, fungi, and yeasts have been studied for extra- and intracellular synthesis of various kind of nanoparticles. A range of biological protocols for nanoparticle synthesis has been reported using microbial biomass, supernatant and its derived components. Moreover, diverse organic molecules of the biological system have significant roles by acting as reducing agents. Moreover, these help in providing natural capping to nanomaterials during synthesis, thereby avoiding the aggregation of nanoparticles and helping them to keep on stable for a long time, thus providing added stability [142]. Therefore, among the microbial system, actinobacterial synthesis of nanomaterials has emerged as an important branch of nanobiotechnology. Due to their rich diversity in nature, actinobacteria have the distinctive potential for the synthesis of various nanoparticles and are regarded as important biofactories for nanomaterial synthesis (Table 10.7). This could be easily scaled up for many biomedical, industrial, and environmental applications [143].

Table 10.7 Nanoparticles synthesized by actinobacteria for anticancer activities

Actinobacterial species	Nanoparticle	Size (nm)	Morphology	Activity	Reference
Streptomyces naganishii (MA7)	Ag	5–50	Spherical	Anticancer	[144]
Nocardiopsis sp. MBRC-1	Ag	45	Spherical	Anticancer	[145]
Streptomyces bikiniensis	Se	17	Nanorod	Anticancer	[146]
Streptomyces minutiscleroticus M10A62	Se	10–250	Spherical	Anticancer	[147]
Streptomyces clavuligerus	Au	8.2	Spherical	Anticancer	[148]
Streptomyces rochei MHM13	Ag	22–85	Spherical	Anticancer	[149]
Streptacidiphilus durhamensis	Ag	8–48	Spherical	Anticancer	[150]
Streptomyces sp. (MA30)	ZnO	17–30	Spherical	Anticancer	[151]
Streptomyces sp. *B5*	Ag, Au, Ag -Au	30.5, 14.5 & 41.5	Spherical	Anticancer	[152]
Nocardiopsis flavascens	Ag	5–50	Spherical	Cytotoxicity	[153]
Streptomyces sp. *B5*	Pt/Ag, Pt/Au, Pt/Ag/Au	10–30	Spherical	Anticancer	[154]
Streptomyces sp. MA30	Fe_3O_4	15–30	Porous	Anticancer	[155]
Streptomyces tuirus DBZ39	Au	27–56	Spherical	Anticancer	[156]

10.13 Mechanism of Nanoparticles Induced Cancer Cell Death

Microbial synthesis of metal nanomaterials offers safe and effective therapeutic agents for cancer treatment. Different metal nanoparticles may show different properties and thus are likely show diverse mechanisms of toxicity against various cancer cells [157]. Active targeting depends on the specific interface of a targeting moiety with surface receptors present on the cancer cells. The cancer cell populations limit the broader applicability of the metal nanoparticles because of their receptor density and distribution. The nanomaterials depend on the general physiological structures found in all tumors, thus present a universal method for anticancer therapy [158]. Major apoptotic mechanism of metal nanoparticles on cancer cells illustrated in Fig. 10.4.

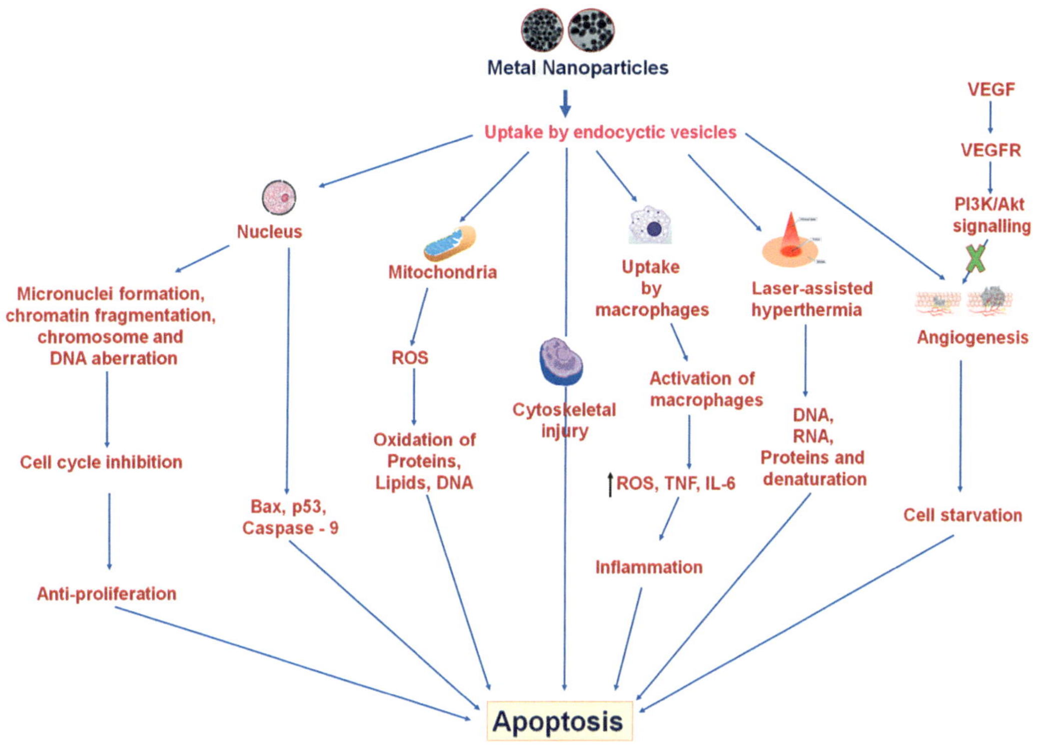

Fig. 10.4 Major mechanism of metal nanoparticles induced cancer programmed cell death (*ROS* reactive oxygen species, *TNF* Tumor necrosis factor, *VEGF* Vascular endothelial growth factor, *VEGFR* Vascular endothelial growth factor receptor and *IL-6* interleukin-6)

10.14 Conclusion

Selected members of the actinobacterial phylum played a vital role in providing novel drugs for cancer therapy for the past 80 years. The salient research findings made in the last two decades revealed that actinobacteria from extreme ecosystems like the deep sea, Desert, caves, marine organisms, and medicinal plants are the tremendous source for novel actinobacteria which in turn produce structurally new molecules with unique anticancer properties. Actinobacteria are also acting as microbial factories to synthesize nanoparticles with unique anticancer properties. This group of bacteria is yet to be explored in detail for anticancer enzymes like L-asparaginase, L-Glutaminase, and others. Pursuing research on extremophilic actinobacteria is worthy of getting novel molecules to fight against cancer.

Acknowledgment Authors thank the authorities of Sathyabama Institute of Science and Technology, Tamil Nadu, India and Periyar University, Salem, Tamil Nadu, India for their research support and encouragement. Authors (MRK, GST, SR and RB) thank the Department of Biotechnology (DBT), New Delhi for their support in the form of research grant [BT/PR41474/NDB/39/760/2020 dated 28.09.2021].

References

1. Bianconi E, Piovesan A, Facchin F, Beraudi A, Casadei R, Frabetti F, Vitale L, Pelleri MC, Tassani S, Piva F, Perez-Amodio S. An estimation of the number of cells in the human body. Ann Hum Biol. 2013;40(6):463–71.
2. Nair A, Chauhan P, Saha B, Kubatzky KF. Conceptual evolution of cell signaling. Int J Mol Sci. 2019;20(13):3292.
3. Mantovani F, Collavin L, Del Sal G. Mutant p53 as a guardian of the cancer cell. Cell Death Differ. 2019;2:199–212.

4. Levine AJ. Targeting therapies for the p53 protein in cancer treatments. Annu Rev Cancer Biol. 2019;3:21–34.
5. Sever R, Brugge JS. Signal transduction in cancer. Cold Spring Harb Perspect Med. 2015;5(4):a006098.
6. Harvey AJ. Predictive biomarkers in oncology. In: Predictive biomarkers in oncology. Cham: Springer; 2019. p. 167–82.
7. Hanahan D, Weinberg RA. Hallmarks of cancer: the next generation. Cell. 2011;144(5):646–74.
8. Armstrong N, Ryder S, Forbes C, Ross J, Quek RG. A systematic review of the international prevalence of BRCA mutation in breast cancer. Clin Epidemiol. 2019;Volume 11:543–61.
9. Lee YC, Lee YC, Li CY, Lee YL, Chen BL. BRCA1 and BRCA2 gene mutations and lung cancer risk: a meta-analysis. Medicina. 2020;56(5):212.
10. Meirson T, Gil-Henn H, Samson AO. Invasion and metastasis: the elusive hallmark of cancer. Oncogene. 2020;39(9):2024–6.
11. WHO. Assessing national capacity for the prevention and control of noncommunicable diseases: report of the 2019 global survey. Geneva: WHO; 2020.
12. Christakis P. Bicentennial: the birth of chemotherapy at Yale: bicentennial lecture series: surgery grand round. Yale J Biol Med. 2011;84(2):169.
13. Schirrmacher V. From chemotherapy to biological therapy: a review of novel concepts to reduce the side effects of systemic cancer treatment. Int J Oncol. 2019;54(2):407–19.
14. Barka EA, Vatsa P, Sanchez L, Gaveau-Vaillant N, Jacquard C, Klenk HP, Clément C, Ouhdouch Y, van Wezel GP. Taxonomy, physiology, and natural products of Actinobacteria. Microbiol Mol Biol. 2016;80(1):1–43.
15. Quispe-Tintaya W, Lee M, Dong X, Weiser DA, Vijg J, Maslov AY. Bleomycin-induced genome structural variations in normal, non-tumor cells. Sci Rep. 2018;8(1):16523.
16. Wang X, Zhang H, Chen X. Drug resistance and combating drug resistance in cancer. Canc Drug Resist. 2019;2(2):141.
17. Bai J, Li Y, Zhang G. Cell cycle regulation and anticancer drug discovery. Cancer Biol Med. 2017;4:348.
18. Kinghorn AD, Carcache de Blanco EJ, Chai HB, Orjala J, Farnsworth NR, Soejarto DD, Oberlies NH, Wani MC, Kroll DJ, Pearce CJ, Swanson SM. Discovery of anticancer agents of diverse natural origin. Pure Appl Chem. 2009;81(6):1051–63.
19. Rayan A, Raiyn J, Falah M. Nature is the best source of anticancer drugs: indexing natural products for their anticancer bioactivity. PLoS One. 2017;12(11):e0187925.
20. Ashraf MA. Phytochemicals as potential anticancer drugs: time to ponder nature's bounty. Biomed Res Int. 2020;2020:8602879.
21. Yadav B, Bajaj A, Saxena M, Saxena AK. In vitro anticancer activity of the root, stem and leaves of Withania somnifera against various human cancer cell lines. Indian J Pharm Sci. 2010;72(5):659.
22. Cragg GM, Newman DJ. Plants as a source of anti-cancer agents. J Ethnopharmacol. 2005;100(1–2):72–9.
23. Efferth T. From ancient herb to modern drug: Artemisia annua and artemisinin for cancer therapy. Semin Oncol. 2017;46:65–83.
24. Tu LY, Pi J, Jin H, Cai JY, Deng SP. Synthesis, characterization and anticancer activity of kaempferol-zinc (II) complex. Bioorganic Med Chem Lett. 2016;11:2730–4.
25. Osman NH, Said UZ, El-Waseef AM, Ahmed ES. Luteolin supplementation adjacent to aspirin treatment reduced dimethylhydrazine-induced experimental colon carcinogenesis in rats. Tumour Biol. 2015;36:1179–90.
26. Vallianou NG, Evangelopoulos A, Schizas N, Kazazis C. Potential anticancer properties and mechanisms of action of curcumin. Anticancer Res. 2015;35(2):645–51.
27. Ali I, Braun DP. Resveratrol enhances mitomycin C-mediated suppression of human colorectal cancer cell proliferation by up-regulation of p21WAF1/CIP1. Anticancer Res. 2014;34(10):5439–46.
28. Hahm ER, Moura MB, Kelley EE, Van Houten B, Shiva S, Singh SV. Withaferin A-induced apoptosis in human breast cancer cells is mediated by reactive oxygen species. PLoS One. 2011;8:e23354.
29. Bhatnagar I, Kim SK. Immense essence of excellence: marine microbial bioactive compounds. Mar Drugs. 2010;8(10):2673–701.
30. Gomes NG, Dasari R, Chandra S, Kiss R, Kornienko A. Marine invertebrate metabolites with anticancer activities: solutions to the "supply problem". Mar Drugs. 2016;14(5):98.
31. Dias N, Vezin H, Lansiaux A, Bailly C. Topoisomerase inhibitors of marine origin and their potential use as anticancer agents. In: DNA binders and related subjects. Cham: Springer; 2005. p. 89–108.
32. Bonnard I, Bontemps N, Lahmy S, Banaigs B, Combaut G, Francisco C, Colson P, Houssier C, Waring MJ, Bailly C. Binding to DNA and cytotoxic evaluation of ascididemin, the major alkaloid from the Mediterranean ascidian *Cystodytes dellechiajei*. Anticancer Drug Des. 1995;10(4):333–46.
33. Dassonneville L, Wattez N, Baldeyrou B, Mahieu C, Lansiaux A, Banaigs B, Bonnard I, Bailly C. Inhibition of topoisomerase II by the marine alkaloid ascididemin and induction of apoptosis in leukemia cells. Biochem Pharmacol. 2000;60(4):527–37.
34. Mohammed KA, Hossain CF, Zhang L, Bruick RK, Zhou YD, Nagle DG. Laurenditerpenol, a new diterpene from the tropical marine alga Laurenciaintricata that potently inhibits HIF-1 mediated hypoxic signaling in breast tumor cells. J Nat Prod. 2004;67(12):2002–7.
35. Schumacher M, Cerella C, Eifes S, Chateauvieux S, Morceau F, Jaspars M, Dicato M, Diederich

M. Heteronemin, a spongean sesterterpene, inhibits TNFα-induced NF-κB activation through proteasome inhibition and induces apoptotic cell death. Biochem Pharmacol. 2010;79(4):610–22.
36. Malaker A, Ahmad SA. Therapeutic potency of anticancer peptides derived from marine organism. Int J Adv Eng Sci Appl Math. 2013;2(4):53–65.
37. Salam N, Jiao JY, Zhang XT, Li WJ. Update on the classification of higher ranks in the phylum Actinobacteria. Int J Syst Evol. 2020;70(2):1331–55.
38. Bérdy J. Thoughts and facts about antibiotics: where we are now and where we are heading. J Antibiot. 2012;65(8):385–95.
39. Amin DH, Abdallah NA, Abolmaaty A, Tolba S, Wellington EM. Microbiological and molecular insights on rare Actinobacteria harboring bioactive prospective. Bull Natl Res Cent. 2020;44(1):1–2.
40. Valliappan K, Sun W, Li Z. Marine actinobacteria associated with marine organisms and their potentials in producing pharmaceutical natural products. Appl Microbiol Biotechnol. 2014;98:7365–77.
41. Tan LT, Chan KG, Lee LH, Goh BH. Streptomyces bacteria as potential probiotics in aquaculture. Front Microbiol. 2016;5(7):79.
42. Ser HL, Tan LT, Law JW, Chan KG, Duangjai A, Saokaew S, Pusparajah P, Ab Mutalib NS, Khan TM, Goh BH, Lee LH. Focused review: cytotoxic and antioxidant potentials of mangrove-derived Streptomyces. Front Microbiol. 2017;1(8):2065.
43. Balagurunathan R, Radhakrishnan M. Biotechnological, genetic engineering and nanotechnological potential of actinomycetes. J Ind Microbiol Biotechnol. 2010:302–436.
44. Radhakrishnan M, Jerrine J, Anbarasu S, Suresh A, Balagurunathan R. Actinobacteria from less explored ecosystems: a promising source for anti TB metabolites. Microbiol Curr Res. 2017:1–29.
45. Manikkam R, Pati P, Thangavel S, Venugopal G, Joseph J, Ramasamy B, Dastager SG. Distribution and bioprospecting potential of actinobacteria from Indian mangrove ecosystems. In: Microbial diversity in ecosystem sustainability and biotechnological applications, vol. 1. Cham: Springer; 2019. p. 319–53.
46. Herold K, Gollmick FA, Groth I, Roth M, Menzel KD, Möllmann U, Gräfe U, Hertweck C. Cervimycin A–D: a polyketide glycoside complex from a cave bacterium can defeat vancomycin resistance. Chem Eur J. 2005;11(19):5523–30.
47. Jiang ZK, Guo L, Chen C, Liu SW, Zhang L, Dai SJ, He QY, You XF, Hu XX, Tuo L, Jiang W. Xiakemycin A, a novel pyranonaphthoquinone antibiotic, produced by the *Streptomyces* sp. CC8-201 from the soil of a karst cave. J Antibiot. 2015;68(12):771–4.
48. Axenov-Gibanov DV, Voytsekhovskaya IV, Tokovenko BT, Protasov ES, Gamaiunov SV, Rebets YV, Luzhetskyy AN, Timofeyev MA. Actinobacteria isolated from an underground lake and moonmilk speleothem from the biggest conglomeratic karstic cave in Siberia as sources of novel biologically active compounds. PLoS One. 2016;11(2):e0149216.
49. Derewacz DK, McNees CR, Scalmani G, Covington CL, Shanmugam G, Marnett LJ, Polavarapu PL, Bachmann BO. Structure and stereochemical determination of hypogeamicins from a cave-derived actinomycete. J Nat Prod. 2014;77(8):1759–63.
50. Jiang L, Pu H, Xiang J, Su M, Yan X, Yang D, Zhu X, Shen B, Duan Y, Huang Y. Huanglongmycin AC, cytotoxic polyketides biosynthesized by a putative type II polyketide synthase from *Streptomyces* sp. CB09001. Front Chem. 2018;6:254.
51. Schulz D, Beese P, Ohlendorf B, Erhard A, Zinecker H, Dorador C, Imhoff JF. Abenquines A–D: aminoquinone derivatives produced by *Streptomyces* sp. strain DB634. J Antibiot. 2011;64(12):763–8.
52. Rateb ME, Houssen WE, Harrison WT, Deng H, Okoro CK, Asenjo JA, Andrews BA, Bull AT, Goodfellow M, Ebel R, Jaspars M. Diverse metabolic profiles of a Streptomyces strain isolated from a hyper-arid environment. J Nat Prod. 2011;74(9):1965–71.
53. Kavitha A, Prabhakar P, Vijayalakshmi M, Venkateswarlu Y. Purification and biological evaluation of the metabolites produced by *Streptomyces* sp. TK-VL_333. Res Microbiol. 2010;161(5):335–45.
54. Wagner M, Abdel-Mageed WM, Ebel R, Bull AT, Goodfellow M, Fiedler HP, Jaspars M. Dermacozines h–j isolated from a deep-sea strain of *Dermacoccus abyssi* from Mariana Trench sediments. J Nat Prod. 2014;77(2):416–20.
55. Huang H, Yao Y, He Z, Yang T, Ma J, Tian X, Li Y, Huang C, Chen X, Li W, Zhang S. Antimalarial β-carboline and indolactam alkaloids from Marinactinospora thermotolerans, a deep sea isolate. J Nat Prod. 2011;74(10):2122–7.
56. Liu D, Lin H, Proksch P, Tang X, Shao Z, Lin W. Microbacterins A and B, new peptaibols from the deep sea actinomycete *Microbacterium sediminis* sp. nov. YLB-01 (T). Org Lett. 2015;17(5):1220–3.
57. Gärtner A, Ohlendorf B, Schulz D, Zinecker H, Wiese J, Imhoff JF. Levantilides A and B, 20-membered macrolides from a Micromonospora strain isolated from the mediterranean deep sea sediment. Mar Drugs. 2011;9(1):98–108.
58. Song Y, Huang H, Chen Y, Ding J, Zhang Y, Sun A, Zhang W, Ju J. Cytotoxic and antibacterial marfuraquinocins from the deep South China sea-derived *Streptomyces niveus* SCSIO 3406. J Nat Prod. 2013;76(12):2263–8.
59. Abdelmohsen UR, Balasubramanian S, Oelschlaeger TA, Grkovic T, Pham NB, Quinn RJ, Hentschel U. Potential of marine natural products against drug-resistant fungal, viral, and parasitic infections. Lancet Infect Dis. 2017;17(2):e30–41.
60. Mitchell SS, Nicholson B, Teisan S, Lam KS, Potts BC. Aureoverticillactam, a novel 22-atom macrocyclic lactam from the marine actinomycete *Streptomyces aureoverticillatus*. J Nat Prod. 2004;67(8):1400–2.

61. Li F, Maskey RP, Qin S, Sattler I, Fiebig HH, Maier A, Zeeck A, Laatsch H. Chinikomycins A and B: isolation, structure elucidation, and biological activity of novel antibiotics from a marine Streptomyces sp. isolate M045, 1. J Nat Prod. 2005;68(3):349–53.
62. Kwon HC, Kauffman CA, Jensen PR, Fenical W. Marinomycins A–D, antitumor-antibiotics of a new structure class from a marine actinomycete of the recently discovered genus "Marinispora". J Am Chem Soc. 2006;128(5):1622–32.
63. Asolkar RN, Jensen PR, Kauffman CA, Fenical W. Daryamides A–C, weakly cytotoxic polyketides from a marine-derived actinomycete of the genus Streptomyces strain CNQ-085. J Nat Prod. 2006;69(12):1756–9.
64. Williams PG, Miller ED, Asolkar RN, Jensen PR, Fenical W. Arenicolides A–C, 26-membered ring macrolides from the marine actinomycete *Salinispora arenicola*. J Org Chem. 2007;72(14):5025–34.
65. Wu SJ, Fotso S, Li F, Qin S, Laatsch H. Amorphane sesquiterpenes from a marine *Streptomyces* sp., 1. J Nat Prod. 2007;70(2):304–6.
66. Martin GD, Tan LT, Jensen PR, Dimayuga RE, Fairchild CR, Raventos-Suarez C, Fenical W. Marmycins A and B, cytotoxic pentacyclic C-glycosides from a marine sediment-derived actinomycete related to the genus Streptomyces. J Nat Prod. 2007;70(9):1406–9.
67. Fu P, Liu P, Li X, Wang Y, Wang S, Hong K, Zhu W. Cyclic bipyridine glycosides from the marine-derived actinomycete *Actinoalloteichus cyanogriseus* WH1-2216-6. Org Lett. 2011;13(22):5948–51.
68. Babadi ZK, Sudarman E, Ebrahimipour GH, Primahana G, Stadler M, Wink J. Structurally diverse metabolites from the rare actinobacterium *Saccharothrix xinjiangensis*. J Antibiot. 2020;73(1):48–55.
69. Iniyan AM, Sudarman E, Wink J, Kannan RR, Vincent SG. Ala-geninthiocin, a new broad spectrum thiopeptide antibiotic, produced by a marine *Streptomyces* sp. ICN19. J Antibiot. 2019;72(2):99–105.
70. Yang T, Yamada K, Zhou T, Harunari E, Igarashi Y, Terahara T, Kobayashi T, Imada C. Akazamicin, a cytotoxic aromatic polyketide from marine-derived *Nonomuraea* sp. J Antibiot. 2019;72(4):202–9.
71. Fu P, Mac Millan JB. Thiasporines A–C, thiazine and thiazole derivatives from a marine-derived *Actinomycetospora chlora*. J Nat Prod. 2015;78(3):548–51.
72. Wu SJ, Fotso S, Li F, Qin S, Kelter G, Fiebig HH, Laatsch H. N-carboxamido-staurosporine and selina-4 (14), 7 (11)-diene-8, 9-diol, new metabolites from a marine *Streptomyces* sp. J Antibiot. 2006;59(6):331–7.
73. Gorajana A, Kurada BV, Peela S, Jangam P, Vinjamuri S, Poluri E, Zeeck A. 1-Hydroxy-1-norresistomycin, a new cytotoxic compound from a marine actinomycete, *Streptomyces chibaensis* AUBN1/7. J Antibiot. 2005;58(8):526–9.
74. Jeong SY, Shin HJ, Kim TS, Lee HS, Park SK, Kim HM. Streptokordin, a new cytotoxic compound of the methylpyridine class from a marine-derived Streptomyces sp. KORDI-3238. J Antibiot. 2006;59(4):234–40.
75. Miller ED, Kauffman CA, Jensen PR, Fenical W. Piperazimycins: cytotoxic hexadepsipeptides from a marine-derived bacterium of the genus Streptomyces. J Org Chem. 2007;72(2):323–30.
76. Manam RR, Teisan S, White DJ, Nicholson B, Grodberg J, Neuteboom ST, Lam KS, Mosca DA, Lloyd GK, Potts BC. Lajollamycin, a nitro-tetraene spiro-β-lactone-γ-lactam antibiotic from the marine actinomycete Streptomyces nodosus. J Nat Prod. 2005;68(2):240–3.
77. Bugni TS, Woolery M, Kauffman CA, Jensen PR, Fenical W. Bohemamines from a marine-derived *Streptomyces* sp. J Nat Prod. 2006;69(11):1626–8.
78. Li DH, Zhu TJ, Liu HB, Fang YC, Gu QQ, Zhu WM. Four butenolides are novel cytotoxic compounds isolated from the marine-derived bacterium, *Streptoverticillium luteoverticillatum* 11014. Arch Pharm Res. 2006;29:624–6.
79. Hohmann C, Schneider K, Bruntner C, Irran E, Nicholson G, Bull AT, Jones AL, Brown R, Stach JE, Goodfellow M, Beil W. Caboxamycin, a new antibiotic of the benzoxazole family produced by the deep-sea strain Streptomyces sp. NTK 937. J Antibiot. 2009;62(2):99–104.
80. Hughes CC, Mac Millan JB, Gaudêncio SP, Jensen PR, Fenical W. The ammosamides: structures of cell cycle modulators from a marine-derived Streptomyces species. Angew Chem Int Ed. 2009;48(4):725–7.
81. Udwary DW, Zeigler L, Asolkar RN, Singan V, Lapidus A, Fenical W, Jensen PR, Moore BS. Genome sequencing reveals complex secondary metabolome in the marine actinomycete *Salinispora tropica*. Natl Acad Sci. 2007;104(25):10376–81.
82. Asolkar RN, Freel KC, Jensen PR, Fenical W, Kondratyuk TP, Park EJ, Pezzuto JM. Arenamides A–C, cytotoxic NFκB inhibitors from the marine actinomycete *Salinispora arenicola*. J Nat Prod. 2009;72(3):396–402.
83. Golinska P, Wypij M, Agarkar G, Rathod D, Dahm H, Rai M. Endophytic actinobacteria of medicinal plants: diversity and bioactivity. Antonie Van Leeuwenhoek. 2015;108:267–89.
84. Janaki T. Anticancer activity of Streptomyces cacaoi subsp cacaoi.M20 against breast cancer (MCF-7) cell lines. Int. J. Chemtech Res. 2019;12(4):108–16. https://doi.org/10.20902/IJCTR.
85. Taechowisan T, Chaisaeng S, Phutdhawong WS. Antibacterial, antioxidant and anticancer activities of biphenyls from Streptomyces sp. BO-07: an endophyte in Boesenbergia rotunda (L.) Mansf A. Food Agric Immunol. 2017;28(6):1330–46.
86. Li J, Zhao GZ, Chen HH, Wang HB, Qin S, Zhu WY, Xu LH, Jiang CL, Li WJ. Antitumour and antimicrobial activities of endophytic streptomycetes

from pharmaceutical plants in rainforest. Lett Appl Microbiol. 2008;47(6):574–80.
87. Salam N, Khieu TN, Liu MJ, Vu TT, Chu-Ky S, Quach NT, Phi QT, Narsing Rao MP, Fontana A, Sarter S, Li WJ. Endophytic actinobacteria associated with *Dracaena cochinchinensis* Lour.: isolation, diversity, and their cytotoxic activities. Biomed Res Int. 2017;2017:1308563.
88. Ezra D, Castillo UF, Strobel GA, Hess WM, Porter H, Jensen JB, Condron MA, Teplow DB, Sears J, Maranta M, Hunter M. Coronamycins, peptide antibiotics produced by a verticillate *Streptomyces* sp. (MSU-2110) endophytic on *Monstera* sp. Microbiol. 2004;150(4):785–93.
89. Igarashi Y, Mogi T, Yanase S, Miyanaga S, Fujita T, Sakurai H, Saiki I, Ohsaki A. Brartemicin, an inhibitor of tumor cell invasion from the actinomycete *Nonomuraea* sp. J Nat Prod. 2009;72(5):980–2.
90. Igarashi Y, Ogura H, Furihata K, Oku N, Indananda C, Thamchaipenet A. Maklamicin, an antibacterial polyketide from an endophytic *Micromonospora* sp. J Nat Prod. 2011;74(4):670–4.
91. Igarashi Y, Miura SS, Fujita T, Furumai T. Pterocidin, a cytotoxic compound from the endophytic *Streptomyces hygroscopicus*. J Antibiot. 2006;59(3):193–5.
92. Castillo U, Harper JK, Strobel GA, Sears J, Alesi K, Ford E, Lin J, Hunter M, Maranta M, Ge H, Yaver D. Kakadumycins, novel antibiotics from Streptomyces sp. NRRL 30566, an endophyte of *Grevillea pteridifolia*. FEMS Microbiol Lett. 2003;224(2):183–90.
93. Caruso M, Colombo AL, Fedeli L, Pavesi A, Quaroni S, Saracchi M, Ventrella G. Isolation of endophytic fungi and actinomycetes taxane producers. Ann Microbiol. 2000;50(1):3–14.
94. Davidson SK, Allen SW, Lim GE, Anderson CM, Haygood M. Evidence for the biosynthesis of bryostatins by the bacterial symbiont "Candidatus Endobugula sertula" of the bryozoan Bugula neritina. Appl Microbiol. 2001;67(10):4531–7.
95. Thakur NL, Jain R, Natalio F, Hamer B, Thakur AN, Müller WE. Marine molecular biology: an emerging field of biological sciences. Biotechnol Adv. 2008;26(3):233–45.
96. Abdelmohsen UR, Bayer K, Hentschel U. Diversity, abundance and natural products of marine sponge-associated actinomycetes. Nat Prod Rep. 2014;31(3):381–99.
97. Abdelmohsen UR, Pimentel-Elardo SM, Hanora A, Radwan M, Abou-El-Ela SH, Ahmed S, Hentschel U. Isolation, phylogenetic analysis and anti-infective activity screening of marine sponge associated actinomycetes. Mar Drugs. 2010;8(3):399–412.
98. Wyche TP, Hou Y, Braun D, Cohen HC, Xiong MP, Bugni TS. First natural analogs of the cytotoxic thiodepsipeptide thiocoraline A from a marine *Verrucosispora* sp. J Org Chem. 2011;76(16):6542–7.
99. Khan ST, Tamura T, Takagi M, Shin-Ya K. Streptomyces tateyamensis sp. nov., Streptomyces marinus sp. nov. and Streptomyces haliclonae sp. nov., isolated from the marine sponge Haliclona sp. Int J Syst Evol. 2010;60(12):2775–9.
100. Ueda JY, Khan ST, Takagi M, Shin-ya K. JBIR-58, a new salicylamide derivative, isolated from a marine sponge-derived Streptomyces sp. SpD081030ME-02. J Antibiot. 2010;63(5):267–9.
101. Schneemann I, Kajahn I, Ohlendorf B, Zinecker H, Erhard A, Nagel K, Wiese J, Imhoff JF. Mayamycin, a cytotoxic polyketide from a Streptomyces strain isolated from the marine sponge *Halichondria panicea*. J Nat Prod. 2010;73(7):1309–12.
102. Wei RB, Xi T, Li J, Wang P, Li FC, Lin.YC, Qin S. Lobophorin C and D, new kijanimicin derivatives from a marine sponge-associated actinomycetal strain AZS17. Mar Drugs. 2011;9(3):359–68.
103. Igarashi Y, Asano D, Sawamura M, In Y, Ishida T, Imoto M. Ulbactins F and G, polycyclic thiazoline derivatives with tumor cell migration inhibitory activity from Brevibacillus sp. Org Lett. 2016;18(7):1658–61.
104. Erba E, Bergamaschi D, Ronzoni S, Faretta M, Taverna S, Bonfanti M, Catapano CV, Faircloth G, Jimeno J, D'incalci M. Mode of action of thiocoraline, a natural marine compound with anti-tumour activity. Br J Cancer. 1999;80(7):971–80.
105. Bae MA, Yamada K, Ijuin Y, Tsuji T, Yazawa K, Uemura D. Aburatubolactam A, a novel inhibitor of superoxide anion generation from a marine microorganism. Heterocycl Commun. 1996;2(4):315–8.
106. Lorente A, Pla D, Canedo LM, Albericio F, Alvarez M. Isolation, structural assignment, and total synthesis of barmumycin. J Org Chem. 2010;75(24):8508–15.
107. Nair V, Schuhmann I, Anke H, Kelter G, Fiebig HH, Helmke E, Laatsch H. Marine bacteria, XLVII–Psychrotolerant bacteria from extreme antarctic habitats as producers of rare bis-and trisindole alkaloids. Planta Med. 2016;82(09/10):910–8.
108. Feling RH, et al. Salinosporamide A: a highly cytotoxic proteasome inhibitor from a novel microbial source, a marine bacterium of the new genus salinospora. Angew Chem Int Ed Engl. 2003;42(3):355–7.
109. Do HN, Nguyen TH. Studies on the prodigiosin production from *Streptomyces coelicolor* in liquid media by using heated *Lactobacillus rhamnosus*. J Appl Pharm Sci. 2014;4(5):021–4.
110. Kawasaki T, Sakurai F, Nagatsuka SY, Hayakawa Y. Prodigiosin biosynthesis gene cluster in the roseophilin producer *Streptomyces griseoviridis*. J Antibiot. 2009;62(5):271–6.
111. Hong B, Prabhu VV, Zhang S, van den Heuvel AP, Dicker DT, Kopelovich L, El-Deiry WS. Prodigiosin rescues deficient p53 signaling and antitumor effects via upregulating p73 and disrupting its interaction with mutant p53rescuing deficient p53 via p73 in cancers. Cancer Res. 2014;74(4):1153–65.
112. Li J, Kim SG, Blenis J. Rapamycin: one drug, many effects. Cell Metabol. 2014;19(3):373–9.

113. Koba M, Konopa J. Actinomycin D and its mechanisms of action. Adv Clin Exp Med. 2005;16:59.
114. Verweij J, Pinedo HM. Mitomycin C: mechanism of action, usefulness and limitations. Anti-Cancer Drugs. 1990;1(1):5–13.
115. Dorr RT. Bleomycin pharmacology: mechanism of action and resistance, and clinical pharmacokinetics. Semin Oncol. 1992;19(2):3–8.
116. Itoh T, Kinoshita M, Wei H, Kobayashi M. Stereostructure of komodoquinone a, a neuritogenic anthracycline, from marine Streptomyces sp. KS3. Chem Pharm Bull. 2003;51(12):1402–4.
117. Itoh T, Kinoshita M, Aoki S, Kobayashi M. Komodoquinone A, a novel neuritogenic anthracycline, from marine Streptomyces sp. KS3. J Nat Prod. 2003;66(10):1373–7.
118. Fitzner A, Frauendorf H, Laatsch H, Diederichsen U. Formation of gutingimycin: analytical investigation of trioxacarcin A-mediated alkylation of dsDNA. Anal Biochem. 2008;390:1139–47.
119. Maskey RP, Helmke E, Fiebig HH, Laatsch H. Parimycin: isolation and structure elucidation of a novel cytotoxic 2, 3-dihydroquinizarin analogue of γ-indomycinone from a marine Streptomycete isolate. J Antibiot. 2002;55(12):1031–5.
120. Schneider K, Keller S, Wolter FE, Röglin L, Beil W, Seitz O, Nicholson G, Bruntner C, Riedlinger J, Fiedler HP, Süssmuth RD. Proximicins A, B, and C—antitumor furan analogues of netropsin from the marine actinomycete Verrucosispora induce upregulation of p53 and the cyclin kinase inhibitor p21. Angew Chem Int Ed. 2008;47(17):3258–61.
121. Romero F, Espliego F, Baz JP, De Quesada TG, Grávalos D, De La Calle FE, Fernåndez-Puentes JL. Thiocoraline, a new depsipeptide with antitumor activity produced by a marine Micromonospora I. Taxonomy, fermentation, isolation, and biological activities. J Antibiot. 1997;50(9):734–7.
122. Baz JP, Canedo LM, Puentes JL, ELIPE MV. Thiocoraline, a novel depsipeptide with antitumor activity produced by a marine Micromonospora II. Physico-chemical properties and structure determination. J Antibiot. 1997;50(9):738–41.
123. Aggarwal BB, Sethi G, Nair A, Ichikawa H. Nuclear factor-κB: a holy grail in cancer prevention and therapy. Curr Signal Transduct Ther. 2006;1(1):25–52.
124. Melisi D, Chiao PJ. NF-κB as a target for cancer therapy. Expert Opin Ther Targets. 2007;11(2):133–44.
125. Butler MS. Natural products to drugs: natural product-derived compounds in clinical trials. Nat Prod Rep. 2008;25:475–16.
126. Maggi M, Scotti C. Enzymes in metabolic anticancer therapy. In: Therapeutic enzymes: function and clinical implications; 2019. p. 173–99.
127. Piątkowska-Jakubas B, Krawczyk-Kuliś M, Giebel S, Adamczyk-Cioch M, Czyż A, Lech-Marańda E, Paluszewska M, Pałynyczko G, Piszcz J, Hołowiecki J. Use of L-asparaginase in acute lymphoblastic leukemia: recommendations of the Polish Adult Leukemia Group. Pol Arch Intern Med. 2008;118(11):664–9.
128. Prabhu GN, Chandrasekaran M. Purification and characterization of an anti-cancer enzyme produced by marine Vibrio Costicola under a novel solid state fermentation process. Braz Arch Biol Technol. 1999;42:363–8.
129. Sharma B, Singh S, Kanwar SS. L-methionase: a therapeutic enzyme to treat malignancies, vol. 2014. Int: Biomed Res; 2014. p. 1.
130. El-Naggar NE, Deraz SF, Soliman HM, El-Deeb NM, El-Ewasy SM. Purification, characterization, cytotoxicity and anticancer activities of L-asparaginase, anti-colon cancer protein, from the newly isolated alkaliphilic Streptomyces fradiae NEAE-82. Sci Rep. 2016;6(1):32926.
131. Nakaew N, Ngoenkam J, Donphraiyon M, Yot-an T, Jompaeng C, Ano-thai B, Sungthong R. Endophytic actinobacteria of herbal rhizomes and their pharmaceutical potential to form L-asparaginase. Acc Microbiol. 2019;1(1A):502.
132. Reda FM. Kinetic properties of *Streptomyces canarius* L-Glutaminase and its anticancer efficiency. Braz J Microbiol. 2015;46:957–68.
133. Awad HM, El-Deen AM, Mostafa ES, Hassabo AA. Biochemical studies and biological activities on L-glutaminase from rhizosphere soil Streptomyces rochei SAH2_CWMSG. Egypt Pharm J. 2019;18(1):27.
134. Singh S, Singh A. Current status of nanomedicine and nanosurgery. Anesth Essays Res. 2013;7(2):237.
135. Rizzo LY, Theek B, Storm G, Kiessling F, Lammers T. Recent progress in nanomedicine: therapeutic, diagnostic and theranostic applications. Curr Opin Biotechnol. 2013;24(6):1159–66.
136. Morigi V, Tocchio A, Bellavite Pellegrini C, Sakamoto JH, Arnone M, Tasciotti E. Nanotechnology in medicine: from inception to market domination. J Drug Deliv. 2012;2012:389485.
137. Etheridge ML, Campbell SA, Erdman AG, Haynes CL, Wolf SM, McCullough J. The big picture on nanomedicine: the state of investigational and approved nanomedicine products. Nanomedicine. 2013;9(1):1–4.
138. Schroeder A, Heller DA, Winslow MM, Dahlman JE, Pratt GW, Langer R, Jacks T, Anderson DG. Treating metastatic cancer with nanotechnology. Nat Rev Cancer. 2012;12(1):39–50.
139. Bae EJ, Park HJ, Park JS, Yoon JY, Kim YH, Choi KH, Yi JH. Effect of chemical stabilizers in silver nanoparticle suspensions on nanotoxicity. Bull Korean Chem Soc. 2011;32(2):613–9.
140. Prabhu P, Patravale V. The upcoming field of theranostic nanomedicine: an overview. J Biomed Nanotechnol. 2012;8(6):859–82.
141. Melancon MP, Stafford RJ, Li C. Challenges to effective cancer nanotheranostics. J Control Release. 2012;164(2):177–82.

142. Singh P, Kim YJ, Yang DC. A strategic approach for rapid synthesis of gold and silver nanoparticles by Panax ginseng leaves. Artif Cells Nanomed Biotechnol. 2016;44(8):1949–57.
143. Manivasagan P, Venkatesan J, Sivakumar K, Kim SK. Actinobacteria mediated synthesis of nanoparticles and their biological properties: a review. Crit Rev Microbiol. 2016;42(2):209–21.
144. Shanmugasundaram T, Radhakrishnan M, Gopikrishnan V, Pazhanimurugan R, Balagurunathan R. A study of the bactericidal, anti-biofouling, cytotoxic and antioxidant properties of actinobacterially synthesised silver nanoparticles. Colloids Surf B: Biointerfaces. 2013;111:680–7.
145. Manivasagan P, Venkatesan J, Senthilkumar K, Sivakumar K, Kim SK. Biosynthesis, antimicrobial and cytotoxic effect of silver nanoparticles using a novel Nocardiopsis sp. MBRC-1. Biomed Res Intl. 2013;2013:287638.
146. Ahmad MS, Yasser MM, Sholkamy EN, Ali AM, Mehanni MM. Anticancer activity of biostabilized selenium nanorods synthesized by *Streptomyces bikiniensis* strain Ess_amA-1. Int J Nanomedicine. 2015;10:3389.
147. Ramya S, Shanmugasundaram T, Balagurunathan R. Biomedical potential of actinobacterially synthesized selenium nanoparticles with special reference to anti-biofilm, anti-oxidant, wound healing, cytotoxic and anti-viral activities. J Trace Elem Med Biol. 2015;32:30–9.
148. Kumar CG, Poornachandra Y, Chandrasekhar C. Green synthesis of bacterial mediated anti-proliferative gold nanoparticles: inducing mitotic arrest (G2/M phase) and apoptosis (intrinsic pathway). Nanoscale. 2015;7(44):18738–50.
149. Abd-Elnaby HM, Abo-Elala GM, Abdel-Raouf UM, Hamed MM. Antibacterial and anticancer activity of extracellular synthesized silver nanoparticles from marine Streptomyces rochei MHM13. Egypt J Aquat Res. 2016;42(3):301–12.
150. Buszewski B, Railean-Plugaru V, Pomastowski P, Rafińska K, Szultka-Mlynska M, Golinska P, Wypij M, Laskowski D, Dahm H. Antimicrobial activity of biosilver nanoparticles produced by a novel *Streptacidiphilus durhamensis* strain. J Microbiol Immunol Infect. 2018;51(1):45–54.
151. Shanmugasundaram T, Balagurunathan R. Bio-medically active zinc oxide nanoparticles synthesized by using extremophilic actinobacterium, Streptomyces sp. (MA30) and its characterization. Artif Cells Nanomed Biotechnol. 2017;45(8):1521–9.
152. Shanmugasundaram T, Radhakrishnan M, Gopikrishnan V, Kadirvelu K, Balagurunathan R. Biocompatible silver, gold and silver/gold alloy nanoparticles for enhanced cancer therapy: in vitro and in vivo perspectives. Nanoscale. 2017;9(43):16773–90.
153. Ranjani A, Gopinath PM, Ananth S, Narchonai G, Santhanam P, Thajuddin N, Dhanasekaran D. Multidimensional dose–response toxicity exploration of silver nanoparticles from *Nocardiopsis flavascens* RD30. Appl Nanosci. 2018;8:699–713.
154. Shanmugasundaram T, Balagurunathan R. Bio-directed synthesis, structural characterisation of platinum based metal nanocomposites (Pt/Ag, Pt/Au, Pt/Ag/Au) and their biomedical applications. Mater Res Express. 2018;5(9):095402.
155. Shanmugasundaram T, Radhakrishnan M, Poongodi A, Kadirvelu K, Balagurunathan R. Bio-inspired synthesis of superparamagnetic iron oxide nanoparticles for enhanced in vitro anticancer therapy. MRS Commun. 2018;8(2):604–9.
156. Mazhari BB, Agsar D, Saiemaldahr MH, AlSoud WA, Adam A, Alrowaily AQ, Elshek I. Anticancer attributes of gold nanoparticles synthesized by novel isolate *Streptomyces tuirus* DBZ39. J Biomed. 2018;1:4.
157. Chugh H, Sood D, Chandra I. Role of gold and silver nanoparticles in cancer nano-medicine. Artif Cells Nanomed Biotechnol. 2018;4:1–1.
158. Uthaman S, Huh KM, Park IK. Tumor microenvironment-responsive nanoparticles for cancer theragnostic applications. Biomater Res. 2018;22:1–1.

Clinical Translation of Microbe-Based Therapies

11

Sangeetha Murthy, Balagurunathan Ramasamy, Sivarajan Anbalmani, and Siddharthan Nagarajan

11.1 Introduction

Every living thing such as plant, animal, human, etc., is born into the globe with a 100% pure one, meanwhile, none of them leave the world without the association of microbes. In particular, different communities of microorganisms live in the human body's genital tracts, gut/gastrointestinal tract (GI), upper airways, skin, mouth, and also other body tissues [1]. Around 100 trillion microbial cells occur in the human body; outnumbering human cells by 10 to 1, they make up only about 1–3% of the human body's mass. The human body act as a harbor for a huge array of microorganisms such as fungi, virus, and parasites among those bacteria have a great role. Each microbiota community regulates the human body as a health and/or disease factor by the influence of the genetic material of the microbe. The collective genomes of the bacteria in a certain environment are known as the microbiome, and they encode approximately three million genes that produce hundreds of metabolites that affect the host's phenotypic and overall health, among other tasks. Dysbiosis, which is caused by an imbalance in the microbial community in the gastrointestinal system, is linked to a number of conditions, including diabetes, obesity, cancer, and *Clostridium difficile* infection. Dysbiosis in the vagina may increase the threat of recurrent infections, pelvic inflammatory disease, HIV transmission, and so on. The microbiota may also impact significantly such as dermatitis disease in the skin and caries disease in the oral [2–7]. The beneficial normal flora of the body involves many physiological functions like participation in nutrient absorption, protection of our body from microbial pathogens, and also enhancement of host immunity. However, the diversity of microbiota can alter by diverse exogenous and endogenous factors like environmental microbes, hygiene, health status, diet, and drugs. The main organs, such as the brain, heart, liver, lungs, and kidneys, depend on the gut bacteria to function properly. These organs lead to malfunction and also the stimulation of various associated diseases may occur due to any disruption to the homeostasis of microbiota. Over a decade ago, a plethora of data in biomedical research showed that modification in gut microbiota plays a major role in the development of numerous diseases and disorders. New therapeutic options for the growth of the gut microbiota have arisen as an emerging necessity in the treatment of many distant and local diseases/disorders, even if we are still at the basic level of progress. At the forefront

S. Murthy
Department of Microbiology, Periyar University, Salem, Tamil Nadu, India

Kriya Biosys Pvt. Ltd., Salem, Tamil Nadu, India

B. Ramasamy (✉) · S. Anbalmani · S. Nagarajan
Department of Microbiology, Periyar University, Salem, Tamil Nadu, India

K. Parthasarathy, R. Manikkam (eds.), *Translational Research in Biomedical Sciences: Recent Progress and Future Prospects*, https://doi.org/10.1007/978-981-97-1777-4_11

of biomedical research are initiatives to investigate and pinpoint the critical role of particular microorganisms [8]. It will result in the translation of mechanistic insights into how normal flora affects health benefits including the successful application of microbe-based therapies. The microbes are being examined for therapeutic uses by the two main categories, that is genetically programmed microbes are used to secrete therapeutics at the locations of disease spot or delivery of therapeutics via systemic absorption by biological barriers and another type, that involves the delivery of therapeutic bacteria to the host for restoring of symbiosis, it leads to the pathogens displacement at the host. The success rate of therapeutic benefit depends upon the appropriate delivery of microbes. The delivery process is influenced by the following factors: Environmental elements such as UV-light, enzymes, and acid, which can increase the microbe viability/efficacy that leads to interrupting the biological secretion of microbes. The physical mechanisms of engraftment and drug diffusion, which are necessary to achieve a proper residence time at the site of action for drug absorption via the duodenum, are impeded by biological barriers such as microbiota, mucus, the duodenum, and lumen contents. A comprehensive comprehension of the interplay of the microbiota, microbial-therapeutic agents, and the host environment has the potential to eliminate the obstacle preventing the logical development of delivery strategies. The present focus of biomedical science is on clarifying the mechanisms of action in delivery approaches for microbe-based medicines in the future. This chapter discusses the critical role that dysbiosis and the gut microbiota play in human health, as well as methods for modifying the gut microbiota through nutrition, probiotics, and formulation and the thoughtful design of next-generation microbial therapies [1–4, 9–12].

11.2 Gut Microbiota's Role in Human Health

Numerous facets of human health, including immunological, metabolic, and neurobehavioral traits, are significantly influenced by gut bacteria. Numerous studies attest to the important role gut microorganisms play in human health (Fig. 11.1). Observational studies in human showed cross-sectional associations of microorganisms with human health traits [13]. Commonly, the quantification of gut microbiota composition is estimated by DNA-based methods—whole genome shotgun sequencing/next-generation 16S ribosomal RNA genes sequencing which inference. Those screenings are used for inference of microbiota functions and metabolomic methods, where are used to measure the metabolic products of the microbiota from stool and serum samples [14–16].

Enhancing the fermentation of non-digestible substrates including dietary fibers and endogenous intestinal mucus are important function of the gut microbiota. Microbes produce short-chain fatty acids (SCFAs) such butyrate, propionate, and acetate as a result of this fermentation process. The most prevalent SCFA, acetate, is a key molecule for bacterial development and plays a crucial function in the control of central appetite in lipogenesis and cholesterol metabolism. Through its interactions with the liver's gut fatty acid receptors, propionate controls gluconeogenesis and satiety signals. Colocytes use butyrate as their primary energy source, which also causes colon cancer cells to undergo apoptosis. Additionally, it triggers intestinal gluconeogenesis, which improves energy homeostasis and glucose levels. Because epithelial cells use β oxidation to consume large amounts of oxygen, butyrate is necessary for them. It is creating a hypoxic environment that keeps the gut's oxygen balance stable and prevents the gut bacteria from

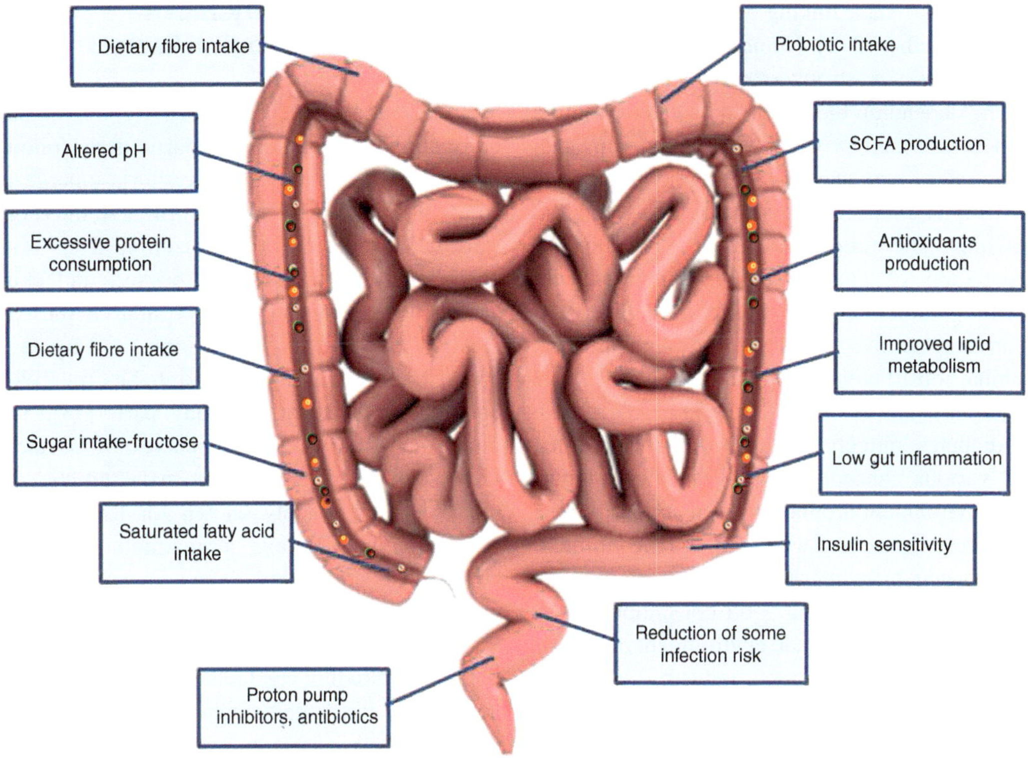

Fig. 11.1 Graphic representation of the role of gut microbiota in human health

becoming dysbiotic. Propionate and butyrate are involved in the regulation of gut hormones and reduce appetite. The unconjugated and secondary bile acids are synthesized by gut microbial enzymes from the end product of bile acid metabolism. They act as metabolic regulators and also signaling molecules to regulate essential host pathways [17–19].

11.3 Microbiota Dysbiosis in Human Diseases

In the past few decades, a tremendous amount of study has examined the dysbiosis of the gut microbiota in humans, which is linked to various diseases (Table 11.1). The study of the human microbiome may advance our understanding of the host-human body's microbial populations. In addition to occurring within an organ, microbe–host interactions have also been found an inter-

Table 11.1 List of microbiota dysbiosis-associated with human diseases

Dysbiosis of the Human microbiota	Diseases/disorders
Gut-Brain	Pneumonia
	Psychiatric disorders
	Autism
	Neurodegenerative disorders
Gut-Lung	Asthma
	Obstructive pulmonary diseases
	Lung cancer
Heart diseases	Heart failure
	Atherosclerosis
Gut-Skin	Psoriasis
	Acne vulgaris
	Skin cancer
Metabolism	Obesity
	T2 diabetes
	Mitochondrial dysfunction
	Cancer

kingdom crosstalk linking automatically diverse organs together [2–5]. Numerous organs, including the brain, gastrointestinal tract, lungs, and others, depend on the gut microbiota to maintain homeostasis and progression of numerous diseases also regulates by gut microbiota via inter-organ connections including gut–brain and gut–lung. The tremendous research revealed the association of gut microbiota dysbiosis with human pathologies such as psychiatric disorders, neurodegenerative disorders, autism, pneumonia, asthma, obstructive pulmonary diseases, acne vulgaris, psoriasis, heart failure, atherosclerosis, T2 diabetes, mitochondrial dysfunction, obesity, and various cancers including skin and lungs. The environment around the human microbiome is actively interacting with it. In the meantime, it is impacted by numerous elements of a host's everyday life, including food consumption and pollutants. The man-made environment including such as building structures, industrial facilities, and transportation vehicles is used for people to live, work and travel. They also utilize very extreme environments like submarines and space stations. The resident microbiomes have been influenced by the built environment such as abundant microbial diversity, unstable environmental conditions, and as well as physiological parameters. Different microbial communities occur on every part of the built environment on the earth's surface, which is collectively called a built environment microbiome. Research evidence concluded that the built environment microbiomes are intensely diverse from the outdoor environments microbiomes in which humans evolved. The interaction of built environment microbiomes with human inhabitants represents a highly interdisciplinary research field. The composition of microbial communities and their function may interact with a human by being extraordinarily complex and highly interconnected. Asthma, skin diseases, and allergies are thought to be becoming more common in industrialized countries due in part to the built environment microbiomes [12–20].

11.3.1 Microbiota Dysbiosis and Physiological Factors

Microbes are first encountered by the human body on the first day of life, particularly following birth when a variety of bacteria emerge to colonize the body of a new-born. The microbes start to develop their colonization from oral, nasopharyngeal membranes, tissues, and skin, gradually reaching the stomach and GI through the oral and salivary microbiome. A very high concentration of microbiome inhabits the colon compared with the other body parts [18]. The more than 1000 different species of bacteria, viruses, and eukaryotes that make up the gut microbiota are widely known for their several advantageous functions in maintaining human homeostasis, including defense against pathogens, GI integrity maintenance, energy harvesting, and host immunity regulation [19]. Many large-scale studies conducted over the past few decades have revealed a connection between gut microbial dysbiosis and a host of human diseases, including cancer, metabolic disorders, cardiovascular disease, chronic renal disease, periodontitis, and dental caries. The naturally occurring physiological changes such as immunological and hormonal gestational balance, pregnancy have an impact on the prevalence of the gut microbiota and their metabolic activity [20]. Estrogen and progesterone in women's bodies influence the proliferation, metabolism, and pathogenicity of microorganisms, which in turn affects the prenatal and postpartum gut microbiota including intestinal motility. According to a recent study, the gut microbiota repertoires of pregnant women differ significantly from those of non-pregnant women according to a variety of parameters, including body mass index, ethnicity, gestational age, state of nutrition, and others [21–23]. The unusual dysbiosis was associated with an increase in blood pressure, proteinuria, aminotransferase, and creatinine levels. Many of the current treatments, including surgery and hormone therapy, are inadequate. When treating endometriosis, taking one or two probiotics has a positive impact on immunological and physiological factors. *Saccharomyces baulardii* is the best example which is used as a new therapeutic technique for endometriosis treatment. Consuming multi-strain probiotics can actually increase intestinal epithelial integration and alter the composition of the gut microbiota [10–14].

11.3.2 Microbiota Dysbiosis in Chronic Kidney Diseases

There is an abundance of research indicating that dysbiosis of the gut microbiota and chronic inflammation in humans are inversely correlated. It was discovered that alterations in the function and composition of the gut microbiota are associated with a systemic inflammatory state and may play a role in the onset of chronic kidney disease (CKD). In addition to playing a role in the onset of CKD, gut dysbiosis is a major risk factor for the disease's progression and the emergence of its side effects, including cardiovascular comorbidities. A recent clinical study has shown that stage 5 CKD-infected patients have an abundance of *Neisseria, Lachnoclostridium, Bifidobacterium,* and *Faecalibacterium.* Some recent animal models confirmed the efficiency of prebiotic intervention in developing the gut microbiota and initiating the direction of new therapeutic methods including microbiota modulators [24–28].

11.3.3 Chronic Liver Disease and Microbiota Dysbiosis

The gut microbiota and liver are connected by a number of intricate processes. Therefore, any alteration to the gut microbiota has the potential to severely impair liver function. The alternation of intestinal absorbency and injured bile acid metabolism caused gut dysbiosis, which leads to systemic inflammation in the liver. The gut dysbiosis development strongly influences the type and severity of the chronic liver disease. Patients with non-alcoholic steatohepatitis and other chronic liver diseases have an imbalance in the Firmicutes/Bacteroidetes ratio (more Firmicutes and less Bacteroidetes), which is widely recognized to have a major impact on maintaining good intestinal homeostasis. Bile salts play a crucial role in fat solubilization and are maintained by microbial dysbiosis, which increases the permeability of the gut microbiota. These outcomes are all favorable to liver disease [29–31].

11.3.4 Carcinogenesis's Dysbiosis of the Microbiota

In healthy individuals, there is a correlation between circadian oscillations and the salivary cytokines and oral bacteria. Coffee and tea consumption, smoking; dental health, and denture use are frequently cited as the main factors influencing the salivary microbiome's composition. Furthermore, the structural and functional changes of gut microbiota have general significance, commonly beyond those related to digestion. About 15–20% of cancers could be caused by tumorigenesis which is associated with microbes. An imbalance in the homeostasis of gut microbes may interfere with the host's ability to maintain health. The human commensal microbiome and gut bacterial populations linked to pathologic circumstances have a role in the etiopathogenesis of malignancies, including lung and prostate carcinomas [32–36].

11.3.5 Microbiota Dysbiosis in Metabolic Syndromes

Numerous metabolic diseases, including obesity, dyslipidemia, and hyperglycemia, are associated with dysbiosis of the gut microbiota. Consuming a high-fat diet is, in fact, one of the best ways to induce dysbiosis of the gut microbiota and metabolic disorders like type 2. In general, dysbiosis of the gut microbiota controls the body's ability to store fat and, in turn, the prevalence of obesity. Excessive fat accumulation and increased sugar consumption have been shown to be important factors in the colonization of the intestine by enterobacteria, including genotoxic and pro-inflammatory *Escherichia coli.* These microbes affect the stability of the DNA of the host cell by DNA double-strand breaks via the production of colibactin, which is a genotoxin, thus exerting a pro-tumorigenic activity. Type 2 diabetes is influenced by the gut microbiota both during its onset and progression. The pathophysiology of type 2 diabetes involves the presence of certain microorganisms, including *Bacteroides, Faecalibacterium, Bifidobacterium, Roseburia,* and *Akkermansia* [37–41].

11.4 Microbial Therapies for Microbiome Modulation

Current clinical studies focus to modulate the microbiome of skin, GI, vaginal tract, and other tissues. The most effective method for inhibition/prevention of disease is altering microbe compositions by first-line antibiotics treatment. Antibiotics are essential components of medical care and have saved many lives. Antibiotic overuse has disrupted the beneficial microbiota and increased the prevalence of antibiotic-resistant/multidrug-resistant bacteria, which has resulted in dysbiosis and unfavorable clinical outcomes in recent times. Pathogens and antibiotic-resistant pathogens can be found in commensal-free environments, and this can frequently lead to more serious infections. This concern has resulted in intense interest in developing alternative strategies to prevent the emergence of antibiotic-resistant pathogens while maintaining the survival rate of commensal/beneficial bacteria [42–44].

11.4.1 Phage-Based Therapy

Phages are viruses that infect and replicate only within bacterial cells, also called bacteriophages. They are abundant in the environment and extremely diverse in morphology, size, and genomic composition. They are found as the most ubiquitous biological agent on earth and are incredibly selective to bacterial strains; commensal/beneficial bacteria are spared while the intestinal pathogen is completely destroyed. This has motivated the scientist to create phage-based treatments to combat diseases that are resistant to antibiotics. Phage-based therapies in clinical translation are expected to be minimized by the difficulties encountered throughout the processes of purification, characterization, and regulation. Furthermore, because of the multipart evolutionary dynamics between the targeted bacteria and the phage, pathogens may evolve a resistance to infection and lysis, which restricts their long-term usage in clinical treatment. Apart from that phage therapy, alternative therapies are developed such as gene editing enzymes, antimicrobial peptides, and inorganic metals. They are not yet widely used in clinical practice due to some limits of those approaches [45–48].

11.4.2 Selective Depletion of Opportunistic Bacterial Pathogens

Opportunistic respiratory pathogens routinely colonize healthy persons' upper respiratory tracts asymptomatically. These pathogens include *Streptococcus pneumoniae, Haemophilus influenzae, Moraxella catarrhalis, Staphylococcus aureus, Pseudomonas aeruginosa*, and *Klebsiella pneumoniae.* In individuals with chronic respiratory disorders, they lead to severe infections and exacerbations in the lower respiratory tract. Moreover, they are the main primary causes for hospital-acquired pneumonia (HAP), and a significant contributing factor to hospital infection-related deaths is their high incidence rate. The multidrug-resistant (MDR) bacterial strains that are frequently discovered in patients' lower airways, including ventilator-associated pneumonia and HAP, make treatment of these infections more challenging. Hence, a significant portion of the research study for the upcoming management of MDR lower airway infections involves the selective depletion of these bacteria in at-risk patients as well as a therapeutic intervention by antibiotic-independent strategies to control and inhibit potentially detrimental lung infections [42–44, 49–51].

11.4.3 Microbiome Modulation to Treat a Respiratory Infection

Respiratory infections such as acute and chronic lower airway disease are foremost reason for morbidity and mortality worldwide. With the continuous development of multidrug-resistant pathogens in respiratory infections, the scientific world is quickly nearing the post-antibiotic era. Furthermore, novel respiratory viruses with the potential to be the most virulent are always emerging; the severe critical respiratory illness coronavirus (COVID-19) is one such example. Changes in the lung and gut microbiome are associated with chronic respiratory syndromes and diseases. These changes are likely to have a role in the progression of infections and diseases as well as an increased vulnerability to respiratory pathogen infection [1–3]. A 10-year interdisciplinary global effort of the Human Microbiome Project (HMP) established that the structure of the healthy human microbiome at various bodily locations, as well as the nature of the connections between alterations in the microbiome and illness or infection. The research revealed a two-way communication channel between the gut and lung microbes. Alterations in the gut microbiota have been linked to respiratory/pulmonary infections and chronic lung illness, according to a number of ongoing clinical and experimental investigations. The microbiome's metabolites are essential to the process [4, 6, 42]. Moreover, pulmonary helminthic and bacterial infections will be prevented when activated immune cells migrate from the colon to the lung. Significantly, the intestinal microbiome may directly stimulate these systems. Chronic bronchitis and emphysema are the chronic obstructive pulmonary disease (COPD). Two major risk factors for COPD stimulation are age and cigarette smoke. These factors are associated with changes in the gut microbial populations, including a decrease in alpha diversity and an increase in Bacteroidetes ratios that lead to dysbiosis. Acute lower respiratory tract infections as well as higher susceptibility to lung infections caused by *Staphylococcus aureus, Streptococcus pneumonia, Pseudomonas aeruginosa,* and *Klebsiella pneumonia*, as well as viral infections such as respiratory syncytial virus and influenza virus, have been associated with intestinal dysbiosis. In order to promote lung immunity, the gut microbiota's activity and composition must be adjusted. This helps prevent respiratory bacterial infections and manage chronic lung illness. According to the International Scientific Association of Probiotics and Prebiotics (ISAPP), a prebiotic is a substrate that a host's microbiota uses to promote the host organism's health. In particular, consumption of non-digestible dietary fiber may promote the formation of bioactive metabolites and short-chain fatty acids (SCFA) from commensal microbiota. An epidemiological study provides compelling evidence of a causal relationship between dietary fiber foods consumption and lung health. By eradicating specific bacterial pathogens with the use of probiotic predatory bacteria, human monoclonal antibodies against bacteria, and strain-specific bacteriophages, the lung microbiota is directly modulated. A probiotic, as defined by the ISAPP, is a live bacterium that, when given in sufficient amounts, benefits the host's health. One of the most popular nutritional supplements is probiotics. It helps to change the microbiome's composition in favor of commensal microbiota, which includes SCFA-producing bacteria and beneficial microorganisms. More research is needed on the selection, quantity, timing, and duration of probiotics. No probiotic has been authorized as a live bio-therapeutic drug as of yet, and probiotic effectiveness is hotly contested for a variety of purposes, including respiratory disorders. Inanimate bacteria or their components that enhance the host organism's health are found in postbiotics. Although the exact immunomodulatory mechanism of postbiotics taken orally or intranasally is yet unknown, it may be partially caused by the induction of immunoglobulin-A and mucosal dendritic cells (Table 11.2). Postbiotics are mixtures of whole and/or fractionated bacterial lysates of common respiratory

Table 11.2 Microbiome-based approaches to prevent/treat respiratory disease

Type	Strategy	Method	Mechanism	Output
Modulation of intestinal microbiota	Prebiotics	Non-digestible dietary fiber	Colonic commensals produce short-chain fatty acids	Modulation of lung immunity
	Dietary probiotics	*Lactobacilli* spp. *Bifidobacterium* spp.	Short-chain fatty acids production	Increase beneficial bacterial taxa
	FMTs	Fecal transplant from healthy donor	Replacement of dysbiotic with healthy microbiota	Healthy microenvironment
Direct modulation of lung microbiota	Postbiotics	Bacterial lysates	Activation of mucosal DCs	IgA induction
	Probiotic bacterial predators	*Bdellovibrio* and *Micavibrio*	*Bdellovibrio* and *Micavibrio*: Attachment to gram pathogen	Pathogens destroyed
	Antibacterial mAbs	Neutralization of virulence factors	Attachment to airway epithelial cells	Complement fixation opsonophagocytosis intercellular killing
	Bacteriophages	Attachment and infection of phage DNA	Production and assembly of new phages	Lysis of airway pathogens

pathogens, and are frequently employed in the treatment of respiratory tract diseases. They exhibit the reduction of acute recurrent respiratory infections occurrence [42, 50–54].

11.4.4 Fecal Transplantation

Fecal transplantation/fecal microbiota transplantation (FMT)/stool transplant is a process that uses direct transfer of the recipient's gut microbiota to normalize the composition and increase a beneficial advantages. The method works by collecting healthy microbiota from the feces of a healthy donor and transferring them to the recipient's colon through colonoscopy, nasogastric tube, and also in capsule form (generally called "poop pills"). It gains a therapeutic benefit for the host. FMT is also called bacteriotherapy or intestinal microbiota transplant. It is described as the "ultimate probiotic" as it contains an abundant quantity and diversity of microbiota than any available probiotic. This therapeutic method has a long history and was first reported in the fourth century in China [55–60]. The human fecal suspension is used to treat severe diarrhea patients through the mouth. The precise mechanism of FMT treating disease is not fully understood it has been regarded since 2013, FMT methods have been approved by the Food and Drug Administration (FDA) in the USA to treat recurring and resistant *Clostridium difficile* infections. FMT has been widely used to treat extragastrointestinal conditions like autism and inflammatory bowel disease. Even though the long-term outcomes of FMT are yet to explored completely, it has a few adverse effects, but modern therapeutics recommend it as a safe therapeutic method. The clinical research looks forward to personalized FMT to treat different patients and diseases in the future [61–68].

11.4.5 Dermal Microbiome Modulation

The outermost layer of all living things is the skin, the biggest organ in the human body. It acts as a protection wall against various external harmful things. The skin has a complex immune system that includes molecular mediators, innate lymphoid cells, resident antigen-presenting cells, immune cells, etc. The skin is a well-known host for microbial communities. The skin's microbiota serves as a barrier to environmental stimuli that respond to life. The symbiotic relationship transforms into a dysbiotic one in response to different stressful circumstances, leading to diseases of the skin and other organs. Changes in the gut microbiome also accompany skin diseases, which are caused by dysbiosis of the skin microbiota. The gastrointestinal tract and skin are both heavily vascularized and extensively colonized by a wide variety of microorganisms that are involved in many aspects of maintaining homeostasis. Numerous investigations verified a bidirectional crosstalk of information between the skin and gut microbes. If conditions fared better, this intimate connection was shown to be linked to a number of skin conditions, including psoriasis, skin cancer, and atopic dermatitis. Compared to FMT techniques, topical cutaneous microbiota modification has received less research attention. The therapy of atopic dermatitis involves the wise development of a microbiota transplant to the skin-wide environment (Table 11.3). *Staphylococcus aureus* is a common causative agent for atopic dermatitis. The coagulase-negative Staphylococcus (CoNS), which is commensal in healthy skin, was isolated from the donor's skin in order to treat patients with *S. aureus*-positive atopic dermatitis. The antimicrobial peptides that CoNS secretes and which show antibacterial properties against *S. aureus* are the mechanism underlying this therapy. In order to treat *S. aureus*-positive patients with atopic dermatitis, CoNS strains were obtained from healthy donors for the clinical investigation. This resulted in a notable decrease in pathogenic *S. aureus* [69–71]. The rational approach toward microbiota modulation shows a promising application in the future. Applying a similar strategy with beneficial microorganisms to different tissues might be feasible. The positive outcome of the phase-1 trial suggests that microbiota transplantation can regulate skin dysbiosis and may be useful in treating fungal infections, burns, and chronic wounds in addition to dermatitis.

Table 11.3 Some examples of clinical trials: microbe-based drugs

Indication	Microbes-Bacteria	Formulation
Dental carries	Genetically modified *Streptococcus* mutant	Topical tooth treatment
Acne vulgaris, hypertension, atopic dermatitis eczema, allergic rhinitis	*Nitrosomonas eutropha*	Topical dermal spray
Eczema	*Staphylococcus hominis*	Topical dermal lotion
Atopic dermatitis	Autologous microbiota transplants	Topical dermal moisturizer
Atopic dermatitis	*Roseomonas mucosa*	Topical dermal spray via atomizer-modified syringe
Recurrent bacterial vaginosis; Recurrent urinary tract infection	Engineered *Lactobacillus* strain	Topical vaginal delivery
Oral mucositis	Genetically modified *Lactococcus lactis* that secretes trefoil factor 1	Mouth rinse
Unresectable hepatic spread	Attenuated strain of *Salmonella typhimurium* which expresses interleukin-2	Oral capsule
Familial adenomatous polyposis	Genetically modified *E. coli* that secretes betacatenin short-hairpin RNA	Oral suspension
Phenylketonuria	Engineered bacteria to convert phenylalanine to trans-cinnamic acid orphan drug status	Oral administration
Hyperammonemia	Engineered bacteria to convert systemic ammonia to arginine	Oral administration

Source: ClincalTrials.gov-identifier

11.4.6 Vaginal Microbiome Modulation

The colony of pathogen, commensal, and symbiotic bacteria that inhabit the vagina is known as the vaginal microbiota (VMB). The VMB is less complex compared with gut microbiota and the diversity of commensal colonization in the vagina is considered to be critical for reproductive health. The VMB is dominated by *Lactobacilli* sp. in the majority of healthy reproductive-age women. The dominant community of *Lactobacilli* sp. plays a key role in protecting against urogenital infections and managing reproductive tract health. The higher microbial diversity and depletion of *Lactobacilli* in the vagina increases the risk of poor gynecologic and obstetric outcomes. As compared to oral delivery, certain delivery challenges will be faced during topical treatment for vaginal tissues. Some of the clinical trials for vaginal microbiome modulation are under process. For example, the formulation of *Lactobacillus crispatus,* as a vaginal topical application was developed by Osel for the modification of the vaginal microbiota in order to treat urinary tract infections and recurrent bacterial vaginosis (Table 11.3). Patients with bacterial vaginosis have demonstrated safety, tolerance, and acceptance of the tropical application approach. In general, the vaginal environment is what attracts healthy and bacterial vaginosis during common illnesses of the female genital tract, like *Chlamydia trachomatis* and *vulvovaginal candidiasis* [72–77]. The composition of vaginal metabolites was significantly altered during genital infections due to changes in the bacterial populations, with the decrease of lactate serving as a common marker/signal for all clinical situations. *Lactobacillus fermentum* and *Lactobacillus acidophilus* were encapsulated and administered as an effervescent tablet to treat *Vulvovaginal candidiasis* [78]. The *Lactobacillus* strains demonstrated significant inhibition against four different Candida species that are associated with vulvovaginal candidiasis. Every clinical study emphasizes how crucial it is to take into account the patient's health, lifestyle, microbiota variability, and even the method of delivering microbiome-modulating treatments for vaginal bacterial infections [79].

11.5 Microbe Based-Delivery Approach

In the pharmaceutical industry, the use of bacteria in drug production is a longstanding and necessary cornerstone. Here, we take a quick look at potential for developing bacterial-based strategies that enhance the delivery system by bringing microenvironment interactions into account. Compared to other techniques, drug-producing bacteria therapies have significantly clearer delivery requirements since the characteristics and site of action of the delivered drug are well-established. Delivery efficiency will be increased by formulation-based strategies that can enhance residence time, increase resistance to environmental stresses, and localize to either infected tissue or the absorption site. Formulation techniques can also be utilized to preserve biological products and bacteria, since most genetically altered strains secrete biological products that have proven particularly challenging to stable and deliver in vivo. Furthermore, since biologics must be fully absorbed, strategies to lengthen the duration that they spend in an appropriate adsorption site—such as the duodenum—will help improve biological delivery [80–85].

11.6 Clinical Outlook

The gut microbiota evolves with the evolution of humans. The dynamic and constant interaction of the host with the GI microenvironment makes it simply changed by various endogen and external factors. Several clinical investigations have shown that a microbe may be able to provide alternative clinical therapies for the treatment of different diseases by secreting and delivering difficult-to-treat medications and by modulating the composition of the microbiota toward symbiosis (Table 11.3). For the advancement of these medicines, it is imperative to take into account the interactions that live-microbe therapies have with their host environment. It has been shown that a key success factor for all other medication types is the necessity of having control over the location, timing, and mode of action of a drug's interaction with the diseased site. A preclinical study has already confirmed that the success criteria such as enhancing distribution at the intended location can be achieved by protecting the microorganisms from environmental stresses, focusing their activity on mucosal surfaces, and directing them toward diseased cells. The mechanism and site of action of formulation-based techniques are known for drug-secreting microorganisms; they can manage residence time, target absorption sites, and boost survival rates. The efficacy of microbiome modulation elements, action site, and enabling particular interactions between the delivery and the source of dysbiosis or disease remain uncertain in the context of microbiome-modulating bacteria and microbe interaction with the host microenvironment. To close this information gap and enable the application of a logical formulation strategy to boost therapeutic microbe efficacy, static and dynamic in vitro models may be necessary. Understanding of pertinent microenvironment interactions and obstacles will grow, and it will become evident how opportunities relate to delivery platforms that might enhance microbial viability, residence time, stability, and efficiency. We envision that current research will make possible: We will identify the strains that are accountable for pushing out particular infections; the investigation of events that, through the use of in vitro model systems, can guide therapeutic design; the creation of a toolset for functionalizing, engineering, and packaging microorganisms so they interact with the surrounding environment in particular ways [86–94].

11.7 Conclusion

Multi-drug resistant bacterial infections are predicted to be on the rise, and by 2050, ten million more people will die from incurable illnesses than from cancer and heart disease put together. Hundreds of millions of people worldwide suffer from respiratory viral infections and chronic lung diseases, which are getting harder to treat as new viral variations appear. Novel therapeutic strategies and preventive measures are desperately needed, with microbiome modification emerging as one possible avenue for intervention. Dietary intake of probiotics, and postbiotics to consciously modify the gut–brain, gut–lung, gut–skin axis, and other metabolisms would be a relatively simple method for controlling so many diseases. With the recent scientific advances in the medical field, the flora-organ interactions are known, and any changes in these axes, such as microbial dysbiosis which constitutes one of the main risk factors in the pathogenesis of many diseases including the metabolic disorders, GI inflammation, cardiovascular-renal disorders, and neurological disorders. Novel diagnostic and screening instruments could be developed to more precisely identify the high-risk group, allowing for the management of such conditions. Continuous research to better understand the difficult host–microbiome communications between individual microbiota members is required. The development of personalized strategies for microbiota modulation in patients will achieve the maximum promising treatment outcome. From a medicinal standpoint, focusing on particular metabolites or components of microorganisms may offer a tool in the management of numerous illnesses. In addition to the conventional and primary option of microbe-based treatments such as probiotics or prebiotics, alternative approaches like phages, microbe-metabolites, and FMT are being studied therapeutically. The preclinical and clinical screenings have numerous limitations that prevent these procedures from being used to manipulate the gut microbiota. Therefore, additional study in this field is required to assess the issues that need to be taken into consideration while treating patients with these approaches. Targeting microbiota modification offers a new or novel therapeutic window for the treatment of many important diseases and disorders, despite all of the current limitations. The drug of tomorrow will come through microbe-based therapies.

References

1. Consortium HMP. Structure, function and diversity of the healthy human microbiome. Nature. 2012;486:207–14.
2. Cho I, Blaser MJ. The human micro biome: at the interface of health and disease. Nat Rev Genet. 2012;13(4):260–70. https://doi.org/10.1038/nrg3182.
3. Foster JA, McVey Neufeld KA. Gut–brain axis: how the microbiome influences anxiety and depression. Trends Neurosci. 2013;36(5):305–12. https://doi.org/10.1016/j.tins.2013.01.005.
4. Shreiner AB, Kao JY, Young VB. The gut micro biome in health and in disease. Curr Opin Gastroenterol. 2015;31(1):69–75. https://doi.org/10.1097/MOG.0000000000000139.
5. Van de Wijgert JHHM, Jespers V. The global health impact of vaginal symbiosis. Res Microbiol. 2017;168(9–10):859–64. https://doi.org/10.1016/j.resmic.2017.02.003.
6. Avila M, Ojcius DM, Yilmaz O. The oral micro biota: living with a permanent guest. DNA Cell Biol. 2009;28(8):405–11. https://doi.org/10.1089/dna.2009.0874.
7. Kong HH, Segre JA. Skin micro biome: looking back to move forward. J Invest Dermatol. 2012;132(3 Pt 2):933–9. https://doi.org/10.1038/jid.2011.417.
8. Murakami T. Absorption sites of orally administered drugs in the small intestine. Expert Opin Drug Discov. 2017;12(12):1219–32. https://doi.org/10.1080/17460441.2017.1378176.
9. Venugopalan V, Shriner KA, Wong-Beringer A. Regulatory oversight and safety of probiotic use. Emerg Infect Dis. 2010;16(11):1661–5. https://doi.org/10.3201/eid1611.100574.
10. Reid G. Probiotics: definition, scope and mechanisms of action. Best Pract Res Clin Gastroenterol. 2016;30(1):17–25. https://doi.org/10.1016/j.bpg.2015.12.001.
11. Kohanski MA, Dwyer DJ, Collins JJ. How antibiotics kill bacteria from targets to networks. Nat Rev Microbiol. 2010;8(6):423–35. https://doi.org/10.1038/nrmicro2333.
12. Vangay P, Ward T, Gerber JS, Knights D. Antibiotics, pediatric dysbiosis, and disease. Cell Host Microbe. 2015;17(5):553–64. https://doi.org/10.1016/j.chom.2015.04.006.
13. Davies J, Davies D. Origins and evolution of antibiotic resistance. Microbiol Mol Biol Rev. 2010;74(3):417–33. https://doi.org/10.1128/MMBR.00016-10.
14. Bull MJ, Plummer NT. The human gut micro biome in health and disease. Integr Med (Encinitas). 2014;13(17–22):1.
15. Rath CM, Dorrestein PC. The bacterial chemical repertoire mediates metabolic exchange within gut microbiomes. Curr Opin Microbiol. 2012;15(2):147–54. https://doi.org/10.1016/j.mib.2011.12.009.
16. Sommer MO, Dantas G. Antibiotics and the resistant microbiome. Curr Opin Microbiol. 2011;14(5):556–63. https://doi.org/10.1016/j.mib.2011.07.005.
17. Reardon S. Bacterial arms race revs up. Nature. 2015;521(7553):402–3. https://doi.org/10.1038/521402a.
18. Kamada N, Chen GY, Inohara N, Nunez G. Control of pathogens and pathobionts by the gut microbiota. Nat Immunol. 2013;14(7):685–90. https://doi.org/10.1038/ni.2608.
19. Young VB. Therapeutic manipulation of the micro biota: past, present, and considerations for the future. Clin Microbiol Infect. 2016;22(11):905–9. https://doi.org/10.1016/j.cmi.2016.09.001.
20. Levy M, Kolodziejczyk AA, Thaiss CA, Elinav E. Dysbiosis and the immune system. Nat Rev Immunol. 2017;17:219–32. https://doi.org/10.1038/nri.2017.7.
21. Edwards SM, Cunningham SA, Dunlop AL, Corwin EJ. The maternal gut microbiome during pregnancy. MCN Am J Matern Child Nurs. 2017;42(6):310.
22. Yang H, Guo R, Li S, Liang F, Tian C, Zhao X, et al. Systematic analysis of gut microbiota in pregnant women and its correlations with individual heterogeneity. Biofilms Microbiomes. 2020;6(1):1–12.
23. Zhang D, Huang Y, Ye D. Intestinal dysbiosis: an emerging cause of pregnancy complications? Med Hypotheses. 2015;84(3):223–6.
24. Yadav B, Prasad N, Saxena A. Gut microbiota dysbiosis and chronic kidney disease. J Ren Nutr Metab. 2020;6(3):70.
25. Jazani NH, Savoj J, Lustgarten M, Lau WL, Vaziri ND. Impact of gut dysbiosis on neurohormonal pathways in chronic kidney disease. Disease. 2019;7(1):21.
26. Li Y, Su X, Zhang L, Liu Y, Shi M, Lv C, et al. Dysbiosis of the gut microbiome is associated with CKD5 and correlated with clinical indices of the disease: a case-controlled study. J Transl Med. 2019;17(1):1–13. https://doi.org/10.1186/s12967-019-1969-1.
27. Li FX, Wang MH, Wang JP, Li RS, Zhang YQ. Alterations to the gut microbiota and their correlation with inflammatory factors in chronic kidney disease. Front Cell Infect Microbiol. 2019;9(6):206.
28. Bryniarski MA, Hamarneh F, Yacoub R. The role of chronic kidney disease-associated dysbiosis in cardiovascular disease. Exp Biol Med. 2019;244(6):514–25. https://doi.org/10.1177/15353-70219-826526.
29. Nicolas S, Blasco-Baque V, Fournel A, Gilleron J, Klopp P, Waget A, et al. Transfer of dysbiotic gut microbiota has beneficial effects on host liver metabolism. Mol Syst Biol. 2017;13(3):921. https://doi.org/10.15252/msb.20167-356.
30. Milosevic I, Vujovic A, Barac A, Djelic M, Korac M, Spurnic AR, et al. Gut liver axis, gut microbiota, and its modulation in the management of liver diseases: a review of the literature. Int J Mol Sci. 2019;20(2):1–16.
31. Albhaisi SAM, Bajaj JS, Sanyal AJ. Role of gut microbiota in liver disease. Am J Physiol Gastrointest Liver Physiol. 2020;318(1):G84–98.

32. Cheng Y, Ling Z, Li L. The intestinal microbiota and colorectal cancer. Front Immunol. 2020;30(11):3100.
33. Sanchez-Alcoholado L, Ramos-Molina B, Otero A, Laborda-Illanes A, Ordonez R, Medina JA, et al. The role of the gut microbiome in colorectal cancer development and therapy response. Cancers. 2020;12(6):1406.
34. Ocariz-Diez M, Cruellas M, Gascon M, Lastra R, Martinez-Lostao L, Ramirez-Labrada A, et al. Microbiota and lung cancer opportunities and challenges for improving immunotherapy efficacy. Front Oncol. 2020;10:1945.
35. Sha S, Ni L, Stefil M, Dixon M, Mouraviev V. The human gastrointestinal microbiota and prostate cancer development and treatment. Investig Clin Urol. 2019;61(Suppl 1):S43–50.
36. Villeger R, Lopes A, Carrier G, Veziant J, Billard E, Barnich N, et al. Intestinal microbiota: a novel target to improve anti-tumor treatment? Int J Mol Sci. 2019;20(18):4584.
37. Wang PX, Deng XR, Zhang CH, Yuan HJ. Gut microbiota and metabolic syndrome. Chin Med J. 2020;133(7):808.
38. Pełka-Wysiecka J, Kaczmarczyk M, Bąba-Kubiś A, Liśkiewicz P, Wroński M, Skonieczna-żydecka K, et al. Analysis of gut microbiota and their metabolic potential in patients with schizophrenia treated with olanzapine: results from a six-week observational prospective cohort study. J Clin Med. 2019;8(10):1605.
39. Agus A, Denizot J, Thevenot J, Martinez-Medina M, Massier S, Sauvanet P, et al. Western diet induces a shift in microbiota composition enhancing susceptibility to Adherent-Invasive E. coli infection and intestinal inflammation. Sci Rep. 2016;6:8.
40. Tronnet S, Floch P, Lucarelli L, Gaillard D, Martin P, Serino M, et al. The genotoxin colibactin shapes gut microbiota in mice. Gut. 2020;8:9.
41. Gurung M, Li Z, You H, Rodrigues R, Jump DB, Morgun A, et al. Role of gut microbiota in type 2 diabetes pathophysiology. EBioMedicine. 2020;51:8.
42. Mindt BC, DiGiandomenico A. Micro biome modulation as a novel strategy to treat and prevent respiratory infections. Antibiotics (Basel). 2022;11(4):474. https://doi.org/10.3390/antibiotics11040474.
43. Gebrayel P, Nicco C, Al Khodor S, et al. Microbiota medicine: towards clinical revolution. J Transl Med. 2022;20:111. https://doi.org/10.1186/s12967-022-03296-9.
44. Ava M, Vargason AM, Anselmo AC. Clinical translation of microbe-based therapies: current clinical landscape and preclinical outlook. Bioeng Transl Med. 2018;3:124–37. https://doi.org/10.1002/btm2.10093.
45. Kutter E, De Vos D, Gvasalia G, et al. Phage therapy in clinical practice: treatment of human infections. Curr Pharm Biotechnol. 2010;11(1):69–86. https://doi.org/10.2174/138920110790725401.
46. Lin DM, Koskella B, Lin HC. Phage therapy: an alternative to antibiotics in the age of multi-drug resistance. World J Gastrointest Pharmacol Ther. 2017;8(3):162–73. https://doi.org/10.4292/wjgpt.v8.i3.162.
47. Reardon S. Phage therapy gets revitalized. Nature. 2014;510(7503):15–6. https://doi.org/10.1038/510015a.
48. Lu TK, Koeris MS. The next generation of bacteriophage therapy. Curr Opin Microbiol. 2011;14(5):524–31. https://doi.org/10.1016/j.mib.2011.07.028.
49. Leung V, Vincent C, Edens TJ, Miller M, Manges AR. Antimicrobial resistance gene acquisition and depletion following fecal microbiota transplantation for recurrent *Clostridium difficile* infection. Clin Infect Dis. 2018;66(3):456–7.
50. Baishya J, Wakeman CA. Selective pressures during chronic infection drive microbial competition and cooperation. NPJ Biofilms Microbiomes. 2019;5:16. https://doi.org/10.1038/s41522-019-0089-2.
51. Hill C. Microbiome and infection: A case for "selective depletion". Ann Nutr Metab. 2021;77(suppl 3):4–9. https://doi.org/10.1159/000516399.
52. Enaud R, Prevel R, Ciarlo E, Beaufils F, Wieërs G, Guery B, et al. The gut-lung axis in health and respiratory diseases: a place for interorgan and interkingdom crosstalks. Front Cell Infect Microbiol. 2020;19(10):9.
53. Grier A, McDavid A, Wang B, Qiu X, Java J, Bandyopadhyay S, et al. Neonatal gut and respiratory microbiota: coordinated development through time and space. Microbiome. 2018;6(1):1–19. https://doi.org/10.1186/s40168-018-0566-5.
54. Chiu YC, Lee SW, Liu CW, Lan TY, Wu LS. Relationship between gut microbiota and lung function decline in patients with chronic obstructive pulmonary disease: a 1-year follow-up study. Respir Res. 2022;23:10.
55. Mattila E, Uusitalo-Seppälä R, Wuorela M, et al. Fecal transplantation, through colonoscopy, is effective therapy for recurrent *Clostridium difficile* infection. Gastroenterology. 2012;142(3):490–6. https://doi.org/10.1053/j.gastro.2011.11.037.
56. Ratner M. Fecal transplantation poses dilemma for FDA. Nat Biotechnol. 2014;32(5):401–2. https://doi.org/10.1038/nbt0514-401.
57. Borody TJ, Khoruts A. Fecal microbiota transplantation and emerging applications. Nat Rev Gastroenterol Hepatol. 2012;9(2):88–96. https://doi.org/10.1038/nrgastro.2011.244.
58. Smits LP, Bouter KE, de Vos WM, Borody TJ, Nieuwdorp M. Therapeutic potential of fecal micro biota transplantation. Gastroenterology. 2013;145(5):946–53. https://doi.org/10.1053/j.gastro.2013.08.058.
59. Kelly CR, Kahn S, Kashyap P, et al. Update on fecal microbiota transplantation 2015: indications, methodologies, mechanisms, and outlook. Gastroenterology. 2015;149(1):223–37. https://doi.org/10.1053/j.gastro.2015.05.008.
60. Rohlke F, Stollman N. Fecal micro biota transplantation in relapsing *Clostridium difficile* infection. Ther Adv Gastroenterol. 2012;5(6):403–20. https://doi.org/10.1177/1756283X12453637.

61. Surawicz CM, Brandt LJ, Binion DG, et al. Guidelines for diagnosis, treatment, and prevention of *Clostridium difficile* infections. Am J Gastroenterol. 2013;108(4):478–98. https://doi.org/10.1038/ajg.2013.4.
62. Bakken JS, Borody T, Brandt LJ, et al. Treating *Clostridium difficile* infection with fecal micro biota transplantation. Clin Gastroenterol Hepatol. 2011;9(12):1044–9. https://doi.org/10.1016/j.cgh.2011.08.014.
63. Kassam Z, Lee CH, Yuan Y, Hunt RH. Fecal micro biota transplantation for *Clostridium difficile* infection: systematic review and met analysis. Am J Gastroenterol. 2013;108(4):500–8. https://doi.org/10.1038/ajg.2013.59.
64. Dubberke ER, et al. Clearance of vancomycin-resistant *Enterococcus* concomitant with administration of a micro biota-based drug targeted at recurrent *Clostridium difficile* infection. Open Forum Infect Dis. 2016;3(3):1–6. https://doi.org/10.1093/ofid/ofw133.
65. Orenstein R, Dubberke E, Hardi R, et al. Safety and durability of RBX2660 (micro biota suspension) for recurrent *Clostridium difficile* infection: results of the PUNCH CD study. Clin Infect Dis. 2016;62(5):596–602. https://doi.org/10.1093/cid/civ938.
66. Khanna S, Pardi DS, Kelly CR, et al. A novel microbiome therapeutic increases gut microbial diversity and prevents recurrent *Clostridium difficile* infection. J Infect Dis. 2016;214(2):173–81. https://doi.org/10.1001/jama.2017.17969.
67. Rao K, Young VB, Malani PN. Capsules for fecal microbiota transplantation in recurrent *Clostridium difficile* infection: the new way forward or a tough pill to swallow. JAMA. 2017;318(20):1979–80. https://doi.org/10.1001/jama.2017.17969.
68. Seekatz AM, Aas J, Gessert CE, et al. Recovery of the gut micro biome following fecal micro biota transplantation. MBio. 2014;5(3):1–14. https://doi.org/10.1128/mBio.00893-14.
69. Cogen AL, Yamasaki K, Muto J, et al. *Staphylococcus epidermidis* antimicrobial d-toxin (phenol-soluble modulin-g) cooperates with host antimicrobial peptides to kill group A *Streptococcus*. PLoS One. 2010;5(1):8557. https://doi.org/10.1371/journal.pone.0008557.
70. Cogen AL, Yamasaki K, Sanchez KM, et al. Selective antimicrobial action is provided by phenol-soluble modulins derived from *Staphylococcus epidermidis*, a normal resident of the skin. J Invest Dermatol. 2010;130(1):192–200. https://doi.org/10.1038/jid.2009.243.
71. Nakatsuji T, Chen TH, Narala S, et al. Antimicrobials from human skin commensal bacteria protect against *Staphylococcus aureus* and are deficient in atopic dermatitis. Sci Transl Med. 2017;9(pii):eaah4680v. https://doi.org/10.1126/scitranslmed.aah4680.
72. Hemmerling A, Harrison W, Schroeder A, et al. Phase 1 dose-ranging safety trial of *Lactobacillus crispatus* CTV-05 (LACTIN-V) for the prevention of bacterial vaginosis. Sex Transm Dis. 2009;36(9):564–9. https://doi.org/10.1097/OLQ.0b013e3181a74924.
73. Hemmerling A, Harrison W, Schroeder A, et al. Phase 2a study assessing colonization efficiency, safety, and acceptability of *Lactobacillus crispatus* CTV-05 in women with bacterial vaginosis. Sex Transm Dis. 2010;37(12):745–50. https://doi.org/10.1097/OLQ.0b013e3181e50026.
74. Stapleton AE, Au-Yeung M, Hooton TM, et al. Randomized, placebo-controlled phase 2 trial of a *Lactobacillus crispatus* probiotic given intravaginally for prevention of recurrent urinary tract infection. Clin Infect Dis. 2011;52(10):1212–7. https://doi.org/10.1093/cid/cir183.
75. Ngugi BM, Hemmerling A, Bukusi EA, et al. Effects of bacterial vaginosis-associated bacteria and sexual intercourse on vaginal colonization with the probiotic *Lactobacillus crispatus* CTV-05. Sex Transm Dis. 2011;38(11):1020–7. https://doi.org/10.1097/OLQ.0b013e3182267ac4.
76. Antonio MA, Meyn LA, Murray PJ, Busse B, Hillier SL. Vaginal colonization by probiotic *Lactobacillus crispatus* CTV-05 is decreased by sexual activity and endogenous Lactobacilli. J Infect Dis. 2009;199(10):1506–13. https://doi.org/10.1086/598686.
77. Murina F, Graziottin A, Vicariotto F, De Seta F. Can *Lactobacillus fermentum* LF10 and *Lactobacillus acidophilus* LA02 in a slow-release vaginal product be useful for prevention of recurrent vulvovaginal candidiasis? A clinical study. J Clin Gastroenterol. 2014;48:102–5. https://doi.org/10.1097/MCG.0000000000000225.
78. Vicariotto F, Del Piano M, Mogna L, Mogna G. Effectiveness of the association of 2 probiotic strains formulated in a slow release vaginal product, in women affected by vulvovaginal candidiasis: a pilot study. J Clin Gastroenterol. 2012;46:S73–80. https://doi.org/10.1097/MCG.0b013e3182684d71.
79. Ceccarani C, Foschi C, Parolin C, et al. Diversity of vaginal microbiome and metabolome during genital infections. Sci Rep. 2019;9:14095. https://doi.org/10.1038/s41598-019-50410-x.
80. Kao D, Roach B, Silva M, et al. Effect of oral capsule–vs colonoscopy-delivered fecal micro biota transplantation on recurrent *Clostridium difficile* infection: a randomized clinical trial. JAMA. 2017;318(20):1985–93. https://doi.org/10.1001/jama.2017.17077.
81. de Araujo Pereira RR, Bruschi ML. Vaginal mucoadhesive drug delivery systems. Drug Dev Ind Pharm. 2012;38(6):643–52.
82. Paderni C, Compilato D, Giannola LI, Campisi G. Oral local drug delivery and new perspectives in oral drug formulation. Oral Surg Oral Med Oral Pathol Oral Radiol. 2012;114(3):e25–34. https://doi.org/10.1016/j.oooo.2012.02.016.
83. Anselmo AC, McHugh KJ, Webster J, Langer R, Jaklenec A. Layerby-layer encapsulation of probiotics for delivery to the microbiome. Adv Mater.

2016;28(43):9486–90. https://doi.org/10.1002/adma.201603270.
84. Ho CL, Tan HQ, Chua KJ, et al. Engineered commensal microbes for diet-mediated colorectal-cancer chemoprevention. Nat Biomed Eng. 2018;2(1):27–37. https://doi.org/10.1038/s41551-017-0181-y.
85. Park GS, Park MH, Shin W, et al. Emulating host-micro biome ecosystem of human gastrointestinal tract in vitro. Stem Cell Rev Rep. 2017;13(3):321–34. https://doi.org/10.1007/s12015-017-9739-z.
86. Smillie CS, Sauk J, Gevers D, et al. Strain tracking reveals the determinants of bacterial engraftment in the human gut following fecal microbiota transplantation. Cell Host Microbe. 2018;23(2):229–40. https://doi.org/10.1016/j.chom.2018.01.003.
87. Overton TW. Recombinant protein production in bacterial hosts. Drug Discov Today. 2014;19(5):590–601. https://doi.org/10.1016/j.drudis.2013.11.008.
88. Riglar DT, Silver PA. Engineering bacteria for diagnostic and therapeutic applications. Nat Rev Microbiol. 2018;16(4):214–25. https://doi.org/10.1038/nrmicro.2017.172.
89. Skalko-Basnet N. Biologics: the role of delivery systems in improved therapy. Biol Targets Ther. 2014;8:107–14. https://doi.org/10.2147/BTT.S38387.
90. Venema K, Van den Abbeele P. Experimental models of the gut micro biome. Best Pract Res Clin Gastroenterol. 2013;27(1):115–26. https://doi.org/10.1016/j.bpg.2013.03.002.
91. May S, Evans S, Parry L. Organoids, organs-on-chips and other systems, and micro biota. Emerg Top Life Sci. 2017;1(4):385–400. https://doi.org/10.1042/ETLS20170047.
92. Kim HJ, Huh D, Hamilton G, Ingber DE. Human gut-on-a-chip inhabited by microbial flora that experiences intestinal peristalsis like motions and flow. Lab Chip. 2012;12(12):2165–74. https://doi.org/10.1039/c2lc40074j.
93. Gupta VK, Paul S, Dutta C. Geography, ethnicity or subsistence-specific variations in human microbiome composition and diversity. Front Microbiol. 2017;8:1162. https://doi.org/10.3389/fmicb.2017.01162.
94. Trieu V, Hwang L, Ng K, D'Cruz O, Qazi S, Fong A. 515P First-in-human Phase I study of bacterial RNA interference therapeutic CEQ508 in patients with familial adenomatous polyposis (FAP). Ann Oncol. 2017;28(suppl-5):mdx393.041. https://doi.org/10.1093/annonc/mdx393.041.

12 Translational Research Platform for Biomedical Sciences: Establishment and Endeavors

Thiyagarajan Sanjeevi

12.1 Introduction

Translational research platform (TRP) for biomedical sciences is a unique facility in the field of translational research at science and technology academics and research institutions. The cooperation of International / National funding agencies in the establishment of this avenue would help in fastening the productization of translational research leads. Because there is no path forward when a study is completed, the integration of scientific advancements into medical technology has experienced a delay [1]. The objectives of TRP in the biomedical field is to facilitate product development, provide regulatory-compliant biotechnological services and serve as a knowledge resource in biomedicals. It is expected that this would in turn improve the human health and healthcare facilities in this country by taking the fruits of research to the ultimate stakeholders, the patients [2]. The TRP would be established as a 'state-of-the-art' research laboratory housing all the major equipment needed for research and product development. It has also mobilized expertise from academia, industry, and regulatory fields.

T. Sanjeevi (✉)
Department of Medical Biotechnology, Aarupadai Veedu Medical College and Hospital, Vinayaka Missions Research Foundation-DU, Puducherry, India
e-mail: thiyagarajan.sanjeevi@avmc.edu.in

12.2 Establishment of a Translational Research Platform

The aim of establishing a center for the "National hub for biomedicals," a translational research platform for biomedical sciences, would be to promote a collaborative and coordinated approach that facilitates the translation of technologies with established proof of concept through multidisciplinary projects in the area of human therapeutics, vaccines, and diagnostics that can be efficiently taken through validation and regulation for product development to commercialization. The platform would serve as a reference center, enhancing national, regional, and international connections and collaborations for the development of human vaccines. It would facilitate the exchange of materials, technology assessment, regulatory processes, and knowledge sharing to support training, consultation, and the commercialization of technologies.

12.3 Key Components of the Translational Research Platform (TRP)

The platform is the key to successful collaborations between fundamental scientific research, clinical practice, and biotech enterprises. It involves the clinical use of novel drugs, chemi-

K. Parthasarathy, R. Manikkam (eds.), *Translational Research in Biomedical Sciences: Recent Progress and Future Prospects*, https://doi.org/10.1007/978-981-97-1777-4_12

cals, and techniques as well as the quality control of research and medical discoveries. Translational research encompasses two main components. On one hand, it involves the translation of new findings, inventions, and technologies generated through basic and preclinical research into clinically applicable solutions. This could include developing new drugs or therapies, designing medical devices or diagnostic tools, or identifying novel treatment approaches based on scientific insights.

On the other hand, translational research also includes policy-based research. This aspect focuses on understanding the social, economic, and policy factors that influence the implementation of new medical technologies and interventions. It considers the broader context in which healthcare operates and aims to address barriers to adoption and dissemination of innovations. Policy-based research may involve studying healthcare systems, evaluating the cost-effectiveness of new interventions, assessing regulatory frameworks, or investigating ethical considerations. It is important to note that the definition and scope of translational research may vary among scientific communities and countries. National socioeconomic conditions, local healthcare priorities, and available resources can influence the specific emphasis and priorities of translational research in different regions. The ultimate goal, however, remains the same: to accelerate the translation of scientific discoveries into tangible benefits for patients and society [3, 4]. The main objective of TRP is to treat a clinical problem more by fostering connections between various stakeholders through "bench-to-bedside and bedside-to-community" research [5]. To achieve formal translation of research leads, translational research platforms act according to the main components depicted in Fig. 12.1.

Fig. 12.1 Key components of Translational Research Platform for Biomedical sciences

12.4 The Mandate and Agendas of TRP

To bridge the gap between academia, basic research, and the medical industry, translational research platforms tend to be;

- Translating clinical techniques identified through potentially beneficial results of biomedical research into products following proper manufacturing and quality standards.
- To provide quality diagnostic services and medical science techniques to the needy, entrepreneurs, and academicians.
- To be a center of information and research techniques in biomedical science.

Funding organizations and regulatory bodies worldwide are currently prioritizing three key objectives within the Translational Research Platform: (1). The identification of basic research findings or innovations with the potential for translation into practical applications. (2). The acceleration of grant approval processes while ensuring adherence to ethical standards and patent regulations. (3). The facilitation of community access to medical therapies or technologies, expediting their availability.

Consequently, these efforts are leading to changes in government health policies. Additionally, awareness campaigns are being initiated at academic and industrial levels, and workforce training and development are being undertaken at various levels. In order to enhance the efficiency of the healthcare system, there is a need for further improvements in the legal and governance structure. To foster the generation of more translational leads and innovations, it is essential to engage multidisciplinary stakeholders at both the national and international levels. These stakeholders encompass the appropriate expertise from academic institutions, industry regulators, policymakers, and relevant organizations.

The field of biomedical science is undergoing revolutionary advancements, reshaping research methodologies. Breakthrough technologies, such as gene and cell-based treatments, nanotechnology, proteomics, genomics, artificial intelligence, and robotics, are redefining the landscape. To progress these novel technologies and therapies, it is crucial to reconsider established research techniques, commencing with fundamental-level basic research and subsequently translating the findings into clinical applications [6].

Having a comprehensive understanding of the initial phases of the Translational Research Platform (TRP) allows other entities to replicate the research component and obtain validation from an independent third party, while the original innovator maintains ownership of the Intellectual Property Rights (IPR). In order to establish a proof of concept methodology, file a patent application, and validate a prototype, it is imperative to employ effective techniques for translation [7, 8]. Therefore, technology transfer and commercialization may make it possible for research results to hit the market more quickly. Hence, to foster innovation, from fundamental research through the supply of potential public healthcare solutions, TRP for biomedical research follows an integrated approach.

12.5 Translational Research Platforms—Global Scenario

Efforts are underway to address the challenges within the TRP and expedite the dissemination of innovative approaches and technologies to the community. This involves the development of various standards, strategies, and regulatory adaptations. In the USA, the National Institutes of Health (NIH) utilizes disease-oriented drug-targeting techniques as part of their translational research initiatives [9]. To accelerate the progress of translational research, the United States Food and Drug Administration (US-FDA) has established a dedicated unit called the Office of Translational Sciences. This unit operates within the Center for Drug Evaluation and Research and serves as a catalyst and support system for basic researchers. Its primary objectives include facilitating technology transfer, streamlining the drug regulatory review process, and providing various resources to expedite translational research initiatives [10].

Also, the US-FDA is promoting expedited approvals for drug-targeted therapy, particularly for cancer and ground-breaking treatments [11]. The United Kingdom has established an impressive Translational Medicine (TM) system within the European Union. The Medical Research Council (MRC) plays a key role in this system by fostering collaboration among multidisciplinary professionals and emphasizing fundamental discoveries derived from basic research. To efficiently generate proof of concept, the British Council's SPARK program has developed a cost-effective strategy that adheres to industrial standards. This collaborative initiative brings together experts from academia and industry to drive innovation in translational medicine [12, 13]. In the field of biomedical research, the United Kingdom has established two distinct categories of research centers known as Comprehensive Biomedical Research Centers (BRCs) and Specialty BRCs. Both types of centers play a vital role in driving forward translational research and its advancement [14]. The program "Translation Together" aims to connect recent breakthroughs in our understanding of human diseases with the development of innovative therapeutic options for patients. Various organizations contribute to this effort, such as LifeArc in the United Kingdom, the European Infrastructure for Translational Medicine in the European Union, and The Centre for Drug Research and Development in Canada [15], Australia's Therapeutic Innovation initiative and the National Center for Advancing Translational Sciences within the National Institutes of Health (NIH) in the USA have initiated collaborative efforts. In the context of research setup in India, the SPARK model is considered the most suitable approach. This model involves professionals from various disciplines, including social sciences, scientific sectors, and subject matter experts from industry (SMEs), who collaborate to establish a Translational Research Platform for biomedical sciences. This methodology prioritizes fundamental research as a key component in the development of new drugs.

12.6 Translational Research Platforms—Indian Scenario

Scientific and biomedical funding agencies of the Indian government have taken different measures to address global translational research in the biomedical sciences. The following lists a few translational research platform projects by Indian groups.

In 2010, the Translational Health Science and Technology Institute was founded on the initiative of the Department of Biotechnology (DBT), the Ministry of Science and Technology (MoST), and the Government of India (GoI). This institution's original mission was to advance fundamental research using a multidisciplinary approach. The main goal was to convert the detected leads into scientific and technological prototypes and encourage inventions and patents by utilizing the scientific leads for healthcare system development. The ultimate goal is to create innovative approaches to disease detection and management. These programs will contribute to the development of an inter-institutional ecosystem in the Biotech Science Cluster, with an emphasis on fostering collaboration between academia, biotech, and industry within significant innovation hubs.

The Biotechnology Industry Research Assistance Council (BIRAC) was established by the Department of Biotechnology (DBT) and the Government of India (GoI) as a non-profit public sector organization. BIRAC's main objective is to provide support and enhance research projects with translational potential. The funding approach focuses on targeted financing, IP management, technology transfer, and partnership programs aimed at fostering innovation excellence among Indian biotech enterprises and helping them gain global recognition.

The funding mechanism is still being developed, and it emphasizes supporting Indian biotech enterprises to excel globally. BIRAC has provided financial and mentoring support to nearly 500 young entrepreneurs, start-ups, and over 500 companies. BIRAC has established collaborations with more than 15 implementing agencies and has formed partnerships with numerous national and international networks. These collaborations involve approximately 700 experts from academia, business, public and private research labs, donor organizations, and other government ministries, collectively working to build India's innovation ecosystem. In 2021, BIRAC launched the Promoting Academic Research Conversion to Enterprise (PACE) program. The primary objective of PACE is to encourage and support academia in transforming technology and intellectual property into viable products or services of societal or national significance, up to the Proof of Concept stage. The subsequent validation of these innovations is conducted in collaboration with industrial partners [16].

The Stanford India Biodesign (SIB) program was operational from 2007 to 2014. In collaboration with Queensland University of Technology in Australia and Hiroshima University in Japan, the SIB innovation program is being implemented by the DBT, GoI, All India Institute of Medical Sciences (AIIMS) in New Delhi, and Indian Institute of Technology, Delhi (IITD). To oversee the program's technical and legal aspects, the DBT introduced the Biotechnology Consortium of India Limited. The primary objective of this program is to educate and empower the next generation of medical technology innovators in India. The key focus is on developing affordable, accessible, and readily available early-stage medical technologies for the Indian population [17]. Over the past decade, this interdisciplinary program has achieved notable progress. It has successfully educated and mentored over 100 medical technology innovators, including doctors, engineers, designers, and young entrepreneurs. Moreover, the program has already produced and validated over 50 prototypes, resulting in the patenting of more than 50 medical devices created by young innovators from IITD and the faculty of AIIMS. Furthermore, 15 technologies have been developed and transferred as a result of this program's efforts [18]. Additionally, nine technologies have been selected to participate in the Start-up India program [19]. Apart from engaging in fundamental biomedical research, the Central Drug Standard Control Organization (CDSCO) in India is actively involved in revising regulations concerning the approval of investigational new drugs, innovations, new interventions, clinical trials, and new medical devices based on the existing requirements. Additionally, to reduce out-of-pocket expenses, multinational corporations are adapting their product offerings to cater to the specific demands of the Indian market, thereby presenting their medical equipment [20].

12.7 Efforts to Translational Research Platform

The activities of the translation research platform are not simply linear; instead, they can be connected through translational bridges that span across disciplines. Although numerous barriers must be overcome at every stage of development, these challenges serve as opportunities for growth and progress [20, 21] The translational research platform encounters various challenges that need to be addressed. These challenges encompass several areas, including: (i) Transitioning from basic non-clinical research to innovation/product development and the creation of diagnostic or prognostic biomarker assays. (ii) Advancing new drug development and interventions. (iii) Conducting clinical research to establish new therapeutic modalities. (iv) Undertaking evidence-based community studies to enhance healthcare policies/programs. (v) Formulating new guidelines for disease prevention at the policymaker level.

The major bottlenecks identified within these challenges include slow regulatory approvals, delayed updates in patent regulations, high costs associated with patents for high-margin products, limited community support, lack of trained personnel, inadequate research funding, and increasing competition from both domestic and foreign companies. It is crucial to address these bottlenecks in order to foster the progress and success of the translational research platform.

The conducted research in basic medical sciences was exploratory, observational, and inno-

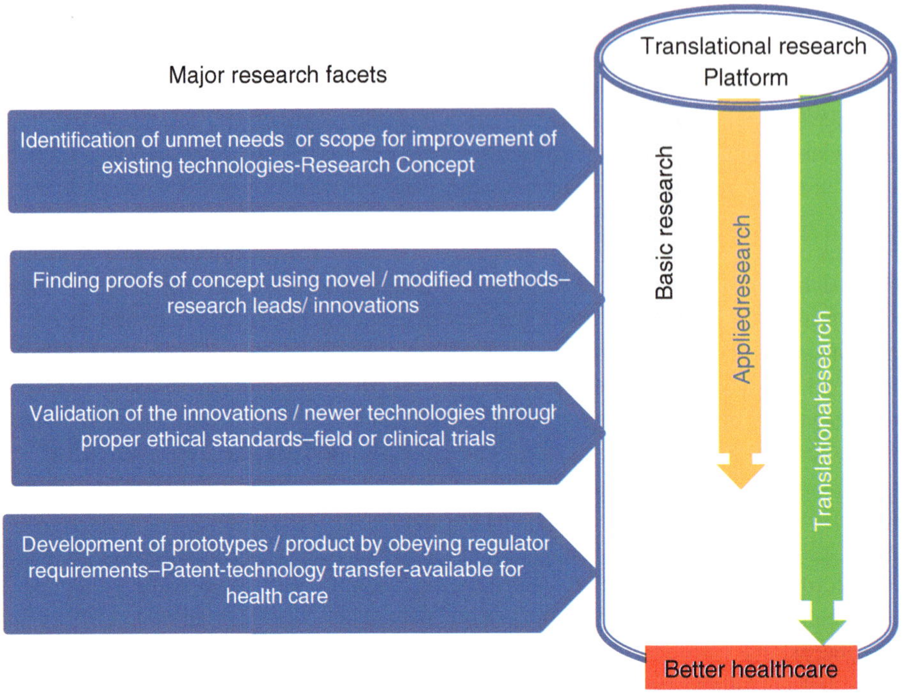

Fig. 12.2 Translational research platform includes all major research facets to deep the arm for better healthcare

vative in nature. While these projects demonstrated reasonable quality, they lacked a crucial component: translation. Some of these studies involved comparative approaches that integrated both basic and clinical sciences. These projects had progressed significantly to the T0 stage (discovery stage, in silico, in vitro) and the T1 stage (animal studies) of translation. However, despite the valuable data obtained, most of them lacked proof of concept, and a significant portion required improved study design. As a result, the observed outcomes did not advance to Phase III in a clinical randomized control trial, hindering the demonstration of proof of concept or potential translational value. Only a limited number of projects managed to reach the T2 stage (product development/patent/proof of concept/prototype development/validation).

The following graphical representation (Fig. 12.2) discusses major research facets housed in the translational research platform to find ways from basic research to translational/clinical research and technologies that become available for medical practices.

12.8 Important Considerations for the Translational Research Platform

The translational research platform emphasizes conducting focused research studies to assess the translational potential of developed prototypes, and this emphasis is reflected in the application for extramural research grants. The initiative adopts a multidisciplinary approach that incorporates statistical evaluations tailored to the study design, ensuring that meaningful insights can be derived from the outcomes. The facility is equipped with up-to-date infrastructure and advanced equipment, enabling faster and more accurate results to be obtained.

Translational research platforms facilitate the testing of developed technologies through both in-house validation and external validation conducted by regulatory compliance agencies at the national and international levels. The scientists involved in these platforms should have a good understanding of the concept of commercialization and technology transfer, particularly regarding the novel or value-added outcomes of their research. To encourage increased patent applications, the translational research platform takes responsibility for the costs associated with obtaining patents for any promising leads emerging from basic research and the development of prototypes. Alternatively, the platform may request this provision from the funding agency supporting a specific research project.

The principal investigators (PIs) within translational research platforms play a crucial role in confirming the findings of basic research and advancing leads toward clinical efficacy. They are encouraged to foster research collaborations with clinicians working in hospitals and clinical institutions. Funding agencies can also facilitate such collaborations by providing support and establishing partnerships with their own institutions or other relevant organizations. Additionally, it is essential for PIs to take the initiative in FDA filings for their research findings, as this is a necessary step for commercializing or marketing their products. In this regard, the funding agency must offer support and facilitate these initiatives to ensure successful outcomes [22].

Principal investigators (PIs) should actively seek opportunities for education and training offered by funding agencies to enhance their knowledge and skills. It is also important for PIs to establish collaborations with industries to facilitate cost-effective scaling up of the developed products. Additionally, there is a need to foster the development of an integrated research network within the institution or among intra-institution setups. Considerable attention should be given to identifying and overcoming barriers that hinder the successful implementation of translational medical approaches. By addressing these barriers, affordable therapies can be effectively delivered to the community [23–25].

The policy of translational research platforms underscores the importance of having well-equipped research facilities and innovative models that incorporate a translational or technology management unit. This unit plays a crucial role in facilitating the successful execution of research studies. It supports activities such as validating leads derived from animal studies, managing clinical trials in regulatory-compliant hospital settings, and overseeing the overall process of clinical trial management [25, 26].

12.9 Conclusion

The establishment of translational research platforms within biomedical sciences is envisioned as a unique initiative by research institutes. This initiative aims to catalyze a paradigm shift that can enhance biomedical and clinical studies through an integrated approach involving researchers and clinicians. By fostering collaboration and innovative thinking, these platforms seek to address patient needs and drive impactful discoveries. The platform emphasizes the importance of conducting fundamental basic research alongside evidence-based, validated, and target-oriented investigations to identify potential leads for translational breakthroughs. To support their endeavors, the platform encourages multidisciplinary scientific experts to seek external research grants for funding.

To bridge the translational gaps and promote fundamental research, funding agencies need to reframe their policies, strategies, and guidelines. By taking proactive steps, they can facilitate the translation of research leads into tangible outcomes. It is essential to expedite translational research to ensure the timely availability of discoveries and primary health technologies in the market at reasonable prices. Conceptualizing and implementing a successful translational research platform require close cooperation among all stakeholders, including researchers, funding agencies, clinicians, providers of intellectual property rights, and industrial partners.

References

1. Bano R, Gupta S, Shekhar C. Translational research in biomedical sciences in India: challenges, observations & national perspectives. Indian J Med Res. 2020;152(4):335–41.
2. Ostergren JE, Hammer RR, Dingel MJ, Koenig BA, McCormick JB. Challenges in translational research: the views of addiction scientists. PLoS One. 2014;9:e93482.

3. Sahu S, Panja S. Current status and challenges of medical device innovations—Indian perspectives. J Intellect Prop Rights. 2017;99:329–35.
4. Wan J. Drug discovery and development in India. BioPharm Int. 2015;28:10–1.
5. Downey LE, Mehndiratta A, Grover A, Gauba V, Sheikh K, Prinja S, et al. Institutionalising health technology assessment: establishing the medical technology assessment board in India. BMJ Glob Health. 2017;2:e000259.
6. Homer-Vanniasinkam S, Tsui J. The continuing challenges of translational research: clinician-scientists' perspective. Cardiol Res Pract. 2012;2012:246710.
7. Kim B. Insight for clinical technology transfer from international environmental and human rights law. J Intellect Prop Rights. 2018;23:7–21.
8. Mann DL, MD, Mochly-Rosen D. Translational medicine: proceed at your own risk. Nat Rev Drug Discov. 2013;12:327–8.
9. Cimino JJ, Ayres EJ, Remennik L, Rath S, Freedman R, Beri A, et al. The National Institutes of Health's Biomedical Translational Research Information System (BTRIS): design, contents, functionality, and experience to date. J Biomed Inform. 2014;52:11–27.
10. U.S. Food & Drug Administration. Office of Translational Sciences https://www.fda.gov/about-fda/center-drug-evaluation-and-research-cder/office-translational-sciences
11. Andrews A, Can FDA. Drug approval keep pace with translational research? Econom Cancer Care. 2013;4:13466.
12. The SPARK model for translational research has proven to be a successful paradigm that can be replicated at other academic institutions. Available from: https://sparkmed.stanford.edu/
13. Kim ES, Omura PMC, Lo AW. Accelerating biomedical innovation: a case study of the SPARK program at Stanford University, School of Medicine. Drug Discov Today. 2017;22:1064–8.
14. Soderquest K, Lord GM. Strategies for translational research in the United Kingdom. Sci Transl Med. 2010;2:53cm28.
15. Top global translational science organizations to catalyze translational innovation through a new initiative—Translation Together. Available from: http://www.translationtogether.org/press_release.pdf
16. Translational Health Science and Technology Institute. Available from: https://thsti.res.in/en/thematic-areas-details/5/multidisciplinar-clinica-an-translationa-research. Accessed 26 Jan 2019.
17. Biotechnology Industry Research Assistance Council Bio-Innovations. PACE. Available from: https://www.birac.nic.in/desc_new.php?id=286
18. Biodesign—A novel Medical Technology Innovation Programme. Available from: https://dbtindia.gov.in/schemes-programmes/research-development/medical-biotechnology/biomedical-engineering-and-biodesign
19. Central Drugs Standard Control Organization. Available from: https://cdsco.gov.in/opencms/opencms/en/Notifications/Circulars/
20. Parrish MC, Tan YJ, Grimes KV, Mochly-Rosen D. Surviving in the valley of death: opportunities and challenges in translating academic drug discoveries. Annu Rev Pharmacol Toxicol. 2019;59:405–21.
21. Vaidya M, Garg S, Singh C, Mahajan M. Changing dimensions of drug patents of Indian pharmaceutical industry. J Intellect Prop Rights. 2018;23:111–8.
22. Kaitin KI. Translational research and the evolving landscape for biomedical innovation. J Investig Med. 2012;60:995–8.
23. Yu D. Translational research: current status, challenges, and future strategies. Am J Transl Res. 2011;3:422–33.
24. Sharma G, Kumar H. Exploring the possibilities of utility models patent regime for grassroots innovations in India. J Intellect Prop Rights. 2018;23:119–30.
25. Gehr S, Garner CC. Rescuing the lost in translation. Cell. 2016;165:765–70.
26. Gillman J, Pillinger M, Plottel CS, Galeano C, Maddalo S, Hochman JS, et al. Teaching translational research to medical students: The New York University School of Medicine's Master of Science in clinical investigation dual-degree program. Clin Transl Sci. 2015;8:734–9.

Advancement in the Molecular Diagnosis of Tuberculosis

13

B. Angayarkanni, Sumant Kumar, Shainaba A. Saadhali, and V. N. Azger Dusthackeer

13.1 Introduction

Mycobacterium tuberculosis (MTB) is an airborne infectious disease that causes tuberculosis (TB), which affects mainly the lungs. Eighty percent of all cases of tuberculosis are pulmonary (PTB). The extrapulmonary form of tuberculosis (EPTB) can affect the colon, meninges, lymph nodes, bones, joints, kidneys, and skin. Depending on the response of the host immune system, exposure to MTB bacilli results in eradication or persistence of the pathogen [1]. TB is the most prevalent infectious cause of mortality in adults' worldwide [2]. According to WHO India represents one-fifth of the global burden of TB. Early and accurate diagnosis is crucial for disease management and improved patient outcomes. With the advent of more recent microscopy, culture, and molecular techniques, diagnostic modalities for tuberculosis have improved significantly over the past few decades (Fig. 13.1). For the purpose of determining a diagnosis, monitoring treatment and stopping the spread of tuberculosis, improved laboratory techniques are essential. In contrast to traditional culture systems, which take several weeks to diagnose TB, molecular detection offers quicker and more affordable ways to identify and confirm resistance to treatment in TB cases. New developments in the molecular diagnosis of tuberculosis, such as the quicker and easier nucleic acid amplification test (NAAT) and whole-genome sequencing (WGS), have sped up the diagnosis and, consequently, TB treatments [3]. There are new methods for improving culture medium, such as culture system improvement, early growth detection, strict oxygen tension control, and MALDI-TOF-MS (matrix-assisted laser desorption/ionisation time-of-flight mass spectrometry) for identification [4]. Most molecular tests have focused on identifying specific nucleic acids to MTB, both in DNA and RNA, using amplification techniques such as polymerase chain reaction (PCR) and identifying gene mutations associated with drug resistance through sequencing or nucleic acid hybridisation [5].

Molecular methods for the detection of tuberculosis (TB) are based on the amplification and detection of specific DNA sequences from the *Mycobacterium tuberculosis* complex, the causative agent of TB. These methods include polymerase chain reaction (PCR) techniques such as real-time PCR (qPCR) and conventional PCR, as well as newer techniques such as loop-mediated isothermal amplification (LAMP) and nucleic acid sequence-based amplification (NASBA) [6, 7].

B. Angayarkanni · S. Kumar · S. A. Saadhali ·
V. N. Azger Dusthackeer (✉)
Department of Bacteriology, ICMR-National Institute for Research in Tuberculosis,
Chetpet, Tamil Nadu, India

K. Parthasarathy, R. Manikkam (eds.), *Translational Research in Biomedical Sciences: Recent Progress and Future Prospects*, https://doi.org/10.1007/978-981-97-1777-4_13

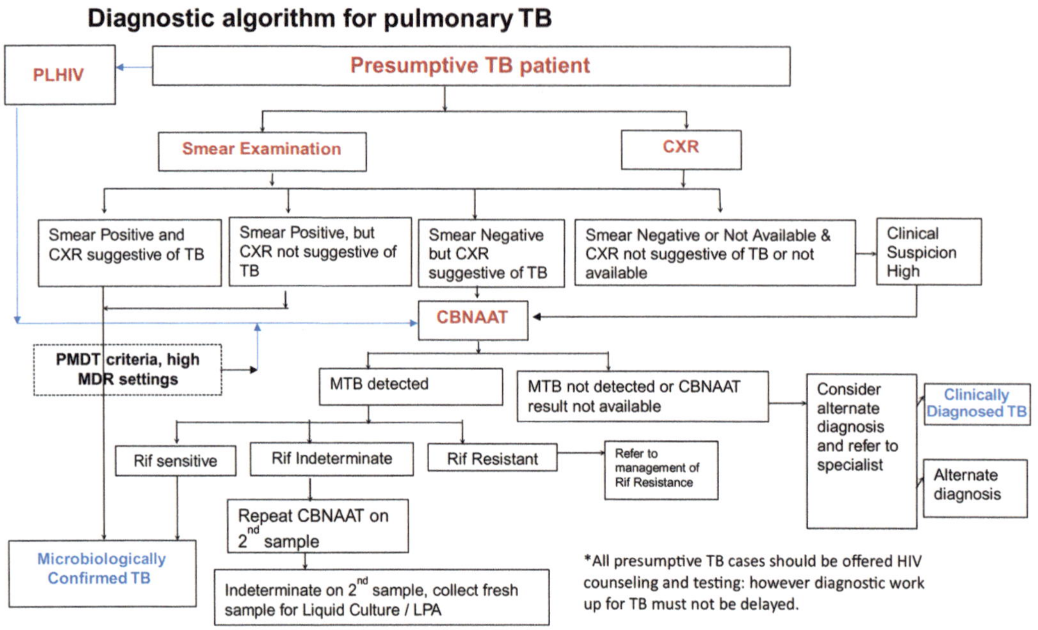

Fig. 13.1 Diagnostic algorithm recommended by Central TB division, India. (Adopted from National TB Elimination Program (NTEP), India)

These molecular methods offer several advantages over traditional TB diagnostic methods including:

1. Speed: molecular methods can provide results within a few hours, whereas sputum culture can take several days or even weeks.
2. Sensitivity: molecular methods can detect TB in patients with low bacterial loads, including those with extrapulmonary TB and those who are HIV positive.
3. Specificity: molecular methods are highly specific for *M. tuberculosis*, reducing the risk of false-positive results.
4. Reduced need for skilled technicians: some molecular methods, such as LAMP, do not require specialised training or equipment and can be performed in low-resource settings.

Therefore, the rapidity provided by the molecular methods has placed them in the first level of screening of the bacillary forms. But the classical phenotype-based method of diagnosing the tubercle bacilli cannot be written-off as it is still the confirmatory testing method and offers an array of advantages which are discussed in following lines. Moreover these are the gold standard methods used for validating the newer molecular methods in most scenarios apart from the use of WGS.

13.2 Direct Method

Direct methods for detecting tuberculosis include acid-fast bacilli (AFB) staining, culture methods, histopathology, and ultrasound imaging [8].

13.2.1 Smear Microscopy

The most popular technique for identifying pulmonary TB is direct sputum smear microscopy, which is available in the majority of primary healthcare labs. This method involves the collection of sputum sample followed by smear preparation and observing the smear under microscope after staining. At least two sputum specimens are required and cannot be collected at ease from the children makes sputum microscopy less favourable. Fortunately, the majority (95–98%) of smear-positive TB patients can be identified by high-quality microscopy. This uses the special capability present among the entire family of mycobacteria, the property of the cell wall which is acid fast and so are resistant to acid treatment after staining with a primary stain. But the degree of fastness varies between species. MTB is resistant to 25% acid and techniques are available for light and fluorescent microscopy. The older method of using strong carbol fuchsin, followed by 25% acid treatment and counter staining with methylene blue is called as the Ziehl-Neelsen method in which the smears can be read using a light microscope but requires heating step during the carbol fuchsin treatment to make the fatty acid layers permeable to the stain in use. Moreover the smears are read using the oil immersion objective. In the Auramine Phenol (AP) method which is a fluorescent based technique where in the heat fixed smears are stained using AP, followed by the decolorising step using 1% acid alcohol and counter staining by 0.1% potassium permanganate. Auramine-O dye or auramine-rhodamine dye are the two main dyes used in the fluorochrome process. When observed under a fluorescence microscope, the hydrochloride dye auramine-O causes stained AFB to exhibit fluorescence (green or yellow). Heating is not necessary, in contrast to the Ziehl-Neelsen procedure, for the stain to penetrate the germs. However, for the acid-fast organisms to adequately pick up the stain, there must be a minimum of 20 min of stain to smear contact time. This method has several advantages; they are more sensitive [9] and the smears can be read using the high-power objective lenses and hence more filed can be scanned in lesser time. But in general, smear microscopy is less sensitive as it requires a minimum of 10,000 bacilli per ml of the specimen for detection.

13.2.2 Culture Methods—Solid Egg-Based Methods

Culture-based methods are more sensitive and can also be used for the detection of drug resistance. Egg-based solid media (Lownstein Jenson, Ogawa) are the most favourite ones where the morphology of MTB results in a typical rough, tough and buff-coloured colonies are characteristics of MTB. The carbon source is glycerol, L-asparagine serves as the nitrogen source and malachite green is used as a contaminant inhibitor. LJ is less expensive than agar-based medium, simpler to prepare, and less prone to contamination during preparation because it is inspissated after being poured in bottles. Mycobacteria toxic materials are neutralised by the medium's high buffer capacity. It has a long shelf life if refrigerated (several weeks). It allows for direct visual recognition of *M. tuberculosis* colonies and contamination growth, just like other solid media. Using liquid media instead of solid media reduces the cultivation time from 12 weeks to 3 or 7 weeks and then they can be stored for longer periods at room temperature. The slow-growing nature of the bacilli makes the method less favourite and the liquid-based systems such as MGIT960, BacTAlert are automated liquid based closed systems where the time to detection is much more reduced than solid based cultures but are very expensive. These techniques involve fluorescent based dyes in the culture medium which offers to detect the growth of the tubercle bacilli in a system that is built with an agitator and incubator.

13.2.2.1 Agar-Based Medium

Middlebrook media: Middlebrook 7H11 and 7H10 medium consists agar as a solidifying agent. Compared to LJ medium, Agar-based media can detect growth more quickly by developing visible small early colonies. On one hand, transparent media can be easier to identify colonial morphology. These media are supplemented with oleic acid, albumin, dextrose, and catalase (OADC) to promote MTB growth and are also suitable for quantitative colony counts, which have been used in phase 2 early bactericidal activity (EBA) trials of TB drugs and drug combinations [10].

13.2.2.2 Nitrate Reduction Test (NRA)

Bacteria utilise nitrate (NO3−) as a terminal electron acceptor or as a source of oxygen during the anaerobic respiration process. In either of these processes, nitrate is first converted to nitrite (NO2−) and then to other by products such as molecular nitrogen gas (N2), ammonia (NH3), hydroxylamine, etc., or it may not be further converted depending on the metabolism of the bacterium or the presence of specific enzymes. These microorganisms are known as nitrate-reducing bacteria (denitrifying bacteria). These bacteria produce the enzymes needed to convert nitrate to nitrite, nitrate reductase. The basis of NRA is the ability of *Mycobacterium tuberculosis* (MTB) to convert nitrate present in the medium to nitrite, which may be identified by a change in colour when Griess reagent is added. The fastest and most accurate way to identify drug resistance in tuberculosis is direct NRA using middle brook 7H11 agar. The nitrate reductase assay (NRA) is one of the methods for rapid detection of resistance. WHO recommends that the NRA be used as a direct test on smear-positive sputum sample or as an indirect test on Mycobacterium tuberculosis isolates grown from conventional solid cultures such as LJ media. Additionally, 1 mg/ml KNO3 was added to the LJ medium as a nitrate source [11].

13.2.2.3 Liquid Culture Systems

The BACTEC MGIT 960 instrument is a fully automated system that detects mycobacteria growth in culture by utilising oxygen. Oxygen molecules act as a quencher to the fluorescence indicator. Following the oxygen reduction induced by aerobically metabolising bacteria within the medium, the ruthenium pentahydrate oxygen sensor embedded in silicon at the bottom of a tube containing 8 ml of modified Middlebrook 7H9 broth fluoresces [12]. It is highly reliable, delivering consistent and reproducible results. It is equipped with advanced sensors and algorithms that monitor the growth of mycobacteria, ensuring accurate and timely detection. The MGIT960 system offers high sensitivity and specificity in TB detection. It can detect as few as 100 mycobacteria per millilitre of the sample, making it highly effective even in cases with a low bacterial burden. Its ability to differentiate between *Mycobacterium tuberculosis* and other non-tuberculous mycobacteria is crucial for accurate diagnosis. When compared to LJ culture, MGIT 960 was found to be a more rapid method of mycobacteria detection and to be highly sensitive (100%), specific (93.3%), and accurate (93.6%) [13]. It can provide results within 2–3 weeks [14]. The automated nature of MGIT960 eliminates subjective interpretation and human error, leading to enhanced diagnostic accuracy. The MGIT960 system is equipped with a built-in susceptibility testing module, enabling the detection of drug resistance in TB bacteria. This feature assists healthcare providers in choosing appropriate treatment regimens, thereby preventing the spread of drug-resistant strains [15, 16]. These systems require power backup round the clock and the use of PANTA to control the normal flora and contaminants present in the specimen. The chances of contamination are higher than those of the solid-based cultures but are quite rapid. The initial investment and maintenance costs associated with the MGIT960 system can be substantial, especially for resource-limited settings. This can restrict its widespread implementation, particularly in regions with limited healthcare resources. The MGIT960 system requires a dedicated laboratory space and access to a stable power supply. Establishing and maintaining the necessary infrastructure can pose challenges, particularly in remote areas or regions with inadequate healthcare facilities. Although the MGIT960 system offers faster results compared to conventional methods, the 2–3 week turnaround time may still be a limitation in urgent cases requiring immediate diagnosis and treatment initiation.

13.2.2.4 MODS Assay

Microscopic Observation Drug Susceptibility assay (MODS) is an approved technique by WHO which does not require any radioactive isotope or florescent indicator like other phenotypic method and this technique is reliable, rapid, and suitable for developing country laboratories [17]. Several research has proved the safety, effective DST for screening of MDR-TB of MODS assay [18]. Moreover first and second line drugs can be used simultaneously in MODS assay in 24 well plates. MODS assays are less expensive in terms of the reagents used when compared with MGIT960, because 0.9 ml of enriched 7H9 medium is used per well in the MODS assay, therefore around 3.6 ml of enriched 7H9 medium is used to determine the first-line drug resistance per sample. For MGIT, more than 7 ml of enriched 7H9 medium are used for primary isolation and there after this much volume is required for each of the drugs for DST.

13.2.2.5 Skin Test: Tuberculin Skin Test

To evaluate if a person has been exposed to MTB, either from a prior TB vaccination or environmental exposure, the tuberculin skin test (TST) is employed. TST is based on the skin reactivation of tuberculin PPD in patients with delayed-type hypersensitivity (DTH). A combination of protein precipitated from modified mycobacterial culture filtrate is known as tuberculin PPD. An immune competent person who has been exposed to MTB experiences an active immune response that leads to the generation of antibodies and memory B cells that will recognise MTB antigens upon reinfection and create MTB antibodies to fend against future TB infections. TST comprises the injection of a small amount of tuberculin fluid containing MTB protein antigen, purified protein derivative, PPD, into the forearm of a patient. Within 48–72 h after injection, PPD reacts with pre-existing antibodies, causing inflammation that results in apparent tissue swelling. The risk that someone has been exposed to MTB increases with the size of the skin oedema. TST can't tell the difference between latent and active TB, though. In addition, those who have received a BCG vaccination to prevent TB will test positive on the TST.

13.3 Indirect Methods

In these methods, the samples collected are incubated for a period of time with appropriate composition of growth supplements that promote the proliferation of TB. Simultaneously, drug susceptibility is checked to select a suitable drug for treatment. A cellular immune response to mycobacterial antigens is required for the diagnosis of long-term bacterial infection (LTBI), which is an indirect method. Indirect tests for diagnosis generally includes immunological and serological tests. Latent tuberculosis infection (LTBI) is described as a condition in which there is a persistent immunological response to stimulation by *M. tuberculosis* antigens but no sign of clinically manifested active TB. Those with LTBI who have negative results from bacteriological tests can opt for the presumptive diagnosis of LTBI which is based on a positive result of a skin (tuberculin skin test, TST) or blood (interferon-gamma release assay, IGRA) test indicating an immunological response to *M. tuberculosis* infection [20].

13.3.1 Interferon-Gamma Release Assays (Igras)

Since IGRAs monitor a patient's immunological response to MTB, they are thought to be more accurate than TSTs Blood samples from people who are thought to have MTB infection are exposed to MTB antigens, if the person is TB-positive, their peripheral blood lymphocytes respond by generating IFN-ɣ. A single test can provide a definitive diagnosis of TB, and these assays are believed to be extremely sensitive. Two more IGRAs have received FDA approval: the QuantiFERON® TB Gold In-Tube test (QFT-GIT) and the T- SPOT® TB test (T-SPOT). The T-SPOT test counts the number of cells actively producing IFN- ɣ, whereas the QFT-GIT test measures the concentration of IFN- ɣ.

13.3.2 QFT-GIT

Whole blood is taken as the test sample to test for single peptides such as the early secretory antigenic target 6 (ESAT-6) as MTB antigens which measures the IFN-ɣ concentration in enzyme linked immuno sorbent assay within the processing time of 24 h and the possible results generated can be positive, negative or intermediate.

13.3.3 T-SPOT

Peripheral blood mononuclear cells (PBMC) blood is taken as a test sample to test for one or both peptides (ESAT-6 and CFP-10) as MTB antigens which measures the number of cells that produce IFN-ɣ in the aptamer-linked DNA immuno sorbent assay within the processing time of 24 h and the possible results generated can be positive, negative or intermediate [19].

13.3.4 Limitations to Phenotypic Methods

The major limitations of liquid and solid DST methods are accuracy, availability, and turnaround time. The DST results may take even more than a month sometimes in culture-based phenotypic assays and this may lead to delay and inaccurate treatment which may increase the resistance proposition. The infrastructure required to carry out phenotypic methods are not available in resource-limited set-ups in many countries. Drugs such as streptomycin, pyrazinamide, and ethambutol suffers from sub-optimal reproducibility. Phenotypic DST is not at all suitable for mixed cultures. There is a fair chance of contamination during the setup of phenotypic DST and also if non-tuberculous mycobacteria is present. This may lead to false-positive results.

13.3.5 Genetic Markers to Identify MTB

1. IS6110: The insertion sequence IS6110 is a widely used genetic marker for MTB. It is a repetitive DNA sequence that is present in multiple copies within the genome of MTB but absent in most other mycobacterial species. The IS6110 element can be detected using polymerase chain reaction (PCR) or other nucleic acid amplification techniques.
2. hsp65: Another frequently used genetic marker for MTB identification is the gene encoding the heat shock protein 65 (hsp65). It encodes a protein that mycobacteria greatly conserve. PCR-based techniques, such as the widely used GenoType MTBDR plus assay, can be used to amplify and detect the hsp65 gene.
3. rpoB: As a genetic marker for MTB detection and medication resistance testing, the RNA polymerase beta subunit (rpoB) gene has been employed. One of the main drugs used to treat tuberculosis, rifampicin, has been linked to certain mutations within the rpoB gene that cause resistance to it. Both species identification and rifampicin resistance data can be obtained using rpoB gene amplification and sequencing.
4. 16S rRNA: The 16S ribosomal RNA (16S rRNA) gene is a conserved region found in the bacterial genome. Specific regions of the 16S rRNA gene can be targeted for amplification and sequencing to identify MTB and differentiate it from other bacteria.
5. Region of Difference (RD) markers: Areas of difference (RD) are genomic regions that are unique to MTB and are absent or markedly different in other mycobacterial species. For PCR-based tests to identify MTB, these RD areas make good targets. RD9, RD12, RD702, and RD750 are a few examples of RD markers.

13.3.6 In-House PCR

PCR is a molecular biology technique that amplifies small amounts of DNA in a sample, making it possible to detect even trace amounts of the target DNA. In-house PCR refers to the use of PCR technology in a laboratory that is part of the same healthcare facility where the sample is collected. This setup allows for faster and more convenient testing, as well as increased cost savings compared to sending samples to an external laboratory.

In the case of tuberculosis (TB), internal PCR is used to detect the DNA of *Mycobacterium tuberculosis*, the bacterium that causes TB [21]. This method is highly sensitive and specific, making it a valuable tool for early diagnosis and prompt treatment of TB.

One of the main benefits of in-house PCR for TB diagnosis is the speed of results. Compared to traditional TB diagnostic methods, such as sputum culture or X-ray, internal PCR can provide results in hours, rather than days or weeks. This fast turnaround time is especially important in areas endemic to tuberculosis, where prompt diagnosis and treatment are crucial to prevent the spread of the disease.

In addition, internal PCR is less prone to contamination and false negative results, compared to sputum culture, and is more accurate than X-ray in detecting TB in people with extrapulmonary TB, such as TB of the lymph nodes, bones, or organs [22, 23].

Despite its many benefits, internal PCR for TB diagnosis is not without limitations. For example, the cost of equipment and reagents can be prohibitive for some healthcare facilities, especially in low-income countries. Additionally, the need for trained personnel to operate and interpret the results of the test can also pose a challenge in resource-limited settings.

13.3.7 Random Fragment Length Polymorphism (RFLP)-PCR for Diagnosis

Random Fragment Length Polymorphism (RFLP)-Polymerase Chain Reaction (PCR) is a diagnostic tool used for the identification of tuberculosis (TB) caused by *Mycobacterium tuberculosis* in human samples. The method is based on the detection of specific genetic regions in the bacterium, which are amplified and fragmented, then analysed to determine the specific strain of TB.

Conventional methods of diagnosis of tuberculosis, such as sputum smear microscopy and culture, are time-consuming and have limitations in terms of sensitivity and specificity. RFLP-PCR, on the other hand, is a highly sensitive and specific diagnostic method that can detect the presence of *M. tuberculosis* in clinical specimens within a few hours. The procedure involves the amplification of specific genetic regions of *M. tuberculosis* using PCR, followed by digestion of restriction enzymes and analysis of the resulting fragments. The pattern of fragments produced can be used to distinguish between different strains of *M. tuberculosis*.

One of the main advantages of RFLP-PCR is its ability to detect TB in a variety of clinical samples, including sputum, bronchoalveolar lavage fluid, and tissues. This makes it a valuable tool in the diagnosis of extrapulmonary TB, which often goes undiagnosed using conventional methods.

Another advantage of RFLP-PCR is its ability to detect TB in immunosuppressed individuals, who may not show typical symptoms of the disease. This is particularly important for patients with HIV, who are at increased risk of developing TB. RFLP-PCR can also be used to monitor the response to treatment and to detect the emergence of drug-resistant strains of *M. tuberculosis*.

However, there are some limitations to the use of RFLP-PCR for the diagnosis of TB. The method requires specialised equipment and expertise and is more expensive than conventional diagnostic methods. In addition, false-positive results can occur if the specimens are contaminated with other species of Mycobacteria.

In conclusion, RFLP-PCR is a highly accurate and precise diagnostic technique for the diagnosis of TB brought on by *M. tuberculosis*. It is an effective tool in the fight against TB since it can find TB in a range of clinical specimens and in immunosuppressed people. However, the process is more expensive than customary diagnostic techniques and calls for specialised equipment and knowledge. For widespread usage in the global TB control effort, more research is required to increase the RFLP-price PCR's and accuracy.

13.3.8 Nucleic Acid Amplification Test (NAAT)

NAAT assays identify the MTB complex organisms by detecting the mycobacterial insertion element IS6110 [24]. Acid-fast bacilli (AFB) smear-positive and AFB smear-negative sputum samples can both be used to find DNA from the *Mycobacterium tuberculosis* complex (MTBC) (deoxyribonucleic acid) in sputum or other respiratory samples. NAA testing comprises a procedure that amplifies (or replicates) the genetic material because the amount of DNA in a sample is so tiny. A typical NAAT method used in laboratory diagnosis is polymerase chain reaction (PCR). The GeneXpert® MTB/RIF test is a PCR that simultaneously identifies MTBC and the genetic mutation that results in resistance to rifampin (RIF). Due to its high sensitivity and specificity, nucleic acid amplification testing (NAAT) has become the preferred method as a potential substitute for the traditional bacteriological diagnosis of tuberculosis (TB), which has a number of drawbacks. A NAAT can detect MTBC genetic material even when very small amounts are present in the tested sample. NAAT results are typically available in 24–48 h. Rapid results enable an earlier diagnosis of tuberculosis, earlier initiation of treatment, a reduced period of infectiousness, and improved patient outcomes.

The nucleic acid amplification test (NAAT) is a highly sensitive and specific diagnostic test that has become an essential tool in the diagnosis of tuberculosis (TB). It is a highly infectious disease that can spread quickly, especially in populations with weakened immune systems, and early and accurate diagnosis is critical to controlling its spread and improving patient outcomes.

NAATs are able to detect very small amounts of *M. tuberculosis* DNA in a patient's sample, making them ideal for the rapid diagnosis of TB, even in patients with early-stage or asymptomatic infections. This is a significant advantage over traditional TB diagnostic tests, such as the sputum smear microscopy test, which can miss up to 50% of cases of TB and can be affected by the presence of concurrent infections or other factors that can interfere with the results [25].

Another advantage of NAAT in the diagnosis of tuberculosis is its specificity, which reduces the risk of false-positive results. This is particularly important in TB-endemic areas where misdiagnosis can lead to inappropriate treatment, further spread of disease, and potential development of drug-resistant strains. NAATs are able to identify the specific subtype of *M. tuberculosis*, providing crucial information for effective treatment and tracking the spread of the disease.

Several commercially available NAATs exist for TB diagnosis, including the polymerase chain reaction (PCR) test. These tests can provide results in just a few hours, allowing for rapid diagnosis and initiation of treatment. Additionally, NAATs can be performed on a variety of sample types (such as urine, blood, and sputum), making them useful for a wide range of diagnostic applications.

13.3.9 XPERT MTB/RIF Assay

The XPERT MTB/RIF assay is a molecular diagnostic test used to detect tuberculosis (TB) and resistance to rifampin, a crucial first-line TB drug. A cartridge based on the GeneXpert Instrument System is used in the nucleic acid amplification-based XpertMTB / RIF assay [26]. This test offers several advantages over traditional TB diagnostic methods, including improved speed, accuracy and versatility.

One of the key benefits of the XPERT MTB/RIF assay is its speed. Results can be obtained in as little as 2 h, making it much faster than traditional TB culture methods which can take several weeks to produce results. This quick turnaround time can help ensure that patients receive timely and effective treatment for their condition.

The XPERT MTB/RIF assay is also highly accurate. Studies have shown that the test has a high level of sensitivity and specificity for detecting TB and rifampin resistance, meaning that it is able to accurately identify TB cases and distinguish between TB and other similar conditions. This helps to reduce the risk of misdiagnosis and ensure that patients receive the correct treatment for their condition. The test is also versatile as it can be performed on a variety of sample types, including sputum, broncho alveolar lavage fluid (BAL), and pleural fluid. This makes it suitable for use in a range of clinical settings, including resource-limited settings where access to laboratory facilities may be limited.

The 81 bp core region of the bacterial RNA polymerase (rpoB) gene, which encodes the enzyme's active site, is the target DNA sequence. Mutations are located in this region in more than 95% of all strains resistant to rifampicin. Furthermore, *M. tuberculosis* specific DNA sequences flank the rpoB core region. Consequently, it is possible to test both *M. tuberculosis* and resistance to rifampicin at the same time [27].

In addition to these benefits, the XPERT MTB/RIF assay is relatively easy to use and requires minimal technical training. This makes it a suitable option for use in a variety of settings, including hospitals, primary care clinics, and low- and middle-income countries. Overall, the XPERT MTB/RIF assay is a highly effective and convenient diagnostic tool for detecting TB and rifampin resistance. Its fast turnaround time, accuracy, versatility, and ease of use make it a valuable tool for improving TB diagnosis and treatment globally.

Steingart et al. [28] has done a meta-analysis and reported that in the low- and middle-income countries GeneXpert MTB/RIF has 89% sensitivity and 99% specificity. The sensitivity is higher in smear-positive cases (98%) than in smear-negative cases (67%). The main limitations of this method are it cannot distinguish between living and dead and so treatment progression cannot be assessed. The sensitivity is lower in case of extrapulmonary and paucibacillary. There is a chance of getting false-positive results in certain silent mutations [29]. The high cost is also one of the limitations. The GeneXpert MTB/RIF Ultra assay is a next generation assay that has higher sensitivity than the previous version.

GeneXpert 10-colour instrument is one of the recent additions by Cepheid wherein the instrument can detect drug resistance to Rifampicin, amikacin, ethionamide, fluoroquinolones, and isoniazid. WHO has recommended the use of this instrument and stated that this is comparable to the existing Xpertsytem in detecting rifampicin resistance (Use of Xpert MTB/RIF and Xpert MTB/RIF Ultra on GeneXpert 10-colour instruments: WHO policy statement. Geneva: World Health Organization; 2021. Licence: CC BY-NC-SA 3.0 IGO).

13.3.10 Line Probe Assays

The line probe assay (LPA) is a molecular diagnostic test that is used to detect the presence of specific genetic mutations in a patient's DNA. The test works by amplifying and then hybridising the target DNA to a set of probes that are attached to a solid support (such as a strip). It is based on the reverse hybridisation theory [30]. It is based on reverse hybridisation theory. If a mutation is present in the target DNA, it will bind to the corresponding probe, causing a visible line to appear on the strip. The presence of *M. tuberculosis* can be seen by looking at the coloured band that appears on the strip.

Advantages of LPA include its high sensitivity and specificity, rapid turnaround time (results are typically available within a few hours), and its ability to detect multiple mutations in a single reaction. This makes it a useful tool for the diagnosis of tuberculosis and human immunodeficiency virus [HIV]), cancers (such as lung and colon cancer), and inherited disorders (such as cystic fibrosis).

In addition to its diagnostic applications, LPA has also been used to monitor the effectiveness of treatments for certain diseases, such as tuberculosis and HIV and for monitoring the development of drug resistance in patients.

There are several different commercial LPA kits available, each with its own specific set of probes designed to detect specific mutations. It is important to choose the correct LPA kit for the intended application, as using the wrong kit may result in false negative or false-positive results.

13.3.11 MTBDR*plus* and MTBDR*sl*

MTBDR*plus* and MTBDR*sl* are line probe assays for rapid screening and DST of tuberculosis. MTBDR*plus* detects isoniazid (katG and inhA) and rifampin (rpoB) resistance, whereas MTBDR*sl* detects ethambutol (embB), aminoglycosides, and cyclic peptides (rrs) and fluoroqinolones (gyrA). The time taken for these two assays are approximately 5 h. Bai et al. in 2016 [31] has done a meta-analysis and reported that the sensitivity and specificity to detect isoniazid resistance is 91% and 99%, respectively. For rifampicin resistance, the sensitivity and specificity is 96% and 98%, respectively, and for MDR, it is 91% sensitivity and 98% specificity. In case of direct smear-negative sputum samples, the early detection percentage for MDR-TB is low [32–34]. GenoTypeMTBDR*sl* 2.0 version is the updated version with higher detection capability of mutations [35–37]. The sensitivity and specificity in detecting fluoroquinolone resistance for direct testing of smear-positive samples are 97% and 98%, respectively, and for smear-negative samples it is 80% and 100%, respectively. In case of second line injectable agents, the sensitivity and specificity for smear-positive samples are 89% and 90%, respectively, whereas for smear-negative, it is 80% and 100%, respectively. Further evaluation should be done for susceptible smear-negative specimens.

13.3.12 Nipro NTM+MDRTB

The Nipro NTM+MDRTB is one of the line probe assays that can identify four species of Mycobacterium, namely *M. tuberculosis*, *M. kansasii*, *M. intracellularle,* and *M. avium*. It also detects resistance to isoniazid (inhA and KatG) and rifampin (rpoB) [38]. The sensitivity and specificity of direct test was reported as 96.5% and 98.5%, respectively, whereas for resistance, the sensitivity and specificity was reported as 94.9% and 97.6%, respectively. Nipro has also designed a test called NiproGenoscholar PZA-TBII line probe assay to detect resistance for pyrazinamide in pncA gene [39].

13.3.13 Anyplex Plus MTB/NTM/MDR-TB and Anyplex II MTB/MDR/XDR Kit

Anyplex plus system is one of the multiplex real-time PCR systems that is used to detect *M. tuberculosis* complex and non-tuberculous mycobacterial species. Resistance to rifampicin (rpoB) and isoniazid (katG and inhA) is also detected in case of *M. tuberculosis*. This assay can be completed in 3 h time. The sensitivity for the detection of Mtb complex is 86.4% and the specificity is 99% [40]. Lower sensitivity is reported in extrapulmonary cases. Anyplex II is a newer version that can identify resistance in rifampicin (rpoB), isoniazid (katG and inhA), aminoglycoside (rrs and eis), and fluoroquinolone (gyrA). When compared with phenotypic DST, this test has lower sensitivity [41].

13.3.14 Truenat MTB, Truenat MTB Plus, and Truenat MTB-RIF Dx

Truenat system is a chip based real-time micro-PCR assay developed in India by Molbio Diagnostics Pvt. Ltd. Truenat MTB and Truenat MTB Plus are diagnostic assays for TB. If the assay is positive, then Truenat MTB-RIF Dx is used to detect resistance for rifampicin. The sensitivity and specificity of Truenat MTB are 88% and 97.2%, respectively, whereas the sensitivity and specificity of Truenat MTB plus are 91.7% and 97.2%, respectively [42]. This assay only requires 0.5 ml of the sputum sample. This can be used as a point of care test as this is portable and battery operated. The total time taken for Truenat MTB Plus followed by MTB-RIF Dx is approximately 2 h. This has an advantage over Xpert system, wherein there are two different chips for Mtb detection and Rifampicin detection and hence this will be more cost effective when compared to Xpert.

13.3.15 Loop-Mediated Isothermal Amplification Technique

LAMP (Loop-mediated isothermal amplification) is a molecular diagnostic technique used to detect the presence of *Mycobacterium tuberculosis*, the causative agent of tuberculosis (TB). It is a rapid, sensitive, and specific method for diagnosing TB, especially in resource-limited settings. LAMP uses specific primers to amplify DNA under isothermal conditions, eliminating the need for thermal cycling and making it a low-cost alternative to traditional PCR-based methods. The results of [43] LAMP can be read visually or by using a fluorescence reader, providing results in as little as 60 min.

13.3.16 Whole-Genome Sequencing (WGS)

Whole-genome sequencing (WGS) is a powerful tool for the diagnosis of *Mycobacterium tuberculosis* (MTB), the causative agent of tuberculosis (TB). It has the potential to revolutionise the diagnosis and management of TB, particularly in resource-limited settings. WGS provides a comprehensive view of the complete genomic makeup of MTB, allowing the detection of genetic variations that are not discernible by traditional diagnostic methods. This information can be used to differentiate between closely related strains, track the spread of tuberculosis, and monitor the emergence of drug-resistant strains [44]. One of the key advantages of WGS is its high resolution, allowing for the identification of mutations that are associated with drug resistance. This is particularly important in the context of TB, where drug resistance is a major challenge to effective treatment. By detecting resistance early, WGS can inform the selection of appropriate treatment regimens, reducing the risk of further spread of drug-resistant tuberculosis. Because MTB must be cultured for several weeks before a substantial amount of DNA can be recovered, WGS has not been used as a standard diagnostic method for TB. Workflow to extract DNA from frozen isolates without re-culturing is significant since slow-growing MTB must be cultured before DNA extraction, which takes a lot of time in WGS [45, 46]. Despite the many benefits of WGS for the diagnosis of MTB, there are also some challenges associated with its implementation. One of the main challenges is the cost, which can be a barrier to widespread adoption, especially in resource-limited settings. Additionally, WGS requires specialised equipment and skilled personnel, which may not be readily available in some regions. In conclusion, WGS has the potential to significantly improve the diagnosis and management of MTB, particularly with regard to the detection of drug-resistant strains and the differentiation between active and latent infections. However, cost and access to equipment and personnel remain barriers to widespread implementation. Further research is needed to address these challenges and make WGS a more accessible and practical diagnostic tool for TB. WGS is becoming more accessible in diagnostic microbiology laboratories as costs decrease and technology advances. Pathogens can be thoroughly characterised at the molecular level to research whole-genome evolution (such as the compensating mechanisms offsetting the fitness cost of resistance mutations), population structure, and phylogeny, as well as for epidemiological applications [47].

13.3.17 Mycobacterial Load Detection Assay

Mycobacterial load detection assays are in-house methodologies that are critical in the management of tuberculosis (TB) and other mycobacterial infections. The assay is used to measure the number of mycobacterial cells in a patient's sample, which is an important predictor of disease progression and response to treatment. The assay can be performed using a variety of methods including culture-based assays, molecular assays, and antibody-based assays. Culture-based assays, such as the Lowenstein–Jensen (LJ) culture method, have been the gold standard for mycobacterial load detection for several decades. However, these assays have significant limitations, including a long turnaround time, low sensitivity, and a requirement for specialised laboratory equipment and personnel. Molecular assays, such as real-time PCR, have emerged as a promising alternative to culture-based methods. These assays are highly sensitive, rapid, and can be performed with relatively simple and inexpensive equipment. However, their accuracy may be influenced by the presence of inhibitors in the patient's sample and the need for accurate and standardised calibration. Antibody-based assays, such as the ELISpot assay, are designed to detect the presence of specific mycobacterial antigens in the patient's sample. These assays are rapid and simple to perform, but their sensitivity and specificity may be limited compared to culture-based and other molecular assays.

13.3.18 Other Advanced Molecular Diagnostic Techniques for TB

1. RFLP: The restriction fragment length polymorphism (RFLP) is a widely used technique for identifying MTB. This is based on the analysis of the differences in the restriction patterns of the MTB genome produced by different restriction enzymes. RFLP is a powerful tool for differentiating between different strains of MTB and has been widely used for epidemiological studies of TB.
2. Spoligotyping: This is another widely used technique that utilises genetic markers for identifying MTB. It is beneficial for laboratories studying population genetics, evolution, molecular epidemiology, and clinical care [48]. It is based on the analysis of the spacers between the direct repeats in the MTB genome. Spoligotyping is a powerful tool for differentiating between different MTB strains and has been widely used for epidemiological studies of TB.
3. MIRU-VNTR: The mycobacterial inter spersed number of tandem repeats in repetitive units (MIRU-VNTR) is a relatively new genetic marker that is used to identify MTB [49]. This marker is based on the analysis of the number of copies of a specific sequence of DNA in the MTB genome. MIRU-VNTR is a powerful tool for differentiating between different MTB strains and has been widely used for epidemiological studies of TB.

13.4 Conclusion

So far, there were several advances with respect to molecular diagnostics of drug resistance in *Mycobacterium tuberculosis*. Yet there are some limitations. The major disadvantage of molecular diagnostics of DST apart from not being a good prognostic indicator is the lack of studies in underling mechanisms of genetics involved in drug resistance, especially for drugs other than rifampicin. But the rapidity offered by the molecular methods are contributing so much that the drastic decrease in the time to detection is very much valuable especially in limiting the spread of the disease and transmission. The prominence in the placement of the molecular methods in the diagnostic algorithm reflects this statement. Generally, mutations that are specific to particular type of resistance are identified and then the molecular mechanism of resistance is studied using sophisticated tools. But in some cases resistance is present due to a cumulative effect of many mutations that act together. Bioinformatics approaches can be used to identify such patterns irrespective of point mutations specified for a particular resistance. For example, machine languages are used to create AI software that are involved in chest radiograph for patients having TB suspicion [50]. Likewise, bioinformatic tools can be used to filter the large data that are generated from whole-genome sequencing. Thus, software that are user friendly and highly streamlined which process automatically the data from whole-genome sequencing and gives us the report of drug resistance that are clinically relevant are needed. The other major limitation is lack of laboratories that have all the expensive instrumentation required for molecular diagnosis of drug-resistant TB. Establishment of many such central facilities will avoid the time taken for transportation of specimen from primary clinic to central facility. Closed cartridge systems are highly recommended over open tube systems for easy procedure with no cross contamination. Finally, as newer molecules having antiTB activity are being discovered now and then, the molecular genotypic determinants of resistance should be analysed and evaluated and should be included in the molecular tests. The resistant strains can be a part of the molecular diagnostic tool in the near future.Contri butionAB, SK and SAS contributed equally for the preparation of this chapter, AD was responsible for the entire flow and critical reviewing of the chapter.

References

1. Yusoof KA, García JI, Schami A, Garcia-Vilanova A, Kelley HV, Wang SH, Rendon A, Restrepo BI, Yotebieng M, Torrelles JB. Tuberculosis phenotypic and genotypic drug susceptibility testing and immunodiagnostics: a review. Front Immunol. 2022;13:870768. https://doi.org/10.3389/FIMMU.2022.870768.
2. Gill CM, Dolan L, Piggott LM, McLaughlin AM. New developments in tuberculosis diagnosis and treatment. Breathe (Sheff). 2022;18(1):210149. https://doi.org/10.1183/20734735.0149-2021.
3. Nurwidya F, DiahHandayani EB, Yunus F. Molecular diagnosis of tuberculosis. Chonnam Med J. 2018;54(1):1. https://doi.org/10.4068/cmj.2018.54.1.1.
4. Ghodbane R, Raoult D, Drancourt M. Dramatic reduction of culture time of Mycobacterium tuberculosis. Sci Rep. 2014;4(1):1–4. https://doi.org/10.1038/srep04236.
5. Balasingham SV, Davidsen T, Szpinda I, Frye SA, Tønjum T. Molecular diagnostics in tuberculosis: basis and implications for therapy. Mol Diagn Ther. 2009;13(3):137–51. https://doi.org/10.1007/BF03256322.
6. Göbel UB. Phylogenetic amplification for the detection of uncultured bacteria and the analysis of complex microbiota. J Microbiol Methods. 1995;23(1):117–28. https://doi.org/10.1016/0167-7012(95)00025-G.
7. Musser JM. Antimicrobial agent resistance in mycobacteria: molecular genetic insights. Clin Microbiol Rev. 1995;8(4):496–514. https://doi.org/10.1128/CMR.8.4.496.
8. Pellegrino R, Viegi G, Vito Brusasco RO, Crapo F, Burgos R, Casaburi AC, et al. Interpretative strategies for lung function tests. Eur Respir J. 2005;26(5):948–68. https://doi.org/10.1183/09031936.05.00035205.
9. Kumar VA, Chandra PS. Auramine phenol staining of smears for screening acid fast bacilli in clinical specimens. J Commun Dis. 2008;40(1):47–52.
10. Joloba ML, Johnson JL, Pei JI, Feng LB, Goldberg SV, Morgan K, Gitta P, et al. What is the Most reliable solid culture medium for tuberculosis treatment trials? Tuberculosis (Edinb). 2014;94(3):311–6. https://doi.org/10.1016/J.TUBE.2014.03.002.
11. Affolabi D, Odoun M, N'diraSanoussi AM, Palomino JC, Kestens L, Anagonou S, Portaels F. Rapid and inexpensive detection of multidrug-resistant *Mycobacterium tuberculosis* with the nitrate reductase assay using liquid medium and direct application to sputum samples. J Clin Microbiol. 2008;46(10):3243–5. https://doi.org/10.1128/JCM.00083 08.
12. Tortoli E, Cichero P, Claudio Piersimoni M, TulliaSimonetti GG, Nista D. Use of BACTEC MGIT 960 for recovery of mycobacteria from clinical specimens: multicenter study. J Clin Microbiol. 1999;37(11):3578–82. https://doi.org/10.1128/JCM.37.11.3578-3582.1999.
13. Hasan M, Munshi SK, BanuMomi MS, Rahman F, Noor R. Evaluation of the effectiveness of BACTEC MGIT 960 for the detection of mycobacteria in Bangladesh. Int J Mycobacteriol. 2013;2(4):214–9. https://doi.org/10.1016/J.IJMYCO.2013.09.001.
14. Balaji S, Ravi Kumar D, Sangamithrai D, Radhika G, Kannan T, Nagarajan P, Thiagarajan V, RadhaKrishnan A, Padmapriyadarsini C, Shanmugam, S. Comparison of performance indicators of MGIT primary culture to assess the impact of implementation of ISO 15189:2012standards. Indian J Tuberc. 2022;69(3):371–3. https://doi.org/10.1016/J.IJTB.2022.03.020.
15. De Almeida I, Da Silva S, Junior H, Figueredo L, Soares V, Carvalho W, Kritski A, Da Costa Fiori M, De Miranda S. The activity-based cost of drug-susceptibility test of *Mycobacterium tuberculosis* through Kit SIRE Nitratase® Plastlabor. Int J Mycobacteriol. 2020;9(1):24–8. https://doi.org/10.4103/ijmy.ijmy_8_20.
16. Siddiqi S, Ahmed A, Asif S, Behera D, Javaid M, Jani J, Jyoti A, Mahatre R, Mahto D, Richter E, Rodrigues C, Visalakshi P, Rüsch-Gerdes S. Direct drug susceptibility testing of Mycobacterium tuberculosis for rapid detection of multidrug resistance using the Bactec MGIT 960 system: a multicenter study. J Clin Microbiol. 2012;50(2):435–40. https://doi.org/10.1128/JCM.05188-11.
17. Caviedes L, Tien-Shun L, Gilman RH, Sheen P, Spellman E, Lee EH, Berg DE, et al. Rapid, efficient detection and drug susceptibility testing of *Mycobacterium tuberculosis* in sputum by microscopic observation of broth cultures. The Tuberculosis Working Group in Peru. J Clin Microbiol. 2000;38(3):1203–8. https://doi.org/10.1128/JCM.38.3.1203-1208.2000.
18. Agarwal A, Katoch CDS, Kumar M, Dhole TN, Sharma YK. Evaluation of microscopic observation drug susceptibility (MODS) assay as a rapid, sensitive and inexpensive test for detection of tuberculosis and multidrug resistant tuberculosis. Med J Armed Forces India. 2019;75(1):58–64. https://doi.org/10.1016/J.MJAFI.2018.03.011.
19. Martínez-Martínez YB, Martínez-Rodríguez HG, Said-Fernández SL. Conventional and molecular diagnosis of drug-sensitive and drug-resistant pulmonary tuberculosis. In: Mycobacterium—research and development. InTech; 2018. https://doi.org/10.5772/intechopen.75004.
20. Castro-Garza J, García-Jacobo P, Lydia G, Rivera-Morales FD, James Q, Russell B, Debra K, Shelly H, Tuhina H, Henry G, Jane B, Itza T, Luna-Cruz A, Javier R, Vargas-Villarreal L, Vera-Cabrera C, Rodríguez-Padilla. Detection of anti-HspX antibodies and HspX protein in patient sera for the identification of recent latent infection by mycobacterium tuberculosis PLOS ONE. 2017;12(8) https://doi.org/10.1371/journal.pone.0181714.
21. Greco S, Rulli M, Girardi E, Piersimoni C, Saltini C. Diagnostic accuracy of in-house PCR

for pulmonary tuberculosis in smear-positive patients: meta-analysis and metaregression. J Clin Microbiol. 2009;47(3) American Society for Microbiology (ASM):569. https://doi.org/10.1128/JCM.02051-08.
22. Kulkarni S, Singh P, Memon A, Nataraj G, Kanade S, Kelkar R, Rajan MGR. An in-house multiplex PCR test for the detection of *Mycobacterium tuberculosis*, its validation and comparison with a single target TB-PCR Kit. Indian J Med Res. 2012;135(5):788. / pmc/articles/PMC3401715/
23. Wei Z, Zhang X, Wei C, Liang Y, Li Y, Zhang X, Xu H, et al. Diagnostic accuracy of in-house real-time PCR assay for *Mycobacterium tuberculosis*: a systematic review and meta-analysis. BMC Infect Dis. 2019;19(1):1–11. https://doi.org/10.1186/S12879-019-4273-Z/FIGURES/5.
24. Tiwari S, Nataraj G, Kanade S, Mehta P. Diagnosis of pediatric pulmonary tuberculosis with special reference to polymerase chain reaction based nucleic acid amplification test. Int J Mycobacteriol. 2015;4(1):48–53. https://doi.org/10.1016/J.IJMYCO.2014.11.063.
25. Niemz A, Boyle DS. Nucleic acid testing for tuberculosis at the point-of-care in high-burden countries. Expert Rev Mol Diagn. 2012;12(7):687. https://doi.org/10.1586/ERM.12.71.
26. Davis JL, Ho C, AdithyaCattamanchi JG, Metcalfe JZ, Pandori M, Banouvong H, et al. The clinical and public health impact of automated nucleic acid testing for TB evaluation in San Francisco. Am J Respir Crit Care Med. 2011:A5314. https://doi.org/10.1164/AJRCCM-CONFERENCE.2011.183.1_MEETINGABSTRACTS.A5314.
27. Lawn SD, Nicol MP. Xpert® MTB/RIF assay: development, evaluation and implementation of a new rapid molecular diagnostic for tuberculosis and rifampicin resistance. Future Microbiol. 2011;6(9):1067–82. https://doi.org/10.2217/FMB.11.84.
28. Steingart KR, Schiller I, Horne DJ, Pai M, Boehme CC, Dendukuri N. Xpert® MTB/RIF assay for pulmonary tuberculosis and rifampicin resistance in adults. Cochrane Database Syst Rev. 2014;2014:CD009593.
29. Mathys V, Van de Vyvere M, De Droogh E, Soetaert K, Groenen G. False-positive rifampicin resistance on Xpert® MTB/RIF caused by a silent mutation in the rpoB gene. Int J Tuberc Lung Dis. 2014;18(10):1255–7.
30. Rossau R, Traore H, de Beenhouwer H, Mijs W, Jannes G, de Rijk P, Portaels F. Evaluation of the INNO-LiPA Rif. TB assay, a reverse hybridization assay for the simultaneous detection of *Mycobacterium tuberculosis* complex and its resistance to rifampin. Antimicrob Agents Chemother. 1997;41(10):2093–8. https://doi.org/10.1128/AAC.41.10.2093.
31. Bai Y, Wang Y, Shao C, Hao Y, Jin Y. GenoType MTBDR plus assay for rapid detection of multidrug resistance in Mycobacterium tuberculosis: a meta-analysis. PLoS One. 2016;11(3):e0150321.
32. Matabane MMZ, Ismail F, Strydom KA, Onwuegbuna O, Omar SV, Ismail N. Performance evaluation of three commercial molecular assays for the detection of *Mycobacterium tuberculosis* from clinical specimens in a high TB-HIV-burden setting. BMC Infect Dis. 2015;15:1–7.
33. Meaza A, Kebede A, Yaregal Z, Dagne Z, Moga S, Yenew B, Diriba G, Molalign H, Tadesse M, Adisse D, Getahun M. Evaluation of genotype MTBDR plus VER 2.0 line probe assay for the detection of MDR-TB in smear positive and negative sputum samples. BMC Infect Dis. 2017;17:1–8.
34. Seifert M, Georghiou SB, Catanzaro D, Rodrigues C, Crudu V, Victor TC, Garfein RS, Catanzaro A, Rodwell TC. MTBDR plus and MTBDRsl assays: absence of wild-type probe hybridization and implications for detection of drug-resistant tuberculosis. J Clin Microbiol. 2016;54(4):912–8.
35. Bang D, Andersen SR, Vasiliauskienė E, Rasmussen EM. Performance of the GenoTypeMTBDRplus assay (v2. 0) and a new extended GenoTypeMTBDRslassay (v2. 0) for the molecular detection of multi-and extensively drug-resistant *Mycobacterium tuberculosis* on isolates primarily from Lithuania. Diagn Microbiol Infect Dis. 2016;86(4):377–81.
36. Gardee Y, Dreyer AW, Koornhof HJ, Omar SV, Da Silva P, Bhyat Z, Ismail NA. Evaluation of the GenoType MTBDRsl version 2.0 assay for second-line drug resistance detection of *Mycobacterium tuberculosis* isolates in South Africa. J Clin Microbiol. 2017;55(3):791–800.
37. Margaryan H, Farnia P, Hayrapetyan A, Mirzoyan A. Molecular genetics of Mycobacterium tuberculosis resistant to aminoglycosides and cyclic peptide testing by MTBDRsl in Armenia. Int J Mycobacteriol. 2016;5:S159–60.
38. Mitarai S, Kato S, Ogata H, Aono A, Chikamatsu K, Mizuno K, Toyota E, Sejimo A, Suzuki K, Yoshida S, Saito T. Comprehensive multicenter evaluation of a new line probe assay kit for identification of Mycobacterium species and detection of drug-resistant *Mycobacterium tuberculosis*. J Clin Microbiol. 2012;50(3):884–90.
39. Willby MJ, Wijkander M, Havumaki J, Johnson K, Werngren J, Hoffner S, Denkinger CM, Posey JE. Detection of *Mycobacterium tuberculosis pncA* mutations by the NiproGenoscholar PZA-TB II assay compared to conventional sequencing. Antimicrob Agents Chemother. 2018;62(1):e01871–17.
40. Sali M, De Maio F, Caccuri F, Campilongo F, Sanguinetti M, Fiorentini S, Delogu G, Giagulli C. Multicenter evaluation of AnyplexPlus MTB/NTM MDR-TB assay for rapid detection of *Mycobacterium tuberculosis* complex and multidrug-resistant isolates in pulmonary and extrapulmonary specimens. J Clin Microbiol. 2016;54(1):59–63.
41. Causse M, Ruiz P, Gutierrez JB, Vaquero M, Casal M. New Anyplex™ II MTB/MDR/XDR kit for detection of resistance mutations in *M. tuberculosis* cultures. Int J Tuberc Lung Dis. 2015;19(12):1542–6.

42. Meaza A, Tesfaye E, Mohamed Z, Zerihun B, Seid G, Eshetu K, Amare M, Sinshaw W, Dagne B, Mollalign H, Diriba G. Diagnostic accuracy of Truenat tuberculosis and rifampicin-resistance assays in Addis Ababa, Ethiopia. PloS One. 2021;16(12):e0261084.
43. Boehme CC, Nabeta P, Henostroza G, Raqib R, Rahim Z, Gerhardt M, Sanga E, et al. Operational feasibility of using loop-mediated isothermal amplification for diagnosis of pulmonary tuberculosis in microscopy centers of developing countries. J Clin Microbiol. 2007;45(6):1936. https://doi.org/10.1128/JCM.02352-06.
44. Walker TM, Ip CLC, Harrell RH, Evans JT, Kapatai G, Dedicoat MJ, Eyre DW, et al. Whole-genome sequencing to delineate *Mycobacterium tuberculosis* outbreaks: a retrospective observational study. Lancet Infect Dis. 2013;13(2):137–46. https://doi.org/10.1016/S1473-3099(12)70277-3.
45. Bjorn-Mortensen K, Zallet J, Lillebaek T, Andersen AB, Niemann S, Rasmussen EM, Kohl TA. Direct DNA extraction from Mycobacterium tuberculosis frozen stocks as a reculture-independent approach to whole-genome sequencing. J Clin Microbiol. 2015;53(8):2716–9. https://doi.org/10.1128/JCM.00662-15.
46. Köser CU, Bryant JM, Jennifer Becq M, Török E, Ellington MJ, Marti-Renom MA, Carmichael AJ, Parkhill J, Smith GP, Peacock SJ. Whole-genome sequencing for rapid susceptibility testing of *M. tuberculosis*. N Engl J Med. 2013;369(3):290–2. https://doi.org/10.1056/NEJMC1215305.
47. Didelot X, Bowden R, Wilson DJ, Peto TEA, Crook DW. Transforming clinical microbiology with bacterial genome sequencing. Nature Rev Genet. 2012;13(9):601. https://doi.org/10.1038/NRG3226.
48. Brudey K, Driscoll JR, Rigouts L, Prodinger WM, Gori A, Al-Hajoj SA, Allix C, et al. *Mycobacterium tuberculosis* complex genetic diversity: mining the fourth international spoligotyping database (SpolDB4) for classification, population genetics and epidemiology. BMC Microbiol. 2006;6(1):1–17. https://doi.org/10.1186/1471-2180-6-23/FIGURES/4.
49. Sun YJ, Bellamy R, Lee ASG, Ng ST, Ravindran S, Wong SY, Locht C, Supply P, Paton NI. Use of mycobacterial interspersed repetitive unit-variable-number tandem repeat typing to examine genetic diversity of *Mycobacterium tuberculosis* in Singapore. J Clin Microbiol. 2004;42(5):1986. https://doi.org/10.1128/JCM.42.5.1986-1993.2004.
50. Lakhani P, Sundaram B. Deep learning at chest radiography: automated classification of pulmonary tuberculosis by using convolutional neural networks. Radiology. 2017;284(2):574–82.

Translational Research in Nanotechnology for Biomedical Applications

14

S. Bharathi, S. Gowrilakshmi,
and M. Radhakrishnan

14.1 Introduction

The Greek word nanos, which means "a dwarf," is the prefix formally approved in 1947 at the 14th meeting of the International Union of Pure and Applied Chemistry to designate the one billionth part (10^{-9}) of a unit. In research literature, the prefix "nano" has become a common word to denote small entities and processes in many domains of modern science. Nanotechnology, nanoencapsulation, nanorobots, nanoscience, nanomagnets, nanoelectronics, and other terminology fall under this category [1]. Nanoparticles (NPs) have an array of shapes, sizes, and properties. They may be conical, spherical, cylindrical, spiral, tubular, or hollow core, with size ranging from 1 to 100 nm in diameter. NPs have distinctive physical, chemical, and biological features as compared to their counterpart particles at higher scales. This may be due to significant higher surface area to volume ratio, chemical reactivity or stability, and improved mechanical strength. These characteristics of nanoparticles have made them useful in a variety of applications [2]. The increasing use of nanotechnology products in biomedicine has sparked the emergence of the hybrid science known as nanobiotechnology [3]. In nanobiotechnology, there are a number of significant uses for nanomaterials, including drug delivery systems, prosthetics, and implants [4]. Due to the fact that the majority of biological systems are nanoscale, nanoparticles integrate well into biomedical equipment [5]. Carbon nanotubes, liposomes, inorganic and metal nanoparticles are the materials most frequently employed in the development of these nanotechnology products [6].

14.2 Classification of Nanoparticles

14.2.1 Carbon-Based NPs

This class of NPs is composed up entirely of carbon atoms. Fullerenes, carbon black nanoparticles, carbon quantum dots, graphene, and carbon nano tubes (CNT) are prominent representatives of this class. The unique characteristics of sp2-hybridized carbon bonds in carbon-based NPs provide extraordinary physicochemical features at the nanoscale [7]. Carbon compounds known

S. Bharathi (✉)
Department of Research Analytics, Saveetha Dental College and Hospitals, Saveetha Institute of Medical and Technical Sciences, Saveetha University, Chennai, Tamil Nadu, India

S. Gowrilakshmi
Department of Zoology, PSG College of Arts & Science (Autonomous), Coimbatore, Tamil Nadu, India

M. Radhakrishnan
Centre for Drug Discovery and Development, Sathyabama Institute of Science and Technology, Chennai, Tamil Nadu, India

K. Parthasarathy, R. Manikkam (eds.), *Translational Research in Biomedical Sciences: Recent Progress and Future Prospects*, https://doi.org/10.1007/978-981-97-1777-4_14

as fullerenes have a symmetrical closed-cage structure. Highly fused spherical particle aggregates with the diameter of 20–70 nm called carbon black. Carbon NPs smaller than 10 nm in size make of discrete, quasi-spherical carbon quantum dots. An allotrope of carbon is graphene, in which carbon atoms arranged in a two-dimensional flat surface forming hexagonal network of honey comb with a typical thickness of 1 nm. CNTs are atoms of carbon arranged as like honeycomb lattice in a hollow cylinder-shaped nanotube constructed of graphene nanofoil. Multi-layered CNTs have a diameter of 100 nm, while single-layer CNTs have a diameter that is as small as 0.7 nm. Nanotube lengths range from a few micrometres to several millimetres [1]. Drug delivery [8], bioimaging [9], photovoltaic devices, energy storage [10], and environmental sensing applications to monitor microbial ecology or to detect pathogenic microbes [11] are merely a few of the uses for carbon-based NPs.

14.2.2 Organic Nanoparticles

This category includes NPs composed of polymers, lipids, proteins, carbohydrates, and other organic substances [12]. Liposomes, dendrimers, micelles, and protein complexes like ferritin are some of the most common instances of this class. Organic NPs are susceptible to electromagnetic and thermal radiation, including heat and light. Moreover, they are frequently made through non-covalent intermolecular interactions, that contribute to their more labile nature and provides a pathway for removal from the body [13]. Among all other nanoparticles the organic nanoparticles are the extensively used in biomedical sector particularly for targeted drug delivery [2].

14.2.3 In Organic Nanoparticles

This class of NPs include that are obtained other than carbon or biological elements. The most common forms of this class are metal-based, metal-oxide, semiconductor, and ceramic nanoparticles.

Metal-based nanoparticles are produced from metals down to nanometric sizes, either destructively or constructively. It is possible to synthesize the nanoparticle form of almost every metal [14]. Gold (Au), Aluminium (Al), silver (Ag), cadmium (Cd), copper (Cu), cobalt (Co), iron (Fe), lead (Pb), and zinc (Zn) are the frequently used metals for the synthesize of NPs. The unique surface plasmon resonance of these metals make them to possess exceptional optical and electrical capacities [15]. In addition, they seems to have notable magnetic, thermal and biological properties. Hence, they play significant role for the development of nanodevices with extensive applications in biomedical, chemical, and pharmacological sectors [2].

In many fields of chemistry, materials science, physics, and biotechnology, metal-oxide nanomaterials (MONs) are intriguing contenders [16]. Unfilled d-shells are a common feature of transition metal ions, facilitate reactive electronic transitions, wide band gaps, better electrical properties, and high dielectric constants [17]. Cerium oxide (CeO_2), silicon dioxide (SiO_2), titanium oxide (TiO_2), aluminium oxide (Al_2O_3), iron oxide (Fe_2O_3), magnetite (Fe_3O_4), and zinc oxide (ZnO) are the most frequently synthesized materials. When compared to their metal counterparts, these nanoparticles exhibit extraordinary qualities [18].

Semiconductor NPs are produced employing substances that display properties of both metals and non-metals (Semiconductor materials). The bandgap tuning is the unique characteristic of semiconductor NPs as compared to bulk semiconductor materials. These NPs are essential parts of photocatalytic, optical and electrical devices [19].

Ceramic NPs are inorganic solids made up of metalloids including titanium, silicon and carbonates, carbides, phosphates of metals, and other inorganic compounds. They can be amorphous, dense, porous, polycrystalline and they are typically produced through heating and subsequent cooling. The high stability and increased load capacity of ceramic NPs make them to be used in biomedical sectors [1].

14.3 Synthesis Strategies of Nanoparticles

The production of nanoparticles involves downsizing—making things smaller—and upscaling—making larger items out of smaller components. The first strategy is known as the "top-down" strategy, whereas the second is known as the "bottom-up" strategy (Fig. 14.1) [20].

14.3.1 Top-Down Approach

Bulk materials are destructed in top-down methods to synthesize nanostructured materials. Thermal decomposition method, mechanical milling, laser ablation, and sputtering are some examples of top-down techniques [21].

14.3.1.1 Thermal Decomposition Method

The use of heat to breakdown compound damages the compound's chemical bond. The temperature at which an element decomposes chemically is known as the decomposition temperature. By performing a chemical reaction to decompose the metal at specified temperatures, nanoparticles are produced [14].

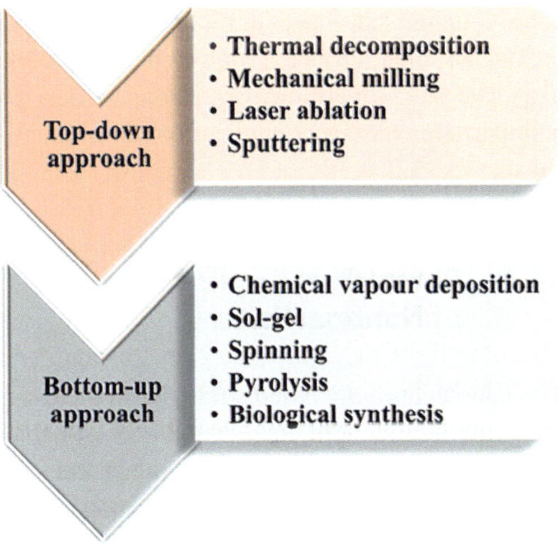

Fig. 14.1 Various methods for the synthesize of nanoparticles

14.3.1.2 Mechanical Milling

An effective way to produce materials at the nanoscale from bulk materials is mechanical milling. In the development of blends of different phases and to create nanocomposites, mechanical milling is a useful technique. Mechanical milling is used to create nanocomposite of aluminium alloys strengthened by oxide and carbide, spray coatings resistant to wear, nanoalloys of nickel/magnesium/aluminium/copper, and many other nanocomposite materials. Carbon nanomaterials obtained by ball milling method has found applications in energy conversion, energy storage, and environmental remediation [22].

14.3.1.3 Laser Ablation

Laser ablation synthesis produces nanoparticles by striking the precursor or source material with a strong laser beam that vapourizes the target material. When reducing metal to nanoparticles, a top-down strategy is much more effective than traditional chemical processes. Laser ablation techniques are used to create stable nanoparticles without the use of any chemicals or stabilizing agents [23, 24].

14.3.1.4 Sputtering

Sputtering produce nanoparticles by bombarding solid surfaces with high-energy particles like plasma or gas and is considered to be a useful technique for creating thin nanomaterial films. There are different methods for sputtering that include the use of magnetrons, radio frequency diodes, and direct current diodes. An evacuated chamber often suitable for sputtering to take place which is later loaded with sputtering gas. In the course of the sputtering deposition process, gaseous ions fiercely hit the target surface and, on the basis of incident gaseous-ion energy, small clusters of atoms are expelled [23].

14.3.2 Bottom-Up Approach

In the bottom-up approach nanoparticles are made from very small building blocks; and hence the other name of this approach is "building-up method." These small building blocks can automatically assemble in the right way because of their precise binding capacities, also known as molecular recognition properties. Self-assembly is essential to bottom-up strategies [25]. Chemical vapour deposition (CVD), sol-gel, spinning, pyrolysis, and biological synthesis are the examples of bottom-up methods.

14.3.2.1 CVD

CVD plays a vital role in the production of carbon related nanomaterials. In this method chemical reaction involving vapour-phase precursors, a thin coating (nanomaterial) is formed on the surface of the substrate. For instance, a substrate is heated to elevated temperatures in an oven during the CVD process for producing carbon nanotubes. A gas that contains carbon (like hydrocarbons) is used as a precursor that is then slowly introduced into the system. When the gas breaks down at elevated temperatures, the carbon atoms are liberated, and as they recombine, they produce carbon nanotubes on the substrate [26].

14.3.2.2 Sol-Gel

This wet chemical process is widely applied in the production of wide range of superior metal-oxide-based nanoparticles. The liquid precursor is transformed into a sol in the formation of the metal-oxide nanoparticles, then this sol is then transformed into a network-like structure called a gel, therefore the name "sol-gel method." The homogeneous nature of the nanomaterial produced, the low operating temperature, and the simplicity in manufacturing of complex nanostructures are some of the advantages of the sol-gel technique [27].

14.3.2.3 Spinning

A spinning disc reactor (SDR) used to produce nanoparticles by this method. The physical temperature can be adjusted using rotating disc present inside a chamber or reactor. To remove oxygen and to avoid chemical reactions, the reactor is often filled with nitrogen or other inert gases. The liquid including water and precursor, is added into the disc that is rotating at different speeds. The spinning of atoms or molecules makes them get precipitated, and the precipitate is collected and dried. The characteristics of nanoparticles produced from SDR rely on a number of operating parameters, which includes disc rotation speed, liquid flow rate, location of feed, liquid/precursor ratio, disc surface, etc. [28].

14.3.2.4 Pyrolysis

Pyrolysis is the most prevalent method to produce nanomaterials on a large scale in industry. Precursors are supplied into the furnace at high pressure through a small opening in either liquid or vapour form, where they burn. The nanoparticles gases are then categorized from the combustion. Some furnaces reach high temperatures for evaporation by using laser and plasma rather than flame. Pyrolysis has the advantages of being a simple, effective, economical, and continuous process with a high yield [29].

14.3.2.5 Biological Synthesis

The production of superior nanomaterials has been made possible by natural processes. The ability of biological systems to serve as a "bio-laboratory" for the creation of pure metal and metal-oxide particles at the nanoscale scale utilize a biomimetic method. Numerous microorganisms have served as environmentally friendly precursors for the synthesis of NPs with potential applications, including bacteria, fungi, yeast, plant extracts, and waste materials [30]. When compared to NPs made by chemical methods, nanoparticles that have a biological molecule coating on their surface are more biocompatible [31]. The biocompatibility of this biosynthesized nanoparticles has wide applications in biomedical sectors [32].

14.4 Biomedical Applications of Nanoparticles

The nanotechnology based strategies in the diagnosis and treatment of disease makes reasonable, modest and convenient path for biomedical sectors. Throughout this chapter, nanoparticles applications were discussed in regard to drug delivery, diagnosis, and therapy (Fig. 14.2 and Table 14.1).

14.4.1 Drug Delivery

The creation of novel therapeutic drug delivery systems (DDS) for multiple applications is crucial and a fundamental requirement to combat various diseases that are related to human health. This includes bioavailability, enhanced/improved bioactivity, therapeutically safer, drug efficacy, targeted delivery, and with an added benefit of overcoming drawbacks of conventional drug formulations/designs. Numerous improved DDS based on nanotechnology have been developed with unique properties for use in medicinal, pharmacological, and cosmetic applications [43].

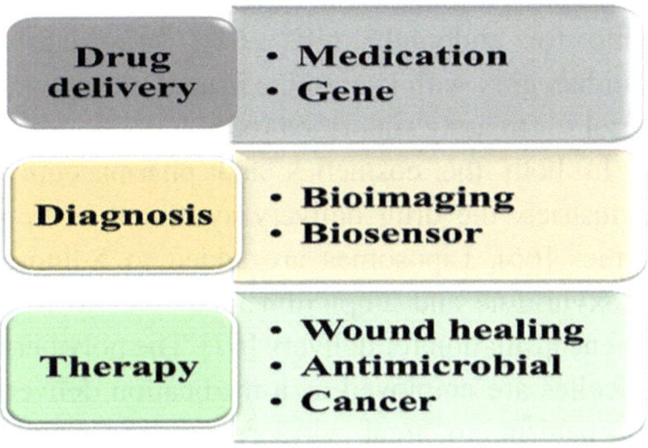

Fig. 14.2 Schematic representation of nanoparticles applications in biomedical sector

14.4.1.1 Medication Delivery

The medication delivery has been improved with the help of nanoparticles by altering the toxicodynamic and biodistribution of the drug [44]. The nanoparticle drug delivery system functions by releasing a specific amount of medication over an extended period of time to the diseased part of the body, protecting healthy cells from drug damage while maintaining the medication's availability in tissue and plasma [45]. The goal of the drug delivery system must meet the following requirements such as localization, prolongation, targeting, and protective interaction to the diseased tissues with that of the drug. The effectiveness of the targeted delivery depends up on the bypassing of the host's defence system and to reach the action site and also reduction of the frequency of the drug consumption by the patient [46].

Various drug delivery agents such as microparticles, lipoproteins, micelles, hydrogels, soluble polymers, microcapsules, liposomes, dendrimers, carbon nanotubes used for drug delivery system to increase safety, efficacy, and tolerability of drug [47]. The efficacy of the

Table 14.1 Application of various nanoparticles in biomedical sector

Nanoparticles	Size (nm)	Applications	References
Fibrin-binding peptide functionalized iron oxide nanoparticles-micelles fibrin (FibPep-ION-micelles)	40	Detecting and imaging thrombus	[33]
3,4-Dihydroxyhydrocinnamic acid (DHCA) functioned iron oxide nanoparticle (IONP) labelled human mesenchymal stem cells (hMSCs)	88.2	Imaging and tracking stem cells	[34]
Mn-nanotexaphyrin	100	Imaging lymph node	[35]
Thermally cross-linked superparamagnetic iron oxide nanoparticles aptamer (TCL-SPION-Apt)	66.4	Imaging prostate cancer cells and chemotherapy	[36]
Micelles with paclitaxel (PTX) and superparamagnetic iron oxide (SPIO)	15–300	Delivering drug and MRI imaging	[37]
Liposomal gadolinium	125	Imaging placenta as blood-pool contrast	[38]
Trimethylamino dextrancoated magnetic iron oxide nanoparticles (TMADM-03)	44	Imaging pancreatic islet graft	[39]
Magnetic nanoparticle-P-selectin binding peptide (MNP-PBP)	50	Imaging post-stroke neuroinflammation	[40]
Alpha(nu)beta(3)-gadolinium (Gd) (paramagnetic particle)	273	Imaging angiogenesis	[41]
Reconstituted high-density lipoprotein gadolinium (rHDL-Gd)	14–17	Imaging and characterizing atherosclerotic plaques	[42]

nanoparticle delivery system lies in the particle size and surface charge. The micro size of the nanoparticles is very much advantageous for higher cellular absorption capability in the target areas [48]. For example, the pore size of the solid tumours will be around 380–780 nm and hence the nanocarrier should be smaller than the vasculature of tumour. This increases the drug concentration in targeted sites and reduces the drug dispersal in the normal tissues [49].

Surface charge of the nanomaterials reflects electrical potential of nanoparticles which gets influenced by the medium and the composition of the surrounding where it gets dispersed. Zeta potential with value of ±30 mV reported as stable on suspension and that prevents the particle aggregation [50]. Drug loading can be done with various processes such as hydrophobic interaction, encapsulation, and covalent conjugation. The dispersion medium, drug's molecular weight, drug interaction with nanomaterials, functional groups on the drug's surface, plays important role in drug delivery [51].

The immune system recognizes nanoparticle drug carriers, which are then phagocytosed and removed from circulation [52]. To accomplish the efficacy of drug targeting, it is essential to keep nanoparticles from opsonizing so they can circulate for an extended period of time. This can be achieved by pre-coating with surfactants and polymers like polyethylene glycol (PEG) [53]. A remarkable achievement of nanotechnology is functionalization or modification of nanoparticles to take the drug for brain beyond the brain barrier [54]. For example, doxorubicin as such cannot penetrate blood brain barrier but by combining with polybutylcyanoacrylate (polysorbate 80 is modified as nanoparticle) improves the transport across blood–brain barrier [55]. When combined with intra-nasal carbamazepine, the nanoparticle carboxymethyl chitosan can cross the blood–brain barrier, increasing the effectiveness of the medication [10]. Alginate nanoparticles containing venlafaxine are also used to treat depression since they deliver the drug to the brain directly through the nasal cavity [56].

Pectin, alginate, and chitosan nanoparticles are possible medication delivery agents for the oral cavity [57]. Chitosan shows muco-adhesive capacity and is used to deliver drugs in tight junctions of epithelial layer at various sites including intestine [58], eye [59], buccal [60], pulmonary [61], and respiratory epithelium [62]. Hydroxypropyl methylcellulose with chitosan nanoparticle helps to deliver ceftazidime antibiotic to eye. It showed good muco-adhesion as well as interaction with ocular mucosa and prolonged the release of drug in the eyes [63]. The permeation effect of antimicrobial drug daptomycin into ocular epithelium was attained by chitosan alginate nanoparticles for antibacterial activity in endophthalmitis. This coated nanoparticle showed potential against pathogen responsible for endophthalmitis [64]. Drug carrier xanthan gum with L-cysteine is used as nanomaterial for treating sialorrhea [65].

In both the cosmetics and pharmaceutical industries, the drug delivery system uses liposomes [66]. Liposomes are added to 5-fluorodeoxyuridine and ampicillin medicines to form an encapsulation for delivery [67]. The polymeric micelles are employed as a medication delivery mechanism to treat vitreoretinopathy, ocular issues, and cancer [68]. Folate loaded with poly-L-lysine dendrimers functions as a highly effective model for the delivery system of drugs to specifically target tumour tissues [69].

Now Food and Drug Administration (FDA) approved lipid systems like liposomes and micelles were a part of the first generation of nanoparticle-based therapies. Inorganic nanoparticles like gold or magnetic nanoparticles incorporated in these liposomes and micelles. These characteristics led to a rise in the usage of inorganic nanoparticles, with a focus on therapeutic, imaging, and drug delivery applications [70]. Silver and gold are commonly used nanomaterials with different structures for drug delivery [71]. For high effectiveness, pH-responsive medicines like Morin may be safely delivered to the target using AuNPs. AuNP-encapsulated morin can reduce tumour growth in xenograft animal models and enhance tumour death [72]. Due to their ability to penetrate cells, cyclic peptide-capped AuNPs are an appealing and effective alternative as a drug delivery mechanism. The hydrophobic residues in the peptides are one way that they differ from standard AuNPs. The peptide's hydrophobic amino acids create a pocket for the drug's noncovalent trapping and hence coupled with anticancer and antiviral drugs [73]. For better medication distribution, Brown et al. [74] linked the anticancer medicine oxaliplatin's active components to AuNPs.

A number of therapeutic compounds, including anti-inflammatory, anti-oxidant, antibacterial, and anticancer substances, were investigated as appropriate carriers for AgNP-based nanosystems in particular [75]. Curcumin-loaded AgNPs hydrogel was created by Ravindra et al. [76], who also investigated its potential uses in drug delivery and antibacterial activities. They concluded that polymer decorated AgNPs are effective drug delivery systems after reporting that these modified AgNPs released the curcumin in a regulated manner and were substantially more active against *Escherichia coli* than standard AgNPs. Due to their inherent anti-platelet, antibacterial, and anti-inflammatory properties, L-lysine conjugated AgNPs show promise for therapeutic applications and are the best option for drug delivery Bonor et al. [77].

The nanomaterial utilized much in the drug delivery system is magnetic nanoparticles. To make the agent effective for drug conjugation or encapsulation into nanoparticles, a biocompatible layer (polymers or gold) is coated above the magnetic nanoparticles. After that, a magnetic field is applied externally to specifically locate the tumour spot. The release of drug is done by pH change, osmolality, enzyme activity or temperature [78]. Initially, nanoparticles were developed as a delivery system for anticancer drugs and vaccines [79]. The recent development in the research has focused on drug delivery to cure chronic diseases such as cardiovascular ailments and diabetes. The most widely used biodegradable polymer nanoparticles are those made of poly (lactic-co-glycolic acid, or PLGA) for drug delivery to the cardiovascular system. For instance, sirolimus that was administered via PLGA nanoparticles that had been treated with gelatin persisted in the body for 50 days. Due to the pressure, administering drugs-coated nanoparticles enter through catheter thereby aids in the penetration of the artery wall. As soon as the pressure is removed, the nanoparticle becomes trapped in the wall and serves as the treatment's drug reservoir [80]. Subcutaneously injected insulin stacked polymeric NPs of 85–185 nm size produced a longer hypoglycaemic effect than free insulin, according to an in vivo investigation on diabetic mice [81]. For the sublingual delivery of insulin, a distinct nanomaterial called biopolymer alginate has shown greater potential than subcutaneous injection [82].

14.4.1.2 Gene Delivery

The optimum approach for treating both inherited and acquired disorders is gene therapy. Recent research has revealed that the delivery of plasmids, double stranded deoxyribonucleic acid (ds DNA), single stranded DNA (ss DNA), small interfering ribonucleic acid (si RNA), and single stranded RNA (ss RNA) using nanoparticles could have excellent therapeutic effects [83]. According to Brown et al. [84], noble metal nanoparticles have special photophysical properties that make them promising carriers for photoactivated gene and medication delivery. The fabrication of small AgNPs embellished with thiol terminated photolabile DNA oligonucleotides has been demonstrated. In comparison to commercial transfection vectors, these DNA-decorated AgNPs were shown to be unique nanocarriers that serve to boost the stability against nucleases, hybridization activity upon photo release, and cellular uptake.

A transferrin-modified cyclodextrin nanoparticle loaded with small interfering RNA (siRNA) has evidenced the effectiveness of nanoparticle-mediated delivery to solid tumours in patients. The siRNA molecules used were uniquely designed to utilize the well-known RNA interference pathway to silence the expression of the M2 subunit of ribonucleotide reductase [85]. In gene therapy techniques, intracellular delivery and subcellular targeting are equally crucial. Multipurpose nanoparticulate systems have great potential to imitate the effectiveness of viral DNA delivery. Several synthetic polymers can be combined to form virus-like particles, some of which may also have surface recognition residues obtained from viral surface residues. In a study, siRNA and doxorubicin were delivered to drug-resistant cancer cells using nonviral polymer-based delivery methods that mimic viruses. It was demonstrated that this multifunctional system mediated enhanced cellular absorption of the siRNA and doxorubicin load. The co-delivered doxorubicin was more effective against the drug-resistant cells because the siRNA delivery decreased the expression of p-glycoprotein [86].

Iron oxide NPs along with polyethylenimine shell was fabricated as gene delivery vehicle by Liu et al. [87] in which siRNA absorbed to NPs. The delivery to targeted cells was reached with the use of magnets. For the transfer plasmid DNA to in vitro models like COS-7 and 293 T cell lines, silica nanoparticles are functionalized with 3-aminopropyltrimethoxysilane was used Bhakta et al. [88]. By encasing the polymerized siRNA in thiolated glycol chitosan (tGC) polymers, Lee et al. [89] produced poly-siRNA-tGC NPs with an average diameter of 370 nm for targeting TNF-α. These particles were found to quickly enter cells and were very successful at in vitro silencing the TNF-α gene. Moreover, in collagen-induced arthritic animals, poly-siRNA particles displayed substantial accumulation at arthritic joint locations.

14.4.2 Diagnosis

14.4.2.1 Bioimaging

The diagnosis of diseases is the most crucial step in medical care. It is preferred that the diagnosis be fast, specific, and accurate to avoid "erroneous negative" events. Without requiring surgery, imaging is a type of non-invasive technique that can detect symptoms or signs in a patient's tissues [90]. Imaging is employed in addition to diagnosis, the investigative approach for toxic responses, drug release and distribution in the body, and to monitor the therapy [91]. Various imaging techniques like computerized tomography (CT), positron emission tomography (PET), magnetic resonance imaging (MRI), ultrasound scan (US), and single-photon emission computerized tomography (SPECT) are used extensively in the field of medical and biochemical research and their imaging resolution is on macroscopic level that is the surface level tissue changes can only be examined [92]. Nevertheless, this technique can only be used to examine of progressing diseases in the late stages and this can be improved by the use of nanotechnologies by improving specificity and resolution by pointing out the site of the diseased area in the tissues [93].

To increase the number of signals, several fluorescent dyes can be added to nanoparticles [94]. The fluorescent nanoparticle imaging can be used for early disease diagnosis, tumour research, enzyme activity, gene detection, cell tracking, real-time monitoring, protein analysis, and element tracing [95]. The nanoparticle made out of high-density lipoprotein combined with Gd3+ chelates will localize the atherosclerotic plaque present in the arterial wall [42]. The nanoparticle ferric oxide is used in many biomedical imaging applications like identification of lymph node, molecular imaging, imaging of blood pool, cell tracking, and diagnosis of cancer [96]. Silver nanoparticle is used to label cancer cells, to check the growth and also helps to tag the red blood cells for the image flow [97]. The nanoparticle made of cholesteryl carbonate γ-butyrolactone-propylene oxide is used in tumour imaging [98]. Technetium-99 labelled albumin nanoparticle used to measure tumour volumes as well as pulmonary shunt in the liver [99]. Gadolinium oxide nanoparticle showed potential for both MRI and CT [100]. NH_4HCO_3 liposomal nanoparticle is used as photoacoustic imaging to detect breast cancer [101]. As endoscopic contrast agents, fluorescent and PEGylated silica nanoparticles (SiNPs) labelled with -L-fucose targeting lectin can be used to detect colorectal polyps, which can lead to colorectal cancer [102].

14.4.2.2 Biosensor

The term sensor denotes the device which could detect the analyte and quantify the biological sample. The stability of sensory surface and the biological system is very essential for the success of the biosensor; hence the stabilization is very crucial between them [103]. In order to meet out this stabilization various designs including physical as well as chemical agents are used [104]. NPs with a bioresponsive shell are coated and can be employed as biosensors [105]. A glucose sensor that immobilizes glucose oxidase on cellulose acetate sheet using gold nanorods for stabilization [106]. For detection of DNA polyaniline nanofibers and carbon nanotubes were used in biosensor [107]. An integrated ZnO surface acoustic wave microfluidics for cancer detection has been developed by Lee et al., [108]. A few graphene-based sensors have been developed for the simultaneous detection of numerous human digestion-related metabolites, such as uric acid and ascorbic acid [109]. Adenosine triphosphate, proteins, hormones, fungal toxins, and hazardous metal ions have all been detected using biosensors based on graphene. Many enzyme' activities, such as trypsin, thrombin, caspase-3, metalloproteinase, and DNA helicase, can also be estimated using graphene oxide biosensors [110].

14.4.3 Therapy

14.4.3.1 Wound Healing Therapy

The chronic wounds result in morbidity, intense pain, infections, hospitalization, and occasionally amputations in addition to function loss. The main causes of chronic wounds, which raise health care expenses, are population ageing, obesity, and diabetes. Because it is not thought to be a life-threatening condition, this disease is frequently not given the importance it deserves in comparison to other illnesses. Almost 40 million people worldwide suffer from chronic wounds, which are a silent epidemic [111]. For physicians, wound healing is constantly becoming more complex, making novel materials and methods extremely attractive. The pharmaceutical and biotechnology industries have seen a radical transformation due to significant advancements in nanotechnology. Moreover, because to their superior adsorption capacity, antibacterial characteristics, and medication loading, nanomaterials have also been widely used in wound healing [112].

Blisters, wound infection, and abscesses are typically treated with silver, a bactericidal agent. For instance, persistent diseases that don't heal are still treated with silver nitrate. Several silver coatings in wound dressings are now available for effective medicine distribution, which play a crucial role during chronic wound illness. One example of this is the wound dressing acticoat, which contains AgNPs with an average size of 15 nm. Anticoat has been proven to have the following beneficial effects, which were seen in the majority of test subjects: wound healing, wound site infection reduction, and pain reduction. Recent clinical trials found that when combined with silver sulphadiazine and chlorhexidine digluconate cream, anticoat may be effective in preventing infections in burns [113]. Bharathi et al. [114] developed a nanobiomaterial containing green synthesized AgNPs with chitosan hydrogel and demonstrated potential in vivo wound healing property using Wistar albino rats.

Unlike AgNPs, AuNPs do not exhibit any antibacterial activity on their own. In order to be effectively used in the biomedical sector, AuNPs should be mixed with the other biomolecules. The crosslinking of AuNPs with collagen makes it simple to combine them with other biomolecules such peptides, growth factors, polysaccharides, and cell adhesion components. These changed AuNPs demonstrated features such as biodegradability and biocompatibility, and henceforth they might be exploited extensively in wound healing [115].

Due to its exceptional antibacterial properties and ability to suppress a wide variety of bacterial strains, CuNPs have received substantial research in the field of wound healing. CuNPs emit Cu2+, which weakens protein structure or modifies enzyme activity, disrupting cell walls and membranes [116]. CuNPs (100 ng/mL) inhibited the growth of *Pseudomonas* biofilms by 94%, outperforming AgNPs in terms of antibacterial potency. *Acinetobacter* in skin wounds was quickly and effectively killed by CuNP-coated wound dressings. By influencing the production of the hypoxia-inducible factor and controlling the secretion of vascular endothelial growth factor, CuNPs increase angiogenesis and aid in the healing of wounds [117]. ZnONPs produce pores on bacterial cell membrane thereby function an promising antibacterial agent. The adherence period of hydrogel based wound dressings on wound is more thereby increase keratinocyte migration and enhance re-epithelialization. A microporous chitosan hydrogel/ZnONPs dressing also demonstrated a high capacity for absorbing wound exudates, facilitated the development of hemostatic blood clots, and exhibited antibacterial activities with minimal cytotoxicity [118].

14.4.3.2 Antimicrobial Therapy

The hunt for new antibacterial drugs capable of resolving the resistance issue has been sparked by the rise in antibiotic-resistant microorganisms. As an alternative to antibiotics, NPs have become more frequently utilized to target pathogenic microbes in recent years. The NPs such as Au, ZnO, MgO, Ag, Ti, Cu exhibit antibacterial activity and showed substitute to antibacterial agents [119]. AuNPs synthesized by trisodium citrate and chlorogenic acid have exhibited antibacterial activity [120]. Gold cuboid nanoparticle with algae showed potential against human pathogens such as *Staphylococcus aureus* and *E. coli* [121]. A report reveals that the pure form of AuNPs was not excellent in antibacterial activity but acted as antibiotic drug carrier. It can be made actively to participate as nanocarrier by loading ampicillin that resist the growth of fungi [122].

AuNPs are used for anti-HIV activity during the early stages of viral replication. According to Kesarkar et al. [123] stable AuNPs in L-cysteine led to improved azidothymidine delivery against the HIV-1Ba-L virus in vitro. The poly-anionic nature enables the binding of positively charged amino acids at the binding location of glycoprotein 120, thereby inhibition occurs. In addition, AuNPs block the reverse transcriptase enzyme of HIV-1 proteins. Conjugated AuNPs with improved HIV activity were also explored by Garrido et al. [124]. At both the pre- and post-stages, AgNPs are highly effective in preventing the emergence of Herpes virus 1 and 2 [125].

The ability of self-assembled nanoparticles made of cationic peptides to cross the blood–brain barrier makes them promising treatments for inflammatory brain diseases like meningitis and encephalitis, which are typically brought on by bacteria like *Bacillus anthrax*, *Bacillus subtilis*, or *Staphylococcus aureus* [126]. Due to the phagocytic nature of macrophages, NPs locally applied to the infection sites may be spontaneously taken up by *Mycobacterium tuberculosis*, *Salmonella typhimurium*, or Methicillin resistant *Staphylococcus aureus*-infected macrophages [127]. Moreover, *Chlamydia trachomatis*-infected mouse fibroblasts and human lung epithelial cells showed enhanced antibiotic efficacy when treated with poly(d-L-lactide-co-glycolide) NPs [128]. ZnO NPs induces cell death of bacteria by producing H_2O_2 and OH^- when exposed under the visible and ultraviolet light [129]. ZnO NPs in combination with ultrasound increases the antibacterial effect in *S. aureus* [130].

AgNPs has an efficient activity of antifungal property against *Fusarium moniliforme*, *Alternaria alternata*, *Penicillium brevicompactum*, *Aspergillus flavus* [131], and antibacterial activity on *Bacillus subtilis*, *Candida albicans*, *Pseudomonas aeruginosa*, *Candida tropicalis*, *Salmonella enterica*, *Vibrio parahaemolyticus*, *Escherichia coli*, *Staphylococcus aureus*, *Bacillus cereus* [132]. CuNPs will damage the nucleic acids and interfere biochemical processes of bacteria [133].

Biofilm microbes gets attached to its own extracellular secreted polymeric matrix [134]. The research studies revealed that the use of antibiotics showed antimicrobial resistance which was due to the group of bacteria in biofilm and not individual bacteria [135]. The removal or clean-up of this biofilm is not achieved completely by normal physicochemical methods [136]. Therefore, a new novel approach of nanotechnology takes the seat to fight and removes the biofilm microbes. The unique properties of nanosized agents with high surface energy, spatial confinement, and large proportion of surface atoms make them to be used as an efficient anti biofilm agent [137] (Table 14.2).

Table 14.2 Antibiofilm activity of nanoparticles against various pathogenic microbes

Nanoparticles	Antibiofilm properties against genus	References
TiO_2	*Bacillus subtilis*	[138]
MgO	*Klebsiella pneumoniae, Escherichia coli*	[139]
Fe_3O_4	*Staphylococcus aureus, Pseudomonas aeruginosa, E. coli*	[140]
CuO	*Candida* sp., *E. coli, P. aeruginosa, K. pneumonia, Proteus vulgaris, S. aureus, B. subtilis*	[141]
ZnO	*P. aeruginosa, Bacillus licheniformis, Bacillus pumilus, E. coli, P. vulgaris*	[142, 143]
Al_2O_3	*Pseudomonas putida, Aeromonas hydrophila*	[144]

Tinospora cordifolia based AuNPs acts as a nanoantibiotic on biofilm control of *Pseudomonas aeruginosa* [145]. Thermosensitive gels made of AuNPs have skin permeability, anti-inflammatory activities, antibacterial and bioavailability ability [115]. Iron oxide NPs reduced the growth of biofilm of *P. aeruginosa* [140], *Enterococcus hirae* [146], *S. aureus*, *E. coli,* and *S. epidermidis* [147]. Selenium NPs synthesized from marine *Streptomyces sp.* found to possess antibiofilm activity against *P. aeruginosa* [148]. TiO_2 NPs acts by inhibiting the bacterial growth by DNA damage, amino acid oxidation, lipid peroxidation and affect protein catalytic site by photocatalysis [149] that reduced the biofilm formation of *Pseudomonas aeruginosa* [150]. TiO_2 NPs are coated on implantable devices such as heart valves or dental implants thereby prevents the attachment and proliferation of *E. coli*, *Streptococcus epidermis,* and *Streptococcus mutans* [151].

14.4.4 Cancer Therapy

Cancer—one of the root causes for ten million peoples' death every year marking the cause as the second place of death in the world. The approach of conventional medical has drawback to discriminate healthy from cancer cells. There are other strategies of targeting shown by the cancer cells which provides efficacy in finding it. Circulatory system only acts as a transport route to deliver the anticancer drugs to the target cancer cells. To overcome this the specific drug delivery system is in need as an alternative method. The targeted drug system of delivery helps to release the drug more to the cancer cell than to the normal cells [78].

14.4.4.1 Anticancer Drug Delivery

Dendrimer system is reported for imaging (fluorescein), localization (folic acid), and delivery of the methotrexate-anticancer drug in vitro [152]. The spherical molecule of nanocrystals like buckminsterfullerene C60 with its derivatives are used for cancer treatment [153]. Colon cancer is treated with chitosan-coated nanoparticles and 5-fluorouracil via oral administration [154]. Lung cancer cells receive the alginate microcapsules filled with the drug cisplatin [155]. Epithelial cell adhesion molecule (EpCAM)-conjugated Mesoporous silica nanoparticles (M-SiNPs) loaded with carboplatin were produced by Qu et al. [156]. When compared to free carboplatin, this M-SiNPs-exhibited selective receptor-mediated cellular internalization targeted to cancer cells induced caspase-3 to rise by two times. Magnetic NPs help to release the drug to specific location and it also increases the drug releasing amount to the target area and minimize the side effects [157].

14.4.4.2 Hyperthermia

The term hyperthermia is concerned about the exposure of the target tissues with high temperature which will not kill the cancer cells directly but makes the cancer cells highly vulnerable to other treatment modalities. Research studies proved that there is a remarkable effect when hyperthermia along with chemotherapy or radiotherapy is used to control tumour and makes the patient survive better [158]. The change in temperature brings elevated blood flow, vascular permeability and creates tumour oxygenation (tissue hypoxia) that leads to intensify the effect of cancer drugs or radiation on the cancer cells [159].

The source to deliver heat to the target area is important in hyperthermia. Various heat energy sources such as radiofrequency, ultrasound, microwave, and laser are used. Conventional hyperthermia is used to generate heat and the application is above the body's surface which decreases when distance is increased from the external source (outside-in hyperthermia). In this method the external radiation energy is dissipated without discrimination to both normal and targeted cells. This heating will lead to the side effects [160]. So, one should find the effective hyperthermic sources that paves a way for the nanoparticle application as hyperthermia agents.

Magnetic nanoparticles are used for the local application of hyperthermia. The principle behind magnetic fluid hyperthermia is the transformation of electromagnetic energy into heat [161]. The four methods of delivering magnetic nanoparticles to the tumour for local hyperthermia treatment are arterial injection, direct injection, in situ implantation, and active targeting. The fluid containing the magnetic nanoparticles must be injected into the tumour's arterial supply in order to use the arterial injection technique [162]. The most popular method is direct injection, which involves injecting the fluid containing the magnetic particles directly into the tumour [163]. To entrap magnetic particles inside tumours, injectable formulations that form hydrogels (chitosan and sodium alginate) and organogels (poly (ethylene-co-vinyl alcohol and cellulose acetate) were used [164]. Another way to get magnetic nanoparticles to the tumour site is through active targeting. Typically, the magnetic nanoparticles are covered in a tumour-specific antibody before being injected into the circulation. The antibodies will bind to the target site since they are tumour-specific [165].

Single walled carbon nanotubes along with radio frequency waves have the ability to penetrate deep into tissue and generate enormous amounts of heat sufficient to trigger apoptosis or necrosis, have been employed to treat deep tissue cancers [166]. The heating of nanoshells within tumours using near-infrared (NIR) region (650–950 nm) absorptions has been demonstrated to be effective in the treatment of superficial cancers. For patients with oropharyngeal cancer, a clinical trial utilizing gold-silica nanoshell hyperthermia after NIR light exposure has been conducted. Due to the significant attenuation of NIR light caused by the body's cellular matrix and biomolecular chromophoric absorptions, NIR photothermal therapy can only be used to treat surface tumours rather than deeper organ-based cancers [167].

14.4.5 Nanotheranostics

According to Sumer and Gao [168] theranostic refers to the combined operation of therapy and diagnosis. This aids in controlling and maintaining nanoparticles in targeted site for diagnostic and therapeutic application. It helps in early detection and administration of medicine for diseases that can be cured [169] (Table 14.3). Gold nanorod is coupled with folic acid and silica (GNR-SiO2-FA), and it has been shown to be effective in photothermal therapy and X-ray radiation therapy. These nanoprobes are made to perform a variety of functions, including imaging, tumour targeting, and selective therapy on gastric cancer cells [177]. Novel probe made of gold nanorod conjugated with matrix metalloprotease used for therapy and cancer diagnosis [178]. Magnetic nanoparticle combined with Pluronic F127 used to provide contrast property in MRI with sustained release of anticancer drug [179]. Heparin-coated iron oxide NPs that were loaded with β -galactosidase and complex polyethyleneimine, used to deliver β-gal to brain tumours [180]. The targeted delivery of siRNA to tumour cells with concurrent hyperthermia-based therapy was described by Park et al. [181] in which magnetic iron cobalt nanoparticles (as a core) and a graphitic carbon (shell) together prevented tumour cells from proliferating and resulted in apoptosis.

Table 14.3 shows some of theranostic nanomedicine

Type of theranosticnanomedicine	Material	Advancement	References
Polymericnanoparticles	Poly(lactide)-Tocopheryl polyethylene glycol 1000 succinate (PLA-TPGS)	Co-delivery of docetaxel and quantum dots	[170]
Dendrimers	Polypropyleni-mine	Delivery of single theranostic agent	[171]
Micelles	Tocopheryl polyethylene glycol 1000 succinate (TPGS)	Delivery of single theranostic agent	[172]
Drug-polymer conjugates	Hydroxypropylmethacrylamide (HPMA)	Cancer imaging and radiochemo-therapy	[173]
Gold nanoparticles	Gold nanoparticles	Stimulus responsive drug release	[174]
Solid lipid nanoparticles	Low-density lipoprotein, cholesterol	Multimodal therapy	[175]
Liposomes	Tocopheryl polyethylene glycol 1000 succinate (TPGS), phospholipids, cholesterol	Co-delivery of docetaxel and quantum dots	[176]

14.5 Conclusion

The biomedical sector has been gaining tremendous advancement with the application of nanotechnology in drug delivery, diagnosis, and therapy. There are still challenges to be solved, though, as with any new technologies. Many of the novel and ostensibly intriguing multifunctional nanoparticles need multistep preparation techniques that are frequently difficult to scale up, and nanoparticles are particularly challenging to standardize in large-scale production. Moreover, there is a need to address the dearth of toxicological information for systems based on nanotechnology, particularly for metal and inorganic nanoparticles.

Acknowledgement Authors are thankful to Dr. K. R. Venkatesan, Principal, Sri Sankara Arts and Science College for providing research facilities.

Conflict of Interest Authors have no conflict of interest

References

1. Joudeh N, Linke D. Nanoparticle classification, physicochemical properties, characterization, and applications: a comprehensive review for biologists. J Nanobiotechnol. 2022;20:262.
2. Ealias AM, Saravanakumar MP. A review on the classification, characterisation, synthesis of nanoparticles and their application. In: IOP conference series: materials science and engineering. IOP Publishing; 2017. p. 32019.
3. Saji VS, Choe HC, Young KWK. Nanotechnology in biomedical applications—a review. Int J Nano Biomater. 2010;3:119–39.
4. Faraji AH, Wipf P. Nanoparticles in cellular drug delivery. Bioorg Med Chem. 2009;17:2950–62.
5. Ramos AP, Cruz MAE, Tovani CB, Ciancaglini P. Biomedical applications of nanotechnology. Biophys Rev. 2017;9(2):79–89.
6. Liu D, Yang F, Xiong F, Gu N. The smart drug delivery system and its clinical potential. Theranostics. 2016;6:1306–23.
7. Maiti D, Tong X, Mou X, Yang K. Carbon-based nanomaterials for biomedical applications: a recent study. Front Pharmacol. 2019;9:1401.
8. Oh WK, Yoon H, Jang J. Size control of magnetic carbon nanoparticles for drug delivery. Biomaterials. 2010;31(6):1342–8.
9. Chandra S, Das P, Bag S, Laha D, Pramanik P. Synthesis, functionalization and bioimaging applications of highly fluorescent carbon nanoparticles. Nanoscale. 2011;3(4):1533–40.
10. Liu M, Zhao F, Zhu D, Duan H, Lv Y, Li L, et al. Ultramicroporous carbon nanoparticles derived from metal–organic framework nanoparticles for high-performance supercapacitors. Mater Chem Phys. 2018;211:234–41.
11. Mauter MS, Elimelech M. Environmental applications of carbon-based nanomaterials. Environ Sci Technol. 2008;42(16):5843–59.
12. Pan K, Zhong Q. Organic nanoparticles in foods: fabrication, characterization, and utilization. Annu Rev Food Sci Technol. 2016;7:245–66.
13. Ng KK, Zheng G. Molecular interactions in organic nanoparticles for phototheranostic applications. Chem Rev. 2015;115(19):11012–42.

14. Salavati-Niasari M, Davar F, Mir N. Synthesis and characterization of metallic copper nanoparticles via thermal decomposition. Polyhedron. 2008;27(17):3514–8.
15. Khan I, Saeed K, Khan I. Nanoparticles: properties, applications and toxicities. Arab J Chem. 2019;12(7):908–31.
16. Vorokhta M, Khalakhan I, Vondráček M, Tomeček D, Vorokhta M, Marešová E, Nováková J, Vlček J, Fitl P, Novotný M, Hozák P, Lančok J, Vrňata M, Matolínová I, Matolín V. Investigation of gas sensing mechanism of SnO_2 based chemiresistor using near ambient pressure XPS. Surf Sci. 2018;677:284–90.
17. Mavrou G, Galata S, Tsipas P, Sotiropoulos A, Panayiotatos Y, Dimoulas A, Evangelou EK, Seo JW, Dieker C. Electrical properties of La_2O_3 and HfO_2/La_2O_3 gate dielectrics for germanium metal-oxide-semiconductor devices. J Appl Phys. 2008;103(1):014506.
18. Yoon KY, Byeon JH, Park JH, Hwang J. Susceptibility constants of *Escherichia coli* and *Bacillus subtilis* to silver and copper nanoparticles. Sci Total Environ. 2007;373:572–5, 572.
19. Gupta SM, Tripathi M. An overview of commonly used semiconductor nanoparticles in photocatalysis. High Energy Chem. 2012;46(1):1–9.
20. Ozin GA, Cademartiri L. Nanochemistry: what is next? Small. 2009;5(11):1240–4.
21. Iravani S. Green synthesis of metal nanoparticles using plants. Green Chem. 2011;13(10):2638–50.
22. Yadav TP, Yadav RM, Singh DP. Mechanical milling: a top down approach for the synthesis of nanomaterials and nanocomposites. Nanosci Nanotechnol. 2012;2(3):22–48.
23. Amendola V, Meneghetti M. Laser ablation synthesis in solution and size manipulation of noble metal nanoparticles. Phys Chem. 2009;11(20):3805–21.
24. Ayyub P, Chandra R, Taneja P. Synthesis of nanocrystalline material by sputtering and laser ablation at low temperatures. Appl Phys A Mater Sci Process. 2001;73:67–73.
25. Blum AS, Soto CM, Wilson CD, Brower TL, Pollack SK, Schull TL, et al. An engineered virus as a scaffold for three-dimensional self-assembly on the nanoscale. Small. 2005;1:702–6.
26. Baig U, Faizan M, Sajid M. Semiconducting graphitic carbon nitride integrated membranes for sustainable production of clean water: a review. Chemosphere. 2021;282:130898.
27. Danks AE, Hall SR, Schnepp Z. The evolution of 'sol–gel' chemistry as a technique for materials synthesis. Mater Horiz. 2016;3:91–112.
28. Ijaz I, Gilani E, Nazir A, Bukhari A. Detail review on chemical, physical and green synthesis, classification, characterizations and applications of nanoparticles. Green Chem Lett Rev. 2020;13:223–45.
29. Kammler HK, Madler L, Pratsinis SE. Flame synthesis of nanoparticles. Chem Eng Tech. 2001;24:583–96.
30. Sharma D, Kanchi S, Bisetty K. Biogenic synthesis of nanoparticles: a review. Arabian J Chem. 2019;12(8):3576–600.
31. Hakim LF, Portman JL, Casper MD, Weimer AW. Aggregation behavior of nanoparticles in fluidized beds. Powder Technol. 2005;160(3):149–60.
32. Huang J, Lin L, Sun D, Chen H, Yang D, Li Q. Bio-inspired synthesis of metal nanomaterials and applications. Chem Soc Rev. 2015;44(17):6330–74.
33. Starmans LW, Moonen RP, Aussems-Custers E, Daemen MJ, Strijkers GJ, Nicolay K, Grull H. Evaluation of iron oxide nanoparticle micelles for magnetic particle imaging (MPI) of thrombosis. PLoS One. 2015;10:0119257.
34. Hachani R, Birchall MA, Lowdell MW, et al. Assessing cell-nanoparticle interactions by high content imaging of biocompatible iron oxide nanoparticles as potential contrast agents for magnetic resonance imaging. Sci Rep. 2017;7(1):7850.
35. Keca JM, Chen J, Overchuk M, et al. Nanotexaphyrin: one-pot synthesis of a manganese texaphyrin-phospholipid nanoparticle for magnetic resonance imaging. Angew Chem Int Ed Engl. 2016;55(21):6187–91.
36. Wang AZ, Bagalkot V, Vasilliou CC, et al. Superparamagnetic iron oxide nanoparticle-aptamer bioconjugates for combined prostate cancer imaging and therapy. Chem Med Chem. 2008;3(9):1311–5.
37. Hu Z, Huang Y, Sun S, Guan W, Yao Y, Tang P, Li C. Visible light driven photodynamic anticancer activity of graphene oxide/TiO_2 hybrid. Carbon. 2012;184:994.
38. Ghaghada KB, Starosolski ZA, Bhayana S, et al. Pre-clinical evaluation of a nanoparticle-based blood-pool contrast agent for MR imaging of the placenta. Placenta. 2017;57:60–70.
39. Oishi K, Miyamoto Y, Saito H, Murase K, Ono K, Sawada M, Watanabe M, Noguchi Y, Fujiwara T, Hayashi S, Noguchi H. *In vivo* imaging of transplanted islets labeled with a novel cationic nanoparticle. PLoS One. 2013;8:57046.
40. Jin AY, Tuor UI, Rushforth D, Filfil R, Kaur J, Ni F, Tomanek B, Barber PA. Magnetic resonance molecular imaging of post-stroke neuroinflammation with a P-selectin targeted iron oxide nanoparticle. Contrast Media Mol Imaging. 2009;4:305–11.
41. Winter PM, Caruthers SD, Kassner A, Harris TD, Chinen LK, Allen JS, Lacy EK, Zhang H, Robertson JD, Wickline SA, Lanza GM. Molecular imaging of angiogenesis in nascent Vx-2 rabbit tumors using a novel $\alpha_v\beta_3$ targeted nanoparticle and 1.5 tesla magnetic resonance imaging. Cancer Res. 2003;63:5838–43.
42. Frias JC, Ma Y, Williams KJ, Fayad ZA, Fisher EA. Properties of a versatile nanoparticle platform contrast agent to image and characterize atherosclerotic plaques by magnetic resonance imaging. Nano Lett. 2006;6(10):2220–4.
43. Iqbal HMN, Rodriguez AMV, Khandia R, Munjal A, Dhama K. Recent trends in nanotechnology-

based drugs and formulations for targeted therapeutic delivery. Recent Patents Inflamm Allergy Drug Discov. 2017;10(2):86–93.
44. Jong WHD, Borm PJ. Drug delivery and nanoparticles:applications and hazards. Int J Nanomedicine. 2008;3(2):133–49.
45. Tiwari G, Tiwari R, Sriwastawa B, et al. Drug delivery systems: an updated review. Int J Pharm Investig. 2012;2(1):2–11.
46. Senapati S, Mahanta AK, Kumar S, Maiti P. Controlled drug delivery vehicles for cancer treatment and their performance. Signal Transduct Target Ther. 2018;3(1):1–19.
47. Rizvi SAA, Saleh AM. Applications of nanoparticle systems in drug delivery technology. Saudi Pharm J. 2018;26(1):64–70.
48. Jain AK, Thareja S. *In vitro* and *in vivo* characterization of pharmaceutical nanocarriers used for drug delivery. Artif Cells Nanomed Biotechnol. 2019;47(1):524–39.
49. Zhang B, Hu Y, Pang Z. Modulating the tumormicroenvironment to enhance tumor nanomedicine delivery. Front Pharmacol. 2017;8:1–16.
50. Kumar A, Dixit CK. Methods for characterization of nanoparticles. In: Advances in nanomedicine for the delivery of therapeutic nucleic acids. Elsevier; 2017. p. 44–58.
51. Din FU, Aman W, Ullah I, et al. Effective use of nanocarriers as drug delivery systems for the treatment of selected tumors. Int J Nanomedicine. 2017;12:7291–309.
52. McMillan J, Batrakova E, Gendelman HE. Cell delivery of therapeutic nanparticles. Prog Mol Biol Transl Sci. 2011;104:563–601.
53. Suk JS, Xu Q, Kim N, Hanes J, Ensign LM. PEGylation as a strategy for improving nanoparticle-based drug and gene delivery. Adv Drug Deliv Rev. 2016;99:28–51.
54. Kumar R, Cristiam F, Chalarca S, et al. Polymeric delivery of therapeutic nucleic acids. Chem Rev. 2021;121:11527–652.
55. He Q, Liu J, Liang J, Liu X, Li W, Liu Z, Ding Z, Tuo D. Towards improvements for penetrating the blood-brain barrier-recent progress from a material and pharmaceutical perspective. Cell. 2018;7(4):24.
56. Haque S, Md S, Sahni JK, Ali J, Baboota S. Development and evaluation of brain targeted intranasal alginate nanoparticles for treatment of depression. J Psychiatr Res. 2014;48(1):1–12.
57. Pistone S, Goycoolea FM, Young A, Smistad G, Hiorth M. Formulation of polysaccharide-based nanoparticles for local administration into the oral cavity. Eur J Pharm Sci. 2017;96:381–9.
58. Artursson P, Lindmark T, Davis SS, Illum L. Effect of chitosan on the permeability of monolayers of intestinal epithelial cells ($Caco^{-2}$). Pharm Res. 1994;11(9):1358–61.
59. De Campos AM, Sánchez A, Alonso MJ. Chitosan nanoparticles: a new vehicle for the improvement of the delivery of drugs to the ocular surface. Application to cyclosporin A. Int J Pharm. 2001;224:159–68.
60. Portero A, Remunan-Lopez C, Criado M, Alonso M. Reacetylated chitosan microspheres for controlled delivery of anti-microbial agents to the gastric mucosa. J Microencapsul. 2002;19:797–809.
61. Al-Qadi S, Grenha A, Carrión-Recio D, Seijo B, Remuñán-López C. Microencapsulated chitosan nanoparticles for pulmonary protein delivery: *in vivo* evaluation of insulin-loaded formulations. J Control Release. 2012;157:383–90.
62. Fernández-Urrusuno R, Calvo P, Remuñán-López C, Vila-Jato JL, Alonso MJ. Enhancement of nasal absorption of insulin using chitosan nanoparticles. Pharm Res. 1999;16:1576–81.
63. Silva MM, Calado R, Marto J, Bettencourt A, Almeida AJ, Gonçalves L. Chitosan nanoparticles as a mucoadhesive drug delivery system for ocular administration. Mar Drugs. 2017;15:370.
64. Silva NC, Silva S, Sarmento B, Pintado M. Chitosan nanoparticles for daptomycin delivery in ocular treatment of bacterial endophthalmitis. Drug Deliv. 2015;22(7):885–93.
65. Laffleur F, Michalek M. Modified xanthan gum for buccal delivery—a promising approach in treating sialorrhea. Int J Biol Macromol. 2017;102:1250–6.
66. Bozzuto G, Molinari A. Liposomes as nanomedical devices. Int J Nanomedicine. 2015;10:975.
67. Mohan A, Narayanan S, Sethuraman S, Krishnan UM. Novel resveratrol and 5-fluorouracil coencapsulated in PEGylated nanoliposomes improve chemotherapeutic efficacy of combination against head and neck squamous cell carcinoma. Biomed Res Int. 2014;2014:424239.
68. Li Q, Lai KL, Chan PS, Leung SC, Li HY, Fang Y, To KK, Choi CHJ, Gao QY, Lee TW. Micellar delivery of dasatinib for the inhibition of pathologic cellular processes of the retinal pigment epithelium. Coll Surf B. 2016;140:278–86.
69. Jain K, Gupta U, Jain NK. Dendronized nanoconjugates of lysine and folate for treatment of cancer. Eur J Pharm Biopharm. 2014;87:500–9.
70. Patra JK, Das G, Fraceto LF, Campos EVR, Rodriguez-Torres MDP, Acosta-Torres LS, Diaz-Torres LA, Grillo R, Swamy MK, Sharma S, Habtemariam S, Shin HS. Nano based drug delivery systems: recent developments and future prospects. J Nanobiotechnol. 2018;16(1):71.
71. Baeza A, Ruiz-Molina D, Vallet-Regi M. Recent advances in porous nanoparticles for drug delivery in antitumoral applications: inorganic nanoparticles and nanoscale metal-organic frameworks. Expert Opin Drug Deliv. 2017;14:783–96.
72. Ding X, Yin C, Zhang W, Sun Y, Zhang Z, Yang E, Sun D, Wang W. Designing aptamer-gold nanoparticle-loaded pH-sensitive liposomes encapsulate morin for treating cancer. Nanoscale Res Lett. 2020;15:1–17.
73. Shirazi AN, Mandal D, Tiwari RK, Guo L, Lu W, Parang K. Cyclic peptide-capped gold nanopar-

ticles as drug delivery systems. Mol Pharm. 2012;10:500–11.
74. Brown SD, Nativo P, Smith JA, Stirling D, Edwards PR, Venugopal B, Wheate NJ. Gold nanoparticles for the improved anticancer drug delivery of the active component of oxaliplatin. J Am Chem Soc. 2010;132:4678–84.
75. Burduşel AC, Gherasim O, Grumezescu AM, Mogoantă L, Ficai A, Andronescu E. Biomedical applications of silver nanoparticles: an up-to-date overview. Nanomaterials (Basel). 2018;8(9):681.
76. Ravindra S, Mulaba-Bafubiandi AF, Rajinikanth V, Varaprasad K, Reddy NN, Raju KM. Development and characterization of curcumin loaded silver nanoparticle hydrogels for antibacterial and drug delivery applications. J Inorg Organomet Polym. 2012;22:1254–62.
77. Bonor J, Reddy V, Akkiraju H, Dhurjati P, Nohe A. Synthesis and characterization of L-lysine conjugated silver nanoparticles smaller than 10 nm. Adv Sci Eng Med. 2014;6(9):942–7.
78. Sun C, Lee JSH, Zhang M. Magnetic nanoparticles in MR imaging and drug delivery. Adv Drug Deliv Rev. 2008;60(11):1252–65.
79. Couvreur P, Kante B, Grislain L, Roland M, Speiser P. Toxicity of polyalkylcyanoacrylate nanoparticles II: doxorubicin-loaded nanoparticles. J Pharm Sci. 1982;71:790–2.
80. Galvin P, Thompson D, Ryan KB, et al. Nanoparticle-based drug delivery: case studies for cancer and cardiovascular applications. Cell Mol Life Sci. 2012;69:389–404.
81. Siddique S, Chow JCL. Gold nanoparticles for drug delivery and cancer therapy. Appl Sci. 2020;10:3824.
82. Patil NH, Devarajan PV. Insulin-loaded alginic acid nanoparticles for sublingual delivery. Drug Deliv. 2016;23:429–36.
83. Kong FY, Zhang JW, Li RF, Wang ZX, Wang WJ, Wang W. Unique roles of gold nanoparticles in drug delivery, targeting and imaging applications. Molecules. 2017;22(9):1445.
84. Brown PK, Qureshi AT, Moll AN, Hayes DJ, Monroe WT. Silver nanoscale antisense drug delivery system for photoactivated gene silencing. ACS Nano. 2013;7:2948–59.
85. Davis ME, Zuckerman JE, Choi CH, et al. Evidence of RNA in humans from systemically administered siRNA via targeted nanoparticles. Nature. 2010;464:1067–70.
86. Xiong XB, Uludag H, Lavasanifar A. Virus-mimetic polymeric micelles for targeted siRNA delivery. Biomaterials. 2010;31:5886–93.
87. Liu XQ, Sun CY, Yang XZ, Wang J. Polymeric-micelle-based nanomedicine for siRNA delivery. Part Part Syst Charact. 2013;30(3):211–28.
88. Bhakta G, Sharma RK, Gupta N, Cool S, Nurcombe V, Maitra A. Multifunctional silica nanoparticles with potentials of imaging and gene delivery. Nanomed Nanotechnol Biol Med. 2011;7(4):472–9.
89. Lee SB, Kim HL, Jeong HJ, Lim ST, Sohn MH, Kim DW. Mesoporous silica nanoparticle pretargeting for PET imaging based on a rapid bioorthogonal reaction in a living body. Angew Chem Int Ed Engl. 2013;52:10549–52.
90. Medina C, Santos-Martinez MJ, Radomski A, Corrigan OI, Radomski MW. Nanoparticles: pharmacological and toxicological significance. Br J Pharmacol. 2007;150:552–8.
91. Sakiyama-Elbert SE, Hubbell JA. Functional biomaterials: design of novel biomaterials. Annu Rev Mater Res. 2001;31:183–201.
92. Cuccurullo V, Di Stasio GD, Mazzarella G, Cascini GL. Microvascular invasion in HCC: the molecular imaging perspective. Contrast Media Mol Imaging. 2018;2018:9487938.
93. Wickline SA, Lanza GM. Nanotechnology for molecular imaging and targeted therapy. Circulation. 2003;107:1092–5.
94. Cai Z, Ye Z, Yang X, Chang Y, Wang H, Liu Y, Cao A. Encapsulated enhanced green fluorescence protein in silica nanoparticle for cellular imaging. Nanoscale. 2011;3(5):1974–6.
95. Dubreil L, Leroux I, Ledevin M, Schleder C, Lagalice L, Lovo C, Fleurisson R, Passemard S, Kilin V, Gerber-Lemaire S, Colle MA, Bonacina L, Rouger K. Multi-harmonic imaging in the second near-infrared window of nanoparticle-labeled stem cells as a monitoring tool in tissue depth. ACS Nano. 2017;11:6672–81.
96. Zhang Z, Mascheri N, Dharmakumar R, et al. Superparamagnetic iron oxide nanoparticle-labeled cells as an effective vehicle for tracking the GFP gene marker using magnetic resonance imaging. Cytotherapy. 2009;11(1):43–51.
97. Chien CC, Chen HH, Lai SF, Hwu Y, Petibois C, Yang CS, Chu Y, Margaritondo G. X-ray imaging of tumour growth in live mice by detecting gold-nanoparticle-loaded cells. Sci Rep. 2012;2:610.
98. Min HS, Son S, You DG, Lee TW, Lee J, Lee S, Yhee JY, Lee J, Han MH, Park JH, Kim SH, Choi K, Park K, Kim K, Kwon IC. Chemical gas-generating nanoparticles for tumor-targeted ultrasound imaging and ultrasound-triggered drug delivery. Biomaterials. 2016;108:57–70.
99. Veres DS, Máthé D, Futó I, et al. Quantitative liver lesion volume determination by nanoparticle-based SPECT. Mol Imaging Biol. 2014;16(2):167–72.
100. Ahmad MW, Xu W, Kim SJ, Baeck JS, Chang Y, Bae JE, Chae KS, Park JA, Kim TJ, Lee GH. Potential dual imaging nanoparticle Gd_2O_3. Sci Rep. 2015;5:8549.
101. Xia J, Feng G, Xia X, Hao L, Wang Z. NH_4HCO_3 gas-generating liposomal nanoparticle for photoacoustic imaging in breast cancer. Int J Nanomedicine. 2017;12:1803–13.
102. Chen Q, Liang C, Sun X, Chen J, Yang Z, Zhao H, et al. H_2O_2-responsive liposomal nanoprobe for photoacoustic inflammation imaging and tumor ther-

anostics via *in vivo* chromogenic assay. Proc Natl Acad Sci USA. 2017;114:5343–8.
103. Jiang Q, Shao F, Gao W, Chen Z, Jiang G, Ho YS. Unified noreference quality assessment of singly and multiply distorted stereoscopic images. IEEE Trans Image Process. 2018;28(4):1866e81:1866.
104. Zuo C, Sun J, Li J, Zhang J, Asundi A, Chen Q. High-resolution transport-of-intensity quantitative phase microscopy with annular illumination. Sci Rep. 2017;7(1):1e22.
105. Banigo AT, Azeez TO, Ejeta KO, Lateef A, Ajuogu E. Nanobiosensors: applications in biomedical technology. In: Nanotechnology applications in Africa: opportunities and constraints IOP Conf. Series: Material Science Engineering, vol. 805; 2020. p. 012028.
106. Ren X, Chen D, Meng X, et al. Amperometric glucose biosensor based on a gold nanorods/cellulose acetate composite film as immobilization matrix. Colloids Surf B Biointerfaces. 2009;72:188–92.
107. Yang T, Zhou N, Zhang Y, et al. Synergistically improved sensitivity for the detection of specific DNA sequences using polyaniline nanofibers and multiwalled carbon nanotubes composites. Biosens Bioelectron. 2009;24:2165–70.
108. Lee DS, Fu YQ, Maeng S, Du XY, Tan SC, Luo JK. Integrated ZnO surface acoustic wave microfluidic and biosensor system. In: Electron devices meeting, IEDM 2007. IEEE International; 2007. p. 851–4.
109. Suvarnaphaet P, Pechprasarn S. Graphene-based materials for biosensors: a review. Sensors. 2017;17(10):2161.
110. Chung C, Kim YK, Shin D, Ryoo SR, Hong BH, Min DH. Biomedical applications of graphene and graphene oxide. Acc Chem Res. 2013;46:2211–24.
111. Blanco-Fernandez B, Castaño O, Mateos-Timoneda MÁ, Engel E, Pérez-Amodio S. Nanotechnology approaches in chronic wound healing. Adv Wound Care. 2021;10(5):234–56.
112. Berthet M, Gauthier Y, Lacroix C, Verrier B, Monge C. Nanoparticle-based dressing: the future of wound treatment? Trends Biotechnol. 2017;35:770–84.
113. Boroumand Z, Golmakani N, Boroumand S. Clinical trials on silver nanoparticles for wound healing. Nanomed J. 2018;5:186–91.
114. Bharathi S, Ramesh B, Kumaran S, Radhakrishnan M, Saravanan D, Sundari MSN. Development of nanobiomaterial for wound healing based on silver nanoparticles loaded on chitosan hydrogel. 3 Biotech. 2021;11:490.
115. Arafa MG, El-Kased RF, Elmazar MM. Thermoresponsive gels containing gold nanoparticles as smart antibacterial and wound healing agents. Sci Rep. 2018;8(1):13674.
116. Kushwaha A, Goswami L, Kim BS. Nanomaterial-based therapy for wound healing. Nanomaterials (Basel, Switzerland). 2022;12(4):618.
117. Oscar LF, MubarakAli D, Nithya C, Priyanka R, Gopinath V, Alharbi NS, Thajuddin N. One pot synthesis and anti-biofilm potential of copper nanoparticles (CuNPs) against clinical strains of *Pseudomonas aeruginosa*. Biofouling. 2015;31:379–91.
118. Kumar PT, Lakshmanan VK, Anilkumar T, Ramya C, Reshmi P, Unnikrishnan A, Nair SV, Jayakumar R. Flexible and microporous chitosan hydrogel/nano ZnO composite bandages for wound dressing: in vitro and in vivo evaluation. ACS Appl Mater Interfaces. 2012;4:2618–29.
119. Vimbela GV, Ngo SM, Fraze C, Yang L, Stout DA. Antibacterial properties and toxicity from metallic nanomaterials. Int J Nanomedicine. 2017;12:3941–65.
120. Zhu S, Shen Y, Yu Y, Bai X. Synthesis of antibacterial gold nanoparticles with different particle sizes using chlorogenic acid. R Soc Open Science. 2020;7(3):191141.
121. Kumar PSM, Ali DM, Saratale RG, et al. Synthesis of nano-cuboidal gold particles for effective antimicrobial property against clinical human pathogens. Microb Pathog. 2017;113:68–73.
122. Brown AN, Smith K, Samuels TA, Lu J, Obare SO, Scott ME. Nanoparticles functionalized with ampicillin destroy multiple-antibiotic-resistant isolates of *Pseudomonas aeruginosa* and *Enterobacter aerogenes* and methicillin-resistant *Staphylococcus aureus*. Appl Environ Microbiol. 2012;78(8):2768–74.
123. Kesarkar R, Oza G, Pandey S, Dahake R, Mukherjee S, Chowdhary A, et al. Gold nanoparticles: effective as both entry inhibitors and virus neutralizing agents against HIV. J Microbiol Biotech Res. 2012;2:276–83.
124. Garrido C, Simpson CA, Dahl NP, et al. Gold nanoparticles to improve HIV drug delivery. Future Med Chem. 2015;7(9):1097–107.
125. Marambio-Jones C, Hoek EM. A review of the antibacterial effects of silver nanomaterials and potential implications for human health and the environment. J Nano Res. 2010;12:1531–51.
126. Ewald C, Kuhn S, Kalff R. Pyogenic infections of the central nervous system secondary to dental affections—a report of six cases. Neurosurg Rev. 2006;29:163–6.
127. Semiramoth N, Meo CD, Zouhiri F, Said-Hassane F, Valetti S, Gorges R, Nicolas V, Poupaert JH, Chollet-Martin S, Desmaele D, Gref R, Couvreur P. Self-assembled squalenoylated penicillin bioconjugates: an original approach for the treatment of intracellular infections. ACS Nano. 2012;6:3820–31.
128. Toti US, Guru BR, Hali M, McPharlin CM, Wykes SM, Panyam J, Whittum-Hudson JA. Targeted delivery of antibiotics to intracellular chlamydial infections using PLGA nanoparticles. Biomaterials. 2011;32:6606–13.
129. Padmavathy N, Vijayaraghavan R. Enhanced bioactivity of ZnO nanoparticles—an antimicrobial study. Sci Technol Adv Mater. 2008;9:035004.
130. Seil JT, Webster TJ. Antibacterial effect of zinc oxide nanoparticles combined with ultrasound. Nanotechnology. 2012;23:495101.

131. Elamawi RM, Al-Harbi RE, Hendi AA. Biosynthesis and characterization of silver nanoparticles using Trichoderma longibrachiatum and their effect on phytopathogenic fungi. Egypt J Biol Pest Control. 2018;28:28.
132. Singh H, Du J, Yi TH. Biosynthesis of silver nanoparticles using Aeromonas sp. THG-FG1.2 and its antibacterial activity against pathogenic microbes. Artif Cells Nanomed Biotechnol. 2017;45(3):584–90.
133. Kim JH, Cho H, Ryu SE, Choi MU. Effects of metal ions on the activity of protein tyrosine phosphatase VHR: highly potent and reversible oxidative inactivation by Cu2+ ion. Arch Biochem Biophys. 2000;382:72–80.
134. Ismail AO, Ajayi SO, Alausa AO, Ogundile OP, Ademosun OT, Antimicrobial and antibiofilm activities of green synthesized silver nanoparticles for water treatment. J Phys Conf Ser. International Conference on Recent Trends in Applied Research (ICoRTAR). 2020;1734:012043.
135. Liu YJ, Bhattarai P, Dai ZF, Chen XY. Photothermal therapy and photoacoustic imaging via nanotheranostics in fighting cancer. Chem Soc Rev. 2019;48:2053–108.
136. Vyas N, Wang QX, Walmsley AD. Improved biofilm removal using cavitation from a dental ultrasonic scaler vibrating in carbonated water. Ultrason Sonochem. 2021;70:105338.
137. Bai X, Gao Y, Liu H, Zheng L. Synthesis of amphiphilic ionic liquids terminated gold nanorods and their superior catalytic activity for the reduction of nitro compounds. J Phys Chem C. 2009;113:17730–6.
138. Raie DS, Mhatre E, Thiele M, Labena A, El-Ghannam G, Farahat LA, Youssef T, Fritzsche W, Kovács ÁT. Application of quercetin and its bio-inspired nanoparticles as anti-adhesive agents against *Bacillus subtilis* attachment to surface. Mater Sci Eng C. 2017;70:753–62.
139. Hayat S, Muzammil S, Rasool MH, Nisar Z, Hussain SZ, Sabri AN, Jamil S. *In vitro* antibiofilm and antiadhesion effects of magnesium oxide nanoparticles against antibiotic resistant bacteria running. Microbiol Immunol. 2017;26:211–20.
140. Thukkaram M, Sitaram S, Kannaiyan SK, Subbiahdoss G. Antibacterial efficacy of iron-oxide nanoparticles against biofilms on different biomaterial surfaces. Int J Biomater. 2014;2014:716080.
141. Azam A, Ahmed AS, Oves M, Khan MS, Memic A. Size-dependent antimicrobial properties of CuO nanoparticles against gram-positive and negative bacterial strains. Int J Nanomedicine. 2012;7:3527–35.
142. Lee KW, Periasamy S, Mukherjee M, Xie C, Kjelleberg S, Rice SA. Biofilm development and enhanced stress resistance of a model, mixed-species community biofilm. ISME J. 2014;8(4):894–907.
143. Ishwarya R, Vaseeharan B, Kalyani S, Banumathi B, Govindarajan M, Alharbi NS, Kadaikunnan S, Al-anbr MN, Khaled JM, Benelli G. Facile green synthesis of zinc oxide nanoparticles using *Ulva lactuca* seaweed extract and evaluation of their photocatalytic, antibiofilm and insecticidal activity. J Photochem Photobiol B Biol. 2018;178:249–58.
144. Chrzanowska N, Załeska-Radziwiłł M. The impacts of aluminum and zirconium nano-oxides on planktonic and biofilm bacteria. Desalin Water Treat. 2014;52:3680–9.
145. Ali SG, Ansari MA, Alzohairy MA, et al. Biogenic gold nanoparticles as potent antibacterial and antibiofilm nano-antibiotics against *Pseudomonas aeruginosa*. Antibiotics (Basel). 2020;9(3):100.
146. Gabrielyan L, Hovhannisyan A, Gevorgyan V, Ananyan M, Trchounian A. Antibacterial effects of iron oxide (Fe_3O_4) nanoparticles: distinguishing concentration-dependent effects with different bacterial cells growth and membrane-associated mechanisms. Appl Microbiol Biotechnol. 2019;103:2773–82.
147. Taylor EN, Webster TJ. The use of superparamagnetic nanoparticles for prosthetic biofilm prevention. Int J Nanomedicine. 2009;4:145–52.
148. Sumithra D, Bharathi S, Kaviyarasan P, Suresh G. Biofabrication of selenium nanoparticles using marine *Streptomyces sp.* and assessment of its antibacterial, antibiofilm, antioxidant, and *in vivo* cytotoxic potential. Geomicrobiol J. 2023;40:485. https://doi.org/10.1080/01490451.2023.2196280.
149. Chorianopoulos NG, Tsoukleris DS, Panagou EZ, Falaras P, Nychas GJE. Use of titanium dioxide (TiO_2) photocatalysts as alternative means for *Listeria monocytogenes* biofilm disinfection in food processing. Food Microbiol. 2011;28:164–70.
150. Rajkumari J, Magdalane CM, Siddhardha B, Madhavan J, Ramalingam G, Al-Dhabi NA, Arasu MV, Ghilan AKM, Duraipandiayan V, Kaviyarasu K. Synthesis of titanium oxide nanoparticles using *Aloe barbadensis* mill and evaluation of its antibiofilm potential against *Pseudomonas aeruginosa* PAO1. J Photochem Photobiol B Biol. 2019;201:111667.
151. Swidan NS, Hashem YA, Elkhatib WF, et al. Antibiofilm activity of green synthesized silver nanoparticles against biofilm associated enterococcal urinary pathogens. Sci Rep. 2022;12:3869.
152. Quintana A, Raczka E, Piehler L. Design and function of a dendrimer-based therapeutic nanodevice targeted to tumor cells through the folate receptor. Pharm Res. 2002;19:1310–6.
153. Chen Z, Mao R. Fullerenes for cancer diagnosis and therapy: preparation, biological and clinical perspectives. Curr Drug Metab. 2012;13(8):1035–45.
154. Jain A, Jain SK. Optimization of chitosan nanoparticles for colon tumors using experimental design methodology. Artif Cells Nanomed Biotechnol. 2016;44:1917–26.
155. Román JV, Galán MA, del Valle EMM. Preparation and preliminary evaluation of alginate crosslinked microcapsules as potential drug delivery system (DDS) for human lung cancer therapy. Biomed Phys Eng Expr. 2016;2:035015.

156. Qu W, Meng B, Yu Y, Wang S. EpCAM antibody-conjugated mesoporous silica nanoparticles to enhance the anticancer efficacy of carboplatin in retinoblastoma. Mater Sci Eng C Mater Biol Appl. 2017;76:646–51.
157. Chatterjee K, Sarkar S, Jagajjanani Rao K, Paria S. Core/shell nanoparticles in biomedical applications. Adv Colloid Interf Sci. 2014;209:8–39.
158. Yang K, Wan J, Zhang S, Tian B, Zhang Y, Liu Z, Yang K, et al. The influence of surface chemistry and size of nanoscale graphene oxide on photothermal therapy of cancer using ultra-low laser power. Biomaterials. 2012;33:2206–14.
159. Zhang H, Wu H, Wang J, et al. Graphene oxide-BaGdF5 nanocomposites for multi-modal imaging and photothermal therapy. Biomaterials. 2015;42:66–77.
160. van der Zee J. Heating the patient: a promising approach? Ann Oncol. 2002;13(8):1173–84.
161. Cherukuri P, Glazer ES, Curley SA. Targeted hyperthermia using metal nanoparticles. Adv Drug Deliv Rev. 2010;62(3):339–45.
162. Tang YD, Zou J, Flesch RCC, Jin T. Effect of injection strategy for nanofluid transport on thermal damage behavior inside biological tissue during magnetic hyperthermia. Int Commun Heat Mass Transf. 2022;133:105979.
163. Peng XH, Qian X, Mao H, Wang AY, Chen ZG, Nie S, Shin DM. Targeted magnetic iron oxide nanoparticles for tumor imaging and therapy. Int J Nanomedicine. 2008;3:311–21.
164. Le Renard PE, Jordan O, Faes A, Petri-Fink A, Hofmann H, Rüfenacht D, Bosman F, Buchegger F, Doelker E. The *in vivo* performance of magnetic particle-loaded injectable, in situ gelling, carriers for the delivery of local hyperthermia. Biomaterials. 2010;31:691–705.
165. Ito A, Shinkai M, Honda H, Kobayashi T. Medical application of functionalized magnetic nanoparticles. J Biosci Bioeng. 2005;100:1–11.
166. Gannon CJ, Patra CR, Bhattacharya R, Mukherjee P, Curley SA. Intracellular gold nanoparticles enhance non-invasive radiofrequency thermal destruction of human gastrointestinal cancer cells. J Nanobiotechnol. 2008;6:2.
167. Gobin AM, Lee MH, Halas NJ, James WD, Drezek RA, West JL. Near-infrared resonant nanoshells for combined. Optical imaging and photothermal cancer therapy. Nano Lett. 2007;7:1929–34.
168. Sumer B, Gao J. Theranostic nanomedicine for cancer. Nanomedicine. 2008;3:137–40.
169. Wun HC, Li TS, Sheng LJ, Kar TSL, Biau FJ, Suan NH, Wei WSY, Sze OY. Emerging Nanotheranostics for 5-fluorouracil in cancer therapy: a systematic review on efficacy, safety, and diagnostic capability. Front Pharmacol. 2022;13:882704.
170. Pan J, Liu Y, Feng SS. Multifunctional nanoparticles of biodegradable copolymer blend for cancer diagnosis and treatment. Nanomedicine (Lond). 2010;5(3):347–60.
171. Taratula O, Schumann C, Naleway MA, et al. A multifunctional theranostic platform based on phthalocyanine-loaded dendrimer for image guided drug delivery and photodynamic therapy. Mol Pharm. 2013;10(10):3946–58.
172. Chandrasekharan P, Maity D, Yong CX. Vitamin E (D-alpha-tocopheryl-co-poly (ethylene glycol) 1000 succinate) micelles-superparamagnetic iron oxide nanoparticles for enhanced thermotherapy and MRI. Biomaterials. 2011;32(24):5663–72.
173. Yuan J, Zhang H, Kaur H, et al. Synthesis and characterization of theranostic poly (HPMA)-c(RGDyK)-DOTA-^{64}Cu copolymer targeting tumor angiogenesis: tumor localization visualized by positron emission tomography. Mol Imaging. 2013;12(3):1–10.
174. Chen WH, Xu XD, Jia HZ. Therapeutic nanomedicine based on dual-intelligent functionalized gold nanoparticles for cancer imaging and therapy in vivo. Biomaterials. 2013;34(34):8798–807.
175. Shuhendler AJ, Prasad P, Leung M, et al. A novel solid lipid nanoparticle formulation for active targeting to tumor $\alpha(v)$ $\beta(3)$ integrin receptors reveals cyclic RGD as a double-edged sword. Adv Healthc Mater. 2012;1(5):600–8.
176. Muthu MS, Kulkarni SA, Raju A, et al. Theranostic liposomes of TPGS coating for targeted co-delivery of docetaxel and quantum dots. Biomaterials. 2012;33(12):3494–501.
177. Huang P, Li Z, Lin J, et al. Photosensitizer-conjugated magnetic nanoparticles for *in vivo* simultaneous magnetofluorescent imaging and targeting therapy. Biomaterials. 2011;32(13):3447–58.
178. Yi DK, Sun IC, Ryu JH, et al. Matrix metalloproteinase sensitive gold nanorod for simultaneous bioimaging and photothermal therapy of cancer. Bioconjug Chem. 2010;21(12):2173–7.
179. Foy SP, Manthe RL, Foy ST, Dimitrijevic S, Krishnamurthy N, Labhasetwar V. Opimaging and magnetic tical field targeting of magnetic nanoparticles in tumors. ACS Nano. 2010;4(9):5217–24.
180. Chertok B, David AE, Yang VC. Magnetically-enabled and MR-monitored selective brain tumor protein delivery in rats via magnetic nanocarriers. Biomaterials. 2011;32(26):6245–53.
181. Park JK, Jung J, Subramaniam P, et al. Graphite-coated magnetic nanoparticles as multimodal imaging probes and cooperative therapeutic agents for tumor cells. Small. 2011;7(12):1647–52.

Huntington's Disease: A Neurodegenerative Disorder

15

Jayasree R, Yoga Mithra S, and Shweta Ravi

15.1 Introduction

Huntington's disease is a rare, progressive, and deadly hero-neurodegenerative illness that causes cognitive, behavioral, and motor impairment. The condition is autosomal dominant, meaning that all it takes to pass it down is one copy of the defective gene. The Huntington (HTT) gene, which codes for the Huntingtin protein, has undergone a mutation that results in an excess of CAG repeats close to its 5′ end [1]. The mutation causes the poly-glutamine in the HTT protein to expand excessively long, which causes neurodegeneration. Those between the ages of 35 and 50 are the group that is most affected. The striatal portion of the ganglia exhibits selective atrophy and cell death as a result of this adult-onset disease [2]. Although the range for those affected is thought to be 36–120 triplet repeats, persons with more than 35 triplet repeats are more likely to have this illness. Most people who have fewer than 35 triplet repeats are unaffected.

While making rounds with his father in a hospital in 1872, Dr. George Huntington found this illness. His systematic research provided a traditional description that is still applied to make the initial clinical diagnosis. The HTT gene was the first gene to be located on a chromosomal locus using anonymous markers in 1983. A global collaborative organized by the Genetic Disease Foundation conducted additional study, and in 1993 they uncovered the genetic underpinnings. Clinical diagnosis of patients with motor dysfunctions is possible through DNA analysis [3]. Genetic testing can be done on those who are susceptible to the disease before any symptoms show. There is currently no cure, however, medication, physical therapy, and speech therapy can control the symptoms. Huntington's illness is being studied for a long-term remedy.

15.2 Causes

The Huntington gene, located on the short arm of chromosome number 4, is mutated in Huntington's disease. A basic chemical code is repeated many times in the Huntingtin protein gene, which contains a biological blueprint [4]. An overview of the development of Huntington's disease is shown in Fig. 15.1 [5]. A little region of chromosome 4 contains excess copies of a specific chemical code in this particular gene deficiency. The CAG trinucleotide, which is composed of the three DNA building elements

J. R (✉) · Y. M. S
Department of Biotechnology, Rajalakshmi Engineering College, Chennai, Tamil Nadu, India
e-mail: jayasree.r@rajalakshmi.edu.in

S. Ravi
Department of Industrial Biotechnology, Government College of Technology, Coimbatore, India

K. Parthasarathy, R. Manikkam (eds.), *Translational Research in Biomedical Sciences: Recent Progress and Future Prospects*, https://doi.org/10.1007/978-981-97-1777-4_15

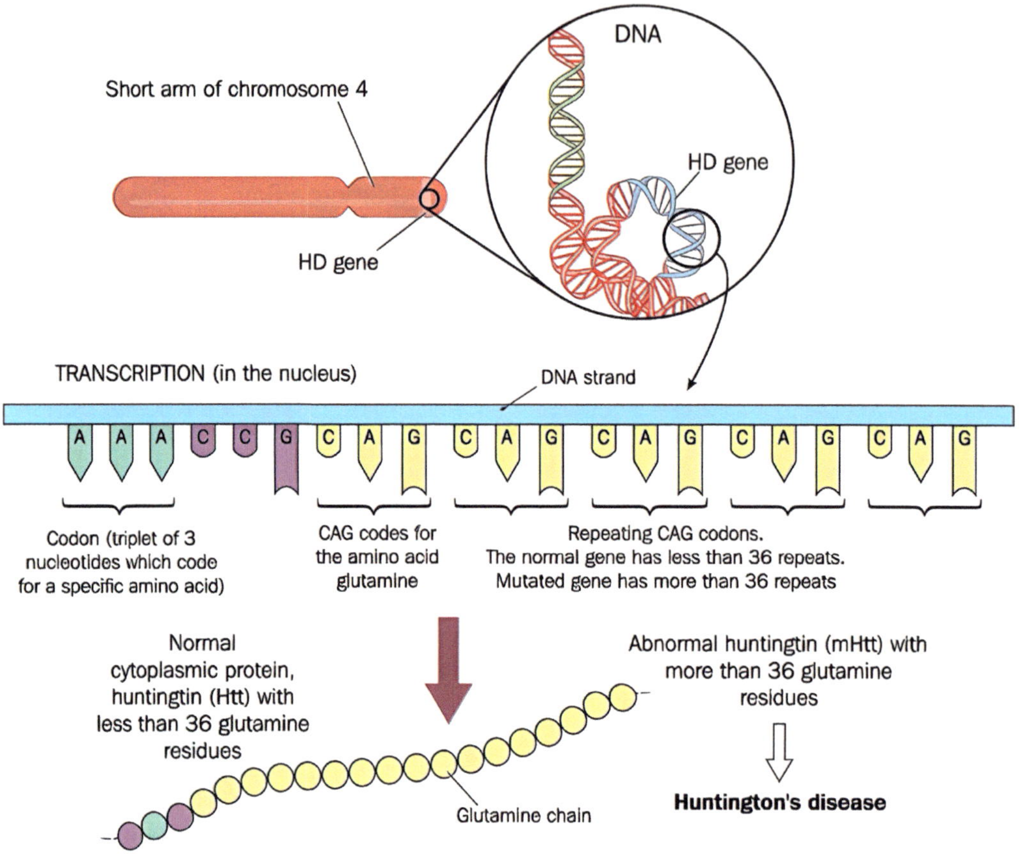

Fig. 15.1 Overview of the development of Huntington's disease (Huntington's disease: California Stem Cell Agency)

cytosine, adenine, and guanine, is the DNA fragment in question. This code is repeated between 17 and 20 times in a normal huntingtin gene [6].

The larger-than-normal size of the mutant gene causes an excessive amount of cytosine, adenine, and guanine to be produced, increasing the repeats' number to above 40. This alteration causes the poisonous huntingtin protein to be produced in an unusually extended form. This long-version protein is broken down into tiny, poisonous fragments that group together and build up in the brain, where they start to harm some brain cells and have an effect on movement, behavior, and cognition—the hallmarks of Huntington's disease [7].

15.3 Types

Juvenile HD and Adult HD are two categories for Huntington's disease based on when it first manifests (Fig. 15.2 [8]). The sooner the disease manifests, the greater the correlation between the amount of HTT repetitions and disease onset.

15.3.1 Juvenile HD

Juvenile HD is defined by symptoms and signs that appear before the age of 20. There are more than 55 duplicates in this instance. These children and teenagers experience epileptic fits, chorea, bradykinetic, motor behavior, behavioral

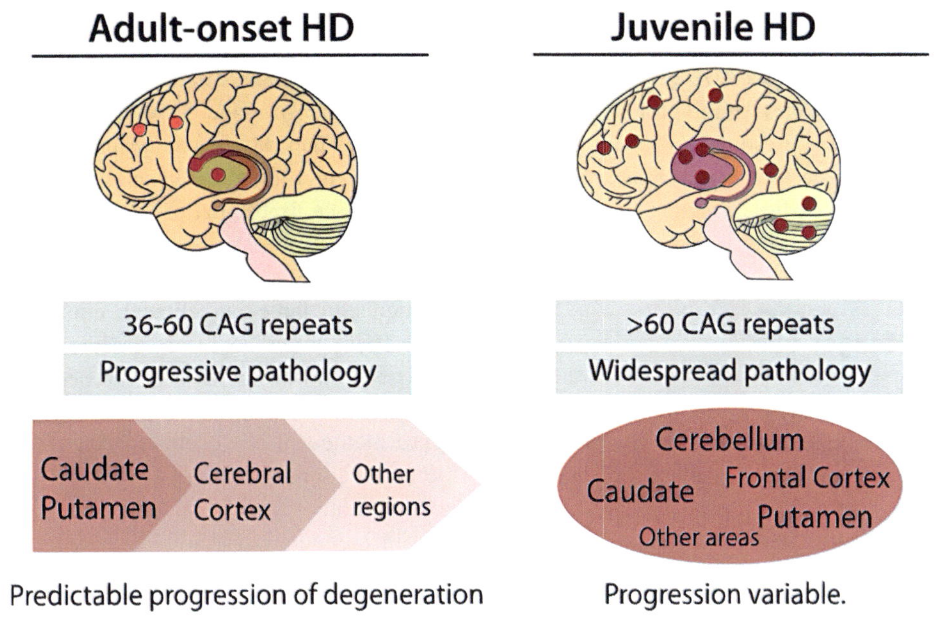

Fig. 15.2 Types of HD. (Monica Bañez-Coronel 2015)

abnormalities, and learning impairments, among other symptoms. Studies show that 75% of people with the condition have a parent who is also affected [9].

15.3.2 Adult (or Late Onset) HD

Adult (or late onset) HD is the most prevalent type of Huntington's disease and strikes persons between the ages of 30 and 50. The length of the repeats is found to be between 40 and 49. Repeat lengths greater than 50 are found in people of the age groups 20–30 years. This type is characterized by its first symptom being gait and balance problems [10].

15.4 Statistics

According to reports, the prevalence of HD varies by ethnicity and area. According to estimates, Huntington's disease affects 4–8 people out of every 100,000 people in much of Europe, India, and some regions of central Asia. According to studies done among Canadians, HD affects 2.4–8.4 people out of every 100,000 people [11].

One in every 100,000 Americans has this disorder, according to data. 16% of cases of Huntington's disease are in children. Finland and Japan have very few cases of Huntington's disease. The data for Africa is not sufficient. The disease is prevalent in populations descended from European immigration at a rate corresponding to those populations' geographic origins [12].

15.5 Pattern of Inheritance

One copy of the defective gene is sufficient to develop Huntington's disease, which is inherited in an autosomal dominant manner. The sick person typically inherits the gene from one of the affected parents. Rarely, a person with the disease does not have a parent who also has it. Although a person with 27–35 CAG repeats in the HTT does not acquire the condition, there is a significant possibility that she will give birth to a kid who does [13]. A person has a 50% probability of spreading the disease to their offspring if they have 40 or more repetitions.

In contrast to other autosomal dominant disorders, only when the condition is inherited from father to child does the size of the CAG repeat increase. This makes Huntington's disease distinct from other autosomal dominant disorders. As a result, under some situations, the disease may manifest earlier, a condition known as anticipation.

15.6 Stages of HD

Based on the patient's functional capacity, the stages are defined. Many scales, like the Disease Rating Scale and the Total Functional Capacity rating scale, have been developed to aid in diagnosis. The Shoulson-Fahn system, Table 15.1 [14], independence in daily activities on a scale from stage 1 to stage 5, with stage 1 having complete functional capacity and stage 5 having severely limited functional capacity. It is based on the functional capacity rating system [15].

The clinical course of a patient is roughly divided into three—preclinical, clinical and at-risk. These stages represent a decrease in independence and an increase in the need for care. Table 15.2 demonstrates the various stages of HD.

Table 15.1 Shoulson-Fahn system [14]

Stage	TFC Score	Years since motor diagnosis	Typical abilities and care level
1	11–13	0–8	Able to work at least part time, may require slight assistance in one of finances, domestic chores or ADL basic functions
2	7–10	3–13	Unable to work, requires some assistance in some basic functions
3	3–6	5–16	Unable to work, requires major assistance in most basic functions
4	1–2	9–21	Requires major assistance in all basic functions and although comprehension may be intact, requires assistance to act
5	0	11–26	Requires major assistance in all basic functions and full time nursing care

Table 15.2 Stages of HD

Stage	Symptoms	Effects
Preclinical stage	Mild symptoms such as anxiety, unusual irritability and difficulty in learning new things and making decisions.	These symptoms are very mild and are often unnoticed and the individual continues in their everyday routine.
Early stage	Involuntary twitches, low coordination, depression, and struggling concentrating or solving problems.	The brain cells are severely damaged. The behavioral or cognitive changes due to neurological damage are hardly noticeable.
Late intermediate stage	Wright issues, difficulty with memory issues with performing motor tasks, falling often, mood swings and depression.	This stage generally carries on for around 5–16 years. Once they reach this stage it becomes harder to reverse it.
Early advanced stage	Psychosis, rigidity, apathy, abnormally slow movements and severe challenges in voluntary movements.	This stage generally begins after about 10 years of the onset of the disease. The patient at this stage requires more advanced care.
Advanced stage	Likely to become immobile, unable to communicate and incapable of performing basic motor functions like swallowing.	This is the final stage, and the patient becomes completely dependent on others.

15.7 Effects

The length of the CAG repeats majorly affects the types of symptoms that are experienced by the patients. The most common symptoms include chorea, gait disturbances, neuropsychiatric effects, etc. The striatum is one of the first parts to be affected due to this disease and subregions of the cortex also appear to be involved [16].

15.7.1 Motor Disturbance

Phases of the motor disturbance are categorized as hyperkinetic and hypokinetic. Early on rate during the Hyperkinetic phase, there is chorea, which later tends to plateau [17]. Dystonia, bradykinesia, balance issues, and abnormal gait are all signs of the hypokinetic phase. While the majority of motor disorders are related to the number of CAG repeats, chorea is not.

15.7.2 Cognitive Disturbance

Impaired emotion identification, processing speed, visuospatial, and executive function are characteristics of the cognitive disorder. HD patients frequently lose the ability to tell what information is important and what can be disregarded [18]. Semantic memory appears to be somewhat intact, despite the fact that memory is undoubtedly diminished. Executive functions are especially linked to cognitive changes.

15.7.3 Neuropsychiatric Disturbance

Apathy, anxiety, depression, irritability, obsessive-compulsive disorder, and psychosis are all examples of neuropsychiatric disturbance [19]. The one symptom that consistently gets worse as the illness does is apathy. Cells become less resilient to random stressors as a result of the HD protein mutation, which lowers their overall viability.

Although it is not a true sign of the disease, aging is thought to be brought on by a deterioration in a number of pathways connected to the neurodegenerative disorder. A further decline in overall cell viability is brought on by aging. Also seen in the patients is an unintentional weight decrease. Despite the fact that chorea and movement disorders are frequently associated with weight loss, the length of the CAG repeats is usually to blame. Autonomic disturbances are the cause of excessive perspiration [17].

15.8 Diagnosis

The diagnosis of the disease is based on the signs and symptoms along with the presence of the HD protein in the parent. Motor, psychiatric and cognitive changes; and the family history of the patient, are the principal clinical features to be observed for the diagnosis. The formal diagnosis is the DNA determination showing at least 36 CAG repeats on the Huntington gene on chromosome 4 [20].

15.8.1 Differential Diagnosis

Differential diagnosis is performed for:

- Clinically affected individuals who are not affected by HD, and
- Evaluating patients who show the signs and symptoms of HD, which are presented as another disease.

Since chorea is the most prominent and common clinical feature of the disease, its differential diagnosis is taken into account. Only about 1% of the chorea-affected patients are diagnosed with HD while a majority of patients have chorea due to a general internal disorder or an iatrogenic disorder [21].

15.8.2 Genetic Testing

Genetic testing for the disease has been performed since 1986 and became more evolved with linkage analysis in 1993. There are three different kinds of genetic testing: diagnostic, presymptomatic, and prenatal.

- *Diagnostic testing*: This is done on patients who may have HD. When the patient's family history is obscured by a parent's death, an adoption, or a novel mutation, confirmation testing is typically helpful [22]. Genetic testing confirms if a patient has the HD gene or not, but it does not prove that they have illness symptoms. Genetic testing that identifies De novo HD genes suggests that the patients' offspring, siblings, and other family members are susceptible to the condition.
- *Presymptomatic testing:* This is done to determine the carrier status of an individual at risk of inheriting the disease. It includes counseling, neurological examination and DNA assay [23]. The primary consideration of this is to inform the at-risk patient about the risks, benefits and alternatives to testing. The patients are informed about the treatment methods that may help them delay the adverse symptoms of the disease.
- *Prenatal testing:* This is done to determine the carrier status of the fetus. Prenatal testing often leads to adverse emotional impacts as they learn that both the mother and the fetus are gene carriers. There is a time constraint on this type of genetic testing as there is little time for preparing the parents for certainties and uncertainties. Pre-implantation genetic diagnosis is a new alternative offered to couples who are gene negative and are expecting to have a baby [24]. By doing this, the moral dilemmas related to pregnancy termination are avoided. At the 8-cell embryo, a single-cell sample is used to make this diagnosis. The PCR is used for gene amplification and for the detection of repeat sizes on each chromosome. The eggs are collected, in vitro fertilized, and examined. Those that test negative for the gene are implanted in the mother.

15.8.3 Neurological Examination

Neurological examination reveals whether an individual exhibits the symptoms of the disease, which gene testing was not able to confirm. Once the patient has undergone this and genetic testing, they should recognize that they are no longer presymptomatic and should start treatment associated with the onset of the disease [10]. Recent MRI research has focused on changes in function and brain imaging because it has been discovered that changes in brain volume and connectivity occur years before clinical manifestations do.

15.9 Treatment

Huntington's disease is now incurable. While there is no cure for the disease, there are medications and therapies that can help control the symptoms.

15.9.1 Medications

The FDA has approved two drugs specifically to manage the movement disorders of Huntington's disease:

- **Tetrabenazine (Xenazine)** treats involuntary, jerky movements or chorea.
- **Deutetrabenazine (Austedo)** also treats the same jerky movements, specifically that of the face and tongue specifically [25].

Other drugs which are also prescribed to suppress the involuntary movements are as follows:

- olanzapine (Zyprexa)
- aripiprazole (Abilify)
- clonazepam (Klonopin)
- haloperidol.

The drugs given to treat the psychiatric disorders like depressions, bipolar disorder, violent outbursts and obsessive-compulsive features include the following:

- fluoxetine (Prozac, Sarafem)
- sertraline (Zoloft)
- citalopram (Celexa)
- quetiapine (Seroquel)
- olanzapine (Zyprexa) [26].

15.9.2 Speech Therapy

The control of the mouth and throat muscles, which are essential for speaking, eating, and swallowing, can considerably be affected by Huntington's disease and result in a variety of serious issues. The capacity to talk effectively can be improved through speech treatment. To lessen the difficulties brought on by this illness, speech therapists also instruct patients how to use communication aids [27]. Also, this treatment can aid in enhancing the flexibility of the swallowing and eating-related muscles.

15.9.3 Physical and Occupational Therapy

This therapy helps to improve the strength, flexibility of a person's muscles and to better the balance of an individual. It includes specialized exercises that the person must repeat on a daily basis. The individual is advised to use supporting devices like wheelchairs and walkers. Additional support devices are fit throughout the person's home [28]. These could be handrails, specialized eating and drinking devices or devices that help the individual to dress and shower.

References

1. McColgan P, Tabrizi SJ. Huntington's disease: a clinical review. Eur J Neurol. 2018;25(1):24–34. https://doi.org/10.1111/ene.13413.
2. Illarioshkin SN, Klyushnikov SA, Vigont VA, Seliverstov YA, Kaznacheyeva EV. Molecular pathogenesis in Huntington's disease. Biochem Mosc. 2018;83(9):1030. https://doi.org/10.1134/S0006297918090043.
3. Kay C, Fisher E, Hayden MR. Epidemiology. In: Bates GP, Tabrizi SJ, Jones L, editors. Huntington's disease. Oxford University Press; 2014.
4. Roos RAC. Huntington's disease: a clinical review. Orphanet J Rare Dis. 2010;5:40. https://doi.org/10.1186/1750-1172-5-40.
5. Huntington's disease: MedlinePlus genetics https://medlineplus.gov/genetics/condition/huntingtons-disease/#causes.
6. Chial H. Huntington's disease: the discovery of the Huntingtin gene. Nat Educ. 2008;1(1):71.
7. Brackenridge CJ, Case J, Chiu E, Propert DN, Teltscher B, Wallace DC. A linkage study of the loci for Huntington's disease and some common polymorphic markers. Ann Hum Genet. 1978;42(2):203–11.
8. Bañez-Coronel M, Ayhan F, Tarabochia AD, et al. RAN translation in Huntington disease. Neuron. 2015;88(4):667–77.
9. Scrimgeour EM, Pfumojena JW. Huntington disease in black Zimbabwean families living near the Mozambique border. Am J Med Genet. 1992;44:762–6.
10. Bates GP, Dorsey R, Gusella JF, Hayden MR, Kay C, Leavitt BR, et al. Huntington disease. Nat Rev Dis Primer. 2015;1:15005.
11. Moher D, Liberati A, Tetzlaff J, Altman DG. PRISMA Group: preferred reporting items for systematic reviews and meta-analyses: the PRISMA statement. PLoS Med. 2009;6:e1000097.
12. Centre for Molecular Medicine and Therapeutics. Published reports of the worldwide prevalence of Huntington's disease. University of British Columbia; 2011.
13. Folstein SE. Huntington's disease: a disorder of families. Baltimore: Johns Hopkins University Press; 1989.
14. Michael Hayden, Eli Eyal, Mark Gordan et al. Use of pridopidine for treating dystonias. WO2018; US2017; 04845.
15. Harper PS. Huntington disease. London: WB Saunders; 1996.
16. Aylward EH, Sparks BF, Field KM, Yallapragada V, Shpritz BD, Rosenblatt A, Brandt J, et al. Onset and rate of striatal atrophy in preclinical Huntington's disease. Neurology. 2004;63(1):66–72.
17. Ghosh R, Tabrizi SJ. Clinical features of Huntington's disease. Adv Exp Med Biol. 2018;1049:128.
18. Brandt J, Folstein SE, Folstein MF. Differential cognitive impairment in Alzheimer disease and Huntington's disease. Ann Neurol. 1988;23:555–61.
19. Kay C, Fisher E, Hayden MR. Epidemiology. In: Bates GP, Tabrizi SJ, Jones L, editors. Huntington's disease. 4th ed. Oxford: Oxford University Press; 2014.
20. Nopoulos PC. Huntington disease: a single-gene degenerative disorder of the striatum. Dialog Clin

Neurosci. 2016;18(1):91–8. https://doi.org/10.31887/DCNS.2016.18.1/pnopoulos.
21. Margolis RL, Ross CA. Diagnosis of Huntington's disease. Clin Chem. 2003;49(10):1726. https://doi.org/10.1373/49.10.1726.
22. Tabrizi SJ, Scahill RI, Durr A, Roos RA, Leavitt BR, Jones R, Landwehrmeyer GB, et al. Biological and clinical changes in premanifest and early stage Huntington's disease in the TRACK-HD study: the 12-month longitudinal analysis. Lancet Neurol. 2011;10(1):31–42.
23. Niccolini F, Haider S, Reis Marques T, Muhlert N, Tziortzi AC, Searle GE, Natesan S, et al. Altered PDE10A expression detectable early before symptomatic onset in Huntington's disease. Brain. 2015;138(Pt 10):3016–29.
24. Quinn L, Busse M. Physiotherapy clinical guidelines for Huntington's disease. Neurodegener Dis Manage. 2012;2:2131. https://doi.org/10.2217/nmt.11.86.
25. Frank S. Treatment of Huntington's disease. Neurotherapeutics. 2014;11(1):153160. https://doi.org/10.1007/s13311013-0244z.
26. Bates G, Tabrizi S, Jones L. Huntington's disease. 4th ed. Oxford: Oxford University Press; 2014.
27. Mestre T, Ferreira J, Coelho MM, Rosa M, Sampaio C. Therapeutic interventions for symptomatic treatment in Huntington's disease. Cochrane Database Syst Rev. 2009;8:CD006456. https://doi.org/10.1002/14651858.CD006456.pub2.
28. Huntington's disease, National Health Service, March 2019. https://www.nhs.uk/conditions/huntingtons-disease/treatment/

Translational Value of Natural Pigments with Reference to Healthcare and Cosmetic Applications

16

Tamil Selvam Saravanan, Venugopal Gopikrishnan, Radhakrishnan Manikkam, Manigundan Kaari, Kishore Kumar Annamalai, Jiaojiao Song, and Kasem Soytong

16.1 Introduction

Colouring has become widely used as a result of the civilisational advancement. Pigments have been used as an essential part of our daily lives because of their numerous applications in a variety of industries, including agriculture, textiles, medicine, food, and cosmetics. Prior to the widespread use of synthetic colours which the natural pigments are accessible replaced for safety. They have been applied to many other uses, such as dyeing leather, fur, and natural fibres like wool, cotton, silk, etc. They are also used to colour as cosmetic items and to make inks, watercolours, and artist's paints. Since Perkin was first created synthetic dyes in 1856, the use of natural colours has decreased. Due to the carcinogenicity of the synthetic dyes product and the effects of disposing of their industrial waste in the environment, the manufacture of some synthetic dyes is well known to be outlawed [1].

Many natural pigments besides fulfilling their function for giving colour are known as interesting bioactive compounds from plants and microorganisms with the potential health benefits. These discovered compounds have shown a wide range of applications in medicine, food, pharmacology, agriculture, and cosmetics [2]. Numerous microbial bioactive pigments have been discovered and many of them show antioxidant, anti-inflammatory, and/or antimicrobial properties [3].

Plant-derived colourants are less harmful and more environmentally friendly than synthetic ones, in addition to being biodegradable and environmental friendly. Some of synthetic dyes were prohibited in certain nations due to their negative effects. Plant-derived colourants can be useful for their additional qualities, such as their antioxidant and antimicrobial activity, which can be significantly advantaged for their applications in the cosmetic, textile, and food industries [4]. Since, unlike higher creatures, microorganisms are

T. S. Saravanan
Department of Biotechnology, Sathyabama Institute of Science and Technology, Chennai, Tamil Nadu, India

V. Gopikrishnan (✉) · R. Manikkam · M. Kaari · K. K. Annamalai
Centre for Drug Discovery and Development, Sathyabama Institute of Science and Technology, Chennai, Tamil Nadu, India

J. Song · K. Soytong
Research Institute of Modern Organic Agriculture (RIMOA), Faculty of Agricultural Technology, King Mongkut's Institute of Technology Ladkrabang (KMITL), Bangkok, Thailand

K. Parthasarathy, R. Manikkam (eds.), *Translational Research in Biomedical Sciences: Recent Progress and Future Prospects*, https://doi.org/10.1007/978-981-97-1777-4_16

known to be a source of readily renewed materials that produce a potentially higher yield and a plentiful source of novel bioactive chemicals [5]. Microorganisms produce a wide range of colours with distinctive properties as a result of their interaction with the environment, most of which are connected to the relationship between the microbe and the ecosystem. A wide variety of microbial pigments including carotenoids, flavins, phenazines, quinones, monascines, violaceins, indigoidines, and melanins have been described recently in a variety of conditions [6, 7].

Even though Actinobacteria often produce colour, it is highly varied process in bacteria. Numerous taxa produce a wide range of colours including *Streptomyces*, *Nocardia*, *Thermomonospora*, *Microbispora*, *Streptosporangium*, *Rhodococcus*, and *Kitasatospora* [8]. Their primary are used in food, cosmetic, and textile industries [9, 10], pigments like melanin, quinones, violaceins, and indigoidines have been found to be effective antibacterial agents.

In order to meet the need for food, it is brought by the expanding global human population, industrial-scale and centralised production systems such as large-scale farming, food processing, and distribution which have been grown during the past few decades [11]. As a result, processing plant-based foods such as fruits, vegetables, cereal grains, nuts, and spices produces a lot of by products, many of which are thrown as trash. It has been observed for the recovery of valuable components both economic and environmental grounds [12]. These processing by-products which total about 190 million tonnes are produced annually global including the damaged raw materials, peels or skins, seeds, brans, husks, hulls, cobs, oilseed cakes, spent grains, and molasses. The massive volume of food waste is generated during manufacturing which examined for the recovery of valuable components for both economic and environmental reasons [13]. This review focuses on the formation of natural pigments, discusses their ecological significance, and offers viewpoints from plants, microorganisms, and other natural sources. The significance of natural pigments and escalating industrial interests are also covered [14].

16.2 Natural Pigments

Natural edible pigments are being used more frequently in food additives, printing, and dyeing in recent years due to customers' is increased and focused on the origin and safety of food. The majority of naturally occurring edible colours come from the secondary metabolites of various animals, plants, and microbes. Common sources of natural culinary colours include cochineal extract, caramel, annatto, paprika, turmeric, and curcumin. The majority of these organic food pigments are beneficial to human health. Natural edible colours can be categorised as carotenoids, iridoids, indoles, polyphenols, anthraquinones, pyridines, and pyrroles, among other categories based on their chemical structures. Clarification of the structural skeleton's biosynthesis pathway in this research can serve as a theoretical foundation for the production of colours using biological processes. Through plant and microbial engineering, it also significantly increased the likelihood of acquiring the naturally occurring edible pigments [15].

16.3 Sources of Natural Pigments

Plants and microbes are known as the two main suppliers of natural pigments. However, employing plant-based pigments has a number of drawbacks including low water solubility and sensitivity to light, heat, and pH. However, in a culture medium, which may even be wasted, microbial pigments can be created swiftly and easily. They are not impacted by the weather in contrast to pigments derived from plants. As a result, the development of microbial pigments are developed research areas with the potential for a range of industrial applications [2]. Microbial pigment manufacturing through fermentation technology is more dynamic and cost-effective than plant and animal sources, producing biodegradable chemicals that could find extensive industrial use as colourants. High production yields, affordable production costs, regulatory approval, pigment characterisation, and resilience to environmental conditions like temperature and light which are necessary for the successful application of microbial pigments [16].

16.4 Microbial Sources of Pigments from Filamentous Fungi, Bacteria and Microalgae

16.4.1 Filamentous Fungi

It is investigated that the filamentous fungi, *Monascus*, *Fusarium*, *Penicillium*, and *Neurospora*, are reported as the new sources of biologically useful natural colours for using in food, feed, and cosmetic products. The manufacture of ethanol, animal feed, and pigments from waste sources can be accomplished using such edible fungi in biorefineries [17]. According to [18], filamentous fungi have been employed in the industrial production of numerous commercially viable goods such as enzymes, antibiotics, feed products, etc. The idea of a biorefinery which involves in turning raw materials into finished goods with additional value that is well-known among scientists. Therefore, research should be done to diversify the current and future facilities for the fermentation-based manufacture of many new and important goods as well as by-products. A few strains of Ascomycestes filamentous fungi are considered as potential pigment producers including *Talaromyces*, e.g., *T. purpurogenus* and *T. atro-roseus* (producing red pigments), *Cordyceps unilateralis* (deep blood red pigment) [14], *Herpotrichia rhodosticta* (orange), *Curvularia lunata*, and *Drechslera* spp. (many different pigments). In order to compete with chemically generated colours, natural-origin pigments, such as filamentous fungi's carotenoids, are valuable bioactive substances [16].

16.4.2 Fungal Pigments as Food Colourants

The majority of research on fungal pigments is investigated for food colourings. Numerous researchers have been known that fungal pigments may be used in a variety of industries, particularly the food industry [19, 20]. Numerous studies have evaluated the possibility of using fungal pigments as food additives or as food colourants in various food products [20]. Some fungi-derived pigments including *Monascus* pigments, pink red from *P. oxalicum*, riboflavin from *Ashbya gossypii*, and beta-carotene from *B. trispora*, have previously been approved for using as food colourings [16, 21–23].

16.4.3 Fungal Pigments as Antimicrobial Agents

According to numerous studies, microbial pigments have significantly known as health advantages over synthetic pigments [24, 25]. Numerous investigations have demonstrated that certain species of the fungi, *Monascus*, *Fusarium*, *Talaromyces*, *Trichoderma*, *Penicillium*, and *Aspergillus* as well as the yeast *R. glutinis* that have released the pigments or pigment extracts to exhibit antibacterial action against certain pathogenic bacteria, yeast, and fungi. All of these investigations by [22, 26, 27] pointed out that the possible application of bioactive pigments as food preservatives or antibacterial additives in the food and pharmaceutical industries. Similarly, the antimicrobial potential of various textiles (cotton, silk, etc.) are dyed with the pigments of fungi (*A. alternata* and *Thermomyces* spp.). The positive outcomes suggested the potential use in producing specific medical products such as bandages, suture threads, face masks, etc. [16, 26, 28].

Chaetomium cupreum CC3003 produced rotiorinols A-C, (−)-rotiorin and *epi*-isochromophilone II, rubrorotiorin which inhibited *Candida albicans* [29]. Rotiorinol is a natural product pigment derived from *C. cupreum* CC3003 that produces rotiorinol, which is red colour and amorphous powder structure. It is significantly inhibited *Rigidophorus microporus* causing rot of Oil palms. The inhibition of mycelial growth after treated with rotiorinol at concentrations of 10, 50, 100, and 250 μg/L which were 29, 49, 97, and 99%, respectively, and the dry mycelial inhibition were 31, 42, 97, and 99%, respectively. ED_{50} of rotiorinol was 26 μg/L. It implies an antibiosis as a control mechanism of *C. cupreum* against *R. microporus* [16].

16.4.4 Fungal Pigments as Antioxidant Agents

The microbial pigments like carotenoids, violacein, and naphthoquinones have reported the potential to be antioxidants [3, 20, 30] who discussed the antioxidant potential of pigments from certain fungi and yeast. *Sanghuangporus baumii*, *Stemphylium lycopersici*, *Penicillium* spp., *Thermomyces* spp., *Chaetomium* spp., and *Trichoderma* spp. (*T. afroharzianum*) are among the fungi whose pigments are evaluated for their antioxidant activity. Studies on these fungi confirmed their promising antioxidant potential and potential applications in the healthcare industry [16, 31, 32].

16.4.5 Fungal Pigments as Cytotoxic Agents

Researchers have been used a variety of techniques to determine the cytotoxic activity of pigments from specific fungal isolates (*F. oxysporum, T. verruculosus*, and *Chaetomium* spp.) including the sour orange seed toxicity assay, the yeast toxicity test (YTT) using *Saccharomyces cerevisiae*, the brine shrimp lethality bioassay and the cell counting kit-8 (CCK-8) assay [9, 33, 34] supported that the potential use of pigments in a variety of businesses related to health and pharmaceuticals. The harmless nature of pigments has been shown their possible use in cosmetics and dyeing which is indicated by a recent study on the evaluation of cutaneous toxicity of pigments of *Thermomyces* spp. and *P. purpurogenum* in Wistar rats [16, 35].

16.4.6 Fungal Pigments as Anticancer Agents

It is well known that some species of fungi produce secondary metabolites against anticancer and antitumor properties. The fungal pigments have been implicated in several investigations as potential cancer treatments. Pigments of Monascus species (*M. purpureus* and *M. pilosus*) such as monascin, ankaflavin, monaphilone A-B, monasphilone A-B, monapilol A-D, and monapurone A-C are proved against anticancer/antitumor, and different types of cancers such as mouse skin carcinoma, human laryngeal carcinoma, human colon adenocarcinoma, human hepatocellular carcinoma, and pulmonary adenocarcinoma [36]. Alterporriol K, Alterporriol L, and Alterporriol M derived from *Alternaria* spp., benzoquinone from *Fusarium* spp., and an unidentified red pigment from *Fusarium chlamydosporum*. In addition, *Monascus* sp. is reported to against anticancer, antitumor or antiproliferative activity, primarily against human breast cancer cell lines, human breast cancer cell lines (MCF-7, MDA-MB-435, and MCF-7 b), whereas hypocrellin D from *S. bambusicola* showed anticancer activity against other cancer cell lines, Bel-7721, A-549, and Anip-973 [16, 37–39].

16.4.7 Fungal Pigments in the Cosmetic Industry

The cosmetics industry is investigated for new kinds of natural pigments to replace synthetic pigments as the market for natural products grows. Fungal pigments are among the natural pigments whose application in cosmetics is rising quickly due to their benefits. There are reported for application of fungal pigments, particularly melanin, carotenoids, lycopene, etc. in cosmetics, sunscreens, sun lotions, sunblocks, face creams, anti-aging facials, etc. [30, 40, 41]. It is noted that some fungal pigments from *Monascus* pigments and *Monascus*-like pigments are ready entered to the market for using in cosmetics including lipsticks, skin conditioners and skin care products [16].

16.4.8 Fungal Pigments in the Textile Industry

The textile industry is the largest industry after agriculture in terms of economic contribution and employment generation. Its majorly depends on synthetic dyes for dyeing different types of fabrics (cotton, silk, and wool). Currently, natural pigments from fungi, with their many advantages (eco-friendly, non-toxic, easy degradation, high colourfastness, high staining capability, etc.) over hazardous synthetic pigments which have proved to be a good alternative to the synthetic dyes in the textile industry. Many investigations are shown that organic pigments produced by fungi as extensive applications in the textile industry [16, 23, 24, 40].

Only a small number of research investigation have known to be using fungal pigments in the textile industry, particularly for dying various kinds of fibres like cotton, silk, and wool. For various types of fabrics including wool, cotton yarn, silk, polyester and nylon. The numerous studies on the dyeing potential of pigments from different species of fungi (*Monascus, Fusarium, Aspergillus, Penicillium, Talaromyces, Trichoderma, Alternaria, Curvularia, Chlorociboria, Scytalidium, Cordyceps, Acrostalagmus, Bisporomyces, Cunningham*) are reported [9, 16, 42, 43]. Studies on the dyeing potential of pigments from wood spalting fungi (red pigment from *S. cuboideum*, yellow pigment from *S. ganodermophthorum*, and green pigment *C. aeruginosa*) are shown the possible use of these pigments for dyeing bleached cotton, spun polyacrylic, spun polyamide (nylon 6.6), worsted wool, spun polyester (Dacron 54), and garment fabrics, because of their high stability and good colourfastness for washing [43]. According to a different study, natural oils cannot be used with these fungal pigments since they had become unstable in them [42]. These fungal pigments exhibit good colour stability, colourfastness qualities, and dye absorbing capability. These fungi-based pigments are also safe for using in human skin and no negative effects for clothing. As a result, there is potential for the use of fungal pigments in the textile and apparel industries [16].

16.4.9 Fungal Pigments in Dyeing Woods or as Colour Modifiers

To increase the commercial value of various types of wood samples, dyes made from the pigment are produced by wood-decaying fungi such as *T. versicolor, X. polymorpha, I. hispidus, S. cuboideum, B. adusta, C. aeruginosa,* and *Arthrographis cuboidea* [44–46]. The presence of blue stain on wood samples from *Pinus* spp. is successfully reduced by using red, green, and yellow pigments derived from *S. cuboideum, S. ganodermophthorum,* and *C. aeruginosa* [16, 44].

16.4.10 Fungal Pigments in (Opto) Electronics

According to a recent study of the (opto) electronic characteristics of blends of the pigment xylindein extracted from *C. aeruginosa*, this pigment has shown a high photostability and electron mobility in amorphous films, suggesting that it may be used to create organic semiconductor materials that are sustainable and long-lasting [16, 47, 48].

16.4.11 Bacterial Pigments

The most prevalent bacterial pigments are carotenoids, aryl polyenes, melanins, phenazines, quinones, tambjamines, prodigiosines, and violacein. In rare circumstances, aryl polyenes are esterified with a dialkylresorcinol system. Many bacterial pigments showed potential medicinal applications, such as antibacterial, antimalarial, and anticancer activities. These pigments are known for their antioxidant and UV protection qualities.

Melanins is ranged in colour from black to brown to olive, carotenoids are ranged in colour from red, yellow, and pink to violet, and actinorhodin-related blue pigments are shown to be the most prevalent pigments which produced by Actinobacteria. Carotenoids are a class of pigments that exhibit antioxidant properties and safety to use as natural colourants in the cosmetic, culinary, pharmaceutical, and textile sectors [49].

16.4.12 Bacterial Pigments in Food Industries

Recombinant DNA technology allows for a multiple-fold boost in bacterial pigment production. Microorganisms produce a variety of pigments including flavin, melanin, monascin, violacein, carotenoids, quinones, and many others [30], which can be used in the modern food industry both as pro stabilisers and colourants due to their free radical scavenging activity [50]. Astaxanthin is a pinkish-red pigment made by the bacteria *Agrobacterium aurantiacum* and *Paracoccus carotinifaciens*. It is reported to be a prime example of a powerful antioxidant when using as a food colouring, not only adds a pleasing hue but also lengthens the shelf life of the item which serve as a preservative [51]. *Bradyrhizobium* spp. produces canthaxanthin which is similar to astaxanthin. Currently, the food sector uses this orange pigment as a powerful antioxidant [49, 52].

16.4.13 Bacterial Pigments in the Cosmetic Industry

Because of the toxicity and carcinogenicity of synthetic colours, the cosmetic industry has likewise shifted to safer substitutes. One of these is bacterial pigments, which are inexpensive but very effective. According to [53], the majority of these pigments are obtained from marine microorganisms or extremophiles. The principal cause of skin ageing is the breakdown of the extracellular matrix in the dermal and epidermal layers, which is mostly regulated by the intrinsic factor (genetics and dietary habits). The external environment, however, smoke, pollution, UV exposure, weather, etc. plays a role in the early ageing of the skin. Carotenoids are the active components found in anti-aging creams among all known pigments.

According to [54], carotenoid is a lipid-soluble pigment that *Deinococcus radiodurans* produces. It has a distinctive orange hue resembling that of a carrot and is highly effective at reducing the generation of ROS, which significantly damages cells. Consequently, it is a component of anti-aging products like provitamin A. High antioxidant content is the reason why cosmetics have an anti-aging effect. Astaxanthin is a pigment made by bacterium *Haematococcus pluvialis* which is well known for its superior antioxidant qualities. These antioxidants consume the free radicals that the cells produce [55]. Myxol and saproxanthin are the other two antioxidants that are most frequently employed in the cosmetics sector. These carotenoid-family pigments were identified from marine bacterial strains that belong to the Flavobacteriaceae family [49, 56].

16.4.14 Bacterial Pigments in Textile Industry

Microbial pigments are currently preferred by the textile industry since they are non-carcinogenic and environmentally safe. Skin reactions and the emission of potentially hazardous substances during synthesis are only way that synthetic colours might hurt your health. Silk, wool, nylon, and acrylics can be dyed using prodigiosins which are vivid red pigments obtained from *Vibrio* species [57]. Prodigiosin is a compound made by *Serratia marcescens* SB08 which is promise as a natural dye for a range of materials, including acrylic, silk, polyester, and cotton [49]. The materials were significantly safer since the dyed pigments from microbes still expressed antimicrobial properties against bacteria like *P. aeruginosa, E. coli,* and *Bacillus subtilis* for human use [49].

16.4.15 Actinobacterial Pigments

Streptomyces is a species of Actinobacteria that produces specialised metabolites with a variety of bioactivities including antioxidant, anticancer, antibiofilm, antifouling, and antibiotic activities. This makes Actinobacteria significant in the field of biotechnology [58, 59]. *Streptomyces* sp. S45 is reported to be a producer of pinkish-brown pigment which shown anti-HIV and anti-TB activities [59, 60]. Compounds of the actinorhodin family from different strains of *Streptomyces coelicolor* showed the potential applications as food colourants or antimicrobial agents [61–65]. The ability of *Streptomyces* to produce antibiofilm/antifouling pigmented extracts and compounds that are effective against micro- and macrofouling organisms [66, 67].

16.5 Pigment Produced by Algae

16.5.1 Red Algae

Red algae generate both chlorophyll and the red protein pigment phycoerythrin. Due to its ability to absorb blue light while reflecting red light [68]. Chromatophores is a covalent bond which formed between the protein and phycobilins. These algal species can carry out photosynthesis since the aforementioned pigment is presented in them [69]. Red algae including Irish moss, *Gracillaria* spp., *Porphyria* spare occasionally used in cosmetics [70].

16.5.2 Green Algae

It produces chlorophyll, a pigment used in photosynthetic processes and able to store light energy. Haemoglobin is the red pigment found in human red blood cells which is similar to this pigment. It moisturises the algal species and provides oxygen to its exposed surface, preventing it from drying out. According to [71] stated that it also possesses anti-inflammatory properties. *Chlorella vulgaris, Ulva lactuca,* and other varieties of green algae are among the ones used in cosmetics. Since beta-carotene is a precursor to vitamin A, it is utilised in dietary supplements and colourants as a nutraceutical [72]. Beta-carotene can be generated from *Dunaliella salina* [70].

16.5.3 Brown Algae

The chloroplast contains fucoxanthin, a brown algal pigment. Additionally, it contains anti-inflammatory qualities, suppresses tyrosinase, and increases collagen formation, a structural protein that helps to lessen or manage skin pigmentation and tends to scatter with age. It also slows down the ageing process of the skin. Additionally, the pigment keeps the skin moisturised and keeps the cells healthy [73]. Examples include *Isochrysis* spp., *Laminaria digilata, Postelsiapa maeformis*, a few species of brown algae used in cosmetics and others [70].

16.6 Industrial Applications of Algal Pigments

16.6.1 Food Industry

In general, phytocyanin dyes are non-toxic and non-carcinogenic. Phycocyanin is used as a food colour for milkshakes, ice cream, chewing gum, soft drinks, alcoholic drinks, desserts, and sweet cakes. It offers a number of benefits, including less expensive production, a higher yield, simpler extraction, and more affordable raw materials [70, 74, 75].

16.6.2 Textile

Algae have colour pigments that utilised as food colouring and the textile industry to dye clothes because they have diversed antibacterial and antioxidant characteristics. Algal pigments could be effectively employed as natural fabric colours rather than synthetic dyes because extraction techniques are practical from an economic, environmental, and health standpoint. There is further worked to be done in the areas of colour characterisation, colour fastness, and dyeing efficiency as well as the antibacterial characteristics of various algal pigments [70, 76].

16.6.3 Pharmaceuticals

Algal metabolites and pigments have been shown in increasing numbers of clinical investigations to provide health advantages, making them a safe and effective alternative to chemically synthesised medications. Contrary to the liver, the human body converts beta-carotene into vitamin A through bodily tissues, preventing the buildup of toxins there. Antioxidant properties are found in beta-carotene. Phycobiliproteins, phycocyanin, phycobilins, and phycoerythrins are examples of pigment and protein complexes generated from microalgae that are commercially available as anti-inflammatory, antioxidant, antiviral, hepato-, nephro-, and neuroprotective medicines [70, 77, 78].

16.6.4 Cosmetics

Algae are used in cosmetics and skin care products due to their great photophysical qualities, high nutritional value, antioxidant nature, and anti-aging components. Algal pigments are used to give soaps vibrant, unusual colours. Due to its long-lasting qualities, algae (macroalgae) is a source of pigments for numerous hair colour products. Microalgae can be used in cosmetics and cosmetic products to achieve benefits like hair, nutritive, skin soothing, anti-inflammatory, antioxidant, skin-elasticity, collagen synthesis, anti-wrinkle, emollient, moisturising, skin softening, tightening effect and stimulates metabolism, skin-conditioning agent, and de-pigmentation [70, 79, 80].

16.6.5 Cancer Studies

Phycobiliproteins, chlorophylls, and carotenoids are related by triggering apoptosis and DNA activation of cancer cells in breast lines, marine pigments such as carotene, fucoxanthin, astaxanthin, violaxanthin, halosynthiaxanthin, lutein, zeaxanthin, and canthaxanthin which are reported to be a powerful antiproliferative effects. Phycoerythrin and phycocyanin glow at a particular wavelength. Phycobilins can be employed as chemicals because of the clear and dependable light that their fluorescence produces. The antibodies are put in the cell solution after being chemically attached to the pigments [70, 81, 82].

16.6.6 Extremophilic Pigments

The potential for biotechnology to improve our lives in exciting new ways is virtually limitless. Many of the chemical processes that result in these chemicals can be fully optimised for efficient and economical outcomes by operating at extremes of temperature, pressure, salinity and pH. There are numerous creatures (extremophiles) that can survive in harsh conditions and are a great source of natural colours [5].

16.6.7 Pigment Production by Cold-Adapted Microbes

Due of the negative impacts that synthetic dyes, there is currently known to be a greater demand for natural pigments made from microorganisms. Therefore, it is essential to look into new potential sources for microorganisms that produce pigment. One such ecosystem is the cryosphere, where microorganisms that create natural colours live as a defence against ecological stressors to jeopardise human life. Exploring these microbes would undoubtedly yield potential sources of new coloured compounds with broader biotechnological applications. These undiscovered bacteria, particularly the novel species, may be concerned as a source of pigments that can be exploited in the production of novel medicinal compounds as well as in the textile and food sectors. To get rid of harmful synthetic dyes, efforts should be made to create colours from these bacteria in a cost-effective manner through strain improvement and optimisation. To avoid causing environmental disruption, sustainable utilisation of these biological resources from the cryosphere should be prioritised. The world community should establish a clear ethical and moral policy for specific concerns concerning possession of these resources. Several cryospheric habitats, such as Antarctica, should be thought of as a collective legacy for humanity. The uses of these pigments derived from cold-adapted microbes would undoubtedly known to be more varied due to their special properties and numerous fresh biotechnology sectors would be undoubtedly launched.

Thirty bacterial strains that can produce carotenoids found in Fildes Peninsula, King George Island, Antarctica, according to [83]. *Planococcus faecalis* produces carotenoids is identified by [84] Antarctic penguin faeces. According to research conducted in Antarctica, heterotrophic bacteria produce carotenoids as a tactical defence against environmental challenges [6]. The psychrotrophic bacterial strain, *Janthinobacterium lividum* was discovered in Alaskan soil and prodigiosin was recovered [85]. According to [5], a number of bacterial strains that produce red pigment were found in a deep ice core taken from the Yuzhufeng Glacier on the Tibetan Plateau. In Antarctic volcanic island sediments [86] described the genes in charge of the 3-oxoacyl-[acyl-carrying protein] reductase (K00059) enzyme's biosynthesis. This enzyme is a member of the type II fatty acid synthesis pathway connected to the creation of prodigiosin.

16.6.8 Pigments Producing Microbes from Himalayan Regions

In the high-altitude glacial habitats, pigmented bacteria were presented in very high concentrations [5, 87–89]. For instance, bacteria that produce colour have been found in ice cores from various depths of the Puruogangri glacier in the Tibetan Plateau [87]. Mount Everest's east Rongbuk glacier yielded a total of 1385 bacterial isolates, of which 84.9% were determined to be pigmented [88]. Further research revealed that the concentrations of culturable and pigment-producing bacteria were higher in the middle of the ice core and successively decreasing in the upper and lower portions. The adaptive response was validated by the large proportion of coloured bacteria in the high-altitude glacier samples. From the ice core samples of the Yuzhufeng glacier, which is located at 3800 masl in the Tibetan Plateau, another study revealed culturable bacteria from four phyla [5].

16.6.9 Natural Pigments from Organic Waste

The recovery of high-added value compounds (like pigments) from vegetable food waste that may be used as food additives (like colourants) which one of the many new business opportunities is being created by approaches influenced by the circular economy model that have been continuously growing globally. Food waste is a problem that affects the entire world and does not appear to be getting any worse, creating problems in the economy, the environment, and society. Furthermore, research towards far safer, natural, and environmentally friendly pigments has been sparked by the connection between synthetic colours and unfavourable effects on human health. Food waste (FW) is a problem that affects the entire world and does not seem to be getting any worse [90]. This raises economic, environmental, and social issues. Since this issue has been ignored for so long, waste is being observed at every stage of the food chain [91].

According to recent estimates, there are 1.6 billion tonnes of FW produced annually, of which 1.3 to 1.6 billion tonnes are edible, with a market value of US $750 million. About 47 million tonnes of FW are produced annually by common families, with the remainder coming from processing (17 million tonnes), catering (10.5 million tonnes), primary production (9.1 million tonnes), and distribution (4.6 million tonnes). FW, which totals $27 billion in the USA, primarily comprises of meat and fish (30%), vegetables (19%), and dairy products (17%). According to estimates is made by [91], the absence of efforts to reduce FW might result in an annual rise of 126 million tonnes or roughly 40%. Only via a valuable food chain control and a better use of the limited resources available can an efficient waste management be achieved. Recent research has concentrated on using vegetal wastes as a source of natural pigments while keeping in mind notions from the Circular Economy.

16.6.10 Extraction Protocols on Microbial Pigments

An effective and ecologically secure extraction technique is ultrasound-assisted extraction (UAE). From among the methods examined, enzymatic UAE produced the maximum yield (92.73 mg/g dry biomass) and extraction efficiency (78%) of the natural food colourant C-phycocyanin from dry biomass of *Arthrospira platensis* [92]. Due to its reproducibility, speed, homogeneous heating, and high extraction yields, microwave aided extraction (MEA) has been regarded as a superior method for isolating microalgae pigments. Water can be utilised as a green solvent in MAE because it is the safest, non-toxic, non-flammable, and noncorrosive solvent available and UAE for efficient extraction of several metabolites from microbial matrices. The CO_2 based supercritical fluid extraction (SFE) approach is served as an alternative to the conventional extraction by organic solvents [93]. SFE has been acknowledged as an environmentally friendly, long-lasting method for the selective separation of molecules, including chemicals that are thermolabile. There have been reported the use of SFE for the extraction of carotenoids from a variety of substrates on a commercial and laboratory scale [94, 95]. Ionic liquids (IL), pulsed electric field (PEF)-assisted extraction and pressurised liquid extraction (PLE; also known as accelerated solvent extraction—ASE) have been mentioned as effective and practical green methods to increase the extraction yield of pigments from microbial biomass.

16.7 Genomics and Metagenomics

Finding gene clusters involved in pigment production may be made easier with the use of a genomics method. The genomic study demonstrated the ability of microbes to create particular secondary metabolites, even when those compounds are silent or criptic in laboratory growth conditions. In fact, it has been found that these categories encompass around 90% of the secondary metabolite biosynthetic gene clusters [96]. Pigment gene clusters have been found in several recent investigations [97, 98]. When compared to closely similar filamentous fungi, the industrial strain *M. purpureus* YY-1's genome information demonstrated adaptation to starch-based diets. According to [99], correlated transcriptomics study also identified the highly expressed genes for pigment creation during carbon shortage, offering important information for industrial applications. The tryptophan genes cluster was discovered using pangenomics study to be crucial for *Pseudomonas fluorescens'* ability to produce blue pigments [100]. The identification and/or confirmation of generated pigments by novel microbes is supported by genomics information, which is also essential for increasing microbial pigment production by genetic modification [2, 101].

Even from uncultured materials, metagenomics analysis of assembled genomes from various microbial phyla allows for the collection of data from unidentified microorganisms. In this regard, the metagenomics research of microbial networks in a community has greatly benefited from the use of next-generation sequencing platforms [102]. With the use of this latter omics methodology, it was possible to identify unique pigments from extremophile bacteria, such as those found in hot springs [103] or marine sources [104] and to circumvent the issue of uncultivable microorganisms. To investigate microorganisms from these harsh conditions, metagenomics may provide advantages over conventional laboratory approaches [105]. Metagenomics can therefore be particularly helpful in the search for new microbial pigments.

16.8 Proteomics and Metabolomics

According to [106], proteomics is recorded as an effective method for identifying proteins on a wide scale and gives a comprehensive overview of all the proteins that an organism expresses overall. Studying proteins involved in pigment synthesis has been done using a comparative proteomics methodology. Although studies primarily focus on plant pigments, the generation of microbial pigments has recently been examined using a proteomics method. The polyextremophilic bacterium *Deinococcus radiodurans* response to oxidative stress, the synthesis of pigments by *Monascus purpureus* under high ammonium chloride concentration, the pigmentation factors in *Pseudomonas fluorescens* ITEM 17298, the air-isolated *Aspergillus* sp. from the International Space Station, and other studies are among them.

All analytical profiling methods that enable the detection of a significant number of metabolites presented in biological samples are included in metabolomics. Metabolomics provides a window on metabolic pathways by combining high throughput analytical chemistry and multivariate data analysis [107]. Untargeted metabolomics approach was chosen as a good methodology in recent studies [108, 109] to seek and study the metabolic routes on pigment formation. In order to identify the biosynthetic enzyme clusters of the producing strains, quantitative proteomics and metabolomics are combined to define connections between abundance of natural products such as pigments and changes in the microbial protein poll.

16.9 Pigment Synthesis Through Genetic Engineering

Previous research has demonstrated that "omics" approaches can aid in understanding the barriers to the manufacture of pigments, and that genetic engineering technologies can be utilised to overcome such barriers and improve pigment production for large-scale applications. Through techniques that activate transcriptionally silent gene clusters and/or recombinant DNA technologies to boost the manufacture of secondary metabolites, it is possible to accomplish the overexpression of gene clusters linked to pigment biosynthesis [110]. The examination of the biosynthesis of microbial secondary metabolites may be supported by the integration of "omics" results with genetic engineering methods, and this can aid in the development of a comprehensive integrated to approach for the identification of bioactive molecules, including pigments.

16.10 Conclusion

Natural pigments have several application possibilities in the food, pharmaceutical, and cosmetics industries since they are safe, renewable and easily accessible. Since numerous microbial pigments exhibit pertinent biological activity, they are enormous potential applications in a variety of fields including medicine. By cultivating coloured microorganisms on waste materials, and improvements in microbial biotechnology are enhanced cultivation techniques and enable optimum pigment outputs. In order to encourage the creation of these pigments for potential usage on a biotechnological scale, the omics science can aid in the knowledge of biosynthetic routes. Future studies should be done to improve the processes for extracting and purifying pigments, looking for methods that are easy to use and can be scaled up while still being safe for the environment. Because the current regulation is frequently based on local cultural tradition, using microbial pigments in foods, nutraceuticals, and cosmetics presents regulatory hurdles. The biggest obstacle to commercialising either native or non-native microbial pigments is the regulatory hurdles and accompanying customer preferences, even if native pigment-producing bacteria represent the stronger regulatory and market acceptance. Additionally, a sufficient toxicity assessment of potential bioactive pigments is required to support the delivery of such natural compounds with positive health effects. Additionally, microbial bioactive pigments have a definite multidisciplinary component that links biotechnology, food and medicinal sciences to produce compounds with both colourant and nutraceutical activities as well as potential health advantages.

Acknowledgement Authors thank the management of Sathyabama Institute of Science and Technology, Tamil Nadu for their Seed grant and encouragement.

References

1. Kiki MJ. Biopigments of microbial origin and their application in the cosmetic industry. Cosmetics. 2023;10:47. https://doi.org/10.3390/cosmetics10020047.
2. Venil CK, Dufossé L, Renuka Devi P. Bacterial pigments: sustainable compounds with market potential for pharma and food industry. Front Sustain Food Syst. 2020;4:100. https://doi.org/10.3389/fsufs.2020.00100.
3. Ramesh C, Vinithkumar NV, Kirubagaran R, Venil CK, Dufossé L. Multifaceted applications of microbial pigments: current knowledge, challenges and future directions for public health implications. Microorganisms. 2019;7(7):186.
4. Brudzyńska P, Sionkowska A, Grisel M. Plant-derived colorants for food, cosmetic and textile industries: a review. Materials. 2021;14(13):3484.

5. Shen L, Liu Y, Wang N, Jiao N, Xu B, Liu X. Variation with depth of the abundance, diversity and pigmentation of culturable bacteria in a deep ice core from the Yuzhufeng Glacier. Extremophiles. 2018;22(1):29–38.
6. Dieser M, Greenwood M, Foreman CM. Carotenoid pigmentation in Antarctic heterotrophic bacteria as a strategy to withstand environmental stresses. Arct Antarct Alp Res. 2010;42(4):396–405.
7. Gao Q, Garcia-Pichel F. Microbial ultraviolet sunscreens. Nat Rev Microbiol. 2011;9(11):791–802. https://doi.org/10.1038/nrmicro2649.
8. Rana S, Salam MD. Antimicrobial potential of actinomycetes isolated from soil samples of Punjab, India. J Microbiol Exp. 2014;1(2):63–8.
9. Chadni Z, Rahaman MH, Jerin I, Hoque KMF, Reza MA. Extraction and optimisation of red pigment production as secondary metabolites from *Talaromyces verruculosus* and its potential use in textile industries. Mycology. 2017;8(1):1–10.
10. Schweiggert RM, Carle R. Carotenoid production by bacteria, microalgae, and fungi. In: Carotenoids in nutrition: therapy, spectroscopy and technology; 2016. p. 217–40. https://doi.org/10.1002/9781118622223.ch12.
11. King T, Cole M, Farber JM, Eisenbrand G, Zabaras D, Fox EM, Hill JP. Food safety for food security: relationship between global megatrends and developments in food safety. Trends Food Sci Technol. 2017;68:160. https://doi.org/10.1016/j.tifs.2017.08.014.
12. Galanakis CM. Recovery of high added-value components from food wastes: conventional, emerging technologies and commercialized applications. Trends Food Sci Technol. 2012;26(2):68–87. https://doi.org/10.1016/j.tifs.2012.03.003.
13. Sharma M, Usmani Z, Gupta VK, Bhat R. Valorization of fruits and vegetable wastes and by-products to produce natural pigments. Crit Rev Biotechnol. 2021;41(4):535. https://doi.org/10.1080/07388551.2021.1873240.
14. Dufossé L, Fouillaud M, Caro Y, Mapari SAS, Sutthiwong N. Filamentous fungi are large-scale producers of pigments and colorants for the food industry. Curr Opin Biotechnol. 2014;26:56. https://doi.org/10.1016/j.copbio.2013.09.007.
15. Shen N, Ren J, Liu Y, Sun W, Li Y, Xin H, Cui Y. Natural edible pigments: a comprehensive review of resource, chemical classification, biosynthesis pathway, separated methods and application. Food Chem. 2023;403:134422.
16. Lagashetti AC, Dufossé L, Singh SK, Singh PN. Fungal pigments and their prospects in different industries. Microorganisms. 2019;7(12):604. https://doi.org/10.3390/microorganisms7120604.
17. Gmoser R, Ferreira JA, Lennartsson PR, Taherzadeh MJ. Filamentous ascomycetes fungi as a source of natural pigments. Fungal Biol Biotechnol. 2017;4(1):4. https://doi.org/10.1186/s40694-017-0033-2.
18. Ferreira JA, Mahboubi A, Lennartsson PR, Taherzadeh MJ. Waste biorefineries using filamentous ascomycetes fungi: present status and future prospects. Bioresour Technol. 2016;215:334. https://doi.org/10.1016/j.biortech.2016.03.018.
19. Lebeau J, Venkatachalam M, Fouillaud M, Petit T, Vinale F, Dufossé L, Caro Y. Production and new extraction method of polyketide red pigments produced by ascomycetous fungi from terrestrial and marine habitats. J Fungi. 2017;3(3):34. https://doi.org/10.3390/jof3030034.
20. Sen T, Barrow CJ, Deshmukh SK. Microbial pigments in the food industry—challenges and the way forward. Front Nutr. 2019;6:7. https://doi.org/10.3389/fnut.2019.00007.
21. Dufossé L. Microbial production of food grade pigments microbial production of food grade pigments. ResearchGate. 2015;44(November).
22. Kim D, Ku S. Beneficial effects of Monascus sp. KCCM 10093 pigments and derivatives: a mini review. Molecules. 2018;23(1):98. https://doi.org/10.3390/molecules23010098.
23. Venkatachalam M, Shum-Chéong-sing A, Caro Y, Dufossé L, Fouillaud M. Ovat analysis and response surface methodology based on nutrient sources for optimization of pigment production in the marine-derived fungus Talaromyces albobiverticillius 30548 submerged fermentation. Mar Drugs. 2021;19(5):248. https://doi.org/10.3390/md19050248.
24. Akilandeswari P, Pradeep BV. Exploration of industrially important pigments from soil fungi. Appl Microbiol Biotechnol. 2016;100(4):1631–43. https://doi.org/10.1007/s00253-015-7231-8.
25. Nagpal N, Munjal N, Chatterjee S. Microbial pigments with health benefits—a mini review. Trends Biosci. 2011;4(2):157.
26. Gunjal A, Bhagat DS. Diversity of actinomycetes in Western Ghats. In: Microbial diversity and ecology in hotspots; 2021. https://doi.org/10.1016/B978-0-323-90148-2.00007-9.
27. Wang W, Liao Y, Chen R, Hou Y, Ke W, Zhang B, Gao M, Shao Z, Chen J, Li F. Chlorinated azaphilone pigments with antimicrobial and cytotoxic activities isolated from the deep sea derived fungus Chaetomium sp. NA-S01-R1. Mar Drugs. 2018;16(2):61. https://doi.org/10.3390/md16020061.
28. Yolmeh M, Hamedi H, Khomeiri M. Antimicrobial activity of pigments extracted from Rhodotorula glutinis against some bacteria and fungi. Zahedan J Res Med Sci. 2016;18(12):e4954. https://doi.org/10.17795/zjrms-4954.
29. Kanokmedhakul S, Kanokmedhakul K, Nasomjai P, Loungsysouphanh S, Soytong K, Isobe M, Kongsaeree K, Prabpai S, Suksamran A. Antifungal Azaphilones from the fungus, *Chaetomium cupreum* CC3003. J Nat Prod. 2006;69:891–5.
30. Narsing Rao MP, Xiao M, Li WJ. Fungal and bacterial pigments: secondary metabolites with wide

applications. Front Microbiol. 2017;8:1113. https://doi.org/10.3389/fmicb.2017.01113.
31. Heo YM, Kim K, Kwon SL, Na J, Lee H, Jang S, Kim CH, Jung J, Kim JJ. Investigation of filamentous fungi producing safe, functional water-soluble pigments. Mycobiology. 2018;46(3):269. https://doi.org/10.1080/12298093.2018.1513114.
32. Poorniammal R, Prabhu S, Sakthi AR. Evaluation of In vitro antioxidant activity of fungal pigments. Pharma Innov J. 2019;8(6):326–30.
33. Malik K, Tokas J, Anand RC. Characterization and cytotoxicity assay of pigment producing microbes. Int J Curr Microbiol App Sci. 2016;5(6):370. https://doi.org/10.20546/ijcmas.2016.506.042.
34. Wang W, Chen R, Luo Z, Wang W, Chen J. Antimicrobial activity and molecular docking studies of a novel anthraquinone from a marine-derived fungus *Aspergillus versicolor*. Nat Prod Res. 2018;32(5):558. https://doi.org/10.1080/14786419.2017.1329732.
35. Poorniammal R, Parthiban M, Gunasekaran S, Murugesan R, Thilagavathi G. Natural dye production from Thermomyces sp fungi for textile application. Indian J Fibre Text Res. 2013;38(3):276–9.
36. Hsu YW, Hsu LC, Liang YH, Kuo YH, Pan TM. Monaphilones A-C, three new antiproliferative azaphilone derivatives from *Monascus purpureus* NTU 568. J Agric Food Chem. 2010;58(14):8211. https://doi.org/10.1021/jf100930j.
37. Fang LZ, Qing C, Shao HJ, Yang YD, Dong ZJ, Wang F, Zhao W, Yang WQ, Liu JK. Hypocrellin D, a cytotoxic fungal pigment from fruiting bodies of the ascomycete Shiraia bambusicola. J Antibiot. 2006;59(6):351. https://doi.org/10.1038/ja.2006.49.
38. Soumya K, Narasimha Murthy K, Sreelatha GL, Tirumale S. Characterization of a red pigment from *Fusarium chlamydosporum* exhibiting selective cytotoxicity against human breast cancer MCF-7 cell lines. J Appl Microbiol. 2018;125(1):148. https://doi.org/10.1111/jam.13756.
39. Zheng L, Cai Y, Zhou L, Huang P, Ren X, Zuo A, Meng X, Xu M, Liao X. Benzoquinone from Fusarium pigment inhibits the proliferation of estrogen receptor-positive MCF.7 cells through the NF-κB pathway via estrogen receptor signaling. Int J Mol Med. 2017;39(1):39–46. https://doi.org/10.3892/ijmm.2016.2811.
40. Sajid S, Akbar N. Applications of fungal pigments in biotechnology. Pesqui Agropecu Bras. 2018;7(2):922–30. https://doi.org/10.19045/bspab.2018.700111.
41. Hill HZ. The function of melanin or six blind people examine an elephant. BioEssays. 1992;14(1):49. https://doi.org/10.1002/bies.950140111.
42. Agurto MEP, Gutierrez SMV, Chen HL, Robinson SC. Wood-rotting fungal pigments as colorant coatings on oil-based textile dyes. Coatings. 2017;7(10):152. https://doi.org/10.3390/coatings7100152.
43. Hinsch EM, Weber G, Chen HL, Robinson SC. Colorfastness of extracted wood-staining fungal pigments on fabrics: a new potential for textile dyes. J Text Appar Technol Manag. 2015;9(3).
44. Hernandez VA, Galleguillos F, Robinson S. Fungal pigments from spalting fungi attenuating blue stain in Pinus spp. Int Biodeterior Biodegrad. 2016;107:154. https://doi.org/10.1016/j.ibiod.2015.11.020.
45. Robinson SC. Developing fungal pigments for "painting" vascular plants. Appl Microbiol Biotechnol. 2012;93(4):1389–94. https://doi.org/10.1007/s00253-011-3858-2.
46. Robinson SC. The fine art of decay. Am Sci. 2014;102(3):206. https://doi.org/10.1511/2014.108.206.
47. Giesbers G, Van Schenck J, Vega Gutierrez S, Robinson S, Ostroverkhova O. Fungi-derived pigments for sustainable organic (opto)electronics. MRS Adv. 2018;3(59):3459. https://doi.org/10.1557/adv.2018.446.
48. Giesbers G, Van Schenck J, Quinn A, Van Court R, Vega Gutierrez SM, Robinson SC, Ostroverkhova O. Xylindein: naturally produced fungal compound for sustainable (Opto)electronics. ACS Omega. 2019;4(8):13309. https://doi.org/10.1021/acsomega.9b01490.
49. Agarwal H, Bajpai S, Mishra A, Kohli I, Varma A, Fouillaud M, Dufossé L, Joshi NC. Bacterial pigments and their multifaceted roles in contemporary biotechnology and pharmacological applications. Microorganisms. 2023;11(3):614. https://doi.org/10.3390/microorganisms11030614.
50. Heer K, Sharma S. Microbial pigments as a natural color: a review. Int J Pharm Sci Res. 2017);8(5).
51. Yokoyama A, Miki W. Composition and presumed biosynthetic pathway of carotenoids in the astaxanthin-producing bacterium Agrobacterium aurantiacum. FEMS Microbiol Lett. 1995;128(2):139. https://doi.org/10.1016/0378-1097(95)00097-O.
52. Surai PF. The antioxidant properties of canthaxanthin and its potential effects in the poultry eggs and on embryonic development of the chick. Part 2. Worlds Poult Sci J. 2012;68(4):717. https://doi.org/10.1017/S0043933912000840.
53. Guillerme JB, Couteau C, Coiffard L. Applications for marine resources in cosmetics. Cosmetics. 2017;4(3):35. https://doi.org/10.3390/cosmetics4030035.
54. Tian B, Hua Y. Carotenoid biosynthesis in extremophilic Deinococcus-Thermus bacteria. Trends Microbiol. 2010;18(11):512–20. https://doi.org/10.1016/j.tim.2010.07.007.
55. Wan M, Hou D, Li Y, Fan J, Huang J, Liang S, Wang W, Pan R, Wang J, Li S. The effective photoinduction of *Haematococcus pluvialis* for accumulating astaxanthin with attached cultivation. Bioresour Technol. 2014;163:26. https://doi.org/10.1016/j.biortech.2014.04.017.
56. Shindo K, Misawa N. New and rare carotenoids isolated from marine bacteria and their antioxidant

activities. Mar Drugs. 2014;12(3):1690. https://doi.org/10.3390/md12031690.
57. Alihosseini F, Ju KS, Lango J, Hammock BD, Sun G. Antibacterial colorants: characterization of prodiginines and their applications on textile materials. Biotechnol Prog. 2008;24(3):742. https://doi.org/10.1021/bp070481r.
58. Selvameenal L, Radhakrishnan M, Balagurunathan R. Antibiotic pigment from desert soil actinomycetes; biological activity, purification and chemical screening. Indian J Pharm Sci. 2009;71:499–504.
59. Manikkam R, Ponnuswamy S, Joseph J, Kumar V. Antitubercular activity of the pigment from forest soil Streptomyces sp.SFA5. Bangladesh J Pharmacol. 2016;11:138–40.
60. Vaishnavi M, Manigundan K, Smalia T, Nandhini SU, Gopikrishnan V, Kumar A, Hanna LE, Radhakrishnan M, Aruni W. Antibacterial and anti-HIV activity of extracellular pigment from Streptomyces Sp. S45 isolated from Sabarimala Forest soil, India. Indian J Exp Biol. 2020;58: 861–8.
61. Zhang H, Zhan J, Su K, Zhang Y. A kind of potential food additive produced by Streptomyces coelicolor: characteristics of blue pigment and identification of a novel compound, λ-Actinorhodin. Food Chem. 2006;95:186–92.
62. Victor TMM, Ndlovu TM, Filho M, Pessela BC, Bull S, Ward AC. Production and evaluation of two antibiotics of *Streptomyces coelicolor* A3(2), prodigiosin and actinorhodin under solid state fermentation, using micro-porous culture. Chem Eng Process Process Intensif. 2022;170:108685.
63. Hobbs G, Frazer CM, Gardner DCJ, Flett F, Oliver SG. Pigmented Antibiotic Production by *Streptomyces coelicolor* A3(2):Kinetics and the Influence of Nutrients. J Gen Microbiol. 1990;136:2291–6.
64. Bystrykh LV, Fernández-Moreno MA, Herrema JK, Malpartida F, Hopwood DA, Dijkhuizen L. Production of actinorhodin-related "blue pigments" by Streptomyces coelicolor A3(2). J Bacteriol. 1996;178:2238–44.
65. Finger M, Sentek F, Hartmann L, Palacio-Barrera AM, Schlembach I, Rosenbaum MA, Büchs J. Insights into *Streptomyces coelicolor* A3(2) growth and pigment formation with high-throughput online monitoring. Eng Life Sci. 2022;23(1):e2100151.
66. Gopikrishnan V, Radhakrishnan M, Shanmugasundaram T, Pazhanimurugan R, Balagurunathan R. Antibiofouling potential of quercetin compound from marine-derived actinobacterium, *Streptomyces fradiae* PE7 and its characterization. Environ Sci Pollut Res. 2016;23:13832–42.
67. Gopikrishnan V, Radhakrishnan M, Shanmugasundaram T, Ramakodi MP, Balagurunathan R. Isolation, characterization and identification of antibiofouling metabolite from mangrove derived *Streptomyces sampsonii* PM33. Sci Rep. 2019;9:12975.
68. Pérez-gálvez A, Viera I, Roca M. Carotenoids and chlorophylls as antioxidants. Antioxidants. 2020;9(6):505. https://doi.org/10.3390/antiox9060505.
69. Holdt SL, Kraan S. Bioactive compounds in seaweed: functional food applications and legislation. In. J Appl Phycol. 2011;23(3):543. https://doi.org/10.1007/s10811-010-9632-5.
70. Ravi BG, Johnson J, Palanisamy A. Algal pigments and its applications—a review. Int J Creat Res Thoughts. 2023;11(3):2320–882.
71. Manivasagan P, Bharathiraja S, Moorthy S, Mondal S, Seo H, Lee KD, Oh J. Critical Reviews in Biotechnology Marine natural pigments as potential sources for therapeutic applications. Crit Rev Biotechnol. 2018;38(5):745.
72. Silvana R. Pengaruh Kualitas Pelayanan Terhadap Kepuasan Konsumen Pada Hotel Pop Di Bandar Lampung. In: Fakultas Ekonomi Dan Bisnis Institute Informatika Dan Bisnis Darmajaya Bandar Lampung. 2020. p. 1.
73. Pereira DM, Valentão P, Andrade PB. Marine natural pigments: chemistry, distribution and analysis. Dyes Pigments. 2014;111:124. https://doi.org/10.1016/j.dyepig.2014.06.011.
74. Pereira T, Barroso S, Mendes S, Amaral RA, Dias JR, Baptista T, Saraiva JA, Alves NM, Gil MM. Optimization of phycobiliprotein pigments extraction from red algae *Gracilaria gracilis* for substitution of synthetic food colorants. Food Chem. 2020;321:126688. https://doi.org/10.1016/j.foodchem.2020.126688.
75. Purwanto EA. Kebijakan Publik Yang Agile Dan Inovatif Dalam Memenangkan Persaingan Di Era Vuca (Volatile, Uncertain, Complex and Ambiguous). Molecules. 2019;9(1).
76. El-Khatib EM, Ali NF, El-Mohamedy RSR. Enhancing dyeing of wool fibers with colorant pigment extracted from green algae. J Chem Pharm Res. 2016;8(2):614–9.
77. Pangestuti R, Kim SK. Biological activities and health benefit effects of natural pigments derived from marine algae. J Funct Foods. 2011;3(4):255. https://doi.org/10.1016/j.jff.2011.07.001.
78. Salehi B, Sharifi-Rad J, Seca AML, Pinto DCGA, Michalak I, Trincone A, Mishra AP, Nigam M, Zam W, Martins N. Current trends on seaweeds: looking at chemical composition, phytopharmacology, and cosmetic applications. Molecules. 2019;24(22):4182. https://doi.org/10.3390/molecules24224182.
79. Morais T, Cotas J, Pacheco D, Pereira L. Seaweeds compounds: an ecosustainable source of cosmetic ingredients? Cosmetics. 2021;8(1):8. https://doi.org/10.3390/COSMETICS8010008.
80. Pereira L. Seaweeds as source of bioactive substances and skin care therapy-cosmeceuticals, algotheraphy, and thalassotherapy. Cosmetics. 2018;5(4):68. https://doi.org/10.3390/cosmetics5040068.

81. Rwigemera A, Mamelona J, Martin LJ. Comparative effects between fucoxanthinol and its precursor fucoxanthin on viability and apoptosis of breast cancer cell lines MCF-7 and MDA-MB-231. Anticancer Res. 2015;35(1):207.
82. Thangam R, Suresh V, Asenath Princy W, Rajkumar M, Senthilkumar N, Gunasekaran P, Rengasamy R, Anbazhagan C, Kaveri K, Kannan S. C-Phycocyanin from Oscillatoria tenuis exhibited an antioxidant and in vitro antiproliferative activity through induction of apoptosis and G 0/G1 cell cycle arrest. Food Chem. 2013;140(1–2):262. https://doi.org/10.1016/j.foodchem.2013.02.060.
83. Vila E, Hornero-Méndez D, Azziz G, et al. Carotenoids from heterotrophic bacteria isolated from Fildes Peninsula, King George Island, Antarctica. Biotechnol Rep. 2019;21:e00306.
84. Kim JH, Kang HJ, Yu BJ, et al. *Planococcus faecalis* sp. Nov., a carotenoid-producing species isolated from stools of Antarctic penguins. Int J Syst Evol Microbiol. 2015;65(10):3373–8.
85. Schloss PD, Allen HK, Klimowicz AK, et al. Psychrotrophic strain of *Janthinobacterium lividum* from a cold Alaskan soil produces prodigiosin. DNA Cell Biol. 2010;29(9):533–41.
86. Centurion VB, Delforno TP, Lacerda-Júnior GV, et al. Unveiling resistome profiles in the sediments of an Antarctic volcanic Island. Environ Pollut. 2019;255:113240.
87. Zhang XF, Yao TD, Tian LD, Xu SJ, An LZ. Phylogenetic and physiological diversity of bacteria isolated from Puruogangri ice core. Microb Ecol. 2008;55(3):476–88.
88. Shen L, Yao T, Xu B, Wang H, Jiao N, Kang S, Liu X, Liu Y. Variation of culturable bacteria along depth in the East Rongbuk ice core. Geosci Front. 2012;3(3):327–34.
89. Panwar AS, Molpa D, Joshi GK. Biotechnological potential of some cold-adapted bacteria isolated from north-western Himalaya. Microbiology (Reading, England). 2019;88(3):343–52.
90. Teigiserova DA, Hamelin L, Thomsen M. Towards transparent valorization of food surplus, waste and loss: clarifying definitions, food waste hierarchy, and role in the circular economy. Sci Total Environ. 2020;706:136033. https://doi.org/10.1016/j.scitotenv.2019.136033.
91. Peira G, Bollani L, Giachino C, Bonadonna A. The management of unsold food in outdoor market areas: food operators' behaviour and attitudes. Sustainability (Switzerland). 2018;10(4):1180. https://doi.org/10.3390/su10041180.
92. Tavanandi HA, Raghavarao KSMS. Ultrasound-assisted enzymatic extraction of natural food colorant C-Phycocyanin from dry biomass of Arthrospira platensis. LWT. 2020;118:108802. https://doi.org/10.1016/j.lwt.2019.108802.
93. Khaw KY, Parat MO, Shaw PN, Falconer JR. Solvent supercritical fluid technologies to extract bioactive compounds from natural sources: a review. Molecules. 2017;22(7):1186. https://doi.org/10.3390/molecules22071186.
94. Goto M, Kanda H, Wahyudiono, & Machmudah, S. Extraction of carotenoids and lipids from algae by supercritical CO2 and subcritical dimethyl ether. J Supercrit Fluids. 2015;96:245. https://doi.org/10.1016/j.supflu.2014.10.003.
95. Kitada K, Machmudah S, Sasaki M, Goto M, Nakashima Y, Kumamoto S, Hasegawa T. Supercritical CO2 extraction of pigment components with pharmaceutical importance from Chlorella vulgaris. J Chem Technol Biotechnol. 2009;84(5):657. https://doi.org/10.1002/jctb.2096.
96. Baltz RH. Gifted microbes for genome mining and natural product discovery. J Ind Microbiol Biotechnol. 2017;44(4–5):573. https://doi.org/10.1007/s10295-016-1815-x.
97. Mandakovic D, Cintolesi Á, Maldonado J, Mendoza SN, Aïte M, Gaete A, Saitua F, Allende M, Cambiazo V, Siegel A, Maass A, González M, Latorre M. Genome-scale metabolic models of Microbacterium species isolated from a high altitude desert environment. Sci Rep. 2020;10(1):5560. https://doi.org/10.1038/s41598-020-62130-8.
98. Xu X, Tian L, Zhang S, Jiang L, Zhang Z, Huang H. Complete genome sequence of Janthinobacterium sp. B9-8, a violacein-producing bacterium isolated from low-temperature sewage. Microb Pathog. 2019;128:178. https://doi.org/10.1016/j.micpath.2019.01.003.
99. Yang Y, Liu B, Du X, Li P, Liang B, Cheng X, Du L, Huang D, Wang L, Wang S. Complete genome sequence and transcriptomics analyses reveal pigment biosynthesis and regulatory mechanisms in an industrial strain, Monascus purpureus YY-1. Sci Rep. 2015;5:8331. https://doi.org/10.1038/srep08331.
100. Andreani NA, Carraro L, Martino ME, Fondi M, Fasolato L, Miotto G, Magro M, Vianello F, Cardazzo B. A genomic and transcriptomic approach to investigate the blue pigment phenotype in Pseudomonas fluorescens. Int J Food Microbiol. 2015;213:88. https://doi.org/10.1016/j.ijfoodmicro.2015.05.024.
101. Varasteh T, Hamerski L, Tschoeke D, Lima AS, Garcia G, Cosenza CAN, Thompson C, Thompson F. Conserved pigment profiles in phylogenetically diverse symbiotic bacteria associated with the corals Montastraea cavernosa and Mussismilia braziliensis. Microb Ecol. 2021;81(1):267. https://doi.org/10.1007/s00248-020-01551-4.
102. Suyal DC, Joshi D, Debbarma P, Soni R, Das B, Goel R. Soil metagenomics: unculturable microbial diversity and its function. In: Mycorrhizosphere and pedogenesis; 2019. https://doi.org/10.1007/978-981-13-6480-8_20.
103. Thiel V, Costas AMG, Fortney NW, Martinez JN, Tank M, Roden EE, Boyd ES, Ward DM, Hanada S, Bryant DA. "Candidates thermonerobacter thiotrophicus," a non-phototrophic member of the Bacteroidetes/Chlorobi with dissimilatory sulfur metabolism in hot spring mat communities. Front

Microbiol. 2019;10:3159. https://doi.org/10.3389/fmicb.2018.03159.
104. Rambo IM, Dombrowski N, Constant L, Erdner D, Baker BJ. Metabolic relationships of uncultured bacteria associated with the microalgae Gambierdiscus. Environ Microbiol. 2020;22(5):1764. https://doi.org/10.1111/1462-2920.14878.
105. Stincone P, Brandelli A. Marine bacteria as source of antimicrobial compounds. Crit Rev Biotechnol. 2020;40(3):3159. https://doi.org/10.1080/07388551.2019.1710457.
106. Aslam B, Basit M, Nisar MA, Khurshid M, Rasool MH. Proteomics: technologies and their applications. J Chromatogr Sci. 2017;55(2):182. https://doi.org/10.1093/chromsci/bmw167.
107. Manchester M, Anand A. Metabolomics: strategies to define the role of metabolism in virus infection and pathogenesis. Adv Virus Res. 2017;98:57. https://doi.org/10.1016/bs.aivir.2017.02.001.
108. Fan M, Lian W, Li T, Fan Y, Rao Z, Li Y, Qian H, Zhang H, Wu G, Qi X, Wang L. Metabolomics approach reveals discriminatory metabolites associating with the blue pigments from Vaccinium bracteatum thunb. Leaves at different growth stages. Ind Crop Prod. 2020;147:112252. https://doi.org/10.1016/j.indcrop.2020.112252.
109. Parrot D, Blümel M, Utermann C, Chianese G, Krause S, Kovalev A, Gorb SN, Tasdemir D. Mapping the surface microbiome and metabolome of Brown seaweed Fucus vesiculosus by amplicon sequencing, integrated metabolomics and imaging techniques. Sci Rep. 2019;9(1):1061. https://doi.org/10.1038/s41598-018-37914-8.
110. Kjærbølling I, Mortensen UH, Vesth T, Andersen MR. Strategies to establish the link between biosynthetic gene clusters and secondary metabolites. Fungal Genet Biol. 2019;130:107–21. https://doi.org/10.1016/j.fgb.2019.06.001.

17 Bacteriophages and Their Lysins as Potent Antibacterials

Balaji Subramanyam, Revathy Kalyanasundaram, Sam Ebenezer Rajadas, and Vanaja Kumar

17.1 Introduction

Bacteriophages (phages) are viruses of bacteria that were reported in the early twentieth century [1]. Phages are widespread and present in almost all environmental samples. Though phage particles can survive outside the host, all bacteriophages are obligate intracellular parasites. Infection is initiated by specific interaction with bacterial cell surface receptors. Using this phenomenon phage-based therapeutics and diagnostics are developed [2, 3]. However, there are a few exceptions with a wide range of host preferences. P1 and Mu are the best-studied phages with such potential to infect and lyse a wide range of bacteria enteric species besides *Escherichia coli*, probably due to changes in the viral G segment region [4–6]. Broad host range could be seen in the phages from marine as well as in other ecosystems as well [7–11].

Phage lysin is an enzyme produced by bacteriophages during the final stage of the life cycle to lyse healthy and vegetative cells of bacteria. Phage lysin is also designated using as lysozyme, endolysin, lysin, muralysin, muramidase, and virolysin. Lysin targets the peptidoglycan (or murein) layer of the bacterial cell wall to cause mechanical damage and osmotic rupture (lysis) [12].

Based on the specificity it is classified as (1) *N*-acetylmuramidases (lysozymes), (2) endo-b-*N*-acetylglucosaminidases, (3) lytic transglycosylases (acts on sugar moiety of peptidoglycan), (4) endopeptidases (acts on the peptide moiety), and (5) *N*-acetyl muramyl-L-alanine amidases (acts on amide bond between both moieties). Among the five muramidases and amidases are highly expressed by the phages. Phage lysin comprises two domains, namely, N-terminal and C-terminal domains that are necessary for its activity. The binding of the substrate is mediated by the C-terminal domain which leads to the catalysis of lysis by the N-terminal domain [13]. Hence, C-terminal domain structural integrity is highly essential for the functioning of the latter [14].

In addition to lysin, another lysis factor called holin is produced by phages at the end of the life cycle. Holin is a membrane protein that accumu-

B. Subramanyam (✉)
Department of Bacteriology, National Institute for Research in Tuberculosis, Chennai, India
e-mail: Subramanyam.nirt@icmr.gov.in

R. Kalyanasundaram · V. Kumar
Department of Bacteriology, National Institute for Research in Tuberculosis, Chennai, India

Centre for Drug Discovery and Development, Sathyabama Institute of Science and Technology, Chennai, India

S. E. Rajadas
Centre for Drug Discovery and Development, Sathyabama Institute of Science and Technology, Chennai, India

K. Parthasarathy, R. Manikkam (eds.), *Translational Research in Biomedical Sciences: Recent Progress and Future Prospects*, https://doi.org/10.1007/978-981-97-1777-4_17

lates during the period of late-protein synthesis and causes lysis of the host cell at a precise genetically programmed time [15]. Holin disrupts the cytoplasmic membrane and creates access of lysin to the murein [16].

This chapter highlights the applications of bacteriophages and their lysins in various fields/ industries. The application of bacteriophages in various industries, the target organisms, and their respective references is tabulated (Table 17.1) for ease of use for readers.

Table 17.1 The application of bacteriophages in various industries, the target organisms and their respective references

S. no	Application	Target organism	References
1	Poultry	*Campylobacter* sp.	Atterbury et al. [17]; Carrillo et al. [18]; Orquera et al. [19]; Firlieyanti et al. [20]; Johnson et al. [21]
		Yersinia enterocolitica	Orquera et al. [19]
		Escherichia coli	Johnson et al. [21]; Huff et al. [22, 23]; Huff et al. [24]; Barrow et al. [25]
		Salmonella sp.	Johnson et al. [21]; Higgins et al. [26]; Higgins et al. [27]; Henriques et al. [28]; Wong et al. [29]; Wall et al. [30]; Albino et al. [31]; Sukumaran et al. [32]
		Listeria monocytogenes	Lang [33]

Table 17.1 (continued)

S. no	Application	Target organism	References
2	Food and dairy	*Escherichia coli*	Waddell [34]; Smith and Huggins [35]; Kudva et al. [36]; Bach et al. [37]; Raya et al. [38]; O'Flynn et al. [39]; Hudson et al. [40]; Pan [41]
		Campylobacter sp.	Carrillo et al. [18]; Wagenaar et al. [42]; Goode et al. [43]
		Salmonella sp.	Leverentz et al. [44]; Whichard et al. [45]; Modi et al. [46]; Guenther et al. [47]; Zinno et al. [48]; Bao et al. [49]; Gouvêa et al. [50]; Mahmoud et al. [51]
		Listeria monocytogenes	Perera et al. [52]; Carlton et al. [53]; Guenther et al. [54]; Akhtar et al. [55]
		Staphylococcus aureus	Synnott et al. [56]; Tabla et al. [57]
		Enterobacter sakazakii	Kim et al. [58]
		Enterobacter sakazakii	Lee et al. [59]
3	Aquaculture	*Vibrio* sp.	Karunasagar et al. [60]; Luo et al. [61]; Zhang et al. [62]; Rong et al. [63]
		Pseudomonas plecoglossicida	Park et al. [64]
		Yersinia ruckeri	Saber et al. [65]
		Fusarium psychrophilum	Madsen et al. [66]
		Lactococcus garvieae	Nakai et al. [67]
		Escherichia coli	Pereira et al. [68]

(continued)

Table 17.1 (continued)

S. no	Application	Target organism	References
4	Agriculture	*Xanthomonas* sp.	Saccardi et al. [69]; Iriarte et al. [70]
		Ralstonia solanacearum	Iriarte et al. [70]; Kalpage and De Costa [71]; Tanaka et al. [72]
		Erwinia amylovora	Schnabel et al. [73]; Gill et al. [74]; Born et al. [75]
		Escherichia coli	Ferguson et al. [76]
		Pseudomonas syringae	Frampton et al. [77]
5	Therapeutic purpose	*Klebsiella* sp.	Kumari et al. [78]; Chadha et al. [79]
		Salmonella sp.	Park et al. [80]; Akhtar et al. [81]
		Staphylococcus aureus	Vaks and Benhar [82]
		Escherichia coli	Maura et al. [83]
		Pseudomonas sp.	Brusina et al. [84]
		Acinetobacter baumannii	Merabishvili et al. [85]
		Cronobacter sp.	Kajsík et al. [86]
6	Water treatment	*Pseudomonas aeruginosa*	Zhang et al. [87]
		Nocardia sp.	Khairnar et al. [88]
		Klebsiella sp.	Maal et al. [89]
		Escherichia coli	Maal et al. [90]
7	Anti-biofilm agent	*Klebsiella pneumoniae*	Verma et al. [91]
		Salmonella sp.	Woolston et al. [92]
		Staphylococcus aureus	Lungren et al. [93]; Yilmaz et al. [94]
		Pseudomonas aeruginosa	Yilmaz et al. [94]
		Mycobacterium smegmatis	Kiefer and Dahl [95]
		Vibrio sp.	Luo et al. [61]
		Citrobacter freundii	Gong et al. [96]

17.2 Bacteriophages in Poultry

Many phages exhibiting promising applications in addressing bacterial infections in poultry caused by pathogens like *Campylobacter, Escherichia coli (E. coli), Listeria,* and *Salmonella* have been identified so far. These pathogens cause spoilage of the meat and human infection upon consumption. Targeted phage-based eradication strategies are employed to encounter *Campylobacter*, a leading cause of foodborne disease, in broiler flocks, leading to a substantial reduction in colonization levels [18]. Phages are used for both the curative treatment of existing *Campylobacter* colonization and the preventive pretreatment of hatched chickens to impede colonization. [42]. NCTC12684, CP8, and CP34 phages were identified to clear *Campylobacter* infections on chicken skin effectively, and their optimal doses for bacterial clearance in broiler chickens were optimized previously to achieve 95% clearance [17–19, 43]. *E.coli* infections in various livestock, including broiler chickens, were mitigated using SPR02 bacteriophages administered via aerosol or intramuscular injection, significantly reducing mortality rates from 50 to 20% [22–24]. Besides enteric infections, *E.coli* bacteremia was also found to be cleared by phages [25]. The FDA-approved bacteriophage preparation LMP-102 demonstrated efficacy against a broad range of *Listeria monocytogenes* strains on ready-to-eat meat and poultry products. In Salmonella control, phages were evaluated to reduce recovery from poultry carcass rinse samples, and studies showcased their effectiveness in reducing intestinal colonization in challenged birds. Additionally, phage therapy demonstrated promise in counteracting *Salmonella* colonization in swine and reducing counts on chicken breast fillets, highlighting the potential of bacteriophages in enhancing poultry safety and product quality [27, 29–31]. Commercially, SalmoFresh™ a phage-antibiotic cocktail was developed for processing chicken breast [32]. Various studies have explored the direct reduction of *S. enteritidis* in broiler chickens using bacteriophages, highlighting their potential impact in poultry settings [97].

17.3 Bacteriophages in Food and Dairy

The persistent rise in the occurrence of meat-associated foodborne diseases attributable to pathogens such as *E. coli, Campylobacter, Salmonella, Listeria*, and others necessitates a thorough examination of the potential contributions of non-antibiotic agents like bacteriophages in mitigating these public health risks. The available data on bacteriophages underscores their pivotal role in addressing outbreaks, serving both as facilitators of rapid detection and effective biocontrol agents [98].

Historical investigations by Smith and Huggins in 1983 revealed that a mixture of two phages protected calves, piglets, and lambs against experimental *E. coli* infections [36, 37]. A mixture comprising six *E. coli* O157-specific bacteriophages significantly reducing its host in the fecal shedding of calves, ground beef, and spinach was later discovered [34, 41]. Furthermore, recent efforts have isolated a novel bacteriophage, CEV1, and assessed its potential to diminish *E. coli* O157:H7 levels in sheep [38]. Other studies have explored the application of phage cocktails, including three different phages, to treat beef contaminated with *E. coli* O157:H7, resulting in promising outcomes [39, 40]. Notably, the phage FAHEc1 has been identified for its ability to infect and eliminate *E. coli* O157 in vitro in beef [99].

Salmonella, a major contributor to food-related illnesses, has witnessed substantial reductions facilitated by bacteriophages. A notable decrease in *Salmonella* levels in meat through phage application was observed in the case of Felix-O1 phage that showed a significant reduction of viable cells *S. typhimurium* on sausages that were previously contaminated experimentally [44, 45]. Likewise, phage SJ2 and P22 are potent enough to eliminate *S. enteritidis* during cheddar production, and its long storage [46, 48]. Additionally, *S. typhimurium* in different ready-to-eat foods has been effectively treated with virulent bacteriophage FO1-E2 [47]. Other isolates, such as lytic phages PA13076, PC2184, ΦSP-1, and ΦSP-3, have exhibited potential as biocontrol agents against *Salmonella* in foods like pressure-cooked chicken meat [49, 50]. In addition, bacteriophages, Salmacey1, Salmacey2, and Salmacey3, from sewage water samples demonstrated their efficacy against various Salmonella serovars isolated from broiler chickens.

ListShield™ a commercially available bacteriophage cocktail phage formulation efficiently reduced the *L. monocytogenes*, load in several in vitro contaminated ready-to-eat foods [52]. A broad host range virulent phage P100 capable of lysing *L. monocytogenes* in soft cheese was also reported [53]. Bacteriophages A511 and P100 were employed against L. monocytogenes in ready-to-eat foods, achieving significant reductions in cell counts [54].

Mastitis poses a widespread problem leading to substantial decreases in milk production. It is predominantly caused by bacteria, especially *Staphylococcus* sp. Given the common problem of antibiotic resistance in *S. aureus*, the efficiency of phages like bacteriophage K, ΦSA012, and ΦSA039 has been notified as capable of bovine mastitis [56, 100]. Evaluations of bacteriophages vB_SauS-phi-IPLA35 (phi-IPLA35) and vB_SauS-phi-IPLA88 (phi-IPLA88) on *S. aureus* Sa9 gave promising outcomes in pasteurized whole milk under simulated cold chain break conditions [57]. Besides treatment, phages are also used in the treatment as stated previously as it is explored to develop a biosensor for the detection of foodborne pathogens using paper immobilized phages [101].

For *Enterobacter sakazakii*, a pathogen associated with reconstituted infant formula milk, bacteriophage ESP 732-1 has proven effective in suppressing its growth, demonstrating efficacy at varying temperatures [58]. *Cronobacter sakazakii*, another foodborne pathogen found primarily in infant milk powder formula, has faced targeted bacteriophage interventions. The phage CR5, isolated from farm soil, exhibited complete lysis of *C. sakazakii* within 2 h in both culture and contaminated milk samples. Interestingly, the host receptor of phage CR5 was identified as the flagellum of *C. sakazakii* [59].

17.4 Bacteriophages in Aquaculture

Aquaculture, encompassing aquatic animals and plants in diverse environments, contributes substantially to global seafood supplies and stands as one of the fastest-growing agricultural sectors. However, fish farming faces significant economic losses due to infections caused by microbial pathogens, including multidrug-resistant bacteria transmitted through water. Bacteriophages, serving as alternatives to antibiotics, are employed to control bacterial infections in aquaculture. Notably, phages targeting fish pathogenic bacteria like *Aeromonas salmonicida, A. hydrophila, Edwardsiella tarda,* and *Yersinia ruckeri* have been identified [102].

In the context of vibrio-related challenges in shrimp hatcheries, bacteriophages could be considered valuable. *Vibrio harveyi* associated with larval shrimp stages affects larval health and causes mortalities. Bacteriophages isolated against *V. harveyi* have shown 85% protective efficiency providing an alternative to antibiotic treatments in shrimp hatcheries [60]. Two lytic phages, P4A and P4F, isolated from seawater, demonstrate significant reductions in Vibrio population density in biofilms formed by Vibrio strain B4F on polyethylene film surfaces [61]. *Vibrio alginolyticus*, a pathogen affecting marine animals like sea cucumbers, faces control through bacteriophages isolated from aquatic market drainpipes, showcasing potential applications in disease management [62]. Similarly, bacteriophage VPp1 was found to reduce *Vibrio parahaemolyticus* in oysters, tested across varying levels of infection (MOI) at different temperature levels [63]. In the case of *Pseudomonas*-related diseases in ayu fish culture, bacteriophages PPpW-3 and PPpW-4 specific to *Pseudomonas plecoglossicida*, the causative agent of bacterial hemorrhagic ascites, exhibited reduced mortality when administered orally through phage-impregnated feed [64].

Pathogens like *Yersinia ruckeri, Flavobacterium psychrophilum, Lactococcus garvieae, and Escherichia coli* affect different fish species. Bacteriophages against these bacterial pathogens have been isolated and applied. Ahmadpour et al. [65] identified phages active against *Y. ruckeri*, while Castillo et al. [103] and Madsen et al. [66] explored host susceptibility dynamics to phage infection with *F. psychrophilum. L. garvieae*-related economic damage in aquaculture is addressed using specific phages, PLgY and PLgW, that enhance fish survival rates [67]. Pereira et al. [68] showcased the efficiency of phages phT4A and ECA2 against *E. coli* for mollusk disease management. Overall, the use of bacteriophages in aquaculture emerges as a promising strategy for controlling bacterial infections and ensuring the sustainability of this vital industry.

17.5 Bacteriophages in Agriculture

Bacterial plant diseases pose a significant economic burden on global agricultural production. Conventional measures rely on chemicals that pose a major threat to the environment. Hence, in recent decades bacteriophages are being explored as an effective alternative to synthetic chemicals [104]. Instead of relying on a single phage for disease prevention, the utilization of a mixture comprising three to eight different phages is preferred to enhance the management of crop pathogens and minimize the risk of developing phage-resistant mutants [105]. To mitigate fruit spot incidence on peaches in orchards caused by *Xanthomonas campestris* pv. pruni, eight bacteriophages were isolated and evaluated for their host range and lytic ability. A lytic phage with the broadest host range was selected [69]. Phages specific for *Ralstonia solanacearum, Xanthomonas perforans*, or *X. euvesicatoria*, either individually or in a mixture were applied to the soil surrounding tomato plants. The most effective control against wilt was observed when the commercial RS5-specific phage mixture (ΦRS5mix) was applied. The biocontrol potential of a mixture of six phages against bacterial wilt in tomatoes caused by *R. solanacearum* was demonstrated against different isolates [71]. For pseudomonas-related diseases, Tanaka et al. [72]

employed a co-application approach, reducing tobacco bacterial wilt caused by *R. solanacearum* as well as *Pseudomonas*. In the case of fire blight infection caused by *Erwinia amylovora* on apple blossoms, Schnabel et al. [73] achieved a significant reduction in disease through the application of a mixture of three phages. Gill et al. [74] further isolated 47 phages capable of lysing *E. amylovora*, demonstrating their efficacy in inhibiting bacterial growth on flower surfaces [75]. The integrated management of bacterial spots in tomatoes involves the formulation of phages with other biological control agents and plant inducers, representing a holistic approach to disease management. This integrated phage-based approach has been officially recommended to tomato growers in Florida, and commercially available bacteriophage mixtures against the pathogen are now accessible [106]. Beyond the agricultural fields, phages are used to prevent spoilages of agri-products, for example, a lytic phage specific for *E. coli* O157:H7 (EcoShield™) is used to reduce cross-contamination in fresh-cut lettuce enhancing food safety practices [76].

17.6 Phage in Therapeutic Purposes

Liposome-entrapped phages Kpn5 and B5055 were tested for wound healing enhancement. The biodistribution of liposome-entrapped phages was observed in various organs within 6 h, while free bacteriophages took 4 h post-administration. However, the former demonstrated a significant reduction in bacterial growth in the skin and liver compared to the free bacteriophage. [78, 79]. Rapid killing of *S. typhimurium* LT2 by lysis caused by P22 phage within 16 h was shown [80]. Two broad range bacteriophages, SEA1 and SEA2, were isolated from animal feces and sewage samples. SEA2 displayed high efficiency in infecting S. typhimurium DT104, while only phage SEA1 could infect *S. montevideo*. These anti-Salmonella phages exhibited high host specificity with few exceptions of lytic phages capable of infecting a wide variety of *Salmonella* [81]. In the realm of antibacterial nanomedicines, chloramphenicol drug-loaded filamentous phage (M13) that inhibited the growth of *S. aureus* was developed [82]. The in vivo bacteriophage targeting of enteroaggregative *E. coli* (EAEC) using the phage O104:H4 55989Str and a cocktail of three virulent bacteriophages was assessed in a mouse intestinal model, mimicking asymptomatic intestinal carriage found in humans [83]. A *Pseudomonas* bacteriophage demonstrated complete elimination of the pathogen within 24 h after a single application, preventing new cases of healthcare-associated *Pseudomonas* infections [84]. Two phages, Acibel004 and Acibel007 were isolated and characterized, from hospital wastewater against multidrug-resistant *Acinetobacter baumannii* [85]. These bacteriophages exhibited high potential for application in bacteriophage-based therapy against infections caused by *A. baumannii* strains. *Cronobacter* spp. is responsible for rare but fatal cases in neonates and immunocompromised infants. It spreads as a foodborne pathogen, especially through contaminated infant milk formulation. A synergistic combination of recombinant human cathelicidin LL-37, an antimicrobial peptide, and bacteriophage Dev-CS-701 lead to a significant reduction in cell numbers in powdered infant formula [86]. Similarly, many bacterial infections including tuberculosis could be treated using phage cocktails.

17.7 Bacteriophages in Water Treatment

The presence of pathogenic bacteria in water bodies necessitates their effective removal to ensure potability after treatment with wastewater filtration systems. Phage treatment against *Pseudomonas aeruginosa* was proposed even a decade before [87]. Stable foaming is a prevalent issue in activated sludge plants globally. While physical and chemical treatment methods are common, biological treatment methods have been less explored. *Nocardia* sp., a major contributor to persistent foam, was targeted using three isolated and characterized Nocardia bacteriophages (NOC1, NOC2, and NOC3) from wastewater samples. These bacteriophages exhibited promising results in controlling foam-producing bacterial growth under laboratory conditions, presenting a potential alternative anti-foaming agent [88].

In another study, novel bacteriophages associated with the Myoviridae and Podoviridae families were isolated and characterized from the Zayandeh-rood River. These phages demonstrated lytic effects on *Klebsiella pneumoniae* and *K. oxytoca*. Municipal sewage treatment with these phages resulted in a 22-fold decrease in coliform MPN from 2400 to 110 after 2 h of incubation. Additionally, bacteriophages derived from the same environment exhibited lytic effects on *E. coli* PTCC1399 and *E. coli* SBSWF27, as well as on the coliform population in sewage water. These findings suggest that lytic *E. coli* phages can effectively reduce coliform populations in sewage, serving as a cost-effective and straightforward alternative to expensive instruments and established methods in traditional wastewater treatment plants [89, 90].

17.8 Bacteriophage as Anti-biofilm Agent

Bacteria commonly establish biofilms in their environments, serving as reservoirs for various microbes and contributing to opportunistic infections. Traditionally, chemical agents are employed to address these biofilms, but recent reports highlight the potential of bacteriophages as effective anti-biofilm agents. Considering various factors stated previously, employing phages are recently attempted to tackle biofilm formation. A combination of antibiotic (ciprofloxacin) and a depolymerase-producing lytic bacteriophage (KPO1K2) is formulated to eliminate biofilm K. pneumoniae [91]. A phage cocktail, SalmoFresh™, comprising six lytic bacteriophages capable of significantly reducing *Salmonella* species' biofilm formation by over 90% [92]. *S. aureus* biofilms on central nervous catheter material was similarly treated using phages [93]. Biofilms of methicillin-resistant *S. aureus* (MRSA) and *P. aeruginosa*, on implants were found to be efficiently cleared using bacteriophages [94]. In marine aquaculture systems, *Vibrio* sp. forms biofilms on polyethylene film surfaces. It could be handled well using lytic phages like P4A and P4F [61]. Biofilms on stainless steels, high-density polyethylene plastic, and rubber templates grown by bacteria *Citrobacter freundii* and *Hafnia* alvei that are designated as sulfide-producing bacteria (SPB) could be controlled using phage treatment. The same applies to the biofilms produced by *Mycobacterium smegmatis* [95, 96].

17.9 Bacteriophage Lysins

Bacteriophage lysins have emerged as valuable tools for targeted bacterial elimination. A noteworthy characteristic of these enzymes is their ability to selectively kill bacteria without affecting the species from which they are derived. These lysins, known as "enzybiotics," possess remarkable heat stability (up to 60 °C) and are easily producible in large quantities, offering a promising avenue for controlling pathogenic bacteria [107, 108].

Lysins have been investigated for their efficacy in mucosal colonization models against *Streptococcus*. In vivo models, with oral colonization for group A *Streptococci* and nasal models with *S. pneumoniae*, demonstrated the effectiveness of lysins in combating these bacteria on mucosal surfaces [109, 110]. Lysin Pal and Cpl-1, derived from a pneumococcal bacteriophage, exhibited effectiveness against *S. pneumoniae* in various models, including bacteremia and topical application, respectively [111, 112]. Notably, it displayed increased killing efficiency against both penicillin-sensitive and resistant strains in vitro [113]. Cpl-1 has also shown success in treating *S. pneumoniae* endocarditis and meningitis in rat models, as well as preventing acute otitis media in mice [114–116].

Phage lysins PlyG and PlyPII have been employed for the detection and killing of *Bacillus anthracis*. PlyG, isolated from the gamma phage, demonstrated specific binding and rapid killing of *B. anthracis*, including both vegetative cells and germinating spores, both in vitro and in vivo.

Additionally, PlyPH is active across a broad pH range, further contributes to the identification and control of *B. anthracis* [117, 118]. Lysins targeting *S. aureus*, such as MV-L from phage ΦMR11 and LysK, LysH5, and endolysin from phage Φ11, have shown significant results. MV-L lysin effectively treated methicillin-resistant *S. aureus* (MRSA) in mouse nasal cavities, leading to the complete elimination [119–122]. Phage lysins Ply118, Ply511, and Ply500 have exhibited activity against *L. monocytogenes*, offering potential applications in food poisoning prevention. Similarly, lysin PlyV12 from phage Φ1 targeting *Enterococcus faecalis* strain V12 demonstrated broad-spectrum lysis of Gram-positive pathogens, including *Staphylococci* and *Streptococci* [123–126]. Moreover, lysins PlyGBS and another GBS phage lysin displayed inhibitory effects on various serotypes of Group B streptococci [127, 128].

17.10 Conclusion

Selecting the appropriate method for applying phages to various materials, including food, poultry, aquaculture, wounds, etc., requires thorough characterization to ensure effectiveness. In situations demanding the eradication of bacterial pathogens in different environments, the utilization of bacteriophages and their lysins emerges as a promising and urgently needed solution for the development of novel antibacterials.

Acknowledgments Authors duly acknowledge Mrs. G. Radhika and Mrs. Devi Sangamithirai, Department of Bacteriology, NIRT, Chennai for their help in reference management.

Disclosures None to declare as authors have no conflict of interest and no financial conflict of interest declared.

References

1. Duckworth DH. Who discovered bacteriophage? Bacteriol Rev. 1976;40:793–802.
2. Hayes W. The genetics of bacteria and their viruses. 2nd ed. London: Blackwell Scientific Publications Ltd; 1968.
3. Welkos S, Schreiber M, Baer H. Identification of *Salmonella* with the O-1 bacteriophage. Appl Environ Microbiol. 1974;28:618–22.
4. Harshey RM. Phage Mu. In: The bacteriophages. Boston: Springer; 1988. p. 193–234.
5. van de Putte P, Cramer S, Giphart-Gassler M. Invertible DNA determines host specificity of bacteriophage Mu. Nature. 1980;286:218–22.
6. Yarmolinsky MB, Sternberg N. Bacteriophage P1. In: The bacteriophages. Boston: Springer; 1988. p. 291–438.
7. Bergh Ø, Børsheim KY, Bratbak G, Heldal M. High abundance of viruses found in aquatic environments. Nature. 1989;340:467–8.
8. Fuhrma JA, Suttle CA. Viruses in marine planktonic systems. Oceanography. 1993;6:51–63.
9. Hennes KP, Simon M. Significance of bacteriophages for controlling bacterioplankton growth in a mesotrophic lake. Appl Environ Microbiol. 1995;61:333–40.
10. Marsh P, Wellington EMH. Phage-host interactions in soil. FEMS Microbiol Ecol. 1994;15:99–107.
11. Torrella F, Morita RY. Evidence by electron micrographs for a high incidence of bacteriophage particles in the waters of Yaquina Bay, oregon: ecological and taxonomical implications. Appl Environ Microbiol. 1979;37:774–8.
12. Borysowski J, Weber-Dąbrowska B, Górski A. Bacteriophage endolysins as a novel class of antibacterial agents. Exp Biol Med. 2006;231:366–77.
13. Loessner MJ. Bacteriophage endolysins—current state of research and applications. Curr Opin Microbiol. 2005;8:480–7.
14. Fischetti VA. Using phage lytic enzymes to control pathogenic bacteria. BMC Oral Health. 2006;6:S16.
15. Gründling A, Manson MD, Young R. Holins kill without warning. Proc Natl Acad Sci U S A. 2001;98:9348–52.
16. Young RY, Wang N, Roof WD. Phages will out: strategies of host cell lysis. Trends Microbiol. 2000;8:120–8.
17. Atterbury RJ, Connerton PL, Dodd CE, Rees CE, Connerton IF. Application of host-specific bacteriophages to the surface of chicken skin leads to a reduction in recovery of *Campylobacter jejuni*. Appl Environ Microbiol. 2003;69:6302–6.
18. Carrillo CL, Atterbury RJ, El-Shibiny A, Connerton PL, Dillon E, Scott A, Connerton IF. Bacteriophage therapy to reduce *Campylobacter jejuni* colonization of broiler chickens. Appl Environ Microbiol. 2005;71:6554–63.
19. Orquera S, Gölz G, Hertwig S, Hammerl J, Sparborth D, Joldic A, Alter T. Control of *Campylobacter* spp. and *Yersinia enterocolitica* by virulent bacteriophages. J Mol Genet Med. 2012;6:273–8.
20. Firlieyanti AS, Connerton PL, Connerton IF. *Campylobacters* and their bacteriophages from chicken liver: the prospect for phage biocontrol. Int J Food Microbiol. 2016;237:121–7.

21. Johnson RP, Gyles CL, Huff WE, Ojha S, Huff GR, Rath NC, Donoghue AM. Bacteriophages for prophylaxis and therapy in cattle, poultry and pigs. Anim Health Res Rev. 2008;9:201–15.
22. Huff WE, Huff GR, Rath NC, Balog JM, Donoghue AM. Prevention of *Escherichia coli* infection in broiler chickens with a bacteriophage aerosol spray. Poult Sci. 2002;81:1486–91.
23. Huff WE, Huff GR, Rath NC, Balog JM, Xie H, Moore PA Jr, Donoghue AM. Prevention of *Escherichia coli* respiratory infection in broiler chickens with bacteriophage (SPR02). Poult Sci. 2002;81:437–41.
24. Huff WE, Huff GR, Rath NC, Balog JM, Donoghue AM. Evaluation of aerosol spray and intramuscular injection of bacteriophage to treat an *Escherichia coli* respiratory infection. Poult Sci. 2003;82:1108–12.
25. Barrow P, Lovell M, Berchieri A. Use of lytic bacteriophage for control of experimental *Escherichia coli* septicemia and meningitis in chickens and calves. Clin Diagn Lab Immunol. 1998;5:294–8.
26. Higgins JP, Higgins SE, Guenther KL, Huff W, Donoghue AM, Donoghue DJ, Hargis BM. Use of a specific bacteriophage treatment to reduce *Salmonella* in poultry products. Poult Sci. 2005;84:1141–5.
27. Higgins SE, Higgins JP, Bielke LR, Hargis BM. Selection and application of bacteriophages for treating *Salmonella enteritidis* infections in poultry. Int J Poult Sci. 2007;6:163–8.
28. Henriques A, Sereno R, Almeida A. Reducing *Salmonella* horizontal transmission during egg incubation by phage therapy. Foodborne Pathog Dis. 2013;10:718–22.
29. Wong CL, Sieo CC, Tan WS, Abdullah N, Hair-Bejo M, Abu J, Ho YW. Evaluation of a lytic bacteriophage, Φ st1, for biocontrol of *Salmonella enterica* serovar *Typhimurium* in chickens. Int J Food Microbiol. 2014;172:92–101.
30. Wall SK, Zhang J, Rostagno MH, Ebner PD. Phage therapy to reduce preprocessing *Salmonella* infections in market-weight swine. Appl Environ Microbiol. 2010;76:48–53.
31. Albino LA, Rostagno MH, Húngaro HM, Mendonça RC. Isolation, characterization, and application of bacteriophages for *Salmonella* spp. biocontrol in pigs. Foodborne Pathog Dis. 2014;11:602–9.
32. Sukumaran AT, Nannapaneni R, Kiess A, Sharma CS. Reduction of *Salmonella* on chicken meat and chicken skin by combined or sequential application of lytic bacteriophage with chemical antimicrobials. Int J Food Microbiol. 2015;207:8–15.
33. Lang LH. FDA approves use of bacteriophages to be added to meat and poultry products. Gastroenterology. 2006;131:1370.
34. Waddell T. Control of *Escherichia coli* O157: H7 infection of calves by bacteriophages. In: 4th international symposium and workshop on STEC (VTEC) infections, Kyoto. 2000. p. 90.
35. Smith HW, Huggins MB. Effectiveness of phages in treating experimental *Escherichia coli* diarrhoea in calves, piglets and lambs. Microbiology. 1983;129:2659–75.
36. Kudva IT, Jelacic S, Tarr PI, Youderian P, Hovde CJ. Biocontrol of *Escherichia coli* O157 with O157-specific bacteriophages. Appl Environ Microbiol. 1999;65:3767–73.
37. Bach SJ, McAllister TA, Veira DM, Gannon VP, Holley RA. Effect of bacteriophage DC22 on *Escherichia coli* O157: H7 in an artificial rumen system (Rusitec) and inoculated sheep. Anim Res. 2003;52:89–101.
38. Raya RR, Varey P, Oot RA, Dyen MR, Callaway TR, Edrington TS, Kutter EM, Brabban AD. Isolation and characterization of a new T-even bacteriophage, CEV1, and determination of its potential to reduce *Escherichia coli* O157: H7 levels in sheep. Appl Environ Microbiol. 2006;72:6405–10.
39. O'Flynn G, Ross RP, Fitzgerald GF, Coffey A. Evaluation of a cocktail of three bacteriophages for biocontrol of *Escherichia coli* O157: H7. Appl Environ Microbiol. 2004;70:3417–24.
40. Hudson JA, Billington C, Wilson T, On SL. Effect of phage and host concentration on the inactivation of *Escherichia coli* O157: H7 on cooked and raw beef. Food Sci Technol Int. 2015;21:104–9.
41. Pan Y. Practical applications of phage-based technologies in food safety. Doctoral dissertation, Purdue University; 2013.
42. Wagenaar JA, Van Bergen MA, Mueller MA, Wassenaar TM, Carlton RM. Phage therapy reduces *Campylobacter jejuni* colonization in broilers. Vet Microbiol. 2005;109:275–83.
43. Goode D, Allen VM, Barrow PA. Reduction of experimental *Salmonella* and *Campylobacter* contamination of chicken skin by application of lytic bacteriophages. Appl Environ Microbiol. 2003;69:5032–6.
44. Leverentz B, Conway WS, Alavidze Z, Janisiewicz WJ, Fuchs Y, Camp MJ, Chighladze E, Sulakvelidze A. Examination of bacteriophage as a biocontrol method for *Salmonella* on fresh-cut fruit: a model study. J Food Prot. 2001;64:1116–21.
45. Whichard JM, Sriranganathan N, Pierson FW. Suppression of *Salmonella* growth by wild-type and large-plaque variants of bacteriophage Felix O1 in liquid culture and on chicken frankfurters. J Food Prot. 2003;66:220–5.
46. Modi R, Hirvi Y, Hill A, Griffiths MW. Effect of phage on survival of *Salmonella enteritidis* during manufacture and storage of cheddar cheese made from raw and pasteurized milk. J Food Prot. 2001;64:927–33.
47. Guenther S, Herzig O, Fieseler L, Klumpp J, Loessner MJ. Biocontrol of *Salmonella typhimurium* in RTE foods with the virulent bacteriophage FO1-E2. Int J Food Microbiol. 2012;154: 66–72.

48. Zinno P, Devirgiliis C, Ercolini D, Ongeng D, Mauriello G. Bacteriophage P22 to challenge *Salmonella* in foods. Int J Food Microbiol. 2014;191:69–74.
49. Bao H, Zhang P, Zhang H, Zhou Y, Zhang L, Wang R. Bio-control of *Salmonella enteritidis* in foods using bacteriophages. Viruses. 2015;7:4836–53.
50. Gouvêa DM, Mendonça RCS, Lopez MES, Batalha LS. Absorbent food pads containing bacteriophages for potential antimicrobial use in refrigerated food products. LWT-Food Sci Technol. 2016;67:159–66.
51. Mahmoud M, Askora A, Barakat AB, Rabie OEF, Hassan SE. Isolation and characterization of polyvalent bacteriophages infecting multi drug resistant *Salmonella* serovars isolated from broilers in Egypt. Int J Food Microbiol. 2018;266:8–13.
52. Perera MN, Abuladze T, Li M, Woolston J, Sulakvelidze A. Bacteriophage cocktail significantly reduces or eliminates *Listeria monocytogenes* contamination on lettuce, apples, cheese, smoked salmon and frozen foods. Food Microbiol. 2015;52:42–8.
53. Carlton RM, Noordman WH, Biswas B, De Meester ED, Loessner MJ. Bacteriophage P100 for control of *Listeria monocytogenes* in foods: genome sequence, bioinformatic analyses, oral toxicity study, and application. Regul Toxicol Pharmacol. 2005;43:301–12.
54. Guenther S, Huwyler D, Richard S, Loessner MJ. Virulent bacteriophage for efficient biocontrol of *Listeria monocytogenes* in ready-to-eat foods. Appl Environ Microbiol. 2009;75:93–100.
55. Akhtar M, Viazis S, Christensen K, Kraemer P, Diez-Gonzalez F. Isolation, characterization and evaluation of virulent bacteriophages against *Listeria monocytogenes*. Food Control. 2017;75:108–15.
56. Synnott AJ, Kuang Y, Kurimoto M, Yamamichi K, Iwano H, Tanji Y. Isolation from sewage influent and characterization of novel *Staphylococcus aureus* bacteriophages with wide host ranges and potent lytic capabilities. Appl Environ Microbiol. 2009;75:4483–90.
57. Tabla R, Martínez B, Rebollo JE, González J, Ramírez MR, Roa I, Rodríguez A, García P. Bacteriophage performance against *Staphylococcus aureus* in milk is improved by high hydrostatic pressure treatments. Int J Food Microbiol. 2012;156:209–13.
58. Kim KP, Klumpp J, Loessner MJ. *Enterobacter sakazakii* bacteriophages can prevent bacterial growth in reconstituted infant formula. Int J Food Microbiol. 2007;115:195–203.
59. Lee JH, Bai J, Shin H, Kim Y, Park B, Heu S, Ryu S. A novel bacteriophage targeting *Cronobacter sakazakii* is a potential biocontrol agent in foods. Appl Environ Microbiol. 2016;82:192–201.
60. Karunasagar I, Shivu MM, Girisha SK, Krohne G, Karunasagar I. Biocontrol of pathogens in shrimp hatcheries using bacteriophages. Aquaculture. 2007;268:288–92.
61. Luo ZH, Yu YP, Jost G, Liu WH, Huang XL, Gu L. Characterization of two bacteriophages for specific treatment of biofilm formed by a *Vibrio* sp. isolated from an abalone farm. Aquac Res. 2016;47:3964–72.
62. Zhang J, Cao Z, Li Z, Wang L, Li H, Wu F, Jin L, Li X, Li S, Xu Y. Effect of bacteriophages on *Vibrio alginolyticus* infection in the sea cucumber, *Apostichopus japonicus* (Selenka). J World Aquacult Soc. 2015;46:149–58.
63. Rong R, Lin H, Wang J, Khan MN, Li M. Reductions of *Vibrio parahaemolyticus* in oysters after bacteriophage application during depuration. Aquaculture. 2014;418:171–6.
64. Park SC, Shimamura I, Fukunaga M, Mori KI, Nakai T. Isolation of bacteriophages specific to a fish pathogen, *Pseudomonas plecoglossicida*, as a candidate for disease control. Appl Environ Microbiol. 2000;66:1416–22.
65. Ahmadpour S, Mardani K, Tukmechi A. Culture and molecular characterization of phages isolated from rainbow trout farms and sewage treatment plants and investigation of their effects on Yersinia ruckeri. Iranian J Fisheries Sciences. 2016;15(1):267–80.
66. Madsen L, Bertelsen SK, Dalsgaard I, Middelboe M. Dispersal and survival of *Flavobacterium psychrophilum* phages in vivo in rainbow trout and in vitro under laboratory conditions: implications for their use in phage therapy. Appl Environ Microbiol. 2013;79:4853–61.
67. Nakai T, Sugimoto R, Park KH, Matsuoka S, Mori KI, Nishioka T, Maruyama K. Protective effects of bacteriophage on experimental *Lactococcus garvieae* infection in yellowtail. Dis Aquat Org. 1999;37:33–41.
68. Pereira C, Moreirinha C, Teles L, Rocha RJ, Calado R, Romalde JL, Nunes ML, Almeida A. Application of phage therapy during bivalve depuration improves *Escherichia coli* decontamination. Food Microbiol. 2017;61:102–12.
69. Saccardi A, Gambin E, Zaccardelli M, Barone G, Mazzucchi U. *Xanthomonas campestris*pv. *pruni* control trials with phage treatments on peaches in the orchard. Phytopathol Mediterr. 1993;32:206–10.
70. Iriarte FB, Obradović A, Wernsing MH, Jackson LE, Balogh B, Hong JA, Momol MT, Jones JB, Vallad GE. Soil-based systemic delivery and phyllosphere in vivo propagation of bacteriophages: two possible strategies for improving bacteriophage persistence for plant disease control. Bacteriophage. 2012;2:e23530.
71. Kalpage MD, De Costa DM. Isolation of bacteriophages and determination of their efficiency in controlling *Ralstonia solanacearum* causing bacterial wilt of tomato. Trop Agric Res. 2015;26:140–51.
72. Tanaka H, Negishi H, Maeda H. Control of tobacco bacterial wilt by an avirulent strain of *Pseudomonas solanacearum* M4S and its bacteriophage. Jpn J Phytopathol. 1990;56:243–6.
73. Schnabel EL, Fernando WGD, Meyer MP, Jones AL, Jackson LE. Bacteriophage of *Erwinia amylovora* and their potential for biocontrol. In: VIII international workshop on fire blight, vol. 489; 1998. p. 649–54.

74. Gill JJ, Svircev AM, Smith R, Castle AJ. Bacteriophages of *Erwinia amylovora*. Appl Environ Microbiol. 2003;69:2133–8.
75. Born Y, Fieseler L, Thöny V, Leimer N, Duffy B, Loessner MJ. Engineering of bacteriophages Y2:: dpoL1-C and Y2:: luxAB for efficient control and rapid detection of the fire blight pathogen, *Erwinia amylovora*. Appl Environ Microbiol. 2017;83:e00341–17.
76. Ferguson S, Roberts C, Handy E, Sharma M. Lytic bacteriophages reduce *Escherichia coli* O157: H7 on fresh cut lettuce introduced through cross-contamination. Bacteriophage. 2013;3:e24323.
77. Frampton RA, Taylor C, Moreno AVH, Visnovsky SB, Petty NK, Pitman AR, Fineran PC. Identification of bacteriophages for biocontrol of the kiwifruit canker phytopathogen *Pseudomonas syringae*pv *actinidiae*. Appl Environ Microbiol. 2014;80:2216–28.
78. Kumari S, Harjai K, Chhibber S. Bacteriophage versus antimicrobial agents for the treatment of murine burn wound infection caused by *Klebsiella pneumoniae* B5055. J Med Microbiol. 2011;60: 205–10.
79. Chadha P, Katare OP, Chhibber S. Liposome loaded phage cocktail: enhanced therapeutic potential in resolving *Klebsiella pneumoniae* mediated burn wound infections. Burns. 2017;43:1532–43.
80. Park SH, Biswas D, Lingbeck J, Koo OK, Ricke SC. Enhancement of chicken macrophage cytokine response to *Salmonella typhimurium* when combined with bacteriophage P22. FEMS Microbiol Lett. 2013;339:137–44.
81. Akhtar M, Viazis S, Diez-Gonzalez F. Isolation, identification and characterization of lytic, wide host range bacteriophages from waste effluents against *Salmonella enterica* serovars. Food Control. 2014;38:67–74.
82. Vaks L, Benhar I. *In vivo* characteristics of targeted drug-carrying filamentous bacteriophage nanomedicines. J Nanobiotechnol. 2011;9:58.
83. Maura D, Galtier M, Le Bouguénec C, Debarbieux L. Virulent bacteriophages can target O104: H4 enteroaggregative *Escherichia coli* in the mouse intestine. Antimicrob Agents Chemother. 2012;56:6235–42.
84. Brusina E, Drozdova O, Zueva L, Akimkin V, Fedorova L. Complex application of bacteriophages as a method of healthcare-associated infections control. Antimicrob Resist Infect Control. 2015;4:P46.
85. Merabishvili M, Vandenheuvel D, Kropinski AM, Mast J, De Vos D, Verbeken G, Noben JP, Lavigne R, Vaneechoutte M, Pirnay JP. Characterization of newly isolated lytic bacteriophages active against *Acinetobacter baumannii*. PLoS One. 2014;9:104853.
86. Kajsík M, Krahulec J, Tóth C, Drahovská H, Stuchlík S, Turňa J. Control of *Cronobacter* in reconstituted infant formula by combined application of cathelicidin LL-37 and bacteriophages. J Food Nutri Res. 2015;54:22–127.
87. Zhang Y, Hunt HK, Hu Z. Application of bacteriophages to selectively remove *Pseudomonas aeruginosa* in water and wastewater filtration systems. Water Res. 2013;47:4507–18.
88. Khairnar K, Pal P, Chandekar RH, Paunikar WN. Isolation and characterization of bacteriophages infecting nocardioforms in wastewater treatment plant. Biotechnol Res Int. 2014;2014:1–5.
89. Maal KB, Delfan AS, Salmanizadeh S. Isolation identification of *Klebsiella pneumonia* and *Klebsiella oxytoca* bacteriophages and their applications in waste water treatment and coliform's phage therapy. Res J Environ Sci. 2014;8:123–33.
90. Maal KB, Delfan AS, Salmanizadeh S. Isolation and identification of two novel *Escherichia coli* bacteriophages and their application in wastewater treatment and coliform's phage therapy. Jundishapur J Microbiol. 2015;8:14945.
91. Verma V, Harjai K, Chhibber S. Structural changes induced by a lytic bacteriophage make ciprofloxacin effective against older biofilm of *Klebsiella pneumoniae*. Biofouling. 2010;26:729–37.
92. Woolston J, Parks AR, Abuladze T, Anderson B, Li M, Carter C, Hanna LF, Heyse S, Charbonneau D, Sulakvelidze A. Bacteriophages lytic for *Salmonella* rapidly reduce *Salmonella* contamination on glass and stainless steel surfaces. Bacteriophage. 2013;3:25697.
93. Lungren MP, Christensen D, Kankotia R, Falk I, Paxton BE, Kim CY. Bacteriophage K for reduction of *Staphylococcus aureus* biofilm on central venous catheter material. Bacteriophage. 2013;3:26825.
94. Yilmaz C, Colak M, Yilmaz BC, Ersoz G, Kutateladze M, Gozlugol M. Bacteriophage therapy in implant-related infections: an experimental study. JBJS. 2013;95:117–25.
95. Kiefer B, Dahl JL. Disruption of *Mycobacterium smegmatis* biofilms using bacteriophages alone or in combination with mechanical stress. Adv Microbiol. 2015;5:699.
96. Gong C, Liu X, Jiang X. Application of bacteriophages specific to hydrogen sulfide-producing bacteria in raw poultry by-products. Poult Sci. 2014;93:702–10.
97. Fiorentin L, Vieira ND, Barioni W Jr. Oral treatment with bacteriophages reduces the concentration of *Salmonella enteritidis* PT4 in caecal contents of broilers. Avian Pathol. 2005;34:258–63.
98. Hagens S, Loessner MJ. Application of bacteriophages for detection and control of foodborne pathogens. Appl Microbiol Biotechnol. 2007;76:513–9.
99. Hudson JA, Billington C, Cornelius AJ, Wilson T, On SLW, Premaratne A, King NJ. Use of a bacteriophage to inactivate *Escherichia coli* O157: H7 on beef. Food Microbiol. 2013;36:14–21.
100. Gill JJ, Pacan JC, Carson ME, Leslie KE, Griffiths MW, Sabour PM. Efficacy and pharmacokinetics of bacteriophage therapy in treatment of subclinical *Staphylococcus aureus* mastitis in lactating dairy cattle. Antimicrob Agents Chemother. 2006;50:2912–8.
101. Anany H, Brovko L, El Dougdoug NK, Sohar J, Fenn H, Alasiri N, Jabrane T, Mangin P, Ali MM, Kannan B, Filipe CD. Print to detect: a rapid and ultrasensi-

tive phage-based dipstick assay for foodborne pathogens. Anal Bioanal Chem. 2018;410:1217–30.
102. Nakai T, Park SC. Bacteriophage therapy of infectious diseases in aquaculture. Res Microbiol. 2002;153:13–8.
103. Castillo D, Christiansen RH, Espejo R, Middelboe M. Diversity and geographical distribution of *Flavobacterium psychrophilum* isolates and their phages: patterns of susceptibility to phage infection and phage host range. Microb Ecol. 2014;67:748–57.
104. Jackson LE, Jones JB. Bacteriophage: a viable bacteria control solution. In: I international symposium on tomato diseases. Vol. 695. 2004. p. 109–18.
105. Balogh B, Jones JB, Momol MT, Olson SM, Obradovic A, King P, Jackson LE. Improved efficacy of newly formulated bacteriophages for management of bacterial spot on tomato. Plant Dis. 2003;87:949–54.
106. Obradovic A, Jones JB, Momol MT, Olson SM, Jackson LE, Balogh B, Guven K, Iriarte FB. Integration of biological control agents and systemic acquired resistance inducers against bacterial spot on tomato. Plant Dis. 2005;89:712–6.
107. Fischetti VA. Bacteriophage lytic enzymes: novel anti-infectives. Trends Microbiol. 2005;13:491–6.
108. O'Flaherty S, Ross RP, Coffey A. Bacteriophage and their lysins for elimination of infectious bacteria. FEMS Microbiol Rev. 2009;33:801–19.
109. Loeffler JM, Nelson D, Fischetti VA. Rapid killing of *Streptococcus pneumoniae* with a bacteriophage cell wall hydrolase. Science. 2001;294:2170–2.
110. Nelson D, Loomis L, Fischetti VA. Prevention and elimination of upper respiratory colonization of mice by group A *streptococci* by using a bacteriophage lytic enzyme. Proc Natl Acad Sci U S A. 2001;98:4107–12.
111. Jado I, López R, García E, Fenoll A, Casal J, García P. Phage lytic enzymes as therapy for antibiotic-resistant *Streptococcus pneumoniae* infection in a murine sepsis model. J Antimicrob Chemother. 2003;52:967–73.
112. Loeffler JM, Djurkovic S, Fischetti VA. Phage lytic enzyme Cpl-1 as a novel antimicrobial for pneumococcal bacteremia. Infect Immun. 2003;71:6199–204.
113. Loeffler JM, Fischetti VA. Synergistic lethal effect of a combination of phage lytic enzymes with different activities on penicillin-sensitive and-resistant *Streptococcus pneumoniae* strains. Antimicrob Agents Chemother. 2003;47:375–7.
114. Entenza JM, Loeffler JM, Grandgirard D, Fischetti VA, Moreillon P. Therapeutic effects of bacteriophage Cpl-1 lysin against *Streptococcus pneumoniae* endocarditis in rats. Antimicrob Agents Chemother. 2005;49:4789–92.
115. Grandgirard D, Loeffler JM, Fischetti VA, Leib SL. Phage lytic enzyme Cpl-1 for antibacterial therapy in experimental pneumococcal meningitis. J Infect Dis. 2008;197:1519–22.
116. McCullers JA, Karlström Å, Iverson AR, Loeffler JM, Fischetti VA. Novel strategy to prevent otitis media caused by colonizing *Streptococcus pneumoniae*. PLoS Pathog. 2007;3:28.
117. Schuch R, Nelson D, Fischetti VA. A bacteriolytic agent that detects and kills *Bacillus anthracis*. Nature. 2002;418:884.
118. Yoong P, Schuch R, Nelson D, Fischetti VA. PlyPH, a bacteriolytic enzyme with a broad pH range of activity and lytic action against *Bacillus anthracis*. J Bacteriol. 2006;188:2711–4.
119. Donovan DM, Lardeo M, Foster-Frey J. Lysis of *Staphylococcal mastitis* pathogens by bacteriophage phi11 endolysin. FEMS Microbiol Lett. 2006;265:133–9.
120. Obeso JM, Martínez B, Rodríguez A, García P. Lytic activity of the recombinant *staphylococcal* bacteriophage ΦH5 endolysin active against *Staphylococcus aureus* in milk. Int J Food Microbiol. 2008;128:212–8.
121. O'Flaherty S, Coffey A, Meaney W, Fitzgerald GF, Ross RP. The recombinant phage lysin LysK has a broad spectrum of lytic activity against clinically relevant staphylococci, including methicillin-resistant *Staphylococcus aureus*. J Bacteriol. 2005;187:7161–4.
122. Rashel M, Uchiyama J, Ujihara T, Uehara Y, Kuramoto S, Sugihara S, Yagyu KI, Muraoka A, Sugai M, Hiramatsu K, Honke K. Efficient elimination of multidrug-resistant *Staphylococcus aureus* by cloned lysin derived from bacteriophage MR11. J Infect Dis. 2007;196:1237–47.
123. Gaeng S, Scherer S, Neve H, Loessner MJ. Gene cloning and expression and secretion of *Listeria monocytogenes* bacteriophage-lytic enzymes in *Lactococcus lactis*. Appl Environ Microbiol. 2000;66:2951–8.
124. Loessner MJ, Schneider A, Scherer S. A new procedure for efficient recovery of DNA, RNA, and proteins from *Listeria* cells by rapid lysis with a recombinant bacteriophage endolysin. Appl Environ Microbiol. 1995;61:1150–2.
125. Loessner MJ, Wendlinger G, Scherer S. Heterogeneous endolysins in *Listeria monocytogenes* bacteriophages: a new class of enzymes and evidence for conserved holin genes within the siphoviral lysis cassettes. Mol Microbiol. 1995;16:1231–41.
126. Yoong P, Schuch R, Nelson D, Fischetti VA. Identification of a broadly active phage lytic enzyme with lethal activity against antibiotic-resistant *Enterococcus faecalis* and *Enterococcus faecium*. J Bacteriol. 2004;186:4808–12.
127. Cheng Q, Nelson D, Zhu S, Fischetti VA. Removal of group B *streptococci* colonizing the vagina and oropharynx of mice with a bacteriophage lytic enzyme. Antimicrob Agents Chemother. 2005;49:111–7.
128. Pritchard DG, Dong S, Baker JR, Engler JA. The bifunctional peptidoglycan lysin of *Streptococcus agalactiae* bacteriophage B30. Microbiology. 2004;150:2079–87.

Translation Research and Herbal Drug Development

18

Muthusamy Sanjivkumar, Tamilselvan Silambarasan, and Kasilingam Nagajothi

18.1 Introduction

Plants are primary producers or autotrophic organisms and they have different bio-chemicals gathered from various parts of their body. These chemicals can be served as therapeutic components to treat various diseases or disorders. Such therapeutically active plants are called as herbs or medicinal plants [1, 2]. Various biotherapeutic components obtained from the medicinal plants are served as a drug, can able to treat, prevent, or cure a dreadful disease. The different groups of plant-based organic chemical constituents or phytochemicals or secondary metabolites have not involved directly in the vital processes of respiration, photosynthesis, solute transport, nutrient assimilation, and protein synthesis [3, 4]. However, the plant-derived components served as herbal remedy used in the traditional folk medicine, which are mainly explored for the production of new active drugs for chemotherapy. We can be used these phyto-components for the overcome of different growing problems originated due to multiple drug resistance and also avoid the toxicity nature of antibiotics [5].

M. Sanjivkumar (✉) · K. Nagajothi
Department of Microbiology, K.R. College of Arts and Science, Kovilpatti, Tamil Nadu, India

T. Silambarasan
School of Allied Health Science, VIMS Hospital Campus, Vinayaka Missions Research Foundation, Salem, Tamil Nadu, India

The increasing significance of plant-based secondary metabolites for human and animal disease management have directed examination toward the search of novel sources of biologically active natural products. These natural derived products have the ability to fight against various health issues of 80% of rural people in the urban area [6, 7]. Today, it is assessed that more than two-thirds of the world's population depend on plant-based secondary metabolites or drugs; more than 7000 plant-based medicinal components have been employed [8, 9]. In the USA, almost 30% of all the prescribed drugs used to comprise one or more plant-derived bioactive compounds. The plant-based pharmaceutical products or herbal drugs are any manufactured medicine attained from resins, aerial and non-aerial parts of the plants, juices, and oil. It may be used either in the form of crude state or as a pharmacological formulation [10]. The role of prominence usage of traditional medicine or healthcare systems will not make any default in the future, because of they are inexpensive, culturally viable, no toxicity, safer to health, respectively, compared to the modern healthcare service, which is more limited and expensive [4, 8].

Scientists categorize the plant-derived biologically active secondary metabolites, based on their presence of chemical constituents such as peptides, polysaccharides, phenolic groups, alkaloids, isoprenoids, saponins, xanthones, glucosinolates, curcumin, resveratrol, anthraqui-

K. Parthasarathy, R. Manikkam (eds.), *Translational Research in Biomedical Sciences: Recent Progress and Future Prospects*, https://doi.org/10.1007/978-981-97-1777-4_18

nones, betaxanthin, betacyanin, lycopene, phytosterols. These chemical groups have high specificity with unique applications and are represents the following plant families like *Moraceae, Orchidaceae, Polygalaceae, Theaceae, Gentianaceae, Hypericaceae, Iridaceae,* and *Asparagaceae,* etc. [11]. Plants can able to produce various secondary metabolites used to protect against different clinical pathogens such as bacteria, viruses, fungi, and protozoa. It helps to boost up our immune systems and used as a blood pressure normalizer as well as food supplements [2, 12]. The plant-derived secondary metabolites have potent biotherapeutic applications and used to treat different diseases like COVID-19, hepatitis, HIV, etc., they also have some pharmaceutical properties such as antimicrobial (antibacterial, antifungal, antiviral), anti-inflammatory, antioxidant, anticancer, anti-biofilm, antidiabetic, antidysenteric, antiulcer, Alzheimer's, Parkinson's diseases, osteoarthritis, cerebrovascular, chronic obstructive pulmonary, and coronary artery diseases [3, 10].

18.1.1 Plant-Derived Bioactive Metabolites

The medicinal properties of plants have been extensively used for human welfare since ancient times, and they also serve as an important source of pharmaceuticals. Natural metabolites such as alkaloids, flavonoids, phenols, steroids, and terpenoids that are structurally unique and bioactive provide a rich resource for the discovery of novel therapeutic approaches [13]. The metabolites they produce are highly potent antifungal, antiviral, antibacterial, cytotoxic, and immunosuppressive. A crucial role may be played by these bioactive metabolites in treating infectious diseases. There is a rich source of natural products derived from plants, also known as secondary or specialized metabolites [14, 15]. In recent years, advances have been made in elucidating the biosynthesis of phenylpropanoids, terpenoids. and alkaloids from medicinal plants as a novel drug.

18.1.1.1 Phenylpropanoids

These compounds are known to be specialized metabolites, including monolignols, lignans, flavonoids, phenolic acids, phenolic acids, stilbenes, derived from the six-carbon aromatic chain phenyl and the three-carbon propene tail. Phenylpropanoids are commonly found in plants and are derived from the six-carbon aromatic chain phenyl and the three-carbon propene tail. Phytoalexins serve as protection against herbivores and pathogens, as well as a number of structural polymers and floral pigments, scent compounds, and signaling molecules that facilitate bio-interactions [12, 16]. UV light radiation and other abiotic stresses act as protection against these molecules. These compounds act as antioxidants, free radical scavengers, anti-inflammatories, and anticancer compounds in many TCM plants, including *Lamiaceae, Fabaceae,* and *Asteraceae.* It is phenylalanine that is the source of the majority of phenylpropanoids [17]. This pathway is known as the general phenylpropanoid pathway because it first requires phenylalanine ammonia lyase (PAL), cinnamate 4-hydroxylase (C4H), and *p*-coumaroyl coenzyme A ligase (4CL) to catalyze three steps. In plants, phenylpropanoids are synthesized from 4CL as a precursor. The transformation of phenylpropanoids is more restricted; it occurs mostly in members of several families. A phenylpropanoid is generally produced by converting L-tyrosine into D-tyrosine. 3,4-dihydroxyphenyllactic acid, one precursor of rosmarinic acid, is produced by this pathway [2, 18].

18.1.1.2 Flavonoids

Flavonoids are a diverse class of secondary metabolites composed of more than 9000 structural variants. The majority of land plants contain them, including vascular plants and some mosses. The compounds are further classified into flavanones, flavones, flavonols, isoflavonoids, anthocyanins, and proanthocyanidins according to their aglycone core. It is derived from condensation of three malonylCoA molecules with one *p*-coumaroyl-CoA to produce a chalcone intermediate [19, 20]. All flavonoids are derived from

1,3-diphenylpropan-1-one (C6–C3–C6). Flavanones are formed from chalcone through chalcone isomerase, and each of these flavanones are converted into various flavones, isoflavones, dihydorflavonols, flavonols, and anthocyanins by their respective enzymes. There is a wide variety of flavonones in folk medicine and each class possesses compounds with pharmaceutical activity. Biosynthesis of flavones in plants is catalyzed by two different flavone synthases (FNS). It was discovered that the first FNS I member in parsley (*Petroselinum crispum*) cellular suspension cultures was a 2-oxoglutarate-dependent dioxygenase. It has been discovered that most of the characterized FNS I enzymes are members of the Apiaceae family, namely, flavanone 2-hydroxylase (F2H), one of the members of the FNS II family. A dehydrase was likely to be involved in catalyzing the formation of flavones in vitro, as 2-hydroxyflavanones were transformed into flavones. The health-promoting properties of isoflavones have been identified from plants. They are the major bioactive ingredients in soybean, *Astragalus*, and *Pueraria lobata*, which are leguminous plants. It is the isoflavone synthase (IFS) that converts flavanones into isoflavones. In plants, more than 1000 prenylated flavonoids have been found. There is a connection between prenylation and flavonoids' diversification. As a result of this prenylation, a covalent bond is formed between the aromatic moiety from schikmate pathway and the prenyl (isoprenoid) chain from isoprenoid pathway. In medicinal plants, numerous prenylated flavonoids are active components, which make them especially useful as lead compounds for medications and functional foods [21].

18.1.1.3 Terpenoids

The terpenoids are composed of five carbon molecules (C_5H_8) called isoprene units. Accordingly, monoterpenes, sesquiterpenes, diterpenes, or combinations of them constitute hemiterpenes, monoterpenes, and monoterpenes, respectively [8, 12]. Oxidation, reduction, isomerization, and conjugation are carried out after the formation of the carbon skeletons. Approximately 36,000 plant specialized metabolites are found in this group, which represents the most abundant class of specialized metabolites [22]. The common precursors of terpenoids, isopentenyl diphosphate (IPP), and dimethylallyl diphosphate (DMAPP) can be synthesized via two separate pathways in plant cells: mevalonic acid (MVA) is synthesized in the cytosol from condensation of acetyl-CoA and mevalonic acid (MEP) is synthesized in the plastid using pyruvate and glyceraldehydes 3-phosphate as substrates. Through the respective prenyltransferases, IPP and DMAPP are condensed into geranyl diphosphate (GPP, C10), farnesyl diphosphate (FPP, C15), and geranylgeranyl diphosphate (GGPP, C20), and then metabolized into terpenes by terpene synthases (TPSs), which determine terpen skeleton structure [3, 5]. As a general rule, sequiterpenes and triterpenes are synthesized by the cytosolic MVA pathway, while monoterpenes, diterpenes, and tetraterpenes are synthesized by the plastid MEP pathway. Despite the fact that there is abundant cross-talk between these two spatially separated IPP pathways, particularly between the plastid and the cytosol [15, 23].

18.1.1.4 Alkaloids

Alkaloid is a nitrogen-containing compound with basic properties. A majority of alkaloids are amino acid derivatives. Decarboxylation or deamination of amino acids is the most common cause of alkaloids' biosynthesis, followed by methylation, hydroxylation, and oxidation, and/or combinations with other compounds [23]. More than 12,000 alkaloids have been identified from plants. There are a wide variety of plants that have these chemicals, but the most abundant families are the Solanaceae, Manispermaceae, Papaveraceae, Berberidaceae, and Fabaceae. A significant aspect of alkaloids is that they possess some bioactivity to varying degrees, often as a result of their nitrogen content [24]. Alkaloids make up a significant portion of drugs, both historically and today. The biosynthesis of natural alkaloids such as morphinan, vindoline, and noscapine has been extensively studied and the pathway has been completely elucidated and it has also been reported that co-expression of enzyme genes can increase alkaloid biosynthesis in plants. There are few reports of biosynthesis of TCM alkaloids such as camptothecin, higenamine, huperzine A, and tetrandrine although these compounds have been used in pharmacy [25, 26].

18.2 Biomedical Efficacy of Plant-derived Bioactive Metabolites

The multiple plant-based secondary metabolites have different pharmaceutical properties such as antimicrobial, anti-biofilm, antioxidant, anticancer, antidiabetic, and anti-inflammatory activities, etc., and schematic diagram also represented in Fig. 18.1. The list of biomedical efficacy of different plant-derived secondary metabolites are summarized in Table 18.1. The biomedical efficacy of plant-based components are as follows

18.2.1 Antimicrobial Properties

The biomedical applications of plant-based phytochemical constituents are of more importance to researchers for developing antimicrobial drugs against various clinical pathogens, which are no toxicity, safe to health, and less expensive [9]. Plants derive secondary metabolites are more effective, potent biotherapeutic properties, and provide significant efficacy of antimicrobial agents. The antibacterial property of aqueous leaves extracts of *Euphorbia cotinifolia* was tested against human clinical pathogenic organisms such as *Bacillus cereus* (20 mm), *Klebsiella pneumoniae* (19 mm), *Enterobacter aerogenes* (21 mm), *Escherichia coli* (23 mm), and *Staphylococcus aureus* (20 mm) using agar well diffusion assay method by Jayalakshmi et al. [1]. Dissanayake et al. [36, 37] achieved the antimicrobial activity of methanol mediated leaf extraction of *Plumbago indica* exhibited the maximum zone of inhibition 19 mm against *E. coli,* 11 mm against *P. aeruginosa,* 24 mm against *S. aureus,* and 21 mm against *B. cereus*, respectively, through agar well diffusion assay method. Similarly, Nyarko et al. [38] demonstrated the antagonistic effect of aqueous plant extract of *Tinospora cordifolia* against various human clinical pathogens like *E. coli* (19 mm) and *S. aureus* (21 mm) using sterile Muller Hinton agar.

In an another study, Qanash et al. [20] performed that the antibacterial efficacy of methonalic leaf extract of *Dovyalis caffra* exhibited maximum zone of growth inhibition against *E.*

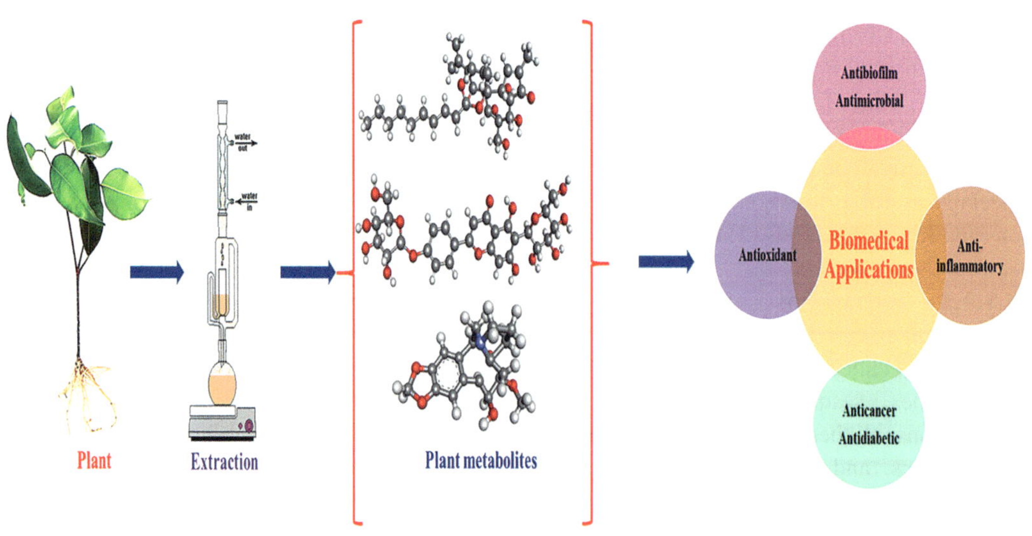

Fig. 18.1 Schematic diagram about the biomedical efficacy of different secondary metabolites extracted from plant bioresources

Table 18.1 List of different biotherapeutic efficacy of bioactive molecules extracted from plant bioresources

Plant sources	Bioactive molecules	Applications	References
Teucrium polium	Polyphenolic groups, flavonoids, monoterpenes	Anti-inflammatory activity	Rahmouni et al. [27]
Eremurus persicus	Polyphenolic groups	Antioxidant activity	Bayrak and Yanardag [28]
Dodonaea viscosa and *Juniperus excelsa*	Anthocyanin, flavonoids and alkaloids	Antioxidant activity and anticancer activity	Rehman et al. [29]
Chelidonium majus and *Corydalis cava*	Isoquinoline, alkaloids, *p*-coumaric acid, chlorogenic acid	Anti-inflammatory, antioxidant, and anti-biofilm activity	Zielinska et al. [16]
Salvia officinalis	12-Methoxy-trans-carnosic acid and carnosol	Anti-biofilm, anti-inflammatory, antioxidant activity	Kerkoub et al. [30]
Zapoteca portoricensis	Flavonoids	Antimicrobial activity and anti-biofilm activity	Agbafor et al. [31]
Fabaceae and *Labiatae*	Tunnins, flavonoids	Antimicrobial activity and anti-biofilm activity	Korir et al. [32]
Ficus indica	Flavonoids, luteolin, quercetin, and apigenin	Anti-inflammatory, antioxidant, and cytotoxic activity	Blando et al. [13]
Cocculus trilobus	Isoquinoline, alkaloids, *p*-coumaric acid	Antimicrobial, antioxidant, and cytotoxic activity	Lu et al. [33]
Lepidium sativum	Alkaloids, 2-pentanoic acid, penta-decadienoic acid	Antimicrobial activity and antioxidant activity	Singh et al. [17]
Acalypha indica, Alpinia galangal	Flavonoids, monoterpenes and alkaloids	Antimicrobial activity and antioxidant activity	Zahidin et al. [18]
Uromyrtus metrosideros	Galloyl glucosides, galloyl-lawsoniaside A	Anti-inflammatory, antimicrobial activity, and anti-biofilm property	Ritmejeryte et al. [34]
Adiantum philippense	7-epiclusianone, tannic acid	Antioxidant activity and anticancer activity	Adnan et al. [35]

coli (20 mm), *Proteus vulgaris* (13 mm), *S. aureus* (24 mm), and *B. subtilis* (22 mm). Mehta et al. [39] attained the maximum zone of growth inhibition of different bacteria like *K. pneumoniae* (19.3 mm), *E. coli* (22.3 mm), and *S. aureus* (25 mm) by using a methane mediated leaf extract of *Bacopa monnieri* through agar well diffusion assay method. Similarly, an antimicrobial properties of ethyl acetate leaf extract of *Ocimum americanum* L. expressed the growth inhibition against the Gram-positive bacteria [*B. cereus* (19 mm) and *S. aureus* (20 mm)] and Gram-negative bacteria [*E. coli* (21 mm) and *K. pneumoniae* (20 mm)] were documented by Ali et al. [40]. Who were also denoted that the highest zone of growth inhibition (26 mm) against *B. cereus* with the MIC value of 62.5 mg/mL. Chebbac et al. [41] showed antagonistic effect of an essential oil extracted from *Artemisia aragonensis* L. exhibited the zone of growth inhibition against *S. aureus* (21 mm), *E. coli* (23 mm), and *B. subtilis* (24 mm), respectively, at 5.37 μg/mL concentration.

Nigussie et al. [42] analyzed an antagonistic efficiency of aqueous leaf extract of *A. indica* expressed the zone of growth inhibition against *S. pyogenes* (21 mm), *S. aureus* (28 mm), *E. coli* (20 mm), *P. aeruginosa* (16 mm), and *K. pneumoniae* (18 mm), respectively, compared with the standard drug cefoxitin (15–24 mm) through agar well diffusion assay method. Mariyammal et al. [43] described the antibacterial activity of hydro alcoholic extract of *Aristolochia tagala* effectively inhibit the growth of bacterial isolates like *P. valgaris* (26.3 mm) and *P. aeruginosa* (19.33 mm). They were also exhibited the maximum zone of growth inhibition against *E. coli* (28 mm) with the MIC vale 10.93 μg/mL. Wahyuni et al. [44] studied the antimicrobial activities of ethyl acetate mediated hardwood extract of *Pterocarpus macrocarpus Kurz* showed the growth inhibition against *B. subtilis* TISTR

1248 (22 mm), *C. albicans* ATCC 10231 (25 mm), *E. coli* ATCC 25922 (24 mm), and *S. aureus* ATCC 25923 (28 mm). Vijay et al. [45] reported the antimicrobial activity of ethanol leaf extract of *Commelina forskaolii* against the bacteria *E. fecalis* (19 mm), *P. aeruginosa* (18.3 mm), *C. albicans* (20 mm), and *A. niger* (19 mm) through agar well diffusion assay method.

Haddad et al. [19] reported that the antibacterial efficiency of methanolic leaf extract of *V. iphionoides* against various clinical bacterial strains with the zone of growth inhibition of *K. pneumoniae* ATCC13883 (19.2 mm), *P. vulgaris* ATCC13315 (18.3 mm), methicillin-resistant *S. aureus* ATCC95047 (22 mm), and *E. coli* ATCC43895 (20 mm), respectively. In an another report, Dissanayake et al. [36, 37] portrayed the antifungal efficiency of methanolic leaf extract of *Plumbago indica* expressed the maximum growth inhibition against *C. albicans* (19.3 mm) under agar well diffusion assay. Chebbac et al. [41] examined the antifungal properties of essential oil extracted from *Artemisia aragonensis* showed the growth inhibition rate against different fungal species are *F. oxysporum* (20 mm), *C. albicans* (21.5 mm), *A. flavus* (19 mm), and *A. niger* (18.3 mm) at the concentration of 5.30 μg/mL, respectively.

18.2.2 Anti-biofilm Activities

Biofilms are a group of microbial consortium, incorporated on the surface of organic polymers. These organisms can able to adhere on the inert or living surfaces, and interface with one another making stronger association. The bacterial association into biofilms offer a major impact of ecological, industrial, sanitary, and health problems. After the formation of biofilm, the bacteria gain more protectiveness against various chemicals, disinfectants, and antibiotics. The formation of microbial biofilm contributes resistance power to antibiotics and tolerance to different immune cells. These problems are overcome by the influences of natural bioactive components obtained from plant origin namely cinnamic acid, eugenol, phenylpropanoid, and cinnamaldehyde [11]. Jang et al. [46] investigated that the anti-biofilm efficacy of plant-derived phytochemical alpha-humulene against *Bacteroides fragilis* under in vitro condition exhibited maximum percentage of inhibition (82.3%) at 8.0 g/mL concentration. In an another study, aqueous leaf extract of *Ginkgo biloba* strongly (86.23%) inhibit the biofilm formation by *Escherichia coli* O157:H7 at 8.0 g/mL concentration under laboratory condition attained by Lee et al. [47]. Roy et al. [21] performed an in vitro anti-biofilm efficacy of aqueous leaf extract of *Moringa stenopetala* against MRSA strain. They were also observed that the maximum percentage of inhibition (84%) of biofilm forming bacteria attained at 1000 μg/mL concentration.

Likewise, Lara et al. [48] documented the anti-biofilm efficiency of dichloromethane mediated seed extract of *Piper regnellii* against methicillin-resistant biofilm forming bacteria *S. aureus* with the percentage of inhibition of 78.42% at 12.5 g/mL concentration. Blando et al. [13] evaluated the anti-biofilm activity of polyphenolic leaf extract of *Opuntia ficus indica* under laboratory condition. They were stated that the leaf extract can able to control the development of *Enterobacteria* sp. and also inhibit (85%) the biofilm formation of *S. aureus* at the concentration rate of 1000 μg/mL. Snoussi et al. [22] reported the anti-biofilm effects aqueous leaf extract of *Allium subhirsutum* through in vitro condition against *S. aureus* showed the percentage of inhibition of 56.21% with the minimum inhibitory concentration of 10 mg/mL. Vijayakumar and Ramanathan [49] demonstrated the anti-biofilm efficacy of 5-hydroxymethylfurfural against various biofilm forming bacteria with the percentage of inhibitions like *Streptococcus pyogenes* (83%), *S. aureus* (82%), *S. epidermidis* (79%), and *S. mutans* (86%), respectively, at 125 μg/mL concentration.

18.2.3 Antioxidant Activities

Oxidative stress is the major causes of cellular aging as well as some chronic diseases and it may occur due to an inequity of radicals and antioxidants. The antioxidants, that are obtain from nature, used to eradicate or neutralize the formation of free radicals by donating an electron. These neutralizing efficacy of antioxidants helps to protect our body from dangerous oxidative stress [15]. More than 8500 different phenolic groups have been identified and characterized from fruits and vegetables are the major sources of natural antioxidants to reduce the formation free oxygen radicals [15, 50]. Many of the medicinal plants (turmeric, tamarind, cardamom, lemon grass, and galangal basil, etc.) are the novel sources of phytochemicals possess antioxidant activities. They consist of different polyphenols and carotenoids such as quercetin, quinic, caffeic, and *p*-coumaric acids showed antioxidant properties [2].

Akgul, et al. [23] determined that the in vitro total antioxidant activity of aqueous leaf extract of *Euphorbia eriophora Boiss* by using 2,2-diphenyl-1-picrylhydrazyl (DPPH) free radical scavenging activity exhibited maximum antioxidant activity of 68.721% at 2 mg/mL concentration. Ayaz et al. [24] studied an in vitro antioxidant activity of aqueous leaves extract of *Persicaria hydropiper* L through DPPH and ABTS (2,2-azino-bis(3-ethylbenzothiazoline-6-sulfonic acid) scavenging activities. Who also denoted that the leaf extract showed high percentage of inhibition 81.84 and 78.79% with the IC_{50} values of 85 and 170 $\mu g{\cdot}mL^{-1,}$ respectively. Yang et al. [50] investigated the antioxidant potential of purified polysaccharides (CPs-1) (0.25–4.0 mg/mL) extracted from Chinese herbal medicine (consist of lotus leaf, hawthorn, *Poria cocos, Lycium barbarum, Semen cassiae*, and *Fagopyrum tataricum*) by using ABTS scavenging activity. They were also denoted that the maximum percentage of antioxidant activity (98.47%) at 4.0 mg/mL concentration. Abdelfattah et al. [51] determined an in vitro antioxidant properties of aqueous bark extract of *Warburgia salutaris* using DPPH and FRAP radical scavenging assays under laboratory condition. Who also observed that the maximum percentage of inhibition were attained 84 and 78% with IC_{50} values of 14.06 and 42.03 μg/mL.

In an another report, Islam et al. [52] analyzed the antioxidant potential of phenolics and flavonoids extracted from aqueous leaf extract of *Wedelia chinensis* through DPPH scavenging assay under laboratory condition. Which expressed highest percentage of DPPH activity 87.2 and 90% with IC_{50} values of 45.20 μg/mL and 25.53 μg/mL, respectively. The antioxidant potential of aqueous leaf extract of *Pholidota cantonensis* showed 78.32% of inhibition against DPPH as well as 82.64% against ABTS at 50 μg/mL concentration was documented by Liu et al. [12]. Similarly, the antioxidant activity of ethanol mediated leaf extract of *Jasminum abyssinicum* under in vitro DPPH assay method showed maximum percentage of inhibition (84.78%) with the IC_{50} of 26.3 μg/mL were reported by Balkrishna et al. [53]. Who also highlighted that the percentage of inhibitions 78.96% for nitric oxide and 83.24% for superoxide dismutase scavenging activities at 50 μg/mL concentration.

Sonter et al. [54] performed the in vitro antioxidant properties of acetone mediated leaf extracts of *Murraya paniculata* through ABTS and hydroxyl radical scavenging activities expressed the highest percentage of inhibition 87.20 and 83.57% with the IC_{50} values of 555.18 and 509.84 μg/mL, respectively. Okello et al. [15] studied the antioxidant potential of secondary metabolites extracted from *Aspilia africana* by DPPH scavenging assay exhibited the high percentage of inhibition of 88.43% with the IC_{50} value of 27.25 μg/mL. DPPH radical scavenging activity of aqueous leaf extract of *Echinops setifer* showed the maximum percentage of inhibition 72.75% was documented by Falah et al. [55]. Similarly, the methanolic leaf extract of *Azanza garckeana* showed the highest percentage of antioxidant activities (92 and 88%) of both DPPH and ABTS activities, respectively with the IC_{50} values of 141.30 and 162.56 μg/mL by Lawal et al. [56].

18.2.4 Anticancer Activities

Cancer is a dreadful disease, hard to cure when its untreated, and subsequently makes death. The secondary metabolites enumerated from the plant bioresources could be used widely as a biotherapeutic agents against cancer disease. More than

75% of anticancer drugs are majorly obtained from plant origin exhibited good pharmacokinetic property against cancerous cells. Al-Dabbas et al. [57] described the cytotoxic efficacy of different solvent leaf extracts of *Varthemia Iphionoides Boiss* against human myelocytic leukemia cell lines (HL-60) under in vitro condition. They were also observed that the maximum cell inhibition of 89.0, 68.4, and 62.3%, respectively, at 200 μg extract/mL concentration. Ghasemzadeh et al. [58] documented that the anticancer efficacy of aqueous flower extract of *E. elatior* against human breast cancer cell lines with the percentage of inhibitions MCF-7 (82%) and MDA-MB-231 (80%) with the IC_{50} values of 173.1 and 196.2 μg/mL, respectively.

Suroowan et al. [59] reported an in vitro cytotoxic efficacy of methnol mediated leaf extract of *Artemisia verlotiorum* showed the percentage cell inhibition 82.01 and 78.30% against both HepG2 and HT29 cancerous cells with the respective IC_{50} values of 722.39 and 792.91 μg/mL. An anticancer activity of ethanolic leaf extract of *V. iphionoides* was examined for breast cancer (MCF7) as well as colon cancer (HT29) cell lines under laboratory condition by Al-Rimawi et al. [14] exhibited the percentage of cell inhibition of 72.8 and 82.4%, respectively. Wen et al. [60] documented that the anticancer activity of flavonoids extracted from *Erythrina suberosa* stem bark against hepatoma (Hep-G2) and breast cancer (MCF-7) cell lines under in vitro conditions exhibited the cell inhibition of 81.3 and 84% respectively. Mykhailenko et al. [61] demonstrated that the cytotoxic efficacy of dry extracts of iridaceae plant against human breast cancer (MCF-7), colon cancer (HCT116), cervical carcinoma (HeLa) cell lines through MTT assay. They were also observed the maximum percentage of cell inhibition 85.2, 79.46 and 88.2%, respectively, with the IC_{50} values of 3.5, 3.6, and 3.8 μg/mL.

18.2.5 Antidiabetic Activities

Now a days, a common metabolic disorder diabetes mellitus affects all the human beings throughout the world, due to hyperglycemia, defects in insulin secretion or action or both. This problem may cause long-term damage, dysfunction, and failure of several organs like kidneys, eyes, nerves, heart, and blood vessels [62]. Various drugs are commonly used for the prevention and control of diabetes (sulfonylureas, biguanides, meglitinides, glitazones, etc.). However, effective research is still going on for creating an alternative therapy against diabetes. The plant-derived bio-metabolites as a source of drug for employing a main role to cure diabetes [63]. In India, different varieties of herbs are found to be suitable for the controlling of diabetes. Based on the ethnobotanical information approximately 800 plants may possess antidiabetic activities. Saranya et al. [7] documented that the antidiabetic activity of aqueous flowers extract of *Cocos nucifera* control the sugar level in the rats which is already induced with streptozotocin at the dose of 300 mg/kg.

In an another study, Wen and Chen [5] observed that the hypoglycemic effect of ethanol mediated leaf extract of *Swertia punicea,* respectively, compared with streptozotocin induced type-II diabetic mice. Kahksha et al. (2022) studied that the secondary metabolites extracted from the plant *Gymnema* species have well-known medical properties such as anti-inflammatory, antidiabetic, antibacterial, anti-hyperlipidemic, and immune-stimulatory. They were also denoted that nearly 27 active pharmacologically important metabolites such as glycosides, saponin, gymnemic acids, and triterpenoid, etc., used for the treatment of type-II diabetes. According to Zhu et al. [64] plant-derived bio-metabolite indole alkaloids play an important role in curing anticonvulsant and antidiabetic activities. Who also observed that the 267 μg/mL of metabolite effective against Type-I diabetes induced rats. In an another report, Vijayanand [65] denoted that the aqueous leaf extracts of *Murraya koenigii* significantly reduced the hypoglycemic effect, respectively, compared to alloxan induced diabetic albino rats at the concentration of doses of 250–500 mg/kg. Ayaz et al. [24] studied an in vitro antidiabetic activity of secondary bioactive metabolites extracted from aqueous leaves extract of *Persicaria hydropiper* L. showed the maximum percentage of enzymes inhibition of α-glucosidase (82%) and α-amylase (80%) at 1000 μg·mL^{-1} concentration.

18.2.6 Anti-inflammatory Activities

A drug that possesses anti-inflammatory efficacy can able to hinder the pathophysiology of inflammation and to reduce the tissue damage [10]. Various plant species belong to *Anacardiaceae* families are *Myracroduo nurundeuva*, *Schinus terebinthifolius,* and *Spondias purpurea* showed a wide range of phytochemicals (phenols, flavonoids, cinnamic acid, and triterpenes) expressed high anti-inflammatory activity [10, 26]. Plant-based flavonoids can able to inhibit the formation of inflammatory mediators through modulating the arachidonic acid pathway as well as inhibiting the activity of different enzymes like NADH oxidase, peroxidases, cyclooxygenase, lipoxygenase, protein kinase, hydrolases, metallopeptidases, and tyrosinases etc. Hence, the flavonoids from plant bioresources showed therapeutic properties and served as a potent drug for minimize the inflammatory activity [66].

In an another research, Cabral et al. [8] demonstrated the anti-inflammatory activity of methanolic leaves extract of *Spondias mombin* at the concentration of 100, 200, 300, and 500 mg/kg, who also observed that the leaf extract (200 mg/kg) showed highest percentage of inhibition (89%) under laboratory condition. Similarly, Mostofa et al. [66] reported that the anti-inflammatory activity of methanolic leaf extract of *Phyllanthus niruri* expressed the percentage of inhibitions 46.80% (100 mg/kg), 55.32% (200 mg/kg), and 69.14% (400 mg/kg), respectively, compared with a standard drug ibuprofen (20 mg/kg). Gupta et al. [25] investigated the anti-inflammatory activity of oils from *Pinus* species through protein denaturation method. They were also found that *P. gerardiana* showed greater anti-inflammatory activity with the IC_{50} value of 221.24 μg/mL than *P. roxburghii* IC_{50} (227.34 μg/mL). The anti-inflammatory properties of oils extracted from *Galagania fragrantissima* and *Origanum tyttanthum* showed the maximum percentage of inhibition (90 and 82%) with the IC_{50} values of 7.34 and 14.78 μg/mL, respectively, denoted by Sharopov et al. [67].

In an another study, Azab et al. [68] observed the anti-inflammatory property of different phytochemicals such as pseudohypericin, amentoflavone, and hyperforin extracted from *Allium cepa showed maximum percentage of inhibition and* decrease the odema quantity in both acute and chronic models. Dinica et al. [69] performed that the anti-inflammatory properties of allantoin extracted from *Symphytum officinale* at the concentrations of 0.25–2 mg/mL, who also observed that the maximum percentage of inhibition (87.20%) at 1 mg/mL concentration, respectively, compared with standard drug diclofenac sodium (85.64%). Abima Shazhni et al. [70] investigated the anti-inflammatory properties of aqueous leaf extract of *Caladium hortulanum* and also inhibited the inflammatory enzyme cyclooxygenase activity by 45.85% at 2 mg/mL concentration. Pant et al. [71] studied the anti-inflammatory properties of acetone mediated extract of stem wood of *Pterocarpus marsupium* expressed the highest percentage of inhibition 52.96% at 200 mg/kg concentration.

18.3 Conclusions

In contrast to synthesized drug molecules, plant secondary metabolites, as well as plant cell and organ cultures are more controllable, environmentally friendly, and sustainable. The above-mentioned data indicate that herbal medicines are biologically active due to several classes of secondary plant metabolites. Plant secondary metabolites are ultimately acting on different molecular targets based on their composition. In addition to enzymes, mediators, transcription factors, and nucleic acids, these targets may also be structural elements. A comprehensive phytochemical study should be conducted before herbal medicines are used to determine the chemical composition of herbs. Thus, the effects of multiple ingredient herbal formulas can be determined pharmacologically and toxicologically, as well as their possible synergistic or antagonistic effects. Hence, although ancient, the identification of secondary plant metabolites and their structural elucidation continues to be a huge and fast-growing field, the methods for separation and analysis of these metabolites are constantly being improved. Those substances that plants secrete as secondary metabolites can be used therapeutically in many ways, such as for the treatment of cardiovascular disease, antidiabetic and antiviral activities. Physiologically, metabolites have gained popularity in recent years because of their importance to human health. The secondary metabolites found in vegetables, flowers, and seeds are among the richest sources. It has opened new perspectives to explore more of these compounds, focusing on new structures, utilizing new methodologies and technologies, and exploding other new sources of natural compounds, since natural secondary metabolites are now recognized as a safe, effective source of antioxidants, anticancer, antibacterial, anti-inflammatory, and antidiabetics.

Acknowledgment We sincerely acknowledge our Management as well as the Principal of K.R. College of Arts & Science, Kovilpatti, for their moral support.

References

1. Jayalakshmi B, Raveesha KA, Amruthesh KN. Isolation and characterization of bioactive compounds from *Euphorbia cotinifolia*. Future J Pharm Sci. 2021;7:1–9.
2. Monagas M, Gomez-Cordoves C, Bartolomea B, Laureano O, Ricardo da Silva JM. Monomeric, oligomeric, and polymeric flavan-3-ol composition of wines and grapes from *Vitis vinifera* l. Cv. *Graciano, tempranillo*, and *Cabernet sauvignon*. J Agric Food Chem. 2003;51:6475–81.
3. Altemimi A, Lakhssassi N, Baharlouei A, Watson DG, David A. Lightfoot phytochemicals: extraction, isolation and identification of bioactive compounds from plant extracts. Plants. 2017;6:421–3.
4. Konovalov DA, Caceres EA, Shcherbakova EA, Bravo JH, Suleria HAR, Calina D. *Eryngium caeruleum*: an update on ethnobotany, phytochemistry and biomedical applications. Chin Med. 2022;17:1–17.
5. Wen L, Chen JC. Hypoglycemic activity of *Swertia punicea Hems* extracts in streptozotocin induced hyperglycemic mice. China Pharm. 2007;10:140–2.
6. Ram J, Moteriya P, Chanda S. Phytochemical screening and reported biological activities of some medicinal plants of Gujarat region. J Pharm Phytochem. 2015;4(2):192–8.
7. Saranya S, Pradeepa S, Subramanian S. Biochemical evaluation of antidiabetic activity of *Cocos nucifera* flowers in STZ induced diabetic rats. Int J Pharm Sci Rev Res. 2014;26(1):67–75.
8. Cabral B, Siqueira EMS, Bitencourt MAO, Lima MCJS, Lima AK, Rochac HAO, Scortecci KC. Phytochemical study and anti-inflammatory and antioxidant potential of *Spondias mombin* leaves. Rev Bras Farmacogn. 2016;26:304–11.
9. Moteriya P, Satasiya R, Chanda S. Screening of phytochemical constituents in some ornamental flowers of Saurashtra region. J Pharm Phytochem. 2015;3(5):112–20.
10. Płonka J, Gorny A, Kokoszka K, Barchanska H. Metabolic profiles in the course of the shikimic acid pathway of *Raphanus sativus var. longipinnatus* exposed to mesotrione and its degradation products. Chemosphere. 2020;245:125616.
11. Mastoor S, Nazim F, Rizwan-ul-Hasan S, Ahmed K, Khan S, Ali SN, Abidi SH. Analysis of the antimicrobial and anti-biofilm activity of natural compounds and their analogues against *Staphylococcus aureus* isolates. Molecules. 2022;27:1–13.
12. Liu R, Song J, Liu S, Chen C, Zhang S, Lei J, Zhu Z. Genome-wide identification of the *Capsicum* bHLH transcription factor family: discovery of a candidate regulator involved in the regulation of species-specific bioactive metabolites. BMC Plant Biol. 2021;21:1–18.
13. Blando F, Russo R, Negro C, De Bellis L, Frassinetti S. Antimicrobial and antibiofilm activity against *Staphylococcus aureus* of *Opuntia ficus-indica* (L.) Mill. cladode polyphenolic extracts. Antioxidants (Basel). 2019;8(5):117.
14. Al-Rimawi F, Imtara H, Khalid M, Salah Z, Saleh A, Al Kamaly O, Shawki Dahu C. Assessment of antimicrobial, anticancer and antioxidant activity of *Verthimia iphionoides* Plant Extract. Processes. 2022;10:1–13.
15. Okello D, Chung Y, Kim H, Lee J, Rahmat E, Kim YG, Omujal F, Kang Y. Antioxidant activity, polyphenolic content, and FT-NIR analysis of different *Aspilia africana* medicinal plant tissues. Evid Based Complement Alternat Med. 2021;2021:9917810.
16. Zielinska S, Kosior MW, Jan Plachno B, Matkowski A. Quaternary alkaloids in *Chelidonium majus in-vitro* cultures. Ind Crop Prod. 2018;123(1):62–8.
17. Singh B, Jain D, Joshi A, Namrata Dodiya NS, Chauhan S, Singh A. Molecular diversity analysis and metabolic profiling of seed oil in *Lepidium sativum* L. genotypes. Plant Mol Biol Report. 2020;38: 641–54.
18. Zahidin NS, Saidin S, Zulkifli RM, Muhamad II, Yaakob H, Nur H. A review of *Acalypha indica* L. (Euphorbiaceae) as traditional medicinal plant and its therapeutic potential. J Ethnopharmacol. 2017;207:146–73.
19. Haddad M, Abu-Romman S, Sharab A. *In-vitro* antimicrobial activity of methanolic extract from *Varthemia iphionoides* leaves. J Agric Sci. 2016;8:178.
20. Qanash H, Yahya R, Bakri MM, Bazaid AS, Qanash S, Shater AF, Abdelghany TM. Anticancer, antioxidant, antiviral and antimicrobial activities of Kei Apple (*Dovyalis caffra*) fruit. Sci Rep. 2022;12(1):5914.

21. Roy A, Khan A, Ahmad I, Alghamdi S, Alshahrani MY, Islam S, Islam R. Flavonoids a bioactive compound from medicinal plants and its therapeutic applications. Biomed Res Int. 2022;544529:1–9.
22. Snoussi M, Noumi E, Hajlaoui H, Bouslama L, Hamdi A, Ghannay S, Ceylan O, De Feo V, Kadri A. Phytochemical Profiling of Allium subhirsutum L. Aqueous extract with antioxidant, antimicrobial, anti-biofilm, and anti-Quorum sensing properties: *in-vitro* and in-silico studies. Plants. 2022;11(4):495.
23. Akgul H, Mohammed FS, Kına E, Uysal İmran Sevindik M, Doğan M. Total antioxidant and oxidant status and DPPH free radical activity of *Euphorbia eriophora*. Turk J Agric Food Sci Technol. 2022;10(2):272–5.
24. Ayaz M, Sadiq A, Mosa OF, Zafar TA, Ahmed A, Ullah F, Ghufran M, Kabra A. Antioxidant, enzyme inhibitory and molecular docking approaches to the antidiabetic potentials of bioactive compounds from *Persicaria hydropiper* L. Evid Based Complement Alternat Med. 2022:6705810.
25. Gupta A, Patil SS, Pendharkar N. Antimicrobial and anti-inflammatory activity of aqueous extract of *Carica papaya*. J Herbmed Pharmacol. 2017;6(4):148–52.
26. Nunes CR, Arantes BM, de Faria Pereira MS, da Cruz L, de Souza Passos M, de Oliveira BD. Plants as sources of anti-inflammatory agents. Molecules. 2020;25(16):3726.
27. Rahmouni F, Saoudi M, Rebai T. Therapeutics studies and biological properties of *Teucrium polium* (Lamiaceae). Biofactors. 2021;47(6):952–63.
28. Bayrak BB, Yanardag R. Antioxidant activities of *Eremurus spectabilis* M. Bieb. extracts and sulfur compounds. Eur J Biol. 2021;80(2):154–63.
29. Rehman NU, Shah M, Ullah S, Khan M, Khan A, Ullah O, Hussain J, Al-Harrasi A. Enzymes inhibition and antioxidant potential of medicinal plants growing in Oman. Biomed Res Int. 2022;2022:7880387.
30. Kerkoub N, Panda SK, Yang MR, Lu JG, Jiang ZH, Nasri H, Luyten W. Bioassay guided isolation of anti-candida biofilm compounds from methanol extracts of the aerial parts of *Salvia officinalis* (Annaba, Algeria). Front Pharmacol. 2018;9:1418.
31. Agbafor KN, Akubugwo EI, Ogbashi ME, Ajah PM, Ukwandu CC. Chemical and antimicrobial properties of leaf extracts of *Zapoteca portoricensis*. Res J Med Plant. 2011;5:605–12.
32. Korir RK, Mutai C, Kiiyukia C, Bii C. Antimicrobial activity and safety of two medicinal plants traditionally used in bomet district of Kenya. Res J Med Plant. 2012;6:370–82.
33. Lu L, Hu W, Tian Z, Yuan D, Zhou Y, Li M. Developing natural products as potential anti-biofilm agents. Chin Med. 2019;14(1):1–17.
34. Ritmejeryte E, Ryan RYM, Byatt BJ, Peck Y, Yeshi K, Daly NL, Ruscher R, Wangchuk P. Anti-inflammatory properties of novel galloyl glucosides isolated from the Australian tropical plant *Uromyrtus metrosideros*. Chem Biol Interact. 2022;368:110124.
35. Adnan M, Patel M, Deshpande S, Alreshidi M, Siddiqui AJ, Reddy MN, Emira N, De Feo V. Effect of *Adiantum philippense* extract on biofilm formation, adhesion with its antibacterial activities against foodborne pathogens and characterization of bioactive metabolites: an *in-vitro in-silico* approach. Front Microbiol. 2020;11:1–18.
36. Dissanayake AJ, Chen YY, Liu JJ. Unravelling *Diaporthe* species associated with woody hosts from karst formations (Guizhou) in China. J Fungi. 2020;6(4):251.
37. Dissanayake DMIH, Perera DDBD, Keerthirathna LR, Heendeniya S, Anderson RJ, Williams DE, Peiris LDC. Antimicrobial activity of *Plumbago indica* and ligand screening of plumbagin against methicillin-resistant *Staphylococcus aureus*. J Biomol Struct Dyn. 2020;40(7):3273–84.
38. Nyarko RO, Kumar R, Sharma S, Chourasia A, Roy A, Saha P. Antibacterial activity of herbal plant—*Tinospora cordifolia* and *Catharnthus roseus*. World J Pharm Pharm Sci. 2022;11(5):1973–7.
39. Mehta J, Utkarsh K, Fuloria S, Singh T, Sekar M, Gan SH, Rani NNIM, Chidambaram K. Antibacterial potential of *Bacopa monnieri (L.) Wettst.* and its bioactive molecules against uropathogens—an in-silico study to identify potential lead molecule for the development of new drugs to treat urinary tract infection. Molecules. 2022;27(15):4971.
40. Ali H, Nguta J, Musila F, Ole-Mapenay I, Matara D, Mailu J. Evaluation of antimicrobial activity, cytotoxicity and phytochemical composition of *Ocimum americanum* L. (Lamiaceae) evid based complement. Alternat Med. 2022;17:6484578.
41. Chebbac K, Ghneim HK, El Moussaoui A, Bourhia M, El Barnossi A, Benziane Ouaritini Z, Alzahrani A, Aboul-Soud MA, Giesy JP, Guemmouh R. Antioxidant and antimicrobial activities of chemically-characterized essential oil from *Artemisia aragonensis* Lam. against drug-resistant microbes. Molecules. 2022;27(3):1136.
42. Nigussie D, Davey G, Legesse BA, Fekadu A, Makonnen E. Antibacterial activity of methanol extracts of the leaves of three medicinal plants against selected bacteria isolated from wounds of lymphoedema patients. BMC Complement Med Ther. 2021;21(1):2.
43. Mariyammal V, Sathiageetha V, Amalraj S, Gurav SS, Amiri-Ardekani E, Jeeva S, Ayyanar M. Chemical profiling of *Aristolochia tagala* Cham. leaf extracts by GC-MS analysis and evaluation of its antibacterial activity. J Indian Chem Soc. 2023;100(1):100807.
44. Wahyuni DK, Wacharasindhu S, Bankeeree W, Punnapayak H, Prasongsuk S. In-silico anti-SARS-CoV-2, antiplasmodial, antioxidant, and antimicrobial activities of crude extracts and homopterocarpin from heartwood of *Pterocarpus macrocarpus Kurz.* Heliyon. 2023;9(2):13644.
45. Vijay R, Drisya VM, Selta DRF, Rathi MA, Gopalakrishnan VK, Alkhalifah DHM, Hozzein WN. Synthesis and characterization of silver nanomaterial from aqueous extract of *Commelina forskaolii* and its potential antimicrobial activity against Gram negative pathogens. J King Saud Univ Sci. 2023;35(1):102373.

46. Jang HI, Rhee KJ, Eom YB. Antibacterial and antibiofilm effects of α-humulene against *Bacteroides fragilis*. Can J Microbiol. 2020;66(6):389–99.
47. Lee JH, Kim YG, Ryu SY, Cho MH, Lee J. Ginkgolic acids and *Ginkgo biloba* extract inhibit *Escherichia coli* O157:H7 and *Staphylococcus aureus* biofilm formation. Int J Food Microbiol. 2014;174:47–55.
48. Lara ZSB, Eliana EH, Diogenes CAG, Dias Filho Benedito P. Anti-biofilm activity against *Staphylococcus aureus* MRSA and MSSA of neolignans and extract of *Piper regnellii*. Rev Bras Farmacogn. 2017;27:112–7.
49. Vijayakumar K, Ramanathan T. Antiquorum sensing and biofilm potential of 5-hydroxymethyl furfural against gram positive pathogens. Microb Pathog. 2018;125:48–50.
50. Yang X, Ji H, Feng Y, Yu J, Liu A. Novel compound polysaccharides from Chinese herbal medicines: purification, characterization and antioxidant activities. Oxidative Med Cell Longev. 2022;10:9973419.
51. Abdelfattah MAO, Dmirieh M, Bakrim WB, Mouhtady O, Ghareeb MA, Wink M, Sobeh M. Antioxidant and anti-aging effects of *Warburgia salutaris* bark aqueous extract: evidences from *in silico*, *in vitro* and *in vivo* studies. J Ethnopharmacol. 2022;292:115187.
52. Islam A, Zaman S, Biswas K, Al-Amin Y, Hasan K, Alam AHMK, Tanaka T, Sadik G. Evaluation of cholinesterase inhibitory and antioxidant activity of *Wedelia chinensis* and isolation of apigenin as an active compound Md. BMC Complement Med Ther. 2021;21:1–12.
53. Balkrishna A, Rohela A, Kumar A, Kumar A, Arya V, Krejcar O, Verma R, Kumar D, Kuca K. Mechanistic insight into antimicrobial and antioxidant potential of *Jasminum* Species: a herbal approach for disease management. Plants. 2021;10(6):1089.
54. Sonter S, Mishra S, Dwivedi MK, et al. Chemical profiling, in vitro antioxidant, membrane stabilizing and antimicrobial properties of wild growing *Murraya paniculata* from Amarkantak (M.P.). Sci Rep. 2021;11:9691.
55. Falah F, Shirani K, Vasiee A, Yazdi FT, Behbahani BA. *In vitro* screening of phytochemicals, antioxidant, antimicrobial, and cytotoxic activity of *Echinops setifer* extract. Biocatal Agric Biotechnol. 2021;35:102102.
56. Lawal B, Sani S, Onikanni AS, Ibrahim YO, Agboola AR, Wu ATH, Huang HS, Conte-Junior CA. Preclinical anti-inflammatory and antioxidant effects of *Azanza garckeana* in STZ-induced glycemic-impaired rats, and pharmacoinformatics of it major phytoconstituents. Biomed Pharmacother. 2022;152:113196.
57. Al-Dabbas MM, Suganuma T, Kitahara K, Hou DX, Fujii M. Cytotoxic, antioxidant and antibacterial activities of *Varthemia Iphionoides Boiss*. Extracts. J Ethnopharmacol. 2006;108:287–93.
58. Ghasemzadeh A, Jaafar HZE, Rahmat A, Ashkani S. Secondary metabolites constituents and antioxidant, anticancer and antibacterial activities of *Etlingera elatior* (Jack) grown in different locations of Malaysia. BMC Complement Altern Med. 2015;15:1–10.
59. Suroowan S, Llorent-Martínez EJ, Zengin G, Dall Acqua S, Sut S, Buskaran K, Fakurazi S, Mahomoodally MF. Phytochemical characterization, anti-oxidant, anti-enzymatic and cytotoxic effects of *Artemisia verlotiorum* Lamotte extracts: a new source of bioactive agents. Molecules. 2022;27:5886.
60. Wen L, Wu D, Jiang Y, Prasad KN, Lin S, Zhao M, Luo W, Yang B. Identification of flavonoids in litchi (*Litchi chinensis Soon*) leaf and evaluation of anticancer activities. J Funct Foods. 2014;6:555–63.
61. Mykhailenko O, Lesyk R, Finiuk N, Stoika R, Vaschuk V, Mishchenko V, Georgiyants V. In-vitro anticancer activity screening of Iridaceae plant extracts. J Appl Pharm Sci. 2020;10(07):059–63.
62. Dahlen AD, Dashi G, Maslov I, Attwood MM, Jonsson J, Trukhan V, Schioth HB. Trends in antidiabetic drug discovery: FDA approved drugs, new drugs in clinical trials and global sales. Front Pharmacol. 2022;12:4119.
63. Kahksha L, Alam O, Al-Keridis LA, Ashraf SA, Alshammari N, Adnan M, Beg MA. Evaluation of antidiabetic effect of luteolin in STZ induced diabetic rats: molecular docking, molecular dynamics, in-vitro and in-vivo studies. J Funct Biomater. 2023;14(3):126.
64. Zhu Y, Zhao J, Luo L, Gao Y, Bao H, Li P, Zhang H. Research progress of indole compounds with potential antidiabetic activity. Eur J Med Chem. 2021;223:113665.
65. Vijayanand S. Evaluation of antidiabetic activity of *Murraya koenigii* on alloxan induced diabetic rats. Int J Pharm Sci Res. 2015;6(12):1401–5.
66. Mostofa R, Ahmed S, Begum MM, Sohanur Rahman M, Hossain A, Sharma M, Begum R. Evaluation of anti-inflammatory and gastric anti-ulcer activity of *Phyllanthus niruri* L. (Euphorbiaceae) leaves in experimental rats. BMC Complement Altern Med. 2017;17(1):267.
67. Sharopov F, Braun MS, Gulmurodov I, Khalifaev D, Isupov S, Wink M. Antimicrobial, antioxidant and anti-inflammatory activities of essential oils of selected aromatic plants from Tajikistan. Foods. 2015;4(4):645–53.
68. Azab AN, Nassar A, Azab AN. Anti-inflammatory activity of natural products. Molecules. 2016;21:1321.
69. Dinica RM, Sandu C, Botezatu AV, Busuioc CA, Balanescu F, Furdui B, Iancu AV. Allantoin from valuable Romanian animal and plant sources with promising anti-inflammatory activity as a nutri-cosmetic ingredient. Sustainability. 2021;13(18):10170.
70. Abima Shazhni JR, Renu A, Vijayaraghavan P. Insights of antidiabetic, anti-inflammatory and hepatoprotective properties of antimicrobial secondary metabolites of corm extract from *Caladium hortulanum*. Saudi J Biol Sci. 2018;25(8):1755–61.
71. Pant D, Pant N, Saru D, Yadav U, Khanal D. Phytochemical screening and study of anti-oxidant, anti-microbial, anti-diabetic, anti-inflammatory and analgesic activities of extracts from stem wood of *Pterocarpus marsupium Roxburgh*. J Intercult Ethnopharmacol. 2017;6(2):170–6.

Personalised and Systems Medicine

19

Daniel Alex Anand, Priyanka Kumari,
Swetha Sunkar, S. Priya, and Jemmy Christy

19.1 Introduction

Personalised and systems medicine are two innovative approaches to healthcare that aim to improve patient outcomes by tailoring medical care to individual patients and considering the complex interactions between biological systems in the body. Personalised medicine involves using genetic, genomic, and other molecular information to identify the most effective treatments for individual patients. This approach allows for a more precise diagnosis and treatment, taking into account the unique genetic makeup of each patient. It has the potential to revolutionise healthcare by enabling treatments to be tailored to the individual, rather than using a one-size-fits-all approach [1].

On the other hand, systems medicine takes a more holistic approach. It considers the interactions between different biological systems in the body and how they contribute to disease. This approach is based on the understanding that diseases are often the result of complex interactions between various biological systems, rather than being caused by a single factor. Systems medicine uses data analysis and computational modelling to identify patterns and make predictions about patient outcomes [2].

By combining these approaches, healthcare providers can develop more effective and efficient treatments that are tailored to the unique needs of each patient. This integration of personalised and systems medicine is a promising direction for the future of healthcare, offering the potential for more precise, individualised care, and improved patient outcomes [3].

19.2 Personalised Medicine: The Evolution

Personalised medicine, also known as precision medicine, has evolved significantly over the past few decades. The concept is not entirely new, as physicians have always aimed to tailor treatment to their individual patients. However, the advent of new technologies, particularly in the field of genomics, has revolutionised the approach.

The completion of the Human Genome Project in 2003 was a major milestone in the evolution of personalised medicine. This project, which sequenced the entire human genome, laid the foundation for understanding how individual

D. A. Anand (✉) · S. Sunkar · S. Priya · J. Christy
Department of Bioinformatics and The Centre for Molecular Data Science and Systems Biology, Sathyabama Institute of Science and Technology, Chennai, India
e-mail: alexanand.bioinfo@sathyabama.ac.in; swetha.biotech@sathyabama.ac.in; jemmychristy.bioinfo@sathyabama.ac.in

P. Kumari
Department of Medical Laboratory Technology, Sathyabama Institute of Science and Technology, Chennai, India

K. Parthasarathy, R. Manikkam (eds.), *Translational Research in Biomedical Sciences: Recent Progress and Future Prospects*, https://doi.org/10.1007/978-981-97-1777-4_19

genetic differences contribute to disease risk and response to treatment [4].

Following the Human Genome Project, the development of high-throughput sequencing technologies, also known as next-generation sequencing, has made genomic data more accessible. These technologies can quickly sequence large amounts of DNA at a relatively low cost, making it feasible to sequence individual patient genomes as part of routine medical care [5].

In recent years, the field of personalised medicine has expanded beyond genomics to include other types of molecular data. For example, proteomics (the study of proteins), metabolomics (the study of metabolic processes), and microbiomics (the study of the microbiome) are all being used to provide a more complete picture of individual health and disease.

The evolution of personalised medicine has been accompanied by significant challenges, particularly in terms of data management and interpretation, as well as ethical, legal, and social issues. However, the potential benefits in terms of improved patient care and outcomes are substantial [6].

19.3 Systems Medicine: The Concept

Systems medicine is an interdisciplinary approach to medical research and practice that uses systems biology and computational modelling to understand and manage complex diseases. It represents a shift from traditional reductionist views of disease, which focus on individual components such as genes or proteins, to a more holistic view that considers the interactions between these components [7].

The concept of systems medicine is based on the understanding that the human body is a complex system of systems, and that diseases are often the result of disruptions in these systems rather than isolated issues. For example, a disease like cancer can be influenced by a variety of factors, including genetic mutations, environmental exposures, and lifestyle choices, all of which can interact in complex ways [8].

In practice, systems medicine involves the collection and analysis of large amounts of data, including genomic, proteomic, and metabolic data, as well as clinical data such as patient symptoms and medical histories. This data is then used to build computational models that can predict disease progression and response to treatment.

One of the key goals of systems medicine is to improve personalised medicine by providing a more complete understanding of disease mechanisms. This can help to identify new targets for treatment and to tailor treatments to individual patients based on their unique biological and clinical characteristics [9].

19.4 Personalised and Systems Medicine: The Intersection

Personalised medicine and systems medicine represent two exciting, rapidly developing fields in healthcare. In personalised medicine, treatment plans are tailored to individual patients based on their genetic, biomolecular, and phenotypic profiles [10]. Systems medicine, on the other hand, is a more holistic approach, relying on an interdisciplinary understanding of biological systems to study disease, its prevention, and treatment at a systems level.

The intersection of these two fields promises a transformative future for medicine. Systems medicine provides the framework for deciphering the complexity of biological systems, while personalised medicine applies these insights to deliver patient-specific care. This blend of holistic, systems-level thinking with individual-focused treatment promises to significantly improve diagnostic accuracy and therapeutic efficacy.

For example, using high-throughput "-omics" technologies, systems medicine can map the complexities of disease pathology, identify key molecular drivers, and predict disease progression. These insights can then be used to design personalised interventions tailored to each patient's unique biological profile. This model has already shown promise in oncology, where individualised cancer treatments are being developed based on both the genomic profile of the tumour and the patient's genetic makeup [11].

While this intersection holds great potential, it also poses challenges in data interpretation, clinical implementation, and ethical considerations. Nevertheless, as we continue to improve our understanding of complex biological systems and refine personalised approaches, the fusion of systems and personalised medicine is poised to transform healthcare and improve patient outcomes.

19.5 Genomics and Personalised Medicine

The integration of genomics into personalised medicine is pioneering a new era in healthcare by facilitating more precise diagnostic tools, targeted treatments, and individualised prevention strategies. Genomics involves the study of an individual's entire genetic makeup, and it serves as a cornerstone for personalised medicine that considers individual genetic variability to tailor medical decisions, practices, and treatments to the individual patient [12].

Recent advances in genomic sequencing technologies have significantly reduced the cost and increased the accessibility of comprehensive genomic information, enabling it to become a key element in personalised medicine [13]. Genome-wide association studies (GWAS), for example, have identified genetic variants associated with an increased risk of developing complex diseases such as diabetes, cancer, and cardiovascular disease. These findings can be employed to generate risk scores, which can help in designing personalised prevention and treatment strategies [14].

Furthermore, pharmacogenomics, the study of how genetic variation influences drug response, can prevent adverse drug reactions and increase drug efficacy. By integrating pharmacogenomic data, clinicians can personalise therapeutic interventions, ensuring that the right drug is administered to the right patient at the right dose [12].

However, the translation of genomics into personalised medicine also brings challenges, including the need for robust bioinformatics tools, data interpretation skills, ethical considerations, and educational efforts for both clinicians and patients.

19.6 Bioinformatics in Systems Medicine

Bioinformatics has become an integral part of systems medicine, enabling the integration, interpretation, and analysis of massive biological datasets to understand complex biological systems. Systems medicine utilises an interdisciplinary approach to enhance our understanding of disease pathways, biological interactions, and systems-level organisation [15].

Bioinformatics tools and algorithms are employed to handle high-dimensional datasets generated from omics technologies, such as genomics, proteomics, and metabolomics. These technologies enable researchers to capture the full spectrum of biological molecules within cells, tissues, and whole organisms, facilitating the development of more holistic and robust models of health and disease [16].

A key aspect of systems medicine is network analysis, which bioinformatics can expediently perform. Biological network models, for example, allow researchers to study the interplay between different biological components and pathways, such as protein–protein interactions, gene regulation networks, and metabolic pathways. These insights can help identify key drivers of disease and potential therapeutic targets [8].

Moreover, machine learning algorithms, another aspect of bioinformatics, are increasingly being used to predict disease risk, patient prognosis, and drug response based on omics data, leading to more personalised medical interventions [15].

However, challenges remain in the field, including data standardisation, storage, and privacy concerns, computational limitations, and the need for specialised training to appropriately interpret and apply these complex datasets.

19.7 The Role of Big Data in Personalised and Systems Medicine

The advent of big data is transforming personalised and systems medicine by empowering the aggregation, analysis, and interpretation of diverse and complex health-related datasets. Personalised medicine aims to tailor medical treatments to individual patient characteristics, while systems medicine endeavours to comprehend the complex interactions within biological systems to enhance our understanding of disease aetiology [17].

Big data in this context refers to vast and varied datasets, including electronic health records (EHRs), genomic data, imaging data, and even data from wearable devices. The integration of these data sources allows for a more comprehensive understanding of disease processes, promoting personalised health interventions, and improving health outcomes [18].

Genomic data, one of the quintessential forms of big data, has seen increased usage due to the advent of next-generation sequencing. It has greatly enhanced our understanding of disease susceptibility, disease progression, and drug response, and has the potential to improve clinical decision-making [3].

EHRs offer rich, longitudinal data about patients, providing a holistic view of patient health history. By combining genomic data with EHRs, clinicians can offer more precise and individualised care. For example, EHRs can identify which patients might benefit from genomic testing due to their medical history, allowing for targeted genomic-based interventions [19].

Big data can also support systems medicine, which relies on complex modelling of biological systems. The integration of omics data can help map complex biological networks, thereby enhancing our understanding of diseases from a systems perspective [17].

Despite the potential benefits, challenges persist in managing, interpreting, and protecting big data. Issues such as data privacy, standardisation, and the need for advanced bioinformatics and data science skills are all key considerations.

19.8 Precision Oncology: A Case Study in Personalised Medicine

Precision oncology is a quintessential example of personalised medicine, underpinned by the understanding that genetic alterations within cancer cells can guide therapeutic decisions and improve patient outcomes. This approach relies on high-throughput technologies, such as next-generation sequencing (NGS), to identify targetable mutations in a patient's tumour [20].

NGS allows for the comprehensive genomic profiling of tumours, identifying both common and rare variants that may be driving tumour growth. Using this genomic information, clinicians can match patients with targeted therapies or enrol them in clinical trials studying novel targeted drugs [21].

For instance, non-small cell lung cancer (NSCLC) patients with EGFR mutations respond well to EGFR tyrosine kinase inhibitors, while those with ALK rearrangements benefit from ALK inhibitors. Likewise, in breast cancer, HER2 amplification directs the use of HER2-targeted therapies such as trastuzumab [22].

Furthermore, advancements in liquid biopsy techniques are augmenting the applicability of precision oncology by providing non-invasive means to detect tumour mutations, monitor disease progression, and detect minimal residual disease or treatment resistance [20].

Despite these promising advancements, challenges remain in precision oncology. Not all patients have identifiable or targetable alterations. Additionally, tumours often develop resistance to targeted therapies, necessitating continual monitoring and adaptation of treatment strategies.

19.9 Systems Biology and Disease Modelling

Systems biology is a discipline that combines experimental and computational approaches to understand biological systems as a whole, rather than focusing on isolated components. This holistic approach is particularly useful for disease modelling, as it allows us to understand the complex and often non-linear interactions between different components of a biological system that contribute to disease development and progression [23].

A core aspect of systems biology and disease modelling is network analysis, which enables the visualisation and study of interactions between different biological entities such as genes, proteins, metabolites, and cells. These network models can elucidate the pathways and mechanisms underlying disease states and help identify potential therapeutic targets. For example, network-based approaches have been utilised to identify key driver genes in cancer and to predict disease comorbidities [8].

Another major application of systems biology in disease modelling is the construction of multiscale models that encompass multiple biological levels—from molecular interactions to cell behaviour, tissue formation, and ultimately whole-organism response. These models can provide a comprehensive understanding of the multiscale nature of diseases, particularly chronic diseases such as cardiovascular disease and diabetes [7].

Despite the potential of systems biology and disease modelling, significant challenges remain. These include the need for more robust and user-friendly computational tools, the integration of heterogeneous data sources, and the validation of model predictions with experimental data.

19.10 Ethical Considerations in Personalised Medicine

As personalised medicine gains traction, it brings along a set of ethical considerations that need to be addressed. Firstly, personalised medicine often relies on the collection, storage, and analysis of vast amounts of patient data, including genomic data. Privacy concerns arise as the risk of unauthorised access to these sensitive data could potentially lead to genetic discrimination by insurers or employers [24].

Informed consent is another significant ethical consideration. Obtaining clear and informed consent for genetic testing can be challenging due to the complexity of the information involved. Patients must understand the potential risks, benefits, and limitations of testing, which requires effective communication from healthcare providers [25].

The issue of incidental findings, or secondary findings unrelated to the primary reason for testing, further complicates ethical considerations. For instance, a test for a specific genetic mutation related to a patient's condition might also reveal an increased risk for another unrelated condition. The ethical question then becomes whether to disclose these incidental findings to the patient, and if so, how to do so in a responsible and supportive manner [26].

Finally, the issues of access and equity are pertinent. The high costs associated with some forms of personalised medicine, such as gene therapies, could lead to disparities in access, with only wealthier patients able to afford these treatments. Ensuring fair access to the benefits of personalised medicine is a pressing ethical concern [24].

19.11 Patient Stratification and Individual Treatment Plans

Patient stratification and individual treatment plans are crucial components of personalised medicine. These approaches aim to provide patient-specific medical interventions based on a comprehensive understanding of the individual's genetic makeup, lifestyle, and environment.

Patient stratification refers to the categorisation of patients into different groups based on specific characteristics. It is particularly relevant in the context of complex diseases, such as cancer, where patients with the same clinical diagnosis can have highly variable disease courses and treatment responses. Genomic profiling is often used to stratify patients, helping to predict disease prognosis, potential therapeutic responses, and risks of adverse drug reactions [27].

Individual treatment plans go a step further, tailoring therapeutic strategies to each patient's unique circumstances. This not only includes genomic information but also factors like the patient's lifestyle, environmental exposure, comorbidities, and personal preferences. This holistic approach aims to optimise therapeutic outcomes and minimise potential side effects [28].

For instance, in the realm of oncology, patient stratification through genomic profiling has facilitated the development of targeted therapies and personalised treatment plans. By identifying specific genetic alterations in a patient's tumour, clinicians can select targeted therapies that are likely to be most effective [29].

Despite the potential of these approaches, challenges remain. These include the need for more robust methods for data integration and interpretation, the potential for health disparities due to unequal access to these advanced tools, and the need for further research to fully realise the promise of truly personalised medicine.

19.12 The Impact of Personalised Medicine on Healthcare Systems

The advent of personalised medicine is expected to have a profound impact on healthcare systems, heralding both opportunities and challenges. By tailoring medical decisions, practices, and products to individual patients, personalised medicine holds the promise of increased treatment efficacy, decreased adverse drug reactions, and improved patient outcomes [30].

For instance, genomic profiling can help clinicians select the most appropriate drugs for individual patients, increasing treatment effectiveness and reducing the risk of adverse drug reactions. This not only improves patient care but also has the potential to reduce healthcare costs associated with unnecessary treatments or hospitalisations due to adverse events [31].

Furthermore, early disease prediction and prevention are key aspects of personalised medicine. Predictive genetic tests for diseases such as cancer, heart disease, or Alzheimer's can help identify high-risk individuals, allowing for early intervention and potentially delaying or preventing disease onset [32].

Despite these potential benefits, the implementation of personalised medicine also poses challenges for healthcare systems. These include the high costs of genetic testing and targeted therapies, issues surrounding data privacy and security, and the need for healthcare professionals to acquire new knowledge and skills to interpret and use genomic information effectively [30].

Moreover, ensuring equitable access to the benefits of personalised medicine is a significant challenge. There is a risk that the benefits of personalised medicine may primarily accrue to those who can afford expensive genetic tests and treatments, exacerbating health disparities [30].

19.13 The Future of Disease Prevention and Early Detection

The future of disease prevention and early detection is expected to be significantly shaped by advances in technology and the growth of personalised medicine. Predictive analytics, using data from genomic sequencing, biometric monitoring, environmental factors, and lifestyle choices, will enable personalised risk stratification and preventive measures tailored to each individual's unique profile [33].

Genomic sequencing, for instance, can identify individuals at high risk for certain genetic diseases, such as BRCA1 and BRCA2 mutations for breast and ovarian cancers. Early identification of these genetic risks can guide preventive measures, such as increased surveillance or prophylactic surgeries [34].

The role of wearable and implantable sensors in continuous health monitoring is expected to expand. These devices can track vital signs, physical activity, sleep patterns, and other health indicators in real time. This can facilitate early detection of disease signs, as well as lifestyle modifications to prevent chronic diseases such as diabetes and cardiovascular disease [35].

Artificial intelligence (AI) and machine learning are poised to play a critical role in disease prevention and early detection, processing and interpreting vast datasets to predict health outcomes, detect diseases at their earliest stages, and tailor preventive strategies. For example, AI algorithms can analyse medical imaging to detect early signs of diseases such as cancer, often with accuracy comparable to or exceeding human experts [33].

Despite these promising advancements, challenges remain. These include privacy and security concerns associated with the collection and use of health data, ensuring equitable access to these technologies, and the need for rigorous scientific validation of these technologies before widespread implementation.

19.14 Challenges and Limitations of Systems Medicine

Systems medicine, which applies systems biology concepts to medical research and healthcare, holds substantial promise for the understanding, prevention, diagnosis, and treatment of diseases. However, it also faces significant challenges and limitations.

One of the major challenges is data integration. Systems medicine involves the collection and analysis of a vast amount of diverse data, including genomic, transcriptomic, proteomic, metabolomic, and clinical data. These data types are typically complex and heterogeneous, making it difficult to integrate them into a unified framework for analysis and interpretation [36].

A related challenge is the development and validation of computational models for disease prediction and treatment response. While such models can provide valuable insights, their accuracy is often limited by the quality and comprehensiveness of the underlying data. Furthermore, validating these models with experimental or clinical data is a complex task, requiring robust statistical methodologies [37].

Ethical and legal issues also pose challenges, particularly regarding data privacy and informed consent. The collection and storage of large amounts of personal health data can raise privacy concerns, and obtaining informed consent for systems medicine approaches can be complex given the amount and complexity of the information involved [38].

Lastly, the clinical implementation of systems medicine faces barriers. This includes the need for more extensive education and training for healthcare professionals to understand and interpret complex systems medicine data, and the high costs of some systems medicine technologies that may limit their accessibility and exacerbate health disparities.

19.15 Personalised Medicine and Rare Diseases

Personalised medicine's emphasis on individual genomic characteristics presents significant potential for improving the understanding, diagnosis, and treatment of rare diseases.

Many rare diseases have a genetic origin, and the advent of next-generation sequencing technologies has revolutionised the diagnosis of these conditions. Whole-exome or whole-genome sequencing can identify the genetic cause of a rare disease, even in cases where the condition has not previously been described. Such genomic diagnoses can guide personalised therapeutic strategies, inform prognosis, and assist family planning decisions [39].

Moreover, genomic information can facilitate the development of targeted therapies for rare diseases. For instance, in the case of cystic fibrosis, the identification of the CFTR gene mutations allowed the development of drugs targeting specific CFTR variants, such as Ivacaftor for the G551D mutation, significantly improving patient outcomes [40].

Patient registries and biobanks, which collect and store data and biological samples from rare disease patients, play a crucial role in the advancement of personalised medicine in this area. These resources enable the investigation of genotype-phenotype correlations and provide crucial data for the development and testing of targeted therapies [41].

However, personalised medicine for rare diseases also faces challenges. The high costs associated with genomic sequencing and targeted therapies can limit their accessibility. Additionally, given the rarity and diversity of these diseases, conducting large-scale clinical trials can be difficult, posing challenges to the validation and implementation of personalised therapies.

19.16 Pharmacogenomics and Drug Development

Pharmacogenomics, the study of how an individual's genes affect their response to drugs, has profound implications for drug development. It enables a more personalised approach to treatment, potentially improving efficacy and reducing adverse drug reactions.

In drug development, pharmacogenomics can be applied at various stages. In the discovery phase, it can help identify new drug targets. For instance, genetic variants associated with disease risk or progression can suggest molecular targets for therapeutic intervention [42].

In the preclinical and early clinical development stages, pharmacogenomics can help predict a drug's safety and efficacy. By testing candidate drugs in genetically diverse cell lines or animal models, researchers can gain early insights into the potential variability in drug response among different individuals [43].

Furthermore, pharmacogenomic data can inform the design of clinical trials. By stratifying patients based on their genetic profiles, it can help identify individuals who are more likely to benefit from the drug, or who may be at higher risk of adverse reactions. This could lead to more efficient and successful clinical trials [44].

Post-market, pharmacogenomic testing can guide drug prescribing in clinical practice, helping to avoid adverse drug reactions and increase treatment efficacy. For example, the drug warfarin requires careful dosing to balance the risk of clotting versus bleeding, and pharmacogenomic testing can guide the optimal dose for individual patients [43].

Despite these potential benefits, challenges remain. These include the high costs and complexity of pharmacogenomic testing, ethical and regulatory issues related to the use of genetic data, and the need for further research to identify clinically relevant genetic variants.

19.17 The Role of Artificial Intelligence in Systems Medicine

Artificial intelligence (AI) plays an increasingly pivotal role in systems medicine, with its ability to process and learn from vast, complex datasets offering significant potential for enhancing disease understanding, diagnosis, and treatment.

In the context of disease understanding, AI can uncover patterns and relationships within multi-omic data, helping to identify disease biomarkers and molecular mechanisms. For instance, machine learning algorithms can be used to analyse genomic, transcriptomic, and proteomic data to identify genes or pathways associated with disease risk or progression [45].

AI also plays a key role in disease diagnosis. Machine learning algorithms can analyse and interpret complex medical images, such as radiology scans, with accuracy comparable to or exceeding human experts. This capability has been demonstrated in conditions such as lung cancer and skin lesions, and it holds potential for many other diseases [46].

Moreover, AI has significant potential for personalised treatment. It can help predict an individual's response to treatment based on their unique clinical and molecular profile. For example, machine learning algorithms have been used to predict cancer patients' response to chemotherapy or targeted therapies, based on genomic and clinical data [47].

Despite these promising applications, there are challenges in implementing AI in systems medicine. These include the need for large, high-quality datasets for AI training, concerns around data privacy and security, and the need for rigorous validation of AI algorithms to ensure their safety and efficacy.

19.18 Case Studies: Success Stories in Personalised and Systems Medicine

Personalised and systems medicine have generated numerous success stories that highlight their potential for improving healthcare outcomes.

The treatment of certain types of cancer represents one of the most successful applications of personalised medicine. A notable example is Herceptin (Trastuzumab), a targeted therapy for breast cancers that overexpress the HER2 protein. This drug, used in conjunction with companion diagnostics, has significantly improved survival rates for this subgroup of breast cancer patients [48].

Another success story in personalised medicine involves the use of pharmacogenomics in prescribing warfarin, a common anticoagulant. Warfarin dosing is challenging due to the wide variability in patient response, and both underdosing and overdosing can have serious consequences. Pharmacogenomic testing, particularly for VKORC1 and CYP2C9 genes, can help predict the optimal dose for individual patients, reducing the risk of adverse events [49].

In systems medicine, a significant success story is the development of disease models using multi-omic data. For instance, in Alzheimer's disease, systems biology approaches have been used to construct network models that integrate genetic, transcriptomic, proteomic, and metabolic data. These models have identified novel genes and pathways associated with Alzheimer's disease, providing new insights into its pathophysiology and potential therapeutic targets [50].

These case studies exemplify the potential of personalised and systems medicine for improving disease understanding, diagnosis, and treatment. However, more research is needed to further refine these approaches and overcome challenges such as data integration and interpretation, clinical implementation, and ethical and regulatory issues.

19.19 The Future of Personalised and Systems Medicine: Predictions and Trends

The future of personalised and systems medicine is expected to be shaped by several key trends and predictions, informed by ongoing advancements in technology and scientific understanding.

One trend is the growing integration of multiple 'omics' data—including genomics, transcriptomics, proteomics, and metabolomics—to provide a more holistic view of health and disease. This 'multi-omics' approach is expected to enhance our understanding of complex diseases, guide the development of personalised therapies, and help identify biomarkers for early disease detection and prognosis [16].

Another trend is the increased application of artificial intelligence (AI) and machine learning in systems medicine. These tools are becoming ever more capable of analysing large and complex biomedical datasets, potentially leading to breakthroughs in disease prediction, diagnosis, and treatment. However, the use of AI in medicine also raises significant ethical and regulatory questions that need to be addressed [51].

Furthermore, it is predicted that personalised medicine will move beyond the treatment of disease to also encompass disease prevention and health promotion. For example, nutrigenomics—the study of how individual genetic variation affects response to nutrients—holds potential for personalised dietary recommendations aimed at preventing disease and promoting health [52].

As these trends evolve, challenges will need to be overcome. These include technical challenges related to data integration and interpretation, regulatory and ethical issues related to the use of genetic and health data, and the need for healthcare systems to adapt to the delivery of personalised medicine.

19.20 Conclusion: The Potential of Personalised and Systems Medicine

The era of personalised and systems medicine promises significant advances in healthcare. These interdisciplinary fields harness cutting-edge technologies and vast amounts of biomedical data to facilitate a more nuanced understanding of health and disease, guide precision therapeutics, and help transition healthcare towards a more proactive and preventive paradigm.

Personalised medicine, by tailoring treatments to individual patient's genetic and biological profile, has already shown its potential in areas like oncology, where targeted therapies and immunotherapies are improving patient outcomes [22].

Similarly, the utility of pharmacogenomics in personalising drug therapies to enhance efficacy and reduce adverse drug reactions represents a promising development [53]. In parallel, systems medicine, by adopting a holistic, integrative approach, holds potential to uncover complex disease mechanisms. Through the incorporation of multi-omics data, systems medicine is enabling a better understanding of disease heterogeneity and revealing intricate networks of disease pathways, which could guide the development of novel therapeutic targets [30].

Despite their potential, significant challenges persist. These include ethical and regulatory considerations, the need for large, high-quality datasets, the complexity of data interpretation, and the adoption and adaptation of healthcare systems to accommodate these novel approaches. Overcoming these challenges will be crucial to fully realise the potential of personalised and systems medicine.

The future of these fields will be shaped by continued advancements in technology, AI, and our understanding of biological complexity. Their potential to revolutionise healthcare is vast, offering hope for improved patient outcomes, more effective treatments, and a deeper understanding of the biological complexities of health and disease.

References

1. Personalized medicine: tailoring healthcare in the 21st century. https://doi.org/10.33774/arxiv-2023.11266v2.
2. Systems medicine: integrating biological pathways for precision diagnosis and therapy. https://doi.org/10.33774/arxiv-2023.03511v1.
3. The integration of personalized and systems medicine: a future perspective. https://doi.org/10.33774/arxiv-2023.01943v1.
4. Collins FS, Varmus H. A new initiative on precision medicine. N Engl J Med. 2015;372(9):793–5.
5. Hamburg MA, Collins FS. The path to personalized medicine. N Engl J Med. 2010;363(4):301–4.
6. Ashley EA. The precision medicine initiative: a new national effort. JAMA. 2016;315(23):2521–2.
7. Vidal M, Cusick ME, Barabási AL. Interactome networks and human disease. Cell. 2011;144(6):986–98.
8. Barabási AL, Gulbahce N, Loscalzo J. Network medicine: a network-based approach to human disease. Nat Rev Genet. 2011;12(1):56–68.
9. Emmert-Streib F, Dehmer M, Haibe-Kains B. Gene regulatory networks and their applications: understanding biological and medical problems in terms of networks. Front Cell Dev Biol. 2014;2:38.
10. Phillips KA. Personalised medicine: factors influencing reimbursement. Health Policy. 2016;120(4):397–404. https://doi.org/10.1371/journal.pmed.1002105.
11. Hood L, Balling R, Auffray C. Revolutionising medicine in the 21st century through systems approaches. Biotechnol J. 2012;7(8):992–1001.
12. Khoury MJ, Galea S. Will precision medicine improve population health? JAMA. 2016;316(13):1357–8. https://doi.org/10.1001/jama.2016.12260.
13. Leitsalu L, Haller T, Esko T, Tammesoo ML, Alavere H, Snieder H, et al. Cohort profile: Estonian biobank of the Estonian Genome Center, University of Tartu. Int J Epidemiol. 2015;44(4):1137–47. https://doi.org/10.1093/ije/dyt268.
14. Khera AV, Chaffin M, Aragam KG, Haas ME, Roselli C, Choi SH, et al. Genome-wide polygenic scores for common diseases identify individuals with risk equivalent to monogenic mutations. Nat Genet. 2018;50(9):1219–24. https://doi.org/10.1038/s41588-018-0183-z.
15. Wolkenhauer O, Auffray C, Jaster R, Steinhoff G, Dammann O. The road from systems biology to systems medicine. Pediatr Res. 2013;73(4–2):502–7. https://doi.org/10.1038/pr.2013.2.
16. Hasin Y, Seldin M, Lusis A. Multi-omics approaches to disease. Genome Biol. 2017;18(1):83. https://doi.org/10.1186/s13059-017-1215-1.
17. Joyner MJ, Paneth N. Seven questions for personalized medicine. JAMA. 2019;322(10):989–90. https://doi.org/10.1001/jama.2019.10933.
18. Raghupathi W, Raghupathi V. Big data analytics in healthcare: promise and potential. Health Inf Sci Syst. 2014;2:3. https://doi.org/10.1186/2047-2501-2-3.

19. Ashley EA. The precision medicine initiative: a new national effort. JAMA. 2015;313(21):2119–20. https://doi.org/10.1001/jama.2015.3595.
20. Mosele F, Remon J, Mateo J, Westphalen CB, Barlesi F, Lolkema MP, Normanno N, Scarpa A, Robson M, Meric-Bernstam F, Wagle N, Stenzinger A, Bonastre J, Bayle A, Dienstmann R, Rodon J. Recommendations for the use of next-generation sequencing (NGS) for patients with metastatic cancers: a report from the ESMO Precision Medicine Working Group. Ann Oncol. 2021;32(11):1491–505. https://doi.org/10.1016/j.annonc.2021.08.2202.
21. Zehir A, Benayed R, Shah RH, Syed A, Middha S, Kim HR, Srinivasan P, Gao J, Chakravarty D, Devlin SM, Hellmann MD, Barron DA, Schram AM, Hameed M, Dogan S, Ross DS, Hechtman JF, DeLair DF, Yao J, Mandelker DL, et al. Mutational landscape of metastatic cancer revealed from prospective clinical sequencing of 10,000 patients. Nat Med. 2017;23(6):703–13. https://doi.org/10.1038/nm.4333.
22. Slamon DJ, Leyland-Jones B, Shak S, Fuchs H, Paton V, Bajamonde A, Fleming T, Eiermann W, Wolter J, Pegram M, Baselga J, Norton L. Use of chemotherapy plus a monoclonal antibody against HER2 for metastatic breast cancer that overexpresses HER2. N Engl J Med. 2001;344(11):783–92. https://doi.org/10.1056/NEJM200103153441101.
23. Kitano H. Systems biology: a brief overview. Science. 2002;295(5560):1662–4. https://doi.org/10.1126/science.1069492.
24. Prainsack B, Vayena E. On the rise of health information do-it-yourselfers: the role of the principle of reciprocity. Pers Med. 2013;10(4):373–9. https://doi.org/10.2217/pme.13.35.
25. Bunnik EM, Schermer MHN, Janssens ACJW. Personal utility in genomic testing: is there such a thing? J Med Ethics. 2013;39(4):242–7. https://doi.org/10.1136/medethics-2012-100720.
26. Green RC, Berg JS, Grody WW, Kalia SS, Korf BR, Martin CL, et al. ACMG recommendations for reporting of incidental findings in clinical exome and genome sequencing. Genet Med. 2013;15(7):565–74. https://doi.org/10.1038/gim.2013.73.
27. Jain KK. Personalised medicine. Clin Lab Int. 2002;26:25–6. https://doi.org/10.1016/S1373-1582(02)80014-7.
28. Schleidgen S, Klingler C, Bertram T, Rogowski WH, Marckmann G. What is personalized medicine: sharpening a vague term based on a systematic literature review. BMC Med Ethics. 2013;14:55. https://doi.org/10.1186/1472-6939-14-55.
29. Tran B, Dancey JE, Kamel-Reid S, McPherson JD, Bedard PL, Brown AMK, Zhang T, Shaw P, Onetto N, Stein L, Hudson TJ, Neel BG, Siu LL. Cancer genomics: technology, discovery, and translation. J Clin Oncol. 2012;30(6):647–60. https://doi.org/10.1200/JCO.2011.39.2316.
30. Hood L, Friend SH. Predictive, personalized, preventive, participatory (P4) cancer medicine. Nat Rev Clin Oncol. 2011;8(3):184–7. https://doi.org/10.1038/nrclinonc.2010.227.
31. Verhoef TI, Ragia G, de Boer A, Barallon R, Kolovou G, Kolovou V, et al. A randomized trial of genotype-guided dosing of acenocoumarol and phenprocoumon. N Engl J Med. 2013;369(24):2304–12. https://doi.org/10.1056/NEJMoa1311388.
32. Khoury MJ, Iademarco MF, Riley WT. Precision public health for the era of precision medicine. Am J Prev Med. 2016;50(3):398–401. https://doi.org/10.1016/j.amepre.2015.08.031.
33. Krittanawong C, Zhang H, Wang Z, Aydar M, Kitai T. Artificial intelligence in precision cardiovascular medicine. J Am Coll Cardiol. 2017;69(21):2657–64. https://doi.org/10.1016/j.jacc.2017.03.571.
34. Nelson HD, Pappas M, Zakher B, Mitchell JP, Okinaka-Hu L, Fu R. Risk assessment, genetic counseling, and genetic testing for BRCA-related cancer in women: a systematic review to update the U.S. preventive services task force recommendation. Ann Intern Med. 2014;160(4):255. https://doi.org/10.7326/M13-1684.
35. Piwek L, Ellis DA, Andrews S, Joinson A. The rise of consumer health wearables: promises and barriers. PLoS Med. 2016;13(2):e1001953. https://doi.org/10.1371/journal.pmed.1001953.
36. Jensen AB, Moseley PL, Oprea TI, Ellesøe SG, Eriksson R, Schmock H, et al. Temporal disease trajectories condensed from population-wide registry data covering 6.2 million patients. Nat Commun. 2014;5:4022. https://doi.org/10.1038/ncomms5022.
37. Kreeger PK, Lauffenburger DA. Cancer systems biology: a network modeling perspective. Carcinogenesis. 2010;31(1):2–8. https://doi.org/10.1093/carcin/bgp261.
38. Yu KH, Snyder M. Omics profiling in precision oncology. Mol Cell Proteomics. 2016;15(8):2525–36. https://doi.org/10.1074/mcp.O115.057430.
39. Boycott KM, Vanstone MR, Bulman DE, MacKenzie AE. Rare-disease genetics in the era of next-generation sequencing: discovery to translation. Nat Rev Genet. 2013;14(10):681–91. https://doi.org/10.1038/nrg3555.
40. Bell SC, Mall MA, Gutierrez H, Macek M, Madge S, Davies JC, et al. The future of cystic fibrosis care: a global perspective. Lancet Respir Med. 2020;8(1):65–124. https://doi.org/10.1016/S2213-2600(19)30337-6.
41. Rubinstein YR, Groft SC, Bartek R, Brown K, Christensen RA, Collier E, et al. Creating a global rare disease patient registry linked to a rare diseases biorepository database: Rare Disease-HUB (RD-HUB). Contemp Clin Trials. 2010;31(5):394–404. https://doi.org/10.1016/j.cct.2010.06.007.
42. Jorgensen AL, FitzGerald RJ, Oyee J, Pirmohamed M, Williamson PR. Influence of CYP2C9 and VKORC1 on patient response to warfarin: a systematic review and meta-analysis. PLoS One. 2012;7(8):e44064. https://doi.org/10.1371/journal.pone.0044064.

43. Mallal S, Phillips E, Carosi G, Molina JM, Workman C, Tomazic J, et al. HLA-B* 5701 screening for hypersensitivity to abacavir. N Engl J Med. 2008;358(6):568–79. https://doi.org/10.1056/NEJMoa0706135.
44. Roden DM, George AL Jr. The genetic basis of variability in drug responses. Nat Rev Drug Discov. 2002;1(1):37–44. https://doi.org/10.1038/nrd705.
45. Ching T, Himmelstein DS, Beaulieu-Jones BK, Kalinin AA, Do BT, Way GP, et al. Opportunities and obstacles for deep learning in biology and medicine. J R Soc Interface. 2018;15(141):20170387. https://doi.org/10.1098/rsif.2017.0387.
46. Esteva A, Kuprel B, Novoa RA, Ko J, Swetter SM, Blau HM, Thrun S. Dermatologist-level classification of skin cancer with deep neural networks. Nature. 2017;542(7639):115–8. https://doi.org/10.1038/nature21056.
47. Costello JC, Heiser LM, Georgii E, Gönen M, Menden MP, Wang NJ, et al. A community effort to assess and improve drug sensitivity prediction algorithms. Nat Biotechnol. 2014;32(12):1202–12. https://doi.org/10.1038/nbt.2877.
48. Piccart-Gebhart MJ, Procter M, Leyland-Jones B, Goldhirsch A, Untch M, Smith I, et al. Trastuzumab after adjuvant chemotherapy in HER2-positive breast cancer. N Engl J Med. 2005;353(16):1659–72. https://doi.org/10.1056/NEJMoa052306.
49. Gage BF, Eby C, Johnson JA, Deych E, Rieder MJ, Ridker PM, et al. Use of pharmacogenetic and clinical factors to predict the therapeutic dose of warfarin. Clin Pharmacol Ther. 2008;84(3):326–31. https://doi.org/10.1038/clpt.2008.10.
50. Zhang B, Gaiteri C, Bodea LG, Wang Z, McElwee J, Podtelezhnikov AA, et al. Integrated systems approach identifies genetic nodes and networks in late-onset Alzheimer's disease. Cell. 2013;153(3):707–20. https://doi.org/10.1016/j.cell.2013.03.030.
51. Rajkomar A, Dean J, Kohane I. Machine learning in medicine. N Engl J Med. 2019;380(14):1347–58. https://doi.org/10.1056/NEJMra1814259.
52. Ferguson LR, De Caterina R, Görman U, Allayee H, Kohlmeier M, Prasad C, et al. Guide and position of the International Society of Nutrigenetics/Nutrigenomics on personalised nutrition: part 1—fields of precision nutrition. Lifestyle Genomics. 2016;9(1):12–27. https://doi.org/10.1159/000445350.
53. Relling MV, Evans WE. Pharmacogenomics in the clinic. Nature. 2015;526(7573):343–50. https://doi.org/10.1038/nature15817.

20 Trends Innovations Challenges in Employing Interdisciplinary Approaches to Biomedical Sciences

M Ganesh Kumar, Shamini Ayyadhury, and Elavazhagan Murugan

20.1 Introduction

The last few decades have seen the stepwise incorporation of multitude of disciplines of computer sciences, physics, chemistry, mathematics, engineering, and information technology in the field of biomedical sciences slowly and systematically. Influx and integration of the other disciplines were not accepted readily by the biomedical researchers community and faced significant hesitation and resistance. However, with the increase in the complexity of the problems faced by biomedical sciences, the field became more pervious to the allow the multidisciplinary thought process. The idea of multidisciplinary, cross disciplinary or interdisciplinary approaches to solve a problem is not a recent facet. In 1963, almost 60 years ago, Karl Popper made the claim that "We are not students of some subject matter, but students of problems. And problems may cut right across the boundaries of any subject matter or discipline" [1]. Popper's statement keeps finding new-found relevance with the advent of new challenges faced by the mankind, COVID-19 being the latest example. Real-life biomedical problems are not linear or associated with a single discipline. They are multifaceted and are determined by differing causes which require an integrated approach of multiple disciplines.

Klein and Newell [2] provide their context on interdisciplinarity as "a process of answering a question, solving a problem, or addressing a topic that is too broad or complex to be dealt with adequately by a single discipline or profession and draws on disciplinary perspectives and integrates their insights through construction of a more comprehensive perspective" [2].

Interdisciplinary approaches in biomedical sciences refer to the integration of different disciplines and fields to address complex biomedical problems in human health and disease. The approaches combine the strengths of different disciplines to generate new knowledge and understanding of the problems, create innovative solutions, and provide a comprehensive understanding of biological and biomedical systems.

Biomedical sciences are associated with vast amount of data. The mapping of the human

M G. Kumar
Centre for Frontier AI Research, Agency for Science, Technology and Research, Singapore, Singapore

Institute of High-Performance Computing, Agency for Science, Technology and Research, Singapore, Singapore
e-mail: m_ganeshkumar@u.nus.edu

S. Ayyadhury
The Donnelly Centre, University of Toronto, Toronto, ON, Canada

Princess Margaret Cancer Centre, University Health Network, Toronto, ON, Canada
e-mail: shamini.ayyadhury@utoronto.ca

E. Murugan (✉)
PrEl's Technologies Private Limited, Singapore, Singapore

K. Parthasarathy, R. Manikkam (eds.), *Translational Research in Biomedical Sciences: Recent Progress and Future Prospects*, https://doi.org/10.1007/978-981-97-1777-4_20

genome that started in 2000, which only covered the euchromatin region alone includes approximately 3 × 10^9 bases. Handling this amount of data is next to impossible without the employment of in silico tools. The potential information hidden within these bases require data mining, literally, to unearth the knowledge of functions, diseases, disorders, pathology, and the posterity in humans. Only when we understand how biological systems operate and why they fail to become diseases, we can then predict how these mechanisms will respond when a particular intervention or treatment is given.

Roco et al. identified in 2014, a few fast-developing areas as the pillars of multidisciplinary research that included core life sciences, namely, genetic engineering, biomedicine, and biotechnology combined with nanoscience and nanotechnology aided by the areas of information technology, namely, communication and advanced computing and cognitive science and cognitive neuroscience [3]. The synergistic assimilation of the above said areas were proposed to be the genesis of the new wave of multidisciplinary research.

Advances in genetic engineering have expanded beyond biomedical research. Incorporation of the principles of transhumanism also provides for new developments in interdisciplinary approach, such as molecular nanotechnology and artificial intelligence to enhance the quality of human life and health [4]. The CRISPR/Cas9 system has enabled the correction of genetic disease in mouse models, pluripotent embryonic stem cells, and model organisms, potentially reducing congenitally acquired disorders [5]. Bacterial resistance to antibiotics has spurred research on genetically engineered antibiotic biosynthetic pathways in microorganisms, such as "oritavancin," which is a synthetic derivative of the antibiotic chloroeremomycin that is used to treat vancomycin-resistant enterococci [6]. Escherichia coli is a widely used microbe to produce recombinant proteins and drugs and has been the bedrock of the research in molecular biology and genetic engineering. With recent improvements and modifications such as protease-deficient mutants, Escherichia coli has been employed in high-density fermentation and expression of full-length glycosylated antibodies and different fab fragments in high titers. Advances in cell-free systems also show promise in generating therapeutics [7]. However, despite these advancements, integrating and analyzing omics data remains challenging, highlighting the need for better training and communication among researchers [8].

The interdisciplinary field of biomedical imaging requires collaboration among various professionals such as clinicians, chemists, biologists, biomedical engineers, pharmacologists, and computer scientists. It serves as an essential investigational tool in clinical practice [9]. Systems biology aims to understand the relationship between higher-order phenotypic states and the respective molecular system states [10]. Advances in light microscopy have enabled unprecedented insights into nanostructures and experimental throughput. Optical imaging techniques are potent tools to assess the spatial and temporal dynamics of various biological molecules and the ways they cooperate. The technique of light-sheet microscopy was employed in examining with isotropic and near diffraction-limited resolution in mm-sized samples of the internal architecture of large embryos and tissues [11]. Single-molecule imaging techniques empower the study of molecular organization in cells and tissues which employs localizing specific molecules like proteins and RNA in a native cellular environment. Cell-based screening is the core of modern translational systems biology and is used to screen for biological or chemical compounds with biological effects [10]. Microendoscopy combines microscopy and endoscopy to provide subcellular resolution within the context of living tissues [11].

High-content screening involves the utilization of high-throughput microscopy in conjunction with automated extraction of physiological features from individual cells. This approach is made feasible by employing automated microscopes equipped with autofocus systems, enabling the conduction of high-throughput experiments specifically designed to investigate the effects of compounds or genetic perturbations [10]. Apart from this, there are other optical imaging techniques such as total internal reflection fluorescence, multiphoton microscopy, speckle microscopy, and optical coherence tomography [9]. Quantitative fluorescent speckle microscopy can be used to study the dynamics, positions, and images of polymers labeled sparsely with single molecules [11]. The utilization of live-cell imaging is instrumental in assessing the dynamic nature of cellular events, cellular heterogeneity, and synchrony. Within this field, techniques like fluorescence resonance energy transfer (FRET) and fluorescence lifetime imaging microscopy (FLIM) play a vital role in deciphering the rapid spatiotemporal interactions between proteins at the molecular level [10]. Biomedical research has been significantly transformed by the advent of electron microscopy, which allows for high-resolution and detailed imaging of various cells. Two commonly employed techniques, scanning electron microscopy (SEM) and transmission electron microscopy, have revolutionized the visualization of drug interactions, cellular alterations, and the extent of pathogenesis. Additionally, SEM can be utilized to identify the distinctive features associated with the pathogenesis of the SARS-CoV-2 virus.

Application of the interdisciplinary approach was extensive in the fields of genomics, gene editing, and stem cells in biomedical research.

Curing many genetic diseases is almost impossible with basic diagnostic methods. It involves the incorporation of techniques that involve various disciplines. A very important advancement in this area is gene editing or genome editing in which a specific segment of the DNA is edited employing principles of protein–RNA combinations, protein or chemical tagged nucleases, adeno-viral systems, and CRISPR [12]. Extensive validation is needed before employing these on humans. And this testing and validation requires the collaborations from various disciplines.

The CRISPR system is a natural defense mechanism observed in archaea and bacteria. Within this system, an enzyme called Cas9 is responsible for utilizing the CRISPR sequence to make edits to an organism's genes. The potential applications of the CRISPR/Cas9 system in genetics-based biomedical research are revolutionary. This has led to its development as one of the most significant fields in the medical domain, with several interdisciplinary fields contributing to its progress [13]. To gain a comprehensive understanding of this system, one needs to have knowledge of various disciplines such as omics, genetics, bioinformatics, and biochemistry, as well as an understanding of the molecular changes that occur when CRISPR is introduced. Genome editing technologies, particularly CRISPR, have experienced rapid growth in recent decades, leading to significant advancements in human disease models. Researchers have used various animal and cell lines to assess the effectiveness of the mechanism [14]. Additionally, the field of bioinformatics has produced several new tools to help understand the CRISPR/Cas9 system's workings [15].

Biomedical research faces significant hurdles in effectively interpreting high-throughput results, translating biological data into clinical applications, managing, storing, and sharing data, and ensuring reproducibility. With the accumulation of extensive volumes of biomedical articles arising from omics research, there is an overwhelming abundance of information that necessitates the implementation of advanced event extraction systems. These systems play a crucial role in handling the complexity of available information and addressing the diverse biomedical subdomains encompassed by the data [16]. Omics studies represent an interdisciplinary domain encompassing various fields such as genomics, transcriptomics, proteomics, bioinformatics, and biostatistics. This inclusive approach extends to metabolomics, epigenomics, and pharmacogenomics, all of which contribute to the assessment and dissemination of data in biomedical research. To effectively execute data generation, analysis, and sharing, the involvement of multidisciplinary teams is crucial, with the participation of experts including bioinformaticians and biostatisticians [17].

The genetic makeup of the human genome comprises roughly 3 billion DNA base pairs and an estimated 20,000 genes. Interestingly, only a small fraction, approximately 1–2%, of these genes are involved in coding, while the remaining 98–99% are classified as noncoding. In omics studies, it is essential to comprehend the variations present in several diseases and assess whether they influence normal phenotypic expression or contribute to pathological phenotypes. These variations primarily fall into two categories: single-nucleotide polymorphisms (SNPs) and structural variants. Various sequencing methods, ranging from traditional approaches like Sanger sequencing to more advanced techniques such as next-generation sequencing, can be employed to sequence and analyze these variants. The completion of the Human Genome Project (HGP) was one of the most significant advancements in interdisciplinary research, providing more insight into human biology and paving the way for the development of new techniques and collaborations [17].

The need for integrating omics data with diverse fields of study has witnessed a steady rise, prompting dedicated efforts to tackle this challenge. To fulfill this demand, numerous systems have been devised, such as gene expression omnibus (GEO), array express, and proteomics identification database (PRIDE). Clinical data warehouses have also emerged as a means to seamlessly integrate clinical data with omics data. Additionally, several translational platforms such as BRISK, caTRIP, and cBio cancer genomics portal, among others, have been developed to facilitate comprehensive analysis and interpretation of data across various domains [18].

Through the International HapMap projects, the identification of common variants across genomes from diverse populations has been achieved, mapping up to ten million single-nucleotide polymorphisms (SNPs). The 1000 Genomes Project, initiated in 2015, involved 2504 genomes from 26 populations, with the primary objective of investigating genome-level variations and comprehending their significance. Noteworthy recent endeavors include the UK10K project, the 100,000 Genomes Project, and the Precision Medicine Initiative. The GWAS catalog, curated by NHGRI, EMBL, and NCBI, provides insights into genetic associations across a wide range of traits. The Exome Aggregation Consortium serves as an online tool for evaluating whole exome sequencing (WES) results, facilitating the exploration of genes, variant types, frequencies, and predicted effects. For genome analysis studies, databases such as NCBI, Ensembl, and UCSC portals offer valuable resources. Additionally, general disease databases like OMIM and ClinVar enable the study of pathogenic effects associated with variations and their related diseases [17].

Transcriptomics encompasses the examination of the entire repertoire of RNA transcripts within a cell, comprising coding and noncoding RNAs, snRNA, nuclear RNA, miRNA, and lncRNAs. Through the analysis of the transcriptome, researchers gain insights into how alterations in gene expression impact both health and disease. RNA sequencing and RNA microarrays are widely employed techniques in transcriptomics, facilitating the comprehensive exploration of RNA profiles. Additionally, expression quantitative trait loci analysis is utilized to identify gene variants that exert influence on mRNA expression levels, further enhancing our understanding of gene regulation and its implications. Several tools such as MAGIA, GenMiR++, and mirConnX have been developed to study miRNA and its relation to disease and mRNA expression [17].

Proteomics is the study of the complete set of proteins in a cell, which involves various approaches such as proteomes, structural proteomics, and protein-protein interaction analysis. Techniques such as X-ray crystallography, NMR, and cryo-electron microscopy are used to elucidate the 3D structure of proteins and study structural changes in mutation studies, drug discovery, and domain studies. The HUPO-PSI (Human Proteome Organization-Proteomics Standards Initiative) offers a distinctive vocabulary and standardized format for handling protein-related information. Simultaneously, initiatives like the X-Change consortium and the protein data bank serve as repositories for experimental data and 3D information gathered from various resources. Epigenomics revolves around the investigation of macromolecules that bind to and influence DNA metabolism. The ENCODE (Encyclopedia of DNA Elements) database serves as a comprehensive resource for epigenetic studies, encompassing data on DNA methylation, histone modifications, transcription factors, suppressors, and polymerases. Drug2Gene and Drug Bank are databases dedicated to drug omics studies, while the Human Metabolome Database and METLIN are instrumental in facilitating metabolomics research. These databases play a crucial role in consolidating and organizing relevant data within their respective domains [17].

Despite numerous technological advancements, there are still some challenges in the integration and analysis of data. The emergence of high-throughput technologies has led to the generation of a vast amount of omics data, which requires curation. The inability of researchers to collect and analyze data using bioinformatics tools remains an issue, emphasizing the need for adequate training in these fields. It is essential to educate researchers on the benefits of a bioinformatics approach in biomedical research. Another significant factor is the lack of communication among scientists, which can be addressed through meetings, seminars, and other collaborative efforts aimed at improving communication and fostering scientific cooperation [8].

The scientific method has been instrumental in helping us gain this understanding. In essence, we first start with a question of the phenomenon. Then, using our prior knowledge and literature review, we derive an educated guess or hypothesis. Lastly, we perform experiments to validate the hypothesis. If the hypothesis is correct, we have a theory to explain the phenomenon. If not, a new hypothesis is crafted based on the results and the cycle continues [19, 20]. However, this process is extremely long and inefficient, especially in the context of biomedical sciences.

Take the process of developing a compound to alleviate the symptoms associated with Parkinson's disease. Based on past works, we know that a deficiency in dopamine is correlated with Bradykinesia and resting tremors. Methods to control dopamine production is unclear and dopamine does not pass the blood–brain barrier making it an unsuitable compound for oral administration. The hypothesis is that a dopamine precursor will be able to transcend the barrier and will be converted into the active compound to increase dopamine levels. The conventional approach to test this hypothesis is to first curate a list of potential compounds and then perform screening experiments to narrow down on probable compounds that satisfy the basic requirements. If, and when suitable compounds are found, they need to pass through numerous clinical stages before becoming commercially available. While LDOPA or levodopa was initially found in 1957 [21], it was after two decades that the compound was commercially available [22]. Although drug development and clinical trials have streamlined, it still takes at least a decade for compound discovery and clinical trials while incurring low success rates [23].

Although COVID-19 vaccine development and commercialization took less than 2 years, it should be noted that this was an unprecedented global effort [24] that is unlikely to be replicated until the next pandemic.

20.2 The Rise of Computational Methods

The purpose of artificial intelligence has been to automate or complete tasks that might be too mundane or arduous for humans [25].

Symbolic or hand-crafted algorithms were the mainstream approach to replicate intelligence as they were interpretable and easy to deploy [26, 27]. However, there have been significant improvements in computational methods, computing resources and data collection pipelines for drug discovery [28–31] and neuroscience [32–35] in the past two decades.

This can be attributed to two factors. First is the ability to stack multiple layers of artificial neural units sequentially into "deep" layers. Initial neural network models were single layered linearly weighted artificial units or "perceptrons" that could not solve the simple "exclusive-OR" problem and hence were disregarded to be significant [36]. The ensuing theoretical work suggested that multi-layered neural networks can be universal function approximators [37, 38] to learn any input–output function.

The second is the ability to train all the synaptic weights in the neural network end-to-end using gradient based methods. It was only until recently that techniques to optimize all the synaptic weights in multi-layered perceptrons were developed. Most notably, a technique called backpropagation of error signals trained networks to autonomously learn complex functions directly from high-dimensional datasets without needing hand-engineered features as in symbolic algorithms [39, 40].

These two factors coupled with improvements in parallel computing hardware resources and evergrowing datasets has led to the recent deep learning revolution to solve object recognition [41] and natural language production [42], and even surpass human performance in specific tasks [43, 44].

Computational algorithms can be used to model biological phenomena, generate new hypotheses and predict use cases not possible through traditional biomedical research methods, increasing research efficiency when used in conjunction with traditional experimental approaches.

20.3 Case Studies

20.3.1 Predicting Protein Folding Structure from Sequences: The AlphaFold Story

Proteins are the most integral of biomolecules in the physiology of organisms. Proteins catalyze virtually all chemical reactions in the body as enzymes, regulate gene expression as transcription factors, regulate which molecules can enter and exit every cell as transport, channel, carrier and other membrane proteins, enhance the immune system as antibodies, and form the major structural components such as the constituents of muscle tissue. The function of a protein is predominantly determined by their structure which is carefully arranged as primary, secondary, tertiary, and quaternary structures in ascension. Primary structure refers to the sequence of amino acids, secondary refers to the local alpha and beta folds that result due to the hydrogen bonding, tertiary refers to the overall or global three-dimensional structure, and the quaternary structure is the combination of various tertiary structures such as a dimer, trimer or a polymer. And together, they define the properties for the protein [45, 46]. The proper folding of the protein and hence the proper alignment of these structures determine the shape, orientation, and conformation of the active site where the protein binds with other proteins and molecules. Enzymes catalyze metabolic processes if the relevant molecules can correctly bind to the enzyme's active sites. Even minute differences in the enzyme's structure affect the efficacy of active site binding. Hence, the tertiary structure of the protein is integral in influencing its function and effectiveness.

The canonical method of determining a protein's tertiary structure has been the likes of X-ray crystallography [47] and cryogenic electromicroscopy [48], and there has been steady global contributions to the Protein Data Bank ("Protein Data Bank: the single global archive for

3D macromolecular structure data," [49]) to make these experimentally elucidated structures available for further analysis. Given that there are at between 18,000 and 22,000 non-modified proteins in the human proteome [50–52], experimentally determining every unique protein's structure [53] is a seemingly impossible task.

20.3.2 The Protein Folding Problem

Predicting the tertiary structure from the primary structure is known as the protein folding problem [54] and has been posted as a biennial scientific challenge called the Critical Assessment of Structure Prediction (CASP) [55] since 1994 [56]. There have been considerable efforts to solve the protein folding problem such as by either creating a symbolic model that captures the physical laws of protein folding [57–60] or a model that learns the patterns of folding through statistical methods [61–64]. Prediction accuracy is determined using the Global Distance Test (GDT) ranging from 0 to 100 which calculates the similarity between the prediction and the true protein structure. The protein folding problem is considered solved if model predictions surpass 90 which is the benchmark set by experimental methods. However, none of the computational methods have been able to come close to experimental benchmarks, with GDT stagnating at about 40 GDT since 2002 [65]. Prediction was worse especially for novel, uncurated protein sequences with no homologous or template structure [55].

20.3.3 Deep Learning Models Solve the Protein Folding Problem

However, in the 2018 CASP13 competition, an algorithm called AlphaFold achieved a significant increase in prediction to 68.5. Similar improvements in prediction accuracies were achieved by other deep learning models though AlphaFold was significantly superior [67]. This was proof that models that employed deep layers of neural networks whose synaptic weights were trained end-to-end by backpropagation of error signals or "deep learning" could handle the complexities involved in protein folding (Fig. 20.1).

In the following 2020 CASP14 competition, the updated AlphaFold2 algorithm solved the protein folding problem by achieving 92.4 GDT [55, 66], a feat that was unimaginable even in 2018. AlphaFold2 is a deep neural network-based model that takes in the novel protein sequence and previously solved homologous protein sequence templates as inputs and predicted the three-dimensional coordinates of each heavy atom. This monumental breakthrough was achieved with two significant model developments.

The first is that AlphaFold is an end-to-end network that performs iterative refinement. End-to-end training allows the model to learn complex features such as physics simulation engine or strategies that might not yet be apparent to humans. This was the same approach taken by AlphaZero which learned complex game strategies of the game Go through self-play to eventually beat multiple Go world champions [68]. Importantly, the same algorithm was able to master other games such as Shogi and Chess [44]. Hence, one algorithm can master many problems. Instead, classical human engineered algorithms like DeepBlue can only solve one specific problem, and a different hand-engineered or symbolic algorithm is needed to solve different problem sets [69]. Iterative refinement is where the initial prediction of the model is recursively fed back to the model during the training process so that the prediction dynamics converges to a stable solution [70, 71]. This "recycling" of initial poor prediction was found to increase prediction accuracy while requiring only a minor increase in training time.

The second is the type of neural network architecture used to process information. While most deep learning architectures use feedforward

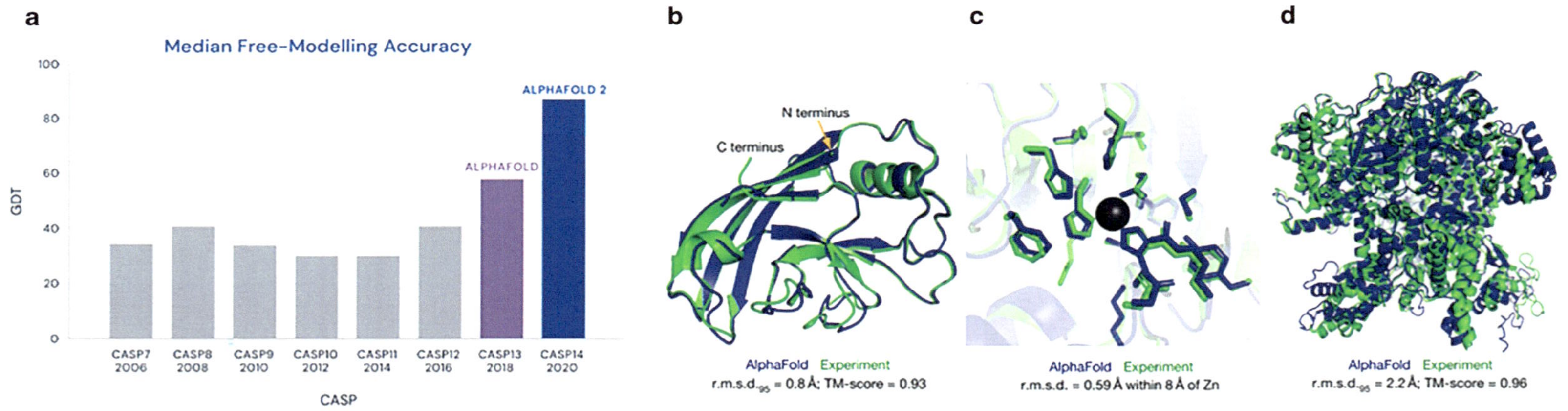

Fig. 20.1 AlphaFold predicts highly accurate protein structures. (**a**) Predicting protein structure folding is considered to be solved if a model achieves above 90.0 GDT. AlphaFold 2 is the current state-of-the-art protein prediction model that achieves a median score of 92.4 GDT overall across all targets with an average error of approximately 1.6 Angstroms. In the most challenging free-modeling category, AlphaFold achieves a mean score of 87.0 GDT. (**b**–**c**) AlphaFold's prediction (blue) of protein structures (**b**) PDB 6Y4F (**c**) PDB 6YJ1 (**d**) PDB 6VR4 which were obtained by experimental methods (green). Figure adapted from Jumper et al. [66]

layers where every neural unit in the model receives linearly weighted inputs, AlphaFold used the transformer architecture which has self-attention mechanisms [72] to identify the relevant contextual information in the input and ignore the rest of the unnecessary information. This was particularly useful to solve the protein folding problem as protein sequences can be extremely long and amino acids that are 300 sequences apart in the primary structure might be close together in the tertiary structure. Transformers can maintain sequential associations despite the length of the sequence unlike recurrent network which struggle with long sequences or feedforward networks which cannot handle sequential information. In fact, transformer models have become the state-of-the-art neural architecture in computer vision [73, 74] and natural language processing [75] such as ChatGPT [42].

20.3.4 The New Age of Predicting Protein Structure

Importantly, AlphaFold has been made publicly available and numerous biomedical research institutes are now using the model to generate a space of hypotheses of their protein of interest within a matter of minutes. For example, there are several notable works such as elucidating the human proteome [76–79], reducing drug discovery time [80–82] and even understanding the COVID-19 pathogen [83–85]. Other applications include improving medicine for malaria or developing enzymes to breakdown plastic waste.

Hence, it is clear that deep learning algorithms such as AlphaFold have changed the landscape of proteomics such that these tools will become as indispensable as a calculator. Biologist can now consider equipping their arsenals with AlphaFold to ask high impact questions. However, it is important to verify the predicted protein structure using experimental methods before moving on to the next phase of drug discovery. Iterating between using computational models to predict and experimental methods to verify will consequently increase the accuracy and efficiency of both approaches respectively.

20.4 Case Study 2: Predicting Neural Computation to Understand Diseases

20.4.1 The Importance of Understanding Brain Computation

The brain is the central control center responsible for a wide range of functions such as sensory processing, cognitive functions including learning and decision-making, emotion and motivation, and motor control [86, 87]. When crucial components in the brain fail to function properly, neurological disorders and mental illnesses can arise. One notable example is dementia, which impacts an estimated 55 million people worldwide, with Alzheimer's disease accounting for 60–70% of cases. Alarmingly, projections suggest that this number will rise to 82 million by 2030 and an astounding 152 million by 2050. It is important to recognize that dementia stands as the seventh leading cause of death globally and plays a substantial role in contributing to disability and dependence. [88]. Hence, understanding how the brain performs its computation and the factors contributing to disease are of significant interest.

Consider the simple delayed matching to sample task (DMS), where a sample stimulus is briefly shown and after a delay period, the subject has to identify the correct target out of several options [89–92]. Given that there are approximately 86 billion neurons in an adult brain and each neuron can potentially synapses to a thousand other neurons [93], fully understanding brain computation is also an impossible problem, especially if we are only endowed with experimental methods.

20.4.2 Decomposing the Problem for Holistic Understanding

Marr argued that if we wanted to understand how a complex system works, we should decompose the problem into three levels of analysis [94], namely,

1. Computation level: What is the problem the system is solving and why is it important?
2. Algorithmic level: What algorithm or software is the system using to solve the problem?
3. Implementation level: How is this algorithm implemented in the physiological hardware?

For example, if we want to understand the phenomenon of flight, looking only at the feathers of a bird will not be sufficient. Similarly, if we want to understand the neural computations for the DMS task, looking only at the neuronal level will not be sufficient. The three levels of analysis is a good starting point towards attaining a holistic understanding of the functional and mechanistic processes that underlie neural computations for a particular computation. Although this method was initially curated to understand vision, it invigorated the field of computational neuroscience and has also been expanded to other domains within biomedical sciences such as computational biology [95, 96].

20.4.3 Developing a Computational Model to Bridge Theory and Experiments

A possible strategy to answer the neural computation question has been to develop the algorithmic level which includes developing neural network based models to bridge the insights from the computational level or psychological theories to the implementation level or experimental results. A suitable artificial model solves the computational problem and the network and can be easily probed to understand the neural computation (Fig. 20.2).

Artificial neural network models are great approximations to biological neural circuits, depending on how it is implemented algorithmically. For instance, approximations can be kept simple by using the perceptron model, where each unit linearly sums the input and has a nonlinear activation function [98]. Alternatively, a more biologically accurate spiking neural model includes the Hodgkin–Huxley model which is a continuous time dynamical system with tuneable parameters to control the sodium and potassium conductance to emulate different action potential dynamics [99]. The perceptron model is computationally inexpensive and hence has been the fundamental unit in most deep learning systems while the Hodgkin–Huxley model replicates the biological properties of individual neurons. There are other classes of artificial neuron types such as leaky rate coded neurons [97, 100] or spike response models [101, 102] that lie between these two polar ends to balance inexpensive computation and biological plausibility.

Next comes the issue of optimizing these artificial neural networks to replicate the computations observed in biological systems. Although there have been works to train the synaptic weights of the neural networks to demonstrate intriguing properties [103–106], these models cannot scale in size to learn complex cognitive behavior. Hence the ability of neural networks to replicate biological performance has been limited [36, 86]. With the advent of deep learning, the synaptic weights of deep neural networks can be easily optimized. This is by computing the cost function or error between the model's prediction and the expected output from a biological system. Then the error is minimized using the principles of gradient descent by backpropagating the error signal to modify the synaptic weights [40, 107]. Neural networks trained by backpropagation can resemble neural representations observed in the visual cortex [108, 109], working memory dynamics in the prefrontal cortex [110–112], place and grid cell-based computation in the hippocampus and entorhinal cortex [113, 114], and causal interactions in the parietal cortex [115]. These neural network models have offered us invaluable insights about the computation and representations that can possibly occur in the brain.

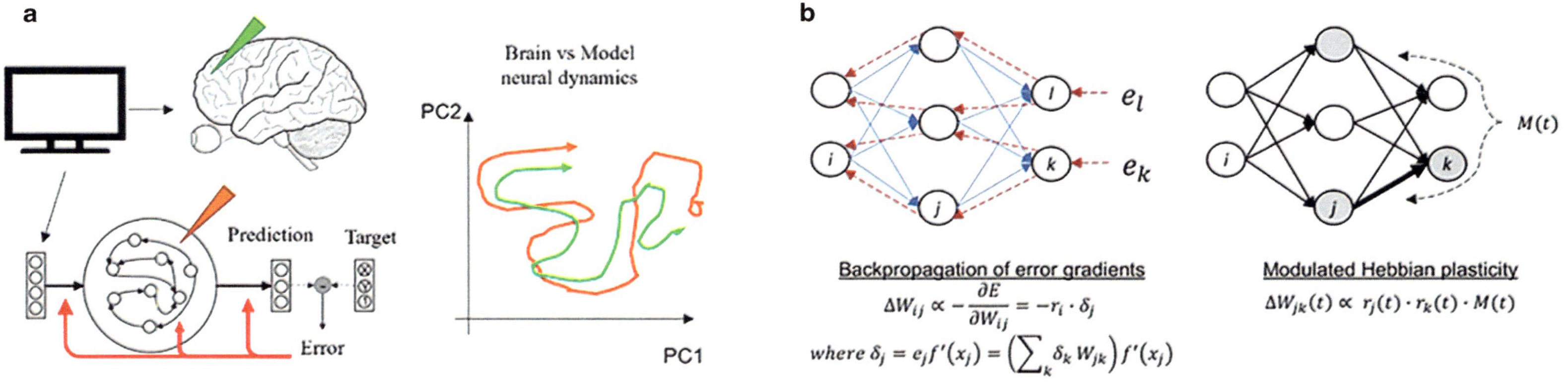

Fig. 20.2 Developing biologically plausible network models to predict brain neural dynamics and computation. (**a**) An animal is trained on an experimental task and invasive electrodes are used to record the neural activity (green probe). A neural network is trained on the same task (red arrows) to replicate the performance of the animal. The model's neural activity can be easily obtained (orange probe). A good animal-to-model correspondence can be determined based on the similarity in neural dynamics. A model that captures the true dynamics can then be used to predict the neural computations for other tasks, reducing the need to train and probe an animal. (**b**) Artificial neural models are currently trained by backpropagating the error signals, which is not biologically plausible. Hebbian plasticity is a biologically plausible learning rule as synaptic plasticity is governed by local and temporal neural activity, replicating the learning computations in the brain. Figure adapted from Kumar et al. [97]

20.4.4 Improving the Biological Plausibility of Deep Learning Models

Training networks using backpropagation is considered to be biologically implausible because it does not use local presynaptic and postsynaptic information to update the synaptic strength and it assumes synaptic weights are the same when the stimulus is passed forward and the error is passed backward through the network [97, 116–119]. Although backpropagation is a great optimization technique to replicate neural representations, it should not be used to make predictions about how biological neural circuits learn a particular function.

To address this limitation, Marr's three levels of analysis has been updated to include the different forms of learning computation as the fourth level such as unsupervised or Hebbian-like learning [120]. Hebbian learning is where the synaptic strength is updated using only presynaptic and postsynaptic activity [121], similar to the principles of Spike Time Dependent Plasticity [122–124], and perhaps modulated by a third global and scalar factor [100, 125] similar to dopamine [126] or acetylcholine [127]. There have been recent advances of neural networks trained by biologically plausible learning rules that can replicate the gradual [97, 128] and rapid [100], [129]) learning behavior of animals with some models also learning representations that are similar to biological experiments [130].

20.4.5 Improving Our Understanding of Neurological Diseases

Once we have a suitable computational neural network model, the artificial neural units and synaptic weights can be easily analyzed using a variety of data analysis techniques [107, 131, 132] to create a space of hypotheses on how neurons compute. Moreover, insights from model analysis can be used to fine-tune the design for animal experiments [133]. Although there are several considerations and knowledge needed to develop a suitable computational model, it is generally the opinion that model development, testing, and evaluation is similar to developing a proof of concept. This process is much faster compared to acquiring, training, and analyzing the animal data, if it even reaches performance criteria.

With an inventory of biologically plausible neural network models and learning rules, we can develop models that explain the neural computation, easily deploy the algorithm for reproducible research and unify the findings across the various experimental results to curate a holistic understanding of how the brain performs various functions. Although we do not have models that explains or predicts complex diseases such as Alzheimer's, there has been momentum in computational psychiatry to achieve this goal within the next decade [134–143].

20.5 Case Study 3: Computer Vision

20.5.1 From Single- to Cross-Modality Interactions in Biomedical Scientific Advancements

The foundations governing the natural and physical sciences were laid by dedicated and niche-centric studies that uncovered the fundamental laws governing the natural order of our universe and biological systems such as elucidating the structure of the double helix structure of DNA to the amino acid biophysical properties that influence the 3-dimensional structure of the protein. These have no doubt led to some of the greatest discoveries in molecular biology that propelled both scientific and medical advancements, some of which have been highlighted in the above discussion. In addition, the discovery of the microscope allowed the expansion of discovery processes into the cellular nature of life and allowed the life sciences to flourish upon the laws of physics and chemistry.

In fact, single modality studies have been instrumental in uncovering the basic rules that drive stable entropic systems and hence for dynamic, community driven hierarchical ecosystems to evolve. Similarly, high-dimensional generation of structural and gene expression datasets would not have been possible if not for the reductionist pursuits of protein domain experimentation and in-cellular technical development [66, 144, 145]. These accomplishments, many originating from the basic sciences, have advanced the field of biomedical research in drug discovery, surgical tool development, and disease screening for patient care and treatment. However, these single modality studies have also simultaneously shown us that no single domain can stand in isolation operating on its own principles.

The importance of cross-domain or interdisciplinary collaborations between the different disciplines has reached an unprecedented height in recent years. And here is an opportune moment for us to transform biomedical research in ways that once could only have been in our imaginations.

One such transforming field that deserves a noteworthy mention is pattern recognition in biological systems and how computer vision and AI can be integrated with high-dimensional molecular networks to facilitate biomedical workflows and translational success.

20.5.2 Computer Vision in Biomedical Research

Computer vision can be considered as the branch of computational science that derives patterns from images and videos and is often referenced as belonging to a sub-category of artificial intelligence. Computer vision algorithms are often composed of highly-interpretable functions called hand-engineered features (i.e., GLCM, granularity spectrum, Fourier transformations), which are often developed upon a-priori knowledge of spatial unit frequencies, directions, and other pattern distributions [146, 147]. However, the complexity of biomedical images benefits from artificial intelligence incorporation, where neural networks learn implicit signature (i.e., pixel, spectral) patterns in a spatial context and learn patterns that are missed by hand-engineered features. These pattern recognition machine learning networks have been applied in the field of cancer, in understanding organ physiology and in aiding surgical development [148] (Fig. 20.3).

Biological medical image analysis includes the analysis of images such as MRI, CT, PET, and histology images. Experts such as radiologists and pathologists who are highly trained professionals have been instrumental in developing international guidelines for clinical classification, diagnosis and treatment courses including surgical processes thus far. However, biomedical images suffer from stochastic patterns in their orientations, morphometry, and texture. Underneath these random, stochastic noise lies true biological structural units, too complex to be quantified or discerned by the human eye but which pattern recognition algorithms from computer vision and newer neural networks can compute. This complexity and the tenacious nature of image analysis coupled with interobserver variability has posed confounding limitations on classification and clinical diagnoses. However, with the limitations of the human eye being increasingly replaced by the power of neural networks capable of finding novel structural patterns, this allows computer vision parameters to pave the way forward where digital images are helping medical professionals diagnose diseases better and faster.

Though AI is influencing the application of computer vision across multiple branches of biomedical research and clinical development, its impact on cancer applications warrants special mention, given the complexity of the genomics of the disease which makes personalized medicine difficult.

Advancements in sequencing technologies have recently supplanted pathology-mediated classification schemes. A high impact example would be how recently WHO changed its guidelines for the grading system of brain cancers based on the molecular profiling of large datasets of patient-derived tumors which proved to show higher concordance with clinically relevant features as compared to pathology based subtyping [149, 150]. In addition to these clinically sensible classification schema, these sequencing studies

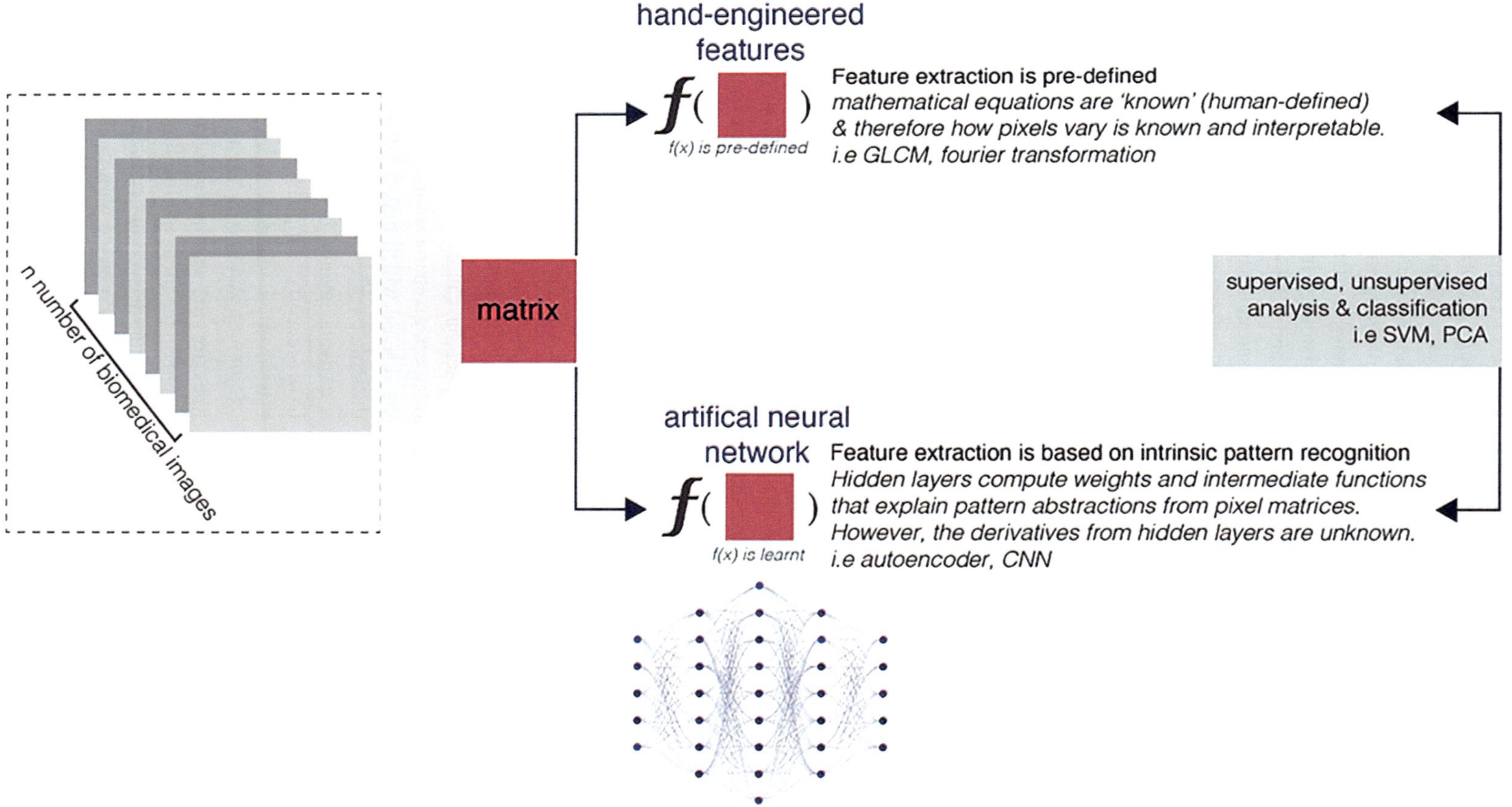

Fig. 20.3 An overview of computer vision pipelines integrated with the rapidly developing AI algorithms. Older and newer algorithms form a spectrum of different modalities that can be used to identify and extract features from images for classification, labeling and identifying parameters that can help develop and guide biomedical applications

have shown us the huge preponderance of genomic alterations in cancer [151–154]. One of the most significant impediments in cancer research and treatment is a direct result of the intra and inter-patient heterogeneity resulting from these alterations. For instance, ambitious single cell sequencing platforms have contributed further towards understanding the cell-types, signaling networks and genomic alterations that drive this heterogeneity and have given us huge libraries of targetable biomarkers with translational value ([155–159]). However, this molecular complexity also makes it harder to understand the relevant functional phenotypes that can benefit clinical workflows, patient care and improving high-throughput target validation for successful biomarker assessment.

Computer vision is proving that pattern recognition in biomedical image analysis can be integrated with high-dimensional molecular datasets to understand phenotypic representations of diseases, demonstrated using MRI brain tumor images trained to predict the biomarkers of high and low grade tumors [160]. This is accomplished through neural networks that extract highly granular features from digital images, allowing differences in structure-texture that is missed by the human visual system [160–162]. Interestingly the very H&E pathology images that were shown to be unreliable previously when analyzed by trained clinicians, could now be fed into large neural networks to pick up patterns in morphometry and texture, that can be used to identify genotype-to-phenotype linkages with high clinical relevance and in evaluating potential therapeutic response [160, 163, 164].

The major area that computer vision and AI are showing an immediate impact is in clinical screening. The progress in this area is adding immense clinical value by improving and speeding up critical diagnosis of various illnesses, shortening pathology workflows and optimizing clinical trial enrollment [165–167]. Histology images provide an important denominator for these gene expression studies, a spatial context, to link gene expression with form and structure [168, 169]. Apart from understanding how molecular signatures translate into tumor structural features, this allows information cross-training between genomics and imaging databases to allow the re-purposing of thousands of images around the globe to be re-analyzed for improved and faster diagnoses [168–170]. This is especially important since it is impractical to set up sequencing facilities in every hospital or clinical facility and doing so might prove to hinder improving patient care instead. For example, clinically relevant biomarkers and gene expression signatures can be approximated through image analysis of breast cancer histology images [165]. Genomic alterations are widespread in many diseased tissues, especially in cancer. And yet the phenotypic outcome of these multiple somatic and copy number variations are unknown and how to best transform these alterations into decision-making steps for personalized medicine is unknown. Histological staining patterns embody underlying structural patterns that are the net result of the underlying genome. By training neural networks on these genomic alterations and whole image slides from patients, we can identify the relevant biomarkers that can be used for clinical trial evaluations and design personalized treatment regiments [163].

These AI-based technologies are not reserved only towards tumor prediction from biomedical images. AI frameworks have been used in supportive frameworks to evaluate different cortical thickness estimators in their abilities to model the subtle nuances of cortical thicknesses, an advancement that will help improve quality of care and assessment in geriatric care [171]. There has been a wide range of integration of computer vision, AI with robotics in developing surgical tools or probes to guide surgery. The 'Raman' spectrum is a popular spectral signature that has been incorporated into surgical probes to identify tumor-normal tissue boundaries during surgeries [172]. The spectral patterns during training are fed into machine learning frameworks in real-time during active surgery and identify the extent or surgical resection that can be pushed beyond the boundaries from MRI scans.

Therefore, these examples serve to highlight the increasing inter-dependence between multiple modalities and how knowledge accumulated over past years are now serving the foundations upon which underlying patterns can be discovered and learnt to formulate a better understanding of normal and diseased physiology as well as to guide in advancing therapeutics.

20.6 Challenges

We have covered significant innovations and applications of interdisciplinary research in biomedical sciences that occurred in the recent past. Due to improvements in computational modeling techniques, we now have powerful tools to predict how inactive protein sequences fold into its active form and also predict the neural computations underlying key neurological processes. But of course, as with new innovations, there will be constraints to push the innovation further.

20.6.1 Manpower Constraints

Most researchers are trained to have deep knowledge in one field and a handful of techniques such as performing animal experiments and analyzing the data. Because of this, most struggle to understand the literature in a different field and apply those techniques to their own problem domain for example, developing computational models to test their hypothesis before conducting animal experiments. Having only a limited pool of researchers trained to perform interdisciplinary research might stifle the creation of new fields like computational psychiatry [173] or lead innovations in their respective field.

20.6.2 Knowledge Constraints

However, pursuing interdisciplinary research takes time away from honing deep knowledge and an expert skill set which is important to determine the limitations within a field. For example, although deep learning models can replicate human performance, the features and representations learned by the network becomes difficult to interpret as a biological network but more importantly, we will not be able to understand how the model arrived as a particular solution. In the case of AlphaFold, it is unclear why the model has low confidence in its own prediction and performs poorly when predicting antibody interactions [66]. To solve the inexplainability problem, we need deep knowledge of theoretical or analytical methods in machine learning [174, 175]. In the case of biomedical sciences, it is difficult to determine causal mechanisms in biological systems unless the relevant techniques are employed [176–178]. However, it is also arguable that such techniques are now available due to innovations through interdisciplinary research.

Hence, the need to balance the constraints posed by disciplinary and interdisciplinary research presents a significant conundrum. Nevertheless, it should become the convention to have both disciplinary and interdisciplinary researchers working collaboratively to solve one problem at a time.

20.7 Conclusion

The concept of incorporating interdisciplinary approaches to biomedical sciences and the collaboration of multiple disciplines must ensure that the final product is greater than the sum of its parts. There are gaps that need to be filled and various disciplines arrive to fill in the gaps. While the parts need to be assembled in a manner to allow a smooth operational prototype, it will take time and a significant number of iterations to arrive there. Interdisciplinary research is not an endgame, but a perpetually evolving process. Biological evolution is driven by changes induced by mutations. Similarly, the growth and success of interdisciplinary research will depend on the influx of new disciplines and technology to the existing paradigms.

References

1. Popper KR. Conjectures and refutations. The growth of scientific knowledge. New York: Routledge & Kegan Paul. 1963.

2. Klein JT, Newell WH. Advancing interdisciplinary studies. In: Handbook of the undergraduate curriculum: a comprehensive guide to purposes, structures, practices, and change; 1997. p. 393–415.
3. Roco MC, Bainbridge WS, editors. Converging technologies for improving human performance: nanotechnology, biotechnology, information technology and cognitive science. Springer Science & Business Media; 2013.
4. Bostrom N. Human genetic enhancements: a transhumanist perspective. J Value Inq. 2003;37:493.
5. Baltimore D, Berg P, Botchan M, Carroll D, Charo RA, Church G, Corn JE, Daley GQ, Doudna JA, Fenner M, Greely HT. A prudent path forward for genomic engineering and germline gene modification. Science. 2015;348(6230):36–8.
6. Baltz RH. Molecular engineering approaches to peptide, polyketide and other antibiotics. Nat Biotechnol. 2006;24(12):1533–40.
7. Huang CJ, Lin H, Yang X. Industrial production of recombinant therapeutics in Escherichia coli and its recent advancements. J Ind Microbiol Biotechnol. 2012;39(3):383–99.
8. Garcia-Milian R, Hersey D, Vukmirovic M, Duprilot F. Data challenges of biomedical researchers in the age of omics. PeerJ. 2018;6:e5553.
9. Sun Z, Ng KH, Ramli N. Biomedical imaging research: a fast-emerging area for interdisciplinary collaboration. Biomed Imaging Interv J. 2011;7(3):e21.
10. Antony PP, Trefois C, Stojanovic A, Baumuratov AS, Kozak K. Light microscopy applications in systems biology: opportunities and challenges. Cell Commun Signal. 2013;11:1–9.
11. Swedlow JR. Innovation in biological microscopy: current status and future directions. BioEssays. 2012;34(5):333–40.
12. Damian M, Porteus MH. A crisper look at genome editing: RNA-guided genome modification. Mol Ther. 2013;21(4):720–2.
13. Han W, She Q. CRISPR history: discovery, characterization, and prosperity. Prog Mol Biol Transl Sci. 2017;152:1–21.
14. Liang P, Zhang X, Chen Y, Huang J. Developmental history and application of CRISPR in human disease. J Gene Med. 2017;19(6–7):e2963.
15. Alkhnbashi OS, Meier T, Mitrofanov A, Backofen R, Voß B. CRISPR-Cas bioinformatics. Methods. 2020;172:3–11.
16. Raja K, Patrick M, Gao Y, Madu D, Yang Y, Tsoi LC. A review of recent advancement in integrating omics data with literature mining towards biomedical discoveries. Int J Genomics. 2017;2017:6213474.
17. Manzoni C, Kia DA, Vandrovcova J, Hardy J, Wood NW, Lewis PA, Ferrari R. Genome, transcriptome and proteome: the rise of omics data and their integration in biomedical sciences. Brief Bioinform. 2018;19(2):286–302.
18. Canuel V, Rance B, Avillach P, Degoulet P, Burgun A. Translational research platforms integrating clinical and omics data: a review of publicly available solutions. Brief Bioinform. 2015;16(2):280–90.
19. Gower B. Scientific method: an historical and philosophical introduction. Psychology Press; 1997.
20. Nola R, Sankey H. Theories of scientific method: an introduction. Routledge; 2014.
21. Carlsson A, Lindqvist M, Magnusson TO. 3, 4-Dihydroxyphenylalanine and 5-hydroxytryptophan as reserpine antagonists. Nature. 1957;180:1200.
22. Tolosa E, Martí MJ, Valldeoriola F, Molinuevo JL. History of levodopa and dopamine agonists in Parkinson's disease treatment. Neurology. 1998;50(6 Suppl 6):S2–10.
23. Sun D, Gao W, Hu H, Zhou S. Why 90% of clinical drug development fails and how to improve it? Acta Pharm Sin B. 2022;12:3049.
24. Thanh Le T, Andreadakis Z, Kumar A, Gómez Román R, Tollefsen S, Saville M, Mayhew S. The COVID-19 vaccine development landscape. Nat Rev Drug Discov. 2020;19:305–6.
25. McCorduck P, Cfe C. Machines who think: a personal inquiry into the history and prospects of artificial intelligence. CRC Press; 2004.
26. Minsky ML. Logical versus analogical or symbolic versus connectionist or neat versus scruffy. AI Mag. 1991;12(2):34.
27. Russell S, Norvig P. Artificial intelligence: a modern approach. 3rd ed. Prentice Hall; 2010.
28. Chen X, Yan CC, Zhang X, Zhang X, Dai F, Yin J, Zhang Y. Drug–target interaction prediction: databases, web servers and computational models. Brief Bioinform. 2016;17(4):696–712.
29. Materi W, Wishart DS. Computational systems biology in drug discovery and development: methods and applications. Drug Discov Today. 2007;12(7–8):295–303.
30. Nantasenamat C, Isarankura-Na-Ayudhya C, Prachayasittikul V. Advances in computational methods to predict the biological activity of compounds. Expert Opin Drug Discov. 2010;5(7):633–54.
31. Stephenson N, Shane E, Chase J, Rowland J, Ries D, Justice N, Zhang J, Chan L, Cao R. Survey of machine learning techniques in drug discovery. Curr Drug Metab. 2019;20(3):185–93.
32. Abbott LF. Theoretical neuroscience rising. Neuron. 2008;60(3):489–95.
33. Itti L, Koch C. Computational modelling of visual attention. Nat Rev Neurosci. 2001;2(3):194–203.
34. Kriegeskorte N, Douglas PK. Cognitive computational neuroscience. Nat Neurosci. 2018;21(9):1148–60.
35. Sterratt D, Graham B, Gillies A, Willshaw D. Principles of computational modelling in neuroscience. Cambridge University Press; 2011.
36. Minsky M, Papert SA. Perceptrons, reissue of the 1988 expanded edition with a new foreword by Léon Bottou: an introduction to computational geometry. MIT Press; 2017.
37. Chen T, Chen H. Universal approximation to nonlinear operators by neural networks with arbitrary

activation functions and its application to dynamical systems. IEEE Trans Neural Netw. 1995;6(4):911–7.
38. Hornik K, Stinchcombe M, White H. Multilayer feedforward networks are universal approximators. Neural Netw. 1989;2(5):359–66.
39. LeCun Y, Bengio Y, Hinton G. Deep learning. Nature. 2015;521(7553):436–44.
40. Rumelhart DE, Hinton GE, Williams RJ. Learning representations by back-propagating errors. Nature. 1986;323(6088):533–6.
41. Krizhevsky A, Sutskever I, Hinton GE. Imagenet classification with deep convolutional neural networks. Commun ACM. 2017;60(6):84–90.
42. Brown T, Mann B, Ryder N, Subbiah M, Kaplan JD, Dhariwal P, Neelakantan A, Shyam P, Sastry G, Askell A, Agarwal S. Language models are few-shot learners. Adv Neural Inf Proces Syst. 2020;33:1877–901.
43. Mnih V, Kavukcuoglu K, Silver D, Rusu AA, Veness J, Bellemare MG, Graves A, Riedmiller M, Fidjeland AK, Ostrovski G, Petersen S. Human-level control through deep reinforcement learning. Nature. 2015;518(7540):529–33.
44. Silver D, Hubert T, Schrittwieser J, Antonoglou I, Lai M, Guez A, Lanctot M, Sifre L, Kumaran D, Graepel T, Lillicrap T. Mastering chess and shogi by self-play with a general reinforcement learning algorithm. arXiv preprint arXiv:1712.01815. 2017.
45. Whitford D. Proteins: structure and function. Wiley; 2013.
46. Buxbaum E, et al. Fundamentals of protein structure and function. Springer. 2007;31.
47. Drenth J. Principles of protein X-ray crystallography. Springer Science & Business Media; 2007.
48. Bai XC, McMullan G, Scheres SH. How cryo-EM is revolutionizing structural biology. Trends Biochem Sci. 2015;40(1):49–57.
49. Protein Data Bank: the single global archive for 3D macromolecular structure data. Nucleic Acids Res. 2019;47(D1):D520–8.
50. Aebersold R, Agar JN, Amster IJ, Baker MS, Bertozzi CR, Boja ES, Costello CE, Cravatt BF, Fenselau C, Garcia BA, Ge Y. How many human proteoforms are there? Nat Chem Biol. 2018;14(3):206–14.
51. Kim MS, Pinto SM, Getnet D, Nirujogi RS, Manda SS, Chaerkady R, Madugundu AK, Kelkar DS, Isserlin R, Jain S, Thomas JK. A draft map of the human proteome. Nature. 2014;509(7502):575–81.
52. Ponomarenko EA, Poverennaya EV, Ilgisonis EV, Pyatnitskiy MA, Kopylov AT, Zgoda VG, Lisitsa AV, Archakov AI. The size of the human proteome: the width and depth. Int J Anal Chem. 2016;2016:7436849.
53. Mitchell AL, Almeida A, Beracochea M, Boland M, Burgin J, Cochrane G, Crusoe MR, Kale V, Potter SC, Richardson LJ, Sakharova E. MGnify: the microbiome analysis resource in 2020. Nucleic Acids Res. 2020;48(D1):D570–8.
54. Dill KA, Ozkan SB, Shell MS, Weikl TR. The protein folding problem. Annu Rev Biophys. 2008;37:289–316.
55. Kryshtafovych A, Schwede T, Topf M, Fidelis K, Moult J. Critical assessment of methods of protein structure prediction (CASP)—Round XIV. Proteins: Struct Funct Bioinformatics. 2021;89(12):1607–17.
56. Moult J, Pedersen JT, Judson R, Fidelis K. A large-scale experiment to assess protein structure prediction methods. Proteins: Struct Funct Bioinformatics. 1995;23(3):ii–v.
57. Anfinsen CB. Principles that govern the folding of protein chains. Science. 1973;181(4096):223–30.
58. Brooks CL III, Gruebele M, Onuchic JN, Wolynes PG. Chemical physics of protein folding. Proc Natl Acad Sci. 1998;95(19):11037–8.
59. Shakhnovich E. Protein folding thermodynamics and dynamics: where physics, chemistry, and biology meet. Chem Rev. 2006;106(5):1559–88.
60. Sippl MJ. Calculation of conformational ensembles from potentials of mena force: an approach to the knowledge-based prediction of local structures in globular proteins. J Mol Biol. 1990;213(4):859–83.
61. Abriata LA, Tamò GE, Dal Peraro M. A further leap of improvement in tertiary structure prediction in CASP13 prompts new routes for future assessments. Proteins: Struct Funct Bioinf. 2019;87(12):1100–12.
62. Brini E, Simmerling C, Dill K. Protein storytelling through physics. Science. 2020;370(6520):eaaz3041.
63. Senior AW, Evans R, Jumper J, Kirkpatrick J, Sifre L, Green T, Qin C, Žídek A, Nelson AW, Bridgland A, Penedones H. Improved protein structure prediction using potentials from deep learning. Nature. 2020;577(7792):706–10.
64. Wang S, Sun S, Li Z, Zhang R, Xu J. Accurate de novo prediction of protein contact map by ultra-deep learning model. PLoS Comput Biol. 2017;13(1):e1005324.
65. Service RF. 'The game has changed.' AI triumphs at protein folding 2020.
66. Jumper J, Evans R, Pritzel A, Green T, Figurnov M, Ronneberger O, Tunyasuvunakool K, Bates R, Žídek A, Potapenko A, Bridgland A. Highly accurate protein structure prediction with AlphaFold. Nature. 2021;596(7873):583–9.
67. Kryshtafovych A, Schwede T, Topf M, Fidelis K, Moult J. Critical assessment of methods of protein structure prediction (CASP)—Round XIII. Proteins: Struct Funct Bioinformatics. 2019;87(12):1011–20.
68. Silver D, Huang A, Maddison CJ, Guez A, Sifre L, Van Den Driessche G, Schrittwieser J, Antonoglou I, Panneershelvam V, Lanctot M, Dieleman S. Mastering the game of Go with deep neural networks and tree search. Nature. 2016;529(7587):484–9.
69. Campbell M, Hoane AJ Jr, Hsu FH. Deep blue. Artif Intell. 2002;134(1–2):57–83.
70. Carreira J, Agrawal P, Fragkiadaki K, Malik J. Human pose estimation with iterative error feedback. In: Proceedings of the IEEE conference on

computer vision and pattern recognition. 2016. pp. 4733–42.
71. Tu Z, Bai X. Auto-context and its application to high-level vision tasks and 3d brain image segmentation. IEEE Trans Pattern Anal Mach Intell. 2009;32(10):1744–57.
72. Vaswani A, Shazeer N, Parmar N, Uszkoreit J, Jones L, Gomez AN, Kaiser Ł, Polosukhin I. Attention is all you need. Adv Neural Inf Proces Syst. 2017;30.
73. Khan S, Naseer M, Hayat M, Zamir SW, Khan FS, Shah M. Transformers in vision: a survey. ACM Comput Surv (CSUR). 2022;54(10s):1–41.
74. Liu Z, Lin Y, Cao Y, Hu H, Wei Y, Zhang Z, Lin S, Guo B. Swin transformer: hierarchical vision transformer using shifted windows. In: Proceedings of the IEEE/CVF international conference on computer vision. 2021. pp. 10012–22.
75. Wolf T, Debut L, Sanh V, Chaumond J, Delangue C, Moi A, Cistac P, Rault T, Louf R, Funtowicz M, Davison J. Transformers: state-of-the-art natural language processing. In: Proceedings of the 2020 conference on empirical methods in natural language processing: system demonstrations. 2020. pp. 38–45.
76. David A, Islam S, Tankhilevich E, Sternberg MJ. The AlphaFold database of protein structures: a biologist's guide. J Mol Biol. 2022;434(2):167336.
77. Porta-Pardo E, Ruiz-Serra V, Valentini S, Valencia A. The structural coverage of the human proteome before and after AlphaFold. PLoS Comput Biol. 2022;18(1):e1009818.
78. Tunyasuvunakool K, Adler J, Wu Z, Green T, Zielinski M, Žídek A, Bridgland A, Cowie A, Meyer C, Laydon A, Velankar S. Highly accurate protein structure prediction for the human proteome. Nature. 2021;596(7873):590–6.
79. Varadi M, Anyango S, Deshpande M, Nair S, Natassia C, Yordanova G, Yuan D, Stroe O, Wood G, Laydon A, Žídek A. AlphaFold Protein Structure Database: massively expanding the structural coverage of protein-sequence space with high-accuracy models. Nucleic Acids Res. 2022;50(D1):D439–44.
80. Binder JL, Berendzen J, Stevens AO, He Y, Wang J, Dokholyan NV, Oprea TI. AlphaFold illuminates half of the dark human proteins. Curr Opin Struct Biol. 2022;74:102372.
81. Ren F, Ding X, Zheng M, Korzinkin M, Cai X, Zhu W, Mantsyzov A, Aliper A, Aladinskiy V, Cao Z, Kong S. AlphaFold accelerates artificial intelligence powered drug discovery: efficient discovery of a novel CDK20 small molecule inhibitor. Chem Sci. 2023;14(6):1443–52.
82. Wong F, Krishnan A, Zheng EJ, Stärk H, Manson AL, Earl AM, Jaakkola T, Collins JJ. Benchmarking AlphaFold-enabled molecular docking predictions for antibiotic discovery. Mol Syst Biol. 2022;18(9):e11081.
83. Arora K, Bist AS. Artificial intelligence-based drug discovery techniques for covid-19 detection. Aptisi Trans Technopreneurship. 2020;2(2): 120–6.
84. Bhatt T, Kumar V, Pande S, Malik R, Khamparia A, Gupta D. A review on COVID-19. In: Artificial intelligence and machine learning for COVID-19; 2021. p. 25–42.
85. Higgins MK. Can we AlphaFold our way out of the next pandemic? J Mol Biol. 2021;433(20):167093.
86. Dayan P, Abbott LF. Theoretical neuroscience: computational and mathematical modeling of neural systems. MIT Press; 2005.
87. Kandel ER, Schwartz JH, Jessell TM, Siegelbaum S, Hudspeth AJ, Mack S, editors. Principles of neural science. New York: McGraw-Hill; 2000.
88. Cahill S. WHO's global action plan on the public health response to dementia: some challenges and opportunities. Aging Ment Health. 2020;24(2):197–99. https://doi.org/10.1080/13607863.2018.1544213. Epub 2019 Jan 2. PMID: 30600688.
89. Funahashi S, Bruce CJ, Goldman-Rakic PS. Mnemonic coding of visual space in the monkey's dorsolateral prefrontal cortex. J Neurophysiol. 1989;61(2):331–49.
90. Lind J, Enquist M, Ghirlanda S. Animal memory: a review of delayed matching-to-sample data. Behav Process. 2015;117:52–8.
91. Miller EK, Erickson CA, Desimone R. Neural mechanisms of visual working memory in prefrontal cortex of the macaque. J Neurosci. 1996;16(16): 5154–67.
92. Robbins TW, Semple J, Kumar R, Truman MI, Shorter J, Ferraro A, Fox B, McKay G, Matthews K. Effects of scopolamine on delayed-matching-to-sample and paired associates tests of visual memory and learning in human subjects: comparison with diazepam and implications for dementia. Psychopharmacology. 1997;134:95–106.
93. Herculano-Houzel S. The human brain in numbers: a linearly scaled-up primate brain. Front Hum Neurosci. 2009;3:31.
94. Marr D. Vision: a computational investigation into the human representation and processing of visual information. MIT Press; 2010.
95. Angermueller C, Pärnamaa T, Parts L, Stegle O. Deep learning for computational biology. Mol Syst Biol. 2016;12(7):878.
96. Noble D. The rise of computational biology. Nat Rev Mol Cell Biol. 2002;3(6):459–63.
97. Kumar MG. Biologically plausible computations underlying one-shot learning of paired associations. ScholarBank@NUS repository. 2022. https://scholarbank.nus.edu.sg/handle/10635/238485.
98. Rosenblatt F. The perceptron: a probabilistic model for information storage and organization in the brain. Psychol Rev. 1958;65(6):386.
99. Hodgkin AL, Huxley AF. A quantitative description of membrane current and its application to conduction and excitation in nerve. J Physiol. 1952;117(4):500.
100. Kumar MG, Tan C, Libedinsky C, Yen SC, Tan AYY. One-shot learning of paired association navigation with biologically plausible schemas. arxiv

preprint arxiv: 2106.03580. 2023. https://arxiv.org/abs/2106.03580.
101. Frémaux N, Sprekeler H, Gerstner W. Reinforcement learning using a continuous time actor-critic framework with spiking neurons. PLoS Comput Biol. 2013;9(4):e1003024.
102. Gerstner W, Kistler WM, Naud R, Paninski L. Neuronal dynamics: from single neurons to networks and models of cognition. Cambridge University Press; 2014.
103. Hopfield JJ. Neural networks and physical systems with emergent collective computational abilities. Proc Natl Acad Sci. 1982;79(8):2554–8.
104. Oja E. Simplified neuron model as a principal component analyzer. J Math Biol. 1982;15:267–73.
105. Rolls ET, Stringer SM, Elliot T. Entorhinal cortex grid cells can map to hippocampal place cells by competitive learning. Netw Comput Neural Syst. 2006;17(4):447–65.
106. Sanger TD. Optimal unsupervised learning in a single-layer linear feedforward neural network. Neural Netw. 1989;2(6):459–73.
107. Yang GR, Wang XJ. Artificial neural networks for neuroscientists: a primer. Neuron. 2020;107(6):1048–70.
108. Kar K, Kubilius J, Schmidt K, Issa EB, DiCarlo JJ. Evidence that recurrent circuits are critical to the ventral stream's execution of core object recognition behavior. Nat Neurosci. 2019;22(6):974–83.
109. Schrimpf M, Kubilius J, Hong H, Majaj NJ, Rajalingham R, Issa EB, Kar K, Bashivan P, Prescott-Roy J, Geiger F, Schmidt K. Brain-score: which artificial neural network for object recognition is most brain-like? BioRxiv. 2018;5:407007.
110. Mante V, Sussillo D, Shenoy KV, Newsome WT. Context-dependent computation by recurrent dynamics in prefrontal cortex. Nature. 2013;503(7474):78–84.
111. Wang JX, Kurth-Nelson Z, Kumaran D, Tirumala D, Soyer H, Leibo JZ, Hassabis D, Botvinick M. Prefrontal cortex as a meta-reinforcement learning system. Nat Neurosci. 2018;21(6):860–8.
112. Yang GR, Joglekar MR, Song HF, Newsome WT, Wang XJ. Task representations in neural networks trained to perform many cognitive tasks. Nat Neurosci. 2019;22(2):297–306.
113. Banino A, Barry C, Uria B, Blundell C, Lillicrap T, Mirowski P, Pritzel A, Chadwick MJ, Degris T, Modayil J, Wayne G. Vector-based navigation using grid-like representations in artificial agents. Nature. 2018;557(7705):429–33.
114. Whittington JC, Muller TH, Mark S, Chen G, Barry C, Burgess N, Behrens TE. The Tolman-Eichenbaum machine: unifying space and relational memory through generalization in the hippocampal formation. Cell. 2020;183(5):1249–63.
115. Suhaimi A, Lim AW, Chia XW, Li C, Makino H. Representation learning in the artificial and biological neural networks underlying sensorimotor integration. Sci Adv. 2022;8(22):eabn0984.
116. Dellaferrera G, Kreiman G. Error-driven input modulation: solving the credit assignment problem without a backward pass. In: International conference on machine learning. PMLR; 2022. pp. 4937–55.
117. Lillicrap TP, Cownden D, Tweed DB, Akerman CJ. Random synaptic feedback weights support error backpropagation for deep learning. Nat Commun. 2016;7(1):13276.
118. Lillicrap TP, Santoro A, Marris L, Akerman CJ, Hinton G. Backpropagation and the brain. Nat Rev Neurosci. 2020;21(6):335–46.
119. Stork. Is backpropagation biologically plausible? In: International 1989 joint conference on neural networks. IEEE; 1989. pp. 241–6.
120. Poggio T. The levels of understanding framework, revised. Perception. SAGE publications Sage UK: London, England. 2012;41;9:1017–23. https://doi.org/10.1068/p7299.
121. Hebb DO. The organization of behavior: a neuropsychological theory. Psychology Press; 2005.
122. Caporale N, Dan Y. Spike timing–dependent plasticity: a Hebbian learning rule. Annu Rev Neurosci. 2008;31:25–46.
123. Dan Y, Poo MM. Spike timing-dependent plasticity of neural circuits. Neuron. 2004;44(1):23–30.
124. Pang KK, Sharma M, Krishna-K K, Behnisch T, Sajikumar S. Long-term population spike-timing-dependent plasticity promotes synaptic tagging but not cross-tagging in rat hippocampal area CA1. Proc Natl Acad Sci. 2019;116(12):5737–46.
125. Frémaux N, Gerstner W. Neuromodulated spike-timing-dependent plasticity, and theory of three-factor learning rules. Front Neural Circuits. 2016;9:85.
126. Montague PR, Dayan P, Sejnowski TJ. A framework for mesencephalic dopamine systems based on predictive Hebbian learning. J Neurosci. 1996;16(5):1936–47.
127. Brzosko Z, Zannone S, Schultz W, Clopath C, Paulsen O. Sequential neuromodulation of Hebbian plasticity offers mechanism for effective reward-based navigation. Elife. 2017;6:e27756.
128. Bellec G, Scherr F, Subramoney A, Hajek E, Salaj D, Legenstein R, Maass W. A solution to the learning dilemma for recurrent networks of spiking neurons. Nat Commun. 2020;11(1):3625.
129. Scherr F, Stöckl C, Maass W. One-shot learning with spiking neural networks. BioRxiv. 2020;19:2020–06.
130. Miconi T. Biologically plausible learning in recurrent neural networks reproduces neural dynamics observed during cognitive tasks. Elife. 2017;6:e20899.
131. Botvinick M, Wang JX, Dabney W, Miller KJ, Kurth-Nelson Z. Deep reinforcement learning and its neuroscientific implications. Neuron. 2020;107(4):603–16.
132. Saxe A, Nelli S, Summerfield C. If deep learning is the answer, what is the question? Nat Rev Neurosci. 2021;22(1):55–67.

133. Gao P, Trautmann E, Yu B, Santhanam G, Ryu S, Shenoy K, Ganguli S. A theory of multineuronal dimensionality, dynamics and measurement. BioRxiv. 2017;5:214262.
134. Collins AG, Brown JK, Gold JM, Waltz JA, Frank MJ. Working memory contributions to reinforcement learning impairments in schizophrenia. J Neurosci. 2014;34(41):13747–56.
135. Hauser TU, Fiore VG, Moutoussis M, Dolan RJ. Computational psychiatry of ADHD: neural gain impairments across Marrian levels of analysis. Trends Neurosci. 2016;39(2):63–73.
136. Hauser TU, Skvortsova V, De Choudhury M, Koutsouleris N. The promise of a model-based psychiatry: building computational models of mental ill health. Lancet Digital Health. 2022;4:e816.
137. Maia TV, Frank MJ. From reinforcement learning models to psychiatric and neurological disorders. Nat Neurosci. 2011;14(2):154–62.
138. Palminteri S, Pessiglione M. Reinforcement learning and Tourette syndrome. Int Rev Neurobiol. 2013;112:131–53.
139. Richardson FM, Thomas MS. The benefits of computational modelling for the study of developmental disorders: extending the Triesch et al. model to ADHD. Dev Sci. 2006;9(2):151.
140. Stein H, Barbosa J, Compte A. Towards biologically constrained attractor models of schizophrenia. Curr Opin Neurobiol. 2021;70:171–81.
141. Véronneau-Veilleux F, Robaey P, Ursino M, Nekka F. A mechanistic model of ADHD as resulting from dopamine phasic/tonic imbalance during reinforcement learning. Front Comput Neurosci. 2022;16:849323.
142. Waltz JA, Frank MJ, Robinson BM, Gold JM. Selective reinforcement learning deficits in schizophrenia support predictions from computational models of striatal-cortical dysfunction. Biol Psychiatry. 2007;62(7):756–64.
143. Ziegler S, Pedersen ML, Mowinckel AM, Biele G. Modelling ADHD: a review of ADHD theories through their predictions for computational models of decision-making and reinforcement learning. Neurosci Biobehav Rev. 2016;71:633–56.
144. Ding J, Adiconis X, Simmons SK, Kowalczyk MS, Hession CC, Marjanovic ND, Hughes TK, Wadsworth MH, Burks T, Nguyen LT, Kwon JY. Systematic comparison of single-cell and single-nucleus RNA-sequencing methods. Nat Biotechnol. 2020;38(6):737–46.
145. Haque A, Engel J, Teichmann SA, Lönnberg T. A practical guide to single-cell RNA-sequencing for biomedical research and clinical applications. Genome Med. 2017;9(1):1–2.
146. Mansour IR, Thomson RM. Haralick texture feature analysis for characterization of specific energy and absorbed dose distributions across cellular to patient length scales. Phys Med Biol. 2023;68(7):075006.
147. Pantic I, Cumic J, Dugalic S, Petroianu GA, Corridon PR. Gray level co-occurrence matrix and wavelet analyses reveal discrete changes in proximal tubule cell nuclei after mild acute kidney injury. Sci Rep. 2023;13(1):4025.
148. Esteva A, Chou K, Yeung S, Naik N, Madani A, Mottaghi A, Liu Y, Topol E, Dean J, Socher R. Deep learning-enabled medical computer vision. NPJ Digit Med. 2021;4(1):5.
149. Louis DN, Perry A, Wesseling P, Brat DJ, Cree IA, Figarella-Branger D, Hawkins C, Ng HK, Pfister SM, Reifenberger G, Soffietti R. The 2021 WHO classification of tumors of the central nervous system: a summary. Neuro-Oncology. 2021;23(8):1231–51.
150. Wen PY, Packer RJ. The 2021 WHO classification of tumors of the central nervous system: clinical implications. Neuro-Oncology. 2021;23(8):1215–7.
151. Frattini V, Trifonov V, Chan JM, Castano A, Lia M, Abate F, Keir ST, Ji AX, Zoppoli P, Niola F, Danussi C. The integrated landscape of driver genomic alterations in glioblastoma. Nat Genet. 2013;45(10):1141–9.
152. Jiang YZ, Ma D, Suo C, Shi J, Xue M, Hu X, Xiao Y, Yu KD, Liu YR, Yu Y, Zheng Y. Genomic and transcriptomic landscape of triple-negative breast cancers: subtypes and treatment strategies. Cancer Cell. 2019;35(3):428–40.
153. Lee E, Iskow R, Yang L, Gokcumen O, Haseley P, Luquette LJ III, Lohr JG, Harris CC, Ding L, Wilson RK, Wheeler DA. Landscape of somatic retrotransposition in human cancers. Science. 2012;337(6097):967–71.
154. Yuan X, Yu G, Hou X, Shih IM, Clarke R, Zhang J, Hoffman EP, Wang RR, Zhang Z, Wang Y. Genome-wide identification of significant aberrations in cancer genome. BMC Genomics. 2012;13:1–4.
155. Cooper J, Ding Y, Song J, Zhao K. Genome-wide mapping of DNase I hypersensitive sites in rare cell populations using single-cell DNase sequencing. Nat Protoc. 2017;12(11):2342–54.
156. Couturier CP, Ayyadhury S, Le PU, Nadaf J, Monlong J, Riva G, et al. Single-cell RNA-seq reveals that glioblastoma recapitulates a normal neurodevelopmental hierarchy. Nat Commun. 2020;11:3406.
157. Neftel C, Laffy J, Filbin MG, Hara T, Shore ME, Rahme GJ, et al. An integrative model of cellular states, plasticity, and genetics for glioblastoma. Cell. 2019;178:835–849.e21.
158. Richards LM, Whitley OK, MacLeod G, Cavalli FM, Coutinho FJ, Jaramillo JE, Svergun N, Riverin M, Croucher DC, Kushida M, Yu K. Gradient of Developmental and Injury Response transcriptional states defines functional vulnerabilities underpinning glioblastoma heterogeneity. Nat Cancer. 2021;2(2):157–73.
159. Shapiro E, Biezuner T, Linnarsson S. Single-cell sequencing-based technologies will revolutionize whole-organism science. Nat Rev Genet. 2013;14(9):618–30.
160. Kalaroopan D, Lasocki A. MRI-based deep learning techniques for the prediction of isocitrate dehydro-

genase and 1p/19q status in grade 2–4 adult gliomas. J Med Imaging Radiat Oncol. 2023;67:492.
161. Moen E, Bannon D, Kudo T, Graf W, Covert M, Van Valen D. Deep learning for cellular image analysis. Nat Methods. 2019;16(12):1233–46.
162. Spiller ER, Ung N, Kim S, Patsch K, Lau R, Strelez C, Doshi C, Choung S, Choi B, Juarez Rosales EF, Lenz HJ. Imaging-based machine learning analysis of patient-derived tumor organoid drug response. Front Oncol. 2021;11:771173.
163. Kather JN, Heij LR, Grabsch HI, Loeffler C, Echle A, Muti HS, Krause J, Niehues JM, Sommer KA, Bankhead P, Kooreman LF. Pan-cancer image-based detection of clinically actionable genetic alterations. Nat cancer. 2020;1(8):789–99.
164. Naik N, Madani A, Esteva A, Keskar NS, Press MF, Ruderman D, Agus DB, Socher R. Deep learning-enabled breast cancer hormonal receptor status determination from base-level H&E stains. Nat Commun. 2020;11(1):5727.
165. Inge LJ, Dennis E. Development and applications of computer image analysis algorithms for scoring of PD-L1 immunohistochemistry. Immuno-Oncol Technol. 2020;6:2–8.
166. Madabhushi A, Lee G. Image analysis and machine learning in digital pathology: challenges and opportunities. Med Image Anal. 2016;33:170–5.
167. Niazi MK, Parwani AV, Gurcan MN. Digital pathology and artificial intelligence. Lancet Oncol. 2019;20(5):e253–61.
168. Levy-Jurgenson A, Tekpli X, Kristensen VN, Yakhini Z. Spatial transcriptomics inferred from pathology whole-slide images links tumor heterogeneity to survival in breast and lung cancer. Sci Rep. 2020;10(1):1.
169. Schmauch B, Romagnoni A, Pronier E, Saillard C, Maillé P, Calderaro J, Kamoun A, Sefta M, Toldo S, Zaslavskiy M, Clozel T. A deep learning model to predict RNA-Seq expression of tumours from whole slide images. Nat Commun. 2020;11(1):3877.
170. Jaber MI, Song B, Taylor C, Vaske CJ, Benz SC, Rabizadeh S, Soon-Shiong P, Szeto CW. A deep learning image-based intrinsic molecular subtype classifier of breast tumors reveals tumor heterogeneity that may affect survival. Breast Cancer Res. 2020;22:12.
171. Rusak F, Santa Cruz R, Lebrat L, Hlinka O, Fripp J, Smith E, Fookes C, Bradley AP, Bourgeat P. Alzheimer's Disease Neuroimaging Initiative. Quantifiable brain atrophy synthesis for benchmarking of cortical thickness estimation methods. Med Image Anal. 2022;82:102576.
172. Desroches J, Jermyn M, Mok K, Lemieux-Leduc C, Mercier J, St-Arnaud K, et al. Characterization of a Raman spectroscopy probe system for intraoperative brain tissue classification. Biomed Opt Express. 2015;6:2380–97.
173. Huys QJ, Maia TV, Frank MJ. Computational psychiatry as a bridge from neuroscience to clinical applications. Nat Neurosci. 2016;19(3):404–13.
174. Erhan D, Bengio Y, Courville A, Vincent P. Visualizing higher-layer features of a deep network. University of Montreal. 2009;1341(3):1.
175. Jacot A, Gabriel F, Hongler C. Neural tangent kernel: convergence and generalization in neural networks. Adv Neural Inf Proces Syst. 2018;31.
176. Hames BD. Gel electrophoresis of proteins: a practical approach, vol. 197. OUP Oxford; 1998.
177. Whisstock JC, Lesk AM. Prediction of protein function from protein sequence and structure. Q Rev Biophys. 2003;36(3):307–40.
178. Yizhar O, Fenno LE, Davidson TJ, Mogri M, Deisseroth K. Optogenetics in neural systems. Neuron. 2011;71(1):9–34.
179. Bhaduri A, Di Lullo E, Jung D, Müller S, Crouch EE, Espinosa CS, Ozawa T, Alvarado B, Spatazza J, Cadwell CR, Wilkins G. Outer radial glia-like cancer stem cells contribute to heterogeneity of glioblastoma. Cell Stem Cell. 2020;26(1):48–63.
180. Popper K. Evolutionary epistemology. In: Open questions in quantum physics: invited papers on the foundations of microphysics; 1985. p. 395–413.
181. Russell SJ. Artificial intelligence a modern approach. Pearson Education, Inc.; 2010.

21 Speciation of Oral Candida Isolates from Patients with Oral Squamous Cell Carcinoma, Oral Potentially Malignant Disorders, and Healthy Subjects Using Phenotypic and PCR-RFLP Methods

Sankar Leena Sankari, Krishnan Mahalakshmi, and Venkatesan Naveen Kumar

21.1 Introduction

Oral squamous cell carcinoma (OSCC) is an epithelial malignancy that accounts for over 0.3 million deaths per year around the globe. With a 62% incidence rate, it stands 12th in the list of common cancers afflicting women and 6th in the same for men worldwide. South-central Asia including Sri Lanka, India, Taiwan, and Pakistan reports a high prevalence of OSCC which is the third highest among various types of cancer [1]. In India, every 20 of 1 lakh population report OSCC [2]. Oral potentially malignant disorders (OPMD) usually precede OSCC in most clinical situations.

OPMD may be regarded as the first detectable clinical change that occurs before an OSCC. The conversion of an oral lesion to a malignant OSCC in the tongue was first reported by Sir James Paget in 1870. World Health Organization (WHO) designates these lesions as "potentially malignant disorder" (OPMD) since the risk of malignant transformation is there. The malignant transformation potential of OPMD lies between 5% and 18% in most of the cases [3]. The prevalence of OPMD has not been widely described and the rates differ based on certain populations. In the Indian subcontinent, the incidence rates of OPMD fall between 0.6/1000 and 30.2/1000 [4]. Quite a few OPMDs can precede the formation of oral carcinoma. The various OPMDs include oral submucous fibrosis (OSMF), leukoplakia, erythroplakia, erythroleukoplakia, palatal lesions in reverse smokers, and oral lichen planus (OLP). Those most encountered are erythroplakia leukoplakia and OSMF. The diagnosis of OPMD is made solely on their varied clinical presentations. Suspicious lesions are subjected to histopathological examination to evaluate the risk of malignant transformation. The histopathological diagnosis of OPMD may range from epithelial hyperkeratosis, hyperplasia or atrophy of the epithelium, dysplasia, carcinoma in situ to a frank OSCC [5].

Oral leukoplakia is characterized as white-colored patches in the oral cavity that are clini-

S. L. Sankari
Department of Oral and Maxillofacial Pathology and Oral Microbiology, Sree Balaji Dental College and Hospital, Bharath Institute of Higher Education and Research, Chennai, Tamil Nadu, India

K. Mahalakshmi (✉)
Department of Microbiology, Sree Balaji Dental College and Hospital, Bharath Institute of Higher Education and Research, Chennai, India

V. N. Kumar
ImmuGenix Biosciences Pvt Ltd, Chennai, Tamil Nadu, India

K. Parthasarathy, R. Manikkam (eds.), *Translational Research in Biomedical Sciences: Recent Progress and Future Prospects*, https://doi.org/10.1007/978-981-97-1777-4_21

cally demarcated as white lesions without the risk of transformation into cancer. They are mostly asymptomatic and often have a benign clinical appearance. Clinical examination for non-scrapable white patches in the mucosal layer that do not fade after stretching should be done to indicate leukoplakia. All the other white lesions were excluded including local trauma. Chemical or physical agents cannot be attributed to leukoplakia excluding tobacco, alcohol, or betel quid [6]. In the Western populations, in general, the palate and the lateral margins of the tongue are involved. The Asian populations have lower buccal vestibule and the buccal mucosa as the most common regions because of betel quid placement. Homogeneous and non-homogeneous leukoplakia are the two main clinical types of leukoplakia. Homogeneous leukoplakias are mostly asymptomatic and present as a uniform thin raised smooth surface. The non-homogeneous leukoplakia has three types (speckled, nodular, and verrucous), which are usually symptomatic. Speckled leukoplakia also commonly known as erythroleukoplakia are mixed white and red lesions. The red areas show atrophy (thinning) of epithelium. A leukoplakia having interspersed red patches (erythroleukoplakia) indicates a likely colonization of *Candida* species which can increase the possibility for dysplasia and/or malignancy [7].

Erythroplakia is characterized as a distinct red velvety lesion with irregular margins. It appears as a keratotic chord-like grid of pale striae on the buccal mucosa and tongue's lateral margins. The most common type is the reticular form when compared to other types such as hypertrophic, atrophic, and erosive. Most patients are either asymptomatic or present with a burning sensation. Malignant transformation of OLP lesions is low when compared to other OPMD. Erosive and atrophic forms have a higher tendency to turn into OSCC when compared to reticular forms. The tongue is the most common site that has high malignant transformation potential. The malignant potential of lichen planus is very low (0.2–1%) [5] with an overall transformation potential of 1.09% [8].

Oral submucous fibrosis (OSMF) is a common chronic insidious lesion in lamina propria leading to fibrous rigidity. The most common etiological factor for OSMF is areca nut chewing besides capsaicin (chilies), and deficiencies of micronutrients like iron and zinc. The early features of OSMF patients include paleness of mucosa, paresthesia, and normal pigmentation loss. When the disease progresses, the mucosa becomes rigid and acquires a leathery texture with fibrous bands being prominent and palpable vertically oriented in the oral mucosa. Furthermore, it restricts the patient from opening the mouth [9, 10].

OPMD are mostly asymptomatic which might result in an undue diagnostic delay. Early detection of OPMD can reduce morbidity and mortality due to OSCC. OPMD and OSCC share common risk factors [5]. Epigenetic risk factors for OSCC may include alcohol, tobacco, microbial infections, nutrition, diet, and immunosuppression [11]. The deep-rooted potential factors for OSSC and OPMD are tobacco consumption in both chewable and non-chewable forms, chewing areca nut, ultraviolet radiation (lip cancer), and alcohol consumption. There are approximately 15% of cases of oral cancer that are not ascribed to any of these common risk factors. Hence it is postulated that other factors like infection and inflammation can have a role [12]. Viruses such as human papilloma viruses, human simplex virus, and Epstein–Barr virus, bacteria like *Fusobacterium* sp., *Porphyromonas gingivalis,* and fungi like *Candida albicans,* are also recognized to cause oral cancer [13, 14]. *C. albicans* is associated with leukoplakia and has been considered as an independent risk factor for OSCC due to its capacity to nitrosylate *N*-benzyl methylamine [14–16].

The name *Candida* derives its origin from the Latin word candid which means white. The principal yeast pathogen, *C. albicans*, itself, was identified in the nineteenth century. *Candida*, a dimorphic yeast-like fungus (Phylum—Ascomycota and Order—Saccharomycetales) comprises of around 200 species. Ninety percent of the infections are mainly caused by *C. albicans*, *Candida krusei*, *Candida tropicalis*,, *Candida glabrata,* and *Candida parapsilosis.* The most frequently isolated species is *C.*

albicans but in recent times, its prevalence is decreasing compared to the other species [17].

Candida is a harmless commensal that can transform into a pathogen and become invasive when there is a disruption of harmony in flora or when the host's immune defense mechanisms are compromised. The commensal to pathogen transition may be attributed to the pathogenic features of the organism. Adhesion of *Candida* to epithelial cells is the major pathogenic factor that prevents or declines the level of clearance by the host's immune system [18]. The potential of *Candida* species to remain on the surface of the oral mucosa of healthy individuals withstanding the mechanical washing of saliva flow towards the esophagus is a vital component contributing to its virulence [19]. *C. albicans* is the most prevalent species that accounts for over more than 80% of all oral yeast isolates. This trend seems to be shifting currently. There is a recent rise in non-albicans *Candida (NAC)* species being implicated in human diseases. The factors that have contributed to this change include factors like immunosuppression and misuse of broad-spectrum antibiotics and antifungal drugs [20].

Candidal growth is favored at the time of the host's immune suppression and also during changes in the O_2 level and pH in the mouth. When commensals like *Candida* gain primacy they lead to an array of infections [21]. Epithelial changes along with *Candida* may further predispose to epithelial dysplasia and malignancy [16]. Statistically significant and correlative transformation of leukoplakia that is superimposed with *Candida* showing dysplasia transforms into malignancy at a higher rate than uninfected leukoplakia [16, 22, 23]. In chronic hyperplastic candidiasis, invasion of candidal hyphae into the oral epithelium induces dysplastic changes leading to oral cancer [21, 24]. In OSCC, a dysbiotic mycobiome dominated by *C. albicans* was observed with alterations in the epithelium of the oral mucosa, such as hyperplasia, atrophy, and dysplasia that can disturb the integrity of the mucosal barrier and promote candidal invasion [25]. *Candida* species could produce nitrosamine compounds that either directly or in conjunction with other chemical carcinogens activate specific proto-oncogenes leading to the initiation of OSCC [26].

As widespread evidence associates *Candida* species with OSCC and OPMD, this chapter describes the methods to measure the incidence of *Candida* and NAC among OSCC, and OPMD patients using phenotypic and genotypic methods.

21.2 Methods

Study Design: In this cross-sectional study, a total of 497 salivary samples were collected from OSCC (n = 97), oral malignancy (n = 200), and healthy volunteers (n = 200) collected over 5 years with approval from the institutional ethical committee.

21.3 Sample Collection and Enumeration of Determination of Colony-Forming Units/mL

Two milliliters salivary samples were collected using the "Draining" method by tilting the patient's head forward ensuring that the sample represents the entire oral cavity [27]. Enumeration of *Candida* load was done as described previously using 10 μL of saliva sample streaked onto Sabouraud's dextrose agar (SDA) plate with aerobic incubation at 37 °C for 1 week. Gram staining was done to check the purity of yeast cells.

21.4 Phenotypic Method of *Candida* Identification

The following phenotypic assays were performed to speciate the candidal colonies.

21.4.1 Germ Tube Test

A yeast colony was inoculated into 500 μL of sterile human serum. The tubes were incubated at 37 °C for 2.5–3 h. The incubated sterile human serum suspension was then examined under the light microscope for the formation of a germ tube. *C. albicans* MTCC 3018 was included as a positive control (Fig. 21.1).

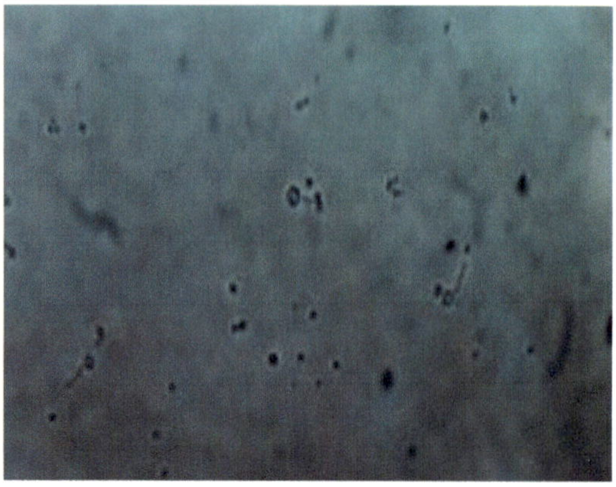

Fig. 21.1 Germ tube formation

21.4.2 Chlamydospore Formation Test

Corn meal agar (Hi media, India) was prepared as per the manufacturer's instructions. One milliliters of tween 80 was added, mixed, and autoclaved at 121°c for 15 min and was poured on plates and allowed to set. A small bit of a single yeast colony was picked up from a fresh SDA plate and a few cuts were made into the agar with the loop in a slanting manner. On top of the cut area, a cover slip was placed. The plates were incubated at 37 °C for 24–72 h. After 72 h the plates were examined under a light microscope (100×, 450×) for the characteristic chlamydospore formation (Fig. 21.2).

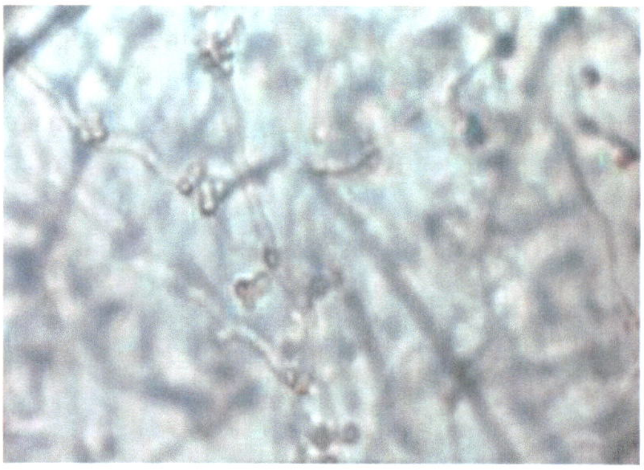

Fig. 21.2 Chlamydospore formation in Corn meal agar

21.4.3 *Candida* Species Identification Using Chromogenic Medium

Procedure

- *Candida* isolates were streaked on HiCrome Candida differential Agar, M1297A (HiMedia, Mumbai, India) and incubated under aerobic conditions at 37 °C for 24–48 h.
- As per the manufacturer's interpretation chart, the colonies were observed and the species were identified based on characteristic color (Fig. 21.3).

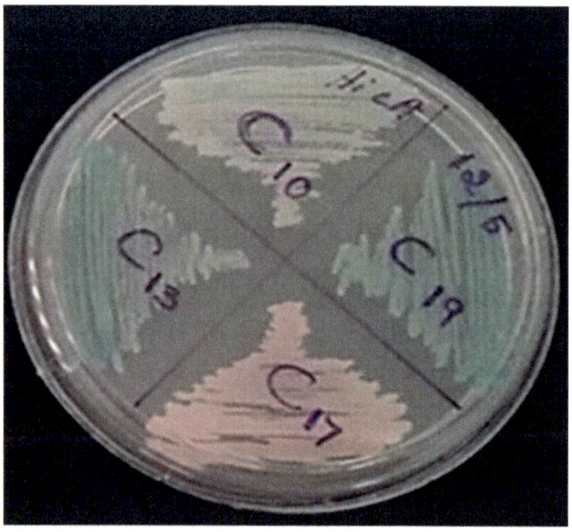

Fig. 21.3 Pink, cream, and green colonies on HiCrome Candida differential Agar

21.4.4 Sugar Fermentation Test

- To further confirm the test isolates sugar fermentation test was carried out, all were tested in a bromocresol purple broth containing 1% sugars.
- Test isolates grown on nutrient agar were matched with 0.5 McFarland standard and 2 mL saline suspension was prepared.
- 0.2 mL of the suspension was added to glucose, maltose, lactose, sucrose, and galac-

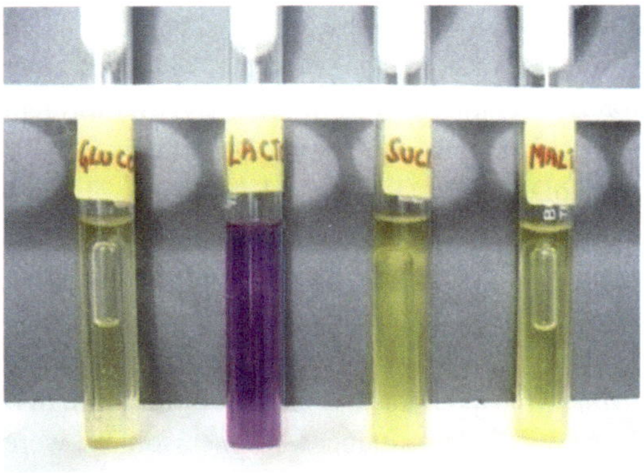

Fig. 21.4 Sugar fermentation showing color changes

tose tubes, and incubated at 37 °C for 7–12 days.
- Acidification of the fermentation broth as evidenced by the color change was observed and noted (Fig. 21.4).

21.4.5 Sugar Assimilation Test

- The capability of the test isolate to assimilate various sugars was assessed by the auxanographic plate method.
- Test isolates were grown initially on sugar-free medium (nutrient agar).
- The yeast cultures from nutrient agar were resuspended into 2 mL of sterile saline (0.85% sodium chloride) and opacity was adjusted to 0.5 McFarland standards.
- 1.5 mL of sterile yeast nitrogen base, 13.5 mL of sterile 2% molten agar was added onto petriplates along with saline suspension.
- Plates were swirled well and allowed to set.
- Discs impregnated with 20% sugar solution (Sucrose, Maltose, Cellobiose, Trehalose Xylose, Raffinose, Mellibiose, Dulcitol, Glucose, Galactose, Inositol, Lactose) were placed on the dried agar plates.
- The plates were incubated aerobically for 48–72 h at 37 °C.
- Following incubation, growth zones around the discs were observed and noted (Fig. 21.5).

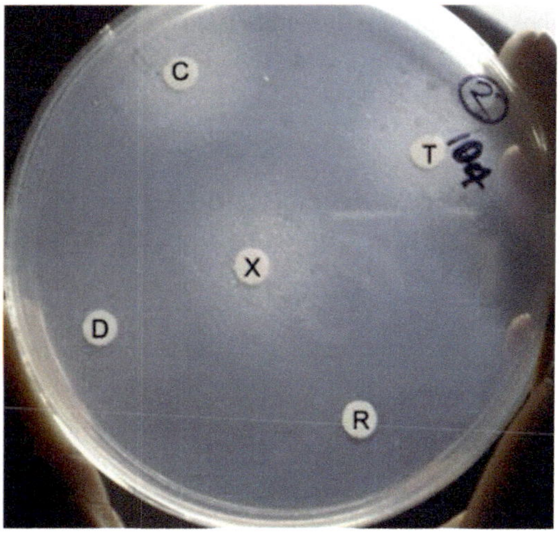

Fig. 21.5 Sugar assimilation test showing growth zones around the discs

21.4.6 Identification by Hi-Candida Identification Kit (KB006, Himedia)

About two to four well-discriminated colonies was considered for homogenous suspension of inoculum preparation in 2–3 mL of sterile saline. The turbidity of the suspension was matched to 0.5 OD at 620 nm.

Under aseptic conditions the kit was opened. Surface inoculation method was done where each well was inoculated with 50 μL of the above inoculum. The kit was incubated at a temperature of 22.5 ± 2.5° C for 24–48 h. The results were interpreted following the manufacturer's instructions.

21.5 Growth Tolerance at 45 °C

The ability of *C. albicans* to tolerate and grow at 45 °C is considered significant to differentiate it from *Candida dubliniensis* (no growth at 45 °C). This test was done with the samples that showed green colonies on HiChrom agar and were positive for germ tube test, chlamydoconidia production. The heat tolerance test was performed on the SDA plate. The inoculated cultures were incubated aerobically at 45 °C. The growth was observed for 10 days.

21.6 Genotypic Method of Identification for *Candida* Species

Genotypic identification was done by PCR-RFLP (restricted fragment length polymorphism) method.

21.6.1 Extraction of DNA

The boiling lysis method was followed for DNA extraction of *Candida* isolates following the protocol as described previously [28]. The supernatant from the culture lysate was considered as a template for PCR assay.

21.6.2 PCR Assay

PCR was carried out using the lysed culture isolates by targeting the ITS1-5.8SrDNA-ITS2 region to genotypically confirm *Candida* isolates [28]. The composition and PCR program are given in Tables 21.1 and 21.2. The PCR products were resolved in 1% agarose gel and observed under UV-transilluminator (Fig. 21.6).

21.6.3 RFLP and ITS Gene Sequencing

To confirm the presence of *Candida* species, each 8.8 μL aliquot of the ITS PCR product underwent digestion with 4 U of MspI at 37 °C for 60 min and then heat-inactivated at 85 °C for 5 min. Subsequently, the digested products were separated using a 2% agarose gel. The resulting restriction patterns were analyzed and compared with those of sequences from the National Center for Biotechnology Information (NCBI) through an *insilico* method, utilizing DNA analysis software pDRAW32 (Version 1.1.140) (Fig. 21.7 and Table 21.3).

To validate the identification of *Candida* species based on RFLP, a representative isolate of each species was sequenced and aligned using BLAST (https://blast.ncbi.nlm.nih.gov/Blast.cgi).The sequences of the isolates were deposited in the NCBI GenBank database (Table 21.4).

Table 21.1 Components of PCR mixture for Genotypic identification of *Candida*

Component	Volume/ concentration
10× PCR buffer with $MgCl_2$	2.5 μL
dNTP mix	0.4 mM
ITS1 (5′-TCCGTAGGTGAACCTGCGG-3′)	10 pM
ITS4 (5′-TCCTCCGCTTATTGATATGC-3′),	10 pM
Taq polymerase	1 U
DNA template	2 μL
Double distilled water	Up to 25 μL

Table 21.2 PCR Program mixture for Genotypic identification of *Candida*

PCR step	Temperature (°C)	Time (s)	No. of cycles
Initial denaturation	94	180	1
Denaturation	94	20	40
Primer annealing	55	30	
Extension	72	45	
Final extension	72	300	1
Hold	12	∞	

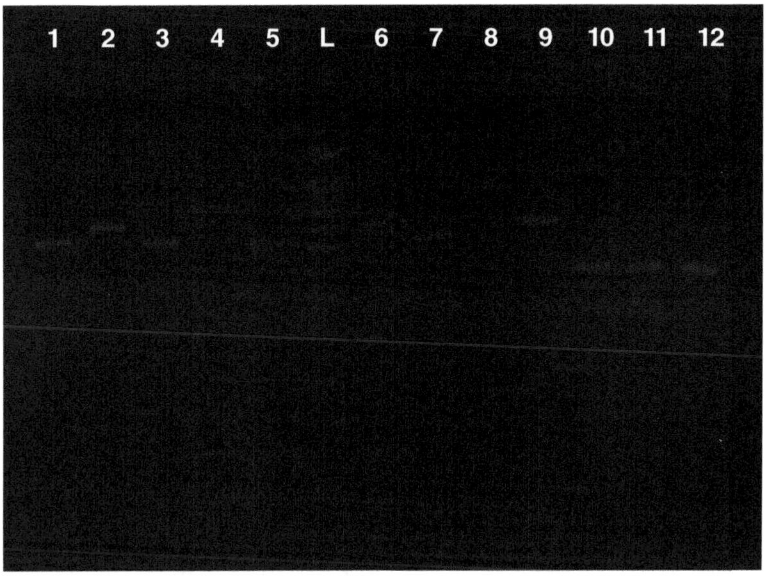

LANE	ISOLATES
1	A116
2	C55
3	B199
4	C78
5	B163
6	A90
7	B197
8	C75S
9	B102
10	B75
11	C89
12	B73

Fig. 21.6 PCR gel picture for *Candida* ITS. *L:100 bp molecular size marker, Lane1: C. albicans, Lane 2: Pichia anomala, Lane 3: Candida tropicalis, Lane 4: Candida kefyr, Lane 5: C. krusei Lane 6: C. guilliermondii, Lane 7: C. orthopsilosis Lane 8: C. glabrata Lane 9: P. anomala Lane10: C. rugosa, Lane 11: C. lusitaniae Lane 12: C. rugosa*

LANE	ISOLATES
1	A116
2	C55
3	B199
4	C78
5	B163
6	A90
7	B197
8	B102
9	C75S
10	B75
11	C89
12	B73

Fig. 21.7 RFLP gel picture for *Candida* its. *L:100 bp molecular size marker, Lane1: C. albicans, Lane 2: Pichia anomala, Lane 3: Candida tropicalis, Lane 4: Candida kefyr, Lane 5: C. krusei Lane 6: C. guilliermondii Lane 7: C. orthopsilosis, Lane 8: C. glabrata, Lane 9: P. anomala, Lane10: C. rugosa, Lane 11: C. lusitaniae, Lane 12: C. rugosa*

Table 21.3 PCR products sizes of ITS1-ITS2 before and after digestion with *Msp I*

Candida species	Size of ITS1-ITS2 (bp)	Restriction product size (bp)
C. albicans	537	239,298
C. glabrata	881	320,561
C. tropicalis	526	186,340
C. krusei	510	250,260
C. guilliermondii	607	82,155,370
C. parapsilosis	520	520
C. famata	639	639
C. lusitaniae	382	118,264
C. anamola	618	618
C. rugosa	399	121,278
C. orthopsilosis	510	510
C. nivarensis	760	205,236,319

Table 21.4 Accession numbers

Accession number	*Candida* species
MN394869	*C. tropicalis*
MN394870	*Clavisporalusitaniae/Candida lusitaniae*
MN394871	*Pichiaanomala formerly C. pelliculosa*
MN394872	*Wickerhamomyces anomalus/C. pelliculosa/Pichia anomala*
MN394873	*Candida albicans*
MN394874	*Candida glabrata*
MN394875	*Clavispora lusitaniae*
MN394876	*Meyerozyma guilliermondii*
MN394877	*Candida krusei/Pichia kudriavzevii*
MN394878	*Candida albicans*

21.7 Findings of the Study

21.7.1 Prevalence of *Candida* Species

The *Candida* species prevalence in all three groups is shown in Fig. 21.8. Non-albicans *Candida* was the most species in all three groups (Fig. 21.9). Figures 21.10, 21.11, and 21.12 show the distribution of NAC in OSCC, OPMD, and health, respectively. Prevalence of *Pichia anomala formerly C. pelliculosa* was 43.5%, 33%, and 21% in health, OPMD, and OSCC respectively, signifying high prevalence in health. The statistically high significance of the odds/risk ratio ($p = 0.001$) for oral Candidal carriage among OSCC (4.25/11.87) and OPMD (3.52/6.99) was observed.

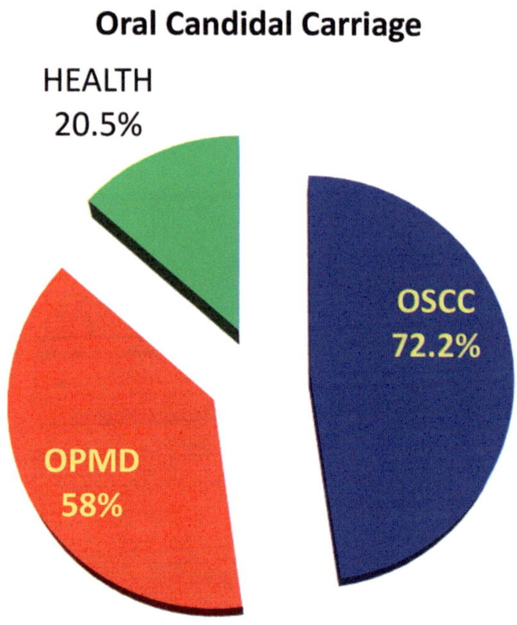

Fig. 21.8 *Candida* species prevalence in OSCC, OPMD, and health

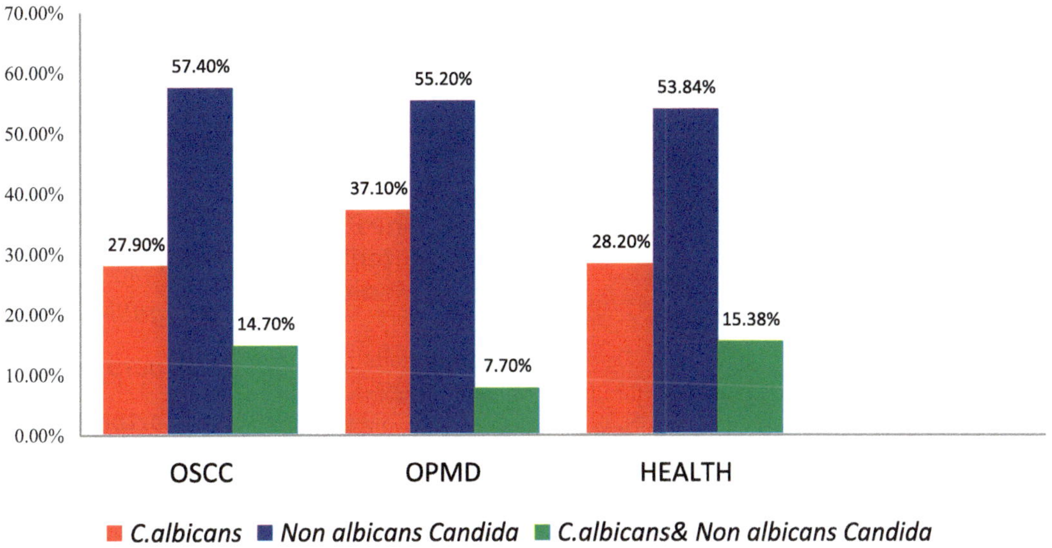

Fig. 21.9 *Candida albicans* and non-*albicans Candida* prevalence

Fig. 21.10 Distribution of non-*albicans Candida* in OSCC

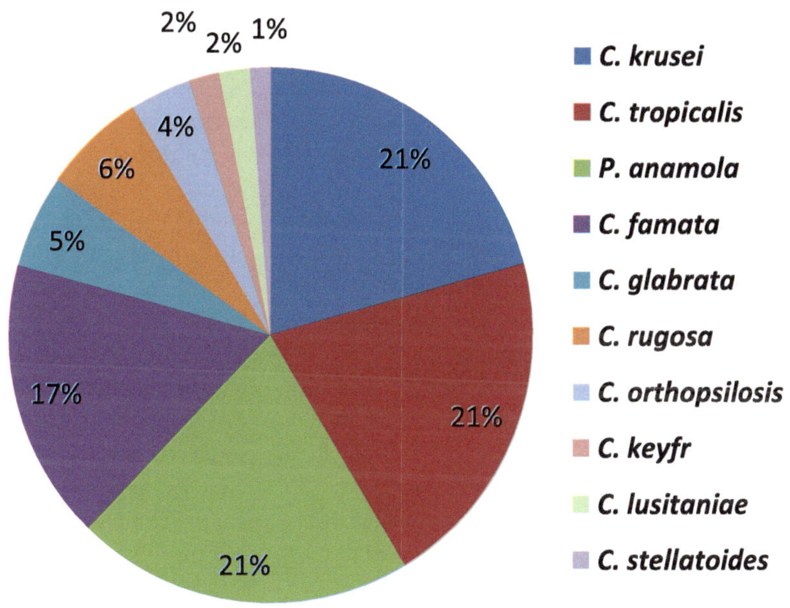

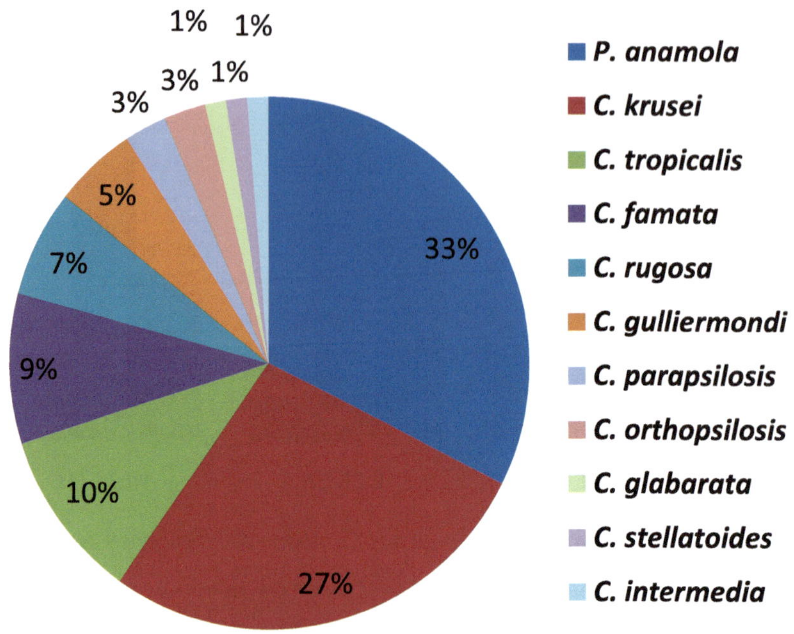

Fig. 21.11 Distribution of non-*albicans Candida* in OPMD

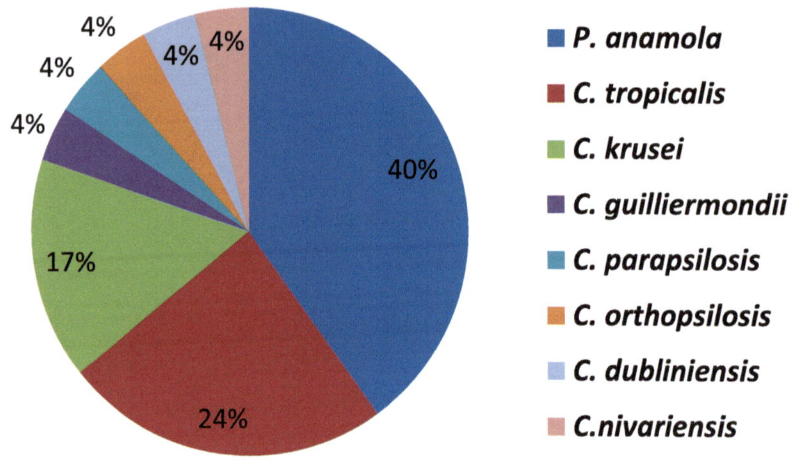

Fig. 21.12 Distribution of non-*albicans Candida* in healthy volunteers

21.8 Discussion

Compared to healthy cohorts (20.5%), extremely significant oral candidal carriage among OSCC (72.2%) (*P* value = 0.000) and OPMD (58.5%) (*P* value = 0.001) was observed. Previously only phenotypic assays were used to identify the species. While this study used both phenotypic and genotypic methods to identify *Candida* species and hence, we have discussed and compared only the studies with comparable genotypic methodology. Non-*albicans Candida* was observed in all three groups (Fig. 21.10). In contrast to previous reports [29, 30], a diversified NAC was observed as the first to report. Interestingly, the present study has identified ten different NAC species by culture method in the saliva of OSCC patients [25]. A high prevalence of *C. krusei, C. tropicalis,* and *P. anomala* formerly *C. pelliculosa* noted in all three groups (OSCC, OPMD, and health) unlike the previous studies [30]. Oral carriage of *P. anomala* was found to decline under OSCC and OPMD conditions concerning health. This observation signifies *P. anamola's* role in health that is in coherence with a study on HIV patients

[31]. Zero prevalence of *Candida famata* was observed in healthy subjects' saliva. In contrast, *C. famata* was found in the saliva of patients with OSCC at 17% and in patients with OPMD at 9%. It is important to note that further research is necessary to fully understand the role of *C. famata* in the development or progression of OSCC and OPMD, as well as its possible implications in the diagnosis and treatment. The present study indicated the presence of *C. parapsilosis, C. guilliermondii*, and *C. dubliniensis*, while a related study did not report these *Candida* species [29]. This diversity of *Candida* species is attributable to the PCR–RFLP identification method.

A very high odds ratio and risk ratio for the prevalence of *Candida* species among OSCC and OPMD patients indicates a strong likelihood of association between *Candida* infection and OSCC/OPMD. The odds of oral Candidal carriage among OSCC were calculated to be 4.25, indicating that individuals with OSCC are 4.25 times riskier to have oral *Candida* infection compared to those without OSCC. This finding supports the notion that *Candida* infection may be a risk factor for the development of OSCC, which is consistent with an earlier study [32]. The high prevalence of NAC in OPMD contrasts with several other studies that solely relied on phenotypic methods for *Candida* species identification. It suggests that the previous studies might have missed detecting non-albicans *Candida* species in OPMD due to limitations in their identification methods [32–34].

The oral Candidal carriage in potentially malignant disorders has been investigated by various authors based on microbiological [35–37], cytological [35, 37], and histopathological studies [33, 36, 37]. NAC was the dominant isolate in our study that was not consistent with previous studies [32, 33]. In the case of OPMD patients with erythroplakia or erythroleukoplakia, the high oral Candidal carriage may be related to factors such as compromised immune function, local tissue changes, or alterations in the oral microenvironment. Compared to previous studies the prevalence of *Candida* species in leukoplakia patients was lower [34, 37, 38]. This information indicates that the prevalence of *Candida* in leukoplakia can vary across different regions. A meta-analysis of 15 leukoplakia studies reveals a 32.2% candidal prevalence [39]. A higher prevalence of *Candida* species in OSMF subjects was observed in this study unlike a few previous reports [34–36, 40, 41]. The authors propose a postulation that in OSMF, changes in the epithelium covering the affected area disrupt the normal physiological barrier. This disruption creates a favorable and conducive environment that promotes the colonization of *Candida* [41].

We observed a higher prevalence of oral Candidal carriage in healthy individuals compared to previous studies [32, 34, 41, 42], but still lower than what has been observed in the populations of Sri Lanka [36] and Poland [43]. It highlights the importance of considering variations in sample collection methods and population demographics when interpreting and comparing research findings on oral yeast carriage. However, it is worth observing that a significant number of subjects (13.4%) in the OSCC group did not have any deleterious habits. This suggests that other factors, including genetic predisposition and immune system status, may play a role in the development of OSCC in these individuals. The presence of high oral Candidal carriage in OSCC patients, as well as in patients with OPMD, can further complicate their condition and add to their morbidity. Oral Candida colonization is a common finding in the general population, but the presence of OSCC or OPMD may disrupt the balance between *Candida* and the host immune response, leading to an overgrowth of *Candida* species.

References

1. Warnakulasuriya S. Global epidemiology of oral and oropharyngeal cancer. Oral Oncol. 2009;45:309–16.
2. Khan Z. An overview of oral cancer in Indian subcontinent and recommendations to decrease its incidence. Cancer. 2012;3(8):WMC003626. https://doi.org/10.9754/journal.wmc.2012.003626.
3. Moro A, Di Nardo F, Boniello R, Marianetti TM, Cervelli D, Gaspardini G. Autofluorescence and early detection of mucosal lesions in patients at risk for oral cancer. J Craniofac Surg. 2010;21:1899–903.
4. Bhargava K, Smith LW, Mani NJ, et al. A follow up study of oral cancer and precancerous lesions in 57,518 industrial workers of Gujarat, India. Indian J Cancer. 1975;12:124–9.

5. Dionne KR, Warnakulasuriya S, Zain RB, Cheong SC. Potentially malignant disorders of the oral cavity: current practice and future directions in the clinic and laboratory. Int J Cancer. 2015;136:503–15. https://doi.org/10.1002/ijc.28754.
6. Axéll T, Pindborg JJ, Smith CJ, van der Waal I. Oral white lesions with special reference to precancerous and tobacco-related lesions: conclusions of an international symposium held in Uppsala, Sweden, May 18–21 1994. International Collaborative Group on Oral White Lesions. J Oral Pathol Med. 1996;25(2):49–54. https://doi.org/10.1111/j.16000714.1996.tb00191.x. PMID: 8667255.
7. Dilhari A, Weerasekera MM, Siriwardhana A, Maheshika O, Gunasekara C, Karunathilaka S, Nagahawatte A, Fernando N. Candida infection in oral leukoplakia: an unperceived public health problem. Acta Odontol Scand. 2016;74(7):565–9. https://doi.org/10.1080/00016357.2016.1220018. Epub 2016 Aug 19. PMID: 27538681.
8. Fitzpatrick SG, Hirsch SA, Gordon SC. The malignant transformation of oral lichen planus and oral lichenoid lesions: a systematic review. J Am Dent Assoc. 2014;145(1):45–56. https://doi.org/10.14219/jada.2013.10. PMID: 24379329.
9. Pindborg JJ, Murti PR, Bhonsle RB, Gupta PC, Daftary DK, Mehta FS. Oral submucous fibrosis as a precancerous condition. Scand J Dent Res. 1984;89:270–4.
10. Pindborg JJ, Bhonsle RB, Murti PR, Gupta PC, Daftary DK, Mehta FS. Incidence and early forms of oral submucous fibrosis. Oral Surg Oral Med Oral Pathol. 1980;50:40–4.
11. Llewellyn CD, Johnson NW, Warnakulasuriya KA. Risk factors for squamous cell carcinoma of the oral cavity in young people—a comprehensive literature review. Oral Oncol. 2001;37(5):401–18. https://doi.org/10.1016/s1368-8375(00)00135-4. PMID: 11377229.
12. Chocolatewala N, Chaturvedi P, Desale R. The role of bacteria in oral cancer. Indian J Med Paediatr Oncol. 2011;31:126–31. Epub 2011/05/18.
13. Scully C. Oral squamous cell carcinoma; from an hypothesis about a virus, to concern about possible sexual transmission. Oral Oncol. 2002;38: 227–34.
14. Cawson RA. Leukoplakia and oral cancer. Proc R Soc Med. 1969;62:610–4.
15. Patil S. Analyzing the association between Candida prevalence, species specificity, and oral squamous cell carcinoma: a systematic review and meta-analysis. Appl Sci. 2020;10(3):1099. https://doi.org/10.3390/app10031099.
16. Barret AW, Kinsmill VJ, Speight PM. The frequency of fungal infection in biopsies of oral mucosal lesions. Oral Dis. 1998;4:26–31.
17. Turner SA, Butler G. The Candida pathogenic species complex. Cold Spring Harb Perspect Med. 2014;4(9):a019778. Published 2014 Sep 2. https://doi.org/10.1101/cshperspect.a019778.
18. Calderone RA, Fonzi WA. Virulence factors of Candida albicans. Trends Microbiol. 2001;9(7):327–35. https://doi.org/10.1016/s0966-842x(01)02094-7. PMID: 11435107.
19. Sitheeque MAM, Samaranayake LP. Chronic hyperplastic candidosis/candidiasis (candidal leukoplakia). Crit Rev Oral Biol Med. 2003;14(4):253–67.
20. Deorukhkar SC, Saini S, Mathew S. Non-albicans Candida infection: an emerging threat. Interdiscip Perspect Infect Dis. 2014;2014:615958. https://doi.org/10.1155/2014/615958. Epub 2014 Oct 22. PMID: 25404942; PMCID: PMC4227454.
21. Mohd Bakri M, Mohd Hussaini H, Rachel Holmes A, David Cannon R, Mary Rich A. Revisiting the association between candidal infection and carcinoma, particularly oral squamous cell carcinoma. J Oral Microbiol. 2010;2:10.3402/jom.v2i0.5780.
22. Samaranayake LP. Host factors and oral candidosis. In: Samaranayake LP, McFarlane TW, editors. Oral candidosis. London: Wright; 1990.
23. McCulough M, Jaber M, Barrett AW, Bain L, Speight P, Porter SR. Oral yeast carriage correlates with presence of oral epithelial dysplasia. Oral Oncol. 2002;38:391–3.
24. Shah N, Ray JG, Kundu S, Sardana D. Surgical management of chronic hyperplastic candidiasis refractory to systemic antifungal treatment. J Lab Physicians. 2017;9(2):136–9. https://doi.org/10.4103/0974-2727.199622.
25. Perera M, Al-Hebshi NN, Perera I, Ipe D, Ulett GC, Speicher DJ, Chen T, Johnson NW. A dysbiotic mycobiome dominated by Candida albicans is identified within oral squamous-cell carcinomas. J Oral Microbiol. 2017;9(1):1385369. https://doi.org/10.1080/20002297.2017.1385369.
26. Field EA, Field JK, Martin MV. Does Candida have a role in oral epithelial neoplasia? J Med Vet Mycol. 1989;27:277–94.
27. Oberg SG, Izutsu KT, Truelove EL. Human parotid saliva protein composition: dependence on physiological factors. Am J Physiol. 1982;242:G231–6.
28. Mohammadi R, Mirhendi H, Rezaei-Matehkolaei A, Ghahri M, Shidfar MR, Jalalizand N, Makimura K. Molecular identification and distribution profile of Candida species isolated from Iranian patients. Med Mycol. 2013;51(6):657–63.
29. Alnuaimi AD, Wiesenfeld D, O'Brien-Simpson NM, Reynolds EC, McCullough MJ. Oral Candida colonization in oral cancer patients and its relationship with traditional risk factors of oral cancer: a matched case-control study. Oral Oncol. 2015;51(2):139–45. https://doi.org/10.1016/j.oraloncology.2014.11.008.
30. Shokohi T, HashemiSoteh MB, SaltanatPouri Z, Hedayati MT, Mayahi S. Identification of Candida species using PCR-RFLP in cancer patients in Iran. Indian J Med Microbiol. 2010;28(2):147–51.
31. Mukherjee PK, Chandra J, Retuerto M, Sikaroodi M, Brown RE, et al. Oral mycobiome analysis of HIV-infected patients: identification of Pichia as an antagonist of opportunistic fungi. PLoS Pathog. 2014;10(3):e1003996. https://doi.org/10.1371/journal.ppat.1003996.

32. Bansal R, Pallagatti S, Sheikh S, Aggarwal A, Gupta D, et al. Candidal species identification in malignant and potentially malignant oral lesions with antifungal resistance patterns. Contemp Clin Dent. 2018;9(Suppl 2):S309–13. https://doi.org/10.4103/ccd.ccd_296_18.
33. Galle F, Colella G, Di Onofrio V, Rossiello R, Angelillo IF, Liguori G. Candida spp. in oral cancer and oral precancerous lesions. New Microbiol. 2013;36:283–8.
34. Saigal S, Bhargava A, Mehra SK, Dakwala F. Identification of candida albicans by using different culture medias and its association in potentially malignant and malignant lesions. Contemp Clin Dent. 2011;2(3):188–93.
35. Anila K, Hallikeri K, Shubhada C, Naikmasur VG, Kulkarni RD. Comparative study of Candida in oral submucous fibrosis and healthy individuals. Rev Odonto Ciênc. 2011;26(1):71–6.
36. Ariyawardana GA, Panagoda J, Fernando HN, Ellepola ANB, Tilakaratne WM. 19. Samaranayake LP. Oral submucous fibrosis and oral yeast carriage—a case control study in Sri Lankan patients. Mycoses. 2007;50:116–20.
37. Vuckovic N, Bokor-Bratic M, Vuckovic D, Picuric I. Presence of Candida albicans in potentially malignant oral mucosal lesions. Arch Oncol. 2004;12(1):51–4.
38. Lipperheide V, Quindós G, Jiménez Y, Pontón J, Bagán-Sebastián JV, Aguirre JM. Candida biotypes in patients with oral leukoplakia and lichen planus. Candida biotypes in leukoplakia and lichen planus. Mycopathologia. 1996;134(2):75–82.
39. Rodriguez-Archilla A, Alcaide-Salamanca MJ. Candida species detection in potentially malignant and malignant disorders of the oral mucosa: a meta-analysis. J Dent Res Rev. 2018;5(2):35–41. https://doi.org/10.4103/jdrr.jdrr_27_18.
40. Kumar RS, Ganvir S, Hazarey V. Candida and calcofluor white: study in precancer and cancer. J Oral Maxillofac Pathol. 2009;13(1):2–8. https://doi.org/10.4103/0973-029X.44575.
41. Kamat MS, Vanaki SS, Puranik RS, Puranik SR, Kaur R. Oral Candida carriage, quantification, and species characterization in oral submucous fibrosis patients and healthy individuals. J Investig Clin Dent. 2011;2(4):275–9. https://doi.org/10.1111/j.2041-1626.2011.00078.x.
42. Odds FC. Candida and Candidosis: a review and bibliography. 2nd ed. London: Bailliere Tindall; 1988. p. 68–92.
43. Zaremba ML, Daniluk T, Rozkiewicz D, Cylwik-Rokicka D, Kierklo A, Tokajuk G, et al. Incidence rate of Candida species in the oral cavity of middle-aged and elderly subjects. Adv Med Sci. 2006;51(Suppl 1):233–6.

Host-Directed Immunotherapy for Tuberculosis

22

Vignesh Sounderrajan, Sam Ebenezer Rajadas, T. Thangam, Sudhanarayani S. Rao, Krupakar Parthasarathy, Rohini Tamilanban, and Shakila Harshavardhan

22.1 Introduction

Mycobacterium tuberculosis (MTB) is one of the leading causes of morbidity and mortality worldwide, with tuberculosis (TB) being a highly contagious infectious disease [1]. The treatment regime for TB involves multiple antibiotics taken for a minimum of 6 months, but this poses challenges to patient compliance due to side effects [2]. Non-adherence to treatment and inadequate prescription practices contribute to the emergence and spread of extensively drug-resistant and multidrug-resistant strains of MTB, requiring more complex and prolonged treatment regimens [3]. Consequently, it is crucial to explore new strategies to control the global TB epidemic.

While the search for novel and more effective antibacterial drugs continues, there is increasing focus on host biological processes involved in TB pathogenesis as potential targets for therapeutic interventions. This new emerging concept, known as host-directed therapy (HDT), is to optimize the host immune responses, enhancing the activation of host antibacterial mechanisms while suppressing harmful inflammation-driven tissue damage [4].

The chronic granulomatous pathology associated with TB leads to severe inflammatory responses in the lungs, resulting in the formation of granulomas. These granulomas serve as physical barriers that impede the penetration of drugs, necessitating prolonged antibiotic therapy. Granuloma formation occurs through the metabolic interaction between host immune cells and MTB, aiming to contain the infection within the lung tissue. However, these inflammatory lesions also limit the entry of antibiotics to target the bacterial populations persist within the central regions of the granulomas. The immune response to TB, disease progression, and severity are significantly influenced by immune metabolic cellular processes and related metabolites.

Immunocompetent patients with an active TB infection often experience an intense pro-inflammatory response that fails to contain the

V. Sounderrajan (✉) · T. Thangam · S. S. Rao · K. Parthasarathy
Centre for Drug Discovery and Development, Sathyabama Institute of Science and Technology, Chennai, India
e-mail: vignesh.irc@sathyabama.ac.in; thangam.t.cddd@sathyabama.ac.in; sudhanarayani.cddd@sathyabama.ac.in; pkrupakar.cddd@sathyabama.ac.in

S. E. Rajadas
Department of Biotechnology, VSB Engineering College, Karur, Karur, India

Centre for Drug Discovery and Development, Sathyabama Institute of Science and Technology, Chennai, India

R. Tamilanban
Department of Microbiology, Mananr Thirumalai Naicker College, Madurai, India

S. Harshavardhan
School of Biotechnology, Madurai Kamaraj University, Madurai, India

K. Parthasarathy, R. Manikkam (eds.), *Translational Research in Biomedical Sciences: Recent Progress and Future Prospects*, https://doi.org/10.1007/978-981-97-1777-4_22

infection and causes severe lung damage. Even after reducing the TB load through antibiotic treatment, many TB-infected patients still suffer from chronic lung inflammation and subsequent pulmonary dysfunction [5]. In addition to the primary goal of eliminating TB, adjunct therapies are needed to address the irreversible chronic lung disorders caused by the infection-induced inflammatory response. Host-directed immunotherapies are designed to guide the host immune system in overcoming this chronic inflammatory disease.

Overall, advancing host-directed therapies and immunotherapies alongside the development of new antibacterial drugs are crucial in combating TB and its associated complications, offering new avenues for the containment of the global TB epidemic.

22.2 Host–Pathogen Interaction of TB

The initial encounter between the TB pathogen and a host occurs when an individual breathes in tiny droplet nuclei, which are produced when pulmonary TB-infected person sneezes, coughs, talks, or sings. These droplet nuclei can remain suspended in the air for varying durations, ranging from minutes to hours, and can be inhaled by people in proximity. Once inside the body, the bacteria spread from the initial infection site to the lungs and then to other parts of the body through the lymphatic system or bloodstream. The apex of the lungs and regional lymph nodes are particularly susceptible to infection and are often targeted by the bacteria [6].

The TB bacteria, after overcoming the defence mechanisms of the upper respiratory tract, encounter alveolar macrophages in the lungs. The interaction between the host and TB is initiated when these alveolar macrophages phagocytose the bacteria, involving several steps.

1. Surface Binding: *M. tuberculosis* binds to macrophages' surfaces.
2. Phagosome-Lysosome Fusion: The phagosome containing TB bacteria fuses with lysosomes, forming a phagolysosome.
3. Mycobacterial Growth Inhibition/Killing: Within the phagolysosome, mechanisms are activated to inhibit or kill the TB bacteria.
4. Recruitment of Immune Cells: Accessory immune cells are recruited, leading to a local inflammatory response.
5. Antigen Presentation: TB antigens are presented to T cells, contributing to the development of acquired immunity.

The binding of TB bacteria to macrophages in the lungs is influenced by both host and pathogen factors. Complement receptors (CR1, CR2, CR3, and CR4) and Mannose Receptors (MR) play a crucial role in the binding process. Cytokines regulate the expression of these receptors on the macrophage surface, thereby controlling the binding of TB bacteria. For example, Interleukin-4 (IL-4) and prostaglandin E2 upregulate CR and MR expression, while interferon-gamma (IFN-γ) downregulates it. Unlike typical phagocytosis, where the engulfed pathogen is degraded by acidic hydrolases upon phagolysosome fusion, TB bacteria-infected phagocytes follow a different pattern. The fusion of phagolysosomes is inhibited, allowing the TB bacteria to survive inside the phagocytes [6].

22.3 Host Immune Response to TB

Host response to TB has been attributed to both the cell-mediated and humoral-mediated immune responses once the innate line of defence is breached by the pathogen.

22.3.1 Cell-Mediated Immune Response to TB

As MTB is an intracellular pathogen that resides and replicates inside host cells. Extensive research has been conducted over several decades to understand the cellular immune response, known as cell-mediated immunity (CMI), against M. tuberculosis infection. CMI plays a critical role in controlling and eliminating MTB from the body. The key components of CMI involved in the immune response against M. tuberculosis include T cells, particularly CD4+ and CD8+ T cells, as well as macrophages and other antigen-presenting cells (APCs). Within a short span of the infection, the influx of CD4+ and CD8+ T cells into the lungs had been demonstrated [7]. The primary effector function of CD4+ T cells is the production of IFN-γ and possibly other cytokines, sufficient to activate macrophages. CD8+ T cells are also capable of secreting cytokines such as IFN-γ and IL-4 and thus may play a role in regulating the balance of Th1 and Th2 cells in the lungs of pulmonary TB-infected individuals [6]. Apoptosis of T cells induced by the TB bacilli augments the spread of the pathogen by causing productive granuloma or disseminative granuloma.

22.3.2 Macrophages and Its Polarization in TB

Macrophages handle the engulfed TB bacilli in many ways, either by the generation of Reactive Oxygen Intermediates (ROI), Reactive Nitrogen Intermediates (RNI) or by mechanisms arbitrated by cytokines. TB non-specific accumulation of hydrogen peroxide (H_2O_2) has been shown in human clinical samples [8]. Activation of phagocytes by IFN-γ and tumour necrosis factor-α (TNF-α), generates nitric oxide (NO) and related RNI through inducible nitric oxide synthase (iNOS2) using L-arginine as the substrate.

Macrophages were found to be capable of efficiently engulfing *M. tuberculosis* but did not generate a subsequent respiratory burst response and were tolerant for intracellular growth of both Bacillus Calmette Gueârin (BCG) and the virulent *M. tuberculosis*. Cytotoxic T Lymphocytes (CTL) activity in TB is highly specific and mediated through HLA class I [9]. The PE_PGRS proteins of *M. tuberculosis* have been recognized as a modulator of apoptosis in infected macrophages. These proteins elicit TLR-2 dependent TNF-α release and TNFR-I further activating MAPKs p38 and JNK. The above finding has also been annexed with the revelation that alteration in the PE-PGRS structure could modulate the innate immune response against TB [10].

Depending on the type of stimulation, macrophages are either polarized to the M1 type or M2 type. M1 exhibits pro-inflammatory activity, while M2 exhibits anti-inflammatory activity. IL-37, an IL-1 family member was found to induce M2 polarization in tuberculosis by inducing arginase 1, TGF-β and IL-10 [11]. Activated B-Cells also induce M2 polarization by secreting type-1 interferons [12]. On the other way, M1 polarization can be induced by NFκB signalling [13]. M1 macrophage promotes granuloma formation and macrophage bactericidal activity in-vitro, while M2 macrophages inhibit these effects [14]. Interleukin 1 Receptor Associated Kinase (IRAK-M) inhibits M2 polarization of U937 cells and causes increased bacillary load [15]. Similarly, a transcription factor, namely, interferon-regulatory factor-5 (IRF-5) was also found to favour the pathogen by polarizing macrophages to M1 type representing it as a transcriptional repressor [16, 17]. M1 macrophages reduce bacillary load, and prolonged existence causes tissue damage, hence as an alternative IL-33, an inducer of M2 is proposed as a therapeutic for severe tuberculosis [18]. *M. tb*-induced B-cells produce type-I interferons, which modulate the macrophages to M2 type [12]. Anti-tuberculosis antibiotics treatment is also known to modulate the polarization of macrophages from M1 to M2-like phenotype. This property could be used as a marker to assess the efficacy of the anti-TB treatment [19]. Such a kind of modulation was also observed in the case of azithromycin treatment post-spinal cord injury [20].

22.3.3 TB Granuloma

Granuloma is the hallmark of TB infection. The granuloma contains mostly blood-derived macrophages, epithelioid cells (differentiated macrophages), and multinucleated giant cells (also known as Langhans giant cells), surrounded by T lymphocytes [21, 22]. This microenvironment limits the replication and spread of TB bacilli [23]. A mature granuloma is often characterized by caseous centre necrotic lesions with low oxygen levels, low pH, and limited nutrients. Lesions in persons with an adequate immune response generally undergo fibrosis and calcification, successfully controlling the infection so that the bacilli are contained in the dormant and healed lesions [24]. This protective structure may become a spot for disseminating the pathogen if the host immune system does not respond in the proper direction. Such a desirable direction of host immune response is achieved with a balance between anti-inflammatory and pro-inflammatory cytokines.

Chemokines and cytokines play a crucial role in granuloma formation and its type. The chemokines binding to the CCR2 receptor (CCL2/MCP-1, CCL12, and CCL13) are important for the early recruitment of macrophages. Osteopontin, produced by macrophages and lymphocytes, promotes the adhesion and recruitment of these cells. CCL19 and, possibly, CCL21 are involved in the recruitment and priming of IFN-γ-producing T cells. CXCL13 is involved in B-cell recruitment and the formation of follicular structures [25]. The expression of the CC and CXC chemokines is deregulated at the transcriptional level in TNF-deficient mice, and the lack of these chemokines prevents the recruitment of macrophages and CD4+ T cells, accounting for the critical role of TNF-α in granuloma formation [26]. Block in the TNF-α regulation leads to the down-regulation of Th1, Th17, and Treg cytokines, which further causes the impairment of granuloma [27].

22.3.4 Humoral Immune Response to TB

Recent studies had shown the importance of the humoral response in TB despite the intracellular nature of the TB pathogen. Mycobacterial antigens inducing a humoral response in humans have been studied, mainly to identify diagnostically relevant antigens. Detection of circulating immune complex-bound antibodies was found to be more sensitive as compared to serum antibodies and these immune complexes were found to contain modulatory activity in TB disease.

There was a report stating the elevated level of anti-F(ab')2γ auto-antibodies in pulmonary TB patients and their household contacts suggesting the significant role of the humoral immune system in TB.

22.3.5 Role of Complement System in TB

The complement system acts in three ways for the immune system. It includes opsonization of pathogens by facilitating phagocytosis, antibody-mediated osmotic lysis of targeted organisms and recruitment of leukocytes by chemokine signalling [28]. It undergoes the pathways of activation, namely, classical, lectin, and alternative pathways. Studies on *M. bovis* have shown the activation of all these pathways through C1q, L-ficolin, and deposition of C3b on the Mycobacterial cell surface [29]. The binding of C3b is also favoured by classical and alternative pathways [30]. In the context of pulmonary TB, pneumocytes and lung residential macrophages act as the sources of complement proteins, however, when dissemination of MTB into the bloodstream occurs serum complement proteins are also being consumed for the cause.

The binding of C3b on *M. tb* enhances the phagocytosis and initiation of the inflammatory response which is argued to be favourable for the pathogen too [30]. The C3b-complement receptor-mediated entry is recognized to be crucial in determining the cellular response and fate of the pathogen in the intracellular environment [31]. Involvement of Factor H in TB pathogenesis has also been demonstrated which on one hand aids opsonization, on the other hand, makes the formation of membrane attack complex to downplay [28, 29]. Contradicting the above finding, the C3b was found to be interfering with the pathogen entry into phagocytes and to be steering the pro-inflammatory cytokine response [32]. Moreover, the C3R-A receptor for iC3b (a breakdown product of C3) has been proven to play no significant role in the outcome and resistance against TB infection [33]. Deficiency in C5 was also shown to be detrimental to the host by decreasing the cytokine production from macrophages and increasing inflammation and mortality [34].

During the pathway towards the formation of the membrane attack complex (MAC), the complement component, namely, C7 gets inserted into the cell membrane of the target. Recently it has been recognized as a cause for higher immunopathology in the progression of TB as revealed through a study on C7 deficient mice showing lesser pathology than the wild-type against the MTB Erdman strain [35].

Though these complement proteins are considered an important role player in TB pathogenesis, still a big lacuna prevails in the studies involving the same for a thorough understanding of the underlying mechanisms.

22.4 Immune Evasion Strategies of MTB

During evolution, MTB has adopted various strategies like inhibition of phagolysosome fusion, resistance to toxic, reactive nitrogen intermediates (RNI), and modulation of antigen presentation by infected macrophages to evade the immune response of the highly developed immune competent host.

MTB secrets strong antagonists to reactive oxygen intermediates (ROI) like catalase and superoxide dismutase and possesses strong free oxygen radical scavengers. Activated macrophages produce RNI through nitric oxide synthase 2 (NOS2)-dependent pathway induced by IFN-γ. It has been shown that *M. tuberculosis* infection in human alveolar macrophages induces nitric oxide (NO) production, however, the levels of NO are negatively correlated with levels of intracellular bacterial growth, causing an increased susceptibility to TB [36]. The products of *noxR1*, *noxR3*, and *ahpC* genes in combination with the dihydrolipoamide dehydrogenase (Lpd), dihydrolipoamide succinyl transferase (SucB), and the thioredoxin-like AhpD had been reported to confer resistance against these RNIs [37]. Additionally, *more* was also reported for conferring resistance against RNI [28]. In a study using the THP-1 cells, it was found that the ESAT-6, CFP-10, and ESAT-6/CFP-10 antigens markedly reduce the macrophage's NO and ROS production with less inducible NO synthase activity and without cytotoxicity [38]. On the other way, these proteins also support the formation of granuloma by inducing the adhesion of macrophages to fibronectin through $\alpha_4\beta_1$ integrin [39].

The maturation of phagosome into phagolysosome is inhibited by MTB, to escape the activity of lysosome. Mannosylated lipoarabinomannan (MLAM), a mycobacterial cell-wall-associated glycolipid was found to stay the endosome-endosome fusion by inhibiting the recruitment of early endosome autoantigen 1 (EEA1) [40]. Arresting of the fusion is also mediated through the tryptophan aspartate rich coat protein (TACO) of *MTB I* [41]. It was also noted that mycobacteria causes retention of Rab5 (Ras-related protein—Rabaptin-5) in the phagosomes for a prolonged period and denies recruitment of Rab7. This enables flourished uptake of nutrients like iron by *Mycobacterium* apart from inhibiting phagosome maturation [42, 43].

MTB has been reported to inhibit MHC class II antigen processing and presentation which is crucial for its recognition and control. This inhibition is characterized by either intracellular sequestration of MHC class II molecules [44], decreased expression of the class II transactivator (CIITA) [45], or inhibition of IFN-g signalling pathways in macrophages [46]. Infected macrophages were also shown to have a limited presentation capability to T-helper cells which result in persistent infection. Modulation of immune response was also augmented by directing the host cells to produce cytokines like TGF-β, IL-10 or IL-6 [47]. MTB was found to block host macrophage apoptosis by using the PPM1A signalling pathway which could be reverted by administrating rifampicin [48]. Other Mycobacterial factors like ManLAM, 25-kDa glycolipoprotein, and 19-kDa lipoprotein were also reported to inhibit IFN-γ dependent [49, 50] and the Toll-Like Receptor 2 dependent MHC Class-II expression [51].

22.4.1 Current Treatment Strategies and Need for HDT in TB

TB treatment strategies often involve combinations of antibiotics that are used over a long time. The standard treatment regimen for drug-sensitive TB, known as a direct follow-up, short course (DOTS), is recommended by the World Health Organization (WHO) and includes a combination of four drugs [52, 53],

1. Isoniazid (INH): An important first-line treatment drug that targets actively growing TB.
2. Rifampicin (RIF): Next important first-line drug that effectively kills TB bacteria and prevents their resistance to other drugs. a hibernation state.
3. Pyrazinamide (PZA): Used during the initial phase of treatment to rapidly kill TB bacteria, especially those in a dormant state.
4. Ethambutol (EMB): A bacteriostatic drug that inhibits the growth of tuberculosis bacteria.

These drugs are called first-line TB drugs. Patients with drug-sensitive TB typically undergo a 2-month period of active treatment during which all four drugs are administered. This was followed by a continued treatment period of 4–6 months, with continued use of INH and RIF only. Compliance with treatment is often supported by directly observed therapy (DOT), in which the healthcare provider ensures that the patient takes the medication as prescribed. In the case of drug-resistant TB, treatment options become more complex. Drug-resistant TB is classified into two main categories: multidrug-resistant TB (MDR-TB) and extensively drug-resistant TB (XDR-TB). MDR-TB is resistant to first-line TB drugs, at least INH and RIF, while extensively drug-resistant TB is resistant to INH, RIF, fluoroquinolones, and at least one second-line injectable drug. Treatment of drug-resistant TB requires a longer duration of treatment (usually 18–24 months) and the use of second-line drugs, which are often more expensive and have more serious side effects. The treatment regimen is individualized based on the results of each patient's drug sensitivity test. In recent years, efforts have been made to develop new drugs and treatment regimens to improve TB treatment outcomes and reduce the duration of treatment. Bedaquiline and delamanid are two new drugs approved to treat drug-resistant tuberculosis, offering hope for more effective and tolerable treatment options [54–57]. However, resistance to these drugs has also been reported recently [58]. Conditions that can affect treatment outcomes are essential elements of comprehensive TB management.

The establishment of infection, progression to disease, and treatment outcome of tuberculosis (TB) are influenced by the complex interaction between the host and Mycobacterium tuberculosis (MTB). When an individual becomes infected with MTB, the immune response primarily aims to contain and control its spread, often leading to dormancy. However, in rare cases, the infection may progress and result in intra-host spread and disease manifestation. Once TB disease develops, the effectiveness of treatment and the resulting pathology largely depends on the host's immune response to the pathogen. Achieving a delicate balance between pro-inflammatory and anti-inflammatory cytokines, as well as the appropriate polarization of macrophages, is crucial. Unfortunately, this balance is not consistently maintained among all individuals, leading to varying levels of disease severity. Some individuals experience severe pathology, while others exhibit minimal symptoms [59].

This emphasizes the necessity for host-directed therapies (HDT) in the management of TB. By targeting the host's immune response and modulating the inflammatory processes, HDT can help optimize treatment outcomes and minimize the detrimental effects of the disease. Recognizing the interplay between the host and MTB, HDT offers a promising approach to improve TB management by addressing the individual variations in immune response and promoting more favourable treatment outcomes. Immunomodulators could potentially play a vital role in HDT as it directs host immune response towards a better outcome (Fig. 22.1).

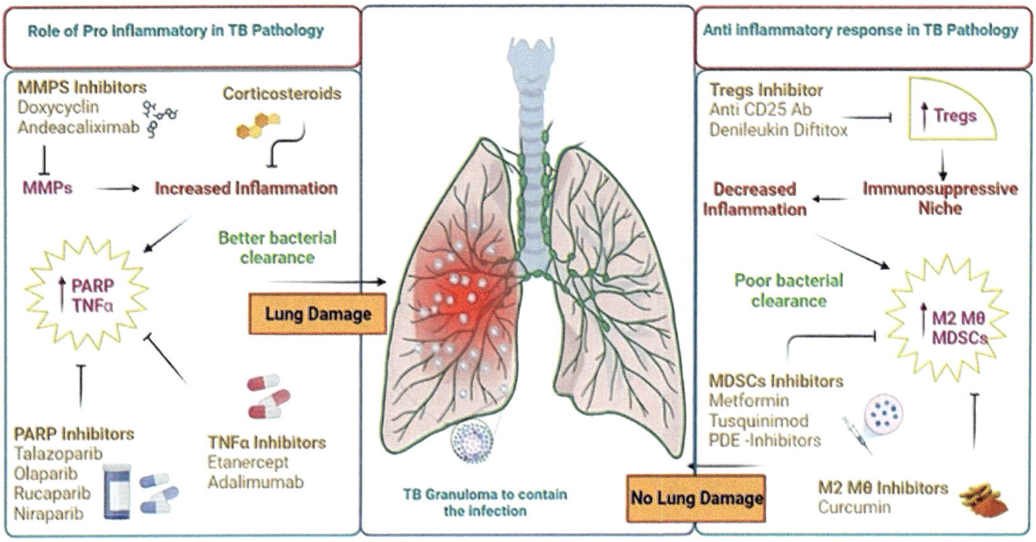

Fig. 22.1 Role of pro-inflammatory and anti-inflammatory immune response in the MTB infected lung and immunomodulatory drug as host-directed immune therapeutics for effective and enhanced bacterial clearance

22.4.2 Immunomodulators in HDT

22.4.2.1 Pro-inflammatory Inhibitors

The high expression of MMPs reported in many degenerative diseases, in the case of TB pathology MMP-1, 3, and 4 are key factors in the remodelling of the damaged lung tissue caused by TB-mediated inflammatory injury in the lung. Few inhibitors for MMP are available which are Marimastat [60], Andecaliximab [61], Doxycyclin [62], and Cipemastat [63]. These MMP inhibitors have many side effects on the host even though it has a role in curtailing the TB burden [64]. TNF α and NF ƙ B promote MMP activity and TB inflammation so the inhibition of these pro-inflammatory cytokines may reduce lung destruction. The drug Etanercept which inhibits the TNF α has shown reduced bacterial load and increased lung recovery [65]. The concern related to this kind of TNF α inhibitor is top adjuvanted with anti-TB drugs. The TNF α antagonist has severe effects where the bacterial containment may reduce and the spread of the bacilli is not admissible. So, it must be given along with the anti-TB drug. Corticosteroids are widely used as an anti-inflammatory agent and for treating many bacterial infections. The chronic inflammatory response to TB results in tissue damage and lung dysfunction. The corticosteroids are used as an adjunct therapy to modulate the immune response to TB [66]. The mechanism behind this is the binding of corticosteroids to the receptors which influence gene transcription and inhibition of humoral immune response and infiltration of innate immune cells. Dexamethasone is the best example of a corticosteroid used to treat TB Meningitis [67]. The use of corticosteroids for TB is in an organ-specific and case-specific manner the dosage differs for extrapulmonary TB while the usage of long-term with a low dosage for Pulmonary TB shows significant clinical outcomes.

PARPs are co-factors for TNF α, NF ƙ B, and MMP which stimulates the inflammatory response and tissue degradation. The inhibitors of PARP(PARP-Is) are used to reduce the inflammation caused by TB in the lungs. The available PARP-Is are Talazoparib, Olaparib, Rucaparib, and Niraparib which have potential applications in cancer therapy and other inflammatory diseases [68] (Table 22.1).

Table 22.1 List of a few pro-inflammatory inhibitors and their role

Sl. no.	HDT role	Drug available
1	MMP inhibitors	Marimastat [60], Andecaliximab [61], Doxicyclin [62], and Cipemastat [63]
2	Corticosteroids	Dexamethasone [67]
3	PARP's inhibitors	Talazoparib, Olaparib, Rucaparib, and Niraparib [68]

22.4.2.2 Biochemical Inhibitor

Cyclooxygenase (COX) and lipoxygenase are the products of Eicosanoid which are the molecules modulate cell signalling and lead to death [69]. A well-balanced eicosanoid level is critical for Mtb management and limiting the production of pro-inflammatory cytokines such as tumour necrosis factor (TNF). Lipoxygenase inhibitors in a TB-susceptible mouse model, inhibiting 5-LOX have been associated with reduced lung pathology, lower type-I IFN production, decreased MTB replication, and increased survival rates [70].

22.4.2.3 Anti-inflammatory Inhibitors

Mycobacterium tuberculosis produces anti-inflammatory molecules which subvert the host immune system for their surveillance and proliferation in the infected host. Likewise, the upregulation of IL 10 in the host that promotes anti-inflammatory responses and ESAT 6 mediates the shifting of the macrophage polarization from M1 to M2. Treg cells, myeloid-derived suppressor cells (MDSCs) and M2-polarized macrophages [71].

22.4.2.4 Myeloid-Derived Suppressor Cells (MDSCs)

MDSCs are activated monocytes and neutrophils regulating the host immune system through their anti-inflammatory property. These MDSCs cells are highly expressed in active TB patients and their response to the drugs is very low which shows the immune dysfunction induced by MTB to suppress the inflammatory response [72]. HDTs are available for inhibiting or depleting the MDSCs population in the host to promote inflammatory response to control the infection. Metformin the drug used for treating diabetes has the potential to suppress the recruitment of MDSCs in the host by modulating the expression and function of HIF-1a, CD39, and CD73 and the AMPK-DACH1-CXCL1 axis. Tasquinimod is an anti-prostate cancer drug which reduces the infiltration of MDSCs by interacting with TLR-4 binding [73]. ATRA (all-trans retinoic acid) also known as tretinoin is a vitamin A derivative and FDA-approved drug extensively used for tumour treatment [74]. Phosphodiesterase inhibitors like Sildenafil which used for hypertension and for in erectile dysfunction. The drug impedes the MDSC's immune suppressive potential by the mechanism of downregulating arginase-1 and nitric oxide synthase-2 (NOS2) in a cGMP-dependent fashion [75].

22.4.2.5 T Cell Regulators in Immunomodulation of TB

T regs are produced in the thymus as a functionally mature T cell subset and in the peripheral of naive T cells, and they have a potential role in maintaining the immunological unresponsiveness to self-antigens and limiting robust immune responses that are detrimental to the tissue during asthma inflammation. T reg cells express the immunosuppressive CD25 and FoxP3 produced by the CD4+ T cell population and CD8+ T cells which also have a potential role in Tuberculosis pathogenesis. The anti-inflammatory cells CD4+ CD25+ FoxP3+ FoxP3+ are regulators of effector T Cell functioning and boost the recruitment and maturation of MDSC and assist in immunosuppression [76]. It is considered that their presence in active TB inhibits antibacterial immune responses and contributes to disease development. Treg levels in the blood and pleural fluid of pulmonary tuberculosis patients were shown to be higher than in healthy controls, and Treg levels were found to return to normal after effective TB chemotherapy.

22.4.2.6 Treg-Depleting Immunotherapies

Anti-CD25 monoclonal antibodies have the property of depleting Tregs and have a role in delayed tumour growth in numerous cancer models. In the in vivo study using a mouse TB model, anti-CD25 antibodies have shown reduced bacillary burdens in the lung and spleen and ameliorated lung histology. A fusion protein Denileukin diftitox (Ontak®), a diphtheria toxin-related IL-2 approved by the FDA for the treatment of refractory cutaneous T cell lymphoma, has been shown to have a significant Treg-depleting effect in murine TB models. In a short-term TB animal model, the reduced recruitment of Treg, and MDSC were noticed in the lungs and spleens with relatively reduced bacterial CFU counts [77].

22.4.2.7 Checkpoint Blockade Immunotherapy

Checkpoint blockade immunotherapy is a novel treatment that uses immune checkpoint inhibitors to treat various types of cancer. The two most widely used checkpoint blockade immunotherapy are anti-PD-1 and anti-CTLA4 antibodies to treat human malignancies. In a study Tregs have been reported to express CTLA-4 in M. tb-infected macaques, implying that checkpoint inhibitor anti-CTLA-4—may offer a viable HDT TB treatment. Still, there is controversy in this that many TB re-activation was reported in cancer patients treated with checkpoint blockade immunotherapy [78]. An extensive study is needed to decipher the potential of checkpoint blockade immune therapy.

22.4.2.8 Anti-IL-10 Targeted Therapies

Many haematopoietic cells produce IL-10, which has a crucial role in suppressing macrophage and dendritic cell (DC) activities, which are necessary for the capture, control, and activation of immune responses MTB [79]. Further, it has the property of M2 macrophage polarization which promotes the anti-inflammatory immune response. The potential IL-10 inhibitors inhibit the conversion of M1 to M2 macrophages [80]. One of the active bioactive compounds present in turmeric, curcumin (diferuloylmethane), has been proven to alter IL-10 levels and the incidence of M2 macrophages. Curcumin has also been found to inhibit M. tb proliferation in THP-1 macrophages and primary alveolar macrophages obtained from healthy human controls in the context of tuberculosis [81].

22.4.2.9 Non-steroidal Anti-inflammatory Drugs (NSAID) as an HDT

The elevated level of prostaglandin in the late stages of M. tb infection (>45 days post-infection in mice) exacerbates TB disease progression by suppressing cell-mediated immunity [82]. NSAIDs are widely used as an analgesic and anti-inflammatory and proven for potential HDT effects. NSAIDs function by decreasing COX activity, preventing the synthesis of pro-inflammatory and immunosuppressive mediators such as prostaglandins and leukotrienes. The significance of using NSAID as HDT engages the inhibition of proinflammatory COX enzymes to downregulate the inflammation to reduce tissue pathology and increases the bactericidal activity. In an early clinical trial, aspirin with dexamethasone has shown to be effective against TB meningitis. The mechanistic action behind this role is by inhibition of thromboxane-A2 and increased levels of protectins. To decrease antibiotic-related joint discomfort, the WHO advises routine inclusion of NSAID as an adjuvant medication to the conventional TB treatment regimen [83].

22.5 Summary

Host-directed immune therapies (HDTs) have emerged as a promising approach to target both inflammatory and anti-inflammatory immune responses. Specifically, HDT drugs that interfere with the pro-inflammatory response have shown potential in mitigating lung tissue damage and improving treatment outcomes in conditions such as TB. By modulating the host immune response, HDTs can enhance the bactericidal effects and promote the clearance of TB without causing significant harm to the host tissue. The appropriate utilization of HDT in TB treatment varies on a case-by-case basis, as there is a delicate balance to be maintained to avoid disrupting the natural immune response to the pathogen. Disrupting the host-pathogen interaction without careful consideration may inadvertently lead to disease progression. Therefore, it is crucial to exercise caution when applying HDTs, ensuring that the benefits of enhanced treatment outcomes outweigh the potential risks of interfering with the host immune response. To minimize TB-related lung tissue damage and mitigate adverse inflammatory responses, several strategies have been emphasized. These include the inhibition of matrix metalloproteinases (MMPs), tumour necrosis factor-alpha (TNFα) antagonists, corticosteroids, and poly (ADP-ribose) polymerase (PARP) inhibition. These interventions aim to attenuate excessive inflammation and prevent tissue damage while enhancing the bactericidal properties of phagocytic cells and promoting the entry of bacilli into the host. Furthermore, HDT holds the potential for preventing the development of active TB in latent individuals. However, it is essential to consider the drawbacks of HDT, such as off-target effects and accompanying side effects. These disadvantages must be carefully weighed against other factors, including storage stability, distribution mode, formulation, and the timing of administration at various stages of Mycobacterium tuberculosis (MTB) infection and disease. In summary, HDTs offer a promising avenue for improving TB treatment outcomes by modulating the immune response. However, their implementation requires a case-specific approach to avoid disturbing the delicate balance between host and pathogen interactions. While HDTs can minimize TB-related lung tissue damage and inflammation, careful consideration must be given to potential off-target effects and side effects. Additionally, factors such as storage stability, distribution mode, formulation, and timing of administration should be considered when considering the use of HDTs in different stages of MTB infection and disease.

References

1. Gagneux S, Small PM. Global phylogeography of Mycobacterium tuberculosis and implications for tuberculosis product development. Lancet Infect Dis. 2007;7(5):328–37.
2. Kolloli A, Subbian S. Host-directed therapeutic strategies for tuberculosis. Front Med (Lausanne) [Internet]. 2017;4:171. https://www.frontiersin.org/articles/10.3389/fmed.2017.00171.
3. Harshavardhan S, Vijayakumar KK, Sounderrajan V, Ramasamy P, Rajadas SE. Chapter 1—Basics of tuberculosis disease and principles of treatment and their effects. In: Rajan M, editor. A mechanistic approach to medicines for tuberculosis nanotherapy [Internet]. Academic; 2021. p. 1–29. https://www.sciencedirect.com/science/article/pii/B9780128199855000115.
4. Krug S, Parveen S, Bishai WR. Host-directed therapies: modulating inflammation to treat tuberculosis. Front Immunol [Internet]. 2021;12:660916. https://www.frontiersin.org/articles/10.3389/fimmu.2021.660916.
5. Young C, Walzl G, Du Plessis N. Therapeutic host-directed strategies to improve outcome in tuberculosis. Mucosal Immunol [Internet]. 2020;13(2):190–204. https://doi.org/10.1038/s41385-019-0226-5.
6. Raja A. Immunology of tuberculosis. Indian J Med Res. 2004;120(4):213–32.
7. Feng CG, Bean AG, Hooi H, Briscoe H, Britton WJ. Increase in gamma interferon-secreting CD8(+), as well as CD4(+), T cells in lungs following aerosol infection with Mycobacterium tuberculosis. Infect Immun. 1999;67(7):3242–7.
8. Selvaraj P, Venkataprasad N, Vijayan V, Prabhakar R, Narayanan P. Alveolar macrophages in patients with pulmonary tuberculosis. Lung India. 1988;6(2):71–4.
9. Passmore JS, Lukey PT, Ress SR. The human macrophage cell line U937 as an in vitro model for selective evaluation of mycobacterial antigen-specific cytotoxic T-cell function. Immunology. 2001;102(2):146–56.
10. Basu S, Pathak SK, Banerjee A, Pathak S, Bhattacharyya A, Yang Z, et al. Execution of macrophage apoptosis by PE_PGRS33 of Mycobacterium tuberculosis is mediated by Toll-like receptor 2-dependent release of tumor necrosis factor-alpha. J Biol Chem. 2007;282(2):1039–50.
11. Huang Z, Gao C, Chi X, Hu YW, Zheng L, Zeng T, et al. IL-37 expression is upregulated in patients with tuberculosis and induces macrophages towards an M2-like phenotype. Scand J Immunol. 2015;82(4):370–9.

12. Benard A, Sakwa I, Schierloh P, Colom A, Mercier I, Tailleux L, et al. B cells producing type I IFN modulate macrophage polarization in tuberculosis. Am J Respir Crit Care Med. 2018;197(6):801–13.
13. Marino S, Cilfone NA, Mattila JT, Linderman JJ, Flynn JL, Kirschner DE. Macrophage polarization drives granuloma outcome during Mycobacterium tuberculosis infection. Ehrt S, editor. Infect Immun. 2015;83(1):324–38.
14. Huang Z, Luo Q, Guo Y, Chen J, Xiong G, Peng Y, et al. Mycobacterium tuberculosis-induced polarization of human macrophage orchestrates the formation and development of tuberculous granulomas in vitro. PLoS One. 2015;10(6):e0129744.
15. Shen P, Li Q, Ma J, Tian M, Hong F, Zhai X, et al. IRAK-M alters the polarity of macrophages to facilitate the survival of Mycobacterium tuberculosis. BMC Microbiol. 2017;17(1):185.
16. Krausgruber T, Blazek K, Smallie T, Alzabin S, Lockstone H, Sahgal N, et al. IRF5 promotes inflammatory macrophage polarization and TH1-TH17 responses. Nat Immunol. 2011;16(12):231.
17. Udalova IA, Krausgruber T, Smallie T, Blazek K, Lockstone H, Sahgal N, et al. IRF5 promotes inflammatory macrophage polarization and Th1/Th17 response to cite this version: HAL Id: hal-00608917. Nat Immunol. 2011.
18. Piñeros AR, Campos LW, Fonseca DM, Bertolini TB, Gembre AF, Prado RQ, et al. M2 macrophages or IL-33 treatment attenuate ongoing Mycobacterium tuberculosis infection. Sci Rep. 2017;7:41240.
19. Wang S, Zhang J, Sui L, Xu H, Piao Q, Liu Y, et al. Antibiotics induce polarization of pleural macrophages to M2-like phenotype in patients with tuberculous pleuritis. Sci Rep. 2017;7(1):14982.
20. Gensel JC, Kopper TJ, Zhang B, Orr MB, Bailey WM. Predictive screening of M1 and M2 macrophages reveals the immunomodulatory effectiveness of post spinal cord injury azithromycin treatment. Sci Rep. 2017;7:40144.
21. Gonzalez-Juarrero M, Turner OC, Turner J, Marietta P, Brooks JV, Orme IM. Temporal and spatial arrangement of lymphocytes within lung granulomas induced by aerosol infection with Mycobacterium tuberculosis. Infect Immun. 2001;69(3):1722–8.
22. Puissegur MP, Botanch C, Duteyrat JL, Delsol G, Caratero C, Altare F. An in vitro dual model of mycobacterial granulomas to investigate the molecular interactions between mycobacteria and human host cells. Cell Microbiol. 2004;6(5):423–33.
23. Frieden TR, Sterling TR, Munsiff SS, Watt CJ, Dye C. Tuberculosis. Lancet. 2003;362(9387):887–99.
24. Dheda K, Booth H, Huggett JF, Johnson MA, Zumla A, Rook GAW. Lung remodeling in pulmonary tuberculosis. J Infect Dis. 2005;192(7):1201–9.
25. Cooper AM, Solache A, Khader SA. Interleukin-12 and tuberculosis: an old story revisited. Curr Opin Immunol [Internet]. 2007;19(4):441–7. https://www.ncbi.nlm.nih.gov/pubmed/17702558.
26. Roach DR, Bean AGD, Demangel C, France MP, Briscoe H, Britton WJ. TNF regulates chemokine induction essential for cell recruitment, granuloma formation, and clearance of mycobacterial infection. J Immunol. 2002;168(9):4620–7.
27. da Silva DAA, da Silva MV, Barros CCO, Alexandre PBD, Timoteo RP, Catarino JS, et al. TNF-alpha blockade impairs in vitro tuberculous granuloma formation and down modulate Th1, Th17 and Treg cytokines. PLoS One. 2018;13(3):e0194430.
28. Gupta A, Kaul A, Tsolaki AG, Kishore U, Bhakta S. Mycobacterium tuberculosis: immune evasion, latency and reactivation. Immunobiology. 2012;217(3):363–74.
29. Carroll MV, Lack N, Sim E, Krarup A, Sim RB. Multiple routes of complement activation by Mycobacterium bovis BCG. Mol Immunol. 2009;46(16):3367–78.
30. Ferguson JS, Weis JJ, Martin JL, Schlesinger LS. Complement protein C3 binding to Mycobacterium tuberculosis is initiated by the classical pathway in human bronchoalveolar lavage fluid. Infect Immun. 2004;72(5):2564–73.
31. Schlesinger LS. Mycobacterium tuberculosis and the complement system. Trends Microbiol. 1998;6(2):47–50.
32. Abdul-Aziz M, Tsolaki AG, Kouser L, Carroll MV, Al-Ahdal MN, Sim RB, et al. Complement factor H interferes with Mycobacterium bovis BCG entry into macrophages and modulates the proinflammatory cytokine response. Immunobiology. 2016;221(9):944–52.
33. Hu C, Mayadas-Norton T, Tanaka K, Chan J, Salgame P. Mycobacterium tuberculosis infection in complement receptor 3-deficient mice. J Immunol. 2000;165(5):2596–602.
34. Actor JK, Breij E, Wetsel RA, Hoffmann H, Hunter RL Jr, Jagannath C. A role for complement C5 in organism containment and granulomatous response during murine tuberculosis. Scand J Immunol. 2001;53(5):464–74.
35. Welsh KJ, Lewis CT, Boyd S, Braun MC, Actor JK. Complement factor C7 contributes to lung immunopathology caused by mycobacterium tuberculosis. Clin Dev Immunol. 2012;2012:429675.
36. Rich EA, Torres M, Sada E, Finegan CK, Hamilton BD, Toossi Z. Mycobacterium tuberculosis (MTB)-stimulated production of nitric oxide by human alveolar macrophages and relationship of nitric oxide production to growth inhibition of MTB. Tuber Lung Dis. 1997;78(5–6):247–55.
37. Bryk R, Lima CD, Erdjument-Bromage H, Tempst P, Nathan C. Metabolic enzymes of mycobacteria linked to antioxidant defense by a thioredoxin-like protein. Science (1979). 2002;295(5557):1073–7.
38. Scghatoleslam A, Hemmati M, Ebadat S, Movahedi B, Mostafavi-Pour Z. Macrophage immune response suppression by recombinant Mycobacterium tuberculosis antigens, the ESAT-6, CFP-10, and ESAT-6/CFP-10 fusion proteins. Iran J Med Sci. 2016;41(4):296–304.

39. Hemmati M, Seghatoleslam A, Rasti M, Ebadat S, Naghibalhossaini F, Mostafavi-Pour Z. Additive effect of recombinant Mycobacterium tuberculosis ESAT-6 protein and ESAT-6/CFP-10 fusion protein in adhesion of macrophages through fibronectin receptors. J Microbiol Immunol Infect. 2016;49(2):249–56.
40. Fratti RA, Backer JM, Gruenberg J, Corvera S, Deretic V. Role of phosphatidylinositol 3-kinase and Rab5 effectors in phagosomal biogenesis and mycobacterial phagosome maturation arrest. J Cell Biol. 2001;154(3):631–44.
41. Schuller S, Neefjes J, Ottenhoff T, Thole J, Young D. Coronin is involved in uptake of Mycobacterium bovis BCG in human macrophages but not in phagosome maintenance. Cell Microbiol. 2001;3(12):785–93.
42. Vergne I, Chua J, Deretic V. Mycobacterium tuberculosis phagosome maturation arrest: selective targeting of PI3P-dependent membrane trafficking. Traffic. 2003;4(9):600–6.
43. Vergne I, Fratti RA, Hill PJ, Chua J, Belisle J, Deretic V. Mycobacterium tuberculosis phagosome maturation arrest: mycobacterial phosphatidylinositol analog phosphatidylinositol mannoside stimulates early endosomal fusion. Mol Biol Cell [Internet]. 2004;15(2):751–60. https://www.ncbi.nlm.nih.gov/pubmed/14617817.
44. Hmama Z, Gabathuler R, Jefferies WA, de Jong G, Reiner NE. Attenuation of HLA-DR expression by mononuclear phagocytes infected with Mycobacterium tuberculosis is related to intracellular sequestration of immature class II heterodimers. J Immunol. 1998;161(9):4882–93.
45. Wojciechowski W, DeSanctis J, Skamene E, Radzioch D. Attenuation of MHC Class II expression in macrophages infected with Mycobacterium bovis BCG involves Class II transactivator and depends on the Nramp1 gene. J Immunol [Internet]. 1999;163(5):2688–96. http://www.jimmunol.org/content/163/5/2688.abstract/.
46. Ting LM, Kim AC, Cattamanchi A, Ernst JD. Mycobacterium tuberculosis inhibits IFN-gamma transcriptional responses without inhibiting activation of STAT1. J Immunol. 1999;163(7):3898–906.
47. Rojas RE, Balaji KN, Subramanian A, Boom WH. Regulation of human CD4(+) αβ T-Cell-receptor-positive (TCR(+)) and γδ TCR(+) T-cell responses to Mycobacterium tuberculosis by interleukin-10 and transforming growth factor β. Kaufmann SHE, editor. Infect Immun [Internet]. 1999;67(12):6461–72. http://www.ncbi.nlm.nih.gov/pmc/articles/PMC97056/.
48. Schaaf K, Smith SR, Duverger A, Wagner F, Wolschendorf F, Westfall AO, et al. Mycobacterium tuberculosis exploits the PPM1A signaling pathway to block host macrophage apoptosis. Sci Rep. 2017;7:42101.
49. Chan J, Fan XD, Hunter SW, Brennan PJ, Bloom BR. Lipoarabinomannan, a possible virulence factor involved in persistence of Mycobacterium tuberculosis within macrophages. Infect Immun [Internet]. 1991;59(5):1755–61. https://www.ncbi.nlm.nih.gov/pubmed/1850379.
50. Wadee AA, Kuschke RH, Dooms TG. The inhibitory effects of Mycobacterium tuberculosis on MHC class II expression by monocytes activated with riminophenazines and phagocyte stimulants. Clin Exp Immunol [Internet]. 1995;100(3):434–9. https://www.ncbi.nlm.nih.gov/pubmed/7774052.
51. Noss EH, Pai RK, Sellati TJ, Radolf JD, Belisle J, Golenbock DT, et al. Toll-like receptor 2-dependent inhibition of macrophage class II MHC expression and antigen processing by 19-kDa lipoprotein of Mycobacterium tuberculosis. J Immunol. 2001;167(2):910–8.
52. Frieden TR. Directly observed treatment, short-course (DOTS): ensuring cure of tuberculosis. Indian J Pediatr [Internet]. 2000;67(2 Suppl):S21–7. http://europepmc.org/abstract/MED/11129903.
53. Sandiford P. WHO's DOTS strategy. Lancet [Internet]. 1999;353(9154):755. https://doi.org/10.1016/S0140-6736(05)76125-0.
54. Caminero JA, Piubello A, Scardigli A, Migliori GB. Bedaquiline: how better to use it. Eur Respir J [Internet]. 2017;50(5):1701670. http://erj.ersjournals.com/content/50/5/1701670.abstract.
55. Deoghare S. Bedaquiline: a new drug approved for treatment of multidrug-resistant tuberculosis. Indian J Pharmacol [Internet]. 2013;45(5):536–7. https://pubmed.ncbi.nlm.nih.gov/24130398.
56. Li Y, Sun F, Zhang W. Bedaquiline and delamanid in the treatment of multidrug-resistant tuberculosis: promising but challenging. Drug Dev Res. 2019;80(1):98–105.
57. World Health Organization. The use of delamanid in the treatment of multidrug-resistant tuberculosis: interim policy guidance. Geneva; 2014.
58. Bloemberg GV, Keller PM, Stucki D, Trauner A, Borrell S, Latshang T, et al. Acquired resistance to bedaquiline and delamanid in therapy for tuberculosis. N Engl J Med [Internet]. 2015;373(20):1986–8. https://pubmed.ncbi.nlm.nih.gov/26559594.
59. Cicchese JM, Evans S, Hult C, Joslyn LR, Wessler T, Millar JA, et al. Dynamic balance of pro- and anti-inflammatory signals controls disease and limits pathology. Immunol Rev [Internet]. 2018;285(1):147–67. https://doi.org/10.1111/imr.12671.
60. Parasa VR, Muvva JR, Rose JF, Braian C, Brighenti S, Lerm M. Inhibition of tissue matrix metalloproteinases interferes with mycobacterium tuberculosis-induced granuloma formation and reduces bacterial load in a human lung tissue model. Front Microbiol [Internet]. 2017;8:2370. https://www.frontiersin.org/articles/10.3389/fmicb.2017.02370.
61. Ordonez AA, Pokkali S, Kim S, Carr B, Klunk MH, Tong L, et al. Adjunct antibody administration with standard treatment reduces relapse rates in a murine tuberculosis model of necrotic granulomas. PLoS One [Internet]. 2018;13(5):e0197474. https://doi.org/10.1371/journal.pone.0197474.

62. Walker NF, Clark SO, Oni T, Andreu N, Tezera L, Singh S, et al. Doxycycline and HIV infection suppress tuberculosis-induced matrix metalloproteinases. Am J Respir Crit Care Med. 2012;185(9):989–97.
63. Urbanowski ME, Ihms EA, Bigelow K, Kübler A, Elkington PT, Bishai WR. Repetitive aerosol exposure promotes cavitary tuberculosis and enables screening for targeted inhibitors of extensive lung destruction. J Infect Dis [Internet]. 2018;218(1):53–63. https://doi.org/10.1093/infdis/jiy127.
64. Shah MA, Yanez Ruiz EP, Bodoky G, Starodub A, Cunningham D, Yip D, et al. A phase III, randomized, double-blind, placebo-controlled study to evaluate the efficacy and safety of andecaliximab combined with mFOLFOX6 as first-line treatment in patients with advanced gastric or gastroesophageal junction adenocarcinoma (GAMMA-1). J Clin Oncol [Internet]. 2019;37(4_Suppl):4. https://doi.org/10.1200/JCO.2019.37.4_suppl.4.
65. Wallis RS, Kyambadde P, Johnson JL, Horter L, Kittle R, Pohle M, et al. A study of the safety, immunology, virology, and microbiology of adjunctive etanercept in HIV-1-associated tuberculosis. AIDS [Internet]. 2004;18(2):257–64. https://journals.lww.com/aidsonline/Fulltext/2004/01230/A_study_of_the_safety,_immunology,_virology,_and.15.aspx.
66. Kadhiravan T, Deepanjali S. Role of corticosteroids in the treatment of tuberculosis: an evidence-based update. Indian J Chest Dis Allied Sci. 2010;52(3):153–8. http://europepmc.org/abstract/MED/20949734.
67. Kumarvelu S, Prasad K, Khosla A, Behari M, Ahuja GK. Randomized controlled trial of dexamethasone in tuberculous meningitis. Tuber Lung Dis [Internet]. 1994;75(3):203–7. https://www.sciencedirect.com/science/article/pii/0962847994900094.
68. Langelier MF, Zandarashvili L, Aguiar PM, Black BE, Pascal JM. NAD+ analog reveals PARP-1 substrate-blocking mechanism and allosteric communication from catalytic center to DNA-binding domains. Nat Commun [Internet]. 2018;9(1):844. https://doi.org/10.1038/s41467-018-03234-8.
69. Kalle AM, Arshad R. Inhibition of bacterial multidrug resistance by celecoxib, a cyclooxygenase-2 inhibitor. Antimicrob Agents Chemother [Internet]. 2011;55(1):439–42. https://doi.org/10.1128/aac.00735-10.
70. Ricciotti E, FitzGerald GA. Prostaglandins and inflammation. Arterioscler Thromb Vasc Biol [Internet]. 2011;31(5):986–1000. https://doi.org/10.1161/ATVBAHA.110.207449.
71. Refai A, Gritli S, Barbouche MR, Essafi M. Mycobacterium tuberculosis virulent factor ESAT-6 drives macrophage differentiation toward the pro-inflammatory M1 phenotype and subsequently switches it to the anti-inflammatory M2 phenotype. Front Cell Infect Microbiol [Internet]. 2018;8:327. https://www.frontiersin.org/articles/10.3389/fcimb.2018.00327.
72. Knaul JK, Jörg S, Oberbeck-Mueller D, Heinemann E, Scheuermann L, Brinkmann V, et al. Lung-residing myeloid-derived suppressors display dual functionality in murine pulmonary tuberculosis. Am J Respir Crit Care Med. 2014;190(9):1053–66.
73. Shen L, Pili R. Tasquinimod targets suppressive myeloid cells in the tumor microenvironment. Oncoimmunology [Internet]. 2019;8(10):e1072672. https://doi.org/10.1080/2162402X.2015.1072672.
74. Nefedova Y, Fishman M, Sherman S, Wang X, Beg AA, Gabrilovich DI. Mechanism of all-trans retinoic acid effect on tumor-associated myeloid-derived suppressor cells. Cancer Res [Internet]. 2007;67(22):11021–8. https://doi.org/10.1158/0008-5472.CAN-07-2593.
75. Leukes V, Walzl G, du Plessis N. Myeloid-derived suppressor cells as target of phosphodiesterase-5 inhibitors in host-directed therapeutics for tuberculosis. Front Immunol [Internet]. 2020;11:451. https://www.frontiersin.org/articles/10.3389/fimmu.2020.00451.
76. Cardona P, Cardona PJ. Regulatory T cells in Mycobacterium tuberculosis infection. Front Immunol [Internet]. 2019;10:2139. https://www.frontiersin.org/articles/10.3389/fimmu.2019.02139.
77. Gupta S, Cheung L, Pokkali S, Winglee K, Guo H, Murphy JR, et al. Suppressor cell–depleting immunotherapy with denileukin diftitox is an effective host-directed therapy for tuberculosis. J Infect Dis [Internet]. 2017;215(12):1883–7. https://doi.org/10.1093/infdis/jix208.
78. Green AM, Mattila JT, Bigbee CL, Bongers KS, Ling Lin P, Flynn JL. CD4+ regulatory T cells in a Cynomolgus macaque model of Mycobacterium tuberculosis infection. J Infect Dis [Internet]. 2010;202(4):533–41. https://doi.org/10.1086/654896.
79. Beamer GL, Flaherty DK, Assogba BD, Stromberg P, Gonzalez-Juarrero M, de Waal Malefyt R, et al. Interleukin-10 promotes Mycobacterium tuberculosis disease progression in CBA/J Mice1. J Immunol [Internet]. 2008;181(8):5545–50. https://doi.org/10.4049/jimmunol.181.8.5545.
80. Huang Z, Luo Q, Guo Y, Chen J, Xiong G, Peng Y, et al. Mycobacterium tuberculosis-induced polarization of human macrophage orchestrates the formation and development of tuberculous granulomas in vitro. PLoS One [Internet]. 2015;10(6):e0129744. https://doi.org/10.1371/journal.pone.0129744.
81. Abdollahi E, Momtazi AA, Johnston TP, Sahebkar A. Therapeutic effects of curcumin in inflammatory and immune-mediated diseases: a nature-made jack-of-all-trades? J Cell Physiol [Internet]. 2018;233(2):830–48. http://europepmc.org/abstract/MED/28059453.
82. Rangel Moreno J, Estrada García I, La Luz D, García Hernández M, Aguilar Leon D, Marquez R, Hernández Pando R. The role of prostaglandin E2 in the immunopathogenesis of experimental pulmonary tuberculosis. Immunology [Internet]. 2002;106(2):257–66. https://doi.org/10.1046/j.1365-2567.2002.01403.x.
83. Kroesen VM, Gröschel MI, Martinson N, Zumla A, Maeurer M, van der Werf TS, et al. Non-steroidal anti-inflammatory drugs as host-directed therapy for tuberculosis: a systematic review. Front Immunol [Internet]. 2017;8:772. https://www.frontiersin.org/articles/10.3389/fimmu.2017.00772.

Healthcare Management Technologies in India: Current Perspectives and Challenges

23

R. Sundari and S. Ajit

23.1 Introduction

Technology has created an impact in every aspect of our life; including health. There is a rapid growth of health care sector. It is estimated that around 1.3 billion patients receive quality health care in India. Jitendra Singh union minister for health quoted that the Indian health care industry will reach $50 billion by 2025. Government plays an active role in improving the healthcare services, making technological advancements and digitalization of health care services [1]. Technologies play a crucial role in effective management of health care services. The Indian health care sector has a number of emerging trends using cutting-edge technology on improving the patient experience [2]. India has made a stunning progress in health parameters including complete eradication of diseases such as smallpox, polio, and guinea worm disease. Effective healthcare management technologies can help healthcare organizations to deliver high-quality care that is accessible, affordable, and patient-centred. By leveraging technology to support and enhance healthcare management, healthcare service providers can improve the efficiency and effectiveness of healthcare delivery, ultimately leading to better health outcomes for patients.

23.2 History of Health Care Management and Evolution of EHR

The history of health care management can be traced back to ancient civilizations where individuals with medical knowledge acted as healers or physicians. However, the formalization of health care management as a distinct field began to take shape during the late nineteenth and early twentieth centuries. Here are some key milestones in the evolution of health care management (http://baytech.com/history-healthcare-technology) (Table 23.1).

R. Sundari (✉)
Xavier Institute of Management & Entrepreneurship, Chennai, India

Department of MBA, St. Joseph's College of Engineering, Chennai, India

S. Ajit
Xavier Institute of Management & Entrepreneurship, Chennai, India

K. Parthasarathy, R. Manikkam (eds.), *Translational Research in Biomedical Sciences: Recent Progress and Future Prospects*, https://doi.org/10.1007/978-981-97-1777-4_23

Table 23.1 Table showing history of health care management and evolution of EHR

1920	Emergence of medical records	• Healthcare professionals documented medical records pertaining to patient care and medication • American Health Information Management Association (AHIMA) standardized medical records
1960	Health information management new approaches	• Computers were used to standardize and share medical records • Dr. Lawrence Weed created the problem-oriented medical record (POMR). The information collected from medical records were organized using POMR • Clinicians assessed patient's medical history and the system allowed verifying diagnosis using third party
1965	Introduction of Medicare and Medicaid	• Record keeping was a priority to keep accurate Health care Information System Development • Medical records were standardized using computers. Sharing, collection and managing patient data became easy • Around 73 hospitals used Healthcare Information technology and found it to be expensive • Mainframe computer was the largest service providers used for medical record keeping • Early adopters of Mainframe computer was The Mayo Clinic in Rochester, Minnesota
Late 1960–early 1970	Healthcare information management systems development	• Lockheed created a computerized physician ordering system for El Camino Hospital called Eclipsys • The University of Utah, 3M and Latter Day Saints Hospital developed health Evaluation through Logical Processing (HELP) a clinical decision support system in collaboration • Regenstrief Institute in Indianapolis created Regenstrief Medical Record System
1980	Modern age of healthcare information technology	• Hospitals invested in computers that touched the patient floor • Doctors could afford to buy personal computers and revolutionized the health care industry • 1982—Dragon Systems developed a voice recognition prototype At hospital level, computers were used for patient registration (check in process), scheduling and billing
1990	Electronic medical records awareness and benefits	• The Institute of Medicine (IOM) started using electronic medical records to study health records • Barriers to adopt electronic health records were security issues, cost and lack of standardization • Patient's medical data were kept on track by Master patient Index (MPI) • The healthcare information exchange (HIE) operated by Indiana Health Information Exchange Indiana Network for Patient Care (INPC) • WHO adopted standard coding ICD-10. The new codes expanded the number of codes that used in medical records
2000	Health Information Technology for Economic and Clinical Health	• President George W. Bush called for computerized health records • The United States Congress by President Barack Obama enacted the Health Information Technology for Economic and Clinical Health (HITECH) Act in 2009 as part of the American Recovery and Reinvestment Act (ARRA). The HITECH Act was designed to promote the adoption and meaningful use of electronic health records (EHRs) by healthcare providers and organizations
2010	EHRs become commonplace	• The Office of the National Coordinator for Health worked with 62 REC across the nation to help healthcare providers migrate to electronic healthcare record systems
2015	Electronic health record adoption	• Interoperability of healthcare providers and patients • Integrated system promoted better decision and reduced medical errors

Table 23.1 (continued)

Present status	Healthcare information technology today	• Artificial intelligence (AI) plays a dominant role in healthcare. AI promotes diagnostic accuracy, decision-making, and streamlining administrative tasks • Telemedicine and remote patient monitoring continue to grow seeking to improve patient care and reduce costs • Increased focus on data analytics in healthcare enables better understanding of patient populations and tailoring care to meet their requirements • Emphasis on interoperability and data sharing improved patient care • Growth of patient engagement tools like patient portals, mobile apps, and other digital tools to engage patients in their own care • Medical devices and wearables provides patient health data more detailed and accurate

23.3 Emerging Trends in Health Care Management

Healthcare industry plays an important role in diagnosing and curing ailments and diseases. The technological advancement in the medical sector has gained an in depth understanding of humanity. Insights about human body was studied with more precision with the advent of technology. The emerging trends in health care industry are presented below.

23.3.1 Artificial Intelligence (AI) in Healthcare

Artificial intelligence (AI) has the potential to revolutionize healthcare by improving patient outcomes, increasing efficiency, and reducing costs. AI technologies can help healthcare providers make diagnoses that are more accurate, provide personalized treatment plans, and identify patient's risk. One of the most significant applications of AI in healthcare is in medical imaging. AI algorithms can analyse medical images such as X-rays, MRIs, and CT scans to detect anomalies with more precision. This can lead to more accurate diagnoses and improve the patient outcomes.AI can also be useful is in drug development. AI algorithms can analyse large amounts of data and identify potential drug that helps in developing new drug for treating diseases that were currently difficult to treat. Chatbots and virtual assistants can be used to provide patients with personalized health advice and support, answer their questions, and provide reminders about medication and appointments.

23.3.2 Integrating Data and Predictive Analysis

Integrating data and predictive analysis is a crucial aspect of leveraging the potential of AI in healthcare. Predictive analysis involves using algorithms and machine learning models to identify patterns in data and make predictions about future events or outcomes. By integrating data from various sources and applying predictive analysis techniques, healthcare providers can make informed decisions about patient care. One important application of predictive analysis in healthcare is in identifying patients who are at risk of developing certain conditions. Another important application of predictive analysis in healthcare is in personalized treatment planning. By analysing data on a patient's medical history, genetics, lifestyle, and other factors, predictive models can recommend personalized treatment plans that are more likely to be effective for that patient. This leads to better patient outcomes and reduced healthcare costs.

23.3.3 Smartphone-Assisted Therapy

Smartphone-assisted therapy, also known as mobile health (mHealth) therapy, is a form of mental health treatment that utilizes mobile apps and other digital tools to deliver therapy and support to patients. With the advent of smartphones and mobile devices, mHealth therapy has the potential to make mental healthcare more accessible and convenient for patients.

23.3.3.1 Types of mHealth Therapy

Cognitive behavioural therapy (CBT) apps: These apps offer users CBT exercises and techniques to help manage symptoms of anxiety and depression.

Mood tracking apps: These apps allow users to track their moods and provide insights into patterns and triggers that may affect their mental health.

Virtual therapy sessions: This session provides virtual therapy through video conferencing or messaging platforms.

Meditation and relaxation apps: These apps offer guided meditation and relaxation exercises to help users manage stress and anxiety.

The key benefits of mHealth therapy is its convenience and accessibility. Patients can access therapy and support whenever and wherever they need it, without the need for in-person appointments. This can be especially beneficial for patients who live in remote areas or have limited mobility.

23.4 Digital Pills

A digital pill, also known as a "smart pill," is a medication that contains an ingestible sensor or a digital device that can track and transmit data about the patient's body. The sensor in the pill detects and transmits data about the patient's vital signs. Healthcare providers monitor patients' conditions and adjust their treatment plans. The technology has the potential to help prevent medical errors, reduce hospitalizations, and improve patient outcomes.

23.5 Digital Symptom Tracking

Digital symptom tracking is the process of using digital tools such as mobile apps or wearable devices to monitor and record a patient's symptoms over time. By tracking symptoms digitally, healthcare providers can obtain a more complete and accurate picture of a patient's health status, that aids in diagnosis, treatment planning, and disease management. Digital symptom tracking is used for a wide range of conditions, including chronic conditions such as diabetes, hypertension, and asthma, as well as mental health conditions such as depression and anxiety. For example, patients with diabetes can use mobile apps to track their blood sugar levels, medication adherence, and diet, and share this information with their healthcare providers to inform treatment decisions.

23.5.1 Benefits of Digital Symptom Tracking

Improved accuracy: Digital tracking can help reduce errors and improve the accuracy of symptom reporting, as patients can record symptoms in real time, rather than relying on recall.

Better patient engagement: Patients feel more engaged and empowered to manage their health through digital tracking.

Personalized treatment: Digital symptom tracking can provide healthcare providers with more comprehensive information about a patient's health status, which can lead to more personalized treatment plans.

Timely intervention: By tracking symptoms in real-time, healthcare providers can intervene early when symptoms worsen, potentially preventing complications or hospitalizations.

It is important to ensure that digital tools used for symptom tracking are secure and comply with privacy laws and regulations.

23.6 Wearable and Implantable Devices

Wearable and implantable devices are digital health tools designed to monitor a patient's health status and collect data on various physiological parameters. These devices are used for a wide range of purposes, such as managing chronic conditions, detecting early warning signs of health issues, and tracking fitness and activity levels. Wearable devices are typically worn on the body, such as on the wrist, chest, or ankle. They can include devices such as fitness trackers, smartwatches, and medical-grade devices that monitor vital signs such as heart rate, blood pressure, and oxygen levels. Implantable devices are surgically implanted into the body and that includes pacemakers, insulin pumps, and other medical devices. These devices are designed to monitor and regulate various bodily functions, such as heart rate and blood sugar levels.

23.6.1 Benefits of Wearable and Implantable Devices in Healthcare

Improved patient outcomes: By providing continuous monitoring of a patient's health status, wearable and implantable devices can enable earlier intervention and improved treatment outcomes.

Increased patient engagement: By giving patients access to real-time data about their health status, wearable and implantable devices can help patients to take a more active role in managing their health.

More efficient care: Wearable and implantable devices can reduce the need for in-person appointments and provide more efficient and streamlined care.

23.7 Telemedicine

Telemedicine is the use of telecommunications technology, such as video conferencing, to provide remote medical care and clinical services. It enables patients to access healthcare services from their homes or other remote locations, eliminating the need for in-person visits to healthcare facilities. Telemedicine are used for a wide range of medical services, such as routine check-ups, consultations, follow-up visits, and remote monitoring of patients with chronic conditions.

23.7.1 Benefits of Telemedicine

Increased access to healthcare: Telemedicine can improve access to healthcare services for patients, living in remote or rural areas, not having mobility or transportation.

Convenience and flexibility: Telemedicine allows patients to receive medical care from the comfort of their own homes, eliminating the need for travel and reducing wait times.

Cost savings: Telemedicine can be less expensive than traditional in-person medical care, as it eliminates the costs associated with travel and facilities.

Improved patient outcomes: Telemedicine has led to improved patient outcomes and increased patient satisfaction.

Not all medical services are provided effectively through telemedicine, some conditions may require in-person care. It is important to ensure that telemedicine is used appropriately and in conjunction with traditional medical care when necessary.

23.8 Healthcare Data Analytics

Healthcare data analytics is the process of using technology and statistical analysis to examine and interpret large amounts of data related to patient health, medical treatments, and healthcare outcomes. The goal of healthcare data analytics is to identify patterns and insights that can be used to improve patient care, increase operational efficiency, and reduce costs. Healthcare data analytics involves collecting and analysing data from various sources, such as electronic health records (EHRs), claims data, and patient-generated data from wearables and other digital health tools. By analysing this data, healthcare providers can gain insights into patient health status, treatment effectiveness, and population health trends.

23.8.1 Benefits of Healthcare Data Analytics

Improved patient outcomes: Healthcare data analytics provides healthcare professionals with insights into patient health status and treatment outcomes, enabling them to make more informed decisions about patient care.

Increased operational efficiency: Healthcare data analytics identifies areas where operational efficiency can be improved, such as reducing wait times or improving patient flow.

Cost savings: Healthcare data analytics can help to identify cost-saving opportunities, such as reducing unnecessary treatments or improving medication adherence.

Population health management: Healthcare data analytics can provide insights into population health trends, enabling healthcare providers to develop targeted interventions to improve the health of specific patient populations.

23.9 Digital Therapeutics

Digital therapeutics (DTx) are evidence-based therapeutic interventions that use digital technology to treat medical conditions and improve patient outcomes. DTx can be used as standalone therapies or in combination with traditional medical treatments. DTx typically involve the use of software or mobile applications (apps) that are designed to deliver therapeutic interventions to patients, such as cognitive behavioural therapy, mindfulness meditation, or physical exercises. These interventions can be tailored to meet the specific needs of individual patients and can be delivered remotely, making them convenient and accessible. DTx can be used to treat a wide range of medical conditions, such as chronic pain, diabetes, hypertension, depression, and anxiety. They are used for disease prevention, such as smoking cessation and weight management.

23.9.1 Benefits of DTx

Improved patient outcomes: DTx can provide patients with evidence-based therapeutic interventions tailored to meet their individual needs, leading to improved treatment outcomes.

Increased accessibility: DTx can be delivered remotely, for patients having difficulty accessing traditional in-person treatments.

Cost savings: DTx reduces the cost burden on patients and healthcare systems.

Personalized care: DTx are tailored to meet the specific needs of individual patients, providing personalized care and improving patient satisfaction.

It is important to ensure that DTx are evidence-based and meet regulatory standards for safety and efficacy.

23.10 Organ Care Technology and Bio Printing

Organ Care Technology (OCT) and Bio printing are two innovative and rapidly evolving fields in the medical industry. OCT is a technology that allows the preservation and transportation of organs in a state that can maintain their viability and function for a longer time than traditional methods. OCT machines use a special solution to perfuse organs, keeping them oxygenated and nourished, while also monitoring and maintaining their temperature and other vital parameters. This technology has the potential to increase the success rate of organ transplantation and reduce the waiting time for patients in need of a transplant.

Bioprinting is a technology that allows the fabrication of biological tissues and organs using 3D printing techniques. The process involves creating a 3D model of the tissue or organ, which is then printed using a biocompatible material and living cells. Bioprinting can be used to create complex and functional tissues, such as skin, bone, and cartilage, and has the potential to revolutionize the field of regenerative medicine.

23.11 Cancer Immunotherapy

Cancer immunotherapy is a type of cancer treatment that uses the body's own immune system to fight cancer cells. The immune system plays a crucial role in defending the body against foreign invaders, including cancer cells. However, cancer cells can sometimes evade the immune system's detection and continue to grow and spread. Immunotherapy works by boosting the body's immune response against cancer cells, making them more visible to the immune system and enhancing the ability of immune cells to attack and destroy cancer cells.

There are several types of cancer immunotherapy, including:

Monoclonal antibodies: These are laboratory-produced molecules that can mimic the immune system's ability to recognize and attack cancer cells. Monoclonal antibodies are designed to target specific proteins on the surface of cancer cells, making them more visible to the immune system.

Checkpoint inhibitors: These drugs block proteins that can inhibit the immune system's ability to attack cancer cells. By blocking these proteins, checkpoint inhibitors can enhance the immune response against cancer cells.

Adoptive cell transfer: This involves removing immune cells from the patient's body, modifying them in the laboratory to enhance their ability to attack cancer cells, and then infusing them back into the patient's body.

Cancer vaccines: These vaccines are designed to stimulate the immune system to recognize and attack cancer cells.

Cancer immunotherapy has shown promise in the treatment of several types of cancer, including melanoma, lung cancer, and certain types of leukaemia and lymphoma. However, immunotherapy can also cause side effects, such as fatigue, fever, and nausea, and it is not effective for all patients.

23.12 Augmented and Virtual Reality in Healthcare

Augmented reality (AR) and virtual reality (VR) are immersive technologies that have the potential to transform healthcare by enhancing medical education and training, improving patient outcomes, and enhancing the overall patient experience.AR is a technology that overlays digital information onto the physical world. In healthcare, AR provides clinicians with real-time information about patients during medical procedures or surgeries. For example, AR superimposes a patient's medical imaging results onto the surgical field to assist the surgeon in performing a procedure. VR is a technology that creates a simulated environment that can be experienced through a headset or other devices. In healthcare, VR is used for medical education and training, pain management, and mental health therapy.

23.12.1 Benefits of AR and VR in Healthcare

Enhanced medical education and training: AR and VR can provide healthcare providers with immersive training experiences that can improve their skills and confidence.

Improved patient outcomes: It provides clinicians with real-time information about patients during medical procedures, improving the accuracy and efficiency of treatment.

Enhanced patient experience: AR distract patients from pain during medical procedures or to provide patients with immersive experiences that can reduce anxiety and improve their overall experience.

Remote healthcare: AR and VR provides remote healthcare services, such as telemedicine or remote patient monitoring.

23.13 Sustainability and Decarbonization

Sustainability and decarbonization are important issues in healthcare, as the healthcare industry is a significant contributor to greenhouse gas emissions and resource consumption.

Ways used by healthcare industry for sustainability and decarbonization includes:

Reducing energy consumption: Healthcare facilities can reduce their energy consumption by implementing energy-efficient technologies, such as LED lighting and efficient heating and cooling systems.

Reducing waste: Healthcare facilities can reduce their waste by implementing recycling programmes, reducing the use of disposable items, and implementing composting programmes.

Sustainable procurement: Healthcare facilities can source sustainable products and materials, such as eco-friendly cleaning products and sustainable building materials.

Transportation: Healthcare facilities can reduce their carbon footprint by promoting alternative modes of transportation, such as walking, biking, and public transit, and by using electric or hybrid vehicles.

Sustainable food: Healthcare facilities can promote sustainable food choices by sourcing local and organic foods, reducing meat consumption, and implementing sustainable food production methods.

Telemedicine: Telemedicine can reduce the need for patients to travel to healthcare facilities, thereby reducing carbon emissions associated with transportation.

It is important for healthcare facilities to work towards sustainability and decarbonization in order to reduce their impact on the environment and to promote public health. By implementing sustainable practices, healthcare facilities can improve the health and well-being of both patients and the planet.

23.14 Big Data Analytics

Big data analytics can help healthcare providers to gain insights into patient health and outcomes, improve care coordination, and develop treatments that are more effective. Applications of big data analytics in healthcare includes personalized treatment plans and medicines based on a patient's unique medical history. The patient data collected is used for drug discovery. It also helps healthcare providers to optimize their operations by analysing data on patient flow, resource utilization, and supply chain management. Big data analytics can help healthcare providers to identify inefficiencies in their operations and reduce costs by optimizing resource allocation and reducing waste.

23.15 Emerging Trends in Mental Health Treatment That Are Gaining Attention and Popularity Brightscout [3]

Digital mental health: The use of technology, such as smartphone apps and online platforms, for mental health treatment and support is becoming more common. These tools can provide users with access to mental health resources and support, as well as digital therapy sessions.

Personalized treatment: Mental health treatment is becoming more personalized, with a focus on understanding the individual needs of each patient. Treatment plans are tailored to each patient's specific symptoms, experiences, and preferences.

Integration of physical and mental health: Mental health treatment is increasingly being integrated with physical health treatment. This approach recognizes the close relationship between mental and physical health and seeks to address both in a holistic manner.

Mind-body approaches: Mind-body approaches, such as yoga, meditation, and mindfulness, are gaining popularity in mental health treatment. These approaches focus on the connection between the mind and body and can help patients reduce stress and improve their overall well-being.

Peer support: Peer support programmes, which connect individuals with others who have experienced similar mental health challenges, are becoming more common. These programmes provide a sense of community and support for individuals who may feel isolated or stigmatized by their mental health condition.

Psychedelic-assisted therapy: The use of psychedelic substances, such as psilocybin and MDMA, in combination with therapy is being explored as a potential treatment for conditions such as depression, anxiety, and post-traumatic stress disorder. Research in this area is ongoing and preliminary results are promising, but more research is needed to understand the potential risks and benefits.

Overall, these emerging trends in mental health treatment reflect a growing recognition of the importance of mental health and the need for more effective and accessible treatments.

Challenges faced by healthcare technologies in India: The challenges faced by healthcare technologies in India was studied by Arshpreet Kaur [4] and are listed below,

Limited Infrastructure: The adoption of advanced healthcare technologies in India is still in development phase due to limited resources and facilities.

Cost: Advanced health care facilities and services are expensive. This sounds true, as majority of the population are low-income groups, who are the most significant portion of population, who are in need of healthcare services.

Lack of Skilled Workforce: There is a shortage of skilled healthcare professionals in India, particularly in the area of healthcare technology. This limits the effective implementation and use of healthcare technologies.

Language and Cultural Barriers: India has a diverse population, with different languages and cultural backgrounds. Delivery and implementation of healthcare technologies is difficult with these barriers.

Limited Access to Healthcare: Access to basic health care facilities is limited to population in rural India. Advanced technologies seem to be an unrealistic goal for certain group of people.

Regulatory Challenges: There are several regulatory challenges faced by healthcare technologies in India, including long approval times and complex regulatory frameworks. This can slow down the development and implementation of new technologies.

Cybersecurity: Cybersecurity infrastructure is still in its developing stage in India. As healthcare technologies become more connected, there is an increased risk of cybersecurity breaches.

Overall, these challenges make it difficult for healthcare technologies to be effectively implemented and utilized in India, particularly for those who need them the most.

23.16 Conclusion

The development and implementation of healthcare management technologies can help to streamline operations, improve patient outcomes, reduce costs, and enhance the overall quality of care. However, there are several challenges that need to be addressed, such as the lack of standardization and interoperability, the shortage of skilled healthcare IT professionals, and the lack of infrastructure and funding to support the development and implementation of healthcare management technologies.

Despite these challenges, there are several promising developments in healthcare technology in India, such as the National Health Stack and the National Digital Health Mission. India needs a robust 4G or 5G connectivity in villages and cities to access the health care services to fulfil the aim of complete patient care. It is important for healthcare organizations and policymakers to continue to invest in the development and implementation of healthcare management technologies, while addressing the challenges that currently exist. By leveraging technology to support and enhance healthcare management, India can improve the efficiency and effectiveness of healthcare delivery, ultimately leading to better health outcomes for its population.

References

1. India Today. Health sector in India to reach $50 billion by 2025: Govt. 2022. https://www.indiatoday.in/health/story/health-sector-in-india-to-reach-50-billion-by-2025-govt-1997596-2022-09-07. Accessed 20 Feb 2023.
2. Awan H. Why is the healthcare industry so important for the world's future. 2021. https://www.youthinsights.org/post/why-is-the-healthcare-industry-so-important-for-the-world-s-future. Accessed 2 Mar 2023.

3. Brightscout. The past present and future of technology in healthcare. 2018. https://www.brightscout.com/insight/the-past-present-and-future-of-technology-in-healthcare. Accessed 25 Jan 2023.
4. Kaur A. 10 problems that healthcare technology can solve for a healthier world. 2022. https://www.netsolutions.com/insights/5-healthcare-problems-which-digital-technologies-can-solve-for-a-fit-and-healthy-world/. Accessed Jan 2023.
5. The history of healthcare technology and the evolution of EHR. 2021. https://www.baytechit.com/history-healthcaretechnology. Accessed 20 Feb 2023.

Translational Research in COPD

24

Supraja. K, Krupakar Parthasarathy, T. Thangam, and T. Palaniappan

24.1 Introduction

Chronic obstructive pulmonary disease (COPD) is defined as a heterogeneous lung condition characterized by chronic respiratory symptoms (dyspnea, cough, sputum production, and/or exacerbations) due to abnormalities of the airways (bronchitis, bronchiolitis) and/or alveoli (emphysema) that cause persistent, often progressive, airflow obstruction [1]. The term COPD has undergone various definitions in the past two decades, indicating that our understanding of this condition is still in its early stages. Advances in diagnostics and molecular methods have slowly unraveled the pathogenesis of COPD. It is now recognized as a syndrome involving multiple organs rather than just a disease state. Globally, the burden of COPD was estimated to be 800 million cases with 3.23 million deaths in 2019. In India, the prevalence has increased from 28.1 million (27.0–29.2) in 1990 to 55.3 million (53.1–57.6) in 2016 [2]. The prevalence has increased from 3.3% (3.1–3.4) to 7.4% (5.0–9.8) in 2021 [3].

Accurately diagnosing COPD is of utmost importance given its multifaceted consequences. The enduring symptoms, reliance on others for daily tasks, the greater burden concerning disability-adjusted life years (DALYs), financial implications for patients and caregivers, emotional distress for individuals and families, and the loss of productivity underscore the criticality of early detection and intervention. In Tamil Nadu, the DALYs associated with COPD are estimated to be 1068 days per 100,000 population, which is three times higher than the DALYs attributed to cardiac disease, emphasizing the significant impact of COPD on the population.

In recent years, there has been significant attention given to understanding the complex pathways involved in airway inflammation, resolution, and repair. The interplay between genes, environmental exposome, and temporal factors has provided new insights into the disease. Adopting a precision medicine approach to this heterogeneous disease will enable tailored therapies for each subgroup, enhancing treatment efficacy.

S. K (✉)
Medway Hospitals, Chennai, Tamil Nadu, India

Medway Institute of Pulmonology, Medway Hospitals, Chennai, Tamil Nadu, India

K. Parthasarathy · T. Thangam
Centre for Drug Discovery and Development, Sathyabama Institute of Science and Technology, Chennai, India
e-mail: pkrupakar.cddd@sathyabama.ac.in; thangam.t.cddd@sathyabama.ac.in

T. Palaniappan
Medway Hospitals, Chennai, Tamil Nadu, India

K. Parthasarathy, R. Manikkam (eds.), *Translational Research in Biomedical Sciences: Recent Progress and Future Prospects*, https://doi.org/10.1007/978-981-97-1777-4_24

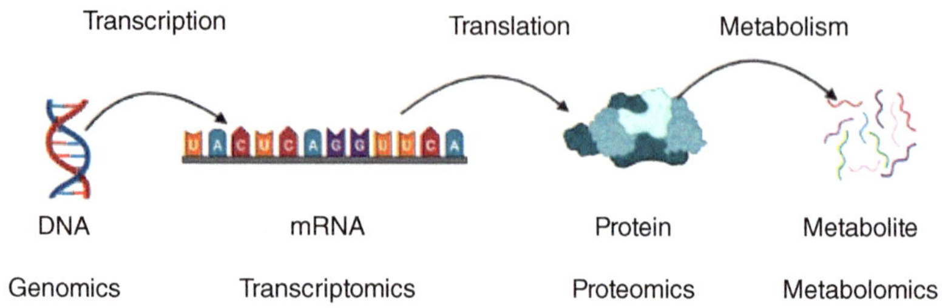

Fig. 24.1 The various stages of nuclear division and the studies associated with it

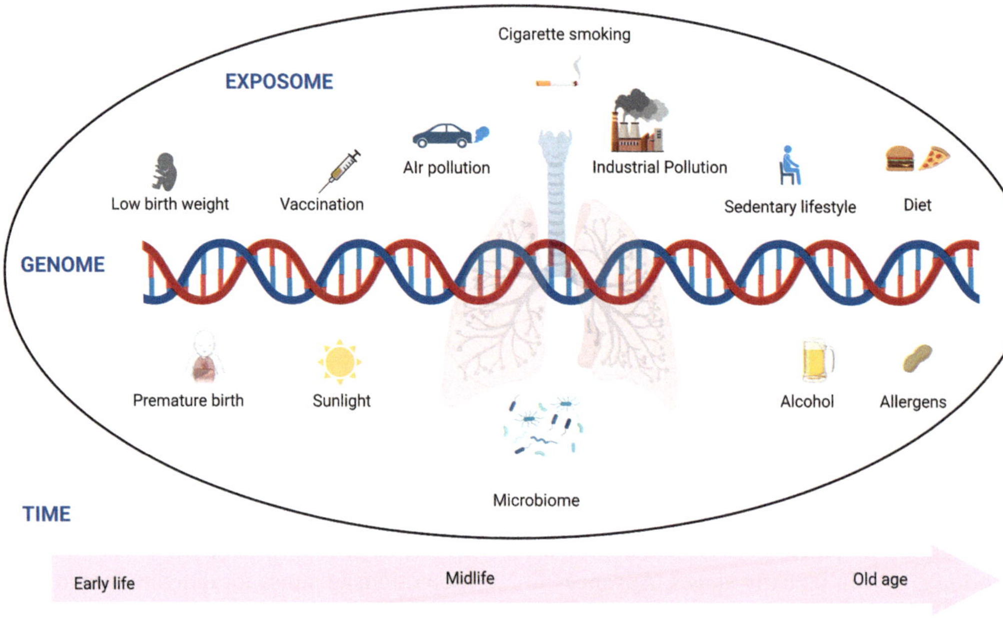

Fig. 24.2 The interplay between genes and environment on the progression of COPD over time

Translational medicine encompasses various disciplines such as genetics, epigenetics, transcriptomics, proteomics, and metabolomics, to facilitate the application of scientific discoveries from the laboratory to clinical practice (Fig. 24.1). This multidisciplinary approach aims to bridge the gap between basic research and patient care, facilitating the transfer of knowledge and advancements in these fields to improve diagnostics, treatments, and outcomes.

24.2 Etiopathogenesis

The concept of gene–environment interplay over time (GET omics) (Fig. 24.2) is gaining recognition as a significant factor in the development of COPD, with extensive studies focusing on the effects of tobacco smoking exposure since Fletcher and Peto's description of the disease's occurrence among young male smokers in London in 1977 [4]. Biomass fuel has also been implicated in low- and middle-income countries.

24.3 Genetics and COPD

Research in the field of COPD genetics has highlighted the significance of gene–environment interactions and identified specific genetic variants and associated genes that contribute to the development and risk of COPD. These findings have provided valuable insights into the underlying mechanisms and potential targets for therapeutic interventions.

Prior to 2008, most studies investigating the interrelation between genetic variants and COPD had limited statistical power and failed to establish a significant relationship, except for variants in GSTM1, TGFB1, TNF, and SOD3 [5]. Alpha-1 antitrypsin (AAT) deficiency had long been recognized as a well-established risk factor for COPD [6]. Early studies examining familial aggregation, linkage analysis, and association studies of heterozygotes for PI deficiency, as well as polymorphisms in EPHX1, GSTM1, and HMOX1, provided evidence suggesting the involvement of gene-environment interactions in COPD development [7–11] (Table 24.1).

Table 24.1 List of early studies with the genes studied and their associated phenotypes

S. No.	Study	Gene	Phenotype Associated
1	Boston Early Onset COPD [8]	Ch 12p, 2,1,19 Ch 1, 12,19 Ch 2q,1, 19,17 TNFα, SFTPB Thr131Ile HMOX1, Ch 19q TGFβ1	FEV1 FVC FEVI/FVC Spirometry
2	National Emphysema Treatment Trial [12]	EPHX1, LTBP4, SFTPB, TGF β1 GSTP1, EPHX1	Exercise capacity, diffusion capacity, dyspnea score, BODE score Upper lobe emphysema in CT
3	Normative ageing study	EPHX1	COPD susceptibility

However, subsequent research has identified ten variants in eight genes (GSTM1 null/present, CHRNA rs16969968, rs8034191, and rs1051730, ADAM33 rs612709, SP-D rs721917, TNF-α rs1800629, VDBP1 F, HMOX1 L allele, and HHIP rs13118928) that have been associated with an increased risk of COPD [13].

In a study conducted by Kang et al. in the Chinese Han population, polymorphism in PTCH1 gene was investigated in relation to COPD. The findings revealed that "A" allele of rs28491365 and "G" alleles of rs10512248 and rs28705285 were associated with an increased risk; conversely, "T/T" genotype of rs34695652 was associated with a decreased risk of COPD [14]. These results suggest that specific genetic variations within the PTCH1 gene may be responsible for COPD susceptibility and could serve as potential indicators for risk assessment in the Chinese Han population. Further research is needed to validate these associations and explore the underlying mechanisms involved.

Genes such as IREB2, MMP12, HHIP, RIN3, CHRNA3, CHRNA5, TGFB2, and FAM13A, which are associated with COPD pathogenesis or nicotine addiction, exhibit established protein–protein interactions, and have related functions in pathobiology [15]. Twenty-five differentially expressed genes (15 from the airway epithelium sample and 10 from whole lung tissue) were strongly differentiated COPD from healthy controls [16].

24.4 GWAS

The initial genome-wide association studies were carried out by Pillai et al. [17] and Wilk et al. [18]. Subsequently, the SpiroMeta consortium [19] and the CHARGE consortium [20] conducted meta-analyses of GWAS focusing on lung function with respect to COPD. The COPD Gene study successfully replicated the associations of certain genomic regions with COPD, including 4q31, 15q25, 4q22, and 14q32. Moreover, they identified associations of 11q22 and 1q41 with severe COPD, as well as 19q13, MIA, and CYP2A6 with smoking-related COPD.

Significant discoveries have been made through whole genome sequencing. Notably, Zhao and colleagues [21] conducted a study utilizing this technique and identified 22 previously unreported loci associated with COPD. Additionally, Prokopenko et al. conducted research that led to the identification of HHIP and SERPINA1 as important functional variants specifically related to severe COPD [22]. These findings represent significant advancements in our comprehension of the genetic underpinnings of COPD and provide potential targets for further investigation and therapeutic interventions.

To date, genetic data has been obtained from multiple sources, including the SpiroMeta consortium, CHARGE consortium, UK Biobank, Lung Exome Evaluation, ECLIPSE, GenKOLS study, COPD Gene study, NETT trial, NAS Study, and International COPD Genetics Consortium. A selected few have been listed below (Table 24.2). These studies have contributed valuable genetic information that enhances our understanding of COPD and its underlying genetic factors. By pooling data from various sources, researchers have been able to conduct comprehensive analyses and investigations into the genetic components of COPD, paving the way for advancements in diagnostics, treatments, and personalized medicine in the field of respiratory health.

Hereditary: The presence of COPD in monozygotic twins was observed in a study done on 22,422 Danish twin pairs [27]. The role of smoking exposure as a confounding factor in familial COPD cases cannot be ruled out. Heritability of COPD have been studied by Palmer [28] and Zhou [29] and was around 37%.

Lung function and genetics: Pulmonary function, respiratory capacity, and exercise capacity have been associated with polymorphisms in EPHX1, LTBP4, SFTPB, and TGFB1 in the NETT trial subjects [12]. Associations have been observed between single nucleotide polymorphisms (SNPs), specifically rs2828103 and rs875033, located on chromosome 6, and early onset COPD [30].

Table 24.2 Genome-wide studies since 2009 till date

S. No	Year	Author	Gene	Phenotype
1	2009	Pillai	CHRNA3/5, IREB2 on Ch 15q25	COPD association
2	2009	Framingham heart study, Wilk [18]	HHIP	FEV1/FVC
3	2010	CHARGE consortium, Hancock [20]	HHIP, FAM13A	FEV1/FVC
4	2010	SpiroMeta consortium, Repapi [19]	FAM 13 A	FEV1/FVC
5	2015	UK BiLEVE [23]	TET2, NPNT, HLA-DQB1/HLA-DQA2, KANSL1, TSEN54 RBM19, TBX5 NCAM 1, TEX41/PABPC1P2, NOL4L, LPPR5, DNAH8	Low FEV1 in never smokers Low FEV1 in heavy smokers Smoking behavior
6	2010	ECLIPSE [24, 25]	CHRNA3/5, IREB2, FAM13A, Ch 19 CHRNA 3/5, HHIP	COPD susceptibility Smoking, emphysema, airflow FEV1/FVC, lean body mass and exacerbation
7	2017	ICGC [26]	TGFβ2, PID1, RARB, **EEFSEC**, FAM13A, GTSCD, TET2, HHIP, HTR4, ADAM 19, **DSP**, AGER, ARMC2, ADGRG6, **SFTPD**, RIN3, THSD4, CHRNA 3/5, IREB2, IL 27, CCDC101, CFDP1, **MTCL1**, RAB4B/ EGLN2/CYP2A6 (bold are new loci identified in this study)	COPD association

Smoking: Cigarette smoking is well-acknowledged as a major risk factor for the development of chronic obstructive pulmonary disease (COPD). Recent studies have revealed a gene–smoking interaction involving the 15q25.1 region (CHRNB4) and the PI∗Z allele in SERPINA, highlighting the role of genetic variations in COPD susceptibility [31].

Interestingly, the occurrence of COPD in both smokers and non-smokers suggests the presence of alternative mechanisms in its pathogenesis. In experimental models, the expression of nine hub genes (COL14A1, SULF1, MOXD1, CXCL12, CHRNA1, COMP, POU2AF1, MMP11, THBS2) was found to be upregulated when exposed to cigarette smoke extract, indicating their potential as biomarkers for assessing the risk of developing COPD [5]. These findings suggest the need for further investigation to enhance our understanding of COPD development and progression in smokers.

Furthermore, the upregulation of these nine hub genes (COL14A1, SULF1, MOXD1, CXCL12, CHRNA1, COMP, POU2AF1, MMP11, THBS2) has been consistently observed in mouse emphysema models and BEAS-2B cells exposed to cigarette smoke extract, reinforcing their potential as biomarkers for assessing COPD risk in smokers. The identification of these upregulated genes provides a promising avenue for studying COPD pathogenesis and improving our ability to predict its development. Additionally, differential methylation in DNA, particularly in the promoter or body regions, has been associated with increased gene expression. This process is often heritable and can be influenced by environmental stimuli, further implicating the role of epigenetic mechanisms in COPD [32, 33]. Further research is necessary to comprehensively investigate these biomarkers and elucidate their roles in COPD pathogenesis, ultimately improving our understanding of this complex disease in smokers.

COPD and Asthma overlap (ACO): Eight novel signal associations (FAM105A, GLB1, PHB, TSLP, ILI7RD, C5orf56, HLA-DQB1) were found for asthma-COPD overlap [34]. These loci may represent type 2 inflammatory response.

Nutrition and COPD genes: Cachexia is defined as weight loss >5% in the last 12 months or body mass index (BMI < 20 kg/m^2). The presence of cachexia is associated with poor outcomes. EFNA2 and BAIAP2 genes have been associated with weight loss in patients with COPD [35].

Functional variants: A total of 22 variants with potential functional effects have been identified from the 82 GWAS loci in lung cell types [36]. Identifying the functional role of these variants in the pathogenesis of COPD will help in targeting future therapies.

Imaging and COPD: Emphysema is a characteristic feature of COPD. Genes associated with emphysema have been studied in the Western population. SNP in the new candidate gene (PIBF1) has been documented in the Korean population in all subjects (healthy and COPD subjects) [37].

Risk scoring: Polygenic risk scoring has been developed for predicting the COPD trajectory. Moll [38] and colleagues have identified a polygenic risk score, which when combined with clinical risk factors, is identified as a risk population. This scoring is also co-related with CT imaging and lung development. This can be applied to the younger generation to predict the risk of developing COPD or its severe forms and implement prevention strategies early on. It is postulated that four genes (DYNC1H1, COL6A5, CR1, and TNFAIP3) could serve as biomarkers for screening for COPD [39]. Through a meta-analysis that encompassed eight cohorts, PPIC and SERPINA 1 were identified as genes associated with severe COPD [40].

24.5 Transcriptomics and COPD

Transcriptomics focuses on the study of the complete set of RNA molecules transcribed from the genome in a specific cell or tissue. Transcriptomics studies in COPD involve the analysis of gene expression (Table 24.3) patterns, alternative splicing events, and non-coding RNA molecules such as microRNAs and have identified key markers involved in lung function, imaging, and response to therapy, molecular pathways and cel-

Table 24.3 Gene symbols of significant transcript probes and their associated outcomes

S. No	Gene symbols	Process involved
1	TMEM 219, ADAP1, SIDT 2, FBP1, TBXAS1, MLLT11, ARID 4B, FCGRT, SLC7A7, TUBA1B	Bronchodilator response
2	ACTB, ACTG1, ARPC2, CFL1, EEF1A1, EIF1, HLA—A, B, C, HMGN2	Exacerbation frequency
3	SEPT6, CRTAP, ME2, NMT, OCIAD2, RPARP-AS1, RPS12, RPS27A, RPS 29, CYFIP2	FEV1/FVC
4	BCL 10, CCDC186, CYBRD1, OSBPL8, RECQL, SLC25A43, SUMO2, TFAM, TMCO3, TOPORS	% Emphysema
5	ME2, FLT3LG, OFD1, PHF1, RASGRP2, RPARP-AS1, RPL30, RPS29, SEPT6, CHST 15	FEV1%

lular processes involved in COPD, including inflammation, oxidative stress, immune response, extracellular matrix remodeling, and apoptosis.

24.6 Metabolomics and COPD

Metabolomics involves the comprehensive analysis of small molecule metabolites, present in biological samples such as blood, urine, or exhaled breath condensate, which are involved in the altered metabolic pathways and act as biomarkers associated with the disease. These metabolites are identified using nuclear magnetic resonance and mass spectroscopy. By comparing the metabolite profiles of COPD patients to healthy individuals, researchers have identified distinct metabolic signatures associated with COPD development, progression, and exacerbations. A study by Zhang et al. showed that theophylline, palmitoylethanolamide, hypoxanthine, and CDH5 were elevated in advanced COPD [41].

Metabolomics studies have highlighted alterations in various metabolic pathways in COPD, including those involved in lipid metabolism, amino acid metabolism, energy metabolism, oxidative stress, and inflammation (Table 24.4) [42–45].

Table 24.4 Metabolic pathways and the associated metabolites significant in COPD

S. No	Metabolic pathway	Biomarker
1	Glycolysis and TCA cycle	Lactate, citrate, hexokinase, phosphofructokinase, pyruvate kinase, arginine, fumarate, glucose, adenosine, glutamine
2	Mitochondrial beta-oxidation and FA metabolism	Linoleic acid, choline, serine, carnitine, acetylcarnitine
3	Lipid metabolism	Betaine, choline, arachidonic acid, sphingolipids, phospholipids, triglycerides
4	Amino acid	L-glutamine, Pyroglutamic acid, tryptophan, tyrosine, Citrulline, creatinine, L-glutamine, L-Norvaline, lysine

Metabolomic profiling has shown promise in identifying potential biomarkers for COPD diagnosis, prognosis, and therapeutic response. These biomarkers can aid in early detection, personalized treatment approaches, and monitoring disease progression.

24.7 Proteomics and COPD

Proteomics, the large-scale study of proteins, focuses on the identification, quantification, and characterization of proteins and their modifications in biological samples. Proteomics analyses have revealed alterations in various protein classes and pathways implicated in COPD, including those related to inflammation, oxidative stress, tissue remodeling, immune response, and protease-antiprotease balance. Thus, they have provided valuable insights into the complex protein networks and pathways involved in the disease pathogenesis, progression, and response to treatment.

The following protein biomarkers have been associated with lung function, imaging, and exacerbation of COPD—sRAGE, IL-6, IL-8, Fibrinogen, CRP, SPD, CC16, APOA1 [46].

24.8 Conclusion

Thus, by integrating findings from genetics, epigenetics, transcriptomics, proteomics, and metabolomics, translational medicine strives to accelerate the translation of research findings into practical applications at the bedside, ultimately benefiting patients and advancing medical practice.

References

1. GOLD-REPORT-2022-v1.1-22Nov2021_WMV. 2022.
2. Gudi N, Mahmood A, Roy MP, Ravishankar NP, Verma A. Burden of COPD among population above 30 years in India: protocol for a systematic review and proposed meta-analysis. Can J Respir Ther. 2021;57:14.
3. Daniel R, Aggarwal P, Kalaivani M, Gupta S. Prevalence of chronic obstructive pulmonary disease in India: a systematic review and meta-analysis. Lung India. 2021;38:506–13.
4. Fletcher C, Peto R. The natural history of chronic airflow obstruction. Br Med J. 1977;1(6077):1645–8.
5. Chen L, Zhu D, Huang J, Zhang H, Zhou G, Zhong X. Identification of hub genes associated with COPD through integrated bioinformatics analysis. Int J COPD. 2022;17:439–56.
6. Laurell CB, Eriksson S. The electrophoretic α1-globulin pattern of serum in α1-antitrypsin deficiency. COPD. 2013;10:3–8.
7. Silverman EK, Chapman HA, Drazen JM, Weiss ST, Rosner B, Campbell EJ, et al. Genetic epidemiology of severe, early-onset chronic obstructive pulmonary disease. Risk to relatives for airflow obstruction and chronic bronchitis. Am J Respir Crit Care Med. 1998;157:1770–8.
8. Silverman EK, Palmer LJ, Mosley JD, Barth M, Senter JM, Brown A, et al. Genomewide linkage analysis of quantitative Spirometric phenotypes in severe early-onset chronic obstructive pulmonary disease. Am J Hum Genet. 2002;70:1229–39.
9. Dahl M, Nordestgaard BG, Lange P, Vestbo J, Tybjærg-Hansen A. Molecular diagnosis of intermediate and severe α1-antitrypsin deficiency: MZ individuals with chronic obstructive pulmonary disease may have lower lung function than MM individuals. Clin Chem. 2001;47(1):56–62.
10. Smith CAD, Harrison DJ. Association between polymorphism in gene for microsomal epoxide hydrolase and susceptibility to emphysema. Lancet. 1997;350(9078):630–3.
11. Harrison DJ, Cantlay AM, Rae F, Lamb D, Smith CAD. Frequency of glutathione S-transferase M1 deletion in smokers with emphysema and lung cancer. Hum Exp Toxicol. 1997;16(7):356–60. [cited 2023 Jun 3].
12. Hersh CP, DeMeo DL, Lazarus R, Celedón JC, Raby BA, Benditt JO, et al. Genetic association analysis of functional impairment in chronic obstructive pulmonary disease. Am J Respir Crit Care Med. 2006;173(9):977–84.
13. Liu C, Ran R, Li X, Liu G, Xie X, Li J. Genetic variants associated with chronic obstructive pulmonary disease risk: cumulative epidemiological evidence from meta-analyses and genome-wide association studies. Can Respir J. 2022;2022:1.
14. Kang X, Guo T, Liu L, Ding SZ, Lei C, Luo H. Association between PTCH1 gene polymorphisms and chronic obstructive pulmonary disease susceptibility in a Chinese Han population: a case-control study. Chin Med J. 2020;133(17):2071–7.
15. Gong L, Bates S, Li J, Qiao D, Glass K, Wei W, et al. Connecting COPD GWAS genes FAM13A controls TGFβ2 secretion by modulating AP-3 transport. Am J Respir Cell Mol Biol. 2021;65(5):532–43.
16. Roessler FK, Benedikter BJ, Schmeck B, Bar N. Novel computational analysis of large transcriptome datasets identifies sets of genes distinguishing chronic obstructive pulmonary disease from healthy lung samples. Sci Rep. 2021;11(1):10258.
17. Pillai SG, Ge D, Zhu G, Kong X, Shianna KV. A genome-wide association study in chronic obstructive pulmonary disease (COPD): identification of two major susceptibility loci. PLoS Genet. 2009;5(3):1000421.
18. Wilk JB, Chen TH, Gottlieb DJ, Walter RE, Nagle MW, Brandler BJ, et al. A genome-wide association study of pulmonary function measures in the Framingham heart study. PLoS Genet. 2009;5(3):e1000429.
19. Repapi E, Sayers I, Wain LV, Burton PR, Johnson T, Obeidat EN, et al. Genome-wide association study identifies five loci associated with lung function. Nat Genet. 2009;42(1):36.
20. Hancock DB, Eijgelsheim M, Wilk JB, Gharib SA, Loehr LR, Marciante KD, et al. Meta-analyses of genome-wide association studies identify multiple loci associated with pulmonary function. Nat Genet. 2009;42(1):30.
21. Zhao X, Qiao D, Yang C, Kasela S, Kim W, Ma Y, et al. Whole genome sequence analysis of pulmonary function and COPD in 19,996 multi-ethnic participants. Nat Commun. 2020;11(1):5182.
22. Prokopenko D, Sakornsakolpat P, Fier HL, Qiao D, Parker MM, McDonald MLN, et al. Whole-genome sequencing in severe chronic obstructive pulmonary disease. Am J Respir Cell Mol Biol. 2018;59(5):614–22.
23. Wain LV, Shrine N, Miller S, Jackson VE, Ntalla I, Artigas MS, et al. Novel insights into the genetics of smoking behaviour, lung function, and chronic obstructive pulmonary disease (UK BiLEVE): a genetic association study in UK biobank. Lancet Respir Med. 2015;3(10):769–81.

24. Pillai SG, Kong X, Edwards LD, Cho MH, Anderson WH, Coxson HO, et al. Loci identified by genome-wide association studies influence different disease-related phenotypes in chronic obstructive pulmonary disease. Am J Respir Crit Care Med. 2010;182(12):1498–505.
25. Siedlinski M, Cho MH, Bakke P, Gulsvik A, Lomas DA, Anderson W, et al. Genome-wide association study of smoking behaviours in patients with COPD. Thorax. 2011;66(10):894–902.
26. Hobbs BD, De Jong K, Lamontagne M, Bossé Y, Shrine N, Artigas MS, et al. Genetic loci associated with chronic obstructive pulmonary disease overlap with loci for lung function and pulmonary fibrosis. Nat Genet. 2017;49(3):426–32.
27. Ingebrigtsen T, Thomsen SF, Vestbo J, Van Der Sluis S, Kyvik KO, Silverman EK, et al. Genetic influences on chronic obstructive pulmonary disease—a twin study. Respir Med. 2010;104(12):1890–5.
28. Palmer L, Knuiman M, Divitini M, Burton P, James A, Bartholomew H, et al. Familial aggregation and heritability of adult lung function: results from the Busselton health study. Eur Respir J. 2001;17(4):696–702.
29. Zhou JJ, Cho MH, Castaldi PJ, Hersh CP, Silverman EK, Laird NM. Heritability of chronic obstructive pulmonary disease and related phenotypes in smokers. Am J Respir Crit Care Med. 2013;188(8):941.
30. Lee YJ, Choi S, Kwon SY, Lee Y, Lee JK, Heo EY, et al. A genome-wide association study in early COPD: identification of one major susceptibility loci. Int J COPD. 2020;15:2967–75.
31. Kim W, Prokopenko D, Sakornsakolpat P, Hobbs BD, Lutz SM, Hokanson JE, et al. Genome-wide gene-by-smoking interaction study of chronic obstructive pulmonary disease. Am J Epidemiol. 2021;190(5):875–85.
32. Eriksson Ström J, Kebede Merid S, Pourazar J, Blomberg A, Lindberg A, Ringh MV, et al. Chronic obstructive pulmonary disease is associated with epigenome-wide differential methylation in BAL lung cells. Am J Respir Cell Mol Biol. 2022;66(6):638–47.
33. Chen YC, Tsai YH, Wang CC, Liu SF, Chen TW, Fang WF, et al. Epigenome-wide association study on asthma and chronic obstructive pulmonary disease overlap reveals aberrant DNA methylations related to clinical phenotypes. Sci Rep. 2021;11(1):5022.
34. John C, Guyatt AL, Shrine N, Packer R, Olafsdottir TA, Liu J, et al. Genetic associations and architecture of asthma-COPD overlap. Chest. 2022;161(5):1155–66.
35. Lakshman Kumar P, Wilson AC, Rocco A, Cho MH, Wan E, Hobbs BD, et al. Genetic variation in genes regulating skeletal muscle regeneration and tissue remodelling associated with weight loss in chronic obstructive pulmonary disease. J Cachexia Sarcopenia Muscle. 2021;12(6):1803–17.
36. Benway CJ, Liu J, Guo F, Du F, Randell SH, Cho MH, et al. Chromatin landscapes of human lung cells predict potentially functional chronic obstructive pulmonary disease genome-wide association study variants. Am J Respir Cell Mol Biol. 2021;65(1):92–102.
37. Sin S, Choi HM, Lim J, Kim J, Bak SH, Choi SS, et al. A genome-wide association study of quantitative computed tomographic emphysema in Korean populations. Sci Rep. 2021;11(1):16692.
38. Moll M, Sakornsakolpat P, Shrine N, Hobbs BD, DeMeo DL, John C, et al. Chronic obstructive pulmonary disease and related phenotypes: polygenic risk scores in population-based and case-control cohorts. Lancet Respir Med. 2020;8(7):696–708.
39. Liu Y, Huang K, Wang Y, Hu E, Wei B, Song Z, et al. Integration of SNP disease association, eQTL, and enrichment analyses to identify risk SNPs and susceptibility genes in chronic obstructive pulmonary disease. Biomed Res Int. 2020;2020:1.
40. Busch R, Hobbs BD, Zhou J, Castaldi PJ, McGeachie MJ, Hardin ME, et al. Genetic association and risk scores in a chronic obstructive pulmonary disease meta-analysis of 16,707 subjects. Am J Respir Cell Mol Biol. 2017;57(1):35–46.
41. Zhang Z, Wang J, Li Y, Liu F, Chen L, He S, et al. Proteomics and metabolomics profiling reveal panels of circulating diagnostic biomarkers and molecular subtypes in stable COPD. Respir Res. 2023;24(1):73.
42. Adamko DJ, Nair P, Mayers I, Tsuyuki RT, Regush S, Rowe BH. Metabolomic profiling of asthma and chronic obstructive pulmonary disease: a pilot study differentiating diseases. J Allergy Clin Immunol. 2015;136(3):571–580.e3.
43. Kilk K, Aug A, Ottas A, Soomets U, Altraja S, Altraja A. Phenotyping of chronic obstructive pulmonary disease based on the integration of metabolomes and clinical characteristics. Int J Mol Sci. 2018;19(3):666.
44. Naz S, Kolmert J, Yang M, Reinke SN, Kamleh MA, Snowden S, et al. Metabolomics analysis identifies sex-associated metabotypes of oxidative stress and the autotaxin–lysoPA axis in COPD. Eur Respir J. 2017;49(6):1602322.
45. Cruickshank-Quinn CI, Jacobson S, Hughes G, Powell RL, Petrache I, Kechris K, et al. Metabolomics and transcriptomics pathway approach reveals outcome-specific perturbations in COPD. Sci Rep. 2018;8(1):17132.
46. Zemans RL, Jacobson S, Keene J, Kechris K, Miller BE, Tal-Singer R, et al. Multiple biomarkers predict disease severity, progression and mortality in COPD. Respir Res. 2017;18(1):117.

Biomaterials and Recent Advancements in Tailoring Approaches

25

Sam Ebenezer Rajadas, Christy Rosaline, Keerthiga Krubanithy, Rohini Tamilanban, and Anis Kumar Mani

25.1 Introduction and History of Biomaterial

Biomaterials encompass a diverse range of natural or artificial materials that can interact with biological systems and are utilized for the treatment, diagnosis, or repair of damaged tissues. Their valuableness extends to applications such as medical devices, drug delivery systems, and tissue engineering. An essential requirement for biomaterials is their ability to provide beneficial effects without causing adverse side effects upon implantation. The field of biomaterials has brought about a revolution in modern medicine by addressing critical medical challenges. These materials must possess biocompatibility, ensuring that they do not elicit negative reactions within the body. Additionally, they need to exhibit suitable mechanical, physical, and chemical properties to fulfil the specific requirements of the intended application. Biomaterials have significantly enhanced patient care by enabling the development of advanced medical devices. Examples include artificial joints, pacemakers, and dental implants, which have greatly improved the quality of life for individuals with various medical conditions. Furthermore, biomaterials play a crucial role in tissue engineering, which involves the creation of functional biological substitutes for damaged tissues or organs. These materials can provide structural support and act as scaffolds for cellular growth, while also facilitating the controlled release of bioactive molecules that promote tissue regeneration. In the realm of drug delivery, biomaterials offer innovative solutions. They can be engineered to provide controlled and targeted release of pharmaceutical agents, optimizing therapeutic outcomes, and minimizing side effects. The rapid growth of the biomaterials field underscores its potential to continue transforming modern medicine and significantly enhance patients' quality of life. Ongoing research and advancements hold promise for further innovations in this exciting discipline.

Evidence for prehistorical biomaterial usage was found in the excavations from the Neanderthal era. Wooden materials were used by them as dental implants. Such evidence was also found in the Egyptian mummies in the form of sutures made of animal tendons. Metallic biomaterials like

S. E. Rajadas (✉)
Centre for Drug Discovery and Development, Sathyabama Institute of Science and Technology, Chennai, Tamil Nadu, India

C. Rosaline
Achira Labs Pvt. Ltd, Bengaluru, Karnataka, India

K. Krubanithy
Centre for Drug Discovery and Development, Sathyabama Institute of Science and Technology, Chennai, Tamil Nadu, India

Department of Biotechnology, VSB Engineering College, Karur, India

R. Tamilanban
Department of Microbiology, Mannnar Thirumalai Naicker College, Madurai, Tamil Nadu, India

A. K. Mani
Department of Biotechnology, VSB Engineering College, Karur, India

K. Parthasarathy, R. Manikkam (eds.), *Translational Research in Biomedical Sciences: Recent Progress and Future Prospects*, https://doi.org/10.1007/978-981-97-1777-4_25

gold and silver were frequently used in Europe during the sixteenth century for dental-related illnesses. Bone fractures were treated using iron strings. However, the terminology of biomaterial got familiarized during the late eighteenth century. Interdisciplinary contribution of various fields of science and medicine has extended the role of biomaterials as medical implants, wound healing, tissue regeneration, drug delivery systems, and molecular probes in biosensors [1, 2]. Development of suitable biomaterials for hip and knee prostheses started in 1920 using cemented ivory ball and successful hip biomaterial was first reported in the year 1968–1972 using polymethyl methacrylate. Similarly, vascular regeneration in case of blood vessel damage was first initiated using a metal tube to connect it. Later insights into the cell attachment and proliferation around the biomaterials have resulted in various porous biomaterials that aid in tissue regeneration [3].

25.2 Classification of Biomaterials

Based on their chemical nature the biomaterials are classified as follows:

1. Polymers.
2. Composites.
3. Bioceramics.
4. Metals.

25.2.1 Composites

Composite biomaterials are prepared by combining two or more distinct constituent materials or phases either on microscopic or larger scales. Cellulose-reinforced composites (CRC) are green composites as it is fabricated using natural materials that have minimal effect on the environment when compared to other composites. These green composites are produced using techniques such as hand lay-up, extrusion, resin-transfer moulding, injection moulding, and compression moulding techniques [4]. These CRCs are widely used in biomedical applications such as skin electronics [4], dental tissue regeneration [5], and wound healing [6].

25.2.2 Polymers

Polymers are repetitive structures of monomeric units that are joint together to form larger structures. The biocompatible, bioactive, biodegradable, and wettable nature of the polymers qualifies them to be a biomaterial [7]. Polymers can be used to prepare biomaterials of many forms such as films, 3D scaffolds, hydrogels, and 3D printed implants [8–11].

25.2.2.1 Natural Polymers

Natural polymeric biomaterials are prepared from natural proteins, polysaccharides, and/or their associated molecules. This includes collagen, fibronectin, fibrin, laminin, keratin, chitosan, alginate, chitin, and various gums [7]. The major advantage is biocompatibility and low chances of graft rejection. The limitations include low mechanical strength, increased chances of microbial contamination, development of allergies, and poor possibilities of establishing tailoring approaches (Table 25.1).

25.2.2.2 Synthetic Polymers

Synthetic polymers (SPs) are prepared using synthetic chemicals. It is considered a good alternative to natural polymers when the patient is allergic. SPs have good mechanical stability and poor immunogenicity with limited biodegradability. However, it can be engineered to be degrad-

Table 25.1 Polymer-biomaterials: types and examples [12]

Natural polymer	• Protein: collagen, fibronectin, fibrin, silk fibroin • Polysaccharides: hyaluronan, alginate, chitosan, chitin
Synthetic polymers	• Alpha polyesters: polyglycolic and polylactic acids • Aliphatic polyesters
Nondegradable polymers	• Poly(ethylene terephthalate) (PET) is used in sutures and meshes • Cotton, silk and linen—nondegradable natural polymers
Degradable polymers	• Polylactic acid (PLA), polylactic acid-co-glycolic acid (PLGA) and polyglycolic acid (PGA)
Ionomers	• Cationic, anionic or zwitterionic monomers

able using various approaches that are discussed later in this chapter. Aliphatic polyester polymers are one such kind. Its degradation is programmable and the degradation products could be easily removed from the physiological system [13]. Other commonly used polymers are polylactic acid (PLA), polyglycolic acid (PGA), polyvinyl alcohol (PVA), polycaprolactone (PCL), and polylactic-co-glycolic acid (PLGA) [7]. These polymers can also be used as drug and vaccine-carrying vehicles [14]. PLA and PGA are combined to form poly alpha-hydroxy esters that are non-immunogenic, non-toxic and have good mechanical strength. It is commonly considered for the fabrication of controlled nano-delivery systems. PGA is synthesized from glycolide produced during sugarcane fermentation [15]. PLGA is a polymer made of lactic acid and glycolic acid forming a stern cord structure. It is used in drug delivery, biosensor construction, and tissue engineering. The desirable properties of PLGA could be easily engineered based on the need by altering the proportion of the monomer components [15]. Numerous surface micropores facilitating nutrient permeability, cell attachment, and proliferation are important advantages of PLGA [16]. Polyanhydride polymers are synthesized by activating aromatic dicarboxylic acids using acetic anhydride under vacuum and heat. Mechanical strength, biocompatibility, and prolonged degradation time are commendable with these polymers [17]. PCL has significant biocompatibility and bioabsorbable nature with sustained degradation capacity [18]. The breakdown products of PCL are found to be cleared from the physiological system through macrophages and giant cells [19]. In contrast, though PVA has all desirable properties, its poor degradation limits its usage as a biomaterial. However, it can be cross-linked with other chemical and biological moieties to synthesize hydrogels [19].

25.2.2.3 Biomedical Foams (BMF)

Biomedical Foams are produced using a variety of materials, including silicone, polyurethane, and other polymers. It has a wide range of medical applications, including wound care, surgical implants, drug delivery, and tissue engineering. The unique properties of biomedical foam make it an ideal material for these applications. For example, biomedical foam can be designed to be biocompatible, meaning that it does not cause an adverse reaction when it interacts with living tissues. Biomedical foam can also be made to be absorbent, elastic, or rigid, depending on the needs of the application. The application of these foams includes porous biomedical and prostheses, 3D platforms, and scaffolds as in vitro cell growth support, and drug delivery [20].

BMF is generally produced using a variety of materials that include metals (titanium) [21], ceramics (hydroxyapatite and α—and β -tricalcium phosphate) [22], polymers (polyurethanes) [23], and composites containing collagen and apatites [22]. These materials are converted to BMFs by traditional (gas foaming, phase separation, and freeze-drying techniques) and advanced manufacturing processes.

25.2.3 Bioceramics

Bioceramic biomaterials are prepared by covalent or ionic binding of metallic and non-metallic elements. Owing to its mechanical properties, these biomaterials are commonly used in implants like hip prostheses, bone grafts, and artificial tendons. Just like any other biomaterials, ceramics also should not be toxic, allergic, or carcinogenic while being functional and compatible [24]. Ceramic biomaterials are classified into three based on the nature of interaction and resorbable nature [25].

1. Inert and Non-absorbable: Alumina, carbon, silicon nitride, and zirconia.
2. Semi-reactive/semi-inert/semi-bioactive: Glass ceramic and hydroxyapatite.
3. Resorbable/biodegradable/non-inert: Calcium aluminate and Calcium phosphate.

25.2.4 Metals

Metallic biomaterials are commonly used where mechanical strength and resistance are needed as in the cases of orthopaedic devices. This includes stainless steel, titanium and its alloys, cobalt-chrome alloys, gold, silver, and platinum. Stainless steel and alloys of titanium and cobalt are used in joint replacements, bone fracture fixations heart valves, dental implants, and coronary stents. Gold is used in dental fillings and crowns. Silver is used in pacemaker wires, sutures, and dental amalgams. Platinum is used in neural stimulation devices.

25.3 Natural Sources of Biomaterials

Biomaterials are produced from several natural sources such as insects, fishes, shells, corals, and animals. Spider's silk component—spidroin is used as biomaterial coating on implants. It enables the attachment and differentiation of cells with surface topology favourable for filopodia protrusion and attachment [26]. Similarly, silk from silkworm act as the source of polylactic acid and collagen [27]. Its cocoon is made of two proteins, fibroin and sericin. The former makes the structural component while the latter acts as a glue to interconnect the former. Fibroin is fibrous and is made of orderly arranged heavy and light chains linked through disulfide bonds at the C-terminal end. Silk fibroins are used as biomaterials in the form of surgical sutures. Besides, recent insights have shown the same to be a potent material for tissue regeneration [28], stem-cell-based tissue engineering [29], wound healing [29], and drug delivery [30]. Though fibroins are a mostly used biomaterial, studies have also shown the usefulness of sericin. Sericin hydrogels fabricated with biological molecules for effective cell proliferation have been developed by tailoring them with human acidic fibroblast growth factor (FGF1) [31].

Interestingly, biomaterials can also be extracted from the eggs. Eggshells, eggshell membranes, and egg white hold various components in them that act as precursors of biomaterials. The calcium carbonate of eggshells is a precursor for hydroxyapatite and calcium phosphate. Collagen and hyaluronic acid can be extracted from egg shell membranes while the egg white is being scientifically examined as a potent hydrogel scaffold [32]. Like eggshells bone regeneration-associated biomaterials can be extracted from mollusc shells, corals, and fish bones [33].

So far animals or their product-associated biomaterial were discussed, however, plants also can provide us with biomaterials. One such is nanocellulose which could be used in drug delivery, 3D cell culturing, bioactive implants, scaffold formation, and in the diagnosis of diseases [4, 34, 35]. Nanocellulose can be extracted from palm tree residues after acid-hydrolysis [36].

25.4 Properties of Biomaterials

The desirable properties of a biomaterial will vary based on the purpose it is used. For example, a biomaterial for hip replacement should have good mechanical strength and the one that is used for drug delivery should have good biodegradability. Hence it is engineered as per the requirements and specifications demanded by the healthcare provider. The general properties of biomaterials are as follows:

1. Physio-chemical properties and
2. Biological properties.

Physio-chemical properties include both surfaces as well as bulk properties. Bulk properties describe its shape-size, mechanical properties, corrosion, degradation, and porosity. Mechanical properties include elasticity, hardness, fracture strength, and fracture toughness. Besides, providing structural stability, mechanical properties were also found to influence the cell behaviours, degradability, and steering of cell-signalling pathways [37]. Surface properties include surface charges, hydrophilicity, surface free energy, surface topography, degradability, and protein absorption [38]. Hydrophilicity determines the interaction of biological molecules and cells with the biomaterial. It is determined by the contact angle exhibited by the water droplet on its surface. Lesser the angle more the hydrophilicity. If the contact angle is above 90°, it could be labelled as hydrophobic material. Surface topography plays a vital role in determining the interaction of cells with biomaterials. It can be controlled by simpler methods like polishing, anodization, and ion implantation methods. The roughness will have a differential impact on different types of cells by favouring one while limiting the other. Increased roughness was found to be good for the proliferation of osteoblast cells while limiting leucocytes, monocytes, and keratinocytes [39–41]. Protein absorption is the primary event that occurs after a biomaterial is implanted. Absorbed protein and its stability influence the cascade of other events like cell adhesion and proliferation [38].

Biological properties determine whether a biomaterial is biocompatible, immunotolerant, and non-toxic. Biocompatibility describes the ability of the biomaterial to exist in the host physiological system without harming or getting rejected by it. The biocompatibility of a biomaterial can be assessed by performing in vitro and in vivo tests. In vitro tests are done on the cell lines by enumerating the total percentage of viable cells after a period of exposure. In addition, the cell proliferation can also be tested using microscopical methods like scanning electron microscope (SEM) and biochemical methods like MTT assay (3-[4,5-dimethylthiazol-2-yl]-2,5 diphenyl tetrazolium bromide). In vitro tests also include hemocompatibility by performing a haemolysis assay. In vivo tests are done on animal models ranging from small invertebrates and insect larvae to vertebrate animals like rabbits. In vivo toxicity tests include sensitization, irritation, intracutaneous reactivity, systemic—Acute toxicity, sub-chronic toxicity, genotoxicity, hemocompatibility, carcinogenicity, toxicokinetics, and immunotoxicity. The immunological response study includes an assessment of acute and chronic inflammation, tissue granulation, and fibrous encapsulation in response to the implanted biomaterial [42].

25.5 Tailoring Approaches

As stated earlier, a perfect biomaterial should mimic the natural biological system and aid in the desirable, selective proliferation of cells without compromising the mechanical and structural properties. Scaffolds are particularly tailored for better biodegradability, biomimicry, bioactivity (cell adhesion and differentiation), and unaltered transport of nutrients and gases. Tailoring of biomaterials is done to achieve such effects in addition to customization of other physio-chemical parameters as per the needs of the specific cases. Predominantly tailoring is done by incorporating biological factors and by modifying the structural parameters that aid in the proliferation of specific cells and the inflow of nutrients for cell growth, respectively [43, 44]. While doing so, the proliferation of undesirable cells is also limited. The geometry of the scaffolds is also found to play a vital role in the regeneration of tissues. Bone regeneration was found to be increased when the scaffolds with concave surfaces are used in contrast to those with convex and planar surfaces [45]. Tailoring approaches also include bioprinting or dispensing of the specific cell onto the specified site of scaffolds to enhance the bio-mimicking property of 3D printing or additive manufacturing processes. Using this method, either individual cells or cell aggregates are dispensed using three categories of technologies, namely, jet-based techniques, robotic dispensing techniques, and laser-induced forward transfer [46].

Bio-contact properties of biomaterials also influence cell attachment and proliferation. It can be engineered through surface engineering methods that are broadly classified as physio-chemical methods and biological methods. The former includes acid etching/oxidation, ionizing irradiation treatments, photolithography, and surface grafting of functional groups while the latter includes decoration of biomaterials surface with biological agents [47]. Biological methods include a coating or immobilization of either cell adhesion proteins (collagen, fibronectin, laminin or vitronectin) or polymer-peptide molecules (poly-Llysine with arginine-glycine-aspartic acid—PLL-RGD complex) [48, 49]. These methods cause increased cell attachment proliferation and migration in experiment set-up using three T3 cells [50]. The elasticity of the biomaterials also influences the regulation of cellular activity, functions, and lineage commitment for tissue generation [51]. Plasticity engineering is done by changing the contents while preparing the reinforced composites. It also helps to attain the desired mechanical strength of the composites as in certain cases polylactic-co-glycolic acid (PLGA) reinforced with titanium oxides is prepared [52]. The bioactivity of the polymers is engineered by three methods that include a direct coating of ECM-derived molecules, functionalization of surfaces with ECM circulating molecules and coating of the surface with antibodies for selective binding of molecules [12]. The porosity of biomaterials plays a vital role in cell attachment, migration, vascularization, and extracellular matrix (ECM) orientation. Porosity determines how far the biomaterials are like the native ECM of the target tissue or organ. It depends on the careful fabrication of the pore size, shape, volume fraction, interconnectivity, and orientation [53]. Porosity also enables easier biodegradation of the biomaterial due to its larger surface-volume ratio and increased biological interactive sites.

25.5.1 Biomaterial Tailoring for Nerve Regeneration

Nerve-related disorders wreak millions of people across the globe irrespective of socio-economical and geographical status causing a reduction in life quality and economic growth [54]. The two parts of the nervous system—peripheral and central systems differ. The peripheral system (PNS) regenerates and gets repaired post-trauma but the central nervous system (CNS) lacks this potential. Neurons do not enter mitosis thereby generation of new cells at the damage site is not possible. However, it can rehabilitate or sprout in certain conditions [54]. This is due to the presence of certain glycoproteins that inhibits regeneration and the absence of limited macrophage infiltration. Macrophages remove the myelin from the nerve damage site causing a delay in regeneration [55]. Until recently, the smaller nerve damage is treated by end-to-end surgical reconnection and the larger damage leaving more gaps between the nerves is treated through autologous nerve grafting [15].

Recent advancements in the arena of tissue engineering have made the treatment easier with more positive outcomes. Through nerve tissue engineering approaches, nerve guidance channels (NGC) are produced. NGCs act like a connection tube that connects the gap in the damaged nerve. Tailoring the biomaterials used for the NGC construction helps in quicker healing by contributing good mechanical strength, biocompatibility, biodegradation, and permeability. These NGCs are prepared using various kinds of synthetic polymers [54]. These polymers by themselves have biomimicking properties and could be engineered to contain biological materials. Laminin-coated collagen-integrated PGA mesh has shown to have delayed degradation and enhanced axonal elongation is one of such kind [56]. Less hydrophilicity of these synthetic polymers is overcome by using overlaying approaches that are used to deposit the biomolecules like heparin, collagen, nerve growth factors, epidermal growth factors, and chitosan [57–59]. This will cause a reduction in the contact angle and increased proliferation of fibroblast and Schwann cells at its surface [60]. Besides previously mentioned biological properties, a biomaterial used in nerve regeneration should also have electrical conduction properties to facilitate the conduction of nerve impulses. Some of the biomaterials like PLGA lack it. The addition of polypyrrole enhanced this property with a significant effect on the growth, and differentiation of hippocampal neurons [61]. Similarly, the PCL-Chitosan coated with gold also should have good conductivity [62].

Certain kinds of porous scaffolds are prepared using mammalian ECM integrated with type-I collagen and or other molecules like laminin, fibrin, fibronectin, and vitronectin are used to mimic the peripheral nerve-associated ECM and to stimulate the regeneration of nerves [63]. To ensure protein permeability, the tube walls are prepared with a pore size of 50 nm larger. The pores must be permeable to myofibroblast while non-permeable to fibrous tissue infiltration to ensure limited scar formation. This is achieved by gradient pore fabrication and control of pore orientation besides pore size [64, 65]. Such a kind of BMFs could be synthesized by spinning technique combined with a lyophilization process done by a centrifugal casting process [66]. The mechanical strength is increased by tailoring the collagen-binding neurotropic factor 3 that incorporates collagen to PPF biomaterial. This resulted in increased mechanical strength when compared to collagen alone.

Neuroinflammation is a major pathological factor associated with diseases related to both the central nervous system and the peripheral nervous system [44]. The components of polymeric biomaterials that are intended to resemble the brain ECM are incorporated with certain functionalized proteins to modulate the inflammatory responses in the brain. Glyco-functionalized type-I collagen such as the neo glycosylated one caused proliferation as well as differentiation of neuroblastoma F11 cells [43] thus paving the way for possible modulation of inflammatory response. Control of inflammation at the site of injury is limited by fabricating the scaffold NGCs with anti-inflammatory agents to enable its sustained release. In a study, NGCs made of poly anhydride polymers are incorporated with salicylic acid resulting in reduced inflammation and reduced scar formation in the experimental mice models.

25.5.2 Biomaterial Tailoring for Dental Illness

Biomaterials are included in the treatment of dental illnesses for quite a long period. It has been used as membranes, hydrogels (injectables), and matrices. Prevention of epithelial cell proliferation and induction of selective periodontal cells to replace defective tissues are the objectives of guided tissue regeneration in periodontal tissue engineering. This is done by using non-resorbable and resorbable membranes made of polytetrafluoroethylene (PTFE) or titanium and polymers (natural or synthetic), respectively [67]. As a tailoring approach, PTFE membranes coated with collagen are implanted with the bone graft from the patient to prevent ridge resorption and promote bone regeneration. High-density PTFE with reduced pore size was also attempted successfully to prevent bacterial infiltration [68]. Similarly, titanium-ceramic composites are used for efficient osteointegration [69]. PEGylated fibrin hydrogels are used to encapsulate dental stem cells to stimulate the proliferation of cells and pulp regeneration in periodontal deformities [70]. But the major drawback with hydrogels is the lack of mechanical and bio-inert properties. Similar to nerve regeneration strategies, proteo-polysaccharide 3D scaffold matrices are also used to induce infiltration and proliferation of dental pulp stem cells [71]. 3D composites prepared with collagen, chondroitin, hydroxyapatite, and tricalcium phosphate exhibited increased adhesion of osteoblasts [72, 73]. Likewise, cell stimulation was also reported in response to mechanical stimulation even though the underlying mechanism is not clear [67].

25.5.3 Biomaterial Tailoring for Wound Healing

The wound healing process involves three major steps: haemostasis, inflammation, proliferation and maturation. Among these, the proliferation includes epidermal resurfacing, fibroplasia, angiogenesis, and the development of ECM. These events influenced by local and systemic factors determine the time taken for wound healing, formation of scars and regeneration of damaged tissues [74, 75]. Hence, this process must be engineered to achieve earlier healing, and less scar formation while limiting the secondary bacterial infections that could otherwise cause additional damage to the tissues. The wound dressing materials and ointments are being tailored with many biological factors that promote fibroplasia while being antimicrobial. One such scientific intervention resulted in the invention of wound dressing material prepared from bacterial cellulose hydrogel incorporated with thymol—a plant-based natural monoterpenoid phenol derivative of p-Cymene. It was shown to cause rapid closure of third degree burns with antimicrobial activity [6] may be due to enhanced adhesion of cells aided by mechanical interlocking [76].

25.5.4 Biomaterial Tailoring for Metabolic Diseases

Diabetes mellitus (DM) is a major metabolism-associated disorder characterized by increased glucose levels in blood initially and in urine at advanced stages of the disease. Based on the mechanism, it is classified into type I and II. Type-I DM is caused by the destruction of β-cells by own immune system—a condition called autoimmunity. Using a tissue engineering approach, the destructed β-cells could be replaced so that the insulin level could be maintained to maintain blood glucose level. Protecting these cells from the body's immune system is a major challenge against this strategy. To prevent the rejection of these cellular transplants, immunoisolation is done by encapsulating the cells with suitable biomaterials like alginate that are semi-permeable. It blocks the β-cell–immune cell interaction thereby preventing auto-immune destruction [77]. However, these cells are still subjected to attack by reactive oxygen species (ROS) a major factor involved in the activation of inflammation and lead to ROS-mediated destruction of transplants. This is circumvented by incorporating cerium oxide nanoparticles (CONPs)—a free radical scavenger with alginates by overlaying it as multiple layers while maintaining the transfer of nutrients and insulin [78].

Prolonged exposure of β-cells to fatty acids causes lipotoxicity followed by impaired autophagy that further led to type-II diabetes. The consequence of impaired autophagy is cell dysfunction caused by the accumulation of intracellular debris containing cell organelles and proteins causing. This is characterized by intracellular lysosomal pH variation. Restoration of lysosomal pH was synthetically done by treating the cells with PLGA nanoparticles by acidification with the observable reversion of β-cells functioning [79].

25.5.5 Biomaterial Tailoring for Cancer Therapy

Besides relying on radiation and chemotherapy, cancer treatment has evolved to the extent of utilizing immunological parameters to treat cancer patients in an efficient way leading to an increased chance of survival. Bioengineering approaches are being carried out tremendously to achieve anti-cancer immunity by proper delivery of immunomodulatory agents to engineer immune cells. This includes the construction of immune-modulating scaffolds [80]. These tailored biomaterials enhance patients' immunity to prevent recurrence and metastasis rather than directly hitting the cancer cells [81] but act as delivery vehicles of immune modulators and immune checkpoint blockade and chimeric antigen receptor T-cells.

It functions in either of the following ways [80],

1. Delivering therapeutics to antigen-presenting cells (APCs).
2. Delivering therapeutics to tumour microenvironment (TME).
3. Engineering of anti-cancer immune cells and
4. Constructing immunomodulatory scaffolds.

The immune modulators include cytokines, adjuvants, antigens, antibodies, and immune checkpoint inhibitors that could be delivered using formulations or delivery systems such as lipids, polymeric and metallic nanoparticles, virus-like particles, scaffolds, and microneedles [80].

25.6 Summary

The use of biomaterials is known for many centuries. The desirable properties of biomaterials vary based on the need from case to case. In general, a biomaterial should be compatible and non-toxic while enabling cell adhesion and proliferation. As the purpose varies, it must be customized or tailored to meet the specific demand. Tailoring is done by changing the surface characteristics, chemical properties, and by incorporating or decorating the biomaterials with biological molecules like chemokines and therapeutic agents.

References

1. National institute of biomedical imaging and bioengineering. Biomaterials. 2017.
2. Vallet-Regí M. Evolution of biomaterials. Front Mater. 2022;9:9. https://doi.org/10.3389/fmats.2022.864016.
3. Ratner BD, Zhang G. 1.1.2- A history of biomaterials. In: Wagner WR, Sakiyama-Elbert SE,

Zhang G, Yaszemski MJ, editors. Biomaterials science. 4th ed. Academic Press; 2020. p. 21–34. https://www.sciencedirect.com/science/article/pii/B9780128161371000027.
4. Khalid MY, Al Rashid A, Arif ZU, Ahmed W, Arshad H. Recent advances in nanocellulose-based different biomaterials: types, properties, and emerging applications. J Mater Res Technol. 2021;14:2601–23. https://www.sciencedirect.com/science/article/pii/S2238785421007924.
5. Kalia S, Dufresne A, Cherian BM, Kaith BS, Avérous L, Njuguna J, et al. Cellulose-based bio- and nanocomposites: a review. Int J Polym Sci. 2011;2011:837875. https://doi.org/10.1155/2011/837875.
6. Jiji S, Udhayakumar S, Rose C, Muralidharan C, Kadirvelu K. Thymol enriched bacterial cellulose hydrogel as effective material for third degree burn wound repair. Int J Biol Macromol. 2019;122:452–60. https://www.sciencedirect.com/science/article/pii/S0141813018350037.
7. Kalirajan C, Dukle A, Nathanael AJ, Oh TH, Manivasagam G. A critical review on polymeric biomaterials for biomedical applications. Polymers (Basel). 2021;13(17):3015. https://www.mdpi.com/2073-4360/13/17/3015.
8. Chen X, Zhou L, Xu H, Yamamoto M, Shinoda M, Kishimoto M, et al. Effect of the application of a dehydrothermal treatment on the structure and the mechanical properties of collagen film. Materials. 2020;13(2):377. https://www.mdpi.com/1996-1944/13/2/377.
9. Yan R, Chen Y, Gu Y, Tang C, Huang J, Hu Y, et al. A collagen-coated sponge silk scaffold for functional meniscus regeneration. J Tissue Eng Regen Med. 2019;13(2):156–73. https://doi.org/10.1002/term.2777.
10. Gao Q, Niu X, Shao L, Zhou L, Lin Z, Sun A, et al. 3D printing of complex GelMA-based scaffolds with nanoclay. Biofabrication. 2019;11(3):035006. https://doi.org/10.1088/1758-5090/ab0cf6.
11. Lin XX, Qing ZG, Jie LX, Pin ZX, Wang W, Jun CZ, et al. Solution blowing of chitosan/PLA/PEG hydrogel nanofibers for wound dressing. Fibers Polym. 2016;17(2):205–11. https://doi.org/10.1007/s12221-016-5800-9.
12. Parisi L, Toffoli A, Ghiacci G, Macaluso GM. Tailoring the interface of biomaterials to design effective scaffolds. J Funct Biomater. 2018;9(3):50. https://www.mdpi.com/2079-4983/9/3/50.
13. Hutmacher DW, Goh JC, Teoh SH. An introduction to biodegradable materials for tissue engineering applications. Ann Acad Med Singap. 2001;30(2):183–91. http://europepmc.org/abstract/MED/11379417.
14. Praphakar RA, Rajadas SE, Vignesh S, Shakila H, Rajan M. Versatile pH-responsive Chitosan-g-Polycaprolactone/Maleic anhydride—isoniazid polymeric micelle to improve the bioavailability of tuberculosis multidrugs. ACS Appl Bio Mater. 2019;2:1931.
15. Houschyar KS, Momeni A, Pyles MN, Cha JY, Maan ZN, Duscher D, et al. The role of current techniques and concepts in peripheral nerve repair. Plast Surg Int. 2016;2016:4175293. https://doi.org/10.1155/2016/4175293.
16. Ferreira CL, Valente CA, Zanini ML, Sgarioni B, Ferreira Tondo PH, Chagastelles PC, et al. Biocompatible PCL/PLGA/polypyrrole composites for regenerating nerves. Macromol Symp. 2019;383(1):1800028. https://doi.org/10.1002/masy.201800028.
17. Ratheesh G, Venugopal JR, Chinappan A, Ezhilarasu H, Sadiq A, Ramakrishna S. 3D fabrication of polymeric scaffolds for regenerative therapy. ACS Biomater Sci Eng. 2017;3(7):1175–94. https://doi.org/10.1021/acsbiomaterials.6b00370.
18. Palamà IE, Arcadio V, D'Amone S, Biasiucci M, Gigli G, Cortese B. Therapeutic PCL scaffold for reparation of resected osteosarcoma defect. Sci Rep. 2017;7(1):12672. https://doi.org/10.1038/s41598-017-12824-3.
19. Chang SH, Lee HJ, Park S, Kim Y, Jeong B. Fast degradable polycaprolactone for drug delivery. Biomacromolecules. 2018;19(6):2302–7. https://doi.org/10.1021/acs.biomac.8b00266.
20. Salerno A, Netti PA. 1- Introduction to biomedical foams. In: Netti PA, editor. Biomedical foams for tissue engineering applications. Woodhead Publishing; 2014. p. 3–39. https://www.sciencedirect.com/science/article/pii/B9780857096968500012.
21. Sumita M, Hanawa T, Teoh SH. Development of nitrogen-containing nickel-free austenitic stainless steels for metallic biomaterials—review. Mater Sci Eng C Mater Biol Appl. 2004;24(6):753–60. https://www.sciencedirect.com/science/article/pii/S0928493104001092.
22. Hoppe A, Güldal NS, Boccaccini AR. A review of the biological response to ionic dissolution products from bioactive glasses and glass-ceramics. Biomaterials. 2011;32(11):2757–74. https://www.sciencedirect.com/science/article/pii/S0142961211000056.
23. Wendels S, Avérous L. Biobased polyurethanes for biomedical applications. Bioact Mater. 2021;6:1083–106.
24. Shekhawat D, Singh A, Banerjee MK, Singh T, Patnaik A. Bioceramic composites for orthopaedic applications: a comprehensive review of mechanical, biological, and microstructural properties. Ceram Int. 2021;47(3):3013–30. https://www.sciencedirect.com/science/article/pii/S0272884220329187.
25. Jiann Chong ET, Ng JW, Lee PC. Classification and medical applications of biomaterials–a mini review. BIO Integr. 2022;4:1.
26. Leal-Egaña A, Lang G, Mauerer C, Wickinghoff J, Weber M, Geimer S, et al. Interactions of fibroblasts with different morphologies made of an engineered spider silk protein. Adv Eng Mater. 2012;14(3):B67–75. https://doi.org/10.1002/adem.201180072.

27. Altman GH, Diaz F, Jakuba C, Calabro T, Horan RL, Chen J, et al. Silk-based biomaterials. Biomaterials. 2003;24(3):401–16. https://www.sciencedirect.com/science/article/pii/S0142961202003538.
28. Preda RC, Leisk G, Omenetto F, Kaplan DL. Bioengineered silk proteins to control cell and tissue functions. In: Gerrard JA, editor. Protein nanotechnology: protocols, instrumentation, and applications. 2nd ed. Totowa, NJ: Humana Press; 2013. p. 19–41. https://doi.org/10.1007/978-1-62703-354-1_2.
29. Wang Y, Kim HJ, Vunjak-Novakovic G, Kaplan DL. Stem cell-based tissue engineering with silk biomaterials. Biomaterials. 2006;27(36):6064–82. https://www.sciencedirect.com/science/article/pii/S0142961206006016.
30. Silva SS, Kundu B, Lu S, Reis RL, Kundu SC. Chinese oak Tasar silkworm Antheraea pernyi silk proteins: current strategies and future perspectives for biomedical applications. Macromol Biosci. 2019;19(3):1800252. https://doi.org/10.1002/mabi.201800252.
31. Wang F, Wang Y, Tian C, Xu S, Wang R, Hou K, et al. Fabrication of the FGF1-functionalized sericin hydrogels with cell proliferation activity for biomedical application using genetically engineered Bombyx mori (B. mori) silk. Acta Biomater. 2018;79:239–52. https://www.sciencedirect.com/science/article/pii/S1742706118304987.
32. Mahdavi S, Amirsadeghi A, Jafari A, Niknezhad SV, Bencherif SA. Avian egg: a multifaceted biomaterial for tissue engineering. Ind Eng Chem Res. 2021;60(48):17348–64. https://doi.org/10.1021/acs.iecr.1c03085.
33. Rubeić M, Krstic AD, Stanković H, Ljupković R, Ranđelović MS, Zarubica AR. Different types of biomaterials: structure and application: a short review. Adv Technol. 2020;9:69.
34. Ullah MW, Rojas OJ, McCarthy RR, Yang G. Editorial: nanocellulose: a multipurpose advanced functional material. Front Bioeng Biotechnol. 2021;1:9. https://doi.org/10.3389/fbioe.2021.738779.
35. Das S, Ghosh B, Sarkar K. Nanocellulose as sustainable biomaterials for drug delivery. Sensors Int. 2022;3:100135. https://www.sciencedirect.com/science/article/pii/S2666351121000565.
36. Mehanny S, Abu-El Magd EE, Ibrahim M, Farag M, Gil-San-Millan R, Navarro J, et al. Extraction and characterization of nanocellulose from three types of palm residues. J Mater Res Technol. 2021;10:526–37. https://www.sciencedirect.com/science/article/pii/S2238785420321037.
37. Wang L, Wang C, Wu S, Fan Y, Li X. Influence of the mechanical properties of biomaterials on degradability, cell behaviors and signaling pathways: current progress and challenges. Biomater Sci. 2020;8(10):2714–33. https://doi.org/10.1039/D0BM00269K.
38. Ball V. 2- Physicochemical properties of biomaterials. In: Vrana NE, Knopf-Marques H, Barthes J, editors. Biomaterials for organ and tissue regeneration. Woodhead Publishing; 2020. p. 19–32. https://www.sciencedirect.com/science/article/pii/B9780081029060000027.
39. Torres FG, Troncoso OP, Gamucci O, Corvaglia S, Brunetti V, Bardi G. Immunological properties of Andean starch films are independent of their nanometric roughness and stiffness. Int J Biol Macromol. 2015;75:460–6. https://www.sciencedirect.com/science/article/pii/S014181301500077X.
40. Jin C, Lee G, Oh C, Kim HJ, Kim HM. Substrate roughness induces the development of defective E-cadherin junctions in human gingival keratinocytes. J Periodontal Implant Sci. 2017;47(2):116–31. https://doi.org/10.5051/jpis.2017.47.2.116.
41. Bobbert FSL, Zadpoor AA. Effects of bone substitute architecture and surface properties on cell response, angiogenesis, and structure of new bone. J Mater Chem B. 2017;5(31):6175–92. https://doi.org/10.1039/C7TB00741H.
42. Anderson JM. 9.19- Biocompatibility. In: Matyjaszewski K, Möller M, editors. Polymer science: a comprehensive reference. Amsterdam: Elsevier; 2012. p. 363–83. https://www.sciencedirect.com/science/article/pii/B9780444533494002296.
43. Russo L, Sgambato A, Lecchi M, Pastori V, Raspanti M, Natalello A, et al. Neoglucosylated collagen matrices drive neuronal cells to differentiate. ACS Chem Neurosci. 2014;5(4):261–5. https://doi.org/10.1021/cn400222s.
44. DiSabato DJ, Quan N, Godbout JP. Neuroinflammation: the devil is in the details. J Neurochem. 2016;139(S2):136–53. https://doi.org/10.1111/jnc.13607.
45. Zadpoor AA. Bone tissue regeneration: the role of scaffold geometry. Biomater Sci. 2015;3(2):231–45. https://doi.org/10.1039/C4BM00291A.
46. Amado S, Morouço P, Pascoal-Faria P, Alves N. Tailoring bioengineered scaffolds for regenerative medicine. In: Dobrzański LA, editor. Biomaterials in regenerative medicine. Rijeka: IntechOpen; 2017. p. 15. https://doi.org/10.5772/intechopen.69857.
47. Vladkova TG. Surface engineered polymeric biomaterials with improved biocontact properties. Int J Polym Sci. 2010;2010:296094. https://doi.org/10.1155/2010/296094.
48. Jaumotte-Thelen S, Dozot-Dupont I, Marchand-Brynaert J, Schneider YJ. Covalent grafting of fibronectin and asialofetuin at surface of poly(ethylene terephthalate) track-etched membranes improves adhesion but not differentiation of rat hepatocytes. J Biomed Mater Res. 1996;32(4):569–82. https://doi.org/10.1002/(SICI)1097-4636(199612)32:4<569::AID-JBM10>3.0.CO.
49. Denizli A, Pişkin E, Dixit V, Arthur M, Gitnick G. Collagen and fibronectin immobilization on PHEMA microcarriers for hepatocyte attachment. Int J Artif Organs. 1995;18(2):90–5. https://doi.org/10.1177/039139889501800208.

50. Nuttelman CR, Mortisen DJ, Henry SM, Anseth KS. Attachment of fibronectin to poly(vinyl alcohol) hydrogels promotes NIH3T3 cell adhesion, proliferation, and migration. J Biomed Mater Res. 2001;57(2):217–23. https://doi.org/10.1002/1097-4636(200111)57:2<217::AID-JBM1161>3.0.CO.
51. Han F, Zhu C, Guo Q, Yang H, Li B. Cellular modulation by the elasticity of biomaterials. J Mater Chem B. 2016;4(1):9–26. https://doi.org/10.1039/C5TB02077H.
52. Fiedler T, Belova IV, Murch GE, Roether JA, Boccaccini AR. Tailoring elastic properties of PLGA/TiO2 biomaterials. Comput Mater Sci. 2012;61:283–6. https://www.sciencedirect.com/science/article/pii/S0927025612002571.
53. Madaghiele M, Salvatore L, Sannino A. 4- Tailoring the pore structure of foam scaffolds for nerve regeneration. In: Netti PA, editor. Biomedical foams for tissue engineering applications. Woodhead Publishing; 2014. p. 101–28. https://www.sciencedirect.com/science/article/pii/B9780857096968500048.
54. Amani H, Kazerooni H, Hassanpoor H, Akbarzadeh A, Pazoki-Toroudi H. Tailoring synthetic polymeric biomaterials towards nerve tissue engineering: a review. Artif Cells Nanomed Biotechnol. 2019;47(1):3524–39. https://doi.org/10.1080/21691401.2019.1639723.
55. Zigmond RE, Echevarria FD. Macrophage biology in the peripheral nervous system after injury. Prog Neurobiol. 2019;173:102–21. https://www.sciencedirect.com/science/article/pii/S030100821830128X.
56. Matsumoto K, Ohnishi K, Kiyotani T, Sekine T, Ueda H, Nakamura T, et al. Peripheral nerve regeneration across an 80-mm gap bridged by a polyglycolic acid (PGA)–collagen tube filled with laminin-coated collagen fibers: a histological and electrophysiological evaluation of regenerated nerves. Brain Res. 2000;868(2):315–28. https://www.sciencedirect.com/science/article/pii/S0006899300022071.
57. Zhang K, Huang D, Yan Z, Wang C. Heparin/collagen encapsulating nerve growth factor multilayers coated aligned PLLA nanofibrous scaffolds for nerve tissue engineering. J Biomed Mater Res A. 2017;105(7):1900–10. https://doi.org/10.1002/jbm.a.36053.
58. Hoveizi E, Tavakol S, Ebrahimi-Barough S. Neuroprotective effect of transplanted neural precursors embedded on PLA/CS scaffold in an animal model of multiple sclerosis. Mol Neurobiol. 2015;51(3):1334–42. http://europepmc.org/abstract/MED/25081586.
59. Haddad T, Noel S, Liberelle B, El Ayoubi R, Ajji A, De Crescenzo G. Fabrication and surface modification of poly lactic acid (PLA) scaffolds with epidermal growth factor for neural tissue engineering. Biomatter. 2016;6(1):e1231276. https://doi.org/10.1080/21592535.2016.1231276.
60. Bolaina-Lorenzo E, Martínez-Ramos C, Monleón-Pradas M, Herrera-Kao W, Cauich-Rodríguez JV, Cervantes-Uc JM. Electrospun polycaprolactone/chitosan scaffolds for nerve tissue engineering: physicochemical characterization and Schwann cell biocompatibility. Biomed Mater. 2017;12(1):015008. https://doi.org/10.1088/1748-605X/12/1/015008.
61. Lee JY, Bashur CA, Goldstein AS, Schmidt CE. Polypyrrole-coated electrospun PLGA nanofibers for neural tissue applications. Biomaterials. 2009;30(26):4325–35. https://www.sciencedirect.com/science/article/pii/S0142961209004633.
62. Saderi N, Rajabi M, Akbari B, Firouzi M, Hassannejad Z. Fabrication and characterization of gold nanoparticle-doped electrospun PCL/chitosan nanofibrous scaffolds for nerve tissue engineering. J Mater Sci Mater Med. 2018;29(9):134. https://doi.org/10.1007/s10856-018-6144-3.
63. Fu SY, Gordon T. The cellular and molecular basis of peripheral nerve regeneration. Mol Neurobiol. 1997;14(1):67–116. https://doi.org/10.1007/BF02740621.
64. Chang CJ, Hsu S, hui. The effect of high outflow permeability in asymmetric poly(dl-lactic acid-co-glycolic acid) conduits for peripheral nerve regeneration. Biomaterials. 2006;27(7):1035–42. https://www.sciencedirect.com/science/article/pii/S0142961205006071.
65. Oh SH, Lee JH. Fabrication and characterization of hydrophilized porous PLGA nerve guide conduits by a modified immersion precipitation method. J Biomed Mater Res A. 2007;80A(3):530–8. https://doi.org/10.1002/jbm.a.30937.
66. Harley BA, Hastings AZ, Yannas IV, Sannino A. Fabricating tubular scaffolds with a radial pore size gradient by a spinning technique. Biomaterials. 2006;27(6):866–74. https://www.sciencedirect.com/science/article/pii/S0142961205005983.
67. Seciu AM, Craciunescu O, Stanciuc AM, Zarnescu O. Tailored biomaterials for therapeutic strategies applied in periodontal tissue engineering. Stem Cells Dev. 2019;28(15):963–73. https://doi.org/10.1089/scd.2019.0016.
68. Antoun H, Sitbon JM, Martinez H, Missika P. A prospective randomized study comparing two techniques of bone augmentation: onlay graft alone or associated with a membrane. Clin Oral Implants Res. 2001;12(6):632–9. https://doi.org/10.1034/j.1600-0501.2001.120612.x.
69. Duraccio D, Mussano F, Faga MG. Biomaterials for dental implants: current and future trends. J Mater Sci. 2015;50:4779–812.
70. Galler KM, Cavender AC, Koeklue U, Suggs LJ, Schmalz G, D'Souza RN. Bioengineering of dental stem cells in a PEGylated fibrin gel. Regen Med. 2011;6(2):191–200. https://doi.org/10.2217/rme.11.3.
71. Seciu AM, Craciunescu O, Zarnescu O. Advanced regenerative techniques based on dental pulp stem cells for the treatment of periodontal disease. In: Manakil J, editor. Periodontology and dental implantology. Rijeka: IntechOpen; 2018. https://doi.org/10.5772/intechopen.78048.
72. Zarnescu O, Craciunescu O, Moldovan L. Collagen-chondroitin sulphate-hydroxyapatite porous compos-

ites: a histochemical and electron microscopy approach. Microsc Microanal. 2010;16(2):137–42. https://www.cambridge.org/core/article/collagenchondroitinsulphatehydroxyapatite-porous-composites-a-histochemical-and-electron-microscopy-approach/6592B7191B7CBBC601CA71D181D96B52.
73. Craciunescu O, Tardei C, Moldovan L, Zarnescu O. Magnesium substitution effect on porous scaffolds for bone repair. Cent Eur J Biol. 2011;6(3):301–11. https://doi.org/10.2478/s11535-011-0012-1.
74. Schultz GS, Chin GA, Moldawer L, Diegelmann RF. Principles of wound healing, vol. 23. Adelaide: University of Adelaide Press; 2011.
75. Rezvani Ghomi E, Khalili S, Nouri Khorasani S, Esmaeely Neisiany R, Ramakrishna S. Wound dressings: current advances and future directions. J Appl Polym Sci. 2019;136(27):47738. https://doi.org/10.1002/app.47738.
76. Pommet M, Juntaro J, Heng JYY, Mantalaris A, Lee AF, Wilson K, et al. Surface modification of natural fibers using bacteria: depositing bacterial cellulose onto natural fibers to create hierarchical fiber reinforced nanocomposites. Biomacromolecules. 2008;9(6):1643–51. https://doi.org/10.1021/bm800169g.
77. Desai T, Shea LD. Advances in islet encapsulation technologies. Nat Rev Drug Discov. 2017;16(5):338–50. https://doi.org/10.1038/nrd.2016.232.
78. Abuid NJ, Gattás-Asfura KM, Schofield EA, Stabler CL. Layer-by-layer cerium oxide nanoparticle coating for antioxidant protection of encapsulated beta cells. Adv Healthc Mater. 2019;8(12):1801493. https://doi.org/10.1002/adhm.201801493.
79. Zeng J, Shirihai OS, Grinstaff MW. Degradable nanoparticles restore lysosomal pH and autophagic flux in lipotoxic pancreatic beta cells. Adv Healthc Mater. 2019;8(12):1801511. https://doi.org/10.1002/adhm.201801511.
80. Wang C, Ye Y, Hu Q, Bellotti A, Gu Z. Tailoring biomaterials for cancer immunotherapy: emerging trends and future outlook. Adv Mater. 2017;29:29.
81. Littman DR. Releasing the brakes on cancer immunotherapy. Cell. 2015;162:1186–90.

Challenges in Pragmatism of Translational Research

26

E. Johnson Christdas

The term research in a philosophical perspective means the pursuit of truth. The instinct of curiosity is driven by the need to find the holistic truth or at least a part. It is always objected towards improving the quality of life. The ultimatum of realizing the truth lies in its utility for the welfare of life. Hence it is an accomplishment of the purpose that results in the translation of research into the utility. Research or the pursuit of truth, when it is well planned and understood, it can be very well done in a scheduled time towards accomplishments of the intended objectives. Records of the research work can be evidenced by the benefits of the research which are nothing but the translated versions of research. In other words, the use of the results of any piece of research is the translation of the research. Such a translation of research gives out transformation in the society. Hence the translational research is the fulfillment of research and that remains as the essential need for perpetuating such attempts to pursue truth. All such attempts are impeded by certain factors that either dilute the quantum of its output or digresses the thought process of the research and its focus.

In this chapter, the pragmatism of research is interpreted as its translations. The impeding challenges for the translation of research are critically analyzed and represented. All through this chapter, the challenges are reviewed and then cognitively addressed to overcome the huddles to succeed in translating research. The investments and the opportunities like effective management of time, money, man power, resources and their effective managements and the mind maps and managerial skills to navigate the projects are to be considered. The policies in practice should always be in accordance with the standards and the regulations prescribed by the governing agencies and should be ethically scrutinized.

The meticulous efforts in performing research are hindered by the aforesaid factors. These factors when they are not constantly or consciously scrutinized, they become the challenges. The onus is on every member of the research community and of mankind to address to these limitations in translating research.

26.1 Time

Time as a factor has a very crucial impact on anything that happens around our existence. The differential value of time is always relative to the environment of any process. Hence the time taken for any process must be as short as possible. More importantly, it should not be any shorter than any shortest possible time. The need of every hour and minute and every fraction of any second must be clearly prioritized across the span of the process

E. Johnson Christdas (✉)
Department of Microbiology, The American College, Madurai, Tamil Nadu, India
e-mail: johnsonchristdas@americancollege.edu.in

K. Parthasarathy, R. Manikkam (eds.), *Translational Research in Biomedical Sciences: Recent Progress and Future Prospects*, https://doi.org/10.1007/978-981-97-1777-4_26

and can be revisited without hesitations to prevent loss of the time. Revamping the priorities and the liberty to exercise it must be a critically available for every careful mind watching it. It would otherwise render all the efforts futile. A process when analogized to a journey must have a realized starting point and should have a fixed destination in order to progress in a particular direction. The research projects that are formulated must be planned with a time stipulation and it can be best done by individuals with prior experiences of handling such journey, like projects. The shortest possible time can be known out of experiences gained by project operators and the attempts to reduce such time consumption can put the holistic efforts at the stakes of failure. Unwarranted attempts to reduce time for any process can result in the failure of translation of any piece of research and that can be a key to futility.

Time as a commonly available intangible component of anyone's life is an integral component of life. This is an asset given to us by nature and this has to be translated into a virtue, a product, or money or any other physical commodity. The time needed for the development of a skill/ any other value must be not only qualitatively assessed. Rather, it would be quantiatively reflected on the quantum of the output. A delicate balance to have an optimal quantity and the best of quality must be the life line of the translation process. Translation of time into a tangible or physical value must be achieved by understanding the importance of it. The time management and decision making are equally important inherent qualities of a leader of a research team. It sets up the hallmark of eligibility for anyone who attempts to translate research. As a matter of fact, this happens to be the first block that challenges the translation of research. It is well analyzed and understood that the time invested to draw the mind-maps of the planned highways must be concordant with the road maps that are created. For these reasons there are project manager appointed to steer the translation of research from the minds of the intellectuals to the bed side of any patient. The project manager/task manager unfortunately are not able to match up the available skill set with the resources and the length of any process. This is relative to the knowledge limitations and obviousness of ineffective management.

With the time as the frame of references, the value of any other factor transiently changes and that impacts on the outcome of any event or a process that is planned. When the time is not managed it shows that the process is an unplanned one. Any event that is planned/organized must be into the control of the research community and this pertains to the translation of knowledge into benefits.

The term translational research is predominantly used in the context of the drug discovery and its utility. Considering the field of medicine, the attempts to design a drug that is most needed for management or prevention of a disease is the objective. When it is made available for public use, it is the tangible translation of research [1]. The availability of the drug should also be accompanied by the knowledge of the drug and the consequences of the use of that drug. The translation of the knowledge or research when managed or controlled with reference to time, the time allotted for achieving the drug availability should include the time of analyzing or estimating the risk and the consequences involved in the use of the drug. When the risk and contraindications are not estimated properly, the translation of such research would invite ill-consequences that may worsen the scenario of the point of translation. Hence the stipulation of time to translate research must be formulated and quantitatively articulated as strategic policies. Such a policy had driven the division of time into various phases of pilot study, clinical trials and field study. The recent pandemic has rendered an experience to revise the existing policies and the strategies in practice. A lack of clear understanding of all the aforesaid facts is one great challenge and that efficiently exerts pressure on the execution of knowledge and it hinders the translation of research.

26.2 Financial Requirements and the Related Constraints

Money as an interchangeable value is not clearly understood by researchers and all otherse who have to meet at cross roads while translating research. There always prevails an imbalance in the realization or the conversion money into any virtue or value. The research and the ideas of doing research are always troubled by the deficit of financial requirements. The only way of stabilizing flow of fund is consistently establishing credibility in whatever is said and done. The flow of money into an organized research laboratory is a need for functionally alive research goal. It is also a basic essential need as in any other flow of life. There goes a popular saying "Money makes many things." This needs to be revisited or revised for the present time as "Money is needed for everything". So in research, the planned, organized well done experiments in the laboratory can be achieved only with the flow of money. In a given span of time of outcome of research has again to be converted into money which must be a relative quantity of work done.

Money/Finance in the absolute idleness will not be useful and this has a greater value when it is interchanged reasonably. This exchange of money should not derail the delicate balance created between the quantum and the quality of any commodity or anything for which the money is exchanged.

On the other hand the flow of money and its interchanged value has to be documented clearly in the order of chronology. This would enable anyone to remember the flow of value around one's objective and can help to steer the project towards the intended translation of research. These are the policies that were written and sometimes only practiced in order to successfully translate research. Contamination or compromise in the quality of this fiscal record maintenance or lethargy towards this practice can be greatly damaging the translation of research. The lack of truth in the fiscal record maintenance can greatly derange the organization and its recognition. The mismatch of reality with the fiscal records sadly is absolved most of the times and thus it becomes the womb of corruption. The mis-appropriations and the mis-managed funds are absolved due to lethargy and such instances are encouraging corruption. As a matter of fact, these are ivy vines masked as prosperity that leads to unjustifiable inflation in economy. This greatly challenges the existence of the society with its values. Such a practice has to be abolished with altruism and ideas of co-existence or inter-dependence. This inter-dependence has long-existed to give birth and nourishment to a civilised, literate society with its values.

It is time for provoking our thoughts to ask ourselves now. Why the huge money or small money granted as a fund for any particular project or a cause is paralleled by experts giving a budget or a guideline for the utilization and with a time stipulation?

In a personal perspective each one of us pay the cost of any commodity. When we desire to buy any product we inspect its quality, credibility, and every value that the paid money confers. This is usual and done by any person in an individualistic perspective. But in a grant that is not to be operated by a single individual this does not happen always. As the grant are received and spent only as installments and not as a whole, it paves a way for the scrutinizing the substantial progress. The report on the proper utility of every portion of money must be periodically scrutinized to steer the recipient of the grant towards the absolute translation of the research from the Bench to the Bed side [2].

In the community of researchers and entrepreneurs and Philanthropist, usually the grants that are offered to any skilled personnel or their teams are celebrated as achievements. The recipients of these funds evolve to be pioneers. These pioneers then become iconic researchers and stalwarts of science in the later years. The stakes that they encountered, their failures and their difficulties are to be presented to everyone. When the stated objective are not achieved, the consequences should put the recipients or the navigators of funds at a risk of execution under criminal procedures. The failure of a grant recipient who had not achieved the least of the stated objective must be executed by criminal procedure codes. Such cases of failure amounts to white collar crimes and the awareness of the consequences of such crimes should potentially put the researchers at stakes. The assignments given to agencies to accomplish the micro-management of the projects must associate identified experts. These are a few of the many facts that destabilize the translation of research pertaining to the flow of money. Hence it is not only the possession of money but also the proper conversion of money into a virtue or any value in the course of practicality of any research idea.

26.3 Man Power and Its Mapping

Any expert is not born but is become, or made. Becoming an expert is only by practicing to gain experience. An experienced personnel becomes an expert and an expertise evolves only out of experience. A daunting task or the daily bread is accomplished only by dedication. Hence in order to be an expert in a daunting task or in a daily bread winning one must have a substantial experience that offers—resistance, tolerance, and fighting instinct to swim against the odds, towards one's dedication. Identifying such dedicated researchers is a very critical and essential need to achieve the translation of research. Identification of such individual generates a confidence to realize the translation of research. The time spent by any expert who participates in a team of research translation from bench to bed side has to be acknowledged with proper monetary emoluments. It must not only empower the researcher financially but also edify him/her with a desire and dedication to sustain one-self in the appointed task. A challenge that seriously impacts translation of research is the appointment of deadlines during micro-management of time. In a team of hierarchical structure with clearly divided labor, it is a basic need to manage time and then fix deadlines that could be achieved. There is always an absence of experience that results in a lacuna during scheduling of deadlines. An actual expert if had evolved out of experience will fix deadlines that are possible by counting on his/her own experience on the task. But when a managerial authority is without any experience on a task has to be only forgiven for lack of experience to appoint deadlines. The fixing of deadlines must be done only after proper mapping of man power and its quality after the sufficient requirements are provided. In reality, the time managers without any experience are at risk of losing money and time. If they are prejudiced in the mapping of man power. Even after mapping and appointing a right person on a right task the personnel must be taken care of by offering the stipulated and other resources. Or else, the digression of tasks and the deficit of resources can result in the damage of the process of translation of research. Such kinds of operation and management can be derogatory for any system and can amount to a gradual and occult collapse. This kind of damage can be best avoided by many strategies at every level of usage of man power, starting from identification of man power and its sustained utility offered along with a sense of gratification and achievements. This can be achieved by revamping of the man power while dividing the labor. The policies and practices of the principles of man power management can be documented, for a professional operation and efficient management of a system. Historical research reports and records can be considered as prototypes for the operations and management of any attempts to translate knowledge.

As a matter of fact, as in the case of drug discoveries and any research in bio-medicine that would take more than a decade. Hence an employee or man power identified must be encouraged to have dedication. It must be intertwined with a personnel's life and identity, because the conversion of research into a product consumes a person's productive number of years. In order to receive it, due acknowledgements must be offered. These are the tokens of encouragement that enables any employees or personnel to dedicate so as to move every switch that navigates the translation of research. To summarize, the experts should have experienced every path and pain of any person in the hierarchical team before mapping timeline, resources, and man power. Otherwise that can greatly challenge the translation of research by digression from the actual progression.

26.4 Evolutionary Growth of Systems

Any successful event will be appreciated and welcome by the world. But the consistency of operating these systems to keep up the achieved rates of success remains a challenge. The modes of operation of any successful system are analyzed and drafted as operational policies for the evolution of many other similar successful systems to translate research. Such prototypes should be set as modules which would also represent the huddles and its failures. The most important policy which is the best of all policies is the Honesty. An honest documentation and representation of the facts gives a picture of our real state of existence. Our journey towards success and the number of milestones and huddles at every point in translation of research can be understood only if there are proper documentation of everything including failures on a daily basis. The word Minute must be literally practiced in the documentation system. Historically, any clinical trial or any drug development which is termed as translational research would require a time span undisturbed by stabilized flow of funds and organized managerial expertise without any digressions. Over the span of time, any systems or an individual must not loose vigor and vibrance in performing the specific assigned role. This is a vital pivot point of management of the identified man power. An expert who is assigned for management of man power should carefully address to it as it is needed for the evolution of any system towards the intended progress. The human resource management is assigned to a ministry of the Government to perform the duties. A national system would miss the mark if this is not done with utmost care. This is one predominant and the most prevalent risk that is challenging the generation of man power for the translation of research. The task—managers and the empowering employees must critically address to this challenge in order to successfully translate research. Exclusive man powers who are pioneers of human resource managements must be assigned at this pivotal point. The claims and needs of the persons employed on various tasks must be clearly defined and then met with the precautions to nourish and nurture the progress of the translation. "Handle with care" at every decision point of translating research must be practiced as a part of mission statement. During the identification of man power one must not choose the faint-hearted at the least.

Anyone attempting or participating in translation of research must be faithful with a vision of the benefits being enjoyed by the mankind. It is clearly understandable now that the vision and the mission statement and the drafted policies and practices have a particular format and that becomes the modes of operation. The vision and mission statement are written to be read in order to be practiced. Whenever these drafts are found only as letters and not in the spirit, the life of any system ends and this penultimately results in failure of translation of research. Sooner or later the missions objective and modes of operation along with the stipulated time line must be informed to every participant in order to be realized. Failing in the preparation of rightly sprinted man power is not a preparation for failure. Rather it is the failure in the acquisition and translation of knowledge.

The growth or the progress towards the defined objectives across timelines has to be analyzed in translational research, in a phased manner. This is the existing model for any translational research (i.e., Phases of research—Pre clinical, Phase I, Phase II, Phase III, Phase IV). The research question or the hypothesis is most of the times forgotten and so the progression towards the framed hypothesis is easily digressed. The longer or the longest timeline stipulated to achieve those framed objective is the greatest of all challenges in the translation of research. This can be overcome by division of labor after mapping the man power. To overcome this challenge, it is a necessity to intermittently revamp and revitalize the process. Such operational quality may energize the system to achieve the objectives

26.5 Policies and Drafted Mandates/and Standards

The practices of the laboratory particularly in a clinical research laboratory are driven and directed by standardized operation methods. The standardized methods or operational protocols are nothing but the outcomes of efforts for organized operations that would ease the labor. In order to achieve the translation of research these

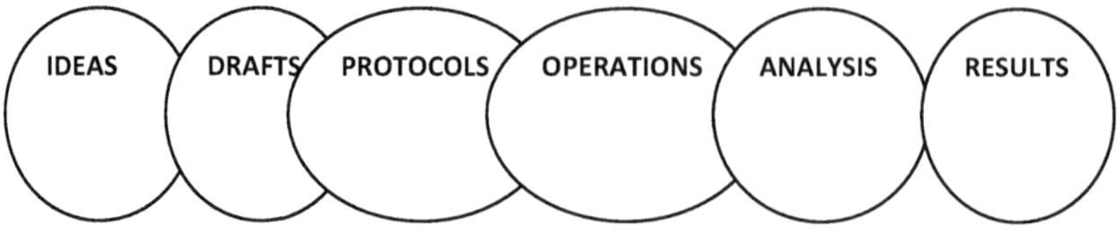

Fig. 26.1 A flow chart for the translation of abstract into understandable results. Each circle can be expanded into its customized

standardized protocols are made as the mandates by and for the effective governance of any system. These standard operating procedures must have been evolved by pioneers of governance and policy makers and planners. The zeal and the pragmatism of these individuals who drafted such strategies or protocols or policies must be disseminated and translated into the hearts and minds of every participant contributing for the achievement of the objectives. These policies are framed and drafted as the formula for achieving the translation, of any research. The drafts are otherwise the translated versions of the success or the formula for the success. The formula existing in letter and not in the spirit can have a devastation of translation of research. The policies have to be revisited in accordance with the evolving technology. But the inclusion of the word mandate becomes mandatory, then it will result in the sub-standards in the place of standards and the under-qualified becomes the quality (Fig. 26.1).

FLOW CHART OF A PATTERN TO TRANSLATE RESEARWCH (TOP DOWN/ BOTTOM UP APPROACH). The process of translation can start at either end or flow in either direction.

An example of the drafted policies are the follow-up op (1) impact factor (2) Citation index (3) Papers published (4) Organization of conferences, etc.

The organizational behavior of any institutionalized efforts is to be translated across the factors mentioned in the circle. A very less or no freedom can be adopted in shuffling the order of these factors. But the flow of the direction can be either way to achieve the translation of research (Fig. 26.1). The flow of the work must be kept alive and the magnitude of work must guide the division of labor across the dedicated and developed man power.

On the whole the progress of the flow of the work must be critically analyzed on a daily basis. In the course of this operation, the basic policy "Honesty" the best policy must be practiced for the realization of research into its application.

Any digression to the work on a daily basis must be analyzed and prevented. The daily digression is a great challenge in realizing the translation of research ideas.

Conclusively, the goals greater or smaller can be achieved with dedication to scheduled plans and strategies and honest documentations on a daily basis and then expanding it across the timeline with the right map of skills. Other challenges like nepotism, favoritism, dishonesty, exploitation of natural systems as models or any other form of white collar crime and corruption are least discussed here. Though these are the challenges to the pragmatism of quality assurance, it must have been well understood by a literate reading. It is summarized that Honesty is the best policy to be practiced at every level of life and that greatly will enable mankind to do research and translate it. To err is human, but mankind can be kind enough to self- identify own errors or at least honestly be grateful to others who help us identify our pitfalls.

References

1. Seyhan AA, Carini C. Are innovation and new technologies in precision medicine paving a new era in patients centric care? J Transl Med. 2019;17:1–28.
2. Rocks INA. Origin promised XX; 1931. p. 183–98.

Enhancement of Neuroimmune Diagnosis by Artificial Intelligence

27

B. Aarthi Rashmi and Harichander Anandaram

27.1 Introduction

There are some ways by which AI can enhance neuroimmune diagnosis: (a) Image Analysis: AI algorithms can analyse neuroimaging data, such as magnetic resonance imaging (MRI) and computed tomography (CT) scans, to aid in diagnosing neuro-immunological disorders. For example, AI algorithms can help identify characteristic patterns of brain lesions in multiple sclerosis or autoimmune encephalitis, which may not be apparent to human radiologists [1]. AI can also assist in detecting subtle changes in brain imaging that may indicate disease progression or response to treatment. Image analysis is extracting meaningful information from digital images using computer algorithms. Image analysis has been revolutionised with machine learning and artificial intelligence (AI). AI algorithms in image analysis can analyse complex ideas and detect patterns, which is crucial in several applications, such as medical diagnosis, self-driving cars, and security surveillance. Convolutional neural networks (CNN) are one of the most widely used AI algorithms for image analysis [2]. CNNs can automatically learn and extract features from images, a crucial step in image analysis. They are instrumental in image recognition tasks, such as object detection and image classification. CNNs apply convolutional filters to input images and pool the resulting features to create a high-level image representation. CNNs have been successful in several applications, including facial recognition, self-driving cars, and medical diagnosis.

Recurrent neural networks (RNN) are another popular AI algorithm used in image analysis. RNNs are particularly useful in analysing sequential data, such as time series or video data. RNNs work by sequentially processing input data and using the output from previous steps to inform the production of the current stage. RNNs have been successful in several applications, including speech recognition, language translation, and video analysis. Generative adversarial networks (GANs) are AI algorithms used in image analysis to generate new images similar to training images. GANs work by pitting two neural networks against each other: one network creates new ideas and the other tries to detect whether the photos are real or fake [3]. This process continues until the generated images are indistinguishable from natural images. GANs have been used in several applications, including image generation, manipulation, and style transfer. Deep belief net-

B. A. Rashmi (✉)
Department of Bioinformatics, Sri Krishna Arts and Science College, Coimbatore, Tamil Nadu, India
e-mail: aarthirashmib@skasc.ac.in

H. Anandaram
Centre for Excellence in Computational Engineering and Networking, Amrita Vishwa Vidyapeetham, Coimbatore, Tamil Nadu, India
e-mail: a_harishchander@cb.amrita.edu

K. Parthasarathy, R. Manikkam (eds.), *Translational Research in Biomedical Sciences: Recent Progress and Future Prospects*, https://doi.org/10.1007/978-981-97-1777-4_27

works (DBNs) are another type of AI algorithm used in image analysis based on hierarchical layers. DBNs can learn complex features and patterns from data by building a layer hierarchy that progressively knows more abstract elements. DBNs have been successful in several applications, including image recognition, speech recognition, and natural language processing. AI algorithms have revolutionised the field of image analysis by enabling the analysis of complex images and patterns. Convolutional neural networks, recurrent neural networks, generative adversarial networks, and deep belief networks are some of the most widely used AI algorithms in image analysis [4]. These algorithms have been successful in several applications, including facial recognition, self-driving cars, medical diagnosis, speech recognition, and image generation. As AI continues to evolve, we expect to see even more powerful AI algorithms for image analysis.

27.2 Biomarker Analysis

AI can analyse complex data from various biomarkers, such as blood tests, cerebrospinal fluid (CSF) analysis, and genetic testing, to aid in diagnosing neuro-immunological disorders. For instance, AI algorithms can identify specific biomarkers associated with certain neurological conditions, helping clinicians make accurate and timely diagnoses. Artificial intelligence (AI) and biomarker analysis are two fields that have seen significant growth in recent years. Combining these two fields has the potential to revolutionise the way we diagnose and treat diseases. This review will explore the current state of AI and biomarker analysis, their potential applications, and the challenges that must be addressed to realise their full potential. Biomarkers are measurable indicators of biological processes or responses to diseases, and their analysis can provide insights into disease progression and treatment response. Traditional biomarker analysis methods such as ELISA and PCR are time-consuming and expensive. AI-based biomarker analysis can streamline the process, reducing the time and cost required for biomarker discovery and validation [5]. AI-based biomarker analysis can be used in various applications, including disease diagnosis, prognosis, and treatment selection. For example, in cancer diagnosis, AI-based biomarker analysis can analyse large amounts of genomic data and identify specific biomarkers associated with different cancer types. This information can then be used to develop personalised treatment plans based on the patient's genomic profile.

AI-based biomarker analysis can also monitor disease progression and treatment response. For example, in multiple sclerosis, AI-based biomarker analysis can monitor cytokine level changes in response to treatment. This information can be used to optimise treatment plans and improve patient outcomes. Despite the potential benefits of AI-based biomarker analysis, several challenges must be addressed. One of the main challenges is the need for more standardisation in biomarker analysis methods [6]. There is a need for standardised protocols and guidelines to ensure the accuracy and reproducibility of biomarker analysis results. Another challenge is the availability of large datasets for AI-based biomarker analysis. The quality and quantity of data are critical for AI-based biomarker analysis, and there is a need for more comprehensive and accessible datasets to support biomarker analysis. AI-based biomarker analysis can revolutionise disease diagnosis, prognosis, and treatment selection. However, several challenges need to be addressed, including more standardisation in biomarker analysis methods and the availability of large datasets. Addressing these challenges will require collaboration between researchers, clinicians, and industry stakeholders to realise the full potential of AI-based biomarker analysis in improving patient outcomes.

27.3 Clinical Decision Support

AI can provide clinical decision support tools to aid clinicians in making informed decisions about diagnosing neuro-immunological disorders. These tools can integrate data from multiple sources, including patient history, clinical examination findings, and laboratory results, and provide evidence-based recommendations to assist clinicians in formulating accurate diagnoses. Artificial intelligence (AI) transforms healthcare by enabling clinicians to make more precise and efficient clinical decisions [7]. Access to AI tools has the potential to revolutionise the healthcare industry by improving patient outcomes, reducing costs, and enhancing clinical workflows. This review article will explore the current state of AI in clinical decision-making and the challenges and opportunities ahead. AI. Machine learning, deep learning, and natural language processing (NLP) are increasingly used in healthcare for clinical decision-making. Machine learning algorithms can analyse large datasets to identify patterns and generate predictions. Deep learning models can process vast amounts of medical imaging data and help diagnose conditions like cancer [8]. NLP can extract insights from unstructured clinical notes and improve diagnosis and treatment plans. AI is used in various clinical settings, including diagnosis, prognosis, treatment planning, and medication management. For example, AI algorithms can analyse electronic health records (EHRs) to predict patient outcomes and identify patients at high risk for readmission. AI can also help physicians personalise treatment plans based on patients' unique characteristics and medical histories.

27.4 Challenges and Opportunities

Despite the numerous benefits of AI for clinical decision-making, several challenges need to be addressed. One of the significant concerns is the ethical use of AI in healthcare. There is a need to ensure that AI systems are transparent, unbiased, and fair and that patient privacy is protected. Another challenge is the need for more standardisation in collecting and sharing healthcare data. Healthcare data are often stored in disparate systems, making it challenging to access and analyse. Data quality and interoperability issues can also affect the accuracy and reliability of AI algorithms. However, these challenges present opportunities for innovation and collaboration. There is a need for industry-wide standards and guidelines for AI in healthcare to ensure its responsible and ethical use. Collaboration between healthcare providers, technology companies, and regulatory bodies can help address data standardisation and interoperability issues. AI can analyse patient-specific data, such as clinical history, imaging findings, and biomarker data, to develop personalised treatment plans [9]. By considering multiple factors, including patient and disease characteristics, AI can help tailor treatment plans to individual patients, resulting in more effective and personalised care. AI can analyse data from various sources, such as imaging data, biomarker data, and patient-reported outcomes, to monitor treatment response in neuro-immunological disorders. AI algorithms can detect subtle changes in disease activity, treatment response, and disease progression, allowing for timely adjustments to the treatment plan.

Artificial intelligence (AI) has the potential to revolutionise how we approach healthcare, including monitoring treatment response. Treatment response monitoring is the process of measuring the effectiveness of treatment over time to determine if it is achieving the desired outcome [10]. AI can aid in this process by analysing large amounts of data and identifying patterns that may be missed by human observation alone. In this review, we will discuss the role of AI in treatment response monitoring and its potential benefits and challenges. One of the primary benefits of AI in treatment response monitoring is its ability to analyse large amounts of data quickly and accurately. This includes data from various sources, such as electronic health records (EHRs), medical imaging, and genetic data. AI algorithms can identify patterns and trends in this data that may be difficult or impossible for humans to detect. For example, AI can identify subtle changes in medical imaging that indicate a treatment is working, even if those changes are not visible to the naked eye.

Another benefit of AI in treatment response monitoring is its ability to personalise treatment plans. AI can analyse patient data to identify individual characteristics affecting treatment response, such as age, sex, and genetic makeup. This information can then be used to tailor treatment plans to each patient, increasing the likelihood of success. However, there are also challenges associated with AI in treatment response monitoring. One challenge is the quality of the data. AI algorithms are only as good as the data they are trained on, so the results may be reliable if the data is complete or accurate. Additionally, there are concerns about the ethical implications of using AI in healthcare. For example, there may be concerns about privacy and data security, as well as the potential for AI to replace human decision-making entirely [11]. Despite these challenges, the potential benefits of AI in treatment response monitoring are significant. By analysing large amounts of data quickly and accurately, AI can help healthcare providers make more informed treatment decisions, leading to better patient outcomes. As AI technology advances, treatment response monitoring will only become more critical.

Drug Discovery and Development: AI can accelerate neuro-immunology's drug discovery and development process. AI can identify potential drug targets, optimise drug candidates, and predict drug efficacy by analysing large datasets, including molecular data, clinical trial data, and electronic health records. This can lead to the development of novel therapeutic interventions for neuro-immunological disorders. Artificial intelligence (AI) has significantly impacted drug discovery, particularly in the early stages of drug development. The traditional drug discovery process involves a lot of trial and error and can be lengthy and expensive [12]. However, AI has the potential to revolutionise this process by streamlining the identification of potential drug candidates and accelerating the development process. One of the most significant benefits of AI in drug discovery is its ability to analyse vast amounts of data quickly and efficiently. This includes data from various sources, such as scientific literature, clinical trials, and genetic information. Machine learning algorithms can analyse this data and identify patterns that may need to be noticed by human researchers. This approach can be instrumental in identifying potential drug targets and designing molecules that can bind to this targets. AI can also help optimise drug design by predicting how molecules behave in different biological systems. This allows researchers to identify potential side effects early in development and adjust the molecule's chemical structure to reduce these risks. AI can also help design more efficient clinical trials by identifying patients more likely to respond to a particular drug.

Several AI-based drug discovery platforms, such as BenevolentAI, Atomwise, and Insilico Medicine, are available. These platforms use machine learning algorithms to analyse data and identify potential drug candidates. These platforms can help to speed up the drug development process by reducing the time and cost required for preclinical testing. While AI has the potential to revolutionise drug discovery, several challenges need to be addressed. One of the biggest challenges is the need for more high-quality data. AI algorithms require vast amounts of high-quality data to identify meaningful patterns and predict outcomes accurately. However, much of the data generated in drug discovery is proprietary and not readily available to researchers outside the pharmaceutical industry. Another challenge is the interpretability of AI models. Machine learning algorithms can be complex and difficult to understand, making it challenging to identify the underlying factors contributing to their predictions [13]. This can make it hard for researchers to validate the results and understand how the AI algorithm arrived at a particular conclusion. AI can revolutionise drug discovery by streamlining the identification of potential drug candidates, optimising drug design, and accelerating the drug development process. While several challenges need to be addressed, the benefits of AI in drug discovery are significant and can improve patient outcomes and reduce healthcare costs in the long term.

Artificial intelligence (AI) has the potential to revolutionise drug development by accelerating the drug discovery process, improving clinical trial efficiency, and reducing costs. In recent years, the application of AI in drug development has gained significant attention from academia and industry. This review will provide an overview of the current state of AI in drug development, its potential benefits, challenges, and prospects. Drug discovery is a complex and expensive process involving identifying and validating drug targets, lead compound identification and optimisation, preclinical and clinical trials, and regulatory approval [14]. AI can facilitate this process by enabling faster and more accurate analysis of large amounts of data from various sources, including genomics, proteomics, and medical records. AI can also be used to predict drug efficacy, toxicity, and side effects and to identify patient subgroups that are more likely to respond to a particular treatment. One of the most significant applications of AI in drug development is identifying new drug targets. AI-based methods can analyse vast amounts of biological data and identify potential targets for a specific disease. This approach can significantly reduce the time and resources required for target identification, and validation.AI can also accelerate drug optimisation by predicting lead compounds' potency, selectivity, and pharmacokinetic properties. Machine learning models can learn from historical data and predict the properties of new compounds, allowing researchers to focus on the most promising candidates.

AI can also improve the efficiency of clinical trials by identifying patient subgroups that are more likely to respond to a particular treatment. This approach, known as precision medicine, can improve the success rate of clinical trials and reduce costs by reducing the number of patients required for a problem. Despite the potential benefits of AI in drug development, there are also several challenges. One of the biggest challenges is the need for high-quality data for training machine learning models [15]. This is particularly true for rare diseases, where limited data may be available. Another challenge is the need for more transparency in AI models, making it difficult to understand how predictions are made and can hinder regulatory approval.AI can transform drug development by enabling faster and more efficient drug discovery, optimisation, and clinical trials. While challenges are still to be overcome, AI will likely play an increasingly important role in drug development in the coming years. The combination of AI and traditional drug development approaches have the potential to bring new treatments to patients faster and more efficiently, improving patient outcomes and reducing healthcare costs.

Artificial intelligence (AI) has revolutionised many fields of medicine, including neurology and immunology. Integrating AI in diagnosis has significantly improved the accuracy and speed of diagnosing various diseases. Neuroimmune diagnosis, which is the diagnosis of neurological and immunological disorders, is one such area that has benefited from using AI. Neuroimmune diagnosis involves identifying and diagnosing diseases such as multiple sclerosis (MS), neuromyelitis optica (NMO), and myasthenia gravis (MG), among others. Traditionally, diagnosis of these disorders involved lengthy and often invasive procedures such as lumbar punctures, biopsies, and blood tests. These procedures were time-consuming, and results often needed to be more conclusive. However, integrating AI in neuroimmune diagnosis has revolutionised the field, making diagnosis faster and more accurate. One of the ways AI is used in neuroimmune diagnosis is through the analysis of medical images such as magnetic resonance imaging (MRI) and computed tomography (CT) scans. AI algorithms can analyse images and detect patterns that are not visible to the human eye, enabling the detection of abnormalities that may be missed in definitive diagnosis [16]. For example, AI algorithms can detect subtle changes in brain scans that indicate the presence of MS, even before symptoms appear. This early detection can lead to earlier treatment and better outcomes for patients. Another way AI is used in neuroimmune diagnosis is by analysing patient data. AI algorithms can analyse large amounts of patient records and medical literature data to identify patterns and predict disease outcomes. For example, AI algorithms can predict the likelihood of relapse in patients with MS based on factors such as age, gender, and disease history. This can help clinicians make more informed treatment decisions and monitoring. AI is also used to develop new diagnostic tools for neuroimmune disorders. For example, researchers are developing AI-based tests that can detect specific biomarkers in blood samples that indicate the presence of MS or other neuroimmune diseases. These tests are faster and less invasive than traditional tests and can provide more accurate results.

27.5 Conclusion

AI has the potential to transform healthcare by improving clinical decision-making, enhancing patient outcomes, and reducing healthcare costs. However, several challenges must be addressed to ensure responsible and ethical use. Collaboration between healthcare providers, technology companies, and regulatory bodies is essential to realising the full potential of AI in clinical decision-making. AI in neuroimmune therapy: A neuro-immunological disorder is diagnosed, and appropriate treatment strategies must be implemented to manage the condition effectively. AI can potentially optimise treatment strategies and enhance therapeutic outcomes in neuro-immunology. Here are some ways AI can aid in neuro-immunotherapy: Neuroimmune disorders are conditions that affect the immune system and the nervous system. These disorders can cause various symptoms, including cognitive and behavioural changes, muscle weakness, and paralysis. Advances in artificial intelligence (AI) have led to significant progress in understanding the pathophysiology of neuroimmune disorders and the development of new diagnostic and treatment approaches. This review will discuss some of AI's recent research findings and applications in neuroimmune disorders.

One of the main challenges in diagnosing neuroimmune disorders is the heterogeneity of clinical presentations. AI techniques can be used to analyse large datasets of clinical and genetic information to identify patterns indicative of a particular disease. For example, machine learning algorithms have been used to classify patients with multiple sclerosis (MS) based on their clinical symptoms and MRI findings. This approach is more accurate than traditional diagnostic methods and can help clinicians make more informed treatment decisions.AI can also be used to develop new treatments for neuroimmune disorders. For example, deep learning algorithms have been used to identify novel drug targets for MS. These algorithms analyse prominent gene expression and protein interaction data datasets to identify molecular pathways involved in the disease's pathophysiology. This approach has led to the development of new drugs that target specific molecules involved in the immune response, which could lead to more effective treatments for MS and other neuroimmune disorders. Another area where AI has shown promise is in predicting disease progression and treatment response. Machine learning algorithms can be trained on longitudinal clinical and imaging data to predict how a patient's symptoms will evolve and which treatments will most likely be effective. This approach could help clinicians personalise treatment plans for individual patients based on their unique disease trajectory and response to treatment.

AI is also being used to develop new diagnostic tools for neuroimmune disorders. For example, researchers have developed a machine learning algorithm that can analyse speech patterns to predict whether a patient has MS. This approach is non-invasive and could be used as a screening tool to identify patients needing further diagnostic testing. In conclusion, AI has the potential to revolutionise our understanding and treatment of neuroimmune disorders. By analysing large datasets of clinical and genetic information, identifying novel drug targets, predicting disease progression and treatment response, and developing new diagnostic tools, AI could help improve outcomes for patients with these challenging conditions. However, further research is needed to validate these approaches and ensure their safety and efficacy in clinical practice. Despite the numerous benefits of AI in neuroimmune diagnosis, its implementation has some challenges. One of the biggest challenges is the need for high-quality data to train AI algorithms. This data must be accurate and diverse to ensure that the AI algorithms can detect patterns across various patients and disease types. Another challenge is the need for ethical and transparent use of AI in diagnosis, including clear guidelines on how AI should be used in clinical practice. In conclusion, integrating AI in neuroimmune diagnosis has significant potential to improve the accuracy and speed of diagnosis, leading to better outcomes for patients with neurological and immunological disorders. As AI evolves and becomes more sophisticated, it will likely play an increasingly important role in neuroimmune diagnosis and treatment. However, ethical and transparent guidelines must be established to ensure that AI is used safely and responsibly.

References

1. Malik N, Solanki A. Simulation of human brain: artificial intelligence-based learning. In: Verma S, Tomar P, editors. Impact of AI technologies on teaching, learning, and research in higher education. IGI Global; 2021. p. 150–60. https://doi.org/10.4018/978-1-7998-4763-2.ch009.
2. Samanci BM, Yildizhan E, Tüzün E. Neuropsychiatry in the century of neuroscience. 2022.
3. Fan J, Fang L, Wu J, Guo Y, Dai Q. From brain science to artificial intelligence. Engineering. 2020;6(3):248–52.
4. Nahirney PC, Tremblay M. Brain ultrastructure: putting the pieces together. Front Cell Dev Biol. 2021;9:629503. https://doi.org/10.3389/fcell.2021.6295035. https://dominoweb.draco.res.ibm.com/reports/rj10404.pdf. Accessed 13 May 2023.
5. Surianarayanan C, Lawrence JJ, Chelliah PR, Prakash E, Hewage C. Convergence of artificial intelligence and neuroscience towards the diagnosis of neurological disorders—a scoping review. Sensors. 2023;23(6):3062. https://doi.org/10.3390/s23063062.
6. Levakov G, Rosenthal G, Shelef I, Raviv TR, Avidan G. From a deep learning model back to the brain—identifying regional predictors and their relation to ageing. Hum Brain Mapp. 2020;41(12):3235–52. https://doi.org/10.1002/hbm.25011 8. https://news.usc.edu/204691/ai-brain-aging-risk-of-cognitive-decline-alzheimers/. Accessed 13 May 2023.
7. Dias R, Torkamani A. Artificial intelligence in clinical and genomic diagnostics. Genome Med. 2019;11:70. https://doi.org/10.1186/s13073-019-0689-8.
8. Toga AW, Clark KA, Thompson PM, Shattuck DW, Van Horn JD. Mapping the human connectome. Neurosurgery. 2012;71(1):1–5. https://doi.org/10.1227/NEU.0b013e318258e9ff.
9. Brown CJ, Hamarneh G. Machine learning on human connectome data from MRI. arXiv preprint arXiv. 2016;1:1611.08699.
10. van der Velde F. Where artificial intelligence and neuroscience meet: the search for grounded architectures of cognition. Adv Artif Intell. 2010;2010:918062. https://doi.org/10.1155/2010/918062.
11. Akinyelu AA, Zaccagna F, Grist JT, Castelli M, Rundo L. Brain tumor diagnosis using machine learning, convolutional neural networks, capsule neural networks and vision transformers, applied to MRI: a survey. J Imaging. 2022;8(8):205. https://doi.org/10.3390/jimaging8080205.
12. Jena B, Nayak GK, Saxena S. An empirical study of different machine learning techniques for brain tumour classification and subsequent segmentation using hybrid texture feature. Mach Vis Appl. 2022;33:6. https://doi.org/10.1007/s00138-021-01262-x.
13. Orhan U, Hekim M, Ozer M. EEG signals classification using the K-means clustering and a multilayer perceptron neural network model. Expert Syst Appl. 2011;38(10):13475–81. https://doi.org/10.1016/j.eswa.2011.04.149.
14. Orimaye SO, Wong JSM, Golden KJ. Learning predictive linguistic features for Alzheimer's disease and related dementias using verbal utterances. In: Proceedings of the workshop on computational linguistics and clinical psychology: from linguistic signal to clinical reality; 2014. p. 78–87.
15. Klöppel S, Stonnington CM, Chu C, Draganski B, Scahill RI, Rohrer JD, Fox NC, Jack CR, Ashburner J, Frackowiak RS. Automatic classification of MR scans in Alzheimer's disease. Brain. 2008;131(3):681–9. https://doi.org/10.1093/brain/awm319.
16. Kotsavasiloglou C, Kostikis N, Hristu-Varsakelis D, Arnaoutoglou M. Machine learning-based classification of simple drawing movements in Parkinson's disease. Biomed Signal Process Control. 2017;31:174–80. https://doi.org/10.1016/j.bspc.2016.08.003.

Opportunities, Challenges in Translational Vaccine Research: Lesson Learnt from Vaccine Development During the CoVID-19 Pandemic

28

Sudhanarayani S. Rao, Vignesh Sounderrajan, T. Thangam, and Krupakar Parthasarathy

28.1 Introduction

The severe acute respiratory syndrome coronavirus type 2 (SARS-CoV-2) has been prevalent globally, triggering an urge to develop a vaccine. Previous research efforts for vaccine development for SARS-CoV can be useful to design vaccines for SARS-CoV-2. Different types of vaccine technologies presently being investigated include whole virus, nucleic acid, and recombinant protein subunit vaccines. Since every vaccine approach has its own share of advantages and disadvantages, multiple approaches need to be evaluated rapidly for safety and efficacy. Cues for vaccine design against SARS-CoV-2 can be obtained by leveraging the existing immunological studies of SARS-CoV [1]. Experiences with previous vaccine development programs such as those for H1N1 have stressed the need for novel development technologies (NGS, reverse genetics) and manufacturing platforms that can be readily adapted to new pathogens by testing prototype pathogens from various viral families [2].

SARS-Coronavirus 2 is a positive-strand RNA virus which belongs to the group of Betacoronaviruses. It has a genome of approximately 29,700 nucleotides and shares 79.5% sequence identity with SARS-CoV [3], SARS CoV-2 has a long ORF1ab polyprotein at the 5′ end, which encode 16 non-structural proteins. The 3′ end of the genome encodes four major structural proteins, including the spike (S) protein, nucleocapsid (N) protein, membrane (M) protein, and the envelope (E) protein. There is a high degree of genetic similarity (89%) between SARS-CoV and SARS-CoV-2 and both viruses bind to the same receptor on human cells, i.e., ACE2 receptor in human lung. The structural proteins of SARS-CoV share a high degree of percentage similarity with those of SARS-CoV-2, i.e., spike (76%), envelope (94.7%), membrane (90.1%), and nucleocapsid (90.6%).

After each dose of the COVID-19 vaccine, the immune system produces antibodies to combat the disease. The COVID-19 vaccines make use of an S protein, a non-lethal variation of the COVID-19 virus's spike-like surface structure. The mRNA that instructs your cells to produce the spike protein seen on the surface of the COVID-19 virus is used to create an mRNA vaccine. The immune system starts producing the spike protein

S. S. Rao · V. Sounderrajan · T. Thangam ·
K. Parthasarathy (✉)
Centre for Drug Discovery and Development, Sathyabama Institute of Science and Technology, Chennai, India
e-mail: sudhanarayani.cddd@sathyabama.ac.in; vignesh.irc@sathyabama.ac.in; thangam.t.cddd@sathyabama.ac.in; pkrupakar.cddd@sathyabama.ac.in

K. Parthasarathy, R. Manikkam (eds.), *Translational Research in Biomedical Sciences: Recent Progress and Future Prospects*, https://doi.org/10.1007/978-981-97-1777-4_28

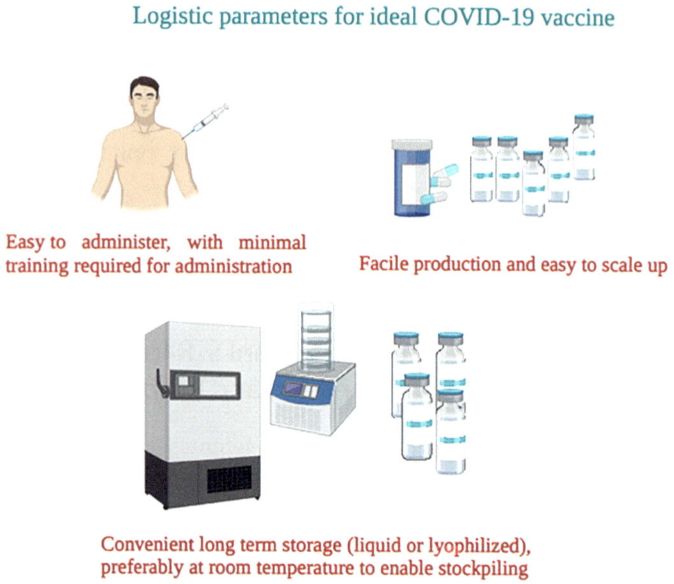

Fig. 28.1 Parameters of an ideal vaccine in terms of logistics

and expressing it on cell surfaces soon after vaccination. The body begins to produce antibodies to the COVID-19 virus as a result. After the protein components are created, the instructions are broken down and eliminated by the cells. The mRNA in the vaccination does not go into the cell's nucleus, which is where DNA is stored. This technique of mRNA is utilized in the Pfizer-BioNTech and Moderna COVID-19 vaccines. In a vector-based vaccine strategy, the SARS CoV-2 virus components are inserted into a modified form of another virus (viral vector). The cells receive instructions from the viral vector to replicate the Spike protein. The immune system reacts when the immune cells display the S proteins on their surfaces by producing antibodies and protective white blood cells. The antibodies will combat the SARS CoV-2 virus each time there is a viral trigger (Fig. 28.1).

28.2 Platforms for Vaccine Development

28.2.1 Inactivated Vaccines

Inactivated vaccines employ a straightforward technology and have been extensively used for development of vaccines against several pathogens. The vaccine candidate, CoronaVac developed by SinoVac is presently under evaluation in clinical trials. The vaccine, composed of a whole virus has been reported to have RBD of the S protein as the main immunogen. Virus plaque CN-2 SARS-CoV-2 was subjected to purification and multiple passages in Vero cells and further inactivated using β- propiolactone. The chemical inactivation inhibits viral membrane fusion in a dose-dependent manner. The vaccine, after stringent purification steps was formulated with an alum adjuvant [4, 5]. The vaccine was initially developed under the name PiCoVacc and demonstrated induction of specific neutralizing antibodies in mice, rats, and non-human primates with no observable antibody-dependent enhancement of infection at the tested doses in the pre-clinical testing phase [5]. The SARS-CoV-2 inactivated vaccination successfully warded off COVID-19, including severe illness and death. The discovery was in line with the outcomes of the vaccine's phase 2 studies [6]. The whole-virion inactivated COVID 19 vaccine (BBV152) (3 mg or 6 mg) combined with a toll-like receptor 7/8 agonist adsorbed to alum (Algel-IMDG) is the indigenous Indian vaccine candidate going by the name "Covaxin," which was developed by Bharat Biotech in partnership with the National Institute of Virology [7].

28.2.2 Non-replicating Viral Vector Vaccines

In the early 2021, the most prominent variant of SARS CoV-2 that was circulating in India was the delta (B.1.617.2) variant which was also classified under the variant of concern. It showed higher transmissibility and reduced vaccine effectiveness when compared to the response by other variants.

The University of Oxford in collaboration with Astra Zeneca has developed a vaccine AZD1222 (formerly ChAdOx1 nCoV-19) whose target antigen is the SARS-CoV-2 S glycoprotein. The vaccine, presently under clinical trials, has a viral vector derived from Chimpanzees (ChAdOx1), which is a weakened version of the adenovirus that causes common cold. Spike protein encoding region was cloned into the vector with an E1 locus modified to infect humans [4]. The vaccine is being evaluated under Phase 2/3 trials in England and India, under the candidate name Covishield, as well as under Phase 3 trials in countries including Brazil, South Africa and USA. The global trials of Astra Zeneca's candidate vaccine was halted to investigate the adverse reaction from a single volunteer but was resumed upon authorization from FDA. The vaccine Ad5-nCoV, which was jointly developed by Cansino and Institute of Biotechnology of the Academy of Military Medical Sciences, is being evaluated under clinical trials. It involved the use of an adenovirus type 5 vector that was replication defective and was modified to carry gene fragments which expressed SARS-CoV-2 S protein [8]. The Ad5 vectors are well studied and can infect dividing, non-dividing cells and are maintained as episomes within a cell. The E1A and E1B essential genes are replaced with a high activity cytomegalovirus immediate early promoter expression cassette. Use of this vector is advantageous as it can be grown into high titer stable stocks. However, limitations include presence of pre-existing neutralizing antibodies to Ad5 vector in some adults [4]. The vaccine is presently under Phase III clinical trials in countries such as Saudi Arabia, Pakistan, and Russia. Johnson & Johnson has developed a vaccine using Janssens's AdVac® adenoviral vector and their PER.C6® cell line technology that has the capacity to produce more than 1 million doses from a 1000 L bioreactor by employing high density suspension culture. The platform uses Ad26 non-replicating vector where E1 and E3 genes are deleted. There is a less likelihood of pre-existing antibodies to the vector, thereby offering an advantage over the use of Ad5 vector [4]. The vaccine is presently under evaluation for Phase III clinical trials and requires a single dose to be administered. The trial has been paused in order to investigate an adverse reaction in a volunteer.

28.2.3 Live-Attenuated Vaccines

Live-attenuated viral vaccines are generated by techniques, e.g., serial passaging in cell culture and codon deoptimization. They offer the advantage of being conventional vaccines with proven, established technology that use simple formulation and elicit strong immune response [4]. Codagenix has collaborated with the Serum Institute of India to develop an attenuated viral vaccine using the codon deoptimization technology, for exploring vaccine strategies for SARS-CoV-2 immunization. Whole virus vaccines have the advantage of inherent immunogenicity and ability to stimulate Toll-like receptors TLR 3, 7/8, and 9 [9, 10].

28.2.4 DNA Vaccines

DNA vaccines use the modern nucleic acid based platform to deliver synthetic or engineered genes into cells for encoding antigenic proteins of the virus, thereby eliciting T-cell and antibody responses [11]. To date, no nucleic acid based vaccines have been approved for human use, but a number of them are in different phases of clinical trials. Although DNA vaccines offer an upper hand with the ease of scaling up, long-term stability and enduring immune responses, they are met with limitations such as need for special tools for delivery or the possibility of variable mucosal immune responses. Inovio Pharmaceuticals, a

US-based company has developed a vaccine candidate that is presently being evaluated in clinical trials. The vaccine is a DNA plasmid encoding S protein delivered by a CELLECTRA® 2000 electroporator and is designed to be injected transdermally followed by electroporation. The platform involved fast, facile design and manufacturing requiring no cold chain for storage or distribution [4]. No serious adverse effects were observed during the Phase I clinical trial, however the trial has been placed on partial hold on account of queries raised on the nature of the delivery device.

28.2.5 RNA Vaccines

RNA vaccines typically consist of an mRNA sequence that encodes a disease specific antigen. Upon delivery into target cells, the encoded antigen is processed and presented to the immune system, eliciting a strong humoral and cell-mediated response. Compared to the production of inactivated, live-attenuated vaccines or subunit vaccines, production of mRNA vaccines is faster and less expensive as the platform does not require use of any living stage of pathogenic virus or bacteria. Most components required for mRNA vaccine production are already available at GMP grade to scale up for commercialization. Conventional mRNA vaccines encode target antigen produced synthetically through a cell-free in vitro enzymatic transcription reaction. The in vitro transcription reaction is mediated by a linearized plasmid DNA encoding the target Ag as template. Self-amplifying mRNA vaccines (saRNA) are alphavirus RNA derivatives with the antigen gene replacing structural protein sequence of the virus. This allows generation of numerous copies of antigen encoding mRNA thereby expressing high levels of the heterologous gene. In vitro transcribed mRNA is further formulated by encapsulation in lipid nanoparticles and delivered into cells. The level of immune response elicited is dependent on additional factors such as delivery vehicle used and route of administration [12].

Individuals with SARS-CoV-2 infection are capable of producing strong neutralizing antibodies (targeting the S protein of SARS-CoV-2) that may prevent SARS-CoV-2 infection in vitro and/or in vivo, according to studies of natural human infection. Based on this understanding, pre-clinical assessments of SARS-CoV-2 mRNA vaccines have focused on evaluating the vaccinations' capacity to elicit strong SARS-CoV-2-binding and neutralizing Ab responses in mice, as a first step in assessing vaccine effectiveness [13]. The first vaccine candidate that was evaluated in human clinical trial for SARS-CoV-2 was mRNA-1273, developed by the National Institute of Allergy and Infectious Disease in collaboration with Moderna. The vaccine was developed within 45 days of publishing of the viral genome of SARS-CoV-2 [10]. RNA and DNA vaccines can be made quickly without culture or fermentation, using synthetic processes, as compared to other types of vaccines. The vaccine was considered superior to conventional vaccines due to its short production cycle, high potency and safety conferred due to absence of actual viral genome. mRNA-1273 vaccine candidate is embedded in lipid nanoparticles which encode SARS-CoV-2 S protein and deliver the antigen to human cells to induce immune responses against SARS-CoV-2. The immune response was promising with specific neutralizing antibodies thereby protecting healthy individuals [8] and the Phase III results have demonstrated 94.5% efficacy.

Another candidate, BNT162 was developed by BioNtech and Pfizer, has SARS-CoV-2 3CLpro, nsp5 and Mpro as antigenic targets. The vaccine was composed of a proprietary lipolex formulation mixed with uridine containing mRNA (uRNA) or nucleoside modified RNA (modRNA) [4]. Clinical trials demonstrated 95% efficacy of the vaccine (as on November 17, 2020) with significantly fewer side effects, fever and fatigue. The trial was also extended to testing on children as young as 12 years of age. Efficacy rates were found to be consistent across gender, age, race, ethnicity demographics, with 94% efficacy being evidenced in adults above 65 years of age. The vaccine is required to be administered in two doses which relies on cold chain storage at low temperatures due to the use of mRNA based platform (Fig. 28.2).

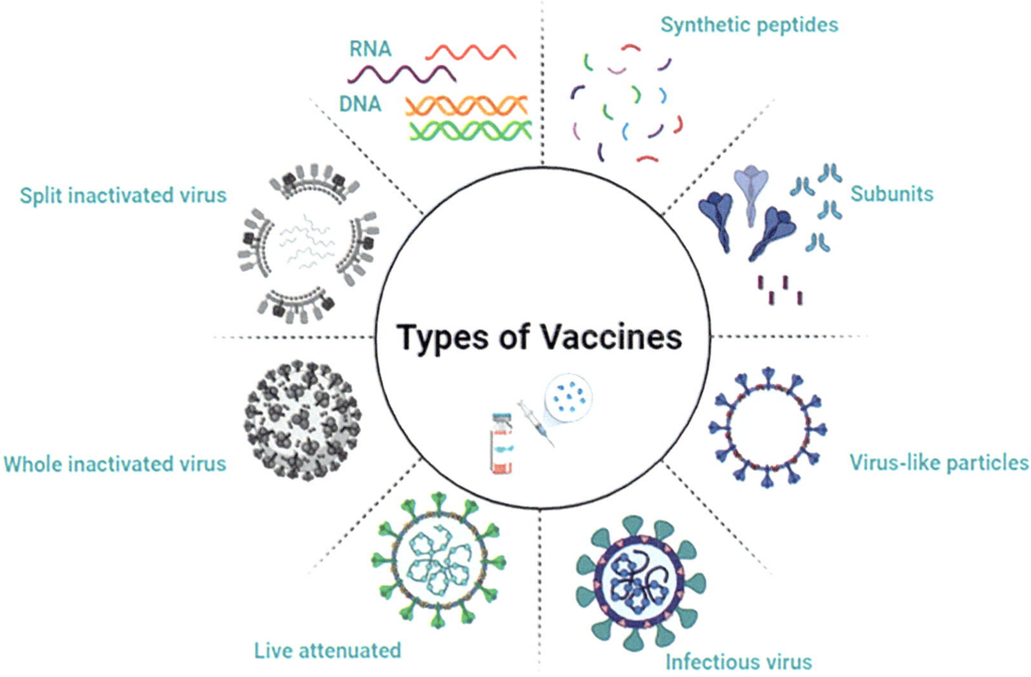

Fig. 28.2 Types of vaccines for SARS CoV-2

28.2.6 Protein Subunit Vaccines

Subunit vaccine candidates of SARS-CoV and SARS-CoV-2 are targeted against S protein to prevent its interaction with ACE2 receptor of human lungs. Several subunit vaccines are in different stages of clinical development. Novavax has developed a vaccine candidate NVX-CoV2373 using immunogenic virus-like nanoparticles based on recombinantly expressed S protein. The vaccine is currently being investigated for safety and efficacy in clinical trials. The vaccine used a stable, perfusion protein expressed in genetically engineered Sf9 insect cells. The expressed recombinant protein was subjected to proper folding and post-translational modifications and incorporated with Novavax's saponin based matrix-M adjuvant as a nanoparticle formulation to elicit enhanced immune responses and increased levels of neutralizing antibodies [4, 8]. Novavax is presently under Phase III clinical trials in UK after receiving promising results in its Phase II blinded-placebo controlled trial. PittCoVacc developed by Pittsburg School of Medicine uses SARS-CoV-2 S protein fragments to stimulate production of specific antibodies. The administration of the vaccine was optimized using a novel technique called the microarray needle, using which more potent immune responses were generated compared to conventional subcutaneous needle injections [8]. University of Queensland, Australia, with funding from CEPI is involved in synthesizing viral surface proteins for effective presentation to immune system using molecular clamp platform. The lead candidate from the university is a recombinant trimeric SARS-CoV-2 spike protein based vaccine [4]. Clover Biopharmaceuticals has produced a vaccine composed of trimerized SARS-CoV-2 S protein using their patented Trimer-tag® technology and GSK's adjuvant system. The trimer subunit vaccine was manufactured using rapid mammalian cell culture based expression system and the trimer-tag, which is an advanced drug development platform used for production of covalently trimerized fusion proteins that can efficiently target previous undruggable pathways [14]. The vaccine candidate by Clover-GSK completed Phase I trials and is under preparation for Phase II.

A subunit vaccine composed of only receptor-binding domain (RBD) of SARS-CoV has been developed by Texas Children's Hospital Center for Vaccine Development. The S protein formulation on alum elicited high levels of protective immunity. RBD vaccines are promising as SARS-CoV and SARS-CoV-2 RBD amino acid sequences are similar by more than 80% and offer the advantage of minimizing host immunopotentiation [9].

As evidenced by the numerous vaccine development programs across the world, the spike protein is the prime candidate around which the vaccines are devised. Spike or its select region such as the RBD or N-terminal domain is most commonly targeted as S protein induces highest neutralizing antibody titers among all the CoV antigens. However, additional antigen targets can be pursued, e.g., nucelocapsid, non-structural proteins, CoVs lacking envelope protein which make promising vaccine candidates or cocktail vaccines. The N protein is also one of the most conserved proteins among SARS and MERS-CoV strains and induces long-lived memory T-cells in humans, making it a promising alternative for providing cross protection and long-term cell-mediated immunity against CoV [15, 16]. Due to the limited information available and patent protection on antigens used in SARS-CoV-2, and the vaccines under development, the exact antigenic details and the expected as well as induced immune responses by the same remains unclear [12]. While the platforms such as inactivated virus, live-attenuated and non-replicating viral vectors employ proven technology utilized over many years, the modern platforms such as DNA, RNA, and protein subunit vaccines offer advantages such as eliminating the direct use of pathogen, facile, and swift scaling up processes. Vaccine candidate that first gains regulatory approval is expected to be safe, efficacious, and available worldwide at a rapid pace, being made available to all strata of people.

28.2.7 COVID-19 Vaccines: The Indian Scenario

Active efforts to contribute to the development of vaccines for COVID-19 are being undertaken by the Government of India, which has pledged 15 million USD to the Global Vaccine Alliance, Gavi. Indian companies and research institutes together have put forth 14 vaccine candidates which are presently in different stages of vaccine development. Four out of the 14 which are presently in the pre-clinical phase are expected to reach clinical trial stages by around October 2020, with an estimated 1 year time period for vaccine to come into markets after procuring approval from regulatory authorities. Although India is effectively contributing to vaccine development globally, its manufacturing might be of most use to address the needs of the ongoing pandemic. This is of great advantage as it would help to meet the global demands once a vaccine is approved and would enable stockpiling to ensure that all countries, both developed and developing, have access to the vaccine. One of the world's largest biotech company with the ability to produce 1.5 billion doses of vaccine annually is India's Pune based Serum Institute of India. The company is presently involved in 3 vaccine development projects; (1) development of its own vaccine for COVID-19, (2) collaboration with UK's Oxford University, (3) collaboration with US-based Codagenix. Despite the risk of one or more of the vaccines not being approved beyond clinical trials, the company has taken up preparatory processes to produce 40–60 million doses by September 2020 to meet the global demands for vaccine production once a vaccine is approved. The collaboration with Codagenix involves a reverse strategy to create live-attenuated vaccine where viral sequences have been changed by swapping optimized codons with non-optimized ones (codon deoptimization process) for attenuation of the virus [10]. The company has also partnered with Oxford University's Jenner Institute to manufacture the Covishield vaccine. Phase I clinical trials of the vaccine has been initiated. Apart from the Serum Institute of India, 5 other Indian companies are contributing their manufacturing and scientific capacities to the global vaccine development program. Zydus Cadilla has two vaccine candidates in the pipeline, a DNA based vaccine against the SARS-CoV-2 spike glycoprotein and a replicating viral vector (Measles virus) expressing undisclosed CoV proteins, among which its plasmid DNA based candidate has reached phase II clinical trials (ZyCoV-D). The vaccine was determined to be safe and immunogenic through pre-clinical toxicity studies and is being developed to possess stability and low cold chain requirements due to use of DNA based platform. Bharat Biotech in association with University of Wisconsin and FluGen are developing a vaccine named CoroFlu which expresses the SARS-CoV-2 S protein, where Bharat Biotech will contribute to the manufacturing of the vaccine as well. Indian Immunologicals has partnered with Griffith University, Australia, to develop an engineered live-attenuated SARS-CoV-2 vaccine. A spike protein subunit vaccine is under development by Indian Institute of Science in collaboration with Mynvax while Biological E is developing a subunit vaccine delivering the RBD of SARS-CoV-2 spike protein. By contributing to the vaccine development as well as manufacture, Indian companies can help bring to light low-cost vaccines to the developing world.

28.2.8 Elucidation of Immune Response: A Critical Factor

Vaccine candidates for SARS-CoV-2 have elicited both humoral and cell-mediated immune responses. Profiling of the type of immune responses is extremely critical in vaccine development as it will determine the measure of immunogenicity, duration of immunity conferred, and effectiveness in target populations. Paucity of information on specific immune responses to SARS-CoV-2 has brought the need to extrapolate data obtained from experimental evaluations performed with SARS-CoV. The T-cell epitopes of SARS-CoV map identically with those of SARS-CoV-2 by 23%, while the B-cell epitopes map identically by 16%. It must be noted, however, that epitopes that elicit a response against SARS-CoV might or might not be effective against SARS-CoV-2 [1] but may provide a direction to identifying potential vaccine targets.

With regard to humoral immune response, studies in pre-clinical mice models indicate that antibodies produced against S protein provide protection from infection. Antibodies generated against N protein of SARS-CoV were highly immunogenic. The antibody response was effective but short-lived in convalescent SARS-CoV patients. The cell-mediated immune response, mediated by T-cells, provided long-term protection of up to 11 years post-infection. Among the immune responses against all the proteins of SARS-CoV, the structural proteins were most immunogenic in PBMC of convalescent patients, as compared to the non-structural proteins. Several DNA vaccine candidates expressing different forms of S proteins have invoked humoral and cellular responses in rhesus macaques, including neutralizing antibodies comparable to convalescent humans and macaques infected with SARS-CoV-2. Vaccination has therefore demonstrated protection against SARS-CoV-2 in non-human primates [17]. Among the structural proteins, S and N proteins produced the highest T-cell responses which were most dominant and long-lasting [1], thereby highlighting their potential as ideal vaccine targets. However, immune responses to other structural proteins or lack of them have not been clearly elucidated and could be investigated further to discover potential vaccine candidates. Screening set of epitopes of SARS-CoV-2 which have been mapped to be identical to SARS-CoV, with no or very low degree of mutation can help guide quick experimental efforts to vaccine development.

28.2.9 Challenges to Vaccine Development for SARS CoV-2

Immunity against the deadly virus requires the development of a vaccine candidate that is safe and effective against multiple variants of the virus. At the same time, it should be affordable and delivered to all the developing and undeveloped nations. Global immunization programs have significant challenges since many first-generation vaccinations are costly and necessitate the use of ultra-cold chains, especially in low- and middle-income nations. Maintaining robust incentives for research and development, coordinating clinical trials, approving safe and effective vaccines promptly, and continuing to monitor their effects as (and after) they are used are the four main challenges identified as obstacles to achieving new vaccines. Importantly, each of these problems will need a bigger public involvement, intergovernmental support, and cooperation in the restructuring of institutions, procedures, and incentives [18].

Conducting clinical trials during a pandemic can be challenging as it is difficult to predict where and when outbreaks will occur and to simultaneously prepare trial sites to coincide with vaccines ready for testing. If multiple vaccines are ready for testing, care must be taken to not burden countries their ethics and regulatory authorities with multiple trials as was the case with therapeutics during Ebola outbreak of 2013–2016 [2].

Lack of or presence of highly limited established animal models for evaluating vaccines, as was the case with SARS and MERS becomes a challenge to vaccine development. The vaccines for SARS and MERS have been evaluated on models such as mouse, hamsters, ferrets, guinea pigs, marmosets, rhesus macaques, and cats. However, models like mice, hamsters, and ferrets could not be developed for the evaluation of MERS vaccines due to the inability of MERS-CoV to replicate in the respiratory tract of these species. In such cases, humanized versions of the experimental models have to be developed in order to mimic the process of receptor binding and immune response [11]. Cytokine storm induced by excessive T-cell responses have been demonstrated to accentuate pathogenesis of COVID-19. T-cell responses elicited by any SARS-CoV-2 vaccine must be well controlled to avoid immunopathology [5]. Immune responses from predictive models of SARS and MERS can be extrapolated but are not established profiles. There are still uncertain/unknown factors such as duration of immunity, similarity of immune response between predictive models and SARS-CoV-2 and whether single dose of vaccine would confer immunity [2]. Extensive additional testing for safety evaluations due to increased infectivity of SARS-CoV vaccines is required following immunization with live or attenuated vaccines. Undesired immunopotentiation occurs when vaccine candidates are administered and may manifest as increased infectivity or eosinophilic infiltration in whole virus vaccines and complete spike protein vaccines. The undesired immunopotentiation must be addressed in any vaccine target product prolife under the safety considerations [9].

Pre-clinical stage vaccine candidates for SARS and MERS have raised concerns about exacerbating lung disease which could occur directly or as a result of Ab-dependent enhancement. The exacerbating lung disease could be an adverse effect associated with Th2 cell response. The SARS-Co-2 Spike protein is a promising target for protection, however, additional challenge includes optimizing Ag design to ensure optimal immune response. Also, it is unclear whether it is most effective to target the full length S protein or to target only the receptor-binding domain [2]. Addressing the needs of target or at-risk population is most critical during a pandemic. The most vulnerable populations include frontline healthcare workers, older age group, and people with comorbidities including chronic conditions such as diabetes, asthma, and hypertension. Vaccine development can be directed toward prioritizing such target populations for clinical trials and licensure. Vaccines that are developed and manufactured for biodefense or global health security during a pandemic yield less profit and require potential stockpiling to provide for immediate needs of target populations [9].

28.2.10 Vaccination for Animals

Animal vaccinations serve to stimulate the immune system without actually spreading the illness. The first COVID-19 vaccine (Carnivac-Cov) for animals has been created by Russian researchers from the Federal Service for

Veterinary and Phytosanitary Surveillance to tackle the threat of animal-to-human transmission and the emergence of mutant variants. The Karnivak-Kov vaccination, widely referred to as a vaccine for carnivore animals [19]. A Vaccine called Ancovax, Specifically designed for animals and has been introduced in the Indian market, which is an inactivated form of the SARS-CoV-2 Delta Virus. The immunity brought on by Ancovax neutralizes both the Delta and Omicron Variants of SARS-CoV-2. The vaccine contains Alhydrogel as an adjuvant along with inactivated SARS-CoV-2 (Delta) antigen. Dogs, lions, leopards, mice, and bunnies could be vaccinated with it [20]. Non-human primates were vaccinated with mRNA-1273 an immunization against SARS-CoV-2 that contains its prefusion-stabilized spike protein, which resulted in strong SARS-CoV-2 neutralizing action, quick protection in the upper and lower airways, and no pathological lung alterations [21].

28.2.11 Conclusion

Unprecedented levels of attention, collaboration, and resource utilization on the part of nations for the development of vaccines against SARS–Cov-2 has allowed us to move swiftly to stop the deaths of people and safeguard livelihoods of millions of people. For a vaccine candidate to be introduced into the market, it nearly takes more than 10 years. Since the developmental stages are usually expensive, it is done gradually, with each step only starting after the previous one has been successfully accomplished. Also, the immune responses against the potential drug have to be closely monitored in the clinical trials. This demanded a radical reconsideration of the conventional vaccination's staggered approach so that the COVID-19 vaccine could be developed considerably faster and more safely. It has been a huge challenge to create COVID-19 vaccinations in 1 year as opposed to ten. New cooperative strategies for science, global production, and distribution were developed to succeed. This involves having multiple collaborations which could accelerate the research at the same time in multi faced dimensions of vaccine research. In order to increase our chances of discovering vaccinations that are effective as well as secure for everyone, vaccine trails should be conducted concurrently around the world, not only in high-income nations. There have already been a few new production facilities erected, and more may be required. This is due to the fact that many current facilities are still required to provide routine immunizations, which must be maintained whenever feasible to reduce the burden of new epidemics. To ensure vaccinations are given equally to all populations, manufacturing facilities must be dispersed around the world. To fight this pandemic, a diverse array of vaccinations is required, therefore we must continue to create new, safe vaccines that are also highly effective, especially those that are simpler or less expensive to produce and administer.

References

1. Ahmed SF, Quadeer AA, McKay MR. Preliminary identification of potential vaccine targets for the COVID-19 coronavirus (SARS-CoV-2) based on SARS-CoV immunological studies. Viruses. 2020;12:254. https://doi.org/10.3390/v12030254.
2. Lurie N, Saville M, Hatchett R, Halton J. Developing covid-19 vaccines at pandemic speed. N Engl J Med. 2020;382:1969.
3. Hu B, Guo H, Zhou P, Shi ZL. Characteristics of SARS-CoV-2 and COVID-19. Nat Rev Microbiol. 2021;19(3):141–54. https://doi.org/10.1038/s41579-020-00459-7.
4. Funk D, Laferrière C, Ardakani A. A snapshot of the global race for vaccines targeting SARS-CoV-2 and the COVID-19 pandemic. Front Pharmacol. 2020;11:937. https://doi.org/10.3389/fphar.2020.00937.
5. Gao Q, Bao L, Mao H, Wang L, Xu K, Yang M, et al. Development of an inactivated vaccine candidate for SARS-CoV-2. Science. 2020;2020:77. https://doi.org/10.1126/science.abc1932.
6. Jara A, Undurraga EA, González C, Paredes F, Fontecilla T, Jara G, Pizarro A, Acevedo J, Leo K, Leon F, Sans C, Leighton P, Suárez P, García-Escorza H, Araos R. Effectiveness of an inactivated SARS-CoV-2 vaccine in Chile. N Engl J Med. 2021;385(10):875–84. https://doi.org/10.1056/nejmoa2107715.
7. Ella R, Vadrevu KM, Jogdand H, Prasad S, Reddy S, Sarangi V, Ganneru B, Sapkal G, Yadav P, Abraham P, Panda S, Gupta N, Reddy P, Verma S, Kumar Rai S, Singh C, Redkar SV, Gillurkar CS, Kushwaha JS, Bhargava B. Safety and immunogenicity of an inac-

tivated SARS-CoV-2 vaccine, BBV152: a double-blind, randomised, phase 1 trial. Lancet Infect Dis. 2021;21(5):637–46. https://doi.org/10.1016/S1473-3099(20)30942-7.
8. Zhang J, Xie B, Hashimoto K. Current status of potential therapeutic candidates for the COVID-19 crisis. Brain Behav Immun. 2020;87:59. https://doi.org/10.1016/j.bbi.2020.04.046.
9. Chen W, Strych U, Hotez PJ, Bottazzi ME. The SARS-CoV-2 vaccine pipeline: an overview. Curr Trop Med Rep. 2020;7:61–4. https://doi.org/10.1007/s40475-020-00201-6.
10. Uddin M, Mustafa F, Rizvi TA, Loney T, Suwaidi HA, Marzouqui AHH, et al. SARS-CoV-2/COVID-19: viral genomics, epidemiology, vaccines, and therapeutic interventions. Viruses. 2020;12:526.
11. Dhama K, Sharun K, Tiwari R, Dadar M, Malik YS, Singh KP, Chaicumpa W. COVID-19, an emerging coronavirus infection: advances and prospects in designing and developing vaccines, immunotherapeutics, and therapeutics. Hum Vaccin Immunother. 2020;16:1232. https://doi.org/10.1080/21645515.2020.1735227.
12. Yi C, Yi Y, Li J. mRNA vaccines: possible tools to combat SARS-CoV-2. Virol Sin. 2020;35:259. https://doi.org/10.1007/s12250-020-00243-0.
13. Bettini E, Locci M. SARS-CoV-2 mRNA vaccines: immunological mechanism and beyond. Vaccine. 2021;9(2):1–20. https://doi.org/10.3390/vaccines9020147.
14. Liu C, Zhou Q, Li Y, Garner LV, Watkins SP, Carter LJ, Smoot J, Gregg AC, Daniels AD, Jervey S, Albaju D. Research and development on therapeutic agents and vaccines for COVID-19 and related human coronavirus diseases. ACS Cent Sci. 2020;2020(6):315–31. https://doi.org/10.1021/acscentsci.0c00272.
15. Schoeman D, Fielding BC. Coronavirus envelope protein: current knowledge. Virol J. 2019;16(69):69. https://doi.org/10.1186/s12985-019-1182-0.
16. Regalado E. Vaccines for SARS-CoV-2: lessons from other coronavirus strains. Infect Dis Ther. 2020;9:255. https://doi.org/10.1007/s40121-020-00300-x.
17. Yu J, Tostanoski LH, Peter L, Mercado NB, McMahan K, Mahrokian SH, et al. DNA vaccine protection against SARS-CoV-2 in rhesus macaques. Science. 2020;2020:806. https://doi.org/10.1126/science.abc6284.
18. Forman R, Shah S, Jeurissen P, Jit M, Mossialos E. Since January 2020 Elsevier has created a COVID-19 resource centre with free information in English and Mandarin on the novel coronavirus COVID- 19. The COVID-19 resource centre is hosted on Elsevier connect, the company' s public news and information. 2020.
19. Chavda VP, Feehan J, Apostolopoulos V. A veterinary vaccine for sars-cov-2: the first covid-19 vaccine for animals. Vaccine. 2021;9(6):7–9. https://doi.org/10.3390/vaccines9060631.
20. Rao SS, Parthasarathy K, Sounderrajan V, Neelagandan K, Anbazhagan P, Chandramouli V. Susceptibility of SARS coronavirus-2 infection in domestic and wild animals: a systematic review. 3 Biotech. 2023;13(1):1–16. https://doi.org/10.1007/s13205-022-03416-8.
21. Corbett KS, Flynn B, Foulds KE, Francica JR, Boyoglu-Barnum S, Werner AP, Flach B, O'Connell S, Bock KW, Minai M, Nagata BM, Andersen H, Martinez DR, Noe AT, Douek N, Donaldson MM, Nji NN, Alvarado GS, Edwards DK, Graham BS. Evaluation of the mRNA-1273 vaccine against SARS-CoV-2 in nonhuman primates. N Engl J Med. 2020;383(16):1544–55. https://doi.org/10.1056/nejmoa2024671.

GPSR Compliance

The European Union's (EU) General Product Safety Regulation (GPSR) is a set of rules that requires consumer products to be safe and our obligations to ensure this.

If you have any concerns about our products, you can contact us on ProductSafety@springernature.com

In case Publisher is established outside the EU, the EU authorized representative is:

Springer Nature Customer Service Center GmbH
Europaplatz 3
69115 Heidelberg, Germany

Batch number: 10731393

Printed by Printforce, the Netherlands